Praise for *Mary, Queen of Scots, and the Murder of Lord Darnley*

"All the elements of a juicy murder mystery are within these pages, including love affairs, political intrigue, and the imprisonment and eventual beheading of Mary Stuart by her suspicious cousin, Elizabeth I of England."
—*Fort Worth Star-Telegram*

"Recommended . . . Weir skillfully analyzes the politics and religious tensions of the time. . . . She adeptly makes her case." —*Library Journal*

"Entertaining popular history that will satisfy fans of Weir's previous bestsellers." —*Publishers Weekly*

"Weir goes to great lengths to isolate the clues and marshal them into a convincing indictment. No stone is left unturned in her investigation, and . . . her book is as dramatic as witnessing firsthand the most riveting court case."
—*Booklist* (boxed and starred review)

ALSO BY ALISON WEIR

Mistress of the Monarchy: The Life of Katherine Swynford,
Duchess of Lancaster

The Lady Elizabeth: A Novel

Innocent Traitor: A Novel of Lady Jane Grey

Britain's Royal Families:
The Complete Genealogy

The Six Wives of Henry VIII

The Princes in the Tower

The Wars of the Roses

The Children of Henry VIII

The Life of Elizabeth I

Eleanor of Aquitaine

Henry VIII: The King and His Court

Queen Isabella

Mary, Queen of Scots, and the Murder of Lord Darnley

MARY, QUEEN OF SCOTS,

AND THE MURDER OF

LORD DARNLEY

ALISON WEIR

BALLANTINE BOOKS NEW YORK

2009 Ballantine Books Trade Paperback Edition

Copyright © 2003 by Alison Weir
Reading Group guide © 2009 by Random House, Inc.

Published in the United States by Ballantine Books,
an imprint of The Random House Publishing Group,
a division of Random House, Inc., New York.

BALLANTINE and colophon are registered trademarks of Random House, Inc.
RANDOM HOUSE READER'S CIRCLE and colophon are trademarks of
Random House, Inc.

Originally published in Great Britain by Jonathan Cape,
a division of Random House Group Limited, London, in 2003.
Subsequently published in hardcover in the United States by Ballantine Books,
an imprint of The Random House Publishing Group, a division of
Random House, Inc., in 2003.

Library of Congress Cataloging-in-Publication Data

Weir, Alison.
  Mary, Queen of Scots, and the murder of Lord Darnley / Alison Weir.
    p. cm.
  ISBN 978-0-8129-7151-4
  1. Darnley, Henry Stuart, Lord, 1545–1567—Death and burial. 2. Mary,
Queen of Scots, 1542–1587—Marriage. 3. Scotland—History—Mary Stuart,
1542–1567. 4. Murder—Scotland—History—16th century. 5. Queens—
Scotland—Biography. I. Title.

DA787.D3 W45 2003
941.105'092—dc21

                                                        2002034467

Printed in the United States of America

www.randomhousereaderscircle.com

6 8 9 7 5

Book design by Richard Oriolo

This book is dedicated to the memory of

JOYCE MASTERTON

and

DAVID KNOWLES,

two great Scots

God will never permit such a mischief to remain hidden.

—WRITTEN BY THE SCOTTISH PRIVY COUNCIL TO CATHERINE DE MEDICI, QUEEN OF FRANCE, ON THE MORNING AFTER DARNLEY'S MURDER

CONTENTS

ACKNOWLEDGMENTS

I should like to express my warmest gratitude to the following, without whom this book would not now be in print: my literary agent, Julian Alexander; my commissioning editors, Will Sulkin (in the U.K.) and Tracy Brown (in the U.S.); and my editorial director, Anthony Whittome. Your interest, encouragement and creative input has been invaluable and is, as ever, greatly appreciated.

Special thanks are also due to my copy editors, Beth Humphries and James Nightingale; Suzanne Dean, art director at Random House, and Gene Mydlowski, art director at Ballantine, for the jacket designs; Sophie Hartley, for the picture research; Neil Bradford, for designing the illustrated section; Roger Walker, for assistance with the map; the staff of Sutton Libraries for their help in obtaining many out-of-print works; and James Cullen, for advice on explosives.

My grateful thanks go also to my family and friends for their kindness and support whilst this book was in preparation, and especially to my dear husband, Rankin, whose unfailing help enabled me to finish it on time.

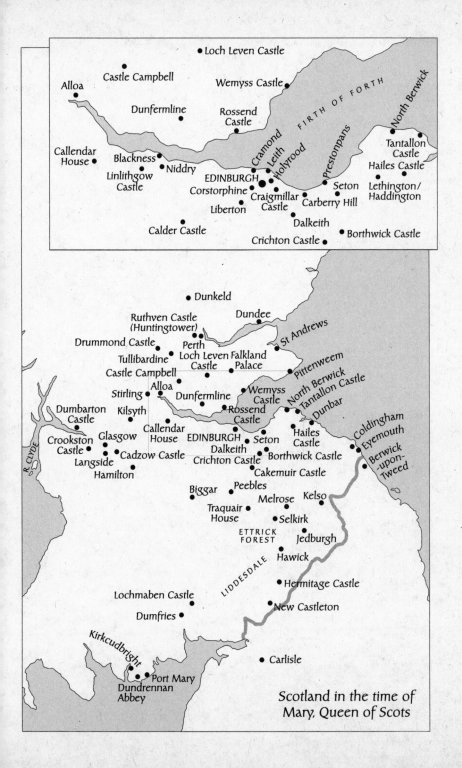

Scotland in the time of
Mary, Queen of Scots

DRAMATIS PERSONAE:
THE SCOTTISH LORDS

1. THE PROTESTANT LORDS

ARGYLL, Archibald Campbell, 5th Earl of (d. 1573). An epileptic, he succeeded to the earldom in 1558. Active in the Reformation Parliament of 1560, but rebuked by John Knox for his religious tolerance. A prominent member of the Privy Council and the most powerful magnate in the Western Highlands. Married to Jean Stewart, natural daughter of James V (divorced 1564).

ARRAN, James Hamilton, Earl of (1537/8–1609). Chatelherault's heir and a fanatical Protestant. Suitor to both Elizabeth I and Queen Mary.

BOTHWELL, James Hepburn, 4th Earl of (c. 1535/6–78). A zealous Protestant but no friend to the Lords of the Congregation. One of the greatest nobels of the period, with a strong power base in East Lothian and the Borders.

BOYD, Robert, 5th Lord (c. 1517–90). A supporter of the Lords of the Congregation, and a member of the Privy Council.

CHATELHERAULT, James Hamilton, Duke of, previously Earl of Arran (c. 1516–75). Head of the House of Hamilton and heir apparent to the Queen. Regent of Scotland during Queen Mary's minority, and head of the Protestant Lords of the Congregation in 1560. Unstable in religion.

CRAWFORD, David Lindsay, 10th Earl of (1524–74). He was loyal to Queen Mary, but had a reputation for recklessness and brutality.

FLEMING, John, 5th Lord (c. 1536–72). His mother was Margaret Stewart, a natural daughter of James IV, and his sister was Mary Fleming, one of the four Maries. He was one of the Queen's most loyal partisans.

GLENCAIRN, Alexander Cunningham, 4th Earl of (c. 1510–74). An ardent reformist and member of the Lords of the Congregation. Religious zeal, rather than self-interest, dictated his actions. A member of the Privy Council.

HERRIES, John Maxwell, 4th Lord (c. 1512–83). An early adherent of the Lords of the Congregation and a friend of John Knox. He later became an active supporter of the Queen.

HUNTLY, George Gordon, 5th Earl of (c. 1535–76). Unlike his father, the 4th Earl (see below), he was a Protestant. A devoted supporter of the Queen and ally of the Earl of Bothwell.

LENNOX, Matthew Stuart, 4th Earl of (1516–71). His religious persuasions were a matter of political pragmatism, but he eventually identified himself with the Protestant cause. He was one of the chief nobles of Scotland, but had been exiled in 1543 for furthering English interests in that country. He married Lady Margaret Douglas, niece of Henry VIII of England; Lord Darnley was their eldest son.

LINDSAY, Patrick, 5th Lord (1521–89). A fanatical but violent adherent of John Knox, he was one of the first Lords to join the reformers.

LIVINGSTON, William, 6th Lord (c. 1528–92). A staunch supporter of the Queen, who stayed at his seat, Callendar House near Falkirk, on several occasions. His sister was Mary Livingston, one of the four Maries.

MAITLAND, Sir William, of Lethington (c. 1528–73). Secretary of State from 1558, and one of the Lords of the Congregation. He married Mary Fleming, one of the four Maries. A subtle, brilliant and devious politician and diplomat.

MAR, John Erskine, 1st Earl of Mar (c. 1510–72). Trained for the Roman Catholic priesthood, he later embraced the reformed faith. He became a member of the Privy Council and the Governor of Edinburgh Castle.

MORAY, James Stewart, Earl of (c. 1531–70). The Queen's half-brother, being the son of James V by Margaret Erskine, sister of the Earl of Mar. He came to prominence in 1560 as one of the leaders of the Lords of the Congregation, and was to play a cental part in the politics of the reign.

MORTON, James Douglas, 4th Earl of (c. 1516–81). Chancellor of Scotland from 1562, and head of the powerful House of Douglas. One of the most zealous of the Lords of the Congregation.

OCHILTREE, Andrew Stewart, 2nd Baron (c. 1520–97). A fervent supporter of the Lords of the Congregation. His friend John Knox married his daughter.

ROTHES, Andrew Leslie, 5th Earl of (c. 1530–1611). One of the foremost Lords of the Congregation. A member of the Privy Council.

RUTHVEN, Patrick, 3rd Lord (c. 1520–66). Although a fanatical Protestant and one of the Lords of the Congregation, he had an evil reputation as a sorcerer. He was a member of the Privy Council.

2. THE CATHOLIC LORDS

ATHOLL, John Stewart, 4th Earl of (d. 1579). Leader of the Catholic nobility, and one of only three Lords who opposed the Protestant Reformation. Member of Queen Mary's Privy Council.

CAITHNESS, George Sinclair, 4th Earl of (c. 1520–82). Although a devout Catholic and a member of the Privy Council, he had a reputation for violence. Briefly imprisoned for murder in 1563. Chiefly concerned with local politics in the far north.

EGLINTON, Hugh Montgomerie, 3rd Earl of (c. 1531–85). Although a Catholic, he supported the Lords of the Congregation. He was a staunch supporter of Queen Mary and upheld her right to hear Mass.

HOME, Alexander, 5th Baron (c. 1528–75). A member of the Privy Council. Preferring to remain neutral in matters of religion, he refused to join the Lords of the Congregation and, later, to attend Mass with the Queen.

HUNTLY, George Gordon, 4th Earl of (c. 1510/14–62). Chancellor of Scotland from 1546. His mother was a natural daughter of James IV. One of the leading Catholic nobles, he had a strong power base in the north-east. His fleeting flirtation with the Lords of the Congregation in 1560 dealt a fatal blow to the Catholic cause in Scotland.

SETON, George, 5th Lord (c. 1532–85). Always a devoted supporter of Mary, he was a member of the Privy Council and Master of the Queen's Household. He remained a staunch Catholic. His sister was Mary Seton, one of the four Maries.

Mary, Queen of Scots, and the Murder of Lord Darnley

PROLOGUE:

KIRK O'FIELD, EDINBURGH,

10 FEBRUARY 1567

FEW SOULS WERE ABROAD IN Edinburgh after midnight on 9 February 1567. Not only was it bitterly cold with a light frosting of snow, but in an age of candles and rushlights, people tended to go to bed earlier than they do now. Anyone found on the streets at the dead of night was likely to be challenged by the watch.

To the south of the city lay a quadrangle of collegiate buildings attached to the adjacent ruined Kirk of St. Mary in the Fields. Here, all appeared to be quiet. An hour or so before midnight, Queen Mary and her retinue had departed from the quadrangle, bound for Holyrood Palace, leaving behind, in his temporary residence, the Old Provost's Lodging, Mary's convalescent consort, King Henry, better known to history as Henry Stuart, Lord Darnley. Darnley had retired for the night as soon as Mary left; he wanted to be up early the next morning. The only sign of life at Kirk o'Field, we are told, was a single light burning in the window of the imposing Duke's House, which belonged to the powerful Hamilton family.

We now know, of course, that all was not quiet at Kirk o'Field on that night, and that the area was in fact the scene of a great deal of conspiratorial activity throughout the evening of the 9th and the small hours of the 10th. Who these conspirators were has been a matter of furious historical debate for four centuries, but what is certain is that, at two o'clock on the morning of 10 February, the Old Provost's Lodging was blasted into rubble by a mighty explosion that reverberated across the city of Edinburgh, awakened most of its inhabitants, and sparked one of the greatest murder mysteries in history. For the chief victim was no less a personage than the King himself.

The reverberations from that explosion were keenly felt by those implicated—rightly or wrongly—in the plot during the months and years that followed, and they have been echoing down the centuries ever since. For over four hundred years, controversy has raged over who murdered Darnley and how he died. Many thought then, and still think now, that Queen Mary was an accessory before the fact to the murder of her husband, for she certainly had sufficient motives for getting rid of him. Yet so did several other people, including most of the Scottish nobility. And Darnley himself, incredible as it may seem, was not above suspicion.

The question of Mary's guilt is crucial, and continues to provoke heated debate. It is time, therefore, for a fresh, objective reappraisal of the mystery of Kirk o'Field. Despite the conflicting nature of the contemporary evidence and the obscuration of centuries of theory, romantic myths, suppositions, speculation, prejudice and uninformed opinion, I believe that it is indeed possible to unravel what actually happened on that long-ago night in Edinburgh, and to point the finger at who was responsible.

ALISON WEIR
Scottish Borders
28 July 2002

INTRODUCTION:
THE CONTROVERSY
AND THE SOURCES

HE MURDER OF LORD DARNLEY is the most celebrated mystery in Scottish history; it has been endlessly recounted by numerous historians and writers, and the question that has most exercised all of them is this: was Mary, Queen of Scots the instigator of, or a party to, the murder of her husband? That is the question that I aim to answer in this book.

The circumstantial evidence against Mary is weighty, but it is not conclusive. Furthermore, there are other suspects. However, most writers focus upon Mary because she was a young and beautiful queen, whose life had already been touched by tragedy, murder and intrigue. Her character is an enigma that has never been solved, and during the four centuries in which she has been the subject of intense scholarly and popular scrutiny, every aspect of her life has become controversial.

Any study of Mary's possible role in Darnley's murder must take into account changing historical perceptions of her over the centuries. After the murder, which led to her enforced abdication and her long imprisonment in England, she became a contentious figure. Scottish Calvinists saw her as an adulteress and murderess, and for political reasons vigorously painted her as such, while Mary's Catholic and loyalist supporters regarded her as a wronged heroine. As memories of the murder faded, and she became the hope of the Counter-Reformation and the focus for Catholic plots against Elizabeth I, Mary herself consciously fostered a pious image, which culminated in her calculated and dramatic appearance as a martyr for her faith at her execution in 1587. English Protestants, it should be remembered, found her an altogether more sinister figure, and not without reason.

Yet Mary's dignified courage as she faced the block has had a profound effect on the way in which most of her biographers have portrayed her; this image has, to a great extent, swept away darker contemporary perceptions of her, and as time passed it helped to enshrine her in romance and legend. Back in the sixteenth and seventeenth centuries, however, observers were more preoccupied with Mary's religious and dynastic significance.

Predictably, most Catholic writers saw Mary as a Catholic martyr. Yet after the accession of her son, James VI of Scotland, to the throne of England in 1603, even Protestant historians began to find praise for her, mindful, no doubt, of King James I's determination to rehabilitate the memories of both his parents. Mary, it was now agreed, had been unfortunate rather than immoral.

It was not until the eighteenth century—when much of the contemporary source material became available for the first time—that Mary was seen as a woman who allowed her emotions to rule her acts and was therefore responsible to a degree for her own destruction. Historians such as David Hume and William Robertson criticised her for succumbing to overt and unwise passions. This view gave rise to a trend, which continued into the nineteenth century, for portraying Mary as the frivolous victim of a licentious upbringing at the French court, whose unrestrained sexual intrigues brought about her downfall. Religion was still a factor: the eminent but prejudiced Victorian historian, James Anthony Froude, was grimly censorious of the Catholic Mary, and shamelessly massaged the facts in order to show her in the worst possible light. At the turn of the century, the controversy over Mary's involvement in Darnley's murder was kept alive by a spirited debate between the historians T.F. Henderson and Andrew Lang.

During the twentieth century, historians were kinder to the Queen of Scots. Thanks to the ongoing reappraisal of contemporary evidence, new theories about Darnley's murder were put forward, and Mary came to be viewed in a more sympathetic light. After Antonia Fraser published what has become the standard biography of the Queen in 1969, most historians have concluded that Mary was an innocent and much wronged victim of the unscrupulous men around her. A virtually lone voice is that of the historian Jenny Wormald, who believes that Mary was an abject failure as both a queen and a woman, and that she was an accomplice in Darnley's murder.

Anyone writing about Mary, Queen of Scots today has to penetrate beyond the several stereotypical images that have evolved throughout the centuries—the adulteress and murderess, the *femme fatale*, the romantic tragic heroine, the religious martyr and the foolish victim of her own passions—to look for the real Mary and attempt to establish some estimation of her true character in order to determine whether or not she was capable of murder.

Central to the issue of Mary's guilt, seemingly, are the controversial Casket Letters. If genuine, they go a long way towards proving her involvement in Darnley's murder, but many have argued that they are forgeries or genuine letters that have been deliberately altered by Mary's enemies. It should be said, however, that Mary's guilt or innocence can be determined by other evidence than the Casket Letters, and that their importance has been somewhat overstated.

As an English historian married for thirty years to a native of Edinburgh, I have long been entranced by Scottish history, and I have visited, on many occasions, most of the places mentioned in this book. It had long been my intention, following on from the success of *The Princes in the Tower*, to write about another historical mystery, and I was delighted to be given the opportunity to take a fresh look at one of Scotland's most celebrated crimes.

I make no apologies for the long build-up to Darnley's murder in this book. It is essential to establish the characters, motives and relationships between the various protagonists, and also to examine the sequence of events leading to Darnley's violent death, in order to arrive at a full understanding of what took place at Kirk o'Field. It is equally important to trace the course of the relationship between Mary and Darnley, and also to examine the history of Mary's policy on religion, because that may well shed light upon the murder.

Nor do I apologise for the length of the text. Every aspect of this case is controversial, and for any study to be credible and exhaustive, each piece of evidence that has a bearing on the conclusion needs to be fully examined and re-evaluated. There is, also, a large cast of suspects whose actions need to be tracked.

Above all, it is vital to become familiar with the bias in contemporary source material, because that is as relevant to solving the mystery of Kirk o'Field as the deeds of those who were there on that fateful night. The chief problem facing the historian is that most of the evidence about Mary comes from hostile later sources that were composed with the specific purpose of proving her guilt, such as propaganda written by the zealous Protestant scholar George Buchanan and by Darnley's father, the Earl of Lennox.

Some scholars did write in Mary's defence, notably John Leslie, Bishop of Ross, who defended her against her Scottish accusers, and the intelligent and able Claude Nau, who became Mary's Secretary in 1575 and wrote his *Memorials* of her reign in Scotland three years later. Nau's informant was probably Mary herself: no one else in her entourage at that time could have had such an intimate knowledge of the details of her life in the 1560s; Nau's work is therefore the closest to an official account that we have.

The memoirs of Mary's third husband, the Earl of Bothwell, which were written in 1568 whilst he was a prisoner in exile in Denmark, have very little to say about Darnley's murder. Bothwell was widely believed to have been the man who plotted Darnley's death, so it is unlikely that he would have revealed anything incriminating, especially in a work that was written "to enable the King of Denmark to get a better and clearer idea of the wickedness and treason of those who are accusing me."[1]

In the circumstances, I have preferred to rely on strictly contemporary sources such as diplomatic reports and letters, circumstantial evidence, and a source known as the *Diurnal of Occurrents*, a diary of events written by an anonymous observer living in Edinburgh, which is generally accurate, if biased against Mary. Where I have used prejudiced contemporary sources, I have done so with caution.

1

THE THREE CROWNS

≈

TO EVERYONE'S DISMAY,[1] THE BABY born to James V of Scotland
and his second wife, Marie de Guise, on 8 December 1542[2] at Linlithgow Palace was a girl. After the deaths of two infant sons in 1541, her father
had hoped for another boy to succeed him, because Scotland needed a man's
strong hand to rule it. For James V was already mortally ill, and following a
crushing defeat by the English at the Battle of Solway Moss on 24 November, he had taken to his bed at Falkland Palace. When news was brought to
him of the birth of his daughter, he turned his face to the wall and, recalling
that the crown had descended to the Stewart dynasty through Marjorie,
daughter of King Robert the Bruce, muttered, "It came from a woman, and
it will end in a woman."[3] Soon afterwards he died, "wherefore there was great
mourning in Scotland."[4]

At only six days old, the infant Mary became Queen of Scots. Scotland
was used to royal minorities, for every one of its monarchs since 1406 had
succeeded as a child. As a result, the nobility had grown in strength and autonomy, having become used to long periods without royal interference during which they enjoyed the unfettered exercise of power. These minorities
had also bred rivalries and factions, as different families struggled for power.

In March 1543, Parliament appointed Mary's cousin and next heir, James

Hamilton, Earl of Arran, as Second Person and Governor of the Realm until the Queen attained her majority at the age of twelve. Arran, then twenty-seven, was a Protestant, and head of the powerful Hamilton clan, whose lands straddled Clydesdale and central Scotland. An English envoy described the Hamiltons as a good looking race, but vicious, faithless and inept.[5] Arran's claim to the succession was not undisputed, because there was uncertainty as to whether his parents had been lawfully married; hence his overriding purpose in life was to establish the legality of his claim. Self-interest and the advancement of his House dictated his political policies, but his indolence, instability and lack of decisiveness lost him the support of many nobles.

The King of England at that time was Henry VIII, and he was resolved to marry his five-year-old son and heir, Prince Edward, to the little Queen of Scots, and thereby unite England and Scotland under Tudor rule. Arran, eager to secure the support of the English King for his claims, was willing to co-operate, and on 1 July 1543 a treaty was concluded at Greenwich, which provided for the marriage of Mary and Edward. Mary was to go to England when she was ten, and be married the following year.

But the Catholic party in Scotland, led by Marie de Guise and Cardinal David Beaton, were opposed to the treaty. They removed Mary from Arran's care, took her to Stirling Castle, and had her crowned there, in the Chapel Royal, on 9 September. In December, a Catholic-dominated Parliament repudiated Mary's betrothal and renewed the ancient alliance between Scotland and France, England's enemy.

Henry VIII was incensed, and in 1544 retaliated by sending an army to Scotland. The savage campaign that followed became known as the "rough wooing": in the course of it, scores of towns, villages and abbeys in the southeast were mercilessly sacked and burned, leaving vast swathes of devastation. Even the city of Edinburgh did not escape Henry's fury: he had ordered his commanders to sack, "burn and subvert it, and put every man, woman and child to the sword."[6] Far from bringing the Scots to heel, the barbarity of the English only strengthened them in their resolve.

In 1543, there had returned to Scotland a man who was to play a prominent role in the drama of Mary, Queen of Scots. Matthew Stuart, 4th Earl of Lennox, whose power base was centred upon Glasgow, had been born in 1516 at Dumbarton, and had succeeded to his earldom at the age of ten, after the murder of his father by Arran's bastard half-brother. This was cause enough for bad blood between Lennox and Arran, but they were also bitter rivals for the succession. Like Arran, Lennox was descended from Mary, daughter of James II, but only in the female line; unlike Arran, he had been born in undisputed wedlock. With such contentious issues dividing them, there could be no friendship between the Lennox Stuarts and the Hamiltons.

In 1531, Lennox had gone to France, where he joined the royal guard, became a naturalised subject of the French King and changed the spelling of his surname from Stewart to Stuart. Twelve years later, to Arran's consternation, he returned to Scotland and began paying court to Marie de Guise. Like most women, she found him handsome, charming and gallant: he was "a strong man of personage, well-proportioned with lusty and manly visage, and carried himself erect and stately, wherefore he was very pleasant in the sight of gentlewomen."[7] A well-educated man, he spoke fluent French and was skilled at playing the lute. The Queen Dowager and Cardinal Beaton believed Lennox to be an ardent Francophile who would support them against the ambitions of Arran. But Lennox was unreliable, treacherous and driven by self-interest, and when Marie refused to marry him, he defected to the English in search of better prospects. In return for his support against the Scots, Henry VIII bestowed on him the hand of his niece, Lady Margaret Douglas.

The wedding took place in July 1544 at St. James's Palace in London. Born in 1515, Margaret was the daughter of Henry VIII's elder sister, Margaret Tudor (widow of James IV and grandmother of Mary, Queen of Scots) by her second husband, Archibald Douglas, Earl of Angus; Margaret was therefore near in blood to the English throne, and a marriage between her and Lennox could only reinforce the dynastic claims of both parties. Yet although their union was politically advantageous, it was also a love match on both sides: he was said to be "far in love,"[8] and in his letters, he addressed his wife as "mine own sweet Madge" or "my Meg," told her she was his "chiefest comfort," and signed himself "Your own Matthieu and most loving husband." Margaret was a devout Catholic, so Lennox, who had been reared in the old faith but recently converted to Protestantism, now tempered his spiritual views to please his wife and King Henry; religion was ever a matter of expediency with him.

Margaret Douglas was a formidable woman. Beautiful, intelligent, domineering and relentlessly ambitious, she had an alarming talent for dangerous intrigue. She had spent much of her youth at the English court and become a great favourite of her uncle the King, but incurred his anger when she twice, in 1536 and 1541, became involved with unsuitable men; on each occasion Henry sent her for a spell in the Tower, a place with which she was to be become all too familiar during the course of her turbulent life. There can be no doubt that Margaret Douglas became the driving force in the Lennoxes' marriage.

In 1545, Lennox led an English army into Scotland in the hope of taking Dumbarton Castle for Henry VIII. It was during this campaign that he ordered the slaughter of eleven child hostages whose Scottish fathers had been forced into his ranks and then defected;[9] this earned him undying notoriety and a perpetually haunted conscience. His offensive ended in failure, and on 1 October the Scottish Parliament attainted him for treason and confiscated all his estates and titles, some of which were given to Arran. Lennox was now the most hated man in Scotland. For the next nineteen years, he remained an exile in England, living on the bounty of Henry VIII. The Lennoxes' chief seat was Temple Newsham in Yorkshire, and they owned another house nearby at Settrington. When in London, they resided at the former royal manor of Hackney. Lennox never abandoned hope of regaining his lost lands and asserting his dynastic claims, his ambitions having been sharpened by his grand marriage and the birth of eight children, who inherited the royal blood of both Scotland and England.

During the 1540s, the impact of the Protestant Reformation began to be felt in Scotland. For decades now, the Catholic Church in Scotland had been morally lax and corrupt, and there had been calls for its reform. Now, religious affiliations became identified with political issues, and two noble factions emerged: the Catholics, who favoured the "auld alliance" with France, and a growing number of Protestants, who wanted closer relations with England, whose King, although a Catholic, had severed links with the Church of Rome and declared himself Supreme Head of the Church of England.

Trouble began when a Protestant heretic, George Wishart, was burned on the orders of Cardinal Beaton in 1546. In reprisal, Wishart's followers brutally murdered Cardinal Beaton, then held out for a year in St. Andrews Castle before the arrival of a French fleet forced them to surrender. Among those taken prisoner was the reformist preacher John Knox, who would one day become one of the prime movers in the Protestant Reformation. He was sentenced to two years as a galley slave.

In 1547, when Henry VIII died and was succeeded by the nine-year-old Edward VI, England became a Protestant state. The Lord Protector, Edward Seymour, Duke of Somerset, was determined to carry on the war against Scotland, and ordered another invasion. On 10 September 1547, the Scots under Arran suffered a devastating defeat at the Battle of Pinkie Cleugh, which enabled the English to occupy south-eastern Scotland. On the day after the battle, the Scots hastily moved their little Queen to Inchmahome Priory for safety, and appealed to the French for aid.

By January 1548, Arran, who had hoped to marry his own son to Mary, was negotiating with King Henry II of France for her marriage to Henry's eldest son, the Dauphin Francis. Mary's maternal uncles, Francis, Duke of Guise and Charles de Guise, Cardinal of Lorraine, were rising men at the French court, and they, foreseeing great advantages to themselves through the marriage of their niece to the heir to the French throne, added their persuasions to Arran's. Henry was more than amenable, as he realised that the match was of far greater benefit to France than Scotland, for it would ultimately bring Scotland under French control, since a wife, even a crowned queen, was always subject to her husband. Given the situation they were in, the Scots 'had little choice in the matter: whether they married Mary to a French or an English prince, they would be under threat of interference by a foreign power. In the circumstances, it seemed safer to ally with an old friend than a hostile enemy, and in February 1548, the Scottish Parliament gave its consent to the marriage. In return, the French promised to send troops to help expel the English garrisons from Scotland. At the end of the month, Mary was moved to the greater safety of Dumbarton Castle.

In June, having cut a swathe through the occupying forces, a French army recaptured the strategic town of Haddington in East Lothian, and there, on 7 July, a treaty was signed formally providing for the marriage of Mary to the Dauphin, with provisions for safeguarding Scotland's future political autonomy.

Arran was now a spent force, although he was to remain Regent for six more years. Real power in Scotland now lay in the hands of the Queen Dowager, who was determined to protect her daughter's interests and preserve her

Catholic kingdom intact. In order to ensure Arran's support, she persuaded the French King to grant him the dukedom of Chatelherault, and promoted his bastard half-brother, John Hamilton, Abbot of Paisley to the office of Archbishop of St. Andrews and Primate of Scotland.

The new Archbishop, who was one day to be accused of involvement in Darnley's murder, was the most able and opportunist politician of all the Hamiltons, and a liberal conservative in religion. Wily and self-seeking, like all his family, "he spent the least part of his time in spiritual contemplations"[10] and led "a life somewhat dissolute"[11] with a "harlot" called Grizzel Sempill, who bore him at least three children, and was the widow of the Provost of Edinburgh. For his sins, Hamilton contracted syphilis, and in 1566 underwent an expensive course of mercury treatment. Marie de Guise ignored the scandals of the Archbishop's private life; she hoped he would be the saviour of the Catholic Church in Scotland.

On 7 August 1548, the five-year-old Mary said goodbye to her mother and her kingdom, and sailed to France. Amongst her attendants were four well-born girls of similar age to her own, all called Mary, who were to be her special companions, and to whom she became especially close: vivacious Mary Livingston, beautiful Mary Beaton, devout Mary Seton and enchanting Mary Fleming.

When Henry II first saw Mary, he declared she was "the most perfect child that I have ever seen."[12] From the first, he treated her as his own daughter, and placed her in the household of his children by his Florentine Queen, Catherine de' Medici. Mary was to grow up in luxurious royal châteaux such as Blois, Chambord and Fontainebleau, surrounded by the art and culture of the Renaissance and the sophisticated, glittering life of the court, where she was petted and pampered by all who came into contact with her, and particularly by her magnificent Guise uncles, who hoped for great things from her in the future, and who guided her in all matters.

Yet the French court was also a moral cesspit, and Mary was exposed from an early age to its promiscuity and corruption. Her own governess bore the King a bastard child. "Here, it is not the men who solicit the women, but the women the men," observed the Queen of Navarre disapprovingly.[13] The court was ruled by the King's mistress, the elegant and cultivated Diane de Poitiers, who was nineteen years his senior yet still beautiful. An affronted Queen Catherine was relegated to the sidelines while Diane was given responsibility for arranging the education of the royal children. From Diane, Mary learned to regard Catherine with contempt, and consequently the Queen "had a great misliking" of her daughter-in-law.[14]

The moral laxity of the court is reflected in two paintings that apparently show a teenaged Mary, the future Queen of France, in the nude. Two figures in the erotic allegorical work *The Bath of Diana*, attributed to Francis Clouet (now in the Musée des Beaux Arts, Rouen) are thought to be portraits of Mary, and she is almost certainly the bare-breasted sitter wearing a ruff and headdress in the portrait of *A Lady at her Toilet* by an artist of the School of Fontainebleau (now in the Worcester Art Museum, Massachusetts).[15] It is not known whether Mary herself posed naked for these pictures, or whether her portrait was superimposed on the body of a nude model, but the portrayal of her in such poses belies the later image she fostered of a prim and virtuous princess.

Even the royal children were tainted by the corruption of the court. Both their grandfathers had died of syphilis, and its effects were now tragically apparent in them. Of the ten children born to Henry II and Catherine de' Medici, Francis was sickly and feeble, Charles suffered from hallucinations, Henry became a homosexual cross-dresser, and Marguerite a nymphomaniac who had an incestuous affair with her brother Hercule.

Mary's closest companion in childhood and youth was her future husband, the ugly little Dauphin Francis, for whom she early on conceived a tender affection. Born in January 1544, he was weak and sickly from birth. His growth was stunted, and he was afflicted not only by a permanently running nose but also, later on, by such terrible eczema that it was reported he had leprosy.[16] As a result, he was shy, moody and difficult, but he soon grew very fond of Mary, and she, in turn, referred to him as her "sweetheart and friend."[17]

Mary was brought up as a devout Catholic, and received a Renaissance education alongside her future husband and his siblings. She was taught sophisticated literary skills and elegant calligraphy. In an age of developing diplomacy, there was great emphasis on languages. French became Mary's first language, and would remain so for the rest of her life; she did retain enough of her native Scots to be able to converse in it as an adult, although she never became proficient at writing it.[18] She also gained "a useful knowledge"[19] of Spanish, Italian, Latin and Greek, but did not begin to learn English until 1568. Mary brought back 240 books from France to replace the royal library at Holyrood Palace in Edinburgh that had been destroyed by the English in 1544, and these were in a wide variety of languages, including Latin and Greek; there were books on history, music, geography, astronomy and theology, a selection of the works of antiquity, and a large number of romances and poetry books in French and Italian, the latter being Mary's preferred reading. The great poet Pierre de Ronsard himself taught her to write quite competent courtly verse.

The young Queen was an intelligent girl with a quick mind, who enjoyed learning for its own sake. Although not an intellectual like her cousin, the future Elizabeth I of England, she read a great deal for pleasure, and "there was hardly any branch of human knowledge of which she could not talk well."[20]

Mary was also taught the traditional feminine accomplishments: many surviving examples of her work testify to her skilled needlework and embroidery, and she was also good at drawing. Dancing became one of her favourite pastimes, and she learned to carry herself with perfect grace and agility in the ballets and masques in which she took part at the French court. She sang beautifully and played the lute, cittern, harp and virginals "reasonably well for a queen."[21] Mary was early on introduced to the pleasures of hunting, hawking and other outdoor pursuits, including archery, pell-mell (croquet) and later, in Scotland, golf; she became an expert and fearless horsewoman, and was never happier than when in the saddle. She also loved fine clothing, dogs, tame birds, long walks, puppet plays from Italy, and games such as cards, dice, chess, billiards and tables (backgammon).

Henry II saw to it that the Scots in Mary's household were gradually replaced by French people. Mary herself began to adopt the French spelling of her surname, Stuart, and always signed herself "Marie." There is little evidence that she received any formal training in political skills, for everyone, herself included, expected her to remain in France. Scotland would be governed by others on her behalf, so there was no necessity for her to be trained specifically for the duties of a queen regnant. Mary's Guise uncles were there to advise if she needed any guidance in matters of state, but she was also growing up in a court where intrigue and brutality were commonplace, and she must have learned something of the Machiavellian nature of Renaissance politics, the manipulation of political factions and the contemporary controversies over religion just by observing what went on around her.

In 1551, two years after the occupying English forces were finally driven out of Scotland, peace was concluded between the two kingdoms. In 1553, Edward VI died, and was succeeded by his Catholic half-sister, Mary I, who was to spend her reign re-establishing the Church of Rome in England and devoutly burning Protestants. In 1554, Marie de Guise finally replaced Chatelherault as Regent of Scotland, and immediately revived the Auld Alliance with France, in the hope of stemming the swelling tide of Protestantism in Scotland. The Queen Dowager strengthened her position by relying on French advisers and French troops, for whom her daughter's subjects were expected to pay, but this only served to alienate the proud and independent Scots, who feared that their country was in danger of ending up as a satellite state of France.

By 1557, the new religion had not only grown in popularity but had also become widely associated with an injured sense of national identity, born out of resentment against unwelcome French interference. That year, five leading Protestant nobles banded together and, calling themselves the Lords of the Congregation of Jesus Christ, allied with militant reformist preachers and signed a bond, or covenant, undertaking to establish the new faith as the national religion of Scotland.

The Lords of the Congregation increased immeasurably in strength in 1558, when Mary's powerful and influential bastard half-brother, the sternly Calvinist Lord James Stewart, joined them with a large following and publicly proclaimed that the Lords of Scotland would embrace the Protestant faith and restore Scotland's independence.

Lord James Stewart, who was to play a momentous and often enigmatic role in Mary's life, had been born around 1531, and was the most able and prominent of the nine bastard children of James V. His mother was Margaret Erskine; at the time of her liaison with James V, she had been married to Sir Robert Douglas of Lochleven. James had petitioned the Pope to have the marriage annulled, so that he could marry his mistress, but in vain. In adulthood, Lord James himself tried unsuccessfully to have his parents' union legalised retrospectively.

Lord James's bastardy was evidently a matter of great bitterness and resentment to him, for it prevented him from wearing the crown of Scotland, a role for which he was eminently suited, both by nature and by ability. He looked like a Stuart king, being tall and dark with a distinctly regal bearing and a commanding presence. Having to give place to his half-sister, a Catholic ruler, and a female at that, cannot have been easy for one who was ambitious, strong-willed, clever and capable, and his jealousy certainly had a profound bearing on the future relations between himself and Mary, which were amicable, and often affectionate, so long as she deferred to his wisdom and judgement. For James was not interested in the outward show of royalty, but in the actual exercise of sovereign power.

Many, then and since, among them Mary herself, have claimed that Lord James never ceased from scheming to seize the Scottish throne, and certainly his record over the coming years would appear to suggest that this was his ultimate aim. Had that been the case, however, it is surprising that he did not grasp the opportunity to usurp the throne on the two occasions when he had the chance to do so.

For centuries, historians have debated whether Lord James was an upright man who acted on principle, or a treacherous villain who cleverly managed to cover his tracks and find unarguably sound pretexts for his actions: indeed, in nearly every instance, his behaviour can be interpreted in both lights. He was a man "whose peculiar art was to appear to do nothing whilst, in truth, he did all."[22] Whenever there was trouble or scandal, he was always absent. And although it was said of him that he "dealt, according to his nature, rudely, homely and bluntly,"[23] he was ruthless, devious, subtle, and cautious in the extreme.

There can be little doubt of the sincerity and consistency of Lord James's stern Calvinist convictions, nor that in his private life he was a model of austere rectitude. No personal scandal ever attached to his name, and he was reputed to be honest, which virtues earned him great popularity with the middle classes. Yet when it came to material things he was greedy, and through steady advancement, the acquisition of ecclesiastical property, and the bounty of his sister, he managed to make himself the richest man in Scotland.

One Protestant lord who refused to join the Lords of the Congregation was the mighty James Hepburn, 4th Earl of Bothwell, who was perhaps the Queen Regent's most staunch supporter and who could not be shifted from his loyalty to the Crown.

Bothwell, whose destiny was to be fatally linked to Mary's, had been born around 1535 and succeeded his father to the earldom and the hereditary office of Lord High Admiral in 1556. The Hepburn territory was centred upon the fertile and rich region of East Lothian, and the family's chief seat was Crichton Castle, eight miles south of Edinburgh. James had been educated in the household of his promiscuous uncle, Patrick Hepburn, Bishop of Moray, at Spynie near Inverness, and in the university schools of Paris. He was a cultivated, literate man, interested in science and warfare, and spoke fluent French and some Latin and Greek.

In 1557, Bothwell had commanded a military force that raided the English border, and for much of his life he would play a major role in suppressing lawlessness in the Scottish Borders. He mortally hated the English and, unlike almost all the rest of the Scottish nobility, would never accept bribes from them, which was commendable as he was always chronically short of money.

Contemporaries referred to Bothwell as "a splendid, rash and hazardous young man,"[24] "high in his own conceit, proud, vicious and vainglorious above measure, one who would attempt anything out of ambition."[25] His enemies said he was "false and untrue as the devil,"[26] the "sink of all horrible sins."[27] Although he was "all his lifetime a faithful servant of the Crown, a man valiant above all others," he was also "audacious, inconstant and changeable."[28]

Bothwell was certainly a volatile, violent and turbulent man, but hardly the "monstrous beast" or "bag of vice"[29] he was made out to be by his foes. Sir Henry Percy, a respected English adversary, was impressed with Bothwell when he met him, and declared he was "very wise, and not the man he was reputed to be. His behaviour was both courteous and honourable."[30]

Bothwell was probably about five feet six inches tall,[31] and of strong, muscular build with dark cropped hair and a moustache. His later enemy, George Buchanan, described him as looking "like an ape in purple," and his language was of a similar lurid colour.[32] Yet women found him irresistible, and his private life was constantly the subject of scandal, for he had an insatiable appetite for sex and a very amoral attitude towards marriage. In 1559, aged twenty-four, he had an affair with his neighbour at Branxholm, Janet Beaton, the Lady of Buccleuch, who was nineteen years his senior, had been married three times, and had seven children. She was also reputed to have resorted to sorcery to preserve her beauty. There is some evidence that she and Bothwell went through some sort of handfasting ceremony, but there is no evidence that they were ever married. After their affair ended, they remained friends.

Bothwell himself was frequently accused by his enemies of practising witchcraft in order to achieve his ambitions, and was said to have become acquainted with the black arts whilst a student in Paris. He was also accused, again mainly by his enemies, of sodomy with men. Mary's apologist, John Leslie, Bishop of Ross, called him vicious and dissolute in his habits, while a hostile English observer wrote, "He was a fit man to be minister to a shamful act, be it either against God or man."[33] Neither accusation is very explicit. But Bothwell's former servant, Paris, later confessed, "I knew his very terrible vices, especially one in which I am said to be so good a minister. I told him it would be his ruin." He recalled Bothwell reminding him, "You covered my dishonour when you were in my service abroad."[34] Paris's confession was extracted under the threat of torture by men who needed to destroy Bothwell's reputation, so little reliance may be based upon it. Nor can we trust the testimony of Dandie Pringle, a servant dismissed by Bothwell for trying to poison him, who told the English Governor of Berwick that the Earl was "as naughty a man as liveth, and much given to that vile and detestable vice of sodomy."[35] A scurrilous ballad by Robert Sempill, written after Bothwell's fall, also accused Bothwell of "beastly buggery,"[36] but may be dismissed as sheer character assassination by an extremist propagandist. However, given the consistency of the accusations, and the variety of people making them, there is at least a possibility that there was some truth in them.

. . .

On 4 April 1558, as the time approached for her marriage to the Dauphin, Mary, probably on the advice of the Guises, signed a secret treaty with Henry II, pledging that, if she died without issue, Scotland would become subject to the French Crown. This amounted to a betrayal of her kingdom and her Scottish heirs, and is proof that she retained little affection for, or pride in, the land of her birth, and that, thanks to the influences around her, she had come to regard it as a mere appendage of France.

Three weeks later, on 24 April, Mary and Francis were married in a magnificent ceremony at Notre-Dame in Paris. The bride was fifteen, the bridegroom fourteen. Although the Venetian ambassador reported that the marriage was consummated on the wedding night,[37] there is some doubt about this. Francis apparently suffered from undescended testicles, and was said to be sexually immature. However, in the late summer of 1559, Mary appeared at court in the floating tunic of a pregnant woman, obviously believing herself to be with child. In the autumn, she was ill, and nothing more is heard of the hoped-for heir to the throne. The Spanish ambassador commented that, if Mary did bear a child, "it will certainly not be the King's."[38]

In England, on 17 November 1558, Mary I died, to the great relief of most of her subjects, and was succeeded by her twenty-five-year-old half-sister, Elizabeth I. Elizabeth was the daughter of Henry VIII by his second wife, Anne Boleyn, whom he had married in defiance of the Pope, who refused to annul Henry's first marriage to Katherine of Aragon, mother of Mary I. It was chiefly for this reason that Henry had broken with Rome; but in the eyes of Catholic Europe, Elizabeth was a bastard and unfit to inherit the throne, and the true successor to Mary I was Mary, Queen of Scots.

The Act of Succession of 1544 and Henry VIII's Will of 1546 laid down that the crown of England was to descend to Edward VI and his heirs, then to Mary I and her heirs, and lastly to Elizabeth I and her heirs. Both Edward and Mary had died childless, and Elizabeth was as yet unmarried, much to the consternation of her advisers. Failing these lines, the throne was to pass to the heirs of Henry VIII's younger sister Mary, and then to anyone else the King might designate. The descendants of his older sister Margaret had been passed over, because Margaret Tudor had relinquished her claim to the English throne on her marriage to James IV in 1503, and because Henry VIII was hoping to annex Scotland to England through the marriage of Mary to Prince Edward.

Mary therefore had no right to the succession under English law, but Henry II ignored this minor detail, and on the day of Elizabeth's accession had Francis and Mary proclaimed King and Queen of England, on the grounds that Elizabeth was a baseborn usurper; the English royal arms were quartered with those of France and Scotland on their shields, and they began styling themselves King and Queen of England, Ireland and Scotland in official documents, much to Elizabeth's fury and alarm, for she feared that Henry might try to enforce Mary's claim by mounting a military offensive against her. There were already French troops on her back doorstep in Scotland.

After the horrors of "Bloody Mary's" reign, however, the majority of Elizabeth's subjects would never have meekly accepted another Roman Catholic ruler, particularly one who was a member of the French royal House, and a Guise at that. Many were of the opinion that a foreigner born outside the realm could not legally inherit the throne, since aliens could not inherit property in England. In the event, Henry II had no immediate intention of making war on Elizabeth, but the real damage caused by his actions was to become apparent in the longer term, for from now on the acquisition of the English crown would be Mary's chief mission in life, more important to her by far than her own kingdom. Mary's pretensions were to permanently sour her relations with Elizabeth, and underpinned all the dealings between them, creating a dangerous climate of resentment and distrust.

Nor were Elizabeth's fears allayed when, in November 1558, the Scottish Parliament agreed that Mary might bestow the Crown Matrimonial on Francis; this effectively made him her heir, in the event of her dying childless, and meant that Scotland might well come under French rule one day.

On 30 June 1559, Henry II was fatally injured when a lance pierced his eye and throat during a tournament held to celebrate the marriage of his daughter Elisabeth to Philip II of Spain. After lingering in agony for ten days, he died on 10 July. Francis and Mary were now King and Queen of France, but Francis's accession signalled a bitter power struggle between the Guises and the Queen Mother, Catherine de' Medici, for political supremacy. Mary, of course, sided with her uncles, thereby incurring the further displeasure of her mother-in-law.

Francis II was crowned at Rheims Cathedral on 18 September 1559; as an anointed monarch in her own right, Mary was a mere observer of the ceremony. Marie de Guise was represented at the coronation by the Earl of Bothwell. Another guest was "a young gentleman who has no beard,"[39] Henry Stuart, Lord Darnley, the twelve-year-old son of the Earl and Countess of Lennox, who had come to offer his parents' congratulations to Francis and Mary on their accession, and also to present a letter petitioning Mary to restore Lennox's lands in Scotland. Although she and Francis received Darnley "with great distinction,"[40] she refused Lennox's request, but sent his son home with a gift of 1,000 crowns.

When Bothwell returned to Scotland after the coronation, the land was in turmoil. The Queen Regent was now involved in a bitter conflict with the Lords of the Congregation; although she had been cautiously supportive of their calls for reform of the Church, she was appalled by the escalating violence and iconoclasm of their movement, and when they began inciting riots and vandalising and desecrating churches and abbeys, she called in French troops to stop them. But this unpopular move only served to strengthen the Lords' resistance, which gathered momentum when the charismatic reformer John Knox returned from exile in May 1559 and allied with Lord James and his Protestant colleagues. Knox's arrival brought more leading nobles over to the Congregation, and his fiery brand of preaching inspired much popular support for the new religion.

During his exile, Knox, a former Catholic priest, had become chaplain to Edward VI. When Mary I succeeded, he fled to Geneva, where he embraced the extreme Protestant views of the Swiss reformer, John Calvin. In 1558, he published a notorious tract against the Catholic Queens, Mary I and Marie de Guise, entitled *First Blast of the Trumpet against the Monstrous Regiment of Women*. In it, he argued that it was against natural and divine law for a woman to hold dominion over men. He was a shrewd, witty man of stern convictions, single-minded and bigoted, "one who neither feared nor flattered any flesh."[41] He loathed any form of frivolity, and severely castigated anyone who indulged in fornication, yet in his fifties he married in succession two sixteen-year-old girls, one of them the daughter of the fervently Calvinist Andrew Stewart, Lord Ochiltree. Knox became Minister of St. Giles's Kirk, the foremost church in Edinburgh, and was given a fine house on the High Street, probably the one still identified as his today, which dates from c. 1490.

The Queen Regent appointed Bothwell her Lieutenant-General, "with special responsibility for affairs of war."[42] Elizabeth I, who had already established the Protestant Church of England, was now secretly supporting the Lords of the Congregation, most of whom were in the pay of the English government. In October, Bothwell intercepted 6,000 crowns that the English had sent to aid the Scottish rebels, and gave them to Marie de Guise. For this, he earned the undying enmity of Lord James, Chatelherault and most of the other Protestant nobles.

In February 1560, the Lords and the English concluded the Treaty of Berwick, whereby Elizabeth agreed to send troops to overthrow the Catholic Regent and drive out the French. In April, an English army laid siege to Leith, which was then held by French troops for Marie de Guise. Later that month, the Lords overthrew the ailing Regent. In her place, Scotland was to be governed on behalf of its absent Queen by a Protestant Great Council comprising Chatelherault, his son, James Hamilton, Earl of Arran, and Lord James: Chatelherault was merely a figurehead—the real power lay with James and Knox. On 11 June, Marie de Guise died of dropsy. When the news reached France, Mary was prostrated with grief for the beloved mother she had not seen for ten years.[43]

Hostilities now ceased, and the Treaty of Leith brought to an end the ancient alliance between Scotland and France. On 6 July, a treaty signed at Edinburgh paved the way for closer and more lasting bonds between Scotland and England. Under its terms, all foreign troops were to leave Scotland, foreigners were to be barred from holding any government office, and the English undertook not to interfere in Scottish affairs; in return, the grateful Scots, on behalf of Queen Mary, recognised Elizabeth as Queen of England, and promised that Mary would renounce her claims to the English throne and succession. The Treaty of Edinburgh was negotiated without Mary's consent, its terms were odious to her, and she would consistently refuse to ratify it, much to Elizabeth's mortification.

In August, the Scottish Parliament met and, in defiance of its lawful sovereign, and without her assent, passed the legislation that would establish the

Protestant Reformation in Scotland. Such legislation was undoubtedly illegal, for Mary refused to ratify it, but it had been enacted in response to popular demand. In an Act opposed by only three peers, without a murmur of protest from Archbishop Hamilton, the Catholic faith was outlawed and the celebration of Mass made a capital offence. When she heard, Mary angrily expressed her disapproval to the English ambassador in Paris: "My subjects of Scotland do their duty in nothing. I am their sovereign, but they take me not so. They must be taught to know their duties."[44] There was talk in Scotland at this time of deposing Mary and replacing her with Lord James, but it came to nothing.

Bothwell, meanwhile, had gone to Denmark, having been sent to Europe to raise support for the late Regent. In Copenhagen, a Norwegian admiral, Christopher Throndssen, offered him the hand of his daughter Anna, with a dowry of 40,000 silver dollars. When Bothwell moved on to Germany and Flanders, Anna went with him and sold her jewellery to finance his travels, for he had spent most of his money in supporting the Regent. Anna and her family later insisted that a marriage had taken place, but this may have been to save face, for there is no record of it, nor of the impecunious Bothwell receiving the dowry, and Anna never styled herself Countess of Bothwell. It seems more likely that she attached herself to Bothwell on the promise of marriage, but that he lost interest in making such a commitment. Anna may have been the mother of his only known bastard, William, to whom Bothwell's mother later willed all her possessions.

The death of Marie de Guise robbed Bothwell of political and financial support in Scotland. He therefore left Anna in Flanders and went to the French court to seek service with Queen Mary and perhaps the restitution of some of the funds he had outlaid. Mary did grant Bothwell an audience, but its outcome is unknown. In the autumn, he rejoined Anna in Flanders.

That November, Francis II fell seriously ill with a virulent inflammation of the middle ear that spread to his brain and caused an abscess.[45] His sufferings were terrible and prolonged, and on 5 December he passed away, aged not quite seventeen. After a post-mortem examination, his physician declared that much of the young King's brain had been destroyed by the abscess. Mary, who had nursed Francis devotedly, was inconsolable at his death;[46] for the third time in less than eighteen months, she was facing the loss of someone dear to her. Again, she donned the *deuil blanc*, the white mourning of French queens, then disappeared into her black shrouded chamber for the customary forty days of seclusion imposed on royal widows.

The throne now passed to Francis's younger brother, the ten-year-old Charles IX, but the reign of the Guises was effectively over; Mary, the instrument of their greatness, was now a childless Queen Dowager, and no longer of great political importance at the French court. Real power now lay in the hands of the hostile Queen Mother, who presently made it perfectly clear that Mary was no longer welcome in France. It was at this point that Mary began to think seriously about returning to her own kingdom.

2

"The Most Beautiful
in Europe"

M ARY HAD TWO OPTIONS OPEN to her: she could make a second marriage with a foreign power, or she could return to Scotland. At first, she barely considered the latter. Her priority was to recover the prestige she felt she had lost through widowhood by marrying a great Catholic king, or a king's son. At eighteen, with her crown and her rich French dowry, she rivalled Elizabeth I as the best match in Europe.

After Mary's period of mourning officially ended in January 1561, she began seriously to consider marriage with Don Carlos, heir to Philip II of Spain. At that time, France and Spain were the two most powerful nations in Christendom, so Don Carlos was a great prize. But Catherine de' Medici, whose daughter Elisabeth had recently married Philip, had no wish to see her eclipsed by Mary, or the influence of the Guises reaching into Spain. She also vehemently opposed their suggestion, put forward as a means of keeping Mary in France, that the Queen of Scots marry her late husband's brother, Charles IX. Instead, the Queen Mother urged Mary to go back to her own kingdom and take up the reins of government there.

Some people thought that Mary should consider an advantageous dynastic marriage nearer home. There were two possible candidates. One was Henry Stuart, Lord Darnley, the fourteen-year-old son of the Earl and Countess of Lennox. Darnley's ambitious parents wasted no time in sending him to France in February 1561 to offer condolences on the death of Francis II and privately to press his suit.[1] Naturally, they took care to keep the true purpose of his visit a secret from Queen Elizabeth, because Darnley had a strong claim to the English throne, and it did not take much to arouse her suspicions. The Catholic Lennoxes had been in high favour with Mary I, and the Countess had then gone out of her way to make life difficult for Elizabeth when the latter was in disgrace; on Elizabeth's accession, it had been made clear to the Lennoxes that they were no longer welcome at court. The Queen feared their ambition, and had spies planted in their household to keep a watch on their movements. In happy ignorance, Lady Lennox was now writing to several Catholic nobles in Scotland in an effort to enlist support for Darnley's marriage to Queen Mary.

Elizabeth would never have approved such a marriage, for Darnley, like Mary, was too near her throne for comfort. The Spanish ambassador in England, Alvaro de Quadra, had told Philip II that, should Elizabeth die, the English Catholics would raise Darnley to royal estate as Henry IX. Yet there were obstacles in the way of him succeeding. His mother had been excluded from the Act of Succession and from Henry VIII's Will, not only because she was a Roman Catholic, but also because there were doubts as to her legitimacy, her parents' marriage having been declared invalid. Nevertheless, she and Darnley, whose claim to the English succession came through her, had both been born in England, and many therefore considered that their line had a better right than Mary Stuart to succeed Elizabeth. Darnley had also inherited rights to the Scottish succession through his father. Marriage to Mary could only reinforce his claims to both kingdoms, and would also boost the Scottish Queen's ambitions in England.

In the event, Mary was not interested in marrying Darnley. She had set her sights on the far greater match with Don Carlos.

The second candidate for Mary's hand was James Hamilton, Earl of Arran, who was five years her senior and had, in 1560, unsuccessfully proposed to Elizabeth I. As Chatelherault's heir, Arran had a strong claim to the Scottish succession, but he did not appeal to Mary as a prospective husband because he was an extreme Protestant and had been one of the most militant leaders of the Reformation. Many Scots, including Knox, were in favour of a marriage between Arran and Mary, but Mary turned him down, with ultimately tragic results.

With no immediate prospect of the great foreign marriage alliance she desired, Mary decided to return to Scotland. Although the Lords of the Congregation had formally invited her to do so, both they, and Queen Elizabeth, would have been happier to see her stay in France; Knox feared that her arrival would signal a religious counter-revolution, while another leading Protestant, William Maitland, foresaw "wonderful tragedies."[2]

In March, Lord James went to France to see Mary and negotiate the conditions for a smooth transfer of power; he was determined to ensure that the arrival of a Catholic queen would not make too many difficulties for the Protestant establishment. Mary made it clear that she would come in a spirit of reconciliation. She would not interfere with the newly founded Protestant Church, but insisted on her right to hear Mass in the privacy of the royal chapels. This seemed a fair compromise, and Lord James promised "to serve her faithfully to the utmost of his power, and returned again to Scotland to prepare the hearts of her subjects against her home-coming."[3]

Soon afterwards, George Gordon, the Catholic Earl of Huntly, sent John Leslie, Bishop of Ross to France to urge Mary to accept Huntly's armed backing and restore the Catholic faith in Scotland by force. Wisely, she declined. Huntly, it turned out, had betrayed his faith by joining the Lords of the Congregation and profiting from the spoils of the Reformation. There was no guarantee that he would not turn his coat again.

In the spring of 1560, the Earl of Bothwell returned to Scotland on the Queen's business, apparently taking Anna Throndssen with him as his mistress. Mary was grateful to him for his unswerving loyalty to her mother, and as he was high in her favour, his enemies in Scotland dared not touch him.

By the summer, Mary was well advanced in preparations for her return, but because she had refused to ratify the Treaty of Edinburgh, Elizabeth declined to issue her with a safe-conduct to journey through England. When she changed her mind, it was too late, and Mary had already put to sea, having sailed from Calais on 14 August. Bothwell, as Lord High Admiral of Scotland, was in command of the fleet that came to fetch her. Over 200 years later, painters of the romantic era would frequently depict Mary being borne off in a ship, gazing wistfully back at France, yet while she certainly retained a lasting affection for the land in which she had grown up, it is clear that she was now determined to look to the future.

At six o'clock on the misty morning of 19 August 1561,[4] Mary's ship docked at the port of Leith, and she set foot in her kingdom for the first time in thirteen years. She was not expected for another few days, and was obliged to take shelter in the house of a local merchant until Lord James and other nobles came to receive her and escort her to Edinburgh. Here, she was warmly welcomed by eager crowds, who cheered as she rode up the High Street (now known as the Royal Mile) to Edinburgh Castle, and later, as she presided over a banquet there, lit bonfires in her honour.

Not everyone was in raptures at her arrival. Knox wrote gloomily: "The very face of Heaven did manifestly speak what comfort was brought into this country with her, to wit, sorrow, dolour, darkness and all impiety. The sun was not seen to shine two days before, nor two days after. That forewarning gave God unto us; but, alas, the most part were blind." Generally, however, the people of Scotland, including many members of the Protestant establishment, welcomed their Queen. "Her Majesty returning was gladly welcomed by the whole subjects," wrote the courtier and diplomat Sir James Melville. "For at first, following the counsel of her friends, she behaved herself humanely to them all." Many were impressed by her beauty, charm and dignity, or felt compassion for her as a young widow. It seemed that she was going to be a success.

Mary would certainly have found Scotland very different from France. It was a much poorer, and more sparsely populated, land, inhabited by about only 5–700,000 people. Its often turbulent nobles were drably dressed[5] compared to their French counterparts, and seemed to be constantly forming rival factions, or engaging in the complicated family feuds that arose from intensive intermarrying or clan warfare. Mostly motivated by self-interest, they ruled their feudalities like independent princes, and resented any interference from the monarch or from central government. Although many still lived in strongly fortified castles, the influence of the French Renaissance, which had featured increasingly in the architecture of the royal palaces since the reign of James IV (1488–1513), was now evident in the houses of the nobility, whose tastes, thanks to the Auld Alliance, were essentially French.

Next in rank below the Lords came the gentry, or lairds, who held their lands directly from the Crown, then the articulate and often outspoken burgesses of the urban merchant class, and finally, at the bottom of the pyramid, the peasantry. Most of Mary's subjects lived in remote villages or farming communities, in rustic hovels. Few received much in the way of education but, thanks to the vision of John Knox, the Reformation Parliament had provided for the foundation of a system of schooling that was to endure for several centuries.

The Scots were a proud and tenacious people. Foreign visitors praised them as courageous warriors, but also found them to be uncouth and lawless, hostile to strangers and inordinately quarrelsome. Their way of life was seen as primitive. The weather was often cold and wet, and the roads, where they existed, were atrocious. The people were ignorant and superstitious, and there was a widespread belief in witchcraft. It appeared that all classes valued money more than honour. However, Scotland was in many respects a civilised land: it boasted three universities, and had thriving trade and cultural links with other countries.

Although Catholics were in the majority, most of the Lords were Protestant, and the city of Edinburgh itself was slowly becoming a bastion of Calvinism. Edinburgh then had a population that has been variously estimated as numbering between 10,000 and 40,000; most were crowded into cramped accommodation in tall tenement blocks in alleyways known as closes or wynds, on either side of the High Street, the impressive wide thoroughfare that led down from Edinburgh Castle, which stood on its high rock at the top, to Holyrood Palace at the bottom, which lay in the shadow of the extinct volcano known as Arthur's Seat. A defensive wall 21 feet high, built in 1450 and replaced in 1513 after the Scots were defeated by the English at the Battle of Flodden, encircled the city, and had eight fortified gateways; one, the crenellated Netherbow Port, straddled the High Street. Below it was the Canongate, along which the former canons of Holyrood Abbey had walked into the city. At night, the city and the wall were patrolled by the 32-strong town watch.

The Flodden Wall, which was not demolished until the eighteenth century, was responsible for the overcrowding in the city. Instead of moving outwards, the citizens preferred to stay safe inside its bounds, and simply kept adding extra levels to their tenement blocks, some of which were fifteen storeys high. Sanitation was non-existent, and the closes were awash with sewage. The Scots might take pride in the High Street itself, but one visitor likened it to "an ivory comb whose teeth on both sides are very foul, though the space between them is clean and sightly."[6] Well-to-do citizens preferred to live in the Canongate, near Holyrood Palace, or below the High Street in the Cowgate, then a select burgh. Another visitor wrote, "There is nothing humble or rustic, but all is magnificent."[7]

Edinburgh was Scotland's capital, its greatest city, and a prosperous, busy market centre. It was also the political hub of the realm, for the Privy Council, Parliament and the Court of Session (the central civil court) met regularly in the new Tolbooth on the High Street, which also served as a prison, and the law courts were situated nearby. Below the castle, on the site now occupied by Princes Street Gardens, lay the Nor' Loch, an artificial lake created by James II as part of a defensive system; this was not drained until the eighteenth century, when the Georgian New Town was built. Until then, Edinburgh was centred upon the High Street and the few surrounding streets. The principal church was the imposing St. Giles with its distinctive crown spire, which stood on the High Street and had enjoyed collegiate status since the fifteenth century, but had recently been stripped of all the trappings of the old faith. Nearby stood the turreted Mercat Cross, where proclamations were made and criminals executed.

When she arrived in Edinburgh, Mary took up residence in Holyrood Palace, which was to be her chief abode, and is still the official Scottish residence of the sovereign. The adjoining former Augustinian abbey of the Holy Rude had been founded by David I in 1128, and by the end of the fifteenth century, after Edinburgh became the capital, its guest house had become a favoured royal residence. In 1500–3, James IV built a royal palace next door to the cloisters to welcome his English bride, Margaret Tudor. Very little remains of this now, because between 1528 and 1536, their son, James V, employed French architects and craftsmen to transform Holyrood into a Renaissance showpiece with a donjon and an elegant west façade. In 1544, during the "rough wooing," the abbey was partially destroyed by the English, and when Mary moved into the damaged palace in 1561, she had to spend some of her French dower on restoration work. At that time, Holyrood Palace was commonly referred to as "the Abbey."

In Mary's day, the royal apartments were housed in the massive rectangular fortified north-west tower built by James V, which was accessed by a stairway leading to an iron drawbridge on the first floor. The walls were thick and the windows small, so the rooms were quite dark. Mary occupied the second-floor chambers that had been assigned to the Queens of Scotland; the empty King's apartments were on the floor below, and were of similar layout. A spiral stair in the north-east turret gave access to all floors, while a privy staircase (now blocked) in the north wall led up from the King's bedchamber to the Queen's.

Mary had a suite of four pine-panelled rooms, which still survive today, although they are not as lofty, since the ceilings on the floor below were raised in the seventeenth century. These rooms comprised a large outer, or presence, chamber, hung with black velvet, where the Queen received ambassadors and dignitaries, a bedchamber and, in the turrets that led off it, two small closets, each no more than 12 feet square. One, with crimson and green hangings, was used as a dining chamber, the other as a stool chamber or dressing room. These rooms were hung with tapestries and hangings brought from France, and lit with silver and gilt chandeliers, and there was a four-poster bed in the bedchamber. The floors were either tiled or covered with rush matting, and the shuttered windows had armorial glass and were protected by iron grilles painted red. The ribbed, oak-panelled ceiling in the presence chamber was decorated with shields bearing the arms of Mary, Francis II, James V and Marie de Guise. Some of the most dramatic events of Mary's life were to take place within these rooms.

Adjoining the tower was a quadrangular range of buildings that housed the beautiful chapel royal, the damaged great hall, and Mary's library. Around a series of lesser courts were ranged the new Council Chamber, where ceremonial events normally took place, the Governor's Tower, the armoury, the mint, a forge, kitchens and other service quarters. The abbey and palace were surrounded by pleasant gardens, an orchard, a lion house, and a deer park in which Mary could exercise her passion for hunting. During her reign, the nave of the ruined abbey was converted into the parish church of the Canongate.[8]

Within the palace grounds still stands a small structure known as Queen Mary's Bath House; this was the only building erected by Mary during her reign in Scotland. Legend has it that she bathed there in white wine in order to preserve her complexion, but the real history of the Bath House is obscure.

. . .

We have no way of knowing what Mary thought of her kingdom as she beheld it anew after her long absence. Some historians have speculated that she compared Scotland with France and found it wanting. She did try to establish a French-style court at Holyrood, which was hardly surprising, as she had known nothing else and other precedents had been forgotten: it was nearly twenty years since a Stuart sovereign had held court in Scotland.

Under Mary, Holyrood became the scene of courtly entertainments and glittering ceremonials, and a magnet for the nobility. The Queen had grand tastes and, like most Renaissance monarchs, realised the importance of a display of magnificence, which she funded from her private income. She patronised poets and musicians, and her *valets de chambre* were all expected to display some musical ability on the lute, viola or trumpet. John Knox was horrified to learn that Mary and her ladies danced at royal balls and banquets, and warned that the palace would turn into a brothel if this devilish practice were allowed to continue; the Queen's abominable way of life, he thundered, was "offensive in the sight of God." The Protestant David Calderwood later wrote that, although Mary showed a grave demeanour in Council, "when she, her fiddlers and other dancing companions got into the house alone, there might be seen unseemly skipping, notwithstanding that she was wearing the deuil blanc. Her common speech in secret was that she saw nothing in Scotland but gravity, which she could not agree well with, for she was brought up in joyousity." Yet Mary did have a more serious side, and set time aside regularly to read Latin with the respected humanist scholar, George Buchanan, who at this time was one of her most fervent admirers.

The Queen's household numbered about 250 persons, mostly French with a few Italians. From 1563, the Master of the Household was George, 5th Lord Seton, the brother of Mary Seton and a leading Catholic noble. Educated in France, he had attended Mary's wedding in 1558, was made a Privy Councillor in 1561, and would remain loyal to her for the rest of his life, often to his own disadvantage.

The four Maries had returned from France with their mistress and still attended her. Knox disapproved of them all, thinking them light of morals and frivolous. In 1562, Mary Livingston married Arthur Erskine of Blackgrange, brother to the future Earl of Mar, and left Mary's service. The beautiful Mary Beaton followed suit in 1566 when she married Alexander Ogilvy of Boyne. Both remained close to the Queen. Mary Fleming, with her charm and sex appeal, was one of the most sought after ladies at court, while Mary Seton, the most pious and unworldly of the four, would never marry, and stayed with her mistress until 1583, when ill health forced her to retire to a convent in France.

Generally, the Scots were impressed with their Queen. She certainly cut a striking figure for, at about six feet tall, she was well above the normal height for a woman, slender, graceful, and dignified in her bearing. She had a pale complexion, frizzy auburn hair, grey or brown slanting, heavy-lidded eyes, an over-long nose inherited from her father and a "very sweet, very lovely"[9] voice; she later acquired "a pretty Scottish accent."[10] Her neck was long, her bosom like marble and her hands delicate.

Ronsard, Brantôme and several other court poets lauded Mary's beauty, and a Venetian ambassador called her "personally the most beautiful in Europe."[11] This cannot have been mere flattery, for even her enemies praised her looks. George Buchanan wrote: "She was graced with surpassing loveliness of form, the vigour of maturing youth, and fine qualities of mind." Lennox called her "a paragon," and even Knox found her features "pleasing." It is therefore disappointing to discover that Mary's surviving portraits (none of which date from her reign in Scotland) do not convey to modern eyes the beauty described by enthusiastic contemporaries. What portraits cannot capture are those indefinable qualities known as charm and sex appeal, and it seems likely that Mary had her full measure of both.

As a widow, Mary normally wore black or white gowns with white veils, but abandoned her weeds for state occasions. In her wardrobe at Holyrood were sixty gowns of cloth of gold or silver, purple or crimson velvet or silk, many adorned with gems or fine embroidery; there were also fourteen cloaks and thirty-three masquing costumes, and her inventories record over 180 fine pieces of jewellery. In Scotland, Mary took to wearing Highland dress, notably long embroidered cloaks of plaid, which was then just a warm material, not tartan as we know it today. She enjoyed dressing up, especially in men's clothes,[12] and going about incognito. Her hair was always beautifully dressed by Mary Seton, and she was fond of wearing wigs in different colours.

Mary was loved and respected by nearly all who served her. To her friends and servants, she was kind, generous and loyal. Ambassadors praised her virtue, her discretion, her modesty and her readiness to be ruled by good counsel.[13] She was spirited, vivacious and brave, majestic yet accessible. But she lacked prudence and common sense and was a notoriously bad judge of character, which resulted in many people taking advantage of her. Ever at the mercy of her emotions, she was highly suggestible, self-absorbed, and subject to storms of hysterical weeping, and periods of nervous prostration that obliged her to take to her bed. "She often weeps when there is little apparent occasion," a contemporary observed.[14] Mary also made the mistake of allowing her heart to rule her head, which on more than one occasion led to tragedy. None of these were desirable qualities in a queen in an age that regarded female rulers as unnatural aberrations, yet in a crisis Mary could keep her wits about her and act decisively, resourcefully and courageously. She functioned best, however, when she had a strong man to lean upon, both politically and personally; unfortunately, most of the men on whom she came to depend used her to further their own ambitions.

Some historians have described Mary as a foolish, passionate woman who was entirely without moral sense, and who was selfish, wilful, reckless, irresponsible and incapable of self-sacrifice. One even called her a nymphomaniac. Her enemies would later emphasise her moral depravity: Buchanan wrote of her "surface gloss of virtue" and Knox compared her to Jezebel. "We call her not a whore," he wrote, "but she was brought up in the company of the vilest whoremongers."

The truth of all this is hard to determine; none was more professedly jealous of her honour than Mary, yet there were undoubtedly occasions when she was constrained by circumstances or the behaviour of others to act in a way that left her open to censure. It is hard to believe that there was no alternative open to her: she was the Queen, and she almost always had powerful supporters willing to help her. Her intrigues show her to have been duplicitous and even ruthless, especially in her later machinations for the English throne; in 1561, Thomas Randolph, the English agent in Edinburgh, warned his superiors never to underestimate Mary, since he had found in her the fruit of the "best practised cunning of France combined with the subtle brains of Scotland."[15] Although she suffered much ill luck, it was often the result of the flaws in her character and her own poor judgement.

All her life, Mary inspired in the imaginations of the male sex a fatal fascination. Knox himself was not immune, but put it down to "some enchantment whereby men are bewitched." A few would be driven to take outrageous liberties, not, it seems, without imagining that they had been given some encouragement, for Mary allowed a certain familiarity in her relationships with her intimates that could easily have been misconstrued as romantic encouragement. It is unlikely that Mary was a nymphomaniac, but she may have inherited her father's promiscuous nature, whether or not she indulged it, and she was no shrinking violet. In 1562, Thomas Randolph was shocked to see one Captain Hepburn casually pass Mary a paper on which were written "ribald verses, and under them drawn the secret members of both men and women in as monstrous a sort as nothing could be more shamefully devised." Randolph was appalled, not only at the Queen's lack of reaction, but at Hepburn's disrespect in showing such an insulting thing to his mistress and the implied slur on her reputation.[16]

It has also been suggested that Mary was sexually frigid, but it is more probable that any reluctance in this sphere was a response to the behaviour of the men with whom she became involved. Yet there is evidence that she did enjoy male attention, but her bad judgement in choosing a husband would ultimately lead to her downfall, for she lacked the perception to spot the defects in a man's character. During her time in Scotland, all her entanglements with men brought disaster.

Although she loved energetic outdoor pursuits, Mary's health was never robust. In 1561, Randolph described her as "a sick, crazed woman."[17] In youth, she had developed anaemia, which was probably the cause of her occasional fainting fits, and at sixteen she was rumoured to be consumptive. From adolescence onwards, until she was forty, she suffered episodes of pain in her side, which may have been of hysterical origin, but are more likely to have been caused by a gastric ulcer. She also suffered from intermittent depression; Randolph attributed this, and her outbursts of weeping, to sexual frustration resulting from her inability to find a suitable husband.[18] It has been suggested that Mary suffered from porphyria, a disease that later affected George III and other members of the Houses of Hanover and Windsor, and which she may have inherited from her father; this would explain many of her symptoms, such as episodic abdominal pain, vomiting, paralysis and mental disturbance, but there is not enough evidence for this diagnosis to be conclusive.

Although dignified, Mary was a most accessible and affable monarch. Like her cousin Elizabeth, she was not above exerting her feminine charm on her male advisers but, unlike Elizabeth, she lacked political experience and mature judgement. Nevertheless, her moderate and conciliatory approach soon found favour with her relieved Protestant Lords. As long as she was willing to heed the counsel of Lord James, they were happy to serve her as their mistress. In return for Mary's compliance, and the honours and rewards she heaped upon him, James ensured her security, kept the turbulent nobility in check and took her part against the disapproving Knox. His relationship with Mary was one of mutual co-operation and fraternal affection.

That Lord James was the power behind the throne during the first four years of Mary's personal rule there can be no doubt. Sir Nicholas Throckmorton, an English diplomat who was familiar with Scottish affairs, stated that the Queen was content "to be ruled by good counsel and wise men." In 1561, William Cecil, Elizabeth's formidably able Secretary of State wrote, "The Queen of Scotland is, I hear, most governed by the Lord James." Soon afterwards, Thomas Randolph echoed, "The Lord James is commander of the Queen." The following year, a Jesuit reported: "The leading men in the government acknowledge the Queen's title, but do not let her use her rights. They have many ways of acting in opposition to her. She is alone, and has not a single protector and good councillor. The men in power are taking advantage of her gentleness. She is well nigh destitute of human aid." In 1562, Cecil informed a colleague that "the whole government rests with the Lord James," and in 1563 another Jesuit noted, "The Lord James rules all. The Queen's authority is nominal only." Mary's partisan, the Bishop of Ross, later recalled that "she had the name and calling, he [James] had the very sway and regiment." In 1568, her supporters accused him of causing the Queen's Majesty to "become subject to him as [if] Her Grace had been a pupil."[19]

Mary relied heavily not only on Lord James, but also on the man whom she retained as her Secretary of State, William Maitland of Lethington.[20] Now aged about thirty-three, he was the son of Sir Richard Maitland, Laird of Lethington in Lauderdale, Keeper of the Privy Seal and a writer and poet of note. The family seat was the fifteenth-century Lethington Castle near Haddington, East Lothian; later it was extensively remodelled and in 1704 renamed Lennoxlove in honour of Frances Stewart, Duchess of Richmond and Lennox, who had once been courted by Charles II. It is now owned by the Duke of Hamilton.

William Maitland, a clever lawyer who had received a Renaissance education at St. Andrews University and later at the French court, was appointed Secretary of State in 1558 by Marie de Guise, who recognised his expertise as a politician and diplomat; in 1559, he had deserted her and joined the Lords of the Congregation. Thereafter, he won over several Lords to their cause, although his motivation was political rather than religious. His ultimate aim was a peaceful union with Protestant England through Elizabeth's recognition of Mary as her heir, and his policies were all directed to that end. Consequently he collaborated closely with his opposite number in England, William Cecil, and, like Lord James, became a pensioner of the English Queen.

Astute, subtle, cunning and cultivated, Maitland was an arch-intriguer and double dealer. Elizabeth I called him "the flower of all the wits in Scotland," but the Scots, seeing in him the pattern of a Machiavellian politician, nicknamed him "Michael Wylie"; Buchanan referred to him as a chameleon, and even Lord James, with whom he was closely associated in the government, disliked and distrusted him. His motives were often obscure: because he covered his traces so well, he was, and remains, something of an enigma, and it is uncertain whether in his dealings with Mary he acted out of loyalty or self-interest; he "held the threads of all the plots"[21] and knew more than he cared to reveal about the great dramas that would unfold during her reign.

Maitland became "the whole guider of [the Queen's] affairs. His advice is followed more than any other."[22] In his opinion, she behaved herself "as reasonably as we can require. If anything be amiss, the fault is rather in ourselves."

Others were more fulsome in their praise. The courtier and diplomat, Sir James Melville, wrote: "The Queen's Majesty, after returning to Scotland, behaved herself so princely, so honourably and discreetly that her reputation spread in all countries." She desired "to hold none in her company but such as were the best quality and conversation, abhorring all vices and vicious persons; and requested me to assist her in case she, being yet young, might forget herself in any unseemly gesture or misbehaviour, that I would warn her thereof. She made me familiar to all her most urgent affairs."

Yet although Sir Thomas Craig claimed that he had often heard Mary "discourse so appositely and rationally in all affairs which were brought before the Privy Council that she was admired by all,"[23] her attendance record at such meetings was poor, and when she was present she sometimes sat there sewing while listening to debates. Most of her time was spent in the company of her largely foreign household. The evidence suggests that her role was mainly formal and ceremonial: she opened and attended Parliament, and went on many progresses throughout her realm, meeting her subjects, exerting her Stuart charm, and administering justice. Knox gained the impression that, rather than attend to state business, Mary preferred archery and hawking. In 1562, the Earl of Bothwell claimed that she "virtually wielded no authority at all."[24]

Had Mary been less obsessed with the English succession, she might have been more successful at restoring royal authority in Scotland. Inevitably, as she gained confidence, she came to resent the tutelage of those formidable allies, Lord James and Maitland, and the other constraints that bound her. It would only be a matter of time before she asserted her independent authority and put her own interests before those of her kingdom, and when that time came, she would reveal herself as dangerously irresponsible and entirely out of tune with the concerns and aspirations of the majority of her subjects. The result would be disaster.

For centuries Scotland had endured an uneasy relationship with her more powerful neighbour, England. From the time of the Norman Conquest in 1066, the Kings of England had repeatedly asserted their unfounded claim to be feudal overlords of Scotland, which nevertheless had its own independent monarchy. In 1290, following the extinction of the ancient royal line, Edward I of England, who had visions of uniting the two kingdoms under English rule, acted as arbitrator between the thirteen claimants to the Scottish throne, and chose one, John Balliol, who would act as his puppet. Scottish resistance led first by William Wallace and then by Robert the Bruce was fierce, and in 1314 Bruce vanquished the English at the Battle of Bannockburn and was able to establish himself firmly on the throne. In 1320, he published the Declaration of Arbroath, affirming Scotland's status as an independent sovereign state. Thereafter, his descendants, the House of Stewart—named after Walter the Steward who had married Bruce's daughter Marjorie; they were the parents of Robert II, the first Stewart king—enjoyed an undisputed succession. In the sixteenth century, however, the dynasty's future rested upon the successful resolution of the political and religious situation in Scotland.

As a young Catholic queen in a turbulent land, Mary faced challenges that would have defeated a far more experienced ruler. She did not understand the Scottish people, and to many of them she must have seemed very alien with her frivolous French ways. In an age of religious intolerance, her willingness to compromise seemed suspect, as indeed it was, for Mary was playing a dangerous double game, professing tolerance of the new faith in Scotland in order to ensure her political survival, whilst assuring the Pope that she intended to restore the Catholic faith in her realm. Although personally devout, she did little to champion the Catholic cause in Scotland during her reign. Her private attendance at Mass gave rise to much resentment, and initially there were even riots in protest against it. Lord James managed to calm the people, but the prejudiced Knox would not be appeased, believing that Mary "plainly purposed to wreck the religion within this realm," and crossed swords with her on several occasions, during which disputes she either spiritedly defended her position or dissolved into tears.

Although for a long time she refused to confirm officially the Acts of the Reformation Parliament, on several occasions Mary issued proclamations reiterating her undertaking not to tamper with the established religion and made generous grants to the Kirk; she even received some instruction in Calvinist doctrines from George Buchanan, but none of this satisfied her critics, nor did it do anything to allay the fears of the Catholics, who had looked to her to bring about a counter-reformation.

Yet Mary still had her sights set on a great Catholic marriage. "The marriage of our Queen was in all men's mouths," wrote Knox. It was her duty to remarry and provide for the succession, but the question of whom she might marry was a matter of great concern, not only in Scotland, but in England also, for Elizabeth was determined to prevent Mary from allying herself with Spain or France and giving a hostile Catholic power a foothold in mainland

Britain; she warned Mary that, if she did so, she, Elizabeth, could not avoid being her enemy. But Mary had dreams of marrying Don Carlos and becoming Queen of Scotland, Spain and—with Spanish help—England. Lord James, however, was determined that she should choose a husband who was acceptable to Elizabeth, preferably one of the Protestant Kings of Sweden or Denmark. Nor were Catherine de' Medici or Mary's uncle, the Cardinal of Lorraine, keen to see Spain aggrandised by a union with Scotland. In desperation, Catherine offered her son, Charles IX, whom Mary rejected as being too young, while the Cardinal urged Mary instead to consider the Archduke Charles of Austria, who had for a long time been fruitlessly negotiating a marriage with Queen Elizabeth. But Mary eventually abandoned all ideas of this match on the grounds that the Archduke was too poor. The Lords then suggested Lord Darnley, but Mary declared "never would she wed with that faction," and continued to pursue the idea of marrying Don Carlos, despite opposition on all sides.

Philip II, however, had reservations about the match. He knew Scotland to be unquiet, and had heard a rumour that Mary had murdered her first husband by poison. More to the point, Don Carlos himself was hopelessly unstable to the point of insanity. At only sixteen, he was morally degenerate, sadistic, severely epileptic, and unprepossessing in his person. His growth was stunted, he had a speech impediment, and he dribbled. But he was set to inherit the greatest throne in Europe, and he was fabulously wealthy. Moreover, King Philip had seen to it that his son's worst defects had remained hidden from public scrutiny. Mary believed him to be a gallant and brave prince who would help her assert her authority in Scotland, champion the Catholic cause and assert her rights in England, and during the next few years, she doggedly persisted in her attempts to bring the reluctant Philip to an agreement.

Her obduracy on this matter did not make for easy relations with her cousin Elizabeth, who was already suspicious of Mary on account of her refusal to ratify the Treaty of Edinburgh, which Mary repeatedly declared she would not do unless Elizabeth recognised her as her heir. "The Queen my mistress," wrote Maitland, "is descended of the blood of England. I fear she would rather be content to hazard all than to forgo her rights."

On a personal level, Elizabeth was jealous of Mary because of her youth, her reputed beauty and the fact that she was now a rival in the European marriage market. On the other hand, Elizabeth felt an affinity with Mary as her kinswoman and a fellow female ruler, and was willing enough to offer her friendship if only Mary would renounce her pretensions to the English crown. Elizabeth would not name a successor for fear of being ousted from her throne; although she privately conceded that she knew of no one with a better title to the succession than Mary, she continually refused publicly to name her her heir. Instead, she advised Mary to win the love of the English by showing herself a friendly neighbour. Nevertheless, the interest that Elizabeth showed in Mary's choice of husband is proof that she realised that Mary had realistic hopes of succeeding in England; she hinted that her recognition of Mary as her heir was dependent on her approval of the man Mary married. Mary's frustration over Elizabeth's unending prevarication, and her persistence in demanding what she regarded as her rights, further soured relations between them. Yet Mary did make efforts to establish friendly relations with her cousin, with some success.

Until now, the two Queens had never met. Several times during the next few years, plans for a meeting would be made, and then scrapped for various political reasons. As it turned out, Mary and Elizabeth would never meet.

3

"POWERFUL CONSIDERATIONS"

~

O^N 6 SEPTEMBER 1561, MARY appointed her Privy Council. Amongst its sixteen members, aside from Lord James and Maitland, were several men who would play a prominent part in her story. Bothwell was one of them. "She was pleased to reward me personally, far more generously and graciously than I deserved," he wrote later, of his appointment and a gift of land that the Queen had given him in recognition of his loyalty to her mother and herself.[1] That autumn, the English agent in Edinburgh, Thomas Randolph, observed a certain rapport between Mary and Bothwell, which was perhaps natural in the circumstances.

The other members of the new Privy Council were the Duke of Chatelherault, the Earls of Huntly, Argyll, Morton, Atholl, Glencairn, Errol, Montrose and Marischal, Lord Erskine, the Lord High Treasurer Robert Richardson, the Clerk Register James MacGill, and the Justice Clerk James Bellenden. Four—Huntly, Errol, Montrose and Atholl—were Catholics; most of the rest were staunch members of the Congregation.

George Gordon, 4th Earl of Huntly was Mary's cousin, his mother having been Margaret Stewart, a bastard daughter of James IV. This powerful and wealthy magnate ruled north-eastern Scotland like an autonomous prince, and was now reappointed Chancellor, an office he had held since

1546. As the leading Catholic noble, Huntly might have led his co-religionists against the Lords of the Congregation, but instead he had briefly defected to the latter and so destroyed all hope of a Catholic revival. Not surprisingly, Mary did not trust him.

Unlike most of his colleagues, John Stewart, 4th Earl of Atholl was an honourable man with high principles, and would remain loyal to Mary until 1567, when her behaviour outraged his sense of propriety. He was no friend to Huntly, but co-operated with both Lord James and Maitland, becoming a friend of the latter. Atholl's wife, Margaret Fleming, a sister of Mary Fleming, was reputed to be a witch and to have the power to cast spells.

Archibald Campbell, 5th Earl of Argyll, whose power base lay in the western Highlands, had been educated at the University of St. Andrews and in 1557 was one of the first to join the Lords of the Congregation. An epileptic, he was married to Mary's only half-sister, Jean Stewart, the natural daughter of James V by Elizabeth Beaton, but the marriage was unhappy because of Argyll's infidelities. Nor, according to Mary, was Lady Argyll "as circumspect in all things as she would wish her to be."[2] The Queen even resorted to asking John Knox to "put them in unity," but his intervention was ultimately unsuccessful, as the couple were divorced in 1573. Both the Earl and Countess stood high in Mary's favour, while Argyll's tolerance of her Catholic observances earned him a rebuke from Knox.

Another active member of the Congregation was Alexander Cunningham, 4th Earl of Glencairn, a man who was motivated more by religious fervour than by political considerations, and was loudly disapproving of Mary's private Masses.

James Douglas, 4th Earl of Morton, the head of the powerful Douglas clan, was to be implicated heavily in Darnley's murder. Now aged about forty-five, he was a cousin of Margaret Douglas, Countess of Lennox, with whom he was involved in a long-standing battle for the disputed earldom of Angus. Morton was a staunch Protestant and a pensioner of Queen Elizabeth. Sir James Melville called him "witty in worldly affairs and policy," but said he had "a crafty head." He was illiterate, sadistic, unscrupulous and avaricious, and Mary was repelled by his uncouth and sometimes brutal manners, yet he was also an able and energetic politician. Morton's promiscuity was notorious, but his private life was tragic: his wife was insane for the last twenty-two years of their marriage, and seven of their ten children had died young.

One of the most aggressive Protestants on the Council was the brutal Patrick, 6th Lord Lindsay of the Byres, who was married to Lord James's half-sister, Euphemia Douglas. This man, who would one day become one of Mary's most virulent enemies, was a creature of Knox and "a raging, furious, rude, ignorant man, nothing differing from a beast."[3] It was he who had incited the mob to protest against Mary's Mass.

It is necessary to examine the tensions and rivalry between certain nobles and to recount the actions of the Earl of Bothwell and his relations with the Queen during the first three years of her reign, in order to lay the basis for an understanding of later events. Despite an outward show of friendship for the Queen's sake, there was bad blood between Bothwell and Lord James, and mutual hatred between Bothwell and the Hamiltons. Lord James was determined to undermine Mary's confidence in Bothwell, and at his instance, Mary made the latter Lieutenant of the Borders in order to remove him from court and avoid clashes between him and the volatile Arran. Bothwell later claimed that the preferment shown him by Mary "incensed my enemies so greatly that they employed every falsity and malicious invention to put me out of favour with the Queen."[4]

The unstable Arran was still cherishing vain hopes of marrying the Queen. In November, a casual remark by the Earl gave rise to an alarming rumour that he was intending to abduct her from Holyrood, which caused a momentary panic at court until it was proved baseless.[5]

In December, Bothwell resolved to discredit Arran. He had learned that the puritanical Earl was secretly having an affair with the daughter of an Edinburgh merchant, Alison Craig, "a good, handsome wench"[6] whom Bothwell himself wished to seduce. One night, Bothwell and his friends, Mary's favourite half-brother Lord John Stewart and her uncle René de Guise, Marquis d'Elbeouf, all masked, arrived at Alison Craig's house, hoping to surprise the couple *in flagrante delicto*, but Arran was not there. Not wishing to lose face, they returned the next night, drunk; when they were refused entry, they broke down the doors and ransacked the house, only to find that Arran had already escaped by a back way.[7]

On Christmas Eve, 300 armed Hamiltons, affronted by the insult to Arran, converged upon the city seeking Bothwell, who in turn raised 500 supporters, intent upon retaliation. Edinburgh was in an uproar. Meanwhile, the General Assembly of the Church of Scotland, outraged by Bothwell's behaviour towards one of its most stalwart supporters, had complained to the Queen. The next day, after Lord James, Argyll and Huntly had managed to disperse the armed factions, Mary reprimanded Bothwell and the other culprits, then sent Bothwell to his castle at Crichton for two weeks in the interests of keeping the peace, and said she trusted that the matter would be forgotten.[8] When the General Assembly demanded that Bothwell and his friends be tried and punished for "this heinous crime," Mary refused, and so, wrote Knox, "deluded the just petition of her subjects."

Bothwell had certainly not forfeited Mary's favour. In January, she went to Crichton Castle for the wedding of his sister Janet to Lord John Stewart. Bothwell hosted the lavish celebrations,[9] while Lord James was also present. On 30 January, Mary secretly created James Earl of Moray; the vast estates that went with the earldom were, however, in the possession of the unsuspecting Earl of Huntly, and it would require a certain diplomacy, if not force, to get them back, hence the secrecy. A week later, Lord James was married by Knox to Agnes Keith, daughter of William, Earl Marischal, in St. Giles's Kirk, and on the same day Mary publicly conferred on him the earldom of Mar, which he resigned soon afterwards in favour of Lord Erskine.

In February, at Bothwell's instigation, and through the mediation of John Knox, Arran and Bothwell were reconciled at Chatelherault's newly built mansion at Kirk o'Field, south of Edinburgh.[10] But Arran was becoming increasingly eccentric. In March, he went to the Queen and accused Bothwell and himself of treasonably plotting to kidnap her and carry her off to Dumbarton Castle so that Arran could, as Bothwell allegedly suggested, use "her person at your pleasure until she agree to whatsoever thing you desire"; then they would murder Lord James and Maitland and seize control of the government. According to Bothwell, Lord James had put Arran up to making these accusations[11] and, as a result of what Bothwell termed "these false suggestions," was able to order them both "into close arrest in the prison of Edinburgh Castle" without benefit of trial.[12] Thomas Randolph, however, reported that Bothwell was "found guilty on his own confession in some points."[13]

For some time, anxious doubts had been expressed about Arran's sanity. Randolph had noticed that he was "drowned in dreams and feedeth himself with fantasies."[14] Now, "he began to rave and speak of devils, witches and such like, fearing that all men about came to kill him."[15] Clearly, he was no longer responsible for his actions, and it is impossible to tell whether or not his accusations against Bothwell were based on truth or were simply the product of a deranged mind. It should be remembered, however, that five years later Bothwell did in fact abduct the Queen and carry her off to one of his castles, and it may be that in 1562, despite his protestations of innocence, he was indeed plotting a similar thing, with a view to overthrowing Lord James.

Chatelherault came to Mary, weeping at the disgrace of his son, but although she received him "with all gentleness,"[16] he was made to surrender Dumbarton Castle. After being declared insane and chained in a dark cell for four years, Arran was released from prison and committed into his mother's care. Utterly mad, he spent forty-seven years in confinement, dying in 1609.

As soon as the Earl of Lennox learned of Mary's return to her kingdom, he sent a messenger to her with a plea for the restitution of his Scottish estates and permission to return to Scotland. In December, Queen Elizabeth got wind of this and other questionable activities from her spies in Yorkshire[17] and, alarmed to hear that the Lennoxes were plotting to marry their son Darnley to Mary, placed the whole family under house arrest in London. In February 1562, the English ports were closed in case Darnley tried to escape,[18] but in April he gave his gaolers the slip; Randolph reported a rumour that he had gone to France.[19] In consequence of this, Lennox was sent to the Tower and his wife and younger son Charles placed under house arrest at Sheen, Surrey. Lennox was interrogated several times by the Privy Council, and in May Cecil drew up a list of fifteen articles against the Countess, but there was little that could be proved against them. Meanwhile, the Council was trying in vain to establish Lady Lennox's illegitimacy.

In June, Lennox made a humble submission to the Queen, but Elizabeth was not inclined to mercy. The following month, his wife appealed to Cecil for his release, as he was "in close prison" and had "a disease which solitariness is most against."[20] Lennox perhaps suffered from claustrophobia, or, it has been suggested, from depression or terrors arising from a guilty conscience over his savage treatment of his young hostages in 1544. Cecil ignored the letter.

· · · ·

In December 1561, disappointed that Mary had not sent any representatives to the Catholic Council of Trent, Pope Pius IV intimated that he thought she would do little for the faith unless pressure was put upon her. That very month, she approved an Act of Parliament for financing the Protestant Kirk out of former Catholic revenues. In June 1562, when a Papal Nuncio, the Jesuit Father Nicholas de Gouda, arrived secretly in Scotland with proposals from the Pope, Mary rejected them all. In Randolph's opinion, she had no intention of oversetting the reformed religion, and this seemed to be confirmed by the action she took against Huntly, the leading Catholic peer, who might have been her ally in any counter-reformation.

In August, Mary embarked on what was ostensibly a progress to the Highlands, but in fact turned out to be a military campaign to destroy the might of the Gordons. This was thought by some to be at the instigation of Lord James, who was proclaimed Earl of Moray that August and was intent on reclaiming the Moray estates, but Mary herself was a prime mover in the matter, and not without provocation: Huntly's son, Sir John Gordon, had been imprisoned for brawling in Edinburgh, and the Huntly clan were determined to avenge the insult. Moreover, Lord John, who had since escaped, was now threatening to abduct the Queen and force her to marry him. After Mary had been refused entry to Inverness Castle, Huntly surrendered, but soon afterwards broke into open rebellion. At the Battle of Corrichie, near Aberdeen, on 28 October, the Gordons were defeated by an army led by the new Earl of Moray: Huntly dropped dead on the battlefield, from either a heart attack or a stroke, and Sir John was later beheaded; the Queen, watching at Moray's insistence, screamed and fainted when the executioner bungled his work. She was also present when Huntly's embalmed corpse was tried and condemned for treason before Parliament in 1563 in Edinburgh. The Huntly estates were then declared forfeit, and the late Earl's heir, Lord George Gordon, who had played no part in the rebellion, was tried for treason and condemned to death, but Mary defied Moray and refused to sign the warrant, so he was imprisoned at Dunbar instead. Morton was made Lord Chancellor in place of Huntly.

The fall of the Gordons left the Protestant party all the more powerful.

Moray had now eliminated or neutralised several of his enemies. Yet Bothwell remained a thorn in his side. At the end of August, Bothwell had escaped from his prison in Edinburgh Castle by prising loose a bar from his window and climbing down the castle rock;[21] then he had made for Hermitage Castle, one of his strongholds in the Borders. From there, he wrote to Mary to "find out what the Queen's real thoughts and intentions were towards me,"[22] but Randolph reported in September, "Anything he can do or say can little prevail. Her purpose is to put him out of the country."[23] Bothwell, however, "discovered that she knew well enough that I had been accused only through motives of personal hatred and envy, but that, for the time being, she was quite unable to give me any help or assistance. But she sent a message to say that I was to do the best I could for myself."[24]

Moray demanded that Bothwell surrender himself on pain of indictment for treason, but Bothwell deemed it prudent to leave Scotland. "I decided to take ship to France, but a tempest drove me to England." Washed up on the Northumbrian coast, he remained in hiding until 7 January, when he was taken prisoner and confined in Tynemouth Castle. It was at this time that Moray and Maitland—and Randolph—began to be concerned about Mary's dealings with Bothwell. On 22 January, Randolph reported that the Lords "suspect the Queen to be more favourable to Lord Bothwell than there be good cause," and that they did not want him to return to Scotland. It was probably with their connivance that, in February 1563, on Queen Elizabeth's orders, he was sent to London, where he was imprisoned in the Tower. At the end of May, he was released on parole, but not immediately allowed to leave England.[25] At this time, Anna Throndssen was granted a safe-conduct by the Scottish government to return to Norway.

By December 1563, Bothwell was in Northumberland, a free man. From now on, he would loyally work for Mary in secret, for it was too dangerous for him to do so openly: he had numerous enemies in Scotland. According to Randolph, Bothwell secretly visited Mary at Dunbar in February 1564, then rode to London carrying letters for her. During 1564, Randolph reported several more secret meetings with Mary in Scotland. All of this implies that Mary was beginning to find Moray's tutelage irksome, and that she was seeking new counsellors. There is no suggestion in any of Randolph's reports, or elsewhere, that she was emotionally involved with Bothwell at this time, or considering him as a future husband.

In November 1562, Lennox had been released from the Tower and allowed to join his wife at Sheen, on condition that he undertook never to "enter into any private bond or practice with any state without the Queen's licence."[26] Lady Lennox was also required to promise that she would never again attempt to marry Lord Darnley to the Queen of Scots. Soon afterwards, the Earl and Countess, and in particular Lord Darnley, who had returned from wherever he had been hiding, were back in favour at court, where Elizabeth could keep an eye on them. Alvaro de Quadra reported to Philip II: "Many people think that, if the Queen of Scots does marry a person unacceptable to this Queen, the latter will declare as her successor the son of Lady Margaret, whom she now keeps in the palace and shows such favour to as to make this appear probable."[27] Darnley's new status at court is evident from the fact that, in June 1564, he was deputed to receive the new Spanish ambassador, Guzman de Silva, and conduct him to his first audience with the Queen.[28]

Meanwhile, there had been a major court scandal in Scotland. Pierre de Boscotel de Chastelard, a gallant French aristocrat and descendant of the Chevalier Bayard, was an accomplished musician and poet who had come from France in Mary's entourage in 1561, but soon afterwards returned in the company of his patron, the son of the Constable of France. Late in 1562, he made his way back to Scotland and, when he passed through London, let it be known that he was going north "to see his lady love."[29]

That lady was Mary herself, for whom Chastelard had apparently conceived a rash and inordinate affection, and she received him with such warmth that he believed his feelings were reciprocated. Thereafter he was often at court; the Queen obviously enjoyed his company and danced with him during the New Year festivities. Soon he was addressing passionate love sonnets to her. The English agent, Thomas Randolph, who was hostile to Mary and had an appetite for scurrilous gossip, claimed afterwards that she permitted too great a degree of familiarity with "so unworthy a creature and abject a varlet,"[30] and Knox, who later wrote an account of the affair, disapproved, relating how "Chastelard was so familiar in the Queen's cabinet that scarcely could any of the nobility have access to her." She "would lie upon Chastelard's shoulder, and sometimes privily she would steal a kiss of his neck. And this was honest enough, for it was the gentle entreatment of a stranger." Nevertheless, it was highly unusual conduct in a queen.

Some writers have argued that Mary's unwise encouragement of Chastelard's attentions was merely part of the ritual game of courtly love, which was accepted behaviour at the French court, but not understood in Scotland. However, when virtuous matrons accepted the homage and addresses of an admirer, they did not normally permit such physical intimacy, and it appears that, by her indiscreet and imprudent dealings with Chastelard, Mary was indeed in danger of compromising her much-vaunted honour.

One evening early in 1563, Chastelard went beyond the bounds of decorum when he secreted himself under the Queen's bed at Holyrood. After he was discovered by her grooms, he was soundly reprimanded and banished from Scotland on Mary's orders.

Undeterred and unhindered, Chastelard followed the Queen on a progress into Fife, where, at Rossend Castle near Burntisland, he again forced his way into her bedchamber while two of her ladies were about to disrobe her, then tried to embrace her; he later claimed he had come to beg forgiveness, but others, including the Queen herself, believed he intended to rape her. Moray, hearing her cries for help, rushed into the room and laid hold of Chastelard. This time, since her honour had been so outrageously compromised and her security threatened, the Queen was in no mood to be merciful, but when she cried, "Thrust your dagger into the villain!" Moray wisely refused, insisting that Chastelard be publicly tried and condemned to death.[31] Mary wondered fearfully if Moray would let Chastelard speak in his defence, to which her half-brother coldly replied, "I shall do, Madam, what in me lieth to save your honour."[32]

On 22 February, after the Queen had refused several pleas for a pardon, Chastelard was beheaded in the market-place at St. Andrews. Mary, against her will, was forced by Moray to be present. The condemned man refused any spiritual comfort on the scaffold, but instead recited Ronsard's "Ode to Death,"[33] then, looking directly at the Queen, he cried out, "O cruel dame!" Knox, anxious to emphasise the scandalous nature of the affair, pointed out that "dame" in this context meant "mistress," and commented, "What that complaint imported, lovers may divine." Knox also recounted how Chastelard "begged licence to write to France the cause of his death, which was for having been found in a very suspicious position. And so received he the reward of his dancing, for he lacked his head, that his tongue should not utter the secrets of our Queen."

In March, however, Maitland informed de Quadra that Chastelard had confessed he had been sent by Mary's Protestant enemies in France to "sully the honour of the Queen" and so wreck her chances of marrying Don Carlos; he had meant to remain all night underneath her bed "and go out in the morning so that he could escape after being seen." According to Chastelard, a "Madame de Curosot" and others whose names Mary would not allow Maitland to entrust to paper had given him his instructions.[34] In Paris, the Venetian ambassador learned from the Guises that Chastelard had been sent by "Madame de Cursolles,"[35] and the story was independently corroborated by the Spanish ambassador in Paris.[36] "Madame de Cursolles" was probably a code name for the wife of the Huguenot leader, Admiral Gaspard de Coligny.[37]

If this is true, then, to a degree, Chastelard had succeeded in his mission and "thereby injured Her Majesty,"[38] for the whole distasteful episode left Mary's reputation somewhat tarnished. She had shown herself not only lax in her conduct, but also vengeful and vicious, belying Brantôme's claim that she never had "the heart to see poor criminals fall under the sword of justice." And, not for the last time, she had unwisely preferred a foreigner above her nobles. Even if her involvement had been entirely innocent, she had, by her foolish behaviour, laid herself open to criticism by her enemies.

Thereafter, to preserve her reputation, the Queen ordered Mary Fleming to sleep in her bedchamber.

Mary had also lost credit with the Catholics. By this time, the Pope was having serious doubts about her commitment to the Catholic cause, and he was given further reason for concern after Easter when she had Archbishop Hamilton imprisoned for saying Mass. Later that year, she approved further legislation benefiting the Protestant Church, while in March 1564, she publicly proclaimed her resolve to maintain religion as she had found it on her return to Scotland. In June that year, the Pope wrote again, urging Mary to promote the Catholic Church in Scotland, but although she replied in October assuring him of her devotion to the faith, in December her Parliament passed another Act against the Mass. Mary had also told the Cardinal of Lorraine that she would send representatives to the Council of Trent, but she failed to keep her word. It was little wonder that King Philip was wary of marrying his son to her.

In the spring of 1563, Mary sent Maitland to London to press her rights to the English succession. There were, however, three obstacles in her way: her continued refusal to ratify the Treaty of Edinburgh, her determination to marry Don Carlos, and the antipathy of most of the English towards her. Elizabeth had fretted for a long time about the prospect of Mary allying with a great Catholic power; now, she came up with a solution that would assure her own security and the friendship of Scotland.

For four years, Elizabeth had been carrying on a very public affair with her Master of Horse, Lord Robert Dudley, to whom Mary had disparagingly referred as "her horsemaster." Dudley was the son and grandson of traitors, and when, in 1560, his wife was found dead with her neck broken, rumour, probably unjustifiably, credited him with her murder and there was a huge scandal, which put paid to his chances of ever marrying Elizabeth, who would never allow herself to be adjudged guilty by association. Nevertheless, their relationship continued, and there was endless speculation as to whether they were really lovers.

Now Elizabeth conceived the idea of making a great personal sacrifice and proposing as a husband for the Queen of Scots Lord Robert, of whose loyalty she was assured and who could be trusted to promote England's interests in Scotland. Lord Robert, however, was against the plan from the first, and horrified at the prospect of having to abandon his ambition to be King Consort of England. But Elizabeth was adamant, and, without naming any names, told Maitland that, if Mary would allow her to choose a husband for her, she might proclaim her her heir. The astute Maitland soon guessed that she was referring to Dudley, but could hardly believe it, since Dudley was so far below Mary in rank and had a dubious reputation. Even Randolph, who had been instructed to pave the way for public acceptance of Dudley in Scotland, was praying that he would not have to disclose to Mary the identity of the husband that Elizabeth was proposing for her. But Elizabeth wanted to keep Mary guessing.

· · · ·

In the autumn of 1563, Don Carlos fell down a staircase and fractured his skull, causing paralysis and blindness. His physicians performed a trepanning operation that restored his faculties but left him insane and subject to violent fits, during one of which he tried to murder his father. None of this was made public, but it was soon known that he was in poor health, and King Philip began to ward off all attempts to negotiate a marriage for his son. At the same time, England and France were doing their best to block a match between Don Carlos and Mary, and she began to realise that her expectations might be frustrated, although she did not entirely give up hope of a happy conclusion.

By February 1564, Mary, at the suggestion of Moray and Maitland,[39] was toying with the idea of marrying Lord Darnley, in the hope of winning the support of the English Catholics. On 14 April, Randolph expressed to Cecil the opinion that she would "at length let fall her anchor between Dover and Berwick, though perchance not in the port that you wish she should."[40] Darnley would be a means to the English succession, and, as far as Mary was concerned, as a Catholic, might support her in her private wish to restore the old faith, and help her to gain the political independence she craved. From now on, "the Queen was beset with reports about him [and] a correspondence was carried on between them on both sides."[41]

In March, Mary was informed by a cringing Randolph that it was Dudley, not Darnley, whom Elizabeth was offering as a husband. Although she received the news patiently and agreed to consider the matter, there can be no doubt that she was deeply affronted and, despite the fact that Moray, Maitland and Knox were in favour of the match, she secretly tried to reopen negotiations for a marriage with Don Carlos. But King Philip finally dashed her hopes in August because of his son's mental state, much to the relief of Queen Elizabeth and the Protestant party in Scotland.

Marriage with Darnley seemed the only alternative, and Mary began seriously to consider it. On 19 September, Sir William Kirkcaldy of Grange informed Randolph that the Scots would never accept Dudley, "but if ye will earnestly press it, ye may cause us to take Lord Darnley."[42] However, Darnley and his family were English subjects and required Elizabeth's permission to visit Scotland, and it was not likely that that would be forthcoming, for she was no fool and had guessed what was afoot. Fortunately, in June 1563, Elizabeth had written asking Mary to reverse the attainder on Lennox and allow him to return to be restored to his estates and settle his affairs in Scotland.[43] Hitherto, Mary had refused this request, but now she relented and informed Lennox that he might come; in some alarm, Elizabeth backtracked and secretly wrote urging Mary to refuse him entry to her kingdom, but Mary had given her word and would not go back on it. Elizabeth had to concede defeat in order to avoid giving offence, and granted Lennox a licence to leave England for three months, although she would not allow Lady Lennox or Darnley to accompany him, but kept them in England as hostages for his good behaviour.

In September, Lennox rode north. Considering his former reputation in Scotland, his reception by his Queen was exceptionally cordial. His rivals, the Hamiltons, were not pleased to see him, but on 27 September, at Mary's behest, he and Chatelherault made a public and utterly insincere show of reconciliation. On 9 October, his restoration in blood was publicly proclaimed in Edinburgh, and it was confirmed by Parliament in December.[44] Lennox managed to win over the Protestants by displaying a renewed interest in the reformed faith and by giving extravagant gifts to members of the Privy Council. He also began cultivating the Catholic nobility. In all these doings, he was preparing the ground for Mary's marriage to his son, who, rumour said, would soon follow him to Scotland, along with Lady Lennox. Randolph reported that there was "a marvellous good liking of the young Lord," and that it was "in all men's mouths" that the Queen had decided to marry him.[45]

On 18 September, Mary had sent Sir James Melville to England to restore good relations with Elizabeth and secretly further Mary's marriage plans. Melville noted that Elizabeth and Dudley were "inseparable" and concluded, quite incorrectly, that Elizabeth had had second thoughts about offering Dudley to Mary. Dudley himself sought him out and declared he had no wish to marry the Queen of Scots, and that the whole idea was a ploy of Cecil's calculated to get rid of him. Elizabeth herself asked Melville if Mary had made up her mind about marrying Dudley, but he answered that such an important decision could not be made until there had been a meeting between the representatives of both monarchs; arrangements were to be made for such a conference to take place at Berwick.

Melville paid a visit to the Spanish embassy and made one last futile attempt to revive the idea of a marriage with Don Carlos, then wrote to Mary confirming that there was no hope of it. Melville also had "a secret charge" to see Lady Lennox in secret "to procure liberty for [Darnley] to go to Scotland, under the pretext of seeing the country and conveying his father back again to England."[46] The Countess welcomed Melville warmly and gave him expensive gifts for Mary, Moray and Maitland, "for she was in good hope that her son would speed better than [Dudley]."[47]

Melville was present when, on 28 September, "with great solemnity," Elizabeth formally created Robert Dudley Earl of Leicester, a strategem calculated to make Mary "think the more of him." It was on this occasion that Melville first saw Darnley, who, "as nearest Prince of the Blood, did bear the sword of honour" before the Queen. After the ceremony was over, Elizabeth asked Melville, "How do you like my new creation?" Melville was carefully diplomatic, but Elizabeth was shrewd and, pointing towards Darnley, said, "And yet ye like better of yonder long lad!" Melville replied, "No woman of spirit would make choice of such a man, that was liker a woman than a man, for he is very lusty [pleasing], beardless and lady-faced." Later, Melville recorded that he had spoken disparagingly because "I had no will that the Queen of England should think I liked Lord Darnley or had any eye or dealing that way." Elizabeth later told him that Darnley "was one of the two that she had in her head to offer our Queen, as born within the realm of England," but Melville wisely did not rise to the bait.[48]

When Melville returned to Scotland, he may have carried with him the famous heart-shaped Lennox (or Darnley) Jewel, which was perhaps a gift from Lady Lennox to her husband, and may well have contained in its elaborate symbolism coded messages that could not be committed to paper. It used to be thought that this was a memorial ring made after the deaths of Darnley and Lennox, but its imagery is still not fully understood, and its style is that of the early 1560s.[49] Its Scots legend, translated, reads, "Who hopes still constantly with patience shall obtain victory in their pretence [i.e., claim]."

Elizabeth, however, was apparently determined to push the Leicester marriage, offering the English succession as bait. In November, the English and Scottish commissioners met at Berwick, where it was made clear that the English Queen would "never willingly consent" to Mary marrying anyone other than Dudley. Moray and Maitland, angry that conditions should be attached to what they believed was Mary's right, walked out of the meeting, then wrote to Cecil insisting that Elizabeth must declare Mary her heir before they would consent to their mistress marrying an Englishman. Elizabeth, predictably, ignored this demand, but still would not abandon the idea of a match between Leicester and Mary, and negotiations dragged futilely on for several more months.

In the autumn of 1564, Elizabeth, at Mary's request, issued Bothwell with a safe-conduct enabling him to journey to France. By November, the Earl was in Paris. His release came as unwelcome news to the Protestant Lords, and Maitland even bribed one John Wemyss to induce Bothwell's servants to poison him, although the attempt failed. In a memorial dated 3 February 1565,[50] Bothwell is listed amongst Lennox's friends, so he presumably supported the Darnley marriage. By 10 February, Bothwell had been appointed Captain of the Scottish Guard in France. He later wrote, "I had received letters from the Queen of Scots for the French King and his Council, which made the request that I should enjoy such status and privileges as are granted to the nobility of my country according to the terms of an ancient treaty between France and Scotland."[51]

Meanwhile, in Scotland, the Queen had a new favourite. In December, her French secretary, Pierre Raullet, was dismissed for accepting English bribes. He was replaced by an ambitious Italian, David Rizzio, one of the Queen's musicians.

David Rizzio (or Riccio), was a native of Piedmont, and probably came of an ancient, patrician family. He had been born around 1533, and had come to Scotland in 1561 in the train of Robertino Solaro, Count Moretta, the Savoyard ambassador. The Queen was impressed with his fine bass voice and expertise on the lute, and persuaded him to remain at her court as part of a musical quartet formed by her *valets de chambre*.

Melville called Rizzio "a merry fellow and a good musician," which probably explains why Mary enjoyed his company. He was witty, discreet and well informed, yet physically ill favoured: his enemies described him as hideously ugly, and it seems he was small, dark, swarthy and in some way deformed. What counted with Mary, though, was his loyalty, and that was never in dispute.

According to Melville, Rizzio "was not very skilful in inditing French letters," and consequently "advices given by the Queen of England were misconstrued," so Mary was often obliged to write her replies "over again by her own hand." Yet for all his shortcomings, Mary came to rely upon him heavily and to take him increasingly into her confidence. As a result, Rizzio grew ever more influential and ever more arrogant and greedy, although, according to Melville, "he had not the prudence how to manage the same rightly."

As a "sly, crafty foreigner" and a Catholic, "Seigneur Davie," as they disparagingly called him, was predictably hated by most of the nobility as an upstart interloper. They bitterly resented "the extraordinary favour" shown him by the Queen, and Moray and Maitland feared, correctly, that Rizzio would supplant them in the Queen's counsels. Because the Italian was so ill qualified for the job he was employed to do, Knox and many Protestant Lords suspected him of being a papal spy, and Melville put it to Mary that he was "a known minion of the Pope," which she did not deny, but the Vatican never acknowledged his existence, and there is no record of him in its archives. Whatever the truth of this, Mary had certainly displayed poor judgement in promoting Rizzio and in openly and tactlessly preferring him over the Lords, who felt that they themselves, by virtue of their birth and status, should have been her natural counsellors.

Early in December 1564, both Mary and Lady Lennox requested Elizabeth to give Darnley leave to go to Scotland to assist his father in the legal settlement of his estates; Lady Lennox assured the Queen that the Earl and his son would return to England within a month. Not believing this for a moment, and knowing that Darnley was really being sent north to earn the Queen of Scots' approval, Elizabeth initially refused to grant this favour; she was, after all, still hoping that Mary would accept Leicester, and Mary was now doing nothing to disabuse her of the idea. In fact, she had almost convinced Elizabeth, Maitland and Randolph that she meant after all to marry Dudley.

Over the next few weeks, Cecil and Leicester did their utmost to persuade Elizabeth to change her mind and let Darnley go to Scotland.[52] Cecil's policy was "to hold the Queen [Mary] unmarried as long as he could"; Darnley would provide a temporary diversion to gain time, and Cecil had persuaded himself that the young man would not dare marry Mary without Elizabeth's consent, especially as his mother would be remaining in England as a hostage for his good behaviour, and Darnley stood to lose everything he owned in England if he defaulted.[53] In Cecil's view, Darnley was a political lightweight and a weathercock where religion was concerned, and in any case would be a less dangerous husband for Mary than a foreign Catholic prince. Cecil was backed by Leicester, who had pressing reasons of his own for wanting Mary to marry Darnley, and did all he could to promote the match, pointing out that Darnley would not dare to place the Lennox lands in England in jeopardy by remaining in Scotland without licence.

A disgruntled Randolph, who had worked tirelessly for eighteen months to promote the Leicester marriage, and had apparently received certain information about Darnley, did not want the latter in Scotland, and warned Cecil on 14 December that Elizabeth would get the blame for "sending home so great a plague into this country."[54] But his remonstrances fell on deaf ears.

In late January, Elizabeth changed her mind and agreed to let Darnley go to Scotland. Her reasons for doing this have never been fully understood. She told the Spanish ambassador in London, Guzman de Silva, that it was because Leicester had refused point blank to marry Mary, and Darnley was the only viable alternative. Melville says it was because Elizabeth had been conned into believing that Mary would marry Leicester; perversely, she now feared losing him, and it was this that made her send Darnley north "in hope that he, being a handsome, lusty youth, should rather prevail, being present, than Leicester, who was absent."[55] Elizabeth knew, however, that a union between Mary and Darnley would pose a dynastic threat to her throne, yet she may have come to agree with Cecil that Darnley himself was less dangerous than she had feared. In fact, he might prove more of a liability to Mary than to Elizabeth, and so cause trouble in Scotland, in which case it would be to Elizabeth's advantage to facilitate the marriage. Yet it would not be politic for her to be seen to encourage it, for she would have it appear that Mary had defied her wishes in rejecting Leicester, and could then use this as a pretext for denying Mary the English succession.

Had Elizabeth not wished Darnley to marry Mary, she would never have let him go to Scotland. The French diplomat, Michel de Castelnau, Sieur de la Mauvissière, was adamant that Elizabeth had "cast her eyes on the young Lord Darnley to make a present of him to the Scottish Queen, and found means to persuade the Queen of Scots, by several powerful considerations, that there was not a marriage in Christendom which could bring her more certain advantages." Later, Castelnau observed, "Her Majesty did not outwardly show the joy and pleasure which was in her heart when I told her that this marriage was advancing apace. On the contrary, she affected not to approve it: which thing, however, did rather hasten than retard it. And yet I am assured [that] she used all her efforts and spared nothing to get this marriage a-going."[56] De Silva also heard a rumour that the match had been arranged "with the concurrence of some of the great people here,"[57] and Cecil himself told Paul de Foix, the French ambassador, in March, that the marriage of the Queen of Scots was an affair in the hands of his mistress.[58] People in Scotland would tell Randolph that Elizabeth had sent Darnley on purpose to match their Queen "poorly and meanly," while Mary herself later came to believe that Elizabeth had deliberately sent Darnley to her, knowing he might well ruin her.

Darnley was given leave of absence for three months, while Lennox's licence was extended for the same period. On 3 February 1565, Darnley left for Scotland. Randolph was horrified to hear that he was on his way, for he had been convinced that his hard work for the Leicester marriage was about to bear fruit, and wrote angrily to Cecil of his fears that "one should come of whom there is so much spoken against. My whole care is to avoid the suspicion that the Queen's Majesty [Elizabeth] was the mean and worker thereof."

Meanwhile, an excited Lady Lennox, seeing the fulfilment of her ambitions within her grasp, was writing to Mary, urging her to take Darnley as her husband, and assuring her that he would be respectful, kind, companionable and utterly loyal. After being entertained at Berwick-upon-Tweed by the English Governor, Francis Russell, Earl of Bedford, Darnley crossed the Scottish border on 10 February. The winter weather was particularly severe, but he pressed on to Dunbar, where he spent the night of 11 February, before proceeding to Haddington. On 12 February, he was entertained by Lord Seton at Seton Palace, then went on to Edinburgh the following day.[59] Here, he spent three days as Randolph's guest. As Cecil had instructed him, Randolph went out of his way to make him welcome and lent him horses. During this time, the Queen's half-brother, Lord Robert Stewart, invited Darnley to dine at Holyrood Palace, and was very impressed with him. Darnley also visited his cousin, the Earl of Morton, and the Earl of Glencairn. Randolph reported that he had won good opinions: "His courteous dealing with all men deserves great praise, and is well spoken of." However, he had caught "a little cold," and did not want his mother informed, as she would be alarmed.[60]

Edinburgh was abuzz, however, with speculation as to the meaning of the ghostly warriors that had been heard fighting in the streets at midnight on the three nights before Darnley's arrival. In a superstitious and credulous age, many regarded them as a warning of what the young Lord's coming portended for Scotland and its Queen.

4

"A Handsome, Lusty Youth"

∼

HENRY STUART WAS THE SECOND of the eight children born to the Earl and Countess of Lennox, and was named after his august godfather, King Henry VIII, and for an older brother who had died in infancy.[1] The name Darnley came from one of the Lennox estates near Glasgow: Lord Darnley was the courtesy title borne by the eldest son of the Earl of Lennox, according to English usage; in Scotland, Darnley would have been styled the Master of Lennox.

There is conflicting evidence for his date of birth, which is traditionally given as 7 December 1545, yet the continuator of Knox's history states that he was not yet twenty-one at the time of his death in February 1567, and in March 1566, Queen Mary's own messenger to the Cardinal of Lorraine stated that Darnley was then nineteen.[2] It is likely, therefore, that he had been born on 7 December 1546.

Darnley first saw the light of day, and spent most of his youth, at his parents' Yorkshire seat, Temple Newsham House, near Leeds, a mansion dating from about 1520, which had been given by Henry VIII to the Lennoxes at the time of their marriage. The house has been much altered since then, but some diapered Tudor brickwork survives on the west front, where the great chamber and main apartments were probably sited in Darnley's day. The rest of the house dates mainly from the seventeenth and eighteenth centuries. An inventory of 1565 refers to "Lord Darnley's Chamber," in which there were tapestries with scenes of hunting and hawking and "one bedstead with gilt posts"; it also reveals that a portrait of Darnley hung in the great chamber alongside others depicting Henry VIII, Mary I, Philip of Spain and the Countess of Lennox.[3]

Of all the children born to the Lennoxes, only two, Henry and Charles (who was born c. 1555/6), survived infancy,[4] therefore Darnley was especially precious to his parents, both of whom doted on him, spoiled him and invested their dynastic hopes in him. Near in blood to the sovereigns of England and Scotland, he was given a Renaissance education befitting a royal prince, and grew up to be just as ambitious as his mother and father, and believing that he was destined for a crown.

Darnley was reared in England as a Roman Catholic. In 1554, aged about eight, he wrote a courteous letter to Mary I, declaring that he wished his "tender years" had not prevented him from fighting against her rebels, and asking her to accept "a little plot of my own planning" called "Utopia Nova." For his pains, the Queen rewarded him with a gold chain, for which he sent a charming note of thanks. The Lennoxes had rather hoped that she would name Darnley her heir, but were destined to be disappointed.

In 1559, after the Lennoxes had fallen from favour on the accession of Queen Elizabeth, Darnley was sent to France to complete his education, and was much praised there for his accomplishments. At some stage, he is said to have translated the works of the classical Roman author Valerius Maximus from Latin into English.

All accounts agree that Darnley was outstandingly good looking. According to Castelnau, it was "not possible to see a more beautiful prince,"[5] while Buchanan called Darnley "the most handsome of our time." He was certainly tall; analysis of a femur alleged on good grounds to be his (now in the museum of the Royal College of Physicians) suggests that his height was between 6'1" and 6'3",[6] which was exceptional in an age in which the average man's height was at most 5'6", and made him a fitting match for the Queen

of Scots, who was herself about six feet tall. Darnley had a slim, strong ath-
letic physique, honed by the sports in which he excelled. He had cropped fair
curly hair and a clean-shaven and handsome, if rather effeminate, face; later,
he grew a short beard and moustache.

Darnley was accomplished in all the traditional aristocratic pursuits. He
was a gifted lute player, a good dancer, a poet and a man of letters who was
proficient in Latin and French,[7] and a keen and expert sportsman, skilled at
swordplay, shooting, horsemanship, hunting, hawking, tennis, golf and pell-
mell (croquet). He had a certain charm, was well versed in courtly manners,
and was described by Randolph as "a fair, jolly young man."[8] "He could speak
and write well, and was bountiful and liberal enough."[9] Indeed, he seemed
"an amiable youth,"[10] and his courtesy and his good looks invariably made a
favourable impression on those who met him.[11]

Yet there was another side to Darnley, the side that was only revealed
when he was bored or thwarted, and to which his loving parents were blind.
For beneath the courtly veneer, he was spoilt, wilful, petulant, immature
and, at his worst, grossly uncouth. And for all his careful education, he
lacked intelligence, depth and sound judgement. Unreliable and unstable,
with a quick, violent temper, he was "haughty, proud and so very weak in
mind as to be a prey to all that came about him. He was inconstant, credulous and facile, unable to abide by any resolutions, capable to be imposed
upon by designing men, and could conceal no secret, let it be either to his
own welfare or detriment."[12] His kinsman Morton said of him that "he was
such a bairn that there was nothing told him but he would reveal it," while
Melville states that he told everything to his servants, "who were not all
honest."

Throughout his adult life, Darnley made enemies not only because of his
arrogance and treachery, but also through his innate selfishness, stupidity and
sheer tactlessness, he being "naturally of a very insolent disposition."[13] To
those who opposed him, he could be ruthless, vengeful and vicious. His ex-
penditure on clothes shows him to have been inordinately vain, and he was
also something of a gourmet. He was sexually promiscuous, "much addicted
to base and unmanly pleasures"[14] and excessively given to drink. His friends
were mostly young men who exerted a bad influence over him. All things considered, it is hard to find much to say in extenuation, except that he was

young and inexperienced, and lacked "good counsel."[15] And when illness and adversity eventually forced him to grow up, acknowledge his shortcomings and try to reform, it was by then far too late.

Such was the young man who arrived in Scotland in February 1565 to woo the unsuspecting Queen of Scots.

5

"Most Unworthy to
Be Matched"

AT THE TIME OF DARNLEY'S arrival in Scotland, Mary and her court were on a progress in Fife, whither he was obliged to follow them in snowy weather. On Saturday, 17 February, Mary received him at Wemyss Castle, a pink sandstone fortress overlooking the Firth of Forth. Randolph, still hoping that she would accept Leicester, reported that the Queen welcomed Darnley with no more than the courtesy due to a cousin, but Melville wrote later, "Her Majesty took well with him and said that he was the lustiest and best proportioned long [tall] man that she had seen."[1] Lennox later claimed that, as soon as she saw Darnley, she was "struck with the dart of love,"[2] but there is no other evidence for this.

Few of the Protestant Lords welcomed the arrival of the reputedly Catholic Darnley, and on 19 February, Randolph reported that Glencairn and Darnley's cousin Morton "much misliked him and wished him away." Later, Lady Lennox secured Morton's support with her renunciation of her claim to the earldom of Angus in Morton's favour, and in the hope of buying friendship, Darnley himself distributed expensive gifts of jewellery to the chief Lords.

On 18 February, Mary left Wemyss Castle for Dunfermline, while Darnley visited his father, Lennox, at Dunkeld before riding south to rejoin the progress. On 24 February, he crossed the Forth with Mary and returned to Edinburgh,[3] and thereafter remained with the court, high in favour with the Queen.

On the day after his arrival at Holyrood, Darnley accompanied Moray to St. Giles's Kirk to hear Knox preach, intent on earning the support of the Earl, in which he was initially successful. Afterwards, he dined with Moray and Randolph, and that evening, at Moray's suggestion, partnered the Queen in a galliard. Mary later recalled that Moray was at this time in favour of a match with Darnley, if only to thwart the dynastic ambitions of the Hamiltons.[4]

Darnley's visit to St. Giles was meant to allay the fears of the Protestants, yet he also attended Mass with the Queen in the chapel royal. For Darnley, religion was a matter of policy, as it was for his father. Although brought up a Catholic, at Queen Elizabeth's court he had practised the reformed faith because it was expedient to do so. He was now prepared to follow both doctrines in order to retain the favour of Queen Mary and her nobles. His contemporaries thought he was "indifferent to religion,"[5] and indeed there is little evidence that he had any deep spiritual convictions.

Darnley's willingness to compromise on religion went some way towards placating those who had been hostile to him. "A great number wish him well," wrote Randolph, but "others doubt him, and deeplier consider what is fit for the state of their country than a fair, jolly young man." Some feared that, if Darnley married the Queen, "it would be the utter overthrow and subversion of them and their Houses."[6] It was not so much his religion that was the stumbling block, as the fact that he was a Lennox Stuart, and a rival of the powerful Hamilton faction.

Darnley, meanwhile, was enjoying the pleasures of the court and the Queen's company. He set himself to charm her by his lute playing and dancing, and made friends with Rizzio. Darnley and Mary shared a passion for riding and hunting, and in the evenings they enjoyed cards, dice and music. Mary was certainly taken with Darnley, but she was still prepared to marry Leicester if Elizabeth, in return, would name her as her successor. Randolph believed that Mary's favour to Darnley and her long talks with him proceeded "rather from her own courteous nature than that anything is meant which some here fear may ensue"; yet he conceded that Mary's emotions were unpredictable, "seeing she is a woman and in all things desires to have her own will."

So far, according to Randolph, Darnley's behaviour was "well liked, and hitherto he so governs himself that there is great praise of him." Buoyed up with his success, he precipitately proposed marriage to Mary, only to be coldly turned down. After she told Melville "how she had refused the ring which he offered unto her," Melville "took occasion to speak in Darnley's favour, that their marriage would put out of doubt their title to the succession."[7] Rizzio also added his persuasions, but to no avail.

Before 5 March, to the dismay of Moray and the Protestant Lords, Bothwell returned to Scotland. Randolph reported that Mary "mislikes his homecoming without her licence,"[8] but when Bothwell, from the security of Hermitage Castle, sent his friend, Sir William Murray of Tullibardine, to plead his cause with the Queen, she listened sympathetically and declared that "she could not hate him." Moray, however, insisted that Bothwell was plotting to kill him and Maitland,[9] and demanded that he be "put to the horn" (i.e., outlawed). But although Mary told Randolph that Bothwell would never receive favour at her hands, the Earl of Bedford, from his vantage point at Berwick, believed that she would not permit him to be exiled.

Moray and Randolph now got two of Bothwell's enemies, Sir James Murray of Purdovis, brother of Tullibardine, and the Earl's former servant, Dandie Pringle, who was now employed by Moray, to tell Mary that, whilst in France, Bothwell had "spoken dishonourably of the Queen," claiming that between them, she and Queen Elizabeth "would not make one honest woman"; as for Mary, she had been her uncle "the Cardinal's whore."[10] What Bothwell had allegedly said was not only a dreadful slur on Mary's honour, but also high treason, and the Queen, shocked, willingly agreed to Moray's demand that the Earl be summoned to Edinburgh to face trial.[11]

For many months now, Mary had been urging Elizabeth to proclaim her her heir. If marriage to Leicester was the price, then Mary was prepared to pay it. On 16 March, Randolph finally delivered Elizabeth's answer, sent ten days earlier, which was that, if Mary agreed to marry Leicester, Elizabeth would advance her title to the succession in every way that she could, but she "could not gratify her desire to have her title determined and published until she be married herself, or determined not to marry."

It was a bitter blow. Too late, Mary saw that she had been duped. In a passion, she "wept her fill" and "used evil speech" of Elizabeth, complaining that she had "abused" her, deceiving her with vain hopes and wasting her time to no purpose.[12] After this, there was no more talk of the Leicester marriage, and no longer a pressing need to keep Elizabeth sweet.

While Moray and Maitland simmered with anger, Mary did "nothing but weep," reported Randolph. He espied her crying as she watched Darnley and her half-brother, Lord Robert Stewart, running at the ring on Leith Sands, and noticed there was "much sadness in her looks." It seemed that her hopes must now be invested in Darnley, which is what Elizabeth had perhaps intended when she effectively scuppered the match with Leicester.

Darnley was about to alienate his most important ally. When Lord Robert Stewart showed him a map of Scotland and pointed out the extent of Moray's vast estates, Darnley tactlessly remarked "that it was too much." Moray, hearing of this, was mightily offended and complained to the Queen. Mary made Darnley apologise, but it was too late,[13] for Moray, alarmed, had realised that, if Darnley became King, he would almost certainly try to curb Moray's power and encourage Mary to free herself from his tutelage. From this time onwards, therefore, Moray was Darnley's enemy, and, in concert with Maitland, Argyll and Chatelherault, strongly opposed any plan for his marriage to Mary, having no intention of allowing his political supremacy, built up over six years, to be eroded. According to Bothwell, "these villains did all they could to stop her, chiefly because they wanted above everything else to prevent her having any children, but also because they wanted no one else to challenge their authority. They realised well enough that any such marriage could only diminish their own influence."[14] Significantly, Bothwell makes no mention of the Lords acting in the interests of the reformed faith.

As yet, it was by no means certain that Darnley was Mary's first choice as a husband. On 24 March, she again attempted to revive negotiations for a union with Don Carlos,[15] but at the same time, aware that there was little hope of success, she agonised over whether or not she should take Darnley. "What to do, or wherein to resolve, she is marvellously in doubt," Randolph wrote on 27 March.

Rizzio, whose influence at this time should never be underestimated, was strongly in favour of a match with Darnley. Rizzio was now Mary's most valued counsellor, and any lord who sought an audience with her had to approach him first, for he controlled access to her. Arrogant, boastful and open to bribery, he swaggered about the court dressed in rich velvets and silks, incurring enmity on all sides. "Some of the nobility would gloom upon him, and some of them would shoulder him and push him aside when they entered the chamber and found him always speaking with Her Majesty," recalled Melville, who tried to warn Rizzio of the folly of his conduct, only to be told that the Queen approved of it. Melville gently attempted to alert Mary to "the inconveniences I did clearly foresee would inevitably follow if she did not alter her carriage to Rizzio, a stranger, and one suspected by her subjects to be a pensioner of the Pope," yet she insisted she would not be restrained but would "dispense her favours to such as she pleased." Melville reminded her "what displeasure had been procured to her by the rash behaviour" of Chastelard. "I told Her Majesty that a grave and comely behaviour towards strangers, not admitting them to too much familiarity, would bring them to a more circumspect and reverend carriage." Once the hearts of her subjects were lost, they might never be regained. Mary thanked him for his advice, but ignored it.[16]

Given the hatred of the Lords, it was in Rizzio's interests to secure the friendship and patronage of Darnley and further the latter's prospects of becoming King. According to Randolph,[17] Rizzio was one of "the chief dealers" in negotiations for the Darnley marriage—the other was Melville—and Buchanan says Rizzio "was also assiduous in sowing seeds of discord between [Darnley] and Moray."

Before long, Rizzio had become Darnley's "great friend at the Queen's hand."[18] It was a friendship of mutual self-interest, for Darnley too needed an advocate, and it was also very warm, for Rizzio, having persuaded Darnley "that it was chiefly by his good offices that the Queen had become attracted to him," was admitted to Darnley's "table, his chamber and his most secret thoughts."[19] On occasions, the two men would "lie in one bed together."[20] This and other evidence, which will be considered later, suggests that the effeminate-looking Darnley, although he certainly chased women, did have bisexual tendencies, which he may have indulged with Rizzio.

Randolph had thought by now to see evidence as to whether or not Mary was attracted to Darnley, but although he wondered "what alteration the sight of so fair a face daily in presence may work on the Queen's heart, hitherto I have espied nothing. I am somewhat suspicious."

Moray was unable to stomach the triangular relationship between Mary,

Darnley and Rizzio. He too was suspicious of the fact that all three were Catholics, and believed that they were plotting to undermine not only his own position, but also the reformed Church. On 3 April, he withdrew from court on the pretext that he did not wish to witness the "ungodly" Catholic ceremonies that the Queen would observe at Easter.[21] Mary was irritated by his disapproval, but, freed from his constant unwelcome advice, realised she would have scope to act independently.

The court now moved north to Stirling Castle, a mighty fortress commanding access to the Highlands. Set upon a steep rock, the castle boasted strong mediaeval defences, but within its walls was a magnificent great hall, erected by James IV, and a luxurious Renaissance palace that had been built by James V in c. 1538–42 and embellished by French and Italian craftsmen. The Queen's apartments boasted large windows, decorated stone fireplaces and a ceiling adorned with carved oak roundels known as the Stirling Heads, many of which survive today. The castle was surrounded with ornamental gardens and a hunting park stocked with deer, boar and wild cattle.

On 5 April, soon after arriving at Stirling, Darnley fell ill with a feverish cold and took to his bed; within two days, "measles came out on him marvellous thick."[22] Mary insisted on helping to nurse him back to health, regardless of the threat of infection; there was shocked amazement in European diplomatic circles when it became known that she had spent an entire night in Darnley's sickroom,[23] notwithstanding the fact that she had "showed herself very careful and anxious about his malady," although it was conceded that "her care was marvellous, great and tender over him."[24]

Darnley's illness marked a turning point in his relationship with Mary, for it inspired in her first sympathy and then something deeper, and made her realise that she did indeed wish to marry him. Melville says that she tried at first to suppress her feelings, but that it was not long before she was so infatuated that she could not bear to be apart from Darnley. "Great tokens of love daily pass" between them, reported Randolph, but it was clear Mary had become entranced by a "fantasy of a man, without regard to his tastes, manners or estate,"[25] in consequence of which she was throwing propriety and discretion to the winds.

Love, or perhaps lust, blinded her to other concerns, not the least of which was the scandal her behaviour was causing, and she was unwilling to listen to those Lords who cautioned her against the marriage, urging that it could only bring discord and divisions to Scotland. Nor would she heed those who warned her that Darnley was not all that he seemed. For him, she would defy Moray, Maitland, Knox, the Hamiltons and even Queen Elizabeth, jeopardising her long-cherished hopes of the English succession. As she began to lavish gifts on Darnley—rich materials for clothing, hats, shoes, shirts, ruffs, nightcaps, trappings of cloth of gold for his horse, feathered bonnets for his fools—the courts of Europe began to bristle with scurrilous rumours and disapproval of a queen thus compromising her reputation.

John Leslie, Bishop of Ross, who was later in Mary's confidence, felt that there was a strong maternal element in her feelings for Darnley; she displayed "very motherly care" while he was ill, and, although "they were not very different in years"—she was 22, he 18—"she was to him not only a loyal prince, but a most careful and tender mother."[26] This would explain her forbearance when the baser side of Darnley's nature began to manifest itself.

Darnley's feelings for Mary are more difficult to determine. His poems express the conventional sentiments of courtly love,[27] but it is uncertain when they were written or to whom they were addressed. He seems to have wanted Mary as a queen rather than as a woman, and to have regarded her as a trophy; his overriding emotion at this time may well have been triumph at the realisation of his ambitions.

Randolph had quickly seen through Darnley, and wrote to Cecil: "What is thought of his behaviour, wit and judgement I would were less spoken than is, or less occasion for all men to enlarge their tongues as they do. Of this I have a greater number of particulars than I may well put in writing, which shall not be secret to you, though I cannot utter them but with great grief of heart." Even Randolph, her enemy, felt pity for the unsuspecting Mary.

Maitland believed that Mary chose Darnley to spite Elizabeth, but she herself was convinced that there were sound political reasons for marrying him. Foremost was the uniting of their claims to the thrones of England and Scotland, which could only strengthen her position and that of any children of the marriage. Secondly, Mary's union with a Catholic would earn her the approval of the Pope and the Kings of France and Spain. Thirdly, she counted on Darnley to help her break free from her thraldom to Moray and Maitland and enable her to exercise the sovereign power that was her right. Yet she failed to envisage how much hostility the marriage would engender amongst her Protestant nobles, especially Moray, who had been the mainstay of her throne, nor did she foresee how it would alienate Queen Elizabeth and create bitter divisions at court.

That was soon evident. By 15 April, Moray had hastened back to court, having heard "more than a bruit" that the Queen meant to "forsake all other offers and content herself with her own choice, despite the dangers like to ensue." Mary was furious to hear that he was joining forces with other opponents of the marriage, and angrily accused him of scheming to "set the crown on his own head."[28] After this, relations between brother and sister deteriorated rapidly.

On 15 April, Randolph got wind of what was afoot and wrote to Cecil that Mary's "familiarity" with Darnley "breeds no small suspicions that there is more intended than merely giving him honour for his nobility." When this report reached London, Elizabeth began to be alarmed. She already regretted allowing Darnley to go to Scotland, and now it looked as if Mary really did mean to marry him.

Having made her decision, Mary sent Maitland to London to break the news formally to Elizabeth and seek her blessing, which she had no reason to think would not be forthcoming. Elizabeth was no doubt gratified that she had diverted Mary from making a foreign alliance, but she was now aware of how deeply her friends the Protestant Lords in Scotland disapproved of any union with Darnley, so she took steps to distance herself from that which she had been instrumental in bringing to pass. Flying into a rage, she told Maitland she was astonished at this "very strange and unlikely proposal" and much offended at Darnley's disobedience, for, as her subject and her cousin, he required her permission to marry, which she was not prepared to give. On her orders, the English Privy Council declared that such a marriage "would be unmeet, unprofitable and perilous to the amity between the Queens and both realms," and offered Mary a free choice "of any other of the nobility in this whole realm."[29] On 20 April, two days after her audience with Maitland, Elizabeth had Lady Lennox placed under house arrest.

By 18 April, Randolph knew for certain that Mary meant to marry Darnley, and reported Chatelherault's fears that the House of Hamilton would be "quite overthrown" once a Lennox Stuart sat on the throne. "The godly cry out that they are undone," wrote Randolph. "No hope now of the sure establishment of Christ's true religion, but all turning to confusion."

Opposition to the marriage rapidly formed in Scotland, and Moray, Chatelherault, Argyll, Glencairn and others signed a bond declaring their resolve to prevent it, complaining that "what [Mary] has taken in hand tends to her own destruction and the overthrow of tranquillity of her realm—and must be helped by sharper means."[30] But the Queen defiantly ignored all their protests. "She is now in utter contempt of her people," observed Randolph, "and so far in doubt of them that, without speedy redress, worse is to be feared."[31]

On 24 April, Elizabeth sent that seasoned diplomat, Sir Nicholas Throckmorton, to Scotland with instructions to prevent or delay Darnley's marriage, but as soon as he had set out, she changed her mind and recalled him. Instead, she wrote commanding Darnley and Lennox to return to England at once, then sent urgently to Randolph, instructing him to stay the order until further notice, which he felt would compound "the suspicion, which is now almost universal, that the sending of Darnley was done of purpose."[32] At the same time, Maitland, still in London, secretly obtained Spanish approval of Mary's proposed marriage from King Philip's ambassador, Guzman de Silva. Later, Philip wrote to Lady Lennox, declaring that he would be glad not only for her son to be King of Scotland, "but also to be King of England, if this marriage is carried through."[33] Elizabeth's fears were not unfounded.

Easter that year was observed at court with unprecedented splendour, and on Easter Monday, Mary and her ladies dressed up as burgesses' wives and went on foot through the town of Stirling, collecting money to pay for the banquet for the Queen's servants.[34]

On that same day, 5–6,000 armed men in Moray's pay were occupying Edinburgh, where an assize met to try Bothwell on 2 May. The presiding judge was Argyll, Moray's ally. Bothwell dared not put in an appearance himself, but was ably defended by his cousin, Sir Alexander Hepburn, Laird of Riccarton. Nevertheless, he was condemned *in absentia* for high treason. The Queen, however, refused to consent to any punishment other than a nominal forfeiture, much to Moray's fury,[35] but in any case it was no longer safe for Bothwell to remain in Scotland, and soon afterwards he returned to France.

Darnley was now recovering from his illness. On 2 May, and again on 10 May, the French ambassador in London reported that he and Mary had already been secretly married;[36] a letter addressed to Cosimo de' Medici alleges the same thing, adding that the ceremony took place in Darnley's apartment at Stirling, which had been fitted up as a Catholic chapel for the occasion.[37] Mary had not yet applied for a papal dispensation, so these reports may refer to a betrothal or handfasting before witnesses, after which a couple were permitted to have sexual relations. As there is little evidence that Mary and Darnley became lovers at this time, the ambassadors' information may well have been inaccurate.

On 3 May, Mary received a letter from Maitland informing her of Elizabeth's fury over her proposed union with Darnley. This came as a shock, but Mary's resolve did not waver and on 6 May she announced to the Lords at Stirling her forthcoming marriage, asking them to sign a document in support of it. When Moray alone refused, on the grounds that Darnley was an enemy to "Christ's true religion," there was "a great altercation" between him and his sister, in which Mary accused him of being a slave to England.[38] "All things now grow too libertine," observed Randolph darkly, "and the Queen taketh upon her to do as she pleases."[39]

On 5 May, Elizabeth finally sent Throckmorton to Scotland with instructions to bring Darnley back to England, or delay the marriage for as long as possible. He was to offer Mary any other Englishman but Darnley, but warn her that Elizabeth would only consider naming her as her successor if she consented to marry Leicester. Maitland was only sorry that Elizabeth had not ordered Sir Nicholas to threaten war in order to awaken Mary to the reality of the situation.

Mary, meanwhile, had sent a letter to Maitland instructing him to inform Queen Elizabeth that "she did mind to use her own choice in marriage, and she would no longer be fed with yea and nay."[40] But Maitland had already left London, and her messenger, John Beaton, met him at Newark. Maitland read the letter, decided that it was too provocative and would seriously jeopardise his pro-English policy, and resumed his journey to Scotland. At Alnwick, he caught up with Throckmorton and the two travelled together the rest of the way. Maitland showed Throckmorton Mary's letter, and Sir Nicholas reported that he had never seen Maitland in such a passion.[41]

Maitland reached Edinburgh on 13 May, having been ordered by Mary to delay Throckmorton's arrival at Stirling. He passed on the message and hastened on to Stirling alone. Mary was justifiably angry with him for having disobeyed her orders, and withdrew her favour from him.[42] Soon afterwards, Randolph commented that Maitland "hath now time enough to make court to his mistress," Mary Fleming.[43]

Elizabeth's blatant interference in Mary's matrimonial affairs had caused the Scottish Lords to close ranks, and on 15 May, a convention of the nobility at Stirling reluctantly agreed to the Queen's marriage to Darnley.[44] "Many consented on condition that no change should be made in the established state of religion."[45] Of the Lords present, only Lord Ochiltree objected. Moray left before the vote was taken. Argyll, in protest, had refused to attend. On the same day, Mary applied to the Pope for a dispensation, since she and Darnley were within the prohibited degrees of consanguinity.

That morning, Throckmorton had arrived at Stirling, only to find the castle gates locked. Presently, two Councillors arrived and ordered him, in the Queen's name, to retire to his lodgings, saying that she would grant him an audience after he had rested. Mary did not want him voicing any official protests until she had publicly committed herself to marrying Darnley. In the afternoon, Mary knighted Darnley and created him Baron Ardmannoch and Earl of Ross, "that her marriage might not seem too unequal."[46] Although he was Queen Elizabeth's subject and owed allegiance only to her, Darnley accepted these Scottish titles and swore fealty to Mary. Elizabeth would rightly interpret this as an act of treason. Mary intended to give Darnley the royal dukedom of Albany, but was holding this in reserve, much to Darnley's private annoyance, until she knew how Elizabeth was going to react to the lesser creations. After his ennoblement, Darnley was allowed to create fourteen knights, who were to form his personal entourage and the core of a new Queen's party. Among them were several Lennox adherents, including Bothwell's friend, Sir William Murray of Tullibardine, a Protestant who in August became Comptroller of the Queen's Household.[47] His advancement suggests that Bothwell was known to support the Darnley marriage.

Later that same day, Mary finally granted Throckmorton an audience, during which he recited Elizabeth's protests against the marriage and demanded the return of Darnley and Lennox, who had "failed in their duty by their arrogant and presumptuous attempts to enterprise such a matter without making Queen Elizabeth privy, being her subjects." Mary retorted that Elizabeth had objected to all her foreign suitors, and, as Darnley was "of the blood royal, she could not see what possible reasonable excuse her good sister could have for interfering." It was obvious that there was no way of dissuading Mary, but she did assure Throckmorton that the wedding would not take place for three months, in order to give Elizabeth time to express her approval of it.[48]

On 21 May, Moray, having so far failed in his attempts to prevent the marriage, signalled his disapproval by withdrawing from court and retiring to his stepfather's castle at Loch Leven in Fife.[49] This was a mistake because, in his absence, Atholl, a Lennox man who was one of the "chief dealers" in the marriage, acted as the Queen's chief Councillor.[50] On the day of Moray's departure, Throckmorton informed Leicester that Mary had been "seized with love in fervented passions than is comely in any mean personage," and was "so far passed in this matter with Lord Darnley as it is irrevocable, and no place left to dissolve the same persuasion by reasonable means; for though the consummation of the marriage be deferred, I am sure it is indissoluble without violence. The only means to stop the marriage is force." He thought Mary "either so captivated by love or cunning, or rather, say truly, by boasting or folly, that she is not able to keep promise with herself," and might therefore further ennoble Darnley despite her concerns about Elizabeth's reaction.[51] His view was echoed by Randolph, who wrote, "She doteth so much that some report she is bewitched: the tokens, the rings, the bracelets are daily worn that contain the sacred mysteries. Shame is laid aside, and all regard of that which chiefly pertaineth to princely honour removed out of sight."[52] If Mary and Darnley were not yet lovers in the physical sense, they were certainly giving a good impression that they were, and not caring who witnessed it.

Throckmorton feared that, through this marriage, Mary would attempt to restore Catholicism in Scotland to the detriment of Elizabeth, and warned Cecil to keep watch on the great Catholic families in the north and prevent Mary from communicating with the Spanish ambassador, a warning that the English Privy Council took seriously. This was all Sir Nicholas could do in the circumstances, and he returned home, despondent because not only had he failed in his mission, but he was convinced that Mary's determination to marry Darnley had been founded on "despite and anger" towards Elizabeth, and "I cannot assure myself that such qualities will bring forth such fruit as the love and usage bestowed on Darnley shows."[53]

Darnley was beginning to reveal his true colours, but Mary was too infatuated to notice. Even Randolph felt pity for

> the lamentable estate of this poor Queen, whom ever before I esteemed so worthy, so wise, so honourable in all her doings, and at this present do find so altered with affection towards the Lord Darnley that she hath brought her honour in question, her estate in hazard, her country to be torn in pieces. Woe worth the time that ever the Lord Darnley did set his foot in this country. This Queen in her love is so transported, and he is grown so proud, that to all honest men he is intolerable, and almost forgetful of his duty to her already, that hath ventured so much for his sake. What shall become of her, or what life with him she shall lead, that taketh already so much upon him to control and to command her, I leave it to others to think.

He had noted a great change in Mary: "Her majesty is laid aside, her wits not what they were, her beauty other than it was, her cheer and countenance changed into I wot not what—a woman more to be pitied than I ever saw." She no longer heeded "the counsel of such as can best advise her, nor giveth ear to any than such who follow her fantasy."[54] It seemed that, in her obsession with Darnley, she was rushing headlong into disaster.

Darnley's conduct was both inappropriate and intolerable. Having expected to receive the dukedom of Albany, he exploded in temper and brandished his dagger at Justice Clerk Bellenden, who had been delegated to inform him of the deferment of this honour.[55] Randolph judged Darnley "the most unworthy to be matched" with Mary, and wrote of the Scots' belief "that God must send him a short end, or themselves a miserable life," opining: "A greater benefit to the Queen's Majesty [Elizabeth] could not have chanced, than to see this dishonour fall upon [Mary], and her so matched where she shall ever be assured that she can never attain to what she so earnestly looked for"—the English succession.[56] It seemed that she had cast aside all rational considerations in order to gratify her passion for Darnley and her need to be revenged upon Elizabeth.

On 23 May, Randolph reported that Chatelherault had paid Darnley a visit in a spirit of reconciliation, but that Darnley had threatened "to knock his pate."[57] By now, Darnley had made many enemies, and they were beginning to align against him.

Nor were the Guises happy about the marriage. The Cardinal of Lorraine had heard rumours about Darnley, and on 23 May wrote to Mary in the hope of dissuading her from marrying such "an amiable prat" ("un gentil huteaudeau"). Mary, however, made it clear to her uncle that she meant to do so, and he conceded defeat, agreeing to support her request for a papal dispensation.[58]

Rizzio, as Randolph reported on 3 June, continued to support the marriage. He "now worketh all [as] chief Secretary to the Queen and only governor to her good man." This was perhaps another reason why "the hatred towards Lord Darnley and his House [was] marvellously great." Mainly, however, it was because Darnley's pride was "intolerable [and] his words not to be borne." To those who dared not answer back, "he spareth not, in token of his manhood, to let blows fly. The passions and furies I hear say he will sometimes be in are strange to believe." Randolph was convinced that the only remedy for the "mischiefs" that would almost certainly follow upon the marriage was for Darnley to "be taken away, or those he hates so supported that what he intends for others may light upon himself."[59] An anonymous Scot asked Randolph whether, if Darnley and Lennox were seized and carried off to Berwick, the English would take custody of them. Randolph replied that they would.

Early in June, Mary summoned a convention of her nobles to meet at Perth "to persuade those present to allow her to marry with Lord Darnley."[60] She knew she could count on the support of several lesser magnates, but needed to secure that of her chief Lords. From Lochleven, Moray sent a message that he was too ill with diarrhoea to attend the convention,[61] which met on 10 June, but in truth he was still implacable in his opposition to the marriage, ostensibly on religious grounds, and he was powerfully backed by Argyll (who also absented himself), Glencairn, Rothes, Ochiltree, Sir William Kirkcaldy of Grange and the Hamiltons.

On the day the convention met, Elizabeth herself commanded Lennox and Darnley, on their allegiance, to return to England. Mary wept when the summons arrived, and Lennox was worried, but Darnley insolently refused to obey, declaring that he "acknowledged no duty or obedience save to the Queen of Scots. I find myself very well where I am, and so purpose to keep me."[62] On 14 June, Mary wrote to Elizabeth, protesting that she had chosen Darnley "to meet her dearest sister's wishes," but when Elizabeth received this letter, she vented her wrath on the messenger, John Hay. Meanwhile, Mary had told Randolph that she now saw what all Scotland had seen, that Darnley had been sent to degrade her by an unworthy marriage, but she cared nothing for that, and would snap her fingers at all who opposed her, and have her way despite them.[63]

On 20 June, in retaliation for Darnley's and Lennox's defiance, and on the advice of Throckmorton, who was concerned about England's security in the face of this new Catholic threat, Elizabeth sent Lady Lennox to the Tower, where she was not even allowed to receive letters from her husband and son. By the end of June, Elizabeth was covertly supporting Moray's party, having instructed Randolph to inform them that her assistance was conditional upon their undertaking only to act "to uphold the true religion [and] support their Queen with good advice." Although she was angry with Mary, she would not countenance rebellion against their lawful sovereign.[64]

Mary was doing her best to build up her own party in order to counteract the threat from Moray. On 23 June, she promised to John, Lord Erskine, a Privy Councillor and Keeper of Edinburgh Castle, the earldom of Mar, which his family had been claiming in vain since 1435, and which had hitherto been held by Moray. The new Earl, a former Catholic priest who had renounced his vows and turned Protestant, was "a true nobleman,"[65] a fair-minded man of integrity who was respected by all, but his wife, Annabella Murray, who was sister to Tullibardine and a Catholic, was detested by Knox, who called her "a very Jezebel." Mar's sister Margaret was Moray's mother, but this did not affect his loyalty to the Queen.

From 25 to 27 June, Mary was a guest of the sinister Patrick, 3rd Lord Ruthven at Ruthven (now Huntingtower) Castle near Perth. Ruthven was

Darnley's uncle by marriage and, although a staunch Protestant, was a strong supporter of Mary's marriage plans and was said to be "stirring coals as hot as fire to have these matters take effect."[66] In 1561, Mary had told Knox that she could not love Ruthven "for I know him to use enchantment," yet in 1563 she admitted him to her Privy Council.[67] He was an educated man, but a highly unsavoury character because of his involvement with the black arts. Yet Mary could not afford to be too nice about such matters: she and Darnley, who seems to have regarded Ruthven in an avuncular light, now needed all the support they could get. On 30 June, Mary appointed the loyal Lord Fleming Lord Great Chamberlain. She knew she could also count on several other Lords, including the appalling Lindsay, who was linked to Darnley by marriage.

That same day, Mary learned that Charles IX and Catherine de' Medici approved of her proposed marriage. Armed with this knowledge, she felt she could go ahead and risk the consequences. But the very next day, Moray, with the backing of Chatelherault, Glencairn and Randolph, was convening a meeting with Argyll and the Protestant Robert, 5th Lord Boyd at Lochleven to formulate a protest against her marriage and plot rebellion. More ominously, Elizabeth now seemed prepared to back them, and at Moray's request, transmitted through Randolph, soon afterwards secretly sent him £3,000, in the hope of ensuring his continuance in power. Knox and other Protestant ministers were already condemning the marriage from their pulpits, and were ready to take up arms if need be to defend the reformed faith.[68]

Word of Moray's activities had reached Mary, along with a warning that, with the connivance of England, he was planning the kidnap and possible assassination of both her and Darnley. That this was not mere rumour is confirmed by Cecil's assumption on 7 July that the plot had been successful: "The bruit is abroad that the Queen of Scotland has been taken by the Earls of Moray and Argyll." Moray was aware that on 1 July, Mary was to travel with Darnley from Perth to Callendar House near Falkirk, to be godmother to the child of Lord Livingston; Moray had been invited to attend, but had declined. Instead, he was planning to ambush the royal party on the way to Callendar and send Mary, Darnley and Lennox as captives to England. Bothwell later claimed that they meant to murder Darnley.[69] Forewarned, Mary left Perth at 5 a.m., accompanied by Atholl, Ruthven, Mar and an escort of 2–300 men, and rode the thirty miles to Callendar without stopping, arriving an hour before Moray had expected her to set out.[70]

On 2 July, however, Randolph reported that it had been Darnley and Rizzio who were plotting against Moray, and that he had stayed away from Perth because he had been warned that he would be slain there. It seems that Moray had himself put this rumour about, in order to deflect suspicion from himself. Of Darnley, Randolph wrote: "What shall become of him I know not, but it is greatly to be feared that he can have no long life among these people." He added that Mary, "being of better understanding," was trying "to frame and fashion him to the nature of her subjects," but it was an impossible task because Darnley was "proud, disdainful and suspicious. A greater plague to her there cannot be. He is of an insolent temper, and thinks that he is never sufficiently honoured. The Queen does everything to oblige him, though he cannot be prevailed upon to yield the smallest thing to please her. He claims the Crown Matrimonial, and will have it immediately. The Queen tells him that it must be delayed till he be of age, and done by consent of Parliament, which does not satisfy him."[71] The Crown Matrimonial was to become a bone of contention between Mary and Darnley, and would permanently sour their relationship. Mary's excuse did not satisfy Darnley, since Francis II had been granted the Crown Matrimonial when he was younger than Darnley, but it was unlikely, given Darnley's conduct and immaturity, that Parliament would agree to it being bestowed on him as yet, for it brought with it the right of succession, in the event of the sovereign dying childless. To Darnley, it represented the pinnacle of his ambition, and he would never rest until it was his.

Having failed in his design against Mary, Moray was preparing to take up arms, and on 6 July, Argyll began raising troops on his behalf. Four days later, Elizabeth sent Moray a letter of encouragement, and Mary one containing a strong warning.

On 9 July, Mary and Darnley went to Seton Palace as the guests of Lord Seton. Situated ten miles east of Edinburgh, near the Firth of Forth, the palace had been largely rebuilt since its sacking by the English in 1544, and boasted fine, lofty state rooms set around a triangular courtyard.[72] On 16 July,

Randolph reported to Elizabeth that Mary and Darnley had been secretly married at Holyrood on 9 July, with "not above seven persons present," and had consummated their marriage that night at Seton. "If true, Your Majesty sees how her promise is kept."

Mary and Darnley stayed two nights at Seton, then returned to Edinburgh Castle, where they hosted a dinner. "That afternoon, [they] walked up and down the town disguised till supper time, and lay that night at the Abbey."[73] Rumours were flying fast; if they had not been secretly married, then they may well have taken part in a betrothal ceremony, and it is more likely that this took place now rather than in May, as the French ambassador had alleged. But although Randolph initially claimed that Mary and Darnley consummated their union at this time, he later declared that, although suspicious men supposed they were lovers, "the likelihoods are so great to the contrary that, if it were possible to see such an act done, I would not believe it." Coming from Mary's enemy, this must be the truth.

On 12 July, and again on the 15th, in order to allay the fears of the Protestants, Mary issued a proclamation declaring that she did not intend to make any alteration in the state of religion. Her second proclamation also summoned her lieges to arms, for she had learned that Moray was now in the west, raising a rebel army with intent to march on Edinburgh. The following day, in an act of defiance against Moray, Mary summoned Bothwell back to Scotland. But Bothwell, then in Paris, never received her letter, for it was intercepted by Bedford at Berwick.

Moray, Argyll, Chatelherault and several other rebel Lords met at Stirling on 18 July, whence they sent a plea to Elizabeth for military aid, which in itself constituted an act of treason. Elizabeth sent them £10,000.

Two days later, Parliament was due to meet, but Mary deliberately did not summon it, not wishing to create a forum for opposition. On 22 July, without consulting her Lords, she at last created Darnley Duke of Albany. Given the political situation, and Elizabeth's hostility,[74] Mary was not minded to wait for a dispensation, and on that same day took the irrevocable step of ordering the marriage banns to be published in St. Giles's Kirk, the Canongate Kirk and the chapel royal at Holyrood. In so doing, she risked making an invalid marriage and jeopardising the legitimacy of any issue of it,[75] but she must have felt that this was the lesser of two evils for, once married, she would be in a far stronger position to deal with her rebels. In order to win the support of the Pope, Mary wrote to him protesting her determination to re-store the Catholic faith in Scotland, ignoring the fact that she had proclaimed her intention to maintain the reformed faith only a week earlier. In this re-solve, she had the support of Darnley, Lennox, Rizzio and the Clerk Register, Sir James Balfour, a friend of Darnley's.[76]

The wedding was set for 29 July. On the evening before, at the Mercat Cross in Edinburgh, Darnley was publicly proclaimed King of Scots,[77] a title that the Queen could not legally grant him without the consent of Parlia-ment, which gave the Lords further cause for anger and resentment. Ac-cording to the Imperial ambassador in England, Mary had conferred royal status upon Darnley because, having "previously been married to one of the greatest kings in Christendom, she therefore intended to wed no one unless he were a king also."[78] In the event, no formal objections to Darnley's title were ever raised.

The stage was now set for the marriage that would dangerously overset the balance of power in Scotland and set afoot a series of events that would lead to disaster for the two people concerned.

6

"THE CHASEABOUT RAID"

~

BETWEEN THE HOURS OF FIVE and six on the morning of Sunday, 29 July 1565,[1] Mary was conveyed by Atholl and a triumphant Lennox to the chapel royal at Holyrood.[2] She was attired in a "great mourning gown of black, with the great white mourning hood, not unlike that which she wore the doleful day of the burial of her husband."[3] The Lords then went to fetch Darnley, who was wearing a magnificent outfit studded with glittering gems. The marriage ceremony was conducted by John Sinclair, Dean of Restalrig (later Bishop of Brechin), Lord President of the Council, according to the Catholic rite. "The words were spoken," then three rings, representing the Trinity, were placed by Darnley on Mary's finger; the middle one was a fine diamond in a red-enamelled setting.[4] This done, "they knelt together and many prayers were said over them." Darnley then kissed his new wife, left her in the chapel to hear Mass—he was careful not to give offence to the Protestants by attending it himself—and went to wait for her in her chamber. Thither Mary repaired after receiving the Sacrament, to symbolically "cast off her care, and lay aside those sorrowful garments, and give herself to a pleasanter life. After some pretty refusal, more for manners' sake than grief of heart, she suffered every man that could approach her to take out a pin, and so, being committed unto her ladies," donned wedding finery. She and Darnley did not immediately go to bed, as they wished "to signify unto the world that it was not lust moved them to marry, but only the necessity of her country, if she will not leave it destitute of an heir."[5]

The newlyweds rested until noon, when they were conducted to the great hall by the Lords, to the sound of trumpets, for their marriage feast, at which they were served sixteen dishes, among them chicken, lamb and game;[6] afterwards there was music and dancing. Morton, Mar and Glencairn were amongst the Protestant Lords present. Later, the King and Queen threw handfuls of gold and silver coins "in great abundance" to the crowds who had gathered outside the palace. In the evening there was a lavish supper, followed by a Latin masque written by George Buchanan and more dancing, "and so they go to bed."[7] Even if she was not a virgin, this was Mary's first experience of sex with a virile man.

For the next three days, according to the disapproving Knox, "there was nothing but balling and dancing and banqueting." Three more masques by Buchanan were performed, each on a different aspect of love. On the day after the wedding, Darnley was again proclaimed King, "but no man said so much as amen, saving his father, that cried out, 'God save His Grace!' "[8] Medals and coins were struck to commemorate the marriage, with Darnley's name given precedence on the latter, as it was to be, by Mary's order, on all state documents.[9] This caused further resentment among the Lords.

The new King did little to win hearts. Randolph reported on 31 July: "His words to all men against whom he conceiveth any displeasure, however unjust it be, are so proud and spiteful that rather he seemed a monarch of the world than he that not long since we have seen and known as the Lord Darnley. He looketh now for reverence to many that have little will to give it to him, and though there are some that do give it to him, they think him little worthy of it." Mary, in "her vehement love borne towards the King,"[10] was blind to his failings, and deferred to him in all things:

All honour that may be attributed to any man by his wife he hath it fully and wholly; all praise that may be spoken of him he lacketh not from herself. All the dignities that she can endow him with are freely given and taken. No man pleaseth her that contenteth not him—what may I say more? She has given over unto him her whole will to be ruled and guided as himself best likes, but she can as little prevail with him in anything that is against his will.

She would have waited to have him proclaimed King until it could be done with the consent of Parliament, but "he would in no case have it deferred one day, and either then or never."[11] The Queen "did him great honour herself, and desired everyone who would deserve her favour to do the like."[12] It was obvious that Mary had "given over to him her whole will, to be ruled and guided as himself best liketh."[13]

For as long as Mary remained a submissive and pliant wife, all was well, "and for a little time [Darnley] was well accompanied, and such as sought favour by him sped best in their suits."[14] Mary asked Melville "to wait upon the King, who was but young, and give him my best counsel, which might help him to shun many inconveniences, desiring me also to befriend Rizzio, who was hated without a cause," and it appears that Darnley was happy to accept Melville as a mentor, at least for a time.[15]

The royal couple spent their short honeymoon at Seton, before returning to Holyrood, where Darnley was assigned the vacant King's apartments on the first floor of the north-west tower, immediately below Mary's rooms and connected to them by a private stair. His antechamber and bedchamber were modernised in the seventeenth century, but his oddly shaped dressing room still survives, although much altered. We know very little about the early married life of Mary and Darnley, although Lennox tells us that the Queen would dress up in male attire, "which apparel she loved oftentimes to be in, in dancings secretly with her husband, and going in masks by night through the streets."[16]

Knox was not deceived by Darnley's politic attendances at St. Giles. In a sermon he preached before the King on 19 August, he delivered a diatribe on the state of a kingdom ruled by "that harlot Jezebel" and claimed that, to punish the people, God had set boys and women to rule over them. Greatly offended and "extremely crabbit," Darnley stormed out of the church and, on his return to Holyrood, refused to eat his dinner. That afternoon, "being troubled with great fury," he went hawking. As a result, Knox was suspended from preaching for fifteen days, during which, unrepentant, he prepared the offending sermon for publication.[17]

. . .

The royal couple had little leisure to themselves. On 1 August, Mary directed her Council to summon Moray to appear before it within six days to explain his conduct, "or be pronounced rebel and pursued under the law."[18] At the same time, Argyll and Chatelherault were sent written warnings not to aid Moray and his confederates, on pain of outlawry.

Mary was doing her best to extend her support base, and on 3 August ordered the release of Huntly's son, Lord George Gordon, from prison and nominally restored him to his father's title. The new Earl of Huntly had embraced the reformed faith during his captivity, but he blamed Moray for the ruin of his House, and was ready to reward the Queen with his loyalty and the support of his following.

In England, Elizabeth reacted to the news of Mary's marriage with fury, for Mary had broken her promise to wait three months and would now, she feared, subvert religion in Scotland and plot to seize the English throne. In a single stroke, Mary had put in jeopardy the amity that Elizabeth, Cecil, Randolph and the Protestant Lords in Scotland had worked for over the past years. In retaliation, Elizabeth confiscated all Lennox's English properties, and ordered Lady Lennox's confinement to be made "hourly more severe."[19] Her Privy Council wanted her to threaten war, but she stayed her hand. Instead, she sent John Tamworth, a gentleman of her Privy Chamber, to express her disapproval to Mary.

When Mary received Tamworth on 5 August, he rehearsed Elizabeth's objections to her marriage and urged her to make peace with Moray for the sake of the friendship between the two kingdoms, but she declared stoutly that she would pursue her rebels "to the uttermost," and sent Tamworth back to London to tell Elizabeth that she desired "her good sister to meddle no further."[20] As for Moray, Tamworth wrote that he was "so mortally hated by the Queen that it was impossible to unite them."[21] Elizabeth had ordered Tamworth not to acknowledge Darnley as King, but when he refused to accept a safe-conduct signed "Henry R.," Mary had him arrested and imprisoned until he agreed to receive it. When Elizabeth heard, she exploded with rage and swore to aid Moray with all the means that God would give her.[22]

Despite the promise of a safe-conduct for himself and eighty followers, Moray failed to respond to Mary's summons, and on 6 August was declared an outlaw and "put to the horn."[23] At the news of this, Moray, along with Ochiltree, Boyd, Kirkcaldy of Grange and Andrew Leslie, 5th Earl of Rothes, rode west to join Argyll[24] and, encouraged by Randolph, appealed to Elizabeth for assistance. In the face of this most serious threat, Mary prepared to take up arms against them. Glencairn now defected to Moray, while Maitland, who was still at court, was, in the opinion of Castelnau (who had recently arrived in Edinburgh), justly regarded with suspicion.[25] When the rebels "sent forth their complaints" throughout Scotland, insisting that they were acting in defence of the Protestant faith and desiring all good subjects to join them in resisting tyranny, for a king had been imposed on them without the assent of Parliament,[26] civil war became inevitable.

What Moray hoped to achieve by rebelling was almost certainly the deposition of Mary, whose mother he had overthrown in 1560. No revolt could have resulted in the annulment of the royal marriage, and the only other object he could have had in view was the removal of Darnley. Either way, the future security and even the lives of the King and Queen were in jeopardy. This was overt treason of the worst kind.

On 14 August, the Crown seized the properties of the rebel Lords, who, the following day, began mobilising their forces near Ayr, clearly in open revolt. A week later, Mary announced her resolve to march against them, and ordered a muster of her lieges; at the same time, to set her subjects' minds at rest, she again proclaimed that they should enjoy liberty of conscience. But she also ordered the civic authorities of Edinburgh to replace their Protestant Provost with her own supporter, Sir Simon Preston of Craigmillar, a Catholic who was at the same time made a Privy Councillor.

Mary was held in some affection by her people, and many rallied to her banner, whilst few were prepared to support the rebels. The Queen also had powerful support in Lennox, Atholl, Huntly, Mar, Home, Fleming, Livingston, Lindsay, Ruthven, Lord Robert Stewart, Morton—of whose loyalty she was suspicious, and perhaps with good cause—and the Earls of Caithness, Erroll, Montrose and Cassilis. Moreover, Queen Elizabeth was of no mind to support Moray in open rebellion against his lawful sovereign. For the first time, Mary appeared to have the upper hand over Moray. She had told Randolph that she would rather lose her crown than not be revenged on him; Randolph conjectured "that there is some heavier matter at her heart against him than she will utter to any,"[27] and it has been suggested that Moray knew too much about her relations with Rizzio, which, in the light of later events, is certainly possible. Randolph certainly remained convinced that there was more to Mary's antagonism towards her brother than most people realised, and he was to reiterate this conviction later on.

On 23 August, Atholl was appointed Lieutenant of the North and sent to deal with his enemy, Argyll, while Lennox was made Lieutenant of the West. Three days later, the Queen, with a helmet on her head, a pistol at her belt and Darnley in gilded armour at her side, led her army out of Edinburgh, bound for Linlithgow, Stirling and Glasgow, in pursuit of Moray.[28]

Mary had already sent another messenger summoning Bothwell back to Scotland, for she had great need of his support at this time. That messenger reached Paris by 27 August, delivered his message and the Queen's pardon for Bothwell's alleged crimes, and went on to Brussels to summon home Francis Yaxley, Darnley's English secretary. Bothwell wasted no time in responding to Mary's cry for help. "He is gone from Paris, no man knows whither," reported Sir Thomas Smith, England's ambassador, to Cecil on 27 August. Cecil, aware that Mary's position would be immeasurably stronger with Bothwell at her command, took steps to prevent his ever reaching Scotland, and sent warships to patrol the coast.

On 30 August, the Queen and her army of 5,000 men left Glasgow in quest of the rebels, undaunted by driving rain and floods. Even Knox expressed admiration for Mary's "man-like" courage, admitting that she was "ever with the foremost." That same day, Moray's forces advanced on Edinburgh. When Mar, as Governor of Edinburgh Castle, sent to ask the Queen if he should fire his cannon on the invaders, thereby risking the lives of "a multitude of innocent persons," she ordered him to do so.[29] Moray nevertheless occupied Edinburgh on 31 August, anticipating that Argyll would arrive with reinforcements in two days' time, and that the citizens of Edinburgh would support him, but here he made a fatal error, for not only did Mar bombard his army continually from the castle,[30] but the people, whose love for Mary he had grossly underestimated, drove out the occupying forces the very next day.[31]

Moray, intent on evading the royal army, retreated south-west towards Dumfries, to await the expected aid from Elizabeth. Randolph looked on in mounting perturbation as it failed to arrive. Argyll, having vengefully plundered Lennox's lands in the west[32] and failed to arrive in Edinburgh at

Moray's hour of need,[33] fled north to the Highlands, while Knox sought refuge in the west. Soon afterwards, the Queen's army, having "rode the whirlwind" across the country, occupied Edinburgh. Not for nothing did the campaign become known as the "Chaseabout Raid."

On 4 September, Mary was back in Glasgow, awaiting reinforcements from the north to deal with the rebels, her lieges having been summoned to rendezvous at Stirling on 30 September.[34] On 6 September Mary and Darnley appointed Lennox Lieutenant of the South-West,[35] and on the same day Argyll's fortress, Castle Campbell, near Dollar, surrendered to the Queen.

Mary had sent William Chisholm, Bishop of Dunblane, to Rome to beseech the Pope for financial aid against her enemies, in return for which she would "restore religion in splendour."[36] On 10 September, Darnley's English secretary, the Catholic Francis Yaxley, who had formerly been in the service of Mary I and had recently returned to Scotland, was sent back to Brussels carrying letters from both the King and Queen asking Philip II for help against the rebels and support in re-establishing the Roman Church in Scotland;[37] there can be little doubt that both hoped, with Spanish aid, to overthrow Elizabeth and establish Mary as the Queen of a united Catholic Britain. It was being said at the English court that Mary's support for Catholicism was becoming increasingly ill concealed; she had released Archbishop Hamilton from prison, and was currently using all her persuasions to make her Protestant nobles attend Mass. Later that year she wrote to James Beaton, Archbishop of Glasgow, her ambassador in Paris, that she might soon be able to do "some good anent restoring the old religion."

There were at this time rumours of a Catholic League between France, Spain and the Papacy against the Protestants in Europe, but there is no evidence that it ever existed, let alone that Mary was contemplating joining it. Yet it was believed in both Spain and Rome that she was sincere in her desire to restore the faith in Scotland; the Pope was so overjoyed at the prospect that he promised to send her 200,000 crowns and urged King Philip to provide her with military assistance. Yet although Philip undertook to send Spanish troops to Scotland, he never did so because he feared the English would retaliate, for which he was unprepared; instead he sent a subsidy of 20,000 crowns. Then the Pope had second thoughts and sent Mary only 40,000 crowns, having decided to withhold the rest until her intentions became clearer.

Moray had reached Dumfries on 6 September, having dispatched several increasingly urgent messages appealing to England for help. The English Council was at that time debating military intervention in Scotland in order to overthrow Darnley, but the French were threatening a counter-invasion on Mary's behalf, and it was prudently decided that there was no just cause to interfere; thus war between the two countries was narrowly avoided.

Mary was travelling around, raising support for a final push against the rebels. She was at Dunfermline Abbey in Fife from 7 to 9 September, then left for St. Andrews, stopping on the way for dinner at Lochleven Castle, where she threatened Moray's mother and stepfather with sequestration, before visiting Falkland Palace.[38] On 12 September, she imposed a bond of obedience on the barons and gentlemen of Fife.[39] After a stay at St. Andrews, she visited Dundee, Perth and Innerpeffray Abbey, then, from 16 to 17 September, lodged once more with Ruthven at Ruthven Castle. She was again at Dunfermline, staying in the Abbey guest house, from 17 to 18 September, before making her way back towards Edinburgh.

Bothwell returned to Scotland on 17 September, having evaded the English warships that had been sent to intercept him. After landing at Eyemouth, he at once made his way to Edinburgh to see the Queen and make plans to settle old scores with his enemy Moray. With him rode a loyal adherent, David Chalmers, who had shared his exile. Chalmers, a lawyer and historian, had been educated for the Church in France, where he first met Bothwell, who later obtained for him the provostry of Creithtown.[40] Randolph wrote spitefully: "To speak good of him for virtue, knowledge, truth or honesty, would be as great a slander to him as reproof to myself."[41] Nevertheless, he later came to enjoy the Queen's favour.

Like Randolph, the Earl of Bedford, Governor of Berwick, was anxious to discredit Mary in every way, and thus propel Elizabeth into aiding Moray, and on 19 September he hinted that Mary was Rizzio's mistress: "What countenance the Queen shows to David I will not write, for the honour due to the person of a queen."[42] This was the first time that such an allegation had been made, and it is not known on what information it was based, but although there is no other hint in any source at this time that anything was amiss between Mary and Darnley, the latter's jealousy of Rizzio made itself manifest only a month later.

It was around this time that Mary conceived a child that was to be born nine months later. She herself apparently believed for a time that conception had taken place earlier than this, for she later stated that on 9 March 1566 she had been seven months pregnant,[43] yet on 4 April 1566 she wrote to Elizabeth: "I am so gross, being well advanced in my seventh month, that I cannot stoop."[44] Some people would later express doubts that the infant was Darnley's child, as will be seen.

The baby was conceived before the dispensation arrived. It was granted in Rome on 25 September and backdated to 25 May, but did not reach Scotland until six weeks later, and it was not made public in case any wished to point out that the royal marriage had been made only on the assumption that it would be granted.

As her army waited at Stirling, Mary returned to Holyrood on 19 September, intending to raise more men to counteract the possible threat of an English invasion. Randolph reported that there was little hope of an accord between Mary and the rebels because "the Queen is determined to deal with them in all extremity," and added that Bothwell had arrived in Scotland to do mischief.

Maitland had now left court and was skulking at Lethington. In his absence, there were two contenders for the vacant office of Secretary: John Leslie, who would become Bishop of Ross in 1566, and Sir James Balfour, both Catholics. Leslie, now thirty-eight, was a learned, gallant and cunning priest and canon lawyer, an opponent of Knox and a Lord of Session, who had been a faithful servant to Marie de Guise and was later to become one of her daughter's closest confidants. He was conscientious and hard-working, but impulsive, quick-tempered, tactless and sometimes lacking in sound judgement, as Mary would one day find to her cost.

Sir James Balfour of Pittendreich is one of the most enigmatic figures in Mary's story, and was to be heavily implicated in the murder of Darnley. Born around 1525, he was the son of Sir Michael Balfour of Montquharie, Fife, a cousin of the Earl of Bothwell, and had been an early convert to Protestantism. With his brother Gilbert he had been implicated in the murder of Cardinal Beaton, and for this had served time on the galleys with Knox. In 1549, he purchased his freedom by reverting to the Catholic faith, for which Knox called him an "apostate and traitor."

After returning to Scotland, Balfour became an outstanding ecclesiastical lawyer and judge. In 1561, Mary appointed him a Lord of Session and Clerk Register of the Council, but he had the reputation of being a notorious blasphemer and cynic who, according to Knox, neither feared God nor loved virtue, and he seems to have used religion merely to further his own interests. He was untrustworthy, treacherous and corrupt, and, like Moray, adept at covering his tracks. The French ambassador Philippe du Croc was later to call him "a true traitor."

Through his wife, Margaret, Balfour inherited Burleigh Castle in Fife, where Darnley, with whom he had speedily ingratiated himself, stayed whilst hunting in the area. In July 1565, Darnley persuaded Mary to admit Balfour to the Privy Council.[45] It was through Darnley that Balfour came to political prominence. Darnley, however, wanted Leslie, the better Catholic, to replace Maitland and, behind the Queen's back, signed an order in Council giving him the office, but Mary, when she found out, cancelled it.[46] In the event, neither got the post.

On or soon after 19 September, Bothwell arrived at Holyrood with men and munitions and, his former alleged offences having been pardoned and forgotten, was warmly received by Mary, who immediately reappointed him Lieutenant-General of the Borders. Darnley, of whose arrogance and lack of tact he had been forewarned, was "very gracious and polite" to him.[47]

Bothwell was easily the most powerful magnate in south-eastern Scotland and, given his enmity towards the English, could be relied upon to defend the border. His appointment made good political sense, for it secured the loyalty of many Border families for the Queen. During his lieutenancy he established his headquarters at Hermitage Castle and proceeded to deal effectively with disorder and lawlessness in the region. He also allied himself with Huntly against their mutual enemy, Moray, and both raised legions of men for the Queen. On 2 October, Bothwell was given back his seat on the Council, and thereafter both he and Huntly attended regularly.

That day saw the first recorded quarrel between Mary and Darnley. It was over the appointment of a Lieutenant-General of the royal army. Darnley wanted Lennox, Mary, Bothwell, "by reason he bears an evil will against Moray, and has promised to have him die or exiled."[48] Mary got her way, which aroused Darnley's resentment against Bothwell, and she had to placate him by agreeing to let Lennox lead their forces into battle. As a result of having to wait a week for Lennox to join it, Mary's army arrived too late to confront the rebels.

At the end of September, Elizabeth had written to inform Moray and his companions that she would never maintain a subject in disobedience to his prince and could give them no further support. In reality, she feared that hostile action on her part might drive Mary into the arms of the French. With his diminishing forces, Moray was in no position to withstand an attack by the royalist army and, on 6 October, as the Queen's forces closed in on Dumfries,[49] he realised his cause was hopeless and fled with his companions into England, in the hope of claiming asylum from Elizabeth. At Carlisle, he received a letter from her offering him her protection "out of her private love and clemency,"[50] which emboldened him to move to Newcastle. Chatelherault had already fled to France, while Argyll was still in hiding in the western Highlands. On 14 October, Moray bitterly complained to Leicester that, due to Elizabeth's "cold feeling," he and his friends were ruined, and they had been brought to "this extremity . . . by following Her Majesty's and her Council's advice."[51]

Mary's victory was a blow to the Protestants and the English, and enhanced her standing in Catholic Europe. She had married the man of her choice, in defiance of her nobles and Queen Elizabeth, and secured the support of Spain, France and the Vatican. She had shown courage and resolve and retained the good will of her people. Yet it was not a complete victory, for Moray and the other rebel Lords were still at large, and would almost certainly continue to make mischief for her. The Pope wrote warning Mary and Darnley not to compromise with the rebels, and enlisted Rizzio's help in ensuring that they remained firm.[52]

Mary owed her triumph in part to the staunch support and leadership of Bothwell, who was now firmly back in favour. On 4 October, Randolph had observed sourly that Bothwell was already taking great things upon himself;[53] nine days later, he reported his increased influence, saying that Mary was "now content to make much of him, to credit him, and to place him in honour above any subject she hath."[54]

In the same letter, Randolph also reported that Mary hated Moray "neither for his religion, nor yet that he would take the crown from her, as she said lately to myself, but that she knoweth he knoweth some such secret fact, not to be named for reverence's sake, that standeth not with her honour, which he so much detesteth, being her brother, that neither can he show himself as he hath done [i.e., affectionate towards her], nor can she think of him but as one whom she mortally hateth." He added that he was sure that "very few know this grief," and that, in order to have this obloquy and reproach to Mary removed, Moray "would quit his country for all the days of his life." Randolph was unable to commit all he knew to paper, but confided the rest to his messenger, Tamworth, who was to take the letter to Cecil.[55] This dispatch was written at a time when Randolph felt it necessary to discredit Mary; he had already hinted at her improper relations with Rizzio, and it has been suggested that this letter may refer to the same thing, which may be said to be corroborated by Darnley's jealousy of Rizzio becoming manifest less than a fortnight later. An alternative explanation is that Moray knew that Mary had long cherished strong feelings for Bothwell, which would explain his violent antagonism. Mary had all along favoured Bothwell and had seen him in secret during the years of Moray's dominance, and as soon as Moray defected she had recalled him. There had been nothing to suggest any attraction between them, but Moray may have been aware that such existed. A third, and surely far-fetched, theory is that Mary and Moray had indulged in an incestuous relationship that had turned sour, but there is not a shred of evidence for this. Given the events that would soon follow, the Rizzio theory is the likeliest explanation.

This is perhaps borne out by the fact that, in London, on the same day that Randolph wrote his dispatch, the French ambassador, Paul de Foix, was informed by Queen Elizabeth that Mary hated Moray because he "would gladly have hanged an Italian named David that she loved and favoured, giving him more credit and authority in her affairs than was consistent with her interest or her honour."[56]

Darnley was certainly resentful of Bothwell, but this was not the reason why, as Randolph reported, "jars are risen between [the Queen] and her husband," for that was over preferments at court. The agent added that he wrote these things "more from grief of heart than that I take pleasure to set forth any purchase of shame, especially such as we ought to reverence if they know their duty. I should trouble you too long if I wrote everything I hear of Darnley's words and doings, and his boasting to his friends here and assurance of them who would, if they knew, be the first to seek revenge in false reports."[57] Cecil informed Sir Thomas Smith that "the young King is so insolent that his father, weary of his government, has departed from the court." Mary's victory, so dearly bought, was proving to be a hollow one.

It was celebrated, however, by a banquet held at Lochmaben Castle, near Dumfries, on 14 October, which was presided over by the King and Queen. The next day, the royal couple, having disbanded most of their army, left for Edinburgh, staying at Callendar House on the way. Bothwell, in command of 1,500 men, remained at Dumfries to guard the western border.

The honeymoon period was over.

7

"THERE IS A BAIT LAID
FOR SIGNOR DAVID"

MARY WAS BACK IN EDINBURGH by 19 October, free of Moray's tutelage and ready to rule Scotland with the support of Darnley and her chief advisers, Atholl, Lennox, Huntly and Bothwell, the only four earls who were willing to attend court regularly. None of them, however, enjoyed the political stature and experience of Moray, and Maitland, with his acute understanding of statecraft, was still out of favour. In his absence, Mary turned to Rizzio and other "crafty vile strangers,"[1] as well as lesser men like Balfour, for counsel and advice. With the majority of the other Lords hostile to Darnley, Lennox, Bothwell and Rizzio, Mary was in a very precarious situation, and her future success depended greatly on Darnley's character and his ability to help her control the nobles, as Moray had done so effectively. A pessimistic Randolph wrote scathingly: "How she, with this kind of government, her suspicion of her people and debate with the chief of her nobility, can stand and prosper passes my wit. To be ruled by the advice of two or three strangers, neglecting that of her chief Councillors, I do not know how it can stand."[2]

Matters were made worse by the fact that, after less than three months of marriage, relations between Mary and Darnley were already deteriorating. Lennox claims that this first became apparent after the Chaseabout Raid,[3] while the *Book of Articles* declares that marital harmony "lasted not above three months." Mary soon became aware of the defects in her husband's character, and had to come to terms with the fact that she had married a "wilful, haughty and vicious"[4] bully who was not only frequently drunk but also essentially weak in character. Far from being her support, he was more likely to provoke the antagonism of the Lords and further alienate them from her. Clearly, she had made a dreadful mistake in marrying him.

No longer was Mary content to play the role of adoring, submissive wife, for it was obvious that Darnley did not return her love and probably never had done. As soon as he returned to Edinburgh, he began making nightly forays to the city's taverns and brothels with young "gentlemen willing to satisfy his will and affections,"[5] without bothering to conceal his activities from his wife, in whom disgust and disillusionment quickly quenched the fires of infatuation. To add to her humiliation, in late 1565 Darnley had an affair with a lady of the Douglas family, and also made a lady of the court pregnant, according to a report by an Italian visitor to Scotland, Pietro Bizari. Darnley's promiscuity, his insolence towards the Queen and his vile temper only served to diminish her respect for him. Too soon, they were drifting apart and spending less and less time in each other's company, Darnley often being away hunting and hawking around Peebles or in Fife.

Darnley's elevation to kingship had turned his head. He believed that his marriage had taken place "with the consent of the nobility, who thought him worthy of the place," and "that the whole kingdom would follow and serve him upon the field, where it was a shame a woman should command. These conceits were continuously buzzing in the young man's head." Mary, however, took the view that "all the honour of majesty he had came from her," and that "she had made choice of him by her own affection only."[6] The Spanish ambassador later opined that Darnley would not have been "led astray" and antagonised the Queen had his mother been present, "as the son respects her more than he does his father,"[7] who was unable to control him.

It was all too apparent that Darnley was unfit for kingship and would never give Mary the vital support that she needed. His arrogance had already alienated the nobility, his loose tongue was a political liability, and he was more interested in the rights and privileges, rather than the duties and obligations, of his position. Although Mary had made every effort to associate him with her in the government of the kingdom, he was not interested in state affairs or the everyday responsibilities of a ruler, and preferred field sports to attending Council meetings. This meant he was not available to sign the official documents that were supposed to bear both his signature and Mary's, which caused unreasonable delays; in the end Mary had to resort to having a stamp of his signature made, which was held by Rizzio and used in the King's absence. Mary was now largely shouldering the burden of government alone,[8] and Darnley's behaviour was giving her enemies a means of making political capital against her. Moray, in exile, was openly lamenting "the extreme folly of his sovereign" which could only lead to the "utter ruin" of Scotland.[9]

Darnley was also disillusioned with his marriage, chiefly because of Mary's adamant refusal to bestow upon him the Crown Matrimonial, which was the thing he wanted above all else. His resentment continued to fester, not only because he felt he was being denied his proper share of royal authority as Mary's equal, but also because he had his eye on the crown, which would be his if Mary died childless after having given him the Crown Matrimonial. But, despite his bitter and frequent complaints and remonstrances, the Queen insisted that he was too young and had yet to prove himself worthy of the honour. In truth, she may have feared that his ambitions implied a threat to her sovereign rights and even her life.

Darnley's other cause for grievance was Rizzio, whom he blamed for Mary's obstinacy over the Crown Matrimonial. Rizzio had been Darnley's friend, but as Darnley's credit with Mary declined, Rizzio's increased and he came to enjoy the political influence that should have been Darnley's, which aroused the latter's bitter resentment and jealousy and put an end to the friendship. Daily, the Queen showed more and more favour to the upstart Italian and spent many of her leisure hours with him, sometimes making music or playing cards late into the night. It was unwise but understandable: her husband was a disappointment and she could not trust most of the Lords who should have been in attendance as her chief advisers, so in her isolation she turned to the faithful Rizzio, in whose lively and witty company she could relax and on whose advice she was beginning to rely heavily.

Yet there were those, Randolph among them, who suspected that her relationship with Rizzio was more than that of monarch and secretary. Darnley, given his wife's behaviour, had every reason to share his suspicions, and certainly did. Randolph was a hostile witness, and although he referred to Rizzio as "a filthy wedlock breaker" who indulged with Mary in "such filthy behaviour whereof I am ashamed to speak," there is no conclusive contemporary evidence that Mary and Rizzio were in fact lovers, although circumstantial evidence makes it a possibility. What is more important is that many people believed, or affected to believe, that they were.

In March 1566, Paul de Foix, the French ambassador in London, reported to Catherine de' Medici that one night, between midnight and 1 a.m., Darnley arrived up the secret stair to Mary's bedchamber and found the door locked. He knocked, but there was no answer and it was only when he shouted that he would break down the door that Mary opened it. At first, it appeared that she was alone, but Darnley's suspicions had been aroused and he went straight to a closet, where he found a quailing Rizzio wearing only a shirt covered by a furred robe.[10] Buchanan, whose brief was to discredit Mary, later wrote of a similar incident in which Darnley, having been informed that Rizzio had gone to Mary's bedchamber one night, went to investigate and found the door bolted on the inside. In this version, Darnley did not force his way in, but spent a sleepless night in an agony of suspicion and jealousy.

But Darnley never alleged any such thing against Mary or Rizzio, even when it was imperative that he justify his conduct, and Lord Ruthven's contemporary eyewitness account does not refer to either incident, stating only that Darnley complained to Mary in March 1566 that he had good reason to be angry because

"since yonder fellow David came in credit and familiarity with Your Majesty, you neither regarded me, entertained me nor trusted me after your wonted fashion. For every day before dinner you were wont to come to my chamber, and passed the time with me, and this long time you have not done so; and when I came to Your Majesty's chamber, you bore me little company except David had been the third person. And after supper Your Majesty used to sit up at cards with David till one or two after midnight. And this is the entertainment I have had of you this long time." Her Majesty answered that it was not a gentlewoman's duty to come to her husband's chamber, but rather the husband's to come to the wife's. The King answered, "How came you to my chamber in the beginning, and ever till within these six months that David fell into familiarity with you? Or am I failed in any sort in my body?"

Randolph and Bedford's account of this quarrel has Darnley saying "that David had more company of her body than he, for the space of two months." When Mary replied that it was not the wife's part to seek out the husband, and that the fault was his own—which was probably true, for it must be remembered that Darnley was not blameless in this affair—he answered "that when he came, she either would not, or made herself sick."[11] Few men would have tolerated such a situation, and in the circumstances it was logical for Darnley to experience intense sexual jealousy. By the double standards of the age, his was the greater grievance.

Lennox's *Narrative* is the only one of the later libels against Mary to give a full account of the Rizzio affair. The others were written under the auspices of the Lords involved, who naturally did not want their role in it publicised. Lennox wrote independently, and much of his information must have come from Darnley himself, whose murder Lennox was doing his best at the time to avenge. Lennox makes much of Darnley's jealousy of Rizzio, "whom the King might see increase in such disordinate favour to his wife, as he [Darnley], being in his lusty years, bearing such great love and affection unto her, began to enter into such jealousy as he thought he could not longer suffer the proceedings of the said David, she using the said David more as a lover than a servant, forsaking her husband's bed and board very often, liking the company of David, as appeared, better than her husband's."[12] This corroborates Ruthven's account of Darnley's complaints.

Rizzio had usurped the Lords' natural privileges, ensured that Maitland was sidelined, and was believed not only to be a papal agent working in secret for the restoration of Catholicism, but also to be blocking any ideas on Mary's part of recalling the exiled Protestant nobles. He aroused more hatred than Darnley ever did, but Mary seemed oblivious to the Lords' boiling resentment. She knew she could trust Rizzio absolutely. Yet in continuing to favour him above all others, she displayed incredible folly and an alarming lack of awareness of aristocratic sensibilities and of the scandal to which she was laying herself open by her conduct, which suggests that she was indeed infatuated with the Italian.

On 18 October, Randolph expressed his outrage that Rizzio, "a stranger, a varlet, should have the whole guiding of Queen and country." As for Mary, "a more wilful woman, and one more wedded to her own opinion, without order, reason or discretion, I never did hear of." Darnley was even worse, and her Councillors were "men never esteemed for wisdom or honesty." Of course, Randolph was prejudiced, but he added, with what seems like a touch of sincerity, that "though I oftentimes set forth her praises wherever I could, she is so much changed in her nature that she beareth only the shape of that woman she was before" and was "hardly recognisable by one who had known her in the happy days when she heeded worthy counsel and her praise ran through all nations." Without Moray's guiding influence, Mary's poor judgement and lack of political sense were becoming all too apparent.

Although Elizabeth had commanded Moray to remain in Newcastle, he had gone hotfoot to London to plead his cause in person, and on 22 October, the Queen agreed to see him in private with Cecil present. She was anxious not to provoke either Mary or the French by appearing to favour the Scottish rebels, and, according to Guzman de Silva, it was arranged at this meeting that she would publicly express her displeasure. The next day, therefore, a charade was staged in which Moray, kneeling before Elizabeth, was severely castigated for having rebelled against his anointed sovereign, in the presence of Paul de Foix, the French ambassador, and all the court. Afterwards, although the Queen had said she would not permit him to remain in England, he was allowed to return unmolested to Newcastle with Elizabeth's assurance that she would mediate with Mary for his return to Scotland. Mary, for her part, rejoiced to hear from Randolph of Moray's humiliation, not realising that it was mere duplicity.[13] From then on, relations between the two Queens were slightly warmer, although Mary adamantly refused to pardon Moray, even in exchange for Lady Lennox's release.[14]

Bothwell returned to Edinburgh at the end of October, and was put in charge of reorganising Scotland's artillery defences and keeping the border secure. But when Mary appointed him as one of her commissioners to negotiate with Bedford for a new peace treaty between England and Scotland, the English withdrew, insulted.

On 31 October, Randolph reported that members of Mary's household had told him "that she is with child. It is argued upon tokens, I know not what, that are annexed to them that are in that case." By 12 November, having spoken to Mary, he was able to announce: "She is with child, and the nurse already chosen. There can be no doubt, and she herself thinks so." Two days later, Mary became unwell, suffering from a grievous pain in her side; while she was confined to bed, Darnley spent nine days hunting in Fife. By 1 December, Mary had recovered and was "taking as much exercise as her body can endure."[15] Her pregnancy had not been officially announced, but most people drew conclusions when, on that day, she chose to travel to Linlithgow in a litter instead of on horseback, as usual.[16] Lennox wrote to inform his wife of their daughter-in-law's pregnancy on 19 December, giving God "most hearty thanks for that the King our son continues in good health and the Queen great with child."[17]

As far as Mary was concerned, her pregnancy was the crowning of her hopes, for her child would inherit the joint claims of its parents to the thrones of Scotland and England, and place her in a very strong position *vis-à-vis* the English succession.

At Linlithgow, Mary was reunited with Darnley, but it may not have been a happy meeting. Far from being overjoyed at the prospect of fatherhood, Darnley must have realised that the coming infant would block for ever his chances of succeeding to the throne, even if Mary did grant him the Crown Matrimonial, for its rights would take precedence in the succession. If, however, the Queen or her infant died in childbirth, Darnley would inherit the throne, but only if he had first secured the Crown Matrimonial. It was imperative now that he do so, and the matter became an obsession with him. But Mary continued to deny him what he wanted, which caused violent arguments between them. Randolph reported: "I cannot tell what misliking of late there hath been between Her Grace and her husband. He presseth earnestly for the matrimonial crown, which she is loath hastily to grant, but willing to keep somewhat in store until she knows how worthy he is to enjoy such a sovereignty."[18]

Soon after the meeting at Linlithgow, Darnley left for Peebles on yet another hunting trip, and had not returned by 20 December, when Lennox set out to look for him. Buchanan alleges that Mary had sent the King to Peebles in the depths of winter with only a small following, and that he nearly perished of starvation, but this story is not corroborated by any contemporary account.

Mary was not pleased by her husband's prolonged absence. On 20 December, Bedford reported: "The Lord Darnley followeth his pastimes more than the Queen is content withal. What it will breed hereafter I cannot say, but in the meantime there is some misliking between them" that was fast becoming public knowledge. When Darnley did return to court he received a very chilly reception.

How serious was the rift was confirmed on 22 December, when the coin giving Darnley precedence was suddenly withdrawn and replaced by a new one, the Mary ryal, on which Mary's name came first. Randolph was certain that the change was indicative of Mary's serious displeasure with her husband.[19] Documents, however, would continue to be issued in the names of King Henry and Queen Mary until Darnley's death.[20]

On Christmas Day, Randolph wrote: "A while ago there was nothing but 'King and Queen,' 'His Majesty and Hers,' but now 'the Queen's husband' is more common. There are also private disorders amongst themselves, but may be lovers' quarrels."[21] Mary's inventories show that her gifts to Darnley, once so numerous, had virtually ceased by the beginning of 1566.[22]

The rebel Lords' moveable goods, confiscated by the Crown, had now been publicly auctioned off. On 1 December, Glencairn, Ochiltree and Boyd were pronounced guilty *in absentia* of *lèse-majesté*, while on 18 December Moray and the remaining rebels were summoned to appear before Parliament in February 1566 to hear the formal forfeiture of their lands and estates. According to Randolph, it was now Darnley, rather than Mary, who was adamant that Moray should never be pardoned.[23]

That Christmas, Darnley made an ostentatious parade of Catholic piety, obviously intended to show that he was more staunch in the faith than the Queen. Randolph informed Cecil, "The Queen's husband never gave greater token of his religion than this last night [Christmas Eve]. He was at Matins and Mass in the morning, before day, and heard the High Mass devoutly upon his knees, though she herself, the most part of the night, sat up at cards and went to bed when it was almost day."[24] After Christmas, Darnley returned to Peebles to join Lennox for another hunting expedition,[25] and did not return until the middle of January.

On 2 January, in Darnley's absence, and much to his disgust when he found out, Mary pardoned Chatelherault for his part in the Chaseabout Raid, on condition that he remain in exile in France for the next five years. One hundred and sixty members of the Hamilton faction received their remission at the same time.[26] The Queen was softening in her attitude to the rebels, and on 24 January Randolph noted that her extremity towards Moray was partly assuaged. Moray, who was running out of money,[27] had written to her pleading to be allowed to return to Scotland, even undertaking to overlook her association with Rizzio. He and his friends had also offered Darnley a very fine diamond as an inducement to obtain Moray's reinstatement,[28] and had also dangled a bribe of £5,000 before Rizzio, only to be told that his price was nothing less than £20,000.[29] All these efforts proved to be in vain, and Moray grew increasingly desperate.

Pope Pius IV had died in December, and on 10 January 1566, his successor, Pius V, a fanatical champion of the faith who was to be an energetic force behind the Counter-Reformation, wrote—somewhat prematurely—praising Mary for her zeal in "restoring the true worship of God throughout your whole realm," exhorting her to complete what she had commenced and congratulating her on her victory over the Protestants.[30] The Pope's letter was delivered in February by Clerneau de Villeneuve, an emissary of the Cardinal of Lorraine, who travelled to Scotland with James Thornton, who had been sent by Archbishop Beaton from Paris to urge Mary to proceed to the utmost against the rebel Lords.[31]

Although, on 10 December, Mary had again promised her subjects liberty of conscience, in a letter to the Pope dated 31 January, she informed him that she planned to restore Catholicism in Scotland and, later on, in England, when the time was ripe and her enemies were neutralised. On the same day she appointed the Bishop of Dunblane her orator at the Vatican, with instructions to ask for spiritual and financial aid from the Holy Father.

Mary had also been expecting monetary support from King Philip, who had granted Francis Yaxley an audience on 13 October. Ten days later, Yaxley had left Brussels with letters of congratulation on Mary's marriage and the subsidy of 20,000 crowns.[32] But Yaxley drowned when his ship was wrecked off Northumberland in January 1566, and the money was seized by the Earl of Northumberland and claimed by Queen Elizabeth as treasure trove.[33] Darnley took Yaxley's servant, Henry Gwynn, into his service.

Cecil was annoyed that no letters had been discovered on Yaxley's body when it was washed ashore, but Philip had prudently written separately to Mary and Darnley via de Silva in London, begging the Queen not to make any attempt on the English throne until he invaded the Netherlands, "where he can with greater facility assist them." Because of the highly sensitive nature of this letter, de Silva was obliged to hold on to it for several months.[34]

On Candlemas Day (2 February), Mary and Darnley attended High Mass together at Holyrood, carrying candles in procession to the chapel royal. Mary "used great persuasions to divers of her nobility to hear Mass with her, and took the Earl of Bothwell by the hand, to procure him in." Bothwell refused, and went off with Huntly to hear Knox preach, at which Mary was somewhat offended.[35] Alarmed at this overt display of Catholicism, Randolph reported on 5 February that Mary had "said openly that she will have Mass free for all men that will hear it." Darnley, Lennox, Atholl and others "now daily resort to it. The Protestants are in great fear, and doubt of what shall become of them. The wisest so much mislike [Darnley's] government that they design nothing more than the return of the Lords."

Two days later, Darnley was again making a great display of Catholic devotion, swearing that he would have Mass celebrated in St. Giles and urging the same in Council, but more (thought Randolph) to test opinion than carry out his boast. Nevertheless, when several Lords resisted his attempts to make them accompany him to Mass, he "gave them all very evil words." Bedford heard that he wanted to shut them all in their rooms until they did as he wished.[36] On the same day, Randolph recorded another rumour that Mary had subscribed to a Catholic League "to maintain papistry throughout Christendom,"[37] while Melville believed that Rizzio "had secret intelligence" with the Vatican.

Mary was doing her best to maintain her pro-Catholic policy, but Darnley may have had an ulterior motive in his overt displays of piety, and was perhaps trying to enlist Catholic support in Scotland, England and abroad for his bid for the Crown Matrimonial. He may also have been trying to convince Mary's Catholic allies that he was more vigorous in the faith than she was, and therefore more likely to be effective in bringing about a counter-reformation in Scotland.

In such a climate, Rizzio's position was growing daily more dangerous. On 29 January, Randolph voiced the opinion that the Italian was the father of Mary's unborn child, and warned Leicester: "Woe indeed to you when a son of David should bear rule over Scotland."[38] Randolph was not the only person, then or later, to express doubts about the baby's paternity. In 1600, Alexander, Lord Ruthven, sneeringly referred to James VI as "thou son of Signor David," and in the early seventeenth century, that same King James earned the nickname "the British Solomon" after Henry IV of France had said he deserved to be called the modern Solomon, since he was the son of David.

In January and February 1566, a plot to do away with Rizzio was hatched by a confederacy of Protestant Lords, who believed that he was the chief obstacle in the way of Moray's return. It is not certain who instigated the conspiracy, and there are essentially four theories about it: the first, according to Melville, was that it was conceived by Morton, Ruthven, Lindsay and the Douglases, who drew Darnley into it by playing on his jealousy of Rizzio and his conviction that it was Rizzio who was preventing his receiving the Crown Matrimonial—this seems the most likely theory; the second theory, according to Ruthven's deathbed account, was that the plot originated with Darnley, who was urged on and abetted by Lennox,[39] which is less probable; the third theory is that Moray was the mastermind behind the plot and carefully orchestrated it from England, which was later alleged by Bothwell and is certainly possible; and the fourth, that it emanated from the clever brain of Maitland, who had every reason to detest the man who had supplanted him, an equal possibility.

One of the prime movers was Morton, who not only desired the return of his co-religionist Moray, but was also bound by ties of blood to Darnley and felt outraged that his kinsman had been ousted from Mary's affections and counsels by a foreign upstart who had got too far above himself and was meddling in matters that were no business of his. Morton was also motivated by a degree of self-interest, for he had heard a rumour that, in the coming

Parliament, the Crown meant to resume possession of certain lands he had improperly obtained, and he had no intention of allowing that to happen.[40]

Anthony Standen, a gentleman of Darnley's household whose younger brother, also Anthony, was the King's cupbearer, told James I years later that "wicked Ruthven" was the chief conspirator,[41] although Ruthven denied this.[42] Ruthven was also related to Darnley, as was Lindsay, who was married to a Douglas. As far as Morton, Ruthven and Lindsay were concerned, therefore, the plot was a bid for familial advancement, for all would have benefited from Darnley receiving the Crown Matrimonial, which they would dangle before him like a carrot, and wielding sovereign power. In addition, these Lords, all Protestants, were anxious to see the return of Moray.[43] Ruthven was to justify the plot by claiming that Rizzio was preventing the return of Moray and, through his dominance over the Queen, excluding Darnley from her counsels.[44]

Ruthven's activities, and Morton's, may have been a front for Moray's machinations. Moray was seeking a return to power. He and other Protestants believed that Rizzio was responsible for the Bill of Attainder against the exiles that would shortly come before Parliament, and which would deprive them of everything they owned. Moray feared this consequence greatly, but the Protestant Lords in the plot were determined to forestall it, and meant at all costs to prevent Parliament from sitting.[45] Ruthven states that the exiled Lords were not drawn into the plot until 20 February, with Morton acting as a link, but Ruthven may not have been aware of any prior involvement on the part of Moray. Moray was a cunning and cautious man, and would have taken care—as he did on other occasions—not to incriminate himself.

Rizzio was not, however, the main target of the conspirators, whose real objective was almost certainly the removal of the Queen from power,[46] the elimination of the threat of a Catholic revival, and the reinstatement of a Protestant government under Moray, with Darnley, wearing the Crown Matrimonial, as a puppet king. Claude Nau, who probably obtained his information from Mary in the 1570s when he served as her Secretary, claims that the "chief design" of these "crafty foxes" was "the elevation of Moray to the throne, and the deprivation of [Darnley] and the Queen." Had Darnley's elimination really been envisaged, Morton and his Douglas connections would surely not have devised or backed the plot, for there would have been little personal advantage in it for them. But Moray's appearance in Edinburgh immediately after the murder argues the fact that the slaying of Rizzio was secondary to the coup that it initiated.

Ruthven, Randolph and Bedford assert that Darnley, "being entered into a vehement suspicion of David, that by him something was committed which was most against the King's honour, and not to be borne of his part, first communicated his mind to George Douglas,"[47] the bastard son of Archibald, 6th Earl of Angus and half-brother to Darnley's mother. Douglas had been pursuing a career in the Church from a young age. In 1546, aged only sixteen, he had been involved in the murder of Cardinal Beaton, and had then seized the lucrative office of Postulate of Arbroath, despite being a lacklustre preacher, a fornicator and a devious and violent ruffian. Now, finding Darnley in great sorrow, "he sought all the means he could to put some remedy unto his grief."[48]

Melville, however, states that it was Douglas who, at the instigation of Morton, Ruthven, Lindsay and others, began spending time in Darnley's company and insidiously "put into his head such suspicion against Rizzio" as would draw him into the plot.[49] Douglas had little love for his Lennox cousins, but everything to gain if he helped his nephew to the Crown Matrimonial, and Darnley, whose complaints had given Mary's enemies an excuse for action, lacked the perspicacity to see that he was being used. His youth and inexperience would render him as wax in the hands of the ruthless, power-hungry men who were closing in on him, and as such he would prove their most dangerous weapon. They would find, however, that it was a two-edged sword.

Douglas asked Darnley why it was that Mary was refusing him the Crown Matrimonial and why she was denying him a share in the government. It was scandalous, because, as a woman, she should give precedence and respect to her husband. What was the reason for the Queen often being closeted late at night with Rizzio? Could the King really be certain that he was the father of her coming child? Darnley, whose suspicions had already been aroused as a result of his own observations, needed little convincing that Mary was being unfaithful to him, and little persuasion that he should seek a bloody revenge, which, by the moral standards of the time, seemed entirely justifiable. He could not live with his terrible suspicions, nor could he suffer existing any longer as a king with no power. But the Crown Matrimonial meant more to him than the fidelity of his wife, and he made it clear that it was the price of his co-operation, whereupon the conspirators told him soothingly that they would make certain he should have it. Thus did they bend him to their will and entice him to join them as their leader, and he was "won to give his consent over easily to the slaughter of Signor David."[50] From then on, Darnley was at the very epicentre of the plot.

The first indication that a conspiracy was afoot came on 9 February 1566 in a letter to Cecil from Maitland, who confided that he saw no certain way to restore matters in Scotland to their former state "unless we chop at the very root—you know where it lieth."[51] The letter suggests that Maitland was in the confidence of the conspirators, and Randolph lists him as one of their number, but the extent of his involvement is obscure, for he was adept at covering his traces. He certainly had a motive for wanting to get rid of Rizzio, for the Italian had usurped many of the functions of the Secretary's office, which Maitland still held, and Maitland was determined that Rizzio should not sabotage his carefully formulated policy of working towards a peaceful union with England, the result of years of hard work. Maitland may have acted on behalf of the exiled Lords, or as a link between them and the conspirators, but there is no proof of this. Nau later claimed that he "was secretly of Moray's party—not so openly, however, that he could be charged therewith."

From its early stages, Cecil, the English Privy Council and Bedford were aware of the plot, but lifted no finger to prevent its execution; for them, the removal of Rizzio was a political necessity. For this reason, perhaps, there is little evidence relating to it in the English State Papers. Nor is there any evidence, other than Blackwood's allegation of 1587, that the plot originated in England, although its outcome would be distinctly to England's advantage. Elizabeth was not made aware of what was to happen until it was too late to prevent it, in case she tried to warn Mary, but, given that Cecil and Bedford knew of the plot, it is inconceivable that Moray did not.

Meanwhile, in what was probably a prearranged move, George Douglas, ostensibly at Darnley's request, had asked Lord Ruthven to help in seeing Rizzio "executed according to his demerits."[52] Ruthven was already suffering from the mortal illness that would kill him,[53] and had been confined to his chamber for at least two months, but that did not prevent him from entering into the conspiracy with ruthless resolve, although he told the untrustworthy and garrulous Darnley he would lift no finger to help him unless he solemnly swore not to reveal anything to the Queen. Darnley agreed without hesitation to this condition.[54]

Ruthven, in turn, brought in Morton, who made his involvement conditional upon Lennox and Darnley giving up all claims to the lands of the earldom of Angus, which he meant to settle on his nephew.[55] This agreed, Morton showed himself sympathetic to the King's plight and expressed shock at Mary's treatment of him, allegedly declaring, "It is a thing contrary to nature that the hen should crow before the cock, and against the law of God that a man should be subject to his wife, the man being the image of God, the woman the image of man."[56] Therefore he, Morton, would do all he could to assist Darnley to take power into his own hands and rid him of the man who had usurped his royal and marital privileges.

Over the next few weeks, the details of the plot were finalised. Rizzio was to be summarily executed, Mary was to be taken prisoner and shut up at Stirling until her child was born, Darnley was to receive the Crown Matrimonial, and Moray and the other exiled Lords were to be recalled, pardoned and reconciled with Darnley, who would thereafter exert himself to maintain the Protestant Church. The plotters were aware that they had to act before Parliament sat in order to avoid the exiled Lords being attainted.

Morton and Ruthven were of the opinion that Rizzio should be slain either in his own chamber or the garden, or while playing tennis, or even publicly hanged, but even these hardened men were appalled to hear Darnley insist that he be slaughtered in the Queen's presence at her own table.[57] This was not only a vicious revenge, but might also serve an even more sinister purpose, that of bringing about, through shock, a miscarriage or even Mary's death in childbirth, along with that of her infant. Given Darnley's determination to secure the Crown Matrimonial, no other construction can be placed upon such a vindictive act. This was the view that Mary herself and many other people later took. Here again Darnley played into the Lords' hands, for they could allege this treason against him at a later date, and the penalty was death. Thus they could rid themselves of him whenever they chose.

As the days went by, many others were brought into the conspiracy: among them were Lennox,[58] a number of Darnley's Catholic friends and Douglas kinsmen, including Sir William Douglas of Lochleven, Moray's half-brother, and Morton's cousin, Archibald Douglas, as well as several of the King's former Protestant enemies, notably Lindsay, Argyll, Ruthven's son, William, Patrick Bellenden, brother of the Justice Clerk, Andrew Ker of Fawdonside, who had fought for Moray during the Chaseabout Raid, and Mar's brother, Arthur Erskine of Blackgrange, as well as a host of minor players. All were united in their hatred and resentment of Rizzio, and·most were intent on making the plot appear as if it had originated with Darnley. Each conspirator envisaged that the coup would result in some benefit to himself.

Knox, who had spoken out frequently against Rizzio, was aware of the conspiracy and apparently gave it his blessing.[59] Those not involved in it included Bothwell, Huntly, Atholl, Balfour, Glencairn, Mar, Seton and Livingston, none of whom was aware of what was going on.

On 10 February, after Mass in the chapel royal, Darnley was ceremonially invested with the Order of St. Michael, the highest order of knighthood that the King of France could bestow. Representing Charles IX was the Sieur de Rambouillet. Before the assembled court, Darnley had the nerve to solemnly swear that, if he ever brought disgrace upon the Order, he would surrender his collar of knighthood to the French King.[60] Afterwards, when Rambouillet asked what arms would be assigned to the new knight, the Queen "bade give him only his due, whereby it was perceived her love waxed cold towards him."[61]

Over the next three days, there were entertainments in honour of the ambassador and his suite, at one of which Mary and her ladies appeared wearing male apparel.[62] Darnley drank to excess, indulged in debauchery, and made several of the Frenchmen hopelessly inebriated.

By 13 February, Randolph knew most of the details of the plot against Rizzio, for on that day he wrote to Leicester:

I know now for certain that this Queen repenteth her marriage, that she hateth the King and all his kin. I know that he knoweth himself that he hath a partaker [i.e., Rizzio] in play and game with him. I know that there are practices in hand contrived between the father and son to come by the crown against her will. I know that, if that take effect which is intended, David, with the consent of the King, shall have his throat cut within these ten days. Many things grievouser and worse are brought to my ears, yea, of things intended against Her Majesty's own person. This Queen to her subjects is now so intolerable that I see them bent on nothing but extreme mischief. There is a bait laid for Signor David, that if he be caught, howsoever his mistress be offended, others will be pleased.

Randolph ended by asking Leicester to keep all this to himself.[63] Cecil and Elizabeth might have condoned the murder of Rizzio, but Elizabeth would hardly be likely to sanction a plot against an anointed queen.

Around this time, Mary, Darnley and some courtiers were entertained at the home of an Edinburgh merchant. At dinner, Darnley again got drunk, but when Mary tried to restrain him from imbibing any more or enticing others to do so, he ignored her and became so abusive that she "left the house in tears." Such quarrels were not uncommon. In fact, Darnley was now holding so many things against Mary—her refusal of the Crown Matrimonial, the withdrawal of the coinage, the softening of her attitude towards the Hamiltons, her reluctance to give him precedence—that there was constant friction between them, and she was "very weary of him." Some even believed that, if Darnley would not be appeased, she would call on Chatelherault to aid her against him.[64]

Rambouillet and his suite arrived at Berwick on 15 February, and the following day, Sir William Drury, Captain of Berwick, reported that one gentleman was still the worse for wear after Darnley had made him drink "acqua composita" (possibly whisky). Drury observed that "all people say that Darnley is too much addicted to drinking," and added, perhaps significantly, that, during a recent visit to the Isle of Inchkeith in the Firth of Forth with Lord Robert Stewart, Lord Fleming and others, Darnley had done something so vicious that it did not bear describing, but he did not get away with it because "too many were witnesses," and when the Queen heard of it, she "withdrew her company from him."[65]

The nature of Darnley's vicious behaviour has been the subject of some speculation. It may not have been any sexual misdemeanour at all, but one explanation is that he took part in a homosexual act. Apart from his effeminate appearance, which may have no bearing on the matter whatsoever, there is some evidence to support the theory that he was bisexual. It has already been noted that, while referring to speculation that Mary and Darnley were lovers before their marriage, Randolph told Bedford not to believe it: "the likelihoods are so great to the contrary that, if it were possible to see such an act done, I would not believe it."[66] Randolph may have written this after witnessing Darnley's behaviour with Rizzio, with whom, as has been seen, he sometimes shared a bed. Knox wrote that Darnley "passed his time in hunting and hawking, and other such pleasures as were agreeable to his appetites, having in his company gentlemen willing to satisfy his will and affections." The use of the words "and affections" surely has a significance that influences the meaning of the sentence. Finally, in the much later *Historie of James the Sext*, Darnley is accused of indulging in "unmanly pleasures." Whatever the truth about his sexuality, he was certainly promiscuous, and either form of behaviour would have aroused Mary's disgust.

So many people were now involved in the plot against Rizzio that something was bound to leak out. Melville heard "dark speeches that we should have news ere Parliament was ended," and tried to warn Mary that there might be unpleasant repercussions if she did not pardon Moray, but she still refused to do so. "What can they do? What dare they do?" she asked indignantly. She told him she herself had heard the rumours, but gave no credit to them, saying, "Our countrymen are great talkers but rarely put their bragging into effect." However, she did reluctantly agree to postpone Parliament until 12 March. Melville then went to Rizzio to alert him to possible trouble, "but he disdained all danger and despised counsel."[67]

Mary had now learned from a captured English spy that Randolph had conveyed English gold to the rebel Lords, and on 19 February she summoned him before the Council, coldly accused him of perfidy and ordered him to leave Scotland within three days. Outraged, he denied the charge, refused to accept a safe-conduct signed by Darnley, and stayed put in Edinburgh. The next day, Mary wrote to Elizabeth, complaining of Randolph's conduct and informing her of his expulsion.[68]

A little light relief from Mary's problems was provided on 24 February, when Bothwell married Huntly's sister, Lady Jean Gordon, thus cementing the political alliance between the two Earls. As they were among the Queen's staunchest adherents, and represented the might of northern and southern Scotland, the marriage had her blessing and, indeed, had been made on her advice; she witnessed the marriage contract, provided the cloth of silver and white taffeta for the bride's dress from her own Wardrobe,[69] and attended the celebrations that followed the Protestant wedding service in the Canongate Kirk in Edinburgh. David Chalmers was a witness.

Jean, then twenty, was a Catholic, and because the bride and groom were within the forbidden degrees of affinity, Archbishop Hamilton had granted a dispensation for the marriage.[70] Jean and Mary had wanted a Catholic marriage ceremony, but Bothwell had overruled them both.[71] One presumes Jean was not too happy about marrying him because she was already in love with Alexander, Lord Ogilvy of Boyne, but, only weeks before, Ogilvy had jilted her and married Mary Beaton.[72] Bothwell had witnessed their marriage contract.

Jean brought with her a rich dowry, which Bothwell used to rescue himself from penury and clear his debts; in return, after it had been redeemed from his creditors, he gave her Crichton Castle, which she retained for life. She was a woman of strong character, well educated and with a good head for business; according to Sir William Drury, she was "a proper and virtuous gentlewoman."

The Earl and Countess spent their honeymoon at Seton. Because Jean insisted on wearing black in mourning for her lost love, there was initially some friction, and Bothwell returned to Edinburgh on his own after a week. But the couple were soon reunited, and thereafter lived mainly at Crichton. Their servants, Cuthbert Ramsay and George Livingston, later testified that they had seen them living peaceably, "friendly and quietly" together. There were, however, no children of the marriage.

On 25 February, Randolph, still hanging on in Edinburgh, informed Cecil that the Queen's marriage to Darnley had failed and that Darnley and Lennox were plotting against Mary and Rizzio; he also reported the astonishing alliance between Darnley and the exiled Lords.[73]

But Morton and Ruthven did not trust Darnley. According to Ruthven, "considering he was a young prince, and having a lusty princess to lie in his arms afterwards, who might persuade him to deny all that was done for his cause and to allege that others persuaded him to the same," the Lords "thought it necessary to have security thereupon." On 1 March, they made him sign a Bond in which he acknowledged that he was the chief author of the plot and assumed full responsibility for the punishment—the word "murder" was not used—of the "wicked, ungodly" Rizzio and of any who might try to prevent it, even though "the deed may chance to take place in the presence of the Queen"; he further promised to protect his fellow plotters from any repercussions of the murder.[74] That day, Darnley wrote to Moray, asking him to travel to Berwick to await the King's summons.[75] On 8 March, Darnley signed a safe-conduct for Moray to return to Scotland, and promised to provide him with an escort headed by Lord Home.

On 2 March, a second Bond, between Darnley and the exiled Lords, was signed at Newcastle, according to which the Lords promised to obtain the Crown Matrimonial for Darnley in return for him securing their pardons and the restoration of their property, and undertaking to maintain the Kirk. Moray was not among the signatories.[76]

Threats of punishment forced Randolph to leave Edinburgh that day; he was conducted under escort across the border to Berwick, and remained there, still in touch with the Queen's enemies and able to keep an eye on Scottish affairs. Elizabeth wrote to Mary criticising her treatment of both Randolph and Moray, and sent money to the latter at Newcastle.[77] But Mary was taking a hard line with those who had opposed her. On 4 March, she formally opened the Parliament that would see her rebels attainted.

Two days later, Randolph and Bedford provided Cecil with details of the Bonds and the names of the chief plotters, and—now that it was too late for her to intervene—asked him to inform Elizabeth of what was intended, telling her that the discord between Mary and Darnley was the result of her denying him the Crown Matrimonial and also "for that he hath assured knowledge of such usage of himself that altogether is intolerable to be borne, which, if it were not over well known, we should both be very loath to think that it could be true. To take away the occasion of slander, he is himself determined to be at the apprehension and execution of him who [has] done him the most dishonour that can be done to any man, much more being as he is." They also claimed that Mary was determined to remove Morton from the office of Chancellor and replace him with Rizzio.[78] There is, however, no official record of Morton's removal from office.

Enclosed with the above was a letter to Elizabeth, informing her that "a matter of no small consequence is about to take place in Scotland" and that the attempt on Rizzio's life was to be carried out "before Tuesday next" (i.e., before 12 March). For fuller details, they referred her to the letter to Cecil. Neither letter would have reached London in time for the Queen to alert Mary to the plot.

On 7 March, Mary, accompanied by Bothwell carrying the sceptre and Huntly the crown, attended the opening session of Parliament in the Tolbooth, in which Moray, Argyll, Glencairn, Rothes, Ochiltree, Boyd and Kirkcaldy of Grange were formally summoned to Edinburgh to be attainted on 12 March. The Queen also intended that Parliament should enact legislation allowing Catholics to practise their religion unhindered. In despite of Mary, Darnley had refused to attend because he was not to be granted the Crown Matrimonial, and spent the day with his cronies in Leith.[79] Moray had already left Newcastle.

On the night of 8 March, Cecil visited Lady Lennox in the Tower and informed her that Rizzio was shortly to be slain.[80] The conspirators had planned to carry out the murder on 12 March but, guessing that Randolph and Bedford had leaked too many details, and fearful of Elizabeth interfering, they decided to strike three days earlier. By now, over 120 people were involved in the conspiracy, among them some of the highest in the land, and there was every chance that some of them might have been loose tongued, yet neither Mary, nor Bothwell, nor Huntly had any inkling of what was afoot. Rizzio may have heard some of the rumours, for he consulted a French astrologer, Jean Damiot, who told him to beware of the bastard. Rizzio assumed he meant Moray, and told Damiot he would make sure that the bastard never again set foot in Scotland.[81] But Moray was not the only bastard involved in the plot—one of its promulgators had been George Douglas, the bastard of Angus. And when Damiot told him to return to his own country, Rizzio retorted, echoing Mary's own sentiments, "Words, nothing but words! The Scots proclaim much, but their threats are not carried out."[82] It would not be long before he found out, in the most horrific manner, how wrong he was.

8

"This Vile Act"

◁━

On the afternoon of Saturday, 9 March 1566, Darnley played tennis with Rizzio.[1] That evening, Rizzio was one of those present at a supper party given by the Queen in her closet at Holyrood Palace.[2] The little room, measuring only about 12 feet by 10 feet, was crowded with guests: Mary's half-sister, Jean, Countess of Argyll; Jean's uncle, Robert Beaton, Laird of Creich, Master of the Queen's Household; Lord Robert Stewart; Sir Arthur Erskine of Blackgrange, Mary's Master of the Horse, Mar's brother and, according to Knox, "the most pestilent papist in the realm"; the Queen's French apothecary; a page, Anthony Standen the Younger; and a groom. Rizzio, who was wearing a splendid gown of furred damask over a satin doublet and russet velvet hose,[3] had not removed his cap, as was customary when a man was in the presence of his sovereign.[4]

Darnley was not present; he and Mary rarely dined together these days. Instead, he was busy admitting the conspirators to the palace. Morton was in charge of setting an armed guard of between 100 and 500 men (estimates vary)[5] around Holyrood, seizing the keys from the porter and securing all the gates and doors, so that none should enter or depart.[6] He also posted about twenty men on the stairs leading up to the Queen's apartments.

At about six or seven o'clock,[7] as Mary and her friends were eating, to everyone's surprise, Darnley emerged from behind the tapestry covering the door from the bedchamber, having come up via the secret stair from his rooms below. He appeared affable enough and said he had already eaten supper. Sitting next to Mary, he put his arm around her. As if on cue, Lord Ruthven suddenly appeared, wearing full armour and looking deathly pale as a result of his illness.

"May it please Your Majesty to let yonder man Davy come forth of your presence, for he has been overlong here," he demanded.

"What offence hath he done?" Mary asked, astonished.

"Great offence!" was the angry reply. "Madam, he has offended your honour, which I dare not be so bold as to speak of. As to the King your husband's honour, he hath hindered him of the Crown Matrimonial, which Your Grace promised him, and has caused Your Majesty to banish a great part of the nobility that he might be made a lord; he has been the destroyer of the commonwealth, by taking bribes, and must learn his duty better."[8] Mary turned to Darnley and asked him what he knew of this matter, but he "denied the same." In great indignation, Mary commanded Ruthven to leave the room or be arrested for treason.[9] He ignored her, and, outraged at such disrespect, Lord Robert, Creich, Erskine, the apothecary and a groom made to seize him, but he drew out his pistol and snarled, "Lay no hands on me, for I will not be handled."[10]

Drawing his dagger, he advanced menacingly on Rizzio, who was cowering behind Mary in the window recess,[11] his dagger in his hand. At that moment, Lindsay and five heavily armed men—George Douglas, Patrick Bellenden, William Ruthven, Andrew Ker of Fawdonside and Henry Yair, a former priest who was now one of Ruthven's retainers—burst into the room. As the conspirators lunged at the Italian, a violent struggle ensued in which the table was overturned and everything on it was sent crashing to the ground; Lady Argyll managed to save a single lighted candle, which, together with the firelight, illuminated the shocking scene. Ruthven manhandled the Queen out of the way and into Darnley's arms, "entreating her not to be afraid" and assuring her "that all that was done was with the King's own deed and assent." He ordered Darnley, "Sir, take the Queen your sovereign and wife to you,"[12] whereupon Darnley kept a strong hold on Mary, despite her struggles, and lifted no finger to help her when Lindsay brutally rammed a chair towards her stomach.

As Ruthven laid hold of Rizzio, George Douglas, seizing Darnley's dagger, thrust it across the Queen's shoulder at the Italian, so close that she could feel the coldness of the steel on her throat. Mary was certain that Rizzio was wounded by this thrust, and Melville states that the dagger was left "sticking in him," but Ruthven, trying to play down the enormity of the crime, later denied that this ever happened, insisting that David had "received never a stroke in Her Majesty's presence." Yet the death warrant for Henry Yair states that "they committed the said slaughter in her presence."[13] It seems likely, therefore, that Rizzio did sustain his first wound in the dining closet.

Anthony Standen later claimed that "one of Ruthven's followers offered to fix his poniard in the Queen's left side"; Standen grabbed it and turned it away from her. Many years afterwards he told James I that he had saved his life and that of his mother.[14] Mary later stated, probably truthfully, although Ruthven denied this also,[15] that Fawdonside had held a loaded pistol to her womb and would have killed her had not his gun "refused to give fire," an act of such blatant treason that she could never bring herself to forgive it. Not unreasonably, she was convinced, and ever remained so, that she and her unborn child were the true targets of the conspirators.

Rizzio was on his knees, clawing at the Queen's skirts[16] or clinging on to her waist[17] and crying, in Italian, "Justice! Justice! Save me, my Lady! I am a dying man. Spare my life!"[18] But Darnley brutally bent back his fingers[19] and the others dragged him away, struggling and screaming, down the privy stair to the King's bedchamber, where there waited a great number of armed men, "so vehemently moved against David that they could not abide any longer." They hauled him back up the stairs, through the Queen's bedchamber and as far as the outer door of the adjoining presence chamber,[20] where, assisted by Lindsay, Morton[21] and over a dozen of the latter's men, they gave vent to a frenzy of bloodlust and savagely stabbed him to death, with either Morton or George Douglas striking the first blow.[22] So furious was the attack that one of the killers was wounded.[23] Care was taken to ensure that Darnley's dagger was left embedded in Rizzio's side,[24] to proclaim the King's involvement in the deed.[25] It is unlikely that Darnley personally took part in the actual act of murder: although Randolph later reported a rumour that "he gave him one blow himself," Ruthven implies that he remained in the dining closet, keeping Mary under restraint. As for the Queen, while all this was going on, she was, in her own words, "struck with great dread" and in "extreme fear of our life."[26]

Some hours later, on Darnley's orders, Rizzio's lacerated body, bearing fifty-six stab wounds,[27] was hurled down the stairs and then thrown across a wooden chest in the porter's lodge by the door. The porter, stripping the fine garments from the body in order to appropriate them for himself, observed, "This was his destiny, for upon this chest was his first bed when he came to this place, and now here he lieth again, a very ingrate and misknown knave." The next day, Rizzio's corpse was hurriedly buried in a pauper's grave in the Canongate cemetery, near the door of Holyrood Abbey.

Shortly after Rizzio's murder, Henry Yair vented his anti-Catholic resentment on Father Adam Black, a Dominican friar of the Queen's household who had once been chaplain to Marie de Guise and had courted danger as a spy under the pseudonym John Noir. He was murdered in his bed, stabbed to death like Rizzio.[28]

After Rizzio had been dragged away, Mary and Darnley removed from the dining closet to her bedchamber.[29] Mary had no way of knowing what had happened outside, or whether her own life was in peril. "She blamed greatly her husband, that was the author of so foul an act,"[30] and when she angrily asked him why he had betrayed her so shamefully by this "wicked deed," he made his speech about Rizzio having enjoyed more of her company—and, according to Randolph and Bedford, her body—than he himself had over the previous six months, and ended, "I am your husband, and you promised me obedience at the day of your marriage, and that I should be participant and equal with you in all things; but you have used me otherwise by the persuasion of David."

"My Lord," replied Mary bitterly, "all the offence that is done me you have the wit [knowledge] thereof, for the which I will be your wife no longer, nor lie with you any more, and shall never like well till I cause you have as sore a heart as I have at this present." As will be seen, this proved an empty threat.

Ruthven, who had returned to the room[31] but said nothing about what had taken place outside, interrupted, "I beseech Your Majesty to be of good comfort, to entertain your husband and use the counsel of the nobility, and then your government will be as prosperous as in any king's days." Then "be-ing sore felled with his sickness," he sat down without leave in the Queen's presence, and called to her servants, "For God's sake, bring me a cup of wine." Mary regarded this as "a great presumption"[32] and, beginning "to rail" at him for his insolence asked, "Is THIS your sickness?" He nodded, saying, "God forbid Your Majesty had such a sickness."

"If I die in childbirth as a result, or my commonwealth perish," said the Queen, "I will leave the revenge thereof to my friends, to be taken of you, Lord Ruthven, and your posterity. I have the King of Spain and the Emperor my great friends, and likewise the King of France, my good brother, with my uncles of Lorraine, besides the Pope's Holiness and many other princes in Italy."

Ruthven replied, "These noble princes are over-great personages to meddle with such a poor man as I am, being Your Majesty's own subject. If anything be done this night that Your Majesty mislikes, the King your hus-band—and none of us—is in the wit [know], which he confessed to be true."[33] Mary had probably already suspected as much.

Meanwhile, the citizens of Edinburgh had been alerted to the distur-bances at Holyrood and sounded the tocsin.[34] The Provost, Sir Simon Pres-ton, and 400 members of the watch, all armed with spears, soon assembled below the Queen's windows, asking to speak with her. Lindsay warned her, "If you speak to them, we will cut you into collops and cast you over the walls."[35] Darnley went to the window, assured the citizens that all was well and that the tumult had resulted from the just punishment of one who had been a papal agent, then ordered them to return to their homes, which they did.[36]

Mary was by now quite distraught, and begged to be told what had be-come of Rizzio, warning the conspirators, "It shall be dear blood to some of you if his be spilt."[37] Ruthven eventually admitted that David had been "put to death" and accused Mary of "taking his counsel for maintenance of the ancient religion, debarring of the Lords who were fugitives, and putting also upon counsel of the Lords Bothwell and Huntly, who were traitors and with whom he [Rizzio] associated himself."[38] Much later, when Lady Argyll told the Queen that she had seen David's mutilated body, Mary was in great dis-tress, but quickly recovered her composure, saying, "No more tears. I will think upon a revenge."[39]

In another part of the palace, Bothwell, Huntly and Atholl were having supper. Hearing some commotion and the war cry, "A Douglas! A Douglas!"[40] they took their servants and went to investigate, but, after an armed confrontation with Morton and his men, Bothwell and Huntly were forced, through the intervention of Ruthven, to return to Bothwell's apartment. Here, Ruthven told them that vengeance had been taken upon Rizzio at the King's own command, and that their enemy Moray was expected in Edinburgh on the morrow. As soon as Ruthven had gone off to reassure Atholl, Bothwell and Huntly, realising that danger threatened them from all sides, escaped through a low back window to "the little garden where the lions were lodged"[41] and rode like the wind for Dunbar Castle. Prior to their departure, they had left with Huntly's mother a message for the Queen that they intended to rescue her. Their escape was to prove crucial.

Some time that evening, the Lords who had been in attendance on Mary prior to the supper party—Atholl, Tullibardine, Maitland, Fleming, Livingston, Balfour and the Bishop of Ross—were permitted to leave the palace, all "in great fear of their lives."[42] Mary later told Archbishop Beaton that the conspirators had intended to hang Balfour because he had worked to keep Moray in exile; Ruthven, however, states that Balfour sought and obtained leave from the King to depart peacefully from Holyrood; it is unlikely that Darnley would have sanctioned the murder of one of his most influential supporters.

Before the evening was out, Mary knew that the Lords meant to hold her in captivity and that she was potentially in great danger. She had also been informed that Moray was on his way back to Edinburgh, and had wondered aloud why Ruthven had been conspiring with this former enemy, only to be told that the King was willing to remit the exiles' offences.[43]

That night, she was confined to her rooms, attended only by the Dowager Countess of Huntly and a few female servants,[44] with eighty Douglas men standing guard outside the palace gates and her bedchamber door, preventing her from communicating with the rest of her household. In command of them was one of Ruthven's followers, Thomas Scott, a lawyer and Under-Sheriff of Perth. Effectively, martial law had been established.

In desperation, and contrary to what she had said earlier, Mary had asked

Darnley to spend the night with her, but Ruthven had made him go to his own rooms on the floor below. The Queen could not sleep, but spent the dark hours pacing up and down, consumed with rage and sorrow.[45] She was certain that the murder "had appeared to be done to destroy both her and her child."[46] Any illusions she had retained about Darnley had been destroyed. Her most faithful servant had been murdered. Her Catholic policy was in ruins. The conspirators had emerged victorious, and she could expect little from them but imprisonment or worse. At best, they would use her as their puppet, to lend a semblance of legality to their rule. She had only one faint hope: that Bothwell would help her escape. She had received the message left with Lady Huntly, but the odds against it seemed overwhelming.

In Darnley's apartments, the conspirators, joined by Lennox, were discussing what to do with the Queen. It was proposed that she "be sent to Stirling under safe-keeping, there to give birth to her child. Lord Lindsay remarked that she would have plenty of pastime there in nursing her baby, singing it to sleep, shooting with her bow in the garden, and doing fancy work. In the meantime, the King could manage the affairs of state along with the nobles."[47] Ruthven added brutally, "If any raise the least difficulty, or cause any uproar by attempting to release her, we will throw her to them piecemeal, from the top of the terrace." Someone reminded him that the Queen's confinement was approaching.

"I feel certain," he said, "and I will stake my life on it, that the baby is only a girl, and there will be no danger. But on this matter we will take counsel with Lords Moray and Rothes, for without them we will do nothing." He and the other Lords warned Darnley: "If you wish to obtain what we have promised you, you must needs follow our advice, as well for your own safety as for ours. If you do otherwise, we will take care of ourselves, cost what it may." They then turned aside and whispered together, "which put the King and his father in great terror, for they did not think their lives safe, and all the more so when, as they were breaking up, they told him that now he must not talk with the Queen save in their presence. They removed his own attendants and left a guard near his chamber."[48]

Darnley now realised, too late, that the Lords had no intention of placing him in authority over them and that they regarded him as expendable; they had clearly "made use of him, only that they might involve him in the disgrace and infamy of an act of such atrocity." "Moved by these considerations and terrors, [he] came up that night by a private stair to the Queen's bedroom. Finding the door locked, he most urgently entreated her to open it, for he had something to tell her which much concerned their mutual safety. But he was not permitted to enter until the next morning,"[49] by which time Mary had realised that she had every chance of drawing him over to her side. As the father of the unborn heir, she could not afford to abandon him before he had recognised the newborn infant as his own, for fear of compromising its legitimacy. She resolved therefore to conceal her distaste and, summoning up her courage, determined to save herself and the child in her womb.

Early the next morning, Mary admitted a contrite and frightened Darnley to her bedchamber. He had "passed that night in perplexity, in terror for his own life,"[50] and now, in tears, he sank to his knees and confessed that he had failed in his duty towards her, having signed a bond with the conspirators in order to procure the Crown Matrimonial.[51] He excused himself, however, on the grounds that he was young and imprudent, blinded by ambition, and had been the dupe of wicked traitors. Taking God to witness that he "never could have thought nor expected that they would have gone to such lengths, and that the murder of Rizzio had never been intended by him. He asked her to take pity on him, their child and herself, begging her for help, because otherwise they would all be speedily ruined." He then handed her a copy of the Bond he had signed with Moray, "telling her that if it were ever known that he had done so, he would be a dead man"—strangely significant words, given the fate that lay in store for him. "Nevertheless, he wished to free his conscience from this burden."[52]

Mary answered severely, "Sire, within the last 24 hours you have done me such a wrong that neither the recollection of our early friendship nor all the hope you can give me of the future can ever make me forget it. I think you may never be able to undo what you have done. You say you are sorry, and this gives me some comfort. Yet I cannot but think that you are driven to it rather by necessity than led by any sentiment of true and sincere affection."[53] Greatly chastened, Darnley "disclosed all that he knew of any man"[54] in the plot. Mary told him, "Since you have placed us both on the brink of the precipice, you must now deliberate how we shall escape the peril."[55]

When he revealed to her the conspirators' plan to imprison her at Stirling until she died,[56] Mary realised that she must avoid leaving Holyrood at all costs. One way was to feign labour. She outlined her plan to Darnley. His part would be to have the guards removed. He, in turn, urged her to pretend to be reconciled to the conspirators, and to promise them pardons if they asked for them. Mary refused, saying her conscience would never allow her "to promise what I do not mean to perform. However, if you think it good, you can promise them whatever you please in my name." Darnley agreed to do this, and quietly left her chamber, undetected.[57]

The traditional theory, accepted by many writers, is that Mary had to use all her powers of persuasion to detach Darnley from the conspirators, yet it is clear that, even before she had a chance to voice any arguments, he had himself become aware that he was in danger from them and approached her first for help against them. It has also been argued that, in inducing Darnley to abandon the conspirators, Mary knew that she was condemning him to a bloody revenge, but we have seen that Darnley had already decided to dissociate himself from them, so the responsibility for any reprisals rests with him alone.

On the morning of 10 March, Darnley, having agreed to pretend to the conspirators that he was still working with them, issued a proclamation in his own name dissolving Parliament, whose members were ordered to leave Edinburgh within three hours or else face treason charges. The immediate threat to the exiled Lords had now been removed, and they could return with impunity.

Early that afternoon, when Darnley again visited Mary, she "made as though she would part with her child."[58] Given what she had gone through, a premature labour would not be unexpected, and Morton and Ruthven had no choice but to accede to Darnley's demand that a midwife and the Queen's French physician be sent for. After examining her, they insisted that she be released from captivity for the sake of her health. The Lords grudgingly agreed to remove some of her guards, and allowed her ladies and other servants to attend her as usual.

Lady Huntly, who was grateful to Mary for restoring her son to his earldom and "right glad to have her revenge on Moray,"[59] had received a message for the Queen from Huntly, in which he suggested that she escape from her window down a rope ladder, which his mother would smuggle in under the cover of a dinner plate. Mary rejected this idea, not only because of her condition, but also because guards were watching out from the room above. Instead, she gave Lady Huntly a letter to Bothwell and Huntly, telling them that, if they and their men would wait for her near Seton, she would try to find a means to join them there on Monday night; she also asked them to warn Mar to hold Edinburgh Castle for her. In the meantime, she would pretend to be ill. As they were talking, Mary was relieving herself upon her close stool, but at that moment a suspicious Lindsay burst in, with no regard for the Queen's privacy, and told the Dowager she was dismissed. As she left, she was perfunctorily searched, but the Queen's letter, concealed under her chemise, remained undetected.[60]

Mary had touched no food since the supper party the previous evening; it was not until 4 p.m. on Sunday that she was able to eat something, but the thuggish Lindsay was again hovering and insisted on inspecting the dishes sent to her in case messages were concealed in them.[61]

All that day, Mary refused to see Morton and Ruthven, but she was willing enough to receive Moray and the other exiled Lords without delay. She intended, if she could, to enlist their support against the conspirators.

Moray, Rothes and Kirkcaldy of Grange had arrived in Edinburgh shortly before Rizzio's murder, but had remained "in hiding in different parts of the town"[62] until the King's proclamation had been issued. Then they could emerge without fear of arrest and, after being "thankfully received" by Darnley at Holyrood,[63] they went to dine at Morton's house off the Canongate. Whilst at table, Moray received a summons from the Queen[64] and hastened to court, arriving at dusk.

His meeting with Mary was an emotional one: she embraced and kissed him, and, weeping, cried, "Oh, my brother, if you had been here I should not have been so uncourteously handled." At this, Moray wept too,[65] "moved with natural affection" towards her.[66] On his knees, he "excused himself to her very earnestly from the charge of having been the chief promoter" of the recent "atrocities,"[67] and expressed shock over Rizzio's murder, which can surely have been no surprise to him; he assured her he had played no part in it, but had come only to do her service. Mary told him that, had it not been for Darnley, she would have recalled him long ago.[68] However, although she accepted his protestations of innocence and promised to "remit all,"[69] when he asked her to pardon the conspirators, she refused. He did not immediately press the point.

Mary did accede to Moray's request that she be reconciled to Darnley, with whom she was still ostensibly on bad terms. She agreed at length to spend the night with him, which aroused the alarm of the Lords, who, perceiving that Darnley "grew effeminate again" under the Queen's influence, feared that he would betray them. Without his nominal authority, their coup would be divested of all semblance of legality and they would be exposed as common traitors. Darnley, however, failed to arrive in Mary's room. At midnight, George Douglas took Ruthven into the King's bedchamber to show him Darnley lying across his own bed in a drunken stupor.[70]

In the morning, Darnley came to Mary's chamber and sat beside her for an hour while she slept. When she awoke, he apologised for not having come to her bed, and tried to caress her. She shook him off, saying she felt sick. He seems to have been deluding himself that, if Mary pardoned the conspirators, all would be well again, and his optimism appeared justified when he asked if she was ready to do so and found her evidently amenable. Naïvely, he hastened off to tell the conspirators the good news. They, however, warned him not to believe her, "by reason she had been trained up from her youth in the court of France, and well in the affairs of intrigue."[71]

That morning, Moray, Rothes and Grange met with Morton, Ruthven and Lindsay, who declared, as Mary later informed Archbishop Beaton, "they thought it most expedient that we should be warded in our castle of Stirling, there to remain till we had approved in Parliament all their wicked enterprises, established their religion and given to the King the Crown Matrimonial and all the whole government of our realm"; if she refused, they were prepared "to put us to death or to detain us in perpetual captivity." Moray apparently gave tacit consent to these measures, but his real agenda was to reestablish himself in power.

The Lords apparently informed Darnley of the meeting, and it seems he went straight to Mary to tell her of their resolve. She spoke sternly to him, "certifying him how miserably he would be handled if he permitted the Lords to prevail." He needed little convincing that his life too was in danger, and was easily persuaded to fall in with Mary's plan to escape, with the help of Bothwell and Huntly, to Dunbar Castle,[72] a secure royal fortress on the coast, twenty-five miles from Edinburgh.

Later that morning, Darnley met with Moray, Morton and Ruthven, and told them that he "had obtained of Her Majesty that the Earls and Lords should come into her presence and she would forgive all things past and bury them out of her mind."[73] None of them believed him.

They were still arguing about it when, after dinner, the Queen's midwife and her French physician came to urge that, in order to avoid a miscarriage, their mistress should be moved "to some sweeter and pleasanter air." The Lords grumbled that this was "but craft and policy," but Darnley insisted that his wife was "a true princess, and that thing she promised he would set his life by the same."[74] He asked Moray to bring them to her later that afternoon.

Towards evening,[75] Mary and Darnley received Moray and the three chief rebel Lords, Morton, Ruthven and Lindsay, in her presence chamber. They all knelt before the Queen, but Moray arose quickly, leaving the rest on their knees, grudgingly begging for pardon. Morton, who was kneeling on the spot where Rizzio had died, noticed that his knee was bloodstained, and observed, "The loss of one mean man is of less consequence than the ruin of many Lords and gentlemen." Mary ignored this, and said she could not forgive them just yet, at which Moray began lecturing her on the merits of clemency. She tartly replied that her subjects had so far given her many opportunities to exercise that virtue; however, if, by their good conduct in the future, these Lords helped "to blot out the past," she would try to forget what they had done.[76]

At this point, the Queen, "fearing that she might be compelled to go further than she intended, made as though she had been suddenly taken ill and was in great pain, as if childbirth was at hand." Calling for the midwife, she retired to her bedchamber in great haste and asked Darnley "to tell the nobles what her intentions were, as had been arranged between them."[77] He informed the suspicious Lords that the Queen had in fact agreed to "put all things in oblivion as if they had never been"[78] and asked them to have their pardons formally drawn up in writing, ready for her signature. They thought this was a trick, but, having questioned the midwife, whom they themselves had appointed, and having been assured that Mary's life was indeed in danger, they proceeded to have the requisite documents drawn up.[79] Ruthven claimed later that, while this was being done, Mary was walking up and down the presence chamber hand in hand with Darnley and Moray for an hour, but she was more likely to have been still in her bedchamber, feigning a threatened miscarriage.[80]

Moray's behaviour suggests that he was not acting in tandem with Morton and the rest. Melville states that it was clear to the conspirators that Moray was "not so frank for them as they expected." His overriding concern was the restoration of his own power, and it was becoming increasingly obvious that the best way to achieve that would be with the co-operation of Mary, who had shown herself pleasantly disposed to him. He could not risk being associated with men whom she regarded as traitors, and as Darnley was apparently playing a double game and might well leave them exposed to charges of treason, he deemed it wise to distance himself from them. That they had gambled all to bring about his return was of little consequence in the face of his ambition, his desire to remain in the good graces of Queen Elizabeth, and perhaps his vision for the future of Scotland.

After supper, Darnley came to collect the written pardons from Morton and Ruthven, saying that the Queen was too ill at present to read anything, but promising to return the documents the next day with her signature. He then insisted that they remove their remaining guards from the palace and leave her in his charge, which they consented to do, realising that "it would not avail them in law if there were the least appearance of restraint upon her."[81] Maitland may have advised them of this, since Randolph claims he had taken pity on Mary and, on her personal plea, agreed to persuade the Lords to remove the guards.

"Whatever bloodshed follows will be on your head," Ruthven told the King grimly. Imprudently, he and his fellow conspirators left the palace and went to Morton's house for supper, without waiting until the Queen had actually signed their pardons.[82]

Bothwell and Huntly had by now received Mary's message and, "being without fear and willing to sacrifice their lives,"[83] they summoned their "best friends, the most loyal of Her Majesty's subjects"[84] and rode to Seton, there to await the Queen. "The plan of the escape was due to the Queen's ingenuity"[85] and, indeed, her courage and resolve. During the evening of 11 March, she enlisted the support of John Stewart of Traquair, the Captain of her Guard, Arthur Erskine, her Master of Horse, and the page Anthony Standen the Younger, all loyal men who could be relied upon to assist her. They agreed to have horses waiting outside the Canongate cemetery at midnight. Finally, Mary left word with one of her ladies for Melville, that he "should be earnest to keep the Earl of Moray from joining with the other Lords."[86]

All the arrangements were now in place but, at the last minute, Darnley demanded that Lennox accompany them, for his father was in terror of what the conspirators might do to him once they found their captive flown. Mary angrily refused on the grounds that Lennox "had been too often a traitor to her and hers to be trusted on an occasion so hazardous as the present": she had always paid Lennox the respect due to a father-in-law, and had even castigated Darnley for not showing proper deference to his parent, but as Lennox had "forgotten himself and joined her enemies, nothing could happen to him but what he deserved." Darnley was her husband, "therefore in her conscience she could not abandon him."[87] In the face of her anger, Darnley backed down.

As twelve o'clock approached, Mary and Darnley, accompanied just by Standen and a gentlewoman, Margaret Carwood, crept down the back stairs, through the service quarters and out of an insecurely fastened back door in the wine cellar,[88] emerging into the Canongate cemetery. They nearly tripped over an earthen mound, and Darnley, sighing, confessed to Mary that it marked the place where Rizzio lay buried. He added ruefully, "In him I have lost a good and faithful servant, the like of whom I shall never find again. I have been miserably cheated." Mary hushed him, for fear that they should be overheard.[89] Lennox later alleged that she warned Darnley "it should go very hard with her, but ere a twelve month was over, a fatter than he should lie beside him,"[90] but this was written with the benefit of hindsight, probably in a deliberate attempt to show that Mary was thinking of doing away with Darnley long before any murder plot was ever hatched; if Mary did say such a thing to Darnley, she may well have been referring to Morton or Ruthven.

Beyond the cemetery, Traquair and Erskine were waiting with four horses. Mary mounted behind Erskine;[91] Darnley was shaking with fear, and had to be steadied by the page, Anthony Standen, who rode pillion behind him. The tension was high as they trotted through the silent streets of Edinburgh, but, once they reached open country, they could canter non-stop to

Seton, which was ten miles to the east. As they neared their destination, Darnley espied a group of horsemen blocking the road and, dreading that it was Morton and Ruthven come for him, cried in panic to Mary, "Come on! Come on! By God's blood, they will murder both you and me if they can catch us." With no regard to her pregnant state, he savagely whipped on her horse and spurred his own, but when, "worn out by fatigue and in great suffering," she pleaded with him "to have some regard to her condition," he replied, "Come on! In God's name, come on! If this baby dies, we can have more." Mary scathingly told him "to push on and take care of himself," which, to the disgust of everyone with them, he did, not caring that he might be abandoning her to the tender mercies of her enemies.[92] It has been suggested that Darnley still had design on the throne and was hoping that hard riding would accomplish what Rizzio's murder had failed to do,[93] but, if so, he was not thinking very logically, since he had alienated all his supporters.

In the event, the sinister-looking horsemen proved to be Bothwell, Huntly, Seton, Fleming, Livingston and other loyal Lords and gentlemen who had heeded Bothwell's summons.[94] They were waiting to escort the Queen to Dunbar, fifteen miles further on. At Seton, they changed horses and Mary "took a horse to herself" for the rest of the way.[95]

At 5 a.m., after five gruelling hours in the saddle, the exhausted royal party reached the safety of Dunbar. It was later reported in Italy that, as soon as they arrived, the Queen insisted on cooking eggs for everyone's breakfast.[96] Whether this is true or not, it aptly illustrates her buoyant mood. In cunningly escaping from her captors with Darnley, she had deprived them, not only of the cloak of legality that had masked their treasonable proceedings, but also of the means of achieving their political goals. With the help of her loyal Lords and gentlemen, she was now ready to fight back and reassert her regal authority.

9

"As They Have Brewed, So Let Them Drink"

THE ROYAL CASTLE OF DUNBAR had stood on its cliff jutting out over the North Sea since at least the thirteenth century, and was one of the most important strategic fortresses in Scotland. Besieged, sacked and reduced on several occasions, it had been mostly rebuilt during the reign of James IV, and its royal chambers were of the same proportions as those inhabited by that monarch in Edinburgh Castle. Here were kept the national arsenal and the kingdom's reserves of gunpowder.[1]

Mary was safe in this mighty stronghold, and it was here that, over the next five days, in response to her summons and Bothwell's efforts in the Borders, her loyal supporters and over 4,000 Borderers gathered.[2] Among them were Atholl, Balfour, Bishop Leslie, Lord Home, John Maxwell, Lord Herries "and an infinity of others."[3] Here too came Glencairn, Rothes and other rebels, seeking and receiving pardon. All pledged themselves to restore their Queen to her throne and overthrow the conspirators. Soon, as word spread, men came flocking from further afield.

When, on the morning of 12 March, the conspirators found the Queen and Darnley gone, they were understandably aghast and dismayed, realising that without the promised pardons they were doomed. Lennox was furious with Darnley for having left him behind, unaware that it was Mary who had refused to allow him to accompany them, and galloped off to Dunbar to take his son to task.[4] That day, Moray and other rebels went to the Tolbooth and publicly protested that they were ready to answer any charges that might be made against them in Parliament, "well knowing that no one could be found who would venture to accuse them."[5] The next day, Morton, Ruthven and Lindsay sent Robert, Lord Sempill, who was not tainted by involvement in the plot, to the Queen to ask her to fulfil her promise to grant them their pardons. Mary refused, and kept Sempill with her.

On 15 March, as a reward for his outstanding services over the past few days, Mary awarded Bothwell the prestigious wardship of the castle and Crown demesne of Dunbar,[6] of which she had deprived Sir Simon Preston, the Provost of Edinburgh, as punishment for his complacency during her captivity.

That same day, Mary dictated a letter to Queen Elizabeth, giving a dramatic account of how "some of our subjects and Council, by their proceedings, have declared manifestly what men they are, as have taken our house, slain our special servant in our own presence and thereafter holden our proper persons captive treasonably, whereby we were constrained to escape to the place where we are for the present, in the greatest danger for our lives and evil estate that ever princes on Earth stood in. Which handling no Christian prince will allow, nor yourself, we believe." She apologised for not writing in her own hand, "but, of truth, we are so tired and ill at ease through riding twenty [sic] miles in five hours of the night with a frequent sickness and evil disposition for the occasion of our child that we could not."[7] In her letter to Charles IX, written a few days later, Mary refers to "the bodily indisposition of our person" and states she is not "in robust health";[8] clearly the events of the past few days had taken their toll on her.

Darnley had been largely shunned by Mary's supporters. "Some would not speak to him or associate with him. Others, especially Lord Fleming, openly found fault with his conduct towards the Queen his wife and all of them who he had consigned to death." Darnley confided to Mary that he feared her Lords would revenge themselves upon him and begged her "to bring about a reconciliation with them. He offered to promise, upon his oath, to enter into a close and perfect friendship with them for the future, and never to abandon them. The Queen exerted herself to the utmost to accomplish this," but without success, for the Lords had had experience of his promises. Moreover, they had risked their lives for him during the Chaseabout Raid, "and in return he had betrayed them to their greatest enemies." Although Mary had permitted Darnley to share her bed, "their obedience was to her alone, and to no other person. For the future, neither his promises nor his orders should move them."[9] From now on, their attitude towards Darnley was to be one of ill-concealed contempt.

On 17 March, the Queen issued a proclamation summoning the local lieges to muster their troops at Haddington on the 18th with provisions for eight days.[10] She also sent orders to Mar to close the gates of Edinburgh "unless the Lords departed out of it."[11] That day, she left Dunbar, "well attended," and arrived in the evening at the abbey of Haddington.[12] On the way, she encountered Melville, and received him with great thanks for his "care of her honour and welfare."[13]

Melville brought with him a letter from Moray, who had been urged by Morton to make his peace with the Queen in order to put himself in a strong enough position to intercede on the conspirators' behalf. Melville, however, had told Moray that, if he dissociated himself from them, "I should procure a pardon to him and all his followers." Moray had no doubt already decided that reconciliation with Mary was a far better move than supporting traitors, and in his letter to her again asked pardon for his offences and assured her "never any more to have to do with such as had committed this vile act, nor intercede for them."[14] Clearly, Moray was determined to be on the winning side. Argyll also sent a message seeking the Queen's favour.[15]

On the morning of the 17th, having heard that the treacherous Darnley had defected to the Queen, and knowing that they were outnumbered and outwitted, Morton, Ruthven, Lindsay, George Douglas and Fawdonside, "being destitute of all assisters,"[16] had fled to England, seething in mortal hatred at the King's perfidy, and thirsty for revenge. In betraying them, Darnley had as good as signed his own death warrant.

Maitland had not been directly involved in Rizzio's murder, but had certainly had foreknowledge of it. Hearing that both Darnley and Bothwell had denounced him to Mary, and that she had ordered him to withdraw to Inverness, Maitland instead sought refuge at Dunkeld with Atholl, whom he hoped would speak for him to the Queen. Failing that, he would try to purchase his pardon from her, although Randolph thought that would "be as hard as may be."[17]

On the night of 17 March, at Haddington, Mary complained bitterly to Melville

> of the King's folly, ingratitude and misbehaviour. I excused the same the best I could, imputing it to his youth, which occasioned him easily to be led away by pernicious counsel, laying the blame upon George Douglas and other bad counsellors; praying Her Majesty, for many necessary considerations, to remove out of her mind any prejudice against him, seeing that she had chosen him herself against the opinion of many. But I could perceive nothing, from that day forth, but great grudges that she entertained in her heart.[18]

Darnley also sought out Melville and asked if Moray had written to him. Melville diplomatically answered that Moray's letter to Mary had been written in haste "and that he esteemed the Queen's and he but one."

"He might also have written to me," grumbled Darnley sulkily. He then asked what was to become of Morton and the rest, whereupon Melville told him he thought they had fled.

"As they have brewed, so let them drink," commented Darnley. It seemed to Melville "that he was troubled he had deserted them, seeing the Queen's favour but cold."[19]

Mary's army now numbered 8,000 men, but it was soon obvious that there would be no obstacles to her return to the capital, and the next day, 18 March, riding with Darnley at the head of her troops and accompanied by Bothwell, Huntly, Home, Seton, Archbishop Hamilton and the Earl Marischal, she made a triumphal entry into Edinburgh. It was only nine days since Rizzio's murder, yet she had already regained control of her realm without bloodshed. This is sure testimony to her popularity with her subjects. The people of Edinburgh welcomed her with great acclaim and escorted her to the residence of Lord Herries on the High Street;[20] on 26 March, she moved to a larger house owned by the Bishop of Dunkeld, which was situated on the Cowgate, behind the present Tron Kirk.[21] She had made it very clear that she had no wish to return to Holyrood for the present, as the horrifying memories it held were yet very fresh; nor did she feel safe there.

Mary was most anxious that arrangements for her security should be tightened, and immediately ordered cannon to be positioned outside Herries's house. She also "raised certain bands of soldiers, by the advice of Bothwell, whom she made General of the said bands, besides the force of the Hamiltons, which she called into her service to wait upon her, being the ancient enemies of the King her husband's House."[22]

Moray, fearing that Mary still believed he had supported the rebel Lords, had retired to Linlithgow, where, in the company of Argyll, he waited to see what she would do. But Mary wisely recognised the need for conciliation and clemency. In order to consolidate her victory, she needed strong aristocratic support, and at present many of her chief Lords were either technically outlaws or fugitive traitors. It was necessary therefore to exercise a degree of pragmatism, and on the day after her arrival in Edinburgh, Mary wisely pardoned some of the conspirators not actively involved in Rizzio's murder, and obliged several others to find surety for their good behaviour. Furthermore, in order to ensure Moray's loyalty and drive a wedge between him and her other enemies, she sent him a message confirming her willingness to pardon him, Argyll and others involved in the Chaseabout Raid, but insisting there would be no forgiveness or mercy for those who killed Rizzio. Moray's pardon was conditional upon him breaking off relations with the conspirators and retiring for the present to Argyll.[23]

"The investigation of David's death was harshly pursued."[24] On 19 or 20 March, the Queen issued a writ summoning Morton, Ruthven, Lindsay, Fawdonside, George Douglas and sixty-three other conspirators to appear before the Privy Council to answer for their crimes, on pain of outlawry. On 20 March, Morton was deposed from the office of Chancellor and replaced by Huntly, whose father had once held the post.[25] Balfour replaced James MacGill as Clerk Register. Atholl, Seton, Livingston and Fleming now made up the backbone of the Privy Council, over which Mary now made a point of presiding frequently. "By that Council, the affairs of the realm were quieted, and for a time, all was at peace. And in this state of calm they might have remained, but for the turbulence of the King, who could not long continue on good terms with anyone."[26]

Bothwell, who had provided such strength and support during the crisis, "now began to be in great favour,"[27] and in effect became for a time Mary's chief adviser. Months afterwards, Mary was still full of praise for his "dexterity," recalling "how suddenly, by his providence, not only were we delivered out of prison, but also the whole company of conspirators dissolved, and we recovered our former obedience. Indeed, we must confess that service done at that time to have been so acceptable to us that we could never to this hour forget it."[28]

Both Moray and Darnley had proved treacherous, but Bothwell had a record of loyalty to the Crown stretching back many years, and was obviously a man upon whom the Queen could rely. Almost alone amongst the Scottish nobility, he never took bribes from a foreign power; this was perhaps one of the reasons why he was unpopular with his peers. However, he commanded the loyalty of the Borderers, who were ever willing to rise at his bidding. Bothwell's influence may perhaps be detected in wise new laws recorded in the *Register of the Privy Council,* which clamped down on counterfeit coinage, the poaching of fish in Scotland's rivers by alien fishermen, and the pardoning of offenders in serious cases.

But the prestige of the Crown, as well as Mary's reputation, had suffered as a result of Rizzio's murder, which had also signalled an end to the Queen's pro-Catholic policies. The fact that Darnley had taken such drastic action against his wife gave rise to suspicions that he had had just cause. Furthermore, the rift between the royal couple was now public property, which in itself was a scandal.

Mary did not help matters when, shortly before 20 March, she had Rizzio's body reburied with Catholic rites in "a fair tomb" in the abbey church of Holyrood, which gave offence to many of her subjects.[29] However, Buchanan was wrong in stating that Rizzio was buried in the royal vault of James V in the chapel royal: his coffin was nowhere to be seen when the vault was opened in the seventeenth century.

Given the embarrassment that now overshadowed her marriage, Mary had to embark on a damage limitation exercise. She could quite lawfully have had Darnley executed for treason, but she needed to ensure that there were no doubts as to the legitimacy of her child, and so, on 20 March, Darnley appeared before the Privy Council and signed a declaration protesting, "upon his honour, fidelity and the word of a prince," that he had "never counselled, commanded, consented, assisted nor approved" Rizzio's murder;[30] he had merely given consent for Moray to return to Scotland, without the Queen's knowledge.[31] On the following day, his innocence was publicly proclaimed at the Mercat Cross in Edinburgh, "and that not without laughter."[32] Randolph commented, "The King has utterly forsaken the conspirators."[33]

This declaration of innocence on Darnley's part was not just for his own benefit, but also to protect Mary's reputation. For, if her husband had not instigated or approved Rizzio's murder, there would be no grounds for suspecting Rizzio of any impropriety with the Queen. The murder could then be imputed to the jealousy of the Lords, who were to take all the blame for it.

For the sake of her unborn child and her reputation, Mary had protected Darnley from the consequences of his treason, and on the surface it appeared that the two were reconciled; Herries says Mary had told the King she would "forgive and forget all." But she felt bitterly hurt and alienated by his connivance in what she was convinced had been a plot against her life, and was also contemptuous of the way in which he had betrayed not only herself but also his fellow conspirators. Understandably, she wanted as little to do with him as possible. As most of her courtiers—Lennox and Atholl excepted—were already shunning him, Darnley was virtually isolated.

On 21 March, Randolph reported, incorrectly, that Moray and Argyll had returned to court. "The Lords of this last attempt have written to him [Moray] no longer to forbear for their cause to agree with the Queen, and, seeing that the other [Darnley] hath left both them and him, that he do not further endanger himself for their cause. Lennox remains sick at Dunbar, much offended with his son." Randolph added that Bothwell had been given, by way of reward, all Maitland's possessions.[34] These included the rich lands of Haddington Abbey, which had once been under Hepburn patronage.

Knox, in whose publicly stated opinion Rizzio's murder was "worthy of all praise,"[35] fled on 21 March to Ayrshire,[36] where he remained for some time, writing his history of the Reformation in Scotland and beseeching God to "destroy that whore in her whoredom."[37]

Elizabeth I could have taken advantage of the situation in Scotland, but she was genuinely horrified and outraged to hear of Rizzio's murder and the Lords' treatment of their anointed sovereign. Immediately she sent Melville's brother Robert north to assure Mary of her support and warn Darnley and Moray that, should they again betray their mistress, they would incur Elizabeth's wrath. In consequence of this, relations between the two Queens were greatly improved, and they resumed their former friendly correspondence. This had not a little to do with the fact that Elizabeth and her ministers were relieved that Rizzio, whom they had suspected to be a papal agent, had been removed, and that Mary had abandoned her pro-Catholic policy.[38]

Philip II, to whom Guzman de Silva sent a detailed if not very accurate report on 23 March, was also shocked by the events in Scotland, but must have been astounded to learn that Darnley, who had made such a display of Catholic piety, had allied himself with heretics.

Another who was greatly troubled by news of the murder was Lady Lennox,[39] who was still in the Tower. Belatedly, Darnley grew fearful that she would be the victim of reprisals in consequence of his conduct, and wrote to Queen Elizabeth to assure her that Lady Lennox had had no knowledge whatsoever of the plot. But Elizabeth refused to accept the letter. She asked the messenger if it were true that Darnley had drawn his dagger in the Queen's presence and, when told he had not, she commented acidly "that she had not believed it, because all the time he was in this country he had never put his hand to a knife."[40]

On 29 March, on Mary's orders, Morton and over sixty other traitors were outlawed. The Queen informed Charles IX: "We have caused all their possessions to be seized [and are] determined to proceed against them with the utmost vigour. To this end, we are satisfied that the King our husband will act in unison with us."[41] The Queen, reported Randolph, "wills that all men who are friends to any of those that were privy to David's death shall pursue them, to do their uttermost to apprehend them."

Moray, however, was playing his usual double game. On 27 March, Bedford had reported to Cecil that Moray "desireth Your Honour's favour" for "his dear friends," Morton and the other fugitive Lords, who, "for his sake, hath given this adventure." Ruthven, Randolph had noted earlier, was "very sick, keeping most to his bed."[42] According to Nau, Darnley also would have liked to see his former allies pardoned, but dared not speak for them to the Queen, who was implacable towards them; as was Bothwell, who lost his temper when Atholl sued for a pardon for his friend Maitland, whose properties Bothwell now held. On 2 April, Randolph reported that matters had "quieted, but Atholl still travails" for Maitland.[43]

Darnley, meanwhile, had given "express orders to all state officials and subjects of the kingdom to organise a thorough search and arrest anyone who had been with the murderers, wherever they might be found, and punish them with death, and anyone discovered to have helped them in secret was to receive corporal punishment. To set an example to others, he had four of those found at the site of the murder arrested,"[44] among them Henry Yair and Thomas Scott. Randolph informed Cecil that the complicity of three of these men was known only to Darnley.[45] Yair and Scott were hanged and quartered, the only conspirators to be executed for Rizzio's murder. The other two, Sir John Mowbray of Barnbougle and William Harlaw, both Lothian Lairds, were reprieved on the scaffold on the orders of the Queen, after Bothwell had petitioned for their lives.[46]

Darnley, who was more deserving of punishment than any of these wretches, was about to receive his come-uppance. The Lords in exile were furious when they heard of his public declaration of innocence; they were determined to set the record straight and, in the process, have their revenge. On 2 April, Morton and Ruthven sent Cecil their account of the conspiracy,[47] and revealed that they had vindictively forwarded to Mary the Bond, in the King's handwriting, in which Darnley acknowledged himself the chief instigator of the plot to punish Rizzio, in the Queen's presence if necessary, and undertook to protect his fellow plotters from any repercussions. Any illusions Mary may have retained about her immature husband being easily led astray by wicked men and being entirely innocent of the murder were now dramatically shattered: "so many sighs she would give that it was a pity to hear her."[48] Moreover, it was clear that, at best, Darnley had spared no thought for her safety; at worst, he had intended the shock to kill her. He had betrayed her, her unborn child, and the men who had plotted for his advancement. This she could not forgive, and from the time she saw the incriminating Bond, Mary and Darnley were virtually estranged.

After Darnley's murder, Lennox claimed, with a view to incriminating Mary, that she told Darnley "that she never trusted to die till she might revenge the death of her servant David, and that she feared the time should come that he himself might be in the like case as David was, and ask mercy many a time, when it should be refused unto him."[49] Yet in April 1566, Mary could not just order Darnley's arrest and execution, as his enemies had hoped she would do, nor could she punish him in any public manner, for she dared not jeopardise her child's right to the succession. Given the rumours that she had had an affair with Rizzio, she needed to maintain a show of solidarity with Darnley and avoid any confrontations until the infant was born and Darnley had acknowledged it as his own. Until then, she resolved to conceal her revulsion and contempt. But there were other, more subtle, ways of punishing a treacherous husband. Darnley found himself excluded, not only from state affairs,[50] but from the mainstream life of the court, and constantly watched, in case he should plot some new mischief. The Queen would never trust him again, and the Lords despised him and wanted nothing to do with him. Humiliatingly, it seemed to be public knowledge that his wife would not sleep with him.[51] Furthermore, he had to live with the certain knowledge that, if the Queen pardoned his enemies and allowed them to return to Scotland, he would be doomed. Darnley reacted to this treatment by sulking and devising wild ideas of revenge. Even in isolation, he was a danger to Mary's security.

Security certainly remained a priority, with the political situation so uncertain. Holyrood's defences had proved easy to breach, so, on 3 April, on the advice of her Council, Mary took up residence in the royal lodging within the stout walls of Edinburgh Castle, one of the greatest fortresses in Scotland. Darnley went with her, but the nobility, including Bothwell, remained in the town.[52] On 15 April, the Council advised the Queen to stay in Edinburgh Castle until after the birth of her child, "to guard against what she had been warned would occur, that the Lords were resolved to take possession of the infant from the moment of its birth."[53]

There had been Bronze Age and Roman settlements on the lofty volcanic rock that dominates the city of Edinburgh; a castle certainly existed by the Dark Ages, but the mediaeval fortress was first built by Malcolm III in the late eleventh century. The tiny chapel dedicated to his wife, St. Margaret, dates from this period, and is the oldest surviving building in the castle precincts. Most of the early fortifications were destroyed by Robert the Bruce in the fourteenth century, but his son, David II, erected a great tower modelled on Edward III's Round Tower at Windsor. The royal lodgings were built in the fifteenth century by James III and James IV on the south-east side of the castle precincts, around what is now called Crown Square; they were renovated in 1566 for Mary and Darnley, whose visit is commemorated by a seventeenth-century carving "MAH 1566" above a doorway in Palace Yard. The Queen's apartments comprised an impressive great hall with a hammer-beam roof, a presence chamber, an inner chamber that served as a bedchamber, and a tiny cabinet leading off it; these rooms had windows commanding spectacular views to the south, but they had been largely un-used for many years because Holyrood had long since become the favoured city residence of the sovereign. Normally, Edinburgh Castle was used to house the Crown Jewels and other treasure, munitions, the national archives, some officers of state and state prisoners. Now a sovereign was in residence again, and the royal chambers were made luxurious with Turkish carpets, oak furniture and damask cushions.[54]

On 4 April (and again on 25 April), Randolph reported a rumour that Mary, having seen the incriminating bond, was "grievously offended" with Darnley and had sent an envoy, James Thornton, to Rome to inquire about the possibility of an annulment of her marriage.[55] If true, this must have been on the grounds that the couple, who were within the forbidden degrees of consanguinity, had married before the dispensation had arrived from Rome, but in such circumstances any children of the union would be illegitimate, and it is unlikely that Mary would have contemplated taking such a risk just now. Thornton did leave Edinburgh around this time, but it was to convey letters from Mary to Elizabeth I and Charles IX.[56]

Randolph also reported that the Queen was "determined the House of Lennox shall be as poor as ever it was." Lennox himself, still ill and "sore troubled in mind," had been forbidden the court,[57] and now lay at Holyrood, where Darnley had visited him only once.[58] There is no record of what passed between them. In 1568, Lennox would assert that Mary had entered into an adulterous affair with Bothwell at this time, despite the fact that she was nearly seven months pregnant: he claimed that while Darnley, "that innocent lamb who meant so faithfully unto her as his wife," had been outcast from her company, "Bothwell waxed so great that he, supplying the place of David, was her love in such sort that she, forgetting her duty to God and her husband, and setting apart her honour and good name, became addicted and wholly assotted unto the said Bothwell."[59]

This affair was supposed to have begun soon after Mary moved into Edinburgh Castle. Bothwell was lodged in the town, but had leave to attend on the Queen at certain times, and was a frequent guest at her dinner table, along with Huntly; contrary to what many writers state, there were opportunities for clandestine dalliance. However, there is no contemporary evidence to support Lennox's allegations, which appear rather ludicrous, given Mary's heavily pregnant state, and are at variance with Buchanan's libel of 1568, which claims that Mary became sexually involved with Bothwell in September 1566. Both documents, significantly, were written at a time when it had become politically imperative to demonstrate that Mary was an adulteress and murderess. Furthermore, Darnley never at this time displayed any jealousy of Bothwell, and Bothwell himself, although newly married, was about to embark, had perhaps already embarked, on a liaison with his wife's sewing maid.

On 4 April, Mary wrote Elizabeth a warm letter of gratitude for her support, asking her not to give succour to the fugitive Lords, and inviting her to stand as godmother to her child.[60] Darnley was furious about this, taking it as a personal insult, for Elizabeth had never recognised him as King of Scots, and he hated her. But Mary and her Council refused to listen; they were laying the foundations for her child's potential future as heir to a united Scotland and England, and needed Elizabeth's goodwill.

Elizabeth, who was ostentatiously going about with a miniature of Mary hanging from a gold chain around her waist, was still expressing outrage at the way Darnley had behaved to his wife and sovereign. On 11 April, she told de Silva, "Had I been in Queen Mary's place, I would have taken my husband's dagger and stabbed him with it!"[61] The following month, she ordered the fugitive Lords to leave England.[62]

Mary was still keeping up the pretence that she and Darnley were reconciled. He was present when the French diplomat, Michel de Castelnau, Sieur de la Mauvissière, arrived in Edinburgh just before Easter, having been sent by the Guises to warn Darnley to behave himself; Darnley also joined the Queen for the Maundy Thursday ceremonies on 12 April.[63] Yet beneath the surface, tensions were simmering. Drury reported that "the displeasure abates not between the King and Queen, but rather increases." Days before, Darnley had ridden secretly to Stirling "for the purpose of renewing the conspiracy with Argyll and Moray."[64] But the Queen's spies were vigilant and warned Mary, who sent Robert Melville after the King with a warning not to revive his treachery. It was a fool's errand anyway, since Moray and Argyll had "such misliking of their King as never was more of man"[65] and were, in fact, already on their way to Edinburgh, intent on reaching a *rapprochement* with the Queen.

They arrived at Edinburgh Castle on 21 April.[66] Moray told Mary that they had "taken up arms in consequence of the King only, against whom they had acted in their own defence—not against her. They had no share in the interests and indignities offered to the Queen in her own palace, nor with the murder of the late David; for these, Lord Ruthven and his accomplices were entirely responsible." Mary admitted "she had no private quarrel with Moray: all had come through the King her husband," and he "was resolved to pardon Moray. The rigour with which she had hitherto acted towards the Earl was chiefly to please her husband," hence she was "easily induced" to agree to a reconciliation,[67] and gave Moray and Argyll permission to stay in Edinburgh Castle with her,[68] intending to keep a close watch on their doings. Moray's wise counsel and political support would be an advantage of which she was sorely in need at this time, and his restoration to power would certainly ease relations with England, but she would never fully trust him again.

Neither would Bothwell, Huntly, the Catholic Bishop Leslie and Darnley, who all immediately allied against Moray. Bothwell and Moray had long been bitter enemies—Moray had once told Lady Argyll that Scotland could not hold them both at the same time; Huntly wanted revenge on Moray for ruining his father; and Darnley was terrified of Moray, believing that he and the exiled Lords "would have their revenge on him, as soon as they could."[69] Together, they tried to convince Mary that Moray was as much to blame for the murder as the fugitive Lords, and urged her to lock him up, at least until her child was born, "alleging that they were assuredly advertised that he and his dependers were resolved to bring in the banished Lords, even at the very time of her child-bearing." But Mary, believing that their accusations arose "only from their own hatred,"[70] refused to listen, declaring that she knew Moray to be well disposed towards her and that she had forgiven him his former offences. Furthermore, in order to prevent any confrontations, she barred Bothwell, Huntly and Moray for a short period from her dinner table. She kept Bothwell sweet by confiding to him that, in the Will she would soon be drawing up, she would be appointing him a member of the Council of Regency in the event of her death in childbirth. Darnley was to be expressly excluded.

Darnley was also determined to prevent the return of Maitland. "The King proposed that the office of Secretary should be given to the Bishop of Ross in the place of Lethington, whom he especially charged with having been a principal in the late conspiracy."[71] When Mary refused to countenance this, Darnley "became exceedingly angry" and sent one of the grooms of his Chamber to tell the Queen "how much he was displeased with her, and that he had primed and made ready his two pistols, which she would find hanging at the back of the bed." Fearing that he might try to shoot himself, Mary went to his bedchamber at once and, "after having stayed with him for some time, she quietly carried off the pistols." Next day, she informed her Council what had happened, "hoping thus to remove from her husband's mind the prejudice which he had conceived against Lethington, and to let them understand the decision at which she had arrived, which they followed."[72]

Darnley's chief objective now "was to play off, by every means in his power, the one party against the other, so that he himself should become stronger than either of them. The Queen had reason to dread this, knowing as she did the inconstancy and treachery which she had found in his character."[73] It was also obvious that Darnley was blind to reality. On 25 April, Randolph reported that Mary wanted all feuds healed, but that there had been discord between her and Darnley, who was being scorned by the nobles. Moray and Argyll showed only contempt for him, and Melville noticed that the King "passed up and down on his own, and few durst bear him company."

Nau later asserted that the Lords "fomented discord between the King and Queen by underhand dealings," in order to keep Moray in power, yet Mary had reason enough to be antagonistic towards Darnley, and clearly had no desire for a true reconciliation. Melville tried to mediate between the royal couple, but became so importunate that the Queen got Moray to reprove him and charge him not to be so familiar with the King in the future. Melville was one of the few people who were sympathetic towards Darnley, and believed him to have "failed rather for want of good counsel and experience than from any bad inclinations. It appeared to be fatal to him to like better of flatterers and ill company than plain speakers and good men."[74]

Whatever her private feelings, Mary gave a convincing show in public of marital felicity, which was necessary in view of her coming confinement. Lennox states that the King and Queen "accompanied in bed as man and wife,"[75] and Castelnau, when he passed through Berwick, told Bedford that they had spent two nights together, and that he had done his best to bring them together.[76] Later, in London, he informed de Silva that they were behaving as a married couple should, and that, after his arrival, the Queen had been more openly affectionate towards Darnley, but he had also noticed that there was suspicion and distrust between them. He added that the King did not "seem bad personally, or in his habits," and passed his time "mostly in warlike exercises. He is a good horseman."[77] Evidently Darnley had been warned to be on his best behaviour.

Childbirth held many risks for women in those days. With the future security of her heir uppermost in her mind, being loath to "trust her child to the keeping of her husband,"[78] Mary's priority was to seek by all means to ensure the tranquillity of her realm.[79] At the end of April, determined to reconcile Moray, Argyll and their ally, the Earl of Glencairn, with Bothwell, Huntly and Atholl, she invited them all to a feast at Edinburgh Castle. Out of courtesy, they acted civilly towards each other, and afterwards worked together as the core of the Privy Council, on which Moray, Argyll and Glencairn were formally reinstated on 29 April, but Mary was aware that their *entente* was purely superficial. Before long, Moray was attempting to remove Bothwell from court and engage him elsewhere by stirring up trouble in the Borders, with the help of Morton and other exiles. Together, they incited lawless clans such as the Kers of Cessford, the Scotts of Buccleuch and the notorious Elliotts, to create disturbances. Not surprisingly, by 27 April, Mary was seriously contemplating retiring to France for three months after the birth of her child and appointing a regency council to govern during her absence.[80] Two days later, she defiantly, and foolishly, recruited Rizzio's eighteen-year-old brother Joseph (Giuseppe) who had come to Scotland in Castelnau's train and was a virtual unknown, as her French Secretary.[81]

In Rome, on 26 April, the Bishop of Dunblane informed the Pope of Rizzio's murder and urged him to assist the Queen of Scots in her present crisis.[82] Mary had also asked the Cardinal of Lorraine for advice about obtaining aid from the Vatican.[83] Clearly, she did not want the Catholic powers to think she had abandoned her policies in favour of the old religion, but she also wanted them to be aware of the difficulties she faced.

But Darnley, who feared the Protestant establishment in Scotland and certainly aimed to win support in Europe, seems to have decided to set himself up as the hope of Catholicism, preferably to the detriment of Mary, and in the expectation of securing the power he had been denied by the collapse of the coup. On 29 April, de Silva informed Philip II: "The King continues his devotion to the ancient religion and hears Mass every day."[84] Philip appears to have thought Mary lukewarm in her efforts to restore Catholicism, for, although he condemned Rizzio's murder, he was no longer so willing to send help to Mary as he had been after the Chaseabout Raid.[85] He was also preoccupied with his planned invasion of his Dutch provinces, in which he intended ruthlessly to suppress the heresy that had taken root there. The knowledge that King Philip would soon be in the Netherlands may have given impetus to Darnley's hopes of enlisting foreign allies in the Catholic—and his own—cause.

On 6 May, in pursuance of this strategy, and forestalling any attempt to make him return his Order of St. Michael, Darnley wrote to Charles IX and Catherine de' Medici, protesting that he had been "greatly wronged by a rumour that makes me guilty of such a horrible crime. But I hope that my innocence, fully accepted by the Sieur de Mauvissière, to whom I have told the truth of all, will not allow you to have any other than a good opinion of me." He entrusted the letter to Castelnau, who was about to leave Scotland.[86]

On 12 May, Pius V wrote to Mary, congratulating her on her escape from "the treason of heretics," which he attributed to the sharp practice of Queen Elizabeth, and announcing that he would be sending a nuncio to Scotland, along with a subsidy.[87] He did not tell the Queen that the Nuncio was to ensure that the money was spent in the Catholic cause, so that she might prevail over her rebels; given her past record, he was not sufficiently convinced of Mary's zeal for the Faith. His Nuncio, Vincenzo Laureo, a Jesuit hardliner who had recently been appointed Bishop of Mondovi,[88] left Rome on 6 June, firstly to visit his new See, and then to pay the first of two visits to the Catholic duchy of Savoy. After that, he intended to travel on to Scotland, although he was well aware that the Protestant establishment would do everything in their power to keep him from setting foot in that land. He carried with him, not only 150,000 gold crowns of the promised subsidy,[89] but also a papal brief implying that the Pope himself meant to go to Scotland and mentioning the support that could be expected for Mondovi's mission from the King of Spain.[90]

Meanwhile, on 12 May, it was reported by an English observer that the Queen's hatred for Darnley was such that he could not safely stay in Scotland;[91] four days later, Sir John Forster at Berwick informed Cecil that Darnley was now planning to leave the country.[92] According to Knox, he was "desolate and half desperate,"[93] but there may have been a more tactical reason for this decision, for, as will be seen, he was bent on going to Flanders. It is surely more than mere coincidence that this was at a time when it became known that King Philip was expected in the Netherlands.

Around 17 May, the Earl and Countess of Bothwell visited Haddington Abbey. Here, Bothwell committed adultery with his wife's serving maid, twenty-year-old Bessie Crawford, the black-haired daughter of a blacksmith.[94] Bothwell sent one of his followers, a local merchant called Patrick Wilson, with an invitation to Bessie to look over the abbey buildings. On Bothwell's orders, Wilson locked her in a lodging in the cloisters. Half an hour later, Bothwell arrived and took the key from him. A porter and two other people heard whispering behind the door, then watched Bothwell leave soon afterwards with loosened breeches, which Wilson helped him fasten. On another occasion, Bessie emerged from a short tryst with the Earl in the abbey tower, with her hair and clothes in disarray.[95] George Dalgleish, Bothwell's tailor, later stated that Lady Bothwell, suspicious of Bessie's relationship with her husband, had sent the girl away. On 11 June, Bothwell conferred the lands of Nether Hailes on his wife, possibly as a peace offering. This early infidelity confirms that Bothwell's marriage was no love match, and that he remained an opportunist where women were concerned.

But Bothwell had little leisure for dalliance, for he had been charged with keeping the Queen's peace in the Borders, which Moray had deliberately disturbed. On Bothwell's advice, Mary now announced a series of royal assizes to check lawlessness in the region, and summoned her lieges to attend her at Peebles on 13 August, to allow her time to recover from her confinement.

On 24 May, Morton, now resident in Alnwick and obviously keeping track of Darnley's movements, reported to Bedford that he had information that the King was "minded to depart to Flanders and such other places as he thinks will best serve for his purpose to complain upon the Queen, for the evil handling and treatment" that he received from her; already, his ship was lying ready at Glasgow. Blinkered by unrealistic ambitions for a crown, Darnley was again dabbling in treason, having learned nothing from past experience. Yet, if his complaints bore fruit, his wife's crown, and the succession of her child, would again be seriously in jeopardy.

Lennox later alleged that Darnley had told him that, towards the end of her pregnancy, "Bothwell was all in all" to Mary, and that, in an attempt to be revenged upon Moray for his rebellion, she had tried to incite him (Darnley) to seduce the virtuous Countess of Moray, saying "I assure you, I shall never love you the worse." When a shocked Lennox warned his son never to be unfaithful to his sovereign, Darnley lied that he had "never offended the Queen my wife in meddling with any other woman in thought, let be in deed." This tale is unlikely: firstly, there is no contemporary evidence to support it, and secondly, Mary and Moray were now on good terms and she needed his support against Darnley. There was no reason why she should wreck the peace she had brought about by instigating a blood feud between her husband and her brother, unless she hoped that Moray, in a jealous rage, would kill Darnley in revenge, and thus rid her of him. But Buchanan, who repeats the tale, does not place this construction on it, and offers the unlikely explanation that Mary "thought by that way to be revenged on three enemies at once, the King, the Earl and his wife, and therewithal to win a colour and cause for divorce, to make empty bed room for Bothwell."[96] This is patently absurd because, not only was Mary about to leave bequests in her Will to Moray and his wife, but elsewhere in his narrative, Buchanan places the commencement of Mary's alleged affair with Bothwell in September 1566; yet he states that this incident occurred "when she was great with child"; furthermore, adultery would not have provided a Catholic with grounds for annulment, and in any case it is very unlikely that Mary was contemplating an annulment at this time.

On 3 June, Mary ceremonially withdrew into seclusion to await her confinement. A midwife, Margaret Asteane, was appointed and provided with a new black gown, the royal bed was hung with blue taffeta and velvet, ten ells of Holland cloth were purchased for the cradle, and the relics of St. Margaret of Scotland were sent for from Dunfermline, in the belief that they would protect the Queen while she was in labour.

On the same day, as well as receiving the Sacrament, as "one who is in proximate danger of death,"[97] Mary made her Will, leaving everything but specific bequests to her child. To Darnley, she left twenty-six items of jewellery, including two watches and the red-enamelled diamond ring that he had placed on her finger on their wedding day. This was the largest of her bequests, and it suggests not only a softening in her attitude towards him, but also an attempt to ensure his future security; Mary would hardly have done this if she were contemplating getting rid of him by annulment, revenge killing or murder, as the later libels allege.[98] The Queen also left items to her Guise relatives, the Earls and Countesses of Moray, Argyll and Huntly, old Lady Huntly, Lady Seton, the four Maries, Arthur Erskine and even the Lennoxes; a ring that Rizzio had given her was willed to his brother Joseph, who was to convey it to a secret beneficiary.

This cannot have been Bothwell, for he was openly to receive two bequests, a table diamond set in black enamel, and a miniature figurine of a mermaid set in diamonds, holding a diamond mirror and a ruby comb.[99] This may well have had a certain significance, for, in the symbolism of the day, a mermaid represented a siren or temptress, whose involvement with mortals was inevitably followed by disaster; in the popular understanding, the word "mermaid" was synonymous with "prostitute." Mary was hardly likely to refer to herself in this context, especially in her Will, therefore it is possible that this bequest bore a subtle warning about Bothwell's involvement with Bessie Crawford and other women who might lead him astray. The Privy Councillors, including Bothwell, all signed a document binding them to honour the Queen's Will.[100]

On 7 June, Randolph reported that Bothwell and Huntly, who must have been concerned about Moray's influence over the Queen, had had their request for lodgings in Edinburgh Castle turned down by Mary, on the advice of Moray.[101] This suggests that Moray's influence had now superseded Bothwell's. Soon afterwards, Randolph was recalled to London, and on 13 June, Elizabeth I dispatched Sir Henry Killigrew to Edinburgh to inform Mary that his Queen "prayed God to send Her Majesty a quick and happy delivery" and had banished the fugitive Lords from her realm.[102] Yet, for all Elizabeth's fine words, they remained unmolested in their northern refuges.[103] Morton was "now in a hard condition," being reduced to near penury, but Mary would not permit his friends to send him money.[104]

Ruthven died at Newcastle on 13 June, having "showed great repentance for his wicked life." Morton witnessed the final ravings of the old warlock, who cried "that he saw Paradise opened and a great company of angels coming to take him"; Nau commented acidly that they were probably "diabolical illusions wrought by evil spirits."[105] The grieving Morton, however, reported that Ruthven's end "was so godly that all men that saw it did rejoice."[106] Ruthven's heir was his son, William, but he could not succeed to the title because of his father's forfeiture.

Two days after Ruthven's death, there were premature rejoicings in Edinburgh as a result of a false report that the Queen had given birth to a son.[107] In fact, Mary's labour did not commence until 18 June, at which time she withdrew from her state bedchamber into the adjoining cabinet, a tiny room with a window overlooking the city. Here, she would be attended only by the midwife and her ladies-in-waiting until after the birth. For the first time in twenty-four years, an heir to Scotland's throne was about to be born.

10

"An Unwelcome Intruder"

⌒

The Queen's labour was protracted and exceptionally painful. As the contractions became more severe, "she began to wish that she had never been married."[1] At one stage, her suffering was so great that Margaret Fleming, Countess of Atholl is said to have resorted to sorcery in an attempt to transfer the Queen's pains to Mary Beaton's aunt, Margaret, Lady Reres.[2] Predictably, Mary's agony abated not one jot and, being warned by her ladies that she and her child were in great peril, she beseeched God to save her baby rather than herself.[3] Melville later recalled that he "lay within the Castle of Edinburgh, praying night and day for Her Majesty's good and happy delivery of a fair son." His prayers were answered when, between nine and eleven[4] on the morning of Wednesday, 19 June 1566, after twenty hours of labour, Mary was delivered of a healthy boy, who was named James and bore the title Duke of Rothesay from birth. Years later, the Queen wrote to Lady Lennox, "I have borne him, and God knoweth with what danger to him and me both."[5]

The birth boosted Mary's popularity, ensured the future of her dynasty, put paid to Darnley's pretensions to the Crown, and immeasurably strengthened the Queen's claim to the English succession. From now on, however, her ambitions were not just for herself, but for her son, and Melville was dispatched within the hour to London to convey the happy news to Elizabeth.

After the Prince was born, "all the artillery of the Castle shot, and bonfires were set forth in all parts for joy of the same."[6] The nobles, rejoicing, gathered in the Queen's state bedchamber to congratulate her and greet the new heir.

At about two in the afternoon, Darnley visited Mary, "and was desirous to see the child." This was a crucial and somewhat humiliating moment for Mary, for her reputation and honour had so far been called into question that she had no choice but to force her husband publicly to recognise the child as his own.

"My Lord," she said, "God has given you and me a son, begotten by none but you." At her words, "the King blushed and kissed the child." This was not sufficient acknowledgement, so Mary took the baby in her arms and, uncovering his face, said, "My Lord, here I protest to God, and as I shall answer to Him at the great Day of Judgement, this is your son, and no other man's son. And I am desirous that all here bear witness, for he is so much your son that I fear it will be the worse for him hereafter."

Mary then spoke to an English envoy, Sir William Stanley: "This is the son whom I hope shall first unite the two kingdoms of Scotland and England."

"Why, Madam," answered Stanley, "shall he succeed before Your Majesty and his father?"

Mary nodded, and said sadly, "It is because his father has broken to [with] me." Darnley asked her, "Sweet Madam, is this your promise that you made, to forgive and forget all?" She answered, "I have forgiven all, but will never forget. What if Fawdonside's pistol had fired? What would have become of the child and me? Or what estate would you have been in? God only knows, but we may suspect!"

"These things are all past," Darnley said tersely.

"Then let them go," retorted Mary.[7] Their bitter discourse struck a jarring note on what should have been a day of triumph. It was obvious that there was no longer any need for Mary to keep up a pretence of reconciliation. Darnley had played his dynastic part, and was no longer of political importance to her. Now she need not see him if she did not wish to.

It seems that Darnley had had no intention of refusing to acknowledge the Prince as his own, for earlier in the day he had written to the Cardinal of Lorraine proudly announcing "an event which, I am sure, will not cause you less joy than ourselves,"[8] and informing him that he and the Queen had both written asking Charles IX to stand godfather to their son.

Soon after the birth, a popular rumour arose that the Queen's baby had been stillborn or had died at birth, and that a changeling had been substituted in order to block Darnley's pretensions to the Crown. Some said they had seen a basket containing a baby being winched up over the castle rock to the Queen's window; others that the Prince was in fact the son of the Earl of Mar, whom he much resembled in looks. However, no one seriously questioned his identity, although the rumours were given apparent credence in 1830, when it was alleged that some bones—not necessarily those of an infant or even a human being—wrapped in woollen cloth (not cloth of gold, as some versions state) had been discovered in a wall during building works at Edinburgh Castle. In 1944, however, this tale was proved to be a fabrication.[9]

On the day after the birth, St. Giles's Kirk in Edinburgh was packed to overflowing with the nobility and the citizens, who had come "to thank God for the honour of having an heir to their kingdom."[10] Two days later, the Queen received the Pope's letter informing her of the sending of a nuncio, and Sir Henry Killigrew, Elizabeth's envoy, reached Edinburgh. Hearing of his coming, the Queen sent him word "that I was welcome and should have audience as soon as she might have any ease of the pain in her breasts"; despite this, he was told she was "in good state for a woman in her case."[11]

The observant Killigrew quickly summed up the political situation and, on the day after his arrival, reported to Cecil, "I find here an uncertain and disquiet sort of men." The Scottish Lords were divided into factions, with Moray, Argyll, Mar and Atholl in one party, and Bothwell and Huntly in the other. Notwithstanding the birth of the Prince, small account was made of Darnley and his father. Bothwell was in the Borders, apparently dealing with a threat "to bring in Morton during [Mary's] childbed," but he had absented himself because he "would not gladly be in danger of the four above-named that lie in [Edinburgh] Castle. Yet it is thought and said that his credit with the Queen is more than all the rest together."[12] Bothwell himself later explained that "it was as much through the faithful service I had rendered the

Queen's mother in her wars, as much as my service to the Queen herself, that I was in such favour. I had on several occasions risked my life and incurred considerable expense, which she had most generously made good to me, both by presents and by the appointments with which Her Majesty has honoured me."[13]

Killigrew also noted that Henry Gwynn, servant to Francis Yaxley, who had drowned in January whilst bringing the subsidy from Philip II, had arrived in Edinburgh with "letters and tokens from Flanders," including Philip's long-delayed reply to Darnley's letter of September 1565, which de Silva had held on to in London, ostensibly because he could not find a safe messenger, although he could of course have entrusted it to James Thornton; clearly, this letter was not meant for Mary's eyes. Evidently Darnley found Philip's words encouraging, even if he perhaps interpreted them to suit his own purposes.

Killigrew concluded his report with a mention of a spy, William Rogers, who had come in secret to Edinburgh. Without a doubt, something suspicious was going on.[14]

Rogers was an escaped felon, who hoped to evade justice and obtain Cecil's favour by acting on his own initiative as a spy for the English government. He stayed only a few days in Scotland before going south, and when he reached Oxford, sent a report to Cecil.[15] In it, he revealed he had won the confidence of Sir Anthony Standen and, through him, gained the favour of Darnley, with whom he had gone hunting and hawking. Rogers had learned that Gwynn had brought Darnley 2,000 crowns from an English merchant, with more to come if he needed it, as well as letters from Lady Lennox and, more ominously, from two English traitors, Arthur and Edward Pole, who themselves had pretensions to the English throne—both were descendants of the Royal House of Plantagenet—and were at present imprisoned in the Tower for inciting an abortive rebellion. In his letter, Arthur Pole had offered to resign his claim to the English throne to Mary and Darnley, but it is unlikely that Mary was told anything of this, for Darnley was formulating grandiose plans of his own. It seems that he not only meant to become the champion of Catholicism in Scotland, but also King of Scots in Mary's place, and then, after deposing Elizabeth, King of a united Britain, which would be achieved with the support of the Catholic powers in Europe and disaffected English Catholics.

It is impossible to assess to what degree this scheme existed only in

Darnley's fevered imagination, or to what extent his supposed allies were involved. At present, it appears he had secured at least the goodwill of Philip II and perhaps the Papacy, and the support of a number of Catholic malcontents in England.

In Scotland, Darnley's chief ally at this time appears to have been Sir James Balfour. On 7 June, Randolph had noted that Balfour was out of favour, and Killigrew now reported, "Balfour's credit [with the Queen] decays" and that Bishop Leslie "manages all her affairs of state."[16]

According to Rogers, a friend of the Pole brothers, Martin Dare, was also in attendance on Darnley. He had been a sea captain in the Scilly Isles, and had nautical skills that would prove useful to the King in time to come. Sir Anthony Standen, however, was removed from the King's orbit when Mary sent him to France to announce the Prince's birth to Charles IX; Standen would not return for a year.[17]

After a lightning journey lasting just over four days, Sir James Melville arrived in London and informed Elizabeth of the safe delivery of Mary's son. The Queen "seemed glad of the birth of the infant," and told de Silva that the birth would prove "a spur to the lawyers" to resolve the matter of Mary's right to the English succession, which would, she assured the ambassador, be decided in the next session of Parliament.[18] Melville had his doubts about this, but when Mary heard, she was jubilant, confidently anticipating that Elizabeth would at last acknowledge her as heir presumptive to the English throne.

Elizabeth told Melville that she would gladly stand godmother to Prince James, but would be unable to go to Scotland herself; in her place, she would send "honourable lords and ladies." She also consented to receive a letter from Darnley pleading for his mother's release from the Tower, an indication that she was thawing towards the Lennox Stuarts.

Mary had also asked Charles IX of France and Emanuel Philibert, Duke of Savoy, to be godparents; on 25 June, in a letter to Philip II, de Silva implied that there were reasons why she had not asked him to act as sponsor or send a representative to the baptism, such reasons being connected possibly with Philip's coolness after Rizzio's murder; however, she had asked the Duke of Savoy "as she considered him a person attached to Your Majesty."[19] As Sir

Walter Raleigh was later to proclaim, "Savoy from Spain is inseparable." Mary had effectively enlisted the might of Catholic Europe to protect the interests of the infant Prince.

Back in Scotland, on 24 June, Mary received Sir Henry Killigrew in her bedchamber. He reported that she was too weak to extend to him more than a formal welcome, but he was allowed to see her child "sucking of his nurse, and afterward as good as naked," and found James to be "well proportioned and like to prove a goodly prince." The Queen, he added, "was so bold immediately after delivery that she has not yet recovered; the few words she spoke were faintly, with a hollow cough."[20]

Darnley's behaviour during Mary's lying-in period was appalling. Nau later wrote of this time, "The King led a very disorderly life." Every night, he left the castle and went out "vagabondising" and drinking heavily with his young male friends in the streets of Edinburgh. He would return at all hours of the night, so that the castle gates had to be unlocked for him, which left Mary feeling "there was no safety, either for herself or her son." Darnley also went off for long rides on his own to the coast, where he would strip and bathe in secluded places, thereby leaving himself vulnerable to attack and his wife "apprehensive of the danger which might follow, because of the ill will which the greater number of the Lords bore towards him." She begged him to be careful "and not to put himself so indiscreetly into the power of his enemies," but he paid very little attention to her.[21] Not surprisingly, Killigrew again reported on 28 June that Darnley was not in favour.[22] In every way, he was a liability and a constant thorn in Mary's side.

Catherine de' Medici, learning of the birth of Prince James, expressed fears that Darnley was "so bad" that she could not be sure if he felt as he should towards his son. Fearful that he might plot with her enemies to seize her child and rule in his name, Mary decided to keep James with her for the present, rather than establish a separate household for him, as was customary for royal children in that era. James spent his first weeks being cared for in his mother's chamber by his wet-nurse, Helena Little, and four rockers, and sleeping in his cradle beside Mary's bed at night, so that she could watch over him herself.[23]

Mary's fears about Darnley's intentions were almost certainly justified, and she was not the only person to entertain suspicions about his activities. On 29 June, de Silva reported that the English ambassador in Paris "was surprised at the friendship the King of Scotland had with Don Francis[co] de Alava," the Spanish ambassador to the French court, and that he had learned "that they were intimate friends in Paris."[24] It is possible that they had never even met, for de Alava did not arrive in Paris until February 1564; however, the short visits he had paid there before then may have coincided with one of Darnley's trips to France. The term "intimate friends" may imply a homosexual connection, but could equally mean that they became confidants in the platonic sense. Regardless of this, the friendship must have been conducted mainly through correspondence, and it is possible, although there is no proof, that Darnley was using de Alava to gain Spanish support for his dynastic schemes.

That Darnley's aims were not widely known in Spanish diplomatic circles is perhaps confirmed by a letter written by the Duke of Alva—soon to be the Spanish Governor of the Netherlands—to Philip II on 29 June, informing him that "Your Majesty, being in Flanders, could more easily encompass that which would further her [Mary's] interests."[25] Alva was not specific, but was probably referring to the furtherance of Mary's claim to the English crown, or to the restoration of the Catholic faith in Britain, and he is hardly likely to have mentioned such things if he had been aware that Philip was supporting Darnley in a plot to dethrone Mary, which is highly unlikely anyway, not least because Philip was counting on the support of the pro-Spanish Guises when he led his invading army along the French border. Nor is there any evidence in contemporary sources that Philip lent support to Darnley's schemes.

Unable to trust those around her, Mary was turning again to Bothwell. On 30 June, she conferred upon him the priory of North Berwick, and by the end of the following month, Bedford was reporting that Bothwell "had a great hand in the management of affairs." Buchanan goes further, of course, claiming that "Bothwell was everything: he alone managed all affairs, and so much did the Queen wish to display her partiality for him that no request was granted unless presented through him." Further evidence of the trust Mary reposed in Bothwell can be found in her dealings with one Christopher Rokesby. Mary believed Rokesby to be a Catholic agent, but he was in fact one of Cecil's spies. Around this time, she granted him a private audience in Edinburgh Castle, during which she rashly revealed to him her dynastic and religious ambitions, which had burgeoned with the birth of her son.

She told him that she was cultivating the support of those English nobles whom she believed "to be of the old religion, which she meant to restore with all expedition. After she had friended herself in every shire in England, she meant to cause wars to be stirred in Ireland, whereby England might be kept occupied; then she would have an army in readiness, and herself with her army to enter England, and she proclaimed Queen." She had asked Spain, France and the Vatican for aid—on 17 July, she would write to the Pope to say she was looking forward to the arrival of the Bishop of Mondovi "with no little longing"—and added that soothsayers had told her "that the Queen of England shall not live this year."[26]

Randolph had earlier reported that Mary had agents in England inciting Catholic support, one of whom had informed her "that the papists are ready to rise in England when she will have them." Given the fact that Alva expected Philip II to support Mary in such an enterprise, and that Philip's arrival in the Netherlands was imminent, the English would have had every cause for alarm. By early August, de Silva was aware that Elizabeth was more suspicious than ever of Mary.[27]

Rokesby advised the Queen to consult her Privy Council, but she told him she preferred to deal with Bothwell, Mar, Melville and himself, and "willed" him "to confer further of these causes with Bothwell, whom I might well perceive was in more secret favour with her than any other." Probably as a result of Rokesby's meeting with Bothwell, Mary became suspicious of the former and ordered his arrest. After letters from Cecil were found in his possession, he was imprisoned in Spynie Palace, the Highland stronghold of Bothwell's uncle, where he remained for nearly two years.[28]

According to Bedford, writing on 4 July, Morton and the other exiles were busy with plans for their repatriation, and soon afterwards Killigrew observed that "many are like to venture all for their relief."[29] Darnley, however, was fiercely opposed to them being pardoned for he feared their return more than anything else; Leicester wrote on 11 June that Darnley and Bothwell were making further efforts to procure a pardon for "the shameless butcher" George Douglas, who, in return, was willing to incriminate Moray and Maitland in the Rizzio plot, which would at a stroke rid them of two of their greatest enemies.[30] But the Queen refused to pardon any of the fugitives, and was instead concentrating her efforts on reconciling her feuding nobles. Hence, she was deaf to the persuasions of Darnley and Bothwell and unwilling to listen to any allegations against her half-brother. On 13 July, Sir John Forster expressed the opinion that she was reluctant to inquire too closely into Moray's guilt. Elizabeth, reading these reports, was also loath to have Moray's role in the Rizzio affair subjected to scrutiny, and had George Douglas put under guard in order to prevent him from returning to Scotland.

On 5 July, William Rogers wrote a second report to Cecil, having been informed by the Standens how Darnley had "said before twenty gentlemen that he was not so ill-loved in England but that forty gentlemen there would serve him, and more soon after conveyance of my Lady's [his mother's] letters"; one Master Poule (or Pole, which perhaps makes him a relative of Arthur Pole) "and divers gentlemen in his company are looked for shortly in Scotland, offering to serve the King at their own charges." Darnley was also in possession of a chart of the Scilly Isles, doubtless given him or drawn up by Martin Dare, and was plotting with some men in the north of England to seize Scarborough Castle "and have all the North at his command." Both the Scillies and Scarborough were strategically placed as bridgeheads for a Spanish invasion of England. Furthermore, Arthur Pole had written claiming that he could raise the west of England in Darnley's cause, and a man surnamed Moon, who was later in Lennox's employ, was regularly bringing the King letters from his friends in that region.[31] Cecil read all this with mounting dismay.

Moray was still apparently stirring up trouble in the Borders and, as rumour had it, covering the conspirators' traces. On 17 July, Bedford reported that William Ker, Abbot of Kelso, had spoken "infamy and words of dishonour" of Glencairn, and hinted at the latter's involvement in Rizzio's murder. As a result, two of the Abbot's kinsmen savagely murdered him, chopping off his head and arms. The chief suspect was his nephew and godson, the young Laird of Cessford, whom Bothwell was sent to apprehend.[32] But it was Moray whom many suspected of being the real culprit.

Mary was now recovering from her confinement, and it was felt that a change of air would greatly benefit her, so around 27/28 July,[33] she left Edinburgh Castle and travelled to Newhaven, where she boarded a boat for Alloa, further up the Forth, having been invited by the Earl of Mar to be his guest at his fourteenth-century family seat, Alloa Tower. According to Bedford[34] and Buchanan, the Queen left Edinburgh early in the morning without telling anyone where she was going. Darnley was "so far out of her books" that he knew nothing of her plans.[35]

Buchanan claims that her boat was manned by notorious pirates, William and Edmund Blackadder, Leonard Robertson and Thomas Dickson, who were all "avowed men and dependants of the Earl Bothwell," who accompanied Mary on her journey; he adds that "honest persons" were astonished that "she should hazard her person among a sort of such ruffians." The tale is suspect, however, because, although, as Lord High Admiral, Bothwell was in charge of the preparations for the trip, he did not travel with Mary, but remained in Edinburgh as Captain of the Prince's Bodyguard; it was Moray, Mar and other leading nobles who made up the Queen's escort.[36] As for William Blackadder, although he and his brother Edmund had received pardons for the crime of murder, on 2 September following, he was appointed "general and universal Searcher to the Crown" with authority to "search, seek, apprehend and take all and sundry pirates, thieves, robbers, rebels and malefactors upon the seas";[37] such a commission would hardly have been granted to a notorious pirate.

As soon as Darnley discovered where Mary had gone, he followed her on horseback via Stirling "as fast as he could, with the hope and purpose of being alone with her, that he might enjoy his conjugal rights."[38] But he was clearly "an unwelcome intruder,"[39] and Buchanan says that Mary ordered him to "depart or do worse. So great was her disdain that she could not suffer him to remain in her company, nor yet would she declare any good cheer in his presence." This may well have been true, because Darnley departed after only a few hours[40] and went to Dunfermline.[41] Buchanan alleges he was "hardly allowed time to refresh his servants." Nau, however, says that Darnley had merely made, "as it were, a passing call," yet reveals that the original arrangement had been "that they should go back to Edinburgh Castle together." Melville and others were of the opinion that Mary, in going to Alloa, "had fled from the King's company." Obviously, the relationship between the royal couple was now fraught with suspicion and resentment, at the very least, and had all but broken down.

At Alloa Tower,[42] Mar laid on dancing, masques and sports for his royal guest. According to Buchanan, Mary "passed several days there, if not in princely magnificence, yet in rather unprincely licentiousness. How she behaved herself I had rather every man should imagine it than hear me declare it," for she "demeaned herself as if she had forgot not only the majesty of a queen but even the modesty of a matron." Buchanan was writing on the erroneous premise that Bothwell was with her, although elsewhere he claims that their alleged affair did not commence until the following month. Lennox, writing independently, incorrectly states that Mary visited Stirling, not Alloa, and that she took her pleasure "in most uncomely manner, abandoning herself to all riotousness, forgetting her princely state and honour."[43] Nau, however, says that Mary remained at Alloa for several days, but "in the company of the ladies of the court" and the Earl of Mar.

Given her recent confinement, and the fact that Buchanan at least was in the business of character assassination, it is unlikely that Mary's stay at Alloa was one long round of hedonistic indulgence. Moreover, official records show that she did not neglect affairs of state whilst there, and Bedford reported that one purpose of her visit had been to meet and make her peace with Maitland, who was certainly in the district on 28 July.[44] She also held a reception for the newly arrived ambassador from France, Philippe (or Philibert) du Croc, whom de Silva heard was "a good Catholic" but "restless or unreliable,"[45] and whom Nau later derided as a "creature" of Catherine de' Medici. Mary was aware of this, and, in order to keep an eye on him, appointed him a temporary gentleman-in-waiting, so that he would be in daily attendance on her.[46] The Scottish Lords, however, seeing this and knowing that du Croc had been "advanced by the House of Guise,"[47] came to regard him as the Queen's man. Melville calls du Croc "a grave, aged, discreet gentleman"; he was certainly a diplomat of many years' experience, and had already served on an embassy to Scotland, back in 1563. Now he had returned, ostensibly to convey Charles IX's official congratulations on the birth of the Prince.

On 31 July, Mary returned to Edinburgh, where, according to Buchanan, "she stayed not in her palace but in the nearby home of a private citizen." But her stay in the capital was not to be tranquil. The bitter feud between Moray and Bothwell had been aggravated by Bothwell's increasing credit with the Queen. Early in August, Bedford informed Cecil that, thanks to Moray's efforts, Morton's friends, notably Lord Home, the Scotts of Buccleuch, the

Kers of Cessford and other Border malcontents, had formed a confederacy against Bothwell, which Bedford meant to support as far as he dared without prejudicing peaceful relations with England.

A few days later, Bedford, whose informant was Kirkcaldy of Grange, reported that Bothwell "hath now, of all men, greatest access and familiarity with the Queen, so that nothing of importance is done without him." Consequently, he was "the most hated man among the noblemen of this realm, and it is said that his insolence is such as David was never more abhorred than he is now." If Bedford was implying that Mary and Bothwell had become involved in an illicit affair, then, given the widespread bad feeling about Bothwell's closeness to the Queen, Darnley would certainly have known about it; but although Bedford states that relations between the Queen and her husband were "rather worse," and that Darnley was jealous of Mary's familiarity with men and women, especially "the ladies of Argyll, Moray and Mar, who keep most company with her," he makes no mention of any jealousy on Darnley's part specifically towards Bothwell. In fact, he states, in the same letter, that Darnley was jealous of Mary's reliance on Moray, and had threatened to kill him, "finding fault that she bears him so much company." Nau says that Darnley, being "naturally of a very insolent disposition," had begun to "threaten all the Lords, especially Moray, whom he told that the Laird of Balfour had promised him [Darnley] that he would kill him [Moray]."

Bedford's use of the word "familiarity" with regard to both men and women indicates that he is not trying to imply a clandestine relationship between Mary and Bothwell. If that had been the case, he would have been more specific about any rumours he had heard. As for Darnley, Bedford added that Mary "eateth but very seldom with him, but lieth not nor keepeth company with him, nor loveth any such as love him," and concluded, "It cannot for modesty, nor with the honour of a queen, be reported what she said of him." Mary "fell marvellously out" with Melville for giving Darnley an Irish water spaniel, and called him a dissembler and flatterer, saying "she could not trust him who would give any thing to such one as she loved not."[48]

Mary warned Moray that Darnley bore him ill will and had told her that he was determined to kill him. Then, before the whole court, she took her husband to task, saying "she would not be content that either he or any other should be unfriendly to Moray," and constraining him to confess to Moray that his enmity had arisen from reports made to him "that Moray was not his friend, which made him speak that of which he repented."[49] After this humiliating interview, Darnley sped off to grumble about his wife to Lennox, complaining that she refused to sleep with him. He told his father that he was contemplating leaving his troubles in Scotland and going abroad.[50] Mary was not deceived by Darnley's apology; she had seen "the great danger" in his antipathy towards Moray, "which was calculated to lead to serious troubles within the kingdom. She contrived, therefore, to be always busy near the King, so as to thwart his project. But in private he did not abandon the idea."[51] Mary was now in the unenviable position of having to spend time in the company of a husband for whom she felt little but contempt and revulsion, and who had outlived his usefulness to her. It is to her credit that, as will be seen, she tried to make the best of it.

Mary has often been blamed for a fatal lack of judgement in placing such reliance upon Bothwell, a man who was hated by Catholics and Protestants alike, and feared by the English, but bitter experience and his own record of loyalty to the Crown had convinced her that he was more worthy of her trust than her own husband and most of her Lords. He had saved her from Rizzio's murderers, and she was full of gratitude towards him. It has been noted that allegations that Mary was having an affair with Bothwell at this time belong to a later period, when her enemies had good political reasons for maligning her character. There is no evidence for such an affair in contemporary sources; sixteenth-century monarchs lived their lives in the public gaze and were surrounded by attendants, some of whom could be bribed for inside information. Foreign ambassadors were avid for the slightest morsel of gossip or scandal, and often made extensive and secret inquiries about the intimate lives of princes: the English in particular would have been grateful for the chance to defame Mary. There had been scurrilous gossip about Mary and Rizzio, pounced on by Randolph, but no one, in the summer and autumn of 1566, claimed that she was on intimate terms with Bothwell.

In his letter of 3 August, Bedford had mentioned that Mary was now reconciled with Maitland. Maitland had not yet been received back at court but was privately assisting Moray and Argyll in their efforts to bring about the restoration of Morton and the other exiles. Castelnau and du Croc were also working "very earnestly and effectually" towards the same end.[52]

·　·　·

Mary paid another visit to Alloa on 3 August, returning to Edinburgh five days later. On 10 August, the Papal Nuncio, the Bishop of Mondovi, arrived in Paris on his way to Scotland, only to find letters from Mary awaiting him, in which she begged him to defer his departure for her kingdom, as seditious people would prevent her from receiving him with the honour he deserved. Her messenger, John Beaton, "a man of high character in every respect,"[53] arrived soon afterwards to offer her apologies. The truth was that Mary had so far failed to "induce the nobles to give free entrance into the kingdom to the Papal Legate; no argument could move [them], especially Moray, to assent."[54] Mary also knew that, if Mondovi came secretly, "great tumults" would result, which would inevitably upset the status quo she was working so hard to maintain. Mondovi sent Beaton back with a portion of the promised subsidy[55] and a stern letter exhorting the Queen to do everything in her power to bring about the restoration of the faith in her realm.[56]

Meanwhile, Bedford had received intelligence of a plot, or "device," against Bothwell, who "hath grown of late so hated that he cannot long continue." Bedford claimed he "might have heard" the "particularities" of the plot, "but, because such dealings like me not, I desire to hear no further thereof."[57] It would have suited the English very well for someone to assassinate Bothwell, therefore Bedford did not intend to intervene. It has been suggested that Moray was behind this plot, which is possible, given his other activities at this time, but if he was, he took care—as he may have done on other occasions—to cover his traces. Rumour also credited Maitland with an attempt to poison Bothwell: Maitland had regained possession of Haddington Abbey, which had been granted to Bothwell after Maitland's disgrace, and the two men were now locked in a bitter dispute about ownership. Some believed that murder was Maitland's way of resolving it, but there is no proof of this.

Mary was making the best of the situation with Darnley. There was no acceptable way out of her marriage, so the sensible course was to re-establish a good rapport with her husband. This meant resuming sexual relations. On 13 August, Darnley received a large payment of money from her treasury,[58] as well as cloth of gold for caparisons for his horse, and a magnificent bed that had belonged to Marie de Guise. This was upholstered in "violet-brown velvet, enriched with cloth of gold and silver, with ciphers and flowers sewn with cloth of gold and silk, furnished with roof and headpiece"; its curtains were of purple damask, its pillows of violet velvet, and its quilt of blue taffeta. The sheets were of the finest Holland linen.[59] The gift of the bed probably marked what was intended to be, on the Queen's part at any rate, a reconciliation. Randolph, in England, heard that "the King and Queen are bedded together, whereby 'tis thought some better agreement may ensue."

On the day after the bed was delivered, Mary and Darnley went on a stag-hunting expedition to the wild moors of Meggetland, which lay south of Peebles, and the nearby Ettrick Forest. They were accompanied by Bothwell, Moray, Huntly, Atholl and Mar:[60] given the ill feeling between some of these nobles, the atmosphere must have been tense.

In Meggetland, Mary and Darnley stayed at Cramalt, in a tower house whose remains now lie beneath a reservoir. Their sport was disappointing, and they were obliged to issue a proclamation prohibiting anyone from shooting the royal deer, which were proving elusive. Nor was the reconciliation working. Buchanan claims that Mary behaved "capriciously, arrogantly and disdainfully" towards Darnley, "openly, in the face of all"; if this is true, his insulting behaviour certainly gave her sufficient provocation. On 19 August, the party stayed at Traquair House, near Innerleithen, as the guests of the Laird, Sir John Stewart, Captain of the Queen's Guard, who had helped the royal couple escape from Holyrood after Rizzio's murder. Traquair was a fortified three-storey tower house that had been a hunting lodge of the Kings of Scots since c.1100 before passing to a junior branch of the Stewart line. Mary and Darnley occupied chambers on the first floor, now the King's Room and a dressing room.[61]

At supper, Darnley asked Mary to accompany him on another stag hunt on the morrow. "Knowing that, if she did so, she would be required to gallop her horse at a great pace, she whispered in his ear that she suspected she was pregnant."[62] This is confirmation in itself that she had resumed sexual relations with Darnley. However, it was far too soon to tell if she had conceived: it was exactly two months since the birth of James, and she had been unwell and estranged from Darnley for much of that time. It may be that, in the interests of happy marital relations, she wished people to think that she and the King had been reconciled for longer than they had. Darnley's reaction shows that she had every cause to think she might be pregnant, but it was unpardonably brutal.

"Never mind," he told her, "if we lose this one, we will make another." It was the same thing he had said to her on that terrible night ride to Dunbar in March, and, seeing the Queen's distress, the Laird rounded on his King and "rebuked him sharply," telling him "he did not speak like a Christian." But Darnley was unrepentant.

"What? Ought we not to work a mare when she is in foal?" he retorted.[63] After this, all hopes of reconciliation faded, and on the way back to Edinburgh, which they reached on 20 August, Mary decided that it might be wiser to place her son in the stronghold of Stirling, in the care of a governor. There was every chance that Darnley might try to force the issue of the Crown Matrimonial, and if he succeeded, James's security, even his life, would be under threat.

From Paris, on 21 August, having no doubt conferred with statesmen and foreign ambassadors, including Francisco de Alava, Mondovi expressed, in a confidential letter to the Cardinal of Alessandria in Rome, his opinion that Mary's difficulties "might be obviated if the King of Spain should come, as it is hoped, with a strong force to Flanders, or, as certain persons of weight believe, if justice were executed against six rebels, who were leaders and originators of the late treason against the Queen, and whose deaths would effectually restore peace and obedience in that kingdom." He then listed their names: Moray, Argyll, Morton, Maitland, Justice Clerk Bellenden and former Clerk Register MacGill, "a man of no family and contriver of all evil." They comprised effectively the core of the Protestant establishment in Scotland. Moray's inclusion on the list shows how widespread was the belief that he was behind the Rizzio plot, and Mondovi's willingness to have him executed for it suggests that he had access to diplomatic intelligence confirming Moray's role in the affair.

With regard to Darnley, Mondovi had learned that he was "an ambitious and inconstant youth, [who] would like to rule the realm, which was the subject of the plot he hatched a few months back, with the purpose of getting himself crowned King. He continues to go to Mass, but maintains strict friendship and intercourse with the heretical rebels, in order to preserve and increase his credit and authority." By all reports, and possibly on the recommendation of de Alava, Darnley was the man to engineer the arrests of the Lords concerned "without any disturbance arising, and with the assured hope that afterwards the holy Catholic religion would soon be restored with ease throughout that kingdom, as no leader of faction would remain. The danger is that the Cardinal of Lorraine and the Queen, in their excessive clemency, would not consent to such an act." The implication was clear: it was Darnley, not Mary, who would act as the champion of Catholicism. The Pope was said to be "delighted" with Mondovi's suggestions.[64]

That August, the French ambassador to Spain reported that Philip's visit to the Netherlands was certain. Men and ships were being assembled for the invasion. On 23 August, de Silva warned that some disturbance or rising was expected before the English Parliament met in the autumn.[65] A week earlier, Darnley's man, Anthony Standen the Elder, had left Scotland;[66] he remained abroad, plotting on behalf of the Catholic cause, until 1605, and may well have initially acted in secret as Darnley's agent. At the end of August, Darnley received another sum of money from the treasury.[67] There has been speculation that he used this and the earlier payment to fund his treasonable schemes, but there is no evidence of this, and Mary herself must have authorised the grants, which were probably made to finance Darnley's household and pleasures and keep him sweet.

On 31 August, Mary and Darnley, attended by an escort of 500 arquebusiers, took Prince James to Stirling Castle, where Mary entrusted him to the keeping of her good friend, the Earl of Mar, who was to be the Prince's Governor. By tradition, the Erskines were guardians of royal heirs—Mar's father had been given charge of Mary as a child—and Stirling was by custom the nursery palace of future kings. James was now assigned his own household, with a luxuriously furnished nursery; for the next four years, he would be "nursed and upbrought" by the Countess of Mar, the Catholic Annabella Murray. Lady Reres now replaced Helena Little as his wet-nurse,[68] and Bothwell was made one of two Captains of his Bodyguard.

Soon afterwards, thanks to the efforts of his friend Atholl and Moray, Maitland arrived at Stirling and was formally welcomed back to court by the

Queen. Mary had agreed to his return "as there was no proof of the charge against [him], trusting more than he deserved to his good qualities and his loyalty to herself."[69] On 4 September, Maitland dined with Mary, who behaved as if she "liked him very well."[70] She knew that Maitland would be far more effective than the Anglophobic Bothwell when it came to negotiating with Elizabeth for recognition of James's rights to the English succession. Naturally, Bothwell was not pleased by this turn of events.

By 6 September, Mary was back in Edinburgh, where she stayed at the Exchequer House in the Cowgate, below St. Giles's Kirk. Here, she attended an audit of the royal finances, "to understand her revenues and arrange for the maintenance of the Prince."[71] She also wished to ascertain her financial position with a view to paying for a lavish christening for her son. Darnley remained at Stirling, having refused to accompany her. The rift between them now seemed irreparable.

11

"No Outgait"

~

ACCORDING TO BUCHANAN, IN SEPTEMBER 1566, Mary began an adulterous affair with Bothwell. He alleges that the chief attraction of the Exchequer House for her was that its "pleasant, almost solitary" gardens gave access to the back door of the residence of David Chalmers, Bothwell's man, who was shortly to be appointed, through Bothwell's good offices, Common Clerk of Edinburgh. "By this door, Bothwell could come and go as he liked." According to Buchanan's scarcely believable and farcical tale, at Bothwell's request, an accommodating Lady Reres, "a most dissolute woman who had been one of Bothwell's whores," smuggled him through the Exchequer House garden and up to the Queen's room, where he "forced her against her will" to have sexual intercourse with him.

On reflection, Mary decided she had, after all, enjoyed the experience, and, "not many days after, desiring [Buchanan supposed] to repay force with force, sent Lady Reres to bring [Bothwell] captive unto her." We are to believe that Mary and Margaret Carwood let the stout Lady Reres "down by a sash over the wall into the next garden. But behold! The sash suddenly broke! Down with a great noise tumbled Lady Reres. But the old warrior, nothing dismayed by the darkness, the height of the wall or her unexpected flight to earth, reached Bothwell's chamber, opened the door, plucked him out of bed—out of his wife's embrace—and led him, half-asleep, half-naked, to the arms of the Queen."

Bothwell's tailor, George Dalgleish, is said by Buchanan to have been a witness and to have given details of the episode in his confession of 1567, but the extant version of this document does not refer to it. Buchanan also claims that Mary "confessed the whole thing" to Moray and his mother at Lochleven in 1567, "as well as to many others," but there is no proof of this. It is hardly likely that Lady Reres would have connived at the rape of her mistress, whose escape she had risked her life to facilitate after Rizzio's murder, and she could not have done so anyway, for she was now lodging in the Prince's household at Stirling as his wet-nurse. Moreover, it was her sister Janet, the Lady of Buccleuch, who had been Bothwell's mistress. It will also be remembered that Lennox had dated the commencement of Mary's alleged affair with Bothwell to before the birth of the Prince.

Some "Notes on David Chambers [sic]," which were later sent to Cecil alleged that Bothwell and his wife were indeed staying in David Chalmers's house at that time, and that Chalmers got his preferments "because he had served Bothwell as a bawd. He was a great dealer betwixt the Queen and Bothwell, so Mr. David's lodging was chosen as a place meet to exercise their filthiness, when the Queen lay in the Exchequer House in the Cowgate."[1] This would appear to corroborate Buchanan, but it was written after 1568, at a time when it was vitally expedient to destroy Mary's reputation and when Buchanan's libel had been circulated in political circles, so it cannot be relied upon as independent evidence.

According to The Book of Articles, which Buchanan drew up against Mary in 1568, "from September 1566, [Bothwell] became so familiar with her, night and day, that at his pleasure he abused her body," while Darnley "was never permitted to remain patiently the space of 48 hours together in her company." If Mary and Bothwell were lovers at this time, then they must have been exceptionally discreet, because no contemporary source mentions such an affair.

Mary was back at Holyrood by 12 September. A week later, Sir John Forster reported that the Privy Council had voted the Queen £12,000 (now equivalent to at least £3.5 million) to cover the expenses of the Prince's christening; this was to be raised by loans from wealthy Edinburgh merchants. Everyone recognised the necessity for putting on a lavish show of splendour and pageantry in order to impress foreign ambassadors who were used to the magnificent courts of Renaissance Europe.

With Scotland's international reputation at stake, the Queen naturally desired a degree of unity amongst her nobles, and around this time she persuaded Maitland and Bothwell to make a public display of reconciliation and friendship in the presence of Moray and Argyll, after which, Maitland resumed his duties as Secretary of State.[2] Mary's willingness to show favour to these leading Protestants may well have made Darnley all the more determined to expose her as a lukewarm supporter of Catholicism.

On 21 September, Mary, restored to good health and in better spirits,[3] left Edinburgh to visit her son at Stirling. The next day, John Beaton arrived from Paris with the subsidy payment and the Nuncio's letter,[4] and the day after, Mary returned to Edinburgh to attend to affairs of state. She had been "desirous that the King should have come along with her,"[5] but Darnley still insisted upon remaining at Stirling. He was in a foul, dejected mood, and revealed to du Croc that he was in such desperation that he was minded to go overseas. Du Croc "could not believe that he was in earnest."[6] It has been conjectured that the discovery that Mary was Bothwell's mistress was enough to make Darnley want to leave Scotland, but, if so, it is surprising that neither he nor Lennox ever referred to it during the days that followed, when they had ample opportunity to do so. It will be remembered that Darnley had not been reticent in his suspicions of Rizzio.

Around 24/26 September, Lennox briefly visited Darnley at Stirling before returning to his estates in Glasgow.[7] The outcome of their meeting was a letter written by Lennox to Mary, informing her that Darnley was so humiliated by the loss of status consequent upon her denying him the Crown Matrimonial that he intended to go abroad, and had a ship lying ready. According to Buchanan, it was anchored in the Firth of Clyde. Buchanan claims that Darnley meant to go to France or Spain, but Nau says that, "by the persuasion of some dissipated youths, who were his chief companions, he had resolved to go secretly to France, and there to support himself upon the Queen's dowry." Lennox told Mary he had tried to dissuade Darnley from going, but had been unable to "make him alter his mind."[8]

When Mary read this letter on 29 September, she resolved to have the matter out immediately with Darnley. His threat to go abroad was not only a public affront to her but also a threat to her security and that of her realm and her heir, and may have been a form of blackmail; in any case, it had to be dealt with. Some writers have speculated that Mary's alarm arose chiefly from fear of the scandal that would ensue if her husband went abroad and she then became pregnant by Bothwell, but of course there is little reliable evidence that she and Bothwell were lovers at this time.

Mary showed Lennox's letter to the Council, who expressed astonishment that the King should "entertain any thought of departing after so strange a manner" from Scotland and his wife, but they had probably not taken into account the humiliation he felt and his mortal fear that Morton and his other deadly enemies would be repatriated. Nor did they know of his dealings with influential Catholics abroad. "Their Lordships therefore took a resolution to talk with the King, that they might learn from himself the occasion of this hasty deliberation of his, that they might thereby be enabled to advise Her Majesty after what manner she should comfort herself in this conjecture."[9]

That evening, to everyone's "amazement," Darnley turned up at the gates of Holyrood, but refused to enter the palace until the Privy Councillors had been dismissed, a stipulation that greatly offended those Lords. At 10 p.m., the Queen had to go out and persuade him that he was insulting her by his behaviour and should come inside. Because of the state he was in, she "conducted him to her own apartment, where he remained all night, abed together," but he resisted her attempts to make him state his grievances. However, he did agree to attend a meeting of the Privy Council in the morning.[10]

Yet they fared little better. Having told the King that he should thank God for such a wise and virtuous wife, the Councillors asked him to account for his behaviour, and inform them how they had offended him. Mary herself took him by the hand and made him "a pretty strong harangue," begging him to tell her if she had given him any cause to leave the kingdom, and declaring that she had "a clear conscience, [and] that all her life she had done no action which could anywise prejudice either his or her honour." But Darnley refused to admit either that he intended to go abroad or that he had any cause for complaint. Du Croc, who was present, bluntly told him that his leaving the country "must affect either his own or the Queen's honour." At this, Darnley "at last declared that he had no ground at all for leaving the country" and that Mary had given him no occasion for discontent. "Thereupon he went out of the chamber of presence, saying to the Queen, 'Adieu, Madame. You shall not see my face for a long space.' After which, he likewise bade [du Croc] farewell, and, turning to the Lords, said, 'Gentlemen, adieu.'"

After his departure, Mary was visibly distressed, but du Croc and the Lords comforted her, saying they were "all of opinion that this was but a false alarm the Earl of Lennox was willing to give Her Majesty." The best advice they could give her was to continue on her present course of wise and virtuous behaviour, for the truth about her marriage would soon be public knowledge.[11] The Lords would hardly have said this to her had she been carrying on with Bothwell, whom they hated.

Against Mary's wishes,[12] Darnley immediately left Holyrood for Glasgow, accompanied by Lennox. From Corstorphine, he wrote to her revealing that he was still in a mind to leave the country since she did not trust him with any regal authority, "nor is at such pains to advance him and make him to be honoured in the nation as she at first did"; furthermore, he complained, the nobility shunned him. On hearing this, the Council declared that they would never consent to his having the disposal of public affairs. Mary herself sent Darnley a letter in which she pointed out that, if his status was diminished,

he ought to blame himself, not her, for that, in the beginning, she had conferred so much honour upon him as came afterwards to render herself very uneasy, the credit and reputation wherein she had placed him having served as a shadow to those who have most heinously offended Her Majesty; but she has, notwithstanding this, continued to show him such respect that, although they who did perpetrate the murder of her faithful servant had entered her chamber with his knowledge, and had named him the chief of their enterprise, yet would she never accuse him thereof.

Furthermore, "if the nobility abandon him, his own deportment towards them is the cause thereof; for if he desire to be followed and attended by them, he must first make them love him."[13] Mary also wrote to Lennox, assuring him that Darnley had no cause for complaint.

The King's behaviour carried serious implications. On 8 October, on

Mary's instructions, the Council sent a full account of her confrontation with him and the correspondence that followed to Catherine de' Medici, just in case Darnley should appeal to the French for support. It was stressed that the Lords would have been joyfully disposed "to pass over in silence the huge injury he does to himself and the Queen's Majesty but, seeing that he himself is the very first person who, by his deportment, will lead discovery to the world, we can do no less than to testify the things that we have both seen and heard [to] all those who are allied to Her Majesty, that by these you may have opportunity to perceive the great trouble and vexation the Queen labours under at present, and the occasion of it."[14]

Soon after his departure, Darnley had sent a message to du Croc, summoning him to meet him halfway between Edinburgh and Glasgow. He had decided to make public his grievances in the hope that the ambassador would use his influence to put matters right. But du Croc "remonstrated to him every thing that I could think of" to dissuade him from leaving Scotland, and came away with the impression that he had succeeded. Darnley, however, arrived in Glasgow more resentful than ever. Nor did he stay there long, for in October he was in Fife, hunting at Burleigh Castle and Kinross, and fishing at Loch Leven.

Late in September, as Mary had anticipated, the Council, with Moray at his most vociferous, refused permission for the Papal Nuncio to come to Scotland.[15] Even the militant Pius V was having doubts as to the wisdom of Mondovi's mission, for he felt that its success was largely dependent upon Philip II being in Flanders, and on 30 September he wrote to the Nuncio to say that, if Philip's arrival was further delayed, he should return to his See.[16] Unknown to him as yet, Mary was still making concessions to the reformed Church: in Council, on 3 October, she agreed that all benefices under 300 marks should go to ministers of the Kirk.[17]

Mary was more preoccupied with the need to establish good order in the Borders[18], and decided to go ahead with the assizes that had been postponed, initially because of her pregnancy and then because of the harvest. On 1 October, she summoned all her Border Lords and freeholders to meet her at Melrose on 8 October, prior to travelling to Jedburgh for a justice eyre, or circuit court, over which she intended to preside on the 9th.[19] Darnley, invited to accompany her, had refused; Lennox claims that Mary's progress to the Borders was a ploy to get away from her husband,[20] but of course he had absented himself from her.

It was essential, in the circumstances, that there was at least a show of unity between the leading nobles and, early in October, according to Moray,[21] the Queen forced him, Argyll, Bothwell and Huntly to "subscribe a bond, which was devised in sign of our reconciliation in respect of the former grudges and displeasures that had been amongst us." Moray claims he "was constrained to make promise before I could be admitted to the Queen's presence or have any show of her favour": evidently Mary had been obliged to use her royal prerogative to bend him to her will. The Bond bound these Lords to fortify and support each other in all their undertakings against their enemies and in refusing to obey the King "when his orders conflicted with the Queen's wishes."[22] This put an end to Bothwell's support of Darnley, and left the latter politically isolated, which is probably what Mary intended.

On 6 October, Bothwell, as Lieutenant of the Borders, left Edinburgh with 300 horse for Liddesdale, one of the most lawless regions in the Borders, to begin rounding up the worst troublemakers, who were to receive judgement at the Queen's justice eyre. Buchanan alleges that the Earl "conducted himself neither according to the place which he held, nor the dignity of his family," yet, as a result of his efforts, members of the violent Armstrong and Johnstone clans were imprisoned in Hermitage Castle. However, the notorious Elliotts, a family of Border reivers, remained at large, so Bothwell now turned his attention to tracking them down.

On 7 October,[23] Mary, accompanied by Moray, Huntly, Atholl, Livingston, Seton, Caithness, Rothes, Maitland, Bishop Leslie and other Lords, as well as a host of household officers, judges, lawyers, clerks, waiting women, servants and men-at-arms, left Edinburgh for Borthwick Castle, the first stop on her progress. As the cavalcade wended its slow way south, Bothwell was engaging in an affray with the Elliotts, in the course of which he was severely wounded by one of them, the vicious outlaw, Jock Elliott of the Park.[24] Having received stab wounds to the forehead, thigh and left hand, "Bothwell was carried to his castle of Hermitage in a condition such as to make his recovery uncertain."[25] But, in his absence, the fortress had been taken over by the thieves and malefactors whom he had imprisoned there, and they would not surrender it until they had been granted their freedom. Bothwell's officers had no choice: "if he had not gotten in at that time, all his company had been slain."[26] So the Earl was carried in, unconscious and bleeding, and "everyone thought he would die." When he regained consciousness, "he thought so himself."[27]

The news spread fast, but became garbled in the telling. On the following day, Henry, Lord Scrope, informed Cecil, from Carlisle, that Bothwell had been slain in the attack.[28] Soon afterwards, it was being reported in Europe that the Queen of Scots had "lost a man she could trust, of whom she had but few."[29]

Surprisingly, Mary had not yet heard of the attack on Bothwell. She left Borthwick on 8 April and travelled via Peebles and Selkirk to Melrose, where she was met by her assembled lieges. On the following day, she arrived in Jedburgh and took up residence in what is now the Spread Eagle Hotel, and it was here that she learned that Bothwell was lying seriously wounded at Hermitage.[30] She did not "fly like a madwoman" immediately to visit him, being unable to restrain her "inordinate affection" and "shameless lust," as Buchanan later alleged, but set up her court in the Tolbooth and, for the next six days, dispensed justice. However, thanks to the escape of the Armstrongs and Johnstones from Hermitage, there were very few cases to be heard, and Moray complained that Mary was far too merciful to those who did come before her, none of whom was sentenced to death as he felt they deserved, but merely fined.[31]

Melville claims that Bothwell and Huntly had planned to murder Moray at Jedburgh, but that Lord Home arrived there with a force of men "and prevented that enterprise." It is more likely, however, that this plot was foiled by Bothwell's incapacity.

On 9 October, Mary summoned one Stephen Wilson, whom she had chosen to act as her messenger to the Papal Nuncio, and instructed him to tell Mondovi that the nobility had agreed to his coming. It is less likely that they had changed their minds than that Mary was playing for time, which was to be granted her, for Wilson, due to unforeseen and near-tragic circumstances, was not to depart for a month.

Du Croc had formed the opinion that Darnley wanted to be and command all, and suffered mainly from wounded pride. Wishing to inform Mary's friends abroad of the truth, the ambassador wrote letters to Archbishop Beaton on 13 October,[32] and to Catherine de' Medici on 16/17 October,[33] recounting the events of late September. Referring to Darnley's threats to go abroad, he wrote, "He has not embarked, but we receive advertisements from day to day that he still holds on to his resolution and keeps a ship in readiness. It is in vain to imagine that he should be able to raise any disturbance, for there is not one person in all the kingdom, from the highest to the lowest, that regards him any further than is agreeable to the Queen. And I never saw Her Majesty so much beloved, esteemed and honoured."

Du Croc also described preparations for the coming baptism, saying that both Protestants and Catholics were enthusiastic about it, but that the fuss being made probably accounted for Darnley's bad behaviour; apparently, he was bitterly jealous of Mary's good relations with the Protestant Lords, and fearful that his reduced status would be apparent to all the foreign dignitaries who attended the christening, which would be intolerable for one of his "lofty and vainglorious" temperament.[34]

In Paris, on 15 October, Mondovi, concerned that Mary had not responded to his letter, sent by John Beaton over a month before, and correctly concluding that she was stalling, met with the Cardinal of Lorraine, but had "great difficulty in persuading him that there ought not to be further delay in doing something signal for the service of God in Scotland." At length, the Cardinal reluctantly agreed to send a gentleman to persuade Mary to admit the Nuncio and "decide on restoring Holy Religion in her kingdom." A week later, Mondovi had a second meeting with the Cardinal, to tell him that the Pope had recalled him to his See; the Cardinal begged him to await the return of his gentleman from Mary's court.[35] There is, however, no trace of any such gentleman being sent to Scotland at this time; circumstances will reveal, however, that the Cardinal probably dispatched someone in late October.[36]

The assizes were completed by 15 October. According to Nau, because it was thought that Bothwell was dying, Mary "was both solicited and advised to pay him a visit at his house, in order that she might learn from him the state of affairs in these districts of which the said Lord was hereditary governor." This is corroborated by a contemporary French narrative,[37] which states that Mary was advised to consult with Bothwell on the state of the Borders.

This made good political sense, because Bothwell bore heavy responsibilities in the Borders and had a unique knowledge of the region, and while he was out of action, others might have to deputise for him. Of course, the Queen could have sent someone else to liaise with Bothwell, but she clearly felt that the unrest in the Borders needed to be quelled urgently, and must have been very concerned that so few had been brought to justice. Furthermore, Bothwell had been dangerously wounded in her service, and she doubtless wished to express personally to him her debt of gratitude. No one at the time suggested that her visit was made for amorous reasons.

Early in the morning of 15 October,[38] the Queen left Jedburgh for Hermitage Castle. There was no suitable accommodation for her and her entourage at this massive, spartan fortress, and in any case her host was very ill, so she made the sixty-mile round trip in a day, despite wet weather, rough roads and reports of robbers in the region. Buchanan, who was eager to prove that Mary's visit was made only in consequence of her lust for Bothwell, and who falsely claims that she flew off to Hermitage as soon as she heard he was wounded, alleges that she took with her "such an escort as no one slightly more honourable would have dared to trust with life and fortune." In fact, it included Moray, Buchanan's patron, Huntly, Maitland and a strong force of soldiers. Moreover, Lennox, who also accused Mary of impropriety with Bothwell, does not refer to any scandal attaching to her trip to Hermitage; had there been, he would certainly have done so.

Hermitage Castle, which lies on remote moorland five miles north of Newcastleton, had been built in 1242; its stout keep dated from the fourteenth century. The castle took its name from a nearby hermit's dwelling on Hermitage Water in Nithsdale, but had a grim history of violence and feuds. The Hepburns had bought this forbidding edifice in 1492, essentially as a military base for controlling the Borders.[39]

According to Lord Scrope, Mary sat by Bothwell's bed for about two hours, with Moray and the others in attendance;[40] Scrope told Cecil that they discussed Border affairs and the justice eyre, and that it was decided that Bothwell would bring other offenders to justice when he had recovered. Mary also conferred an official post on Bothwell's kinsman, George Sinclair. Then the royal party returned to Jedburgh through Liddesdale. Between Hermitage and Priesthaugh, according to tradition, Mary's horse slipped in a bog that is today known as the Queen's Mire, and she was thrown to the muddy ground. She also lost her watch. The party were forced to stop at a farmhouse near Hawick so that her clothes could be repaired and dried.[41] Mary's servants marvelled at her stamina on the long ride, but she told them she "could find it in her heart to do anything that a man dare do, if her strength would serve her."[42]

Scrope informed Cecil that, on the day after her return, Mary sent "a mass of writing" to Bothwell from Jedburgh.[43] This would appear to confirm that the object of their meeting had been to discuss business. But the arduous journey took its toll on Mary and, on 17 October,[44] she fell seriously ill, suffering initially from the old pain in her side, "which confined her to bed";[45] she then developed a transient fever, which was rapidly followed, on the first day alone, by more than sixty episodes of violent, prolonged vomiting of blood,[46] which intermittently reduced her to unconsciousness.

It is difficult now to determine the nature of Mary's illness, which has been diagnosed by some as a nervous or psychosomatic collapse as a reaction to the stress of the past months. The Venetian ambassador in Paris reported that "the illness was caused by her dissatisfaction at a decision made by the King to go to a place 25 or 30 miles distant without assigning any cause for it; which departure so afflicted this unfortunate Princess, not so much for the love she bears him, as from the consequences of his absence, reducing her to this extremity."[47] Other possible diagnoses are a haemorrhage from a stomach ulcer, haematemesis (i.e., the vomiting of blood as a result of changes in the stomach wall due to an ulcer or acute dyspepsia), or to porphyria, which can give rise to such symptoms. Buchanan maliciously and ludicrously attributes Mary's illness to her "having gratified her unlawful passions" with Bothwell. Whatever it was, its effects were so alarming that Maitland and many others believed the Queen's life to be in danger.

Inevitably, there was talk of poison. A Venetian envoy voiced this suspicion to the Doge in November, adding, "By whom, and with what design this great wickedness has been perpetrated, Your Serenity, who remembers past affairs, may form your own judgement."[48] Nau, perhaps reiterating Mary's own suspicions, states that, "from the frequency and the violence of the vomiting within the period of a single day, it was suspected that she had been poisoned, particularly as among the matter ejected from the stomach was found a lump of green substance, very thick and hard."

As Mary lay sick, "news came that the Prince was so ill that his life was despaired of, but, after having been made to vomit, he recovered."[49] Not so his mother, for on the third day she lost both her sight and her power of speech "and had a very severe fit of convulsions."[50]

Around 21 October, four days after Mary had fallen ill, Bothwell had himself carried to Jedburgh on a horse litter.[51] On the 26th, de Silva reported from London that the Earl was "still in danger from his wounds,"[52] but however ill Bothwell felt, every day that he was absent gave Moray a chance to usurp his influence; moreover, should the Queen die, Bothwell meant to ensure that he was there to hear her final wishes. Buchanan states that Mary had Bothwell brought to Jedburgh and lodged in a chamber below hers. "When he arrived, their meetings and behaviour were beyond all propriety." But Buchanan incorrectly places Bothwell's arrival before Mary's illness, which he attributes to "her exertions by day and night."[53]

At Jedburgh, Bothwell improved steadily, and on 25 October Leslie was able to write that he "convalesces well of his wounds"; by that date, he was able to attend a meeting of the Privy Council.[54] However, he would be scarred on the forehead for life, and his wounds would continue to trouble him for some time.

Du Croc was with the court at Jedburgh, and on 23 October he sent a messenger, Alexander Bog, to inform Catherine de' Medici that Mary's life was in danger. Bog also carried a letter for Archbishop Beaton from the Council, instructing him to tell the King and Queen Mother of France that, the previous night, Mary had had "some fits of swooning, which put men in some fear; nevertheless, we see no tokens of death." On 24 October, Mary "got some relief,"[55] and du Croc wrote to Beaton: "We begin to have more hope of the Queen, and for the present the doctors have no fears. I assure you Her Majesty is well looked after. God knows how all the Lords who are here occupy themselves. You may imagine the trouble they are in and the distress of this poor kingdom. The King is at Glasgow, and has never come here. If he has been informed by someone and has had time enough to come if he wished, it is a fault which I cannot excuse."[56]

Maitland informed Beaton that Bog's message was more desperate than it should have been, as, although she had been "sorely handled, and looked herself for nothing but death," Mary was "well relieved of the extremity of her sickness" and now, "praised be God, we think her out of all danger." He added that

> the occasion of the Queen's sickness, so far as I understand, is thought and displeasure, and I trow, by what I could wring further of her own declaration to me, the root of it is the King. For she has done him so great honour, contrary to the advice of her subjects, and he, on the other part, has recompensed her with such ingratitude and misuses himself so far towards her that it is a heartbreak for her to think he should be her husband, and how to be free of him she sees no outgait. I see betwixt them no agreement, nor no appearance that they shall well agree thereafter. I am assured that it has been her mind this good while.[57]

In her extremity, Mary had lowered her guard and revealed her desperation at the prospect of being tied to Darnley for life. There had been unsubstantiated rumours that she had sent to Rome for an annulment after Rizzio's death, but this is the first evidence that she had seriously considered ways of freeing herself from her husband.

The optimism expressed by Beaton and Maitland about Mary's health was premature. At 10 p.m. that evening, "Her Majesty swooned again and failed in her sight; her feet and knees were cold, which were handled by extreme rubbing, drawing and other cures, by the space of four hours, that no creature could endure greater pain, and through the vehemence of this cure, Her Majesty got some relief."[58]

Believing she was dying, Mary summoned the Lords and du Croc, and made her final dispositions, declaring that the crown must pass to her son, not to Darnley, "not doubting that the King his father would wrong him as to the succession of the crown," and entrusting Moray with charge of the Prince and "the principal part of the government." Moray was also to ensure that James was "nourished in the fear of God and all virtues" and that "no evil company be near him during his youth." In an obvious reference to Darnley, she beseeched God to mend one "whom I have advanced to a great degree of honour and pre-eminence among others; who, notwithstanding, has used ingratitude towards me, which has engendered the displeasure that presently most grieves me, and is also the cause of my sickness." She remitted to God the exiled traitors, but urged that, if they returned to Scotland, the Lords would not suffer them to come near her son. She asked Moray to be as tolerant of Catholics as she had been of Protestants, then asked pardon for sins that had arisen from "the fragility of my nature" and, finally, protested that she died in the Catholic religion. As she "disposed herself as one at the point of death," Bishop Leslie offered up prayers for her.[59]

That night, Mary slipped into a coma and became so stiff and cold that everyone thought she had died. Her servants threw open the windows "to let her spirit go free," her ladies ordered mourning clothes, her Privy Councillors, including Bothwell,[60] prepared for her funeral and issued an edict to safeguard public order, while Moray, with unseemly haste, "started to lay hands on her silver plate and jewels."[61] But Arnault, the Queen's French surgeon and "a perfect man of his craft," noticed that one of Mary's arms had not completely stiffened, and worked frantically to revive her. He tightly bandaged her limbs and extremities, massaged her body vigorously for three hours, forced wine down her throat, and gave her some medicine and an enema of wine and herbs, "the evacuations produced by which were considered by the physicians to be very suspicious."[62] Gradually, Mary's sight and speech were restored, then she began to sweat, and "from that time, she gradually recovered."[63]

Up to 27 October, Darnley was "hawking and hunting" in Glasgow and the west of Scotland,[64] perhaps unaware of Mary's illness; there is no record of any messenger being sent to inform him. On the 22nd, Robert Melville had reported that the King was still threatening to leave the country because the Queen had not agreed to his demand that she dismiss Maitland, Bellenden and MacGill.[65]

It appears that Darnley finally learned that Mary was sick on 27 October because, on that day, he suddenly set off for Edinburgh and the Borders; both Knox and Buchanan claim he travelled with the utmost haste to his wife's bedside.

He arrived at Jedburgh on the 28th, but did not stay long. In the *Diurnal of Occurrents*, Buchanan and Lennox all state that he was offended by a hostile reception from Mary and her nobles, which is hardly surprising, given that most of them, including Mary herself, believed him to have been the cause of her illness. Certainly, his visit did nothing to improve relations between him, Mary and the Lords. After spending only one night in Jedburgh—in one account, Buchanan claims he stayed in the lodgings of Lord Home, in another he states he slept in the bed of the Bishop of Orkney—Darnley rode north to Edinburgh, and thence to Stirling.[66] Buchanan says "his departure seemed the more shameful because, at the same time, Bothwell was openly transferred from the house where he had been lodging to the Queen's apartments"—which contradicts his earlier account.

By 30 October, Mary was well enough to order material for a new dress. Buchanan alleges that, around this time, she and Bothwell, "though not yet fully recovered, returned to their former pastime, and that blatantly"—so blatantly, in fact, that no one else noticed it. Buchanan also states that "the world in the same days began to speak of it," but there were many people present at Jedburgh, and no other contemporary source, not even Lennox, mentions such flagrant behaviour.

On 30 October, Mary's convalescence was disrupted by a fire that destroyed part of her lodgings, and she and her entourage were obliged to move to a "bastel" (fortified) tower owned by the Kers of Ferniehurst, which was perhaps that which survives today and is known as Mary, Queen of Scots' House. This was one of six fortified houses built in the fifteenth century after Jedburgh Castle was demolished. In Mary's day, it had four storeys, a thatched roof, gables, turrets, tiny windows and a garden.[67] The service quarters were on the ground floor, but the upper floors could be accessed only by an outside stair. There was a banqueting room, forechamber and garderobe on the first floor, and bedchambers and a guard room above. The Queen paid Lady Ferniehurst £40 for the use of the house.

Queen Elizabeth, fearing the intervention of Philip II in Flanders, was now finding the prospect of an alliance with Scotland attractive, and had instructed Cecil to draw up instructions for an embassy in which it was to be intimated that Elizabeth was prepared to acknowledge Mary as her heir. On 31 October, Elizabeth asked the Countess of Argyll, a Protestant, to stand proxy for her at James's christening.[68] At the beginning of November, the Comte de Brienne arrived in Scotland to represent Charles IX at the ceremony.[69] In his train was the son of du Croc, who may have acted as the Cardinal of Lorraine's messenger to Mary,[70] for he already held a post in her household and could therefore easily gain access to her. It was probably one of these men who informed Mary that Papal support would be dependent upon her agreeing to execute Moray and the other leading Protestants listed by Mondovi.

Meanwhile, on 29 October, King Philip had ordered the Duke of Alva to make ready for war on the Netherlands, which was probably what Darnley was waiting for. Darnley's grievances had already reached the ears of the Nuncio in Paris, who reported on 4 November: "He cannot obtain from the Queen the authority he had before the late tumults, that is, to sit by the side of his wife in Council and in public places [and] set his name with hers in treaties and public affairs."[71] But Darnley was about to have his revenge in full measure.

Mary was making slow progress, but on or just before 1 November,[72] she received a letter from, or about, Darnley[73] that, according to Buchanan, caused her "miserably to torment herself, wailing wretchedly as if she would have fallen again into her former sickness." She told Moray, Maitland and Huntly that, "unless she might by some means or other be despatched of the King, she would never have any good day, and if by no other way, she would attain it, rather than she would abide to live in such sorrow she would slay herself." Buchanan put these words into Mary's mouth with the aim of demonstrating that she was in a frame of mind in which she could contemplate murdering Darnley, but there is independent corroboration of her reaction to the letter, for by 13 November, de Silva in London had been given details of it by Mary's messenger, Stephen Wilson, who left Scotland around 8 November and arrived in London on the 13th. De Silva informed his master that Mary "had heard that her husband had written to Your Majesty, the Pope, the King of France and the Cardinal of Lorraine that she was dubious in the faith."[74] Knox confirms this, and states that Darnley had also complained "of the state of the country, which was all out of order, all because that Mass and Papacy were not again erected, giving the whole blame thereof to the Queen as not managing the Catholic cause aright."

This was the first concrete evidence of Darnley's dealings abroad, and the first intimation that Mary had received of the extent of his duplicity, and it is hardly surprising that she was devastated by his embarrassing betrayal. She had certainly not done as much for the Catholic faith in Scotland as she could have done, and in some respects she had actively undermined it, but she was in an impossible political situation and had made a virtue of necessity in order to ensure her own survival. Of the two of them, she was personally by far the more genuinely devout, while Darnley bent with the wind, but, by his condemnation of her lack of zeal, he meant to show himself in the best possible light as the champion of Catholicism in Britain. Mary was ignorant of the wider implications of his calumnies, but she was all too aware that they had the power to ruin her credit with the Catholic rulers of Europe; in the case of Philip II and Catherine de' Medici, they seem to have succeeded, for hereafter neither offered much support to Mary, even though Philip later denied that he had ever received from Darnley any letter detrimental to her.[75]

Mary was desperate to repair the damage her husband had caused. De Silva told Philip that she had asked him

> to assure Your Majesty that, as regards religion, she will never, with God's help, fail to uphold it. Although she has entrusted this man [Wilson] to assure me verbally in the matter, she has in addition written to me as regards her steadfastness in the Faith, and I believe, from all that has ever been heard of the Queen, she is as faithful in religion as she professes to be. It seems to me, however, difficult to believe that her husband should have taken such a course, and it must be some French device to sow discord.[76]

Stephen Wilson left Jedburgh around 8 November. He was to go not only to London to reassure de Silva of his Queen's zeal for the faith, but also to Paris and Rome in order to restore Mary's credit with Charles IX, Catherine de' Medici and the Pope, and to inform Pius that the Nuncio *would* be received in Scotland with all honour. Mondovi was to be told, however, that he could only be received under some colour other than that of religion. Wilson arrived in Paris around 20 November.[77]

Because the Nuncio had been "compelled to linger in France, for the

Queen cannot devise any way of receiving him with the respect which is due to himself, to the Papal See and to her own dignity without occasioning very great tumults," the Pope had decided to send secretly to Scotland a fanatical Jesuit priest, Father Edmund Hay, a Scot who was Rector of the Jesuit College in Paris, to assess the situation and persuade Mary to agree to Mondovi's conditions. Mary had almost certainly been apprised of these by now, and the knowledge that she was expected to put to death her half-brother and many of her foremost advisers in return for papal help must have plunged her into even greater turmoil.

Father Hay knew all about the Queen's illness, and had no doubts about her "heroic constancy in her adherence to the Catholic religion," but he was well aware of "the dangers which hang over my head" and the political constraints that bound the Queen, which it was his mission to make her surmount. "May God grant that she may lay to heart this fatherly correction, and that it may lead her to carry out with greater diligence the work which hitherto she has only begun."[78]

On 7 November, Elizabeth instructed Bedford to propose a new treaty by which Mary's rights to the English succession might be secured.[79] This, however, was at variance with what she had told her Parliament two days earlier, when she warned them that any limitation of the succession would mean "some peril unto you and certain danger unto me."[80] However, on the 9th, she snapped that Parliament must cease urging her to marry and be content with her promise to acknowledge Mary as her successor. Mary, too trusting as ever, was joyfully to believe that Elizabeth was sincere.

Mary left Jedburgh for Kelso on 9 November, travelling by litter and accompanied by Moray, Bothwell and other Lords, and a train of 1,000 horse. Maitland informed Cecil that she was perfectly restored to health,[81] but later reports contradict this. Nevertheless, she was determined to complete her progress through the Borders.

Mary spent the nights of 9 and 10 November at Kelso,[82] and held another justice eyre there. The time for the Prince's baptism was approaching, and Elizabeth's ambassador, the Earl of Bedford, was already on his way, but on 11 November, de Silva wrote that there was no news of the envoy from

Savoy.[83] The Duke had in fact written to Mary a day earlier announcing that he would be sending Robertino Solaro, Count Moretta, to stand proxy for him.[84] Moretta, a staunch Catholic, was a seasoned diplomat who had visited Scotland in 1561 and knew Mary; he may also have met Mondovi during the latter's two visits to Savoy. His movements during the next weeks have led some historians to speculate that he had a secret mission that was perhaps connected with Darnley's schemes, and it has also been suggested that he was a Spanish spy. Certainly, some suspicion attaches to his behaviour.

Mary left Kelso for Hume Castle, the seat of Lord Home, on 11 November.[85] Her reluctance to consent to the Nuncio's demands had already been communicated to him, for, on the 12th, he reported that, while the Queen was anxious to receive the balance of the subsidy, she was not prepared to agree to the attached conditions. He added that Father Hay was to be accompanied to Scotland by the Bishop of Dunblane, and that both were determined to discover whether Mary really would be able to keep her promise to receive the Nuncio, whilst giving "courage to the Queen to prosecute the holy cause."[86]

Between 12 and 15 November, Mary visited Langton Castle, home of the Cockburns, and Wedderburn, another of Lord Home's properties. On the 15th, as she passed Berwick, Sir John Forster, its Deputy Governor, crossed the border to pay his respects, and the English guns fired a salute in her honour. The occasion was sadly marred when Forster's horse suddenly reared and kicked Mary in the thigh.[87] Mary made light of the incident, but Forster was deeply embarrassed and begged her forgiveness, which she readily gave, although she was in pain for the next two days.

Forster and his men escorted Mary part of the way to Eyemouth, where she stayed on 16 November. On the next night, she was at Coldingham Priory. Buchanan hints at some further scandal while the Queen was there, alleging that "Lady Reres passed through the guard, was recognised and was allowed to pass. Whom she was with, and where she went at that time of night, was not unknown to the Queen."[88] Buchanan seems to be hinting that Lady Reres was once more acting as procuress, but, again, there is no corroboration of his tale.

Mary reached Dunbar on 18 November, and Tantallon Castle, a Douglas stronghold, the following day. On the 20th, she arrived at Craigmillar Castle, three miles south of Edinburgh;[89] here, according to Maitland, she intended "to stay until her passing next to Stirling to the baptism, which is deferred to December 12 because of the long tarrying of the ambassador of Savoy."[90] It was here also that the fateful train of events that led to Darnley's murder would be set in motion.

12

"Unnatural Proceedings"

CRAIGMILLAR CASTLE LAY IN THE parish of Liberton, and dated from the early thirteenth century but, by Mary's day, thanks to considerable rebuilding, it was a spacious, luxurious residence, large enough to accommodate the entire court. It commanded an elevated position looking out across Edinburgh and the Forth, and its lands extended as far as the royal hunting park of Holyrood. It had been in the hands of the Preston family since c.1374, and its present owner was the elderly Sir Simon Preston, a wealthy merchant, member of Parliament, Privy Councillor and that same Provost of Edinburgh who had briefly fallen from favour for his failure to aid Mary on the night of Rizzio's murder. Although Knox described him as "a man of very wicked life and no religion," he had otherwise distinguished himself by his loyalty and service to the Queen, which is why she had forgiven him and come to stay with him. She was probably lodged in the recently built range of buildings surrounding the courtyard to the east of the fifteenth-century central tower, which were ornamented with Renaissance features.

In Mary's state of health, Craigmillar was a far more attractive residence in which to recuperate than Holyrood with its horrific memories. Yet her stay here was to be far from tranquil for, at the end of November, Darnley arrived unannounced and pleaded with her to resume conjugal relations.[1] Mary could not bring herself to have anything to do with him; Buchanan claims that she even refused to give him money for his day to day expenses unless he returned to Stirling, and says that "this greatly increased people's suspicion, already aroused by the Queen's daily familiarity with Bothwell." There is still no supporting evidence of this in contemporary sources; even Lennox merely claims that Mary used Darnley "but strangely."

Nau says that, after leaving Jedburgh, Mary had "gradually recovered until she returned to Edinburgh, where she vomited a great quantity of corrupt blood, and then the cure was complete." This probably took place on 2 December, for on that date, according to du Croc,[2] the Queen was "in the hands of the physicians, not at all well." Such was her mental anguish at the time that du Croc was convinced that

> "the principal part of the disease consists of a deep grief and sorrow. Nor does it seem possible to make her forget the same. Still she repeats these words, 'I could wish to be dead.' The injury she received is exceeding great, and Her Majesty will not soon forget it." The ambassador did not expect, "on several accounts, any good understanding between [the King and Queen], unless God especially put His hand in it. I shall name only two reasons against it: the first is, the King will never humble himself as he ought; the other, that the Queen cannot perceive him speaking with any noblemen but presently she suspects some plot among them."

Since Rizzio's murder, she had, with good reason, become paranoid. That she was aware of Darnley's latest treasonable schemes is most unlikely, but she certainly knew him well enough to realise that, left to his own devices, he was dangerous.

On 3 December, a disappointed Darnley left Craigmillar for Dunbar. After his departure, his relieved wife, now physically restored to health, threw herself with energy into preparations for the christening. But her mental state undoubtedly remained fragile.

In Paris, Mondovi had received word from the Cardinal of Lorraine's gentleman that Mary would not, after all, consent to his going to Scotland because "she could not stain her hands with the blood of her subjects" and dared not risk offending Elizabeth, who had "begun to show herself a friend"; on 3 December, the Nuncio informed the Vatican of this,[3] yet on that very day, Father Hay and the Bishop of Dunblane sailed from Dieppe for Scotland, not knowing that their mission was destined for failure before it had even begun.

Darnley had only been gone a matter of hours when he sent a message asking du Croc to meet with him "half a league" outside Edinburgh. The ambassador complied and the two men talked for a long while. Afterwards, du Croc reported to Beaton: "Things go still worse and worse. I think he intends going away tomorrow, but I am assured that he is not to be present at the baptism." This was serious, and an outrageous public insult to his wife, because the King's absence would undoubtedly cast doubts once more on James's paternity and undermine the unity that Mary had worked so hard in recent months to achieve. Du Croc felt that Darnley hoped he would sort out his problems for him, but in the face of such obduracy, there was little the ambassador could do. In the event, Darnley did not go abroad, but rode to Dunbar and thence, after a few days, to Stirling.[4] Mary herself planned to go there for the baptism, which was set for 12 December.[5]

It seems likely that du Croc informed Mary and her Lords of Darnley's intentions, and that it was this knowledge that precipitated what happened next. For soon after the King's departure, and probably on 4, 5 or 6 December, a conference was held to discuss the problem of Darnley, who was becoming more than a liability, and an increasing embarrassment to everyone. We know about this mainly from a document entitled "The Protestation of Huntly and Argyll,"[6] which Mary and her advisers drew up in England on 5 January 1569 to be sent to those two Lords with a request that they sign and attest to it as a true record of what had taken place at Craigmillar. The information in it must have come from Huntly and Bothwell. This document never reached its intended recipients: it was intercepted by Cecil's spies and taken to Westminster. Naturally Mary was eager to exonerate herself from all blame for Darnley's murder, and conversely to emphasise Moray's role, but she could hardly have expected Huntly and Argyll to put their signatures to a blatant distortion of the facts, as some of her detractors have suggested. Moreover, this document is supported by other evidence.

According to the Protestation, the chief Lords in attendance on Mary at Craigmillar were Moray, Bothwell, Maitland, Huntly and Argyll. One morning, as Huntly and Argyll lay in bed,[7] Moray and Maitland came into their chamber, where Maitland, lamenting the banishment of the Earl of Morton, Lords Lindsay and Ruthven, with the rest of their faction, said that the occasion of the murder of David was for to trouble and impeach the Parliament wherein Moray and others should have been forfeit and declared rebels; and, seeing that the same was chiefly for the welfare of Moray, it should be esteemed ingratitude if he and his friends, in reciprocal manner, did not enterprise all that were in their puissance for relief of the said banished. Wherefore they thought that we should have been as desirous thereto as they were.

Huntly and Argyll agreed "to do all that was in us for their relief, providing that the Queen's Majesty should not be offended thereat." Maitland averred "that the best way to obtain Morton's pardon was to promise to the Queen's Majesty to find any means to make divorcement betwixt Her Grace and the King her husband, who had offended Her Highness so highly in many ways." It is significant that this came from Maitland, to whom Mary had confided at Jedburgh her desperation to escape from her intolerable marriage.

Argyll said he "knew not how that might be done," but Maitland, with Moray listening, answered, "My Lord, care you not thereof. We shall find the means well enough to make her quit of him, so that you and my Lord of Huntly will only behold the matter, and not be offended thereat." Turning to Huntly, Maitland and Moray reiterated what had been said, "promising, if we would consent to the same, that they should find the means to restore us in our own lands and offices,[8] and they to stand good friends unto us, and cause Morton, Ruthven and the rest to do the like in time coming." Huntly and Argyll assured them that they would not put any obstacles in the way of a divorce, which "might be profitable and honourable both for them and us, and especially where the pleasure, will and contentment of the Queen consisted."

Thereupon, Moray, Maitland, Argyll and Huntly went to Bothwell's chamber "to understand his advice on this thing proposed, wherein he gainsaid not more than we."

It is clear from this that Bothwell was not the originator of this plot to rid Mary of Darnley. It was Moray and Maitland who devised it, and who may have intended, even at this early stage, to make Bothwell, whom they hated and resented, their scapegoat, and perhaps make an occasion for getting rid of him too. As a loyal subject, Bothwell must have shared the Lords' revul-

sion against Darnley, and his Scottish pride, like theirs, would have been outraged at the public embarrassment that the King was causing. It has also
been alleged that he readily chose to support his former enemies in their
schemes because he already had ambitions to marry the Queen, but that
must have come later, after he had had time to reflect on the implications of
a royal divorce.

After Bothwell had agreed to the plan, the five Lords sought out Mary.
Maitland reminded her "of a great number of grievous and intolerable offences the King, ungrateful of the honour received of Her Highness, had
done to Her Grace, and continuing every day from evil to worse," and proposed that, "if it pleased Her Majesty to pardon Morton, Ruthven and Lindsay with their company, they should find the means, with the rest of the
nobility, to make divorcement betwixt Her Highness and the King her husband, which should not need Her Grace to meddle therewith." He added,
ominously, that Mary should "take heed to make resolution therein, as well
for her own easement as well of the realm," for Darnley had already troubled
Her Grace and them all, and, "remaining with Her Majesty, would not cease
till he did her some other evil turn."

The other Lords all brought pressure to bear on Mary to make her agree
to Maitland's proposals. At length, she said she might consent on two conditions: "one, that the divorcement were made lawfully; the other, that it was
not prejudicial to her son; otherwise Her Highness would rather endure all
torments and abide the perils that might chance her. Bothwell answered that
he doubted not but the divorcement might be made without prejudice in any
way of my Lord Prince," reminding Mary that he had succeeded to his earldom despite his parents having been divorced.

After further discussion, it was proposed—by whom is not known—that,
after the divorce, Mary and Darnley should live in different parts of the country, or he should retire abroad. Mary said that, in case Darnley changed his
mind about that arrangement, it might be better if she herself went to live in
France until such time as he came to terms with the divorce. That she should
suggest such an impractical and unrealistic solution suggests that she was
now living in fear of Darnley.

Mary was still having doubts about the effect a divorce would have on
James's legitimacy, but Maitland smoothly reassured her, "Madame, fancy
you not we are here of the principal of Your Grace's nobility and Council, that

shall find the means that Your Majesty shall be quit of him without prejudice of your son. And albeit that my Lord of Moray here present be little less scrupulous for a Protestant nor Your Grace is for a Catholic, I am assured he will look through his fingers thereto, and will behold our doings, saying nothing to the same."

Mary could have interpreted this speech in more than one way. They had been talking about divorce, and she could have understood it to mean that Moray would not interfere if her Lords sanctioned her applying to the Pope for an annulment. Yet the only ground on which one could have been obtained was consanguinity, for which Mary had already obtained a dispensation; however, the fact that it had not been granted until after the wedding made the union technically invalid, and, since the marriage had not been made in ignorance of any impediment, the legitimacy of its issue would be brought seriously into doubt were an annulment to be sought, which was what Mary feared. Therefore Maitland and the other Lords could not have resorted to this means without prejudicing James's title to the succession.

Maitland, however, had not specifically referred to divorce, but merely to finding a means of ridding Mary of Darnley without prejudice to James. There were only a few options open, since neither Mary nor Darnley would have acknowledged the validity of a Protestant divorce, and a separation sanctioned by the Catholic Church, for which the only possible ground could be Darnley's adultery, would prevent either party from remarrying, since both would still be united in the eyes of God.

One option was to have Darnley arrested and charged with treason, which he had committed more than once and for which the penalty was death. Leslie was to claim that, even if Darnley was Mary's "head in wedlock, yet was he otherwise subject to her, as to his principal and supreme governess, and to her laws, by the due and ordinary process and course whereof he might justly have been convicted, condemned and executed, as well for the murder committed upon her secretary, in whose body his dagger was found stabbed, as for the imprisoning of the Queen and attempting to move her from civil government, to intrude himself thereto, and for divers others the like pageants by him played." But, as the law then stood in Scotland, a king could not technically be guilty of treason; secondly, even if this could be circumvented, the arrest of the father of the Prince just as the foreign ambassadors were arriving for the christening would create a humiliating and potentially explosive scandal: Darnley was, after all, of the blood royal of England. The only other option, therefore, was murder.

Mary must have understood that Maitland was not just referring to divorce, for she answered firmly, "I will that you do nothing by which any spot may be laid to my honour or conscience, and therefore I pray you rather let the matter be in the estate as it is, abiding till God of his goodness put remedy thereto, than you, believing to do me service, may possibly turn to my hurt and displeasure." She was, it seems, prepared to wait until either she or Darnley died, rather than permit her Lords to remove her husband by underhand means, and the fact that she insisted that nothing be done that was detrimental to her honour proves that she feared that it might be.

Unperturbed, Maitland replied, "Madame, let us guide the matter amongst us, and Your Grace shall see nothing but good and approved by Parliament." This rather patronising conclusion to the conversation implied that such an issue would be better resolved by men than left to a woman's limited understanding, but it must have been clear to Mary that there was no way of freeing herself from Darnley without endangering the succession or compromising her good name. Moreover, she cannot have come away from this meeting without some impression that the Lords intended to get rid of her husband by fair means or foul; unwittingly, she had already told them that she was prepared to wait until death solved the problem of Darnley.

There is ample corroboration of the Protestation in other sources. Although Huntly and Argyll never had a chance to sign that document, they were among the signatories to a paper drawn up by Mary's Scottish supporters in 1568, which states that, at Craigmillar, the Lords "caused make offers to our Sovereign Lady, if Her Grace would give remission to them that were banished, to find causes of divorce, either for consanguinity, in respect they alleged the dispensation was not published, else for adultery; or to get [Darnley] convicted of treason because he consented to Her Grace's retention in ward; or what other ways to dispatch him; which altogether Her Grace refused, as is manifestly known."[9] The Protestation, however, is not so specific regarding Mary's rejection of "other ways" to dispatch Darnley.

Leslie states that the Lords offered to procure a divorce if the Queen pardoned Morton, but that "she would not consent to it, though she were moved thereto by a great number of her nobility, and by such as [later became] her greatest adversaries." Nau claims that the Lords "fomented discord between the King and Queen by underhand dealings, and then recommended a divorce in order to deprive them of all lawful succession." This is the interpretation that Mary herself had chosen to place upon events by the 1570s.

Buchanan, in *The Book of Articles* of 1568, written before the Protestation was drawn up, states that, when Mary came to Craigmillar, "in the audience of Moray, Huntly, Argyll and the Secretary"—Bothwell is not mentioned—she referred again to her wish to be rid of the King. In this account, however, it is Mary, and not Maitland, who suggests a divorce on the grounds of consanguinity, and Buchanan says that someone else, not Mary, voiced the objection that, if such a divorce were granted, the Prince "should be declared bastard, since neither the King nor she contracted that marriage as ignorant of the degree of consanguinity wherein they stood." Hearing this, the Queen "utterly left that opinion of divorce." A similar account is in Buchanan's *Detectio* of 1571.

Lennox, however, says nothing of this discussion, since his source for much of his *Narrative* was Darnley himself. What Lennox does say, which Buchanan omits, is that, at Craigmillar, the Council resolved to have Darnley imprisoned after the baptism. The fact that this never happened is perhaps proof enough that it was never an issue, but it may have been one of the proposed solutions to the problem of what to do about Darnley.

When, in 1569, Moray learned of the contents of the Protestation, he denied that anything was said in his presence at Craigmillar "tending to any unlawful or dishonourable end." At that time, however, Moray had good reason for wishing to dissociate himself from what had taken place there.

It has been suggested that the Lords meant all along to embroil their Catholic Queen in a plot to do away with Darnley and thus bring about her downfall, leaving them free to rule in the name of her infant son, whom they would raise as a Protestant. There is no proof of this, but it is certainly possible, for not only was it the ultimate outcome of the Darnley plot, but it would not have been the first time that the Lords had attempted to overthrow or undermine Mary. Now that she had a son, there was more justification than ever for them to do so. Although the evidence suggests that, in December 1566, their chief aim was the restoration of the exiled Lords, there may well have been a wider aspect to their plan that was not discussed with Bothwell. What is likely is that the discussions that took place at Craigmillar were the beginnings of the plot that led to Darnley's murder, and that the prime movers were Maitland and Moray.

It was later asserted by both Lennox and Leslie—writing on behalf of both sides—that the Lords plotted the assassination of the King at Craigmillar, and indeed, it is hard to believe that the matter was not touched upon in private by the five nobles who had brought up the matter of divorce with the Queen. Lennox claimed that the time and manner of Darnley's murder were devised at Craigmillar, but this may be discounted because the evidence strongly suggests that these arrangements were made much nearer the time. Leslie states categorically that Moray, Bothwell and others, at Craigmillar, "consulted and devised this mischief." Furthermore, the "Protestation of Huntly and Argyll" concludes: "We judge in our consciences, and hold for certain and truth, that Moray and [Maitland] were authors, inventors, devisers, counsellors and causers of the murder, in what manner and by whatsoever persons the same was executed."

These Lords had little reason to love Darnley, and had bitterly resented him almost from the first. He was a Catholic, a troublemaker and an embarrassment, and the Queen's desperation to be rid of him was welcome news to them, which is why they appeared so overtly sympathetic towards her. In fact, they were eager to exploit her marital problems to their own advantage. Neither they nor their fellow nobles would have wished to see a reconciliation between the royal couple, for this would inevitably have seen Darnley restored to ascendancy over them, which was an intolerable prospect. The Protestant Lords hated him for his betrayal of the fugitive Lords, and Moray and Maitland had long had personal scores to settle with him. They may well have considered that it was worth risking the penalties for high treason in order to do away with him.

There is good evidence that, whilst at Craigmillar, several Lords entered into a Bond for the murder of Darnley, much as they had done for the murder of Rizzio, who had also fallen foul of them. No such Bond has survived, but one of Bothwell's followers, James Ormiston, confessed, just before his execution in 1573, that he had been shown and read the bond by Bothwell in April 1567. Bothwell had told him that the Bond was his security, and when Ormiston expressed doubts about this, the Earl replied, "Tush, Ormiston, ye need not take fear of this, for the whole Lords have concluded the same long since in Craigmillar, all that were there with the Queen, and none dare find fault with it." Six years later, displaying a remarkable memory, Ormiston quoted the substance of the text of the Bond, which read:

> It was thought expedient and most profitable for the Commonwealth, by the whole nobility and Lords underscribed, that such a young fool and proud tyrant should not reign or bear rule over them; and that, for divers causes therefore, that these all had concluded that he should be put off by one way or another; and whosoever should take the deed in hand, or do it, they should defend and fortify as themselves.

Ormiston added that the bond had been drawn up "a quarter of a year before the deed was done"[10] and signed by Huntly, Argyll, Bothwell, Maitland and Sir James Balfour.[11] It should be said that, by 1573, all of these men had fallen foul of the government in one way or other, and that it is highly likely that this was an edited list of signatories.

Ormiston stated that Bothwell had told him that the subtle, devious lawyer, Sir James Balfour, was enlisted to draw up the Bond, which seems likely; according to Nau, who must have got his information from Mary, who had seen the Bond and doubtless recognised the handwriting, it was written out by Alexander Hay, one of the Clerks of the Council. In the original text, Balfour is unlikely to have used the word murder, as seems clear from Ormiston's statement.

The fact that, between 5 and 10 December 1566, Balfour's brother Robert was granted by the Queen the provostry of Kirk o'Field,[12] the house where Darnley was to be murdered, has been seen by some historians as sinister, yet it is almost certain that it was not until several weeks later that this house was chosen as a lodging for the King, after others had been rejected.

In December 1567, another of Bothwell's men, John Hepburn of Bolton, stated in his confession that Bothwell had shown him a Bond that listed "some light causes against the King, such as his behaviour contrar the Queen." This document was signed by Huntly, Argyll, Maitland and Bothwell: when asked if he had seen Balfour's name, Hepburn denied it, but declared he would warrant that Balfour was the principal deviser of the deed; this part of his confession was suppressed by the government, and does not appear in the official record.[13] It would have been strange for Balfour to have instigated the plot against Darnley, his fellow Catholic and friend, unless of course he wished to dissociate himself from the disgraced King, or unless he was playing a double game, which is possible. There have been several theories that Balfour was in fact acting in concert with Darnley to destroy the Protestant establishment in Scotland, and that he was luring them into a trap. It is important to bear this in mind when charting Balfour's movements over the next weeks.

Hepburn added that, on the night of Darnley's murder, "he thought that no man durst say it was evil done, seeing the handwriting and acknowledging the Queen's mind thereto." He seems to have inferred from what he had seen—or been told by Bothwell—that Mary had given her consent to the murder, but, had there been any evidence of this in the original document, the Lords, and later Buchanan, would certainly have made use of it to destroy her.

A third adherent of Bothwell, John Hay of Talla, stated on the scaffold in January 1568 that Huntly, Argyll, Maitland and Balfour had all entered into a Bond to murder Darnley.

Nau says that the murder of Darnley was the result of the bond, and that Moray, Huntly, Bothwell, Maitland and Balfour "protested that they were acting for the public good of the realm, pretending that they were freeing the Queen from the bondage and misery into which she had been reduced by the King's behaviour. They promised to support each other and to avouch that the act was done justly and lawfully by the leading men of the Council. They had done it in defence of their lives, which would be in danger, they said, if the King should get the upper hand and secure the government of the realm, at which he was aiming."

According to Nau, Bothwell gave the Craigmillar Bond to Mary in June 1567, just prior to her capture by the Lords. In 1580, Balfour claimed that it was in his possession, but was unable to produce it as evidence at Morton's trial the following year. He had probably been bluffing in order to gain favour with Morton's accusers, for the Lords had almost certainly taken the incriminating document from Mary years before and destroyed it.

In his answer to the Protestation, Moray wrote, "In case any man will say and affirm that ever I was present when any purposes were holden at Craigmillar in my audience, tending to any unlawful or dishonourable end, or that ever I had subscribed any bond there, or that any purpose was holden anent the subscribing of any bond by me to my knowledge, I avow they speak wickedly and untruly, which I will maintain against them, as becomes an honest man, to the end of my life."[14] He was not saying that a Bond had not been drawn up at Craigmillar, merely that he had not subscribed to it. But Bishop Leslie and Nau were both certain that he had signed it. Neither Ormiston nor Hepburn listed Moray among the signatories, but their confessions had been edited by a government that had its own interests and reputation to preserve.

Maitland had said that Moray would "look through his fingers," and although Moray was afterwards to protest that he had never done nor approved of anything that was unlawful, he must have known about the plot against Darnley, and may even have initiated it, but he remained detached from it. Yet, of all those involved, he was to be the chief beneficiary.

Mary, it appeared, would also benefit from the removal of her husband, and there is no doubt that she had compelling reasons for wanting to be rid of him. Many, then and now, have seen her despair at being chained to Darnley and her bitter resentment against him as strong enough motives for having him killed or approving a plot to kill him. In 1568, Lennox, anxious to bring Mary to justice for the unlawful killing of his son, claimed that, although Mary had pardoned and forgiven many of those involved in Rizzio's murder, she "yet continued still in her deadly hatred towards her husband, till she had his life. Shortly after her coming to Craigmillar, she with her accomplices invented and resolved the time and manner of the most horrible murder of her most innocent and loving husband." The flaws in this latter statement are only too apparent, as we have seen.

Hepburn thought that the Queen had given her consent to the murder, but his confession was extorted by a government whose business it was to demonstrate that Mary was guilty. He may well have spoken in good faith, having been reassured by Bothwell that the Queen had given her approval, but this is not sufficient evidence to prove that she had. Mary must have guessed that the Lords were plotting something criminal, or at least sinister, or she would not have warned them not to compromise her honour or her conscience; yet her concern did not extend to warning Darnley that he might be in danger. She must therefore have been truly desperate to be rid of him, and so bitter towards him that she did not care what befell him.

It has often been alleged that Mary's chief motive for wishing to be rid of

MARY, QUEEN OF SCOTS
"The most beautiful in Europe."

FRANCIS II & MARY, QUEEN OF SCOTS
Francis was Mary's "sweetheart and friend."

JAMES STEWART, EARL OF MORAY
"At deeds of treachery and blood,
Moray looked through his fingers."

JOHN KNOX
"He neither feared nor flattered
any flesh."

SIR WILLIAM MAITLAND OF
LETHINGTON
His contemporaries called him
"the Scottish Machiavelli."

JAMES DOUGLAS, EARL OF MORTON
"The most accomplished and
perfidious scoundrel."

HENRY STUART,
LORD DARNLEY
"He was so weak in
mind as to be a prey
to all that came
about him."

MEDAL STRUCK TO
COMMEMORATE THE
MARRIAGE OF
MARY AND DARNLEY
"She has given over unto
him her whole will to
be ruled and guided as
himself best likes."

DOUBLE PORTRAIT OF MARY AND DARNLEY
Marital harmony "lasted not above three months."

DAVID RIZZIO
He was often
with the Queen
"privately and
alone."

HOLYROOD PALACE
In this tower, in
Mary's apartments,
was enacted one of
the bloodiest deeds
of her reign.

MARY'S BEDCHAMBER IN HOLYROOD PALACE
The open door leads to the supper room. The entrance to the secret stairway from Darnley's room below is concealed in the wall behind the bed-curtains.

THE MURDER OF RIZZIO
"Justice! Justice! Save me, my Lady, I am a dying man!"

THE OLD PALACE IN
EDINBURGH CASTLE
Mary retreated here
after Rizzio's murder.

THE BIRTH CHAMBER OF
JAMES VI, EDINBURGH
CASTLE
Here was born Mary's son.
The frieze and panelling
are of later dates.

Darnley was her wish to marry her lover, Bothwell. According to Buchanan, after the birth of her son, "her secret criminal intentions began to show themselves. Having by one way or another got rid of the King, she would marry
Bothwell. And lest she herself be suspected of the crime, she began gradually
to sow the seeds of discord between the King and the Lords, to drive them into
a deadly feud." After the Craigmillar conference, "she never left her intention
of destroying the King, as may well be perceived from what followed." There is
no reliable evidence to support this statement, and, since Darnley himself was
doing a pretty good job of alienating the Lords, there was little need for Mary to
whip up a feud between them. Furthermore, there is no credible testimony that
she was involved in an affair with Bothwell at this time, and not one of the
Lords, nor any other contemporary observer, saw Mary's growing distaste for
Darnley as a consequence of her supposed passion for Bothwell. However,
there can be little doubt that Bothwell now played a very important role in
Mary's life, and that she relied on him heavily. It would not be surprising, given
the events that were to take place after Darnley's death, if there was already
some sexual or emotional chemistry between them.

Buchanan also alleges that Mary "was incited to this [murder] by letters
from the Pope and the Cardinal of Lorraine." Certainly these men were inciting her to do murder, yet not to eliminate her husband, whose much-
publicised devotion to Catholicism would have precluded their urging such
a course, but to do away with most of the Protestant establishment in Scotland.

With the christening approaching, the problem of Darnley had to be shelved
for the moment, although the Lords did not cease to work for the return of
the exiles.[15] On 7 December, Mary left Craigmillar for Edinburgh, where she
intended to finalise the arrangements for the baptism,[16] which was to be delayed because the Savoyard ambassador, Moretta, had still not arrived in
Scotland. After three nights at Holyrood, the Queen travelled on to Stirling.
On the way, she bruised her breast whilst riding[17] and was in some discomfort when she arrived at the castle on 12 December.

Darnley was already at Stirling when Mary arrived, but she had pre-
empted any refusal of his to become involved in the baptismal preparations
by appointing Bothwell to take charge of them and to receive the ambassa-

dors, which was "scarcely liked with the rest of the nobility."[18] It was later alleged, in *The Book of Articles*, that Mary had a secret passage between her chamber and the great hall at Stirling constructed at this time, "thinking to have had access at all times by that mean to Bothwell, whom purposely she caused to be lodged at the north end of the great hall, as the unperfected work this day testifies, for they departed forth of Stirling before it could be perfect." There are no building accounts to confirm this statement, and it is unlikely that a great noble such as Bothwell would have been lodged at the service end of the hall without some contemporary commenting on the fact; furthermore, it should be noted that the bridge giving access to the royal palace was at the south end of the 38.5-metre-long hall, and that the construction of a secret passage between one end and the other would have been a considerable undertaking that would have attracted much attention.

Melville says that, at this time, Mary was "still sad and pensive" and brooding on Rizzio's murder, which was quite understandable, since she was being urged to pardon those who had committed it. "So many sighs would she give that it was pity to hear her, and few there were to endeavour to comfort her." At length, after a supper at which she had sat sighing and refusing to eat, despite the pleas of Moray and Mar, she walked with Melville in the park at Stirling and unburdened herself of her grief. Melville comforted her by saying that her friends in England would soon help her to forget her enemies in Scotland, who were "unworthy of her wrath" anyway. He praised her "excellent qualities in clemency, temperance and fortitude," and told her she "should not suffer her mind to be possessed with the remembrance of offences, but should rather bend her spirit by a princely and womanly behaviour, whereby she might best gain the hearts of the whole people, both here and in England." He warned her to desist from the pursuit of further revenge, "whereupon may ensue more desperate enterprises," and reminded her that she had repented of not heeding his warnings before the murder of Rizzio. "I pray God the like repentance fall not out again too late," he concluded.[19]

Mary was also fearful of another conspiracy against her, and her Privy Council issued an edict forbidding anyone to bring firearms into the court.[20] The Queen could not forget how Ker of Fawdonside had pressed his pistol against her belly on the night of Rizzio's murder. Now, it seems, her fears were centred upon Darnley. Both Lennox and Buchanan refer to her dismissing the majority of his servants, but if this is true, she may have deemed it necessary to do so, in case they were plotting with him.

Lennox says that, in the absence of those servants, he appointed a number of his own dependants and followers to wait on Darnley at the baptism. Their arrival disconcerted and worried Mary, who expressed her disapproval and told Darnley that "there were too many Lennox men there, and if they were without the castle, they should not come in again. He answered they should go where he went, and if they were without the castle, and he with them, they should either enter with him, or he would make an entry for them."[21] Melville also mentions this quarrel. Afterwards, Mary spoke sharply to Robert Cunningham, leader of the Lennox men,[22] presumably to warn him of what would happen to him and his followers if there was any trouble, but she did not go as far as to send them away, probably for fear of provoking further trouble.

According to *The Book of Articles,* Bothwell was so afraid of the Lennox men that he caused a dozen of his armed servants to watch in his bedchamber while he slept, and Mary, responding to his terror, summoned fifteen arquebusiers to the castle to act as Bothwell's bodyguard; Mar, however, refused to let them in. However, this account presupposes that Bothwell was Mary's lover at this time and that his fear arose from guilt.

Given Darnley's defiance, it is hardly surprising that Mary should thereafter have tried to isolate him from the rest of the court. Both Lennox and Buchanan claim she did her best to prevent the nobles from having anything to do with him, but, according to Lennox, this only "inflamed their hearts the more against her," so that the King's "lamentable" case "won thereby the whole hearts of the nobility," which is patently untrue, since several of them were plotting his removal. Lennox also alleges that Mary would have laid murderous hands on Darnley but for the imminent arrival of the foreign ambassadors, which obliged her to dissemble and defer the matter. On one occasion, though, she allegedly dropped her husband a hint of her intentions: during one of their quarrels, when Darnley grew red in the face at her "sharp words," she told him that, "if he were a little daggered and had bled as much as my Lord Bothwell had lately done, it would make him look the fairer."[23]

Buchanan says that Mary deprived Darnley of "any kind of expenses" and ordered him to be confined to "an obscure, narrow room," but, although there is some evidence in de Silva's dispatches that Darnley was short of money at this time,[24] it is clear that he came and went as he pleased, and it is unthinkable that Mary would have so shabbily treated the father of her child at a time when she was worried that he would not attend the baptism and would thereby disgrace her before the foreign ambassadors. Buchanan also claims that, much to Darnley's distress, Mary had his silver plate taken away and replaced with pewter vessels, but elsewhere he contradicts himself, saying that the plate was removed after Darnley left Stirling.

More credibly, Buchanan states that the Queen forbade her husband to communicate with the ambassadors, "under pretext that his garments were not prepared." Lennox says that he was not permitted to speak to them unless Mary was present, and claims that this was to prevent him from informing them of "her unnatural proceedings towards him," but in fact it suggests that Mary was apprehensive that Darnley might either attempt to spread word of his grievances abroad, to her great embarrassment, or, worse still, would try to intrigue with foreign powers. Altogether, it appears that Mary was very afraid of Darnley and what he might do.

On 13 December, perhaps—it has been argued—with a view to enlisting the support of the Protestant establishment for the dissolution of her marriage to Darnley and the means by which she was to secure this, Mary approved further measures to aid the Kirk. A week later, she granted lavish gifts to the reformed Church.[25]

It was by a stroke of irony that Father Hay and the Bishop of Dunblane arrived in Edinburgh on 13 December. Learning that the Queen was at Stirling, they proceeded there immediately, but she was too busy with preparations for the christening to see them. Nor is it likely that she would have wanted to, for she must have known that they would do their utmost to persuade her to agree to Mondovi's proposals. There is, indeed, no reliable evidence that Mary did speak with either Hay or the Bishop during their stay in Scotland; they, in turn, were under orders to report back to the Nuncio within a few days. On 23 December, Father Hay wrote to Mondovi, promising that he would soon be with him.[26]

On 14 December, the ambassadors gathered for the christening. Moretta had still not arrived, and the Queen had decided that the ceremony should go ahead without him.

Darnley had threatened to leave Stirling two days before the baptism, but showed no sign of departing. However, he kept to his own apartments,[27] sulking because he had not been consulted over the choice of godparents. He was not present when, on 16 December, Mary received the Earl of Bedford in audience and was presented with Queen Elizabeth's christening gift of a richly enamelled, gem-encrusted gold font weighing 28 pounds.[28] During this audience, Bedford, to Mary's great joy, informed her that his mistress wished to arrange a conference to discuss Mary's claim to the English succession. At last, it seemed that her title was to be acknowledged, and she agreed to send some of her Councillors to "treat, confer and accord" with her royal cousin. Elizabeth's friendship was also apparent in a letter she wrote to Darnley at this time, exhorting him to obey the Queen of Scots in all things.

The Prince was christened, with full Catholic rites and appropriate splendour, on 17 December in the chapel royal at Stirling, and given the names Charles James, the former in honour of the King of France.[29] The Catholic ceremony, conducted by Archbishop Hamilton, drew adverse comment from alarmed Protestants, and several Lords, including Bedford, Moray, Argyll, Huntly and Bothwell, waited at the door of the chapel until it was over. Mary had provided new suits of clothing for her chief nobles: Moray's was green, Argyll's red and Bothwell's blue.[30] The King of France's ambassador carried the baby, attended by Atholl, Seton and other Scottish Catholic nobles, as well as by du Croc, who was standing in for the ambassador of Savoy.[31] The only part of the traditional rite that was omitted was that in which the priest customarily spat saliva into the infant's mouth: Mary had expressly forbidden the syphilitic Archbishop Hamilton, whom she referred to as "a pocky priest," to do this. At the end of the ceremony, the Countess of Argyll, acting as proxy for Bedford and Queen Elizabeth, took the baby, earning herself the severe censure of the Kirk.[32]

"The Queen behaved herself admirably well all the time of the baptism, and showed so much earnestness to entertain all the goodly company in the best manner that this made her forget in a good measure all her former ailments."[33] For three days, Mary presided over the lavish festivities that had been devised to enhance Scotland's prestige in the eyes of the world: there were banquets, masques, pageants, dancing, a bull hunt and a spectacular firework display. George Buchanan wrote a Latin masque, in which he extolled Mary's virtues, while many of the other entertainments were devised or mounted by Mary's favoured, able and witty valet, Sebastien Pagez, a native of Auvergne and an accomplished musician, singer and cook.[34] A ballet of his contriving gave great offence to some of the English visitors, for it depicted them as satyrs with tails, and Mary and Bedford had to employ all their diplomatic skills to defuse the situation.

Darnley was conspicuous by his absence. He kept to his apartments throughout the celebrations.[35] Buchanan claims he had been forbidden to attend, and Lennox that Mary asked him not to, but du Croc's evidence makes it clear that this was Darnley's own decision. On the day of the baptism, the King sent several times to du Croc,

> desiring me to come and see him, or to appoint him an hour that he might come to me in my lodgings; so that I found myself at last obliged to signify to him that, seeing he was in no good correspondence with the Queen, I had it in charge from the Most Christian King [Charles IX] to have no conference with him, and I caused tell him likewise that, as it would not be very proper for him to come to my lodgings, because there was such a crowd of company there, so he might know that there were two passages to it, and if he should enter by the one, I should be constrained to go out by the other. His bad deportment is incurable, nor can there ever be any good expected of him, for several reasons which I might tell you, were I present with you.

Du Croc may have been referring to Darnley's possible homosexual activities, or he may even have suspected, without much concrete evidence to go on, that the King was again plotting against the Queen. Charles IX and Catherine de' Medici may well have heard something of this in Paris, hence the orders to du Croc to have no dealings with Darnley. Certainly it seems as if Darnley was hoping to air his grievances and enlist at least du Croc's sympathy, if not his support for his nefarious schemes; it is hardly likely, as Lennox implies, that he wanted du Croc to obtain Mary's favour for him, for he had done his best to irrevocably alienate her by not attending the baptism.

Whatever du Croc had in mind when he wrote this letter, it was certainly too sensitive to be committed to paper. He concluded: "I cannot pretend to foretell how all may turn, but I will say that matters cannot subsist long as they are without being accompanied by sundry bad consequences."[36]

Historians have long speculated about Darnley's reasons for not attending the baptism. Du Croc believed that he stayed away because he did not want his obviously diminished status and others' contempt for him to be apparent to the foreign ambassadors. According to Nau, Darnley feared that Bedford, as Queen Elizabeth's representative, would refuse to acknowledge him as King of Scots, a fear that was probably well founded:[37] on the day of the baptism, the King had gone out by a back door "to take the air" and encountered a member of Bedford's suite who "did him reverence"; this was reported to Bedford, who later reprimanded the man for disobeying Elizabeth's order not to recognise Darnley as King of Scots.[38] More sinisterly, Darnley may have wished to cast doubts on the paternity of the Prince by his non-attendance, thereby emphasising his own right to the Crown Matrimonial. It has been pointed out that kings did not always attend their sons' christenings—Henry VIII did not attend Edward VI's—but the fact that Darnley's absence drew adverse comment is proof that it was considered strange. Moreover, it was an unforgivable insult to his wife, whose honour he had publicly demeaned in the most humiliating manner.

Mary managed to retain her composure for as long as was necessary, but in private she was "pensive and melancholy," and on 20 December, the day after the baptismal festivities came to an end, du Croc, responding to her summons, found her "weeping sore" on her bed, complaining of "a grievous pain in her side" and the enduring discomfort from her swollen breast. The ambassador came away with the worrying conviction that "she will give us some anxiety yet"—he could not think otherwise while she continued so depressed. "I am much grieved for the many troubles and vexations that she meets with," he added.[39] There can be little doubt that Darnley was the chief cause of her distress, nor that it was exacerbated by the prospect of the exiles' return. But worse was yet to come.

William Hiegait was the Town Clerk of Glasgow, a city at the heart of the Lennox landed interests. Some time in December, he thought fit to warn one William Walker, a servant of Archbishop Beaton who, by virtue of this connection, had access to the Queen, that he had heard that "the King, by the assistance of some of our nobility, should take the Prince and crown him; and, being crowned, as his father, should take upon him[self] the government."[40] In order to accomplish this, Darnley would have needed foreign aid, since he and Lennox did not have sufficient men or resources to effect such a coup, nor would any of the chief nobles of Scotland have supported them. Of course, such a grandiose scheme could have existed only in Darnley's imagination, but he had definitely been in contact with the Catholic powers in Europe in order to destroy Mary's reputation as an advocate of her faith, and his dealings with them may have gone further than that. There has been speculation that Hiegait had been involved in Darnley's plotting, but had thought better of it and decided that it was in his interests to warn the Queen what was afoot, although he was later to warn Darnley of a plot against him; at the very least, he appears to have been two-faced and duplicitous. Darnley's plans had perhaps reached the point where maintaining discretion was no longer possible, which is how Hiegait had heard such detailed rumours of what Darnley was intending.

Hiegait also told Walker that "the King could not content and bear with some of the noblemen that were attending in our court, but either he or they behoved to leave the same."[41] This must refer to those Lords who were working for the return of the exiles, Darnley's mortal enemies. The fact that Darnley did leave court soon afterwards gives credence to Hiegait's words. Neither Lennox nor Buchanan, however, says anything about Darnley's ambitions, but it is inconceivable that they did not know of them: Buchanan was a Lennox man, and Lennox must have been heavily involved in his son's schemes. Their silence argues Lennox's complicity.

Unaware as yet of the full extent of her husband's treachery, but goaded by his appalling behaviour, Mary had, it seems, decided after all to seek an annulment. On 23 December, in defiance of the Kirk, she restored Archbishop Hamilton to his consistorial jurisdiction,[42] which had been abolished in 1560 and which gave him the power to adjudicate in matrimonial cases. The fact that she took this extraordinary—and unlawful—step indicates just how desperate she was to be free of Darnley; it was almost certainly to pre-empt censure for this that she had bestowed bounteous gifts on the Church of Scotland just three days earlier. Furthermore, the Archbishop, being a Hamilton, would be only too delighted to dissolve the marriage between the Queen and the son of his family's long-standing enemy, Lennox, and he would certainly be more sympathetic and accommodating than the far more scrupulous Pope over the matter of James's legitimacy. Canon law, however, decreed that marriages of royal persons could be dissolved only by the Pontiff himself,[43] but if Mary was not aware of this, Archbishop Hamilton should have been. In all, this was a highly injudicious and unwise step on Mary's part.

The timing of the Archbishop's restoration also argues that Mary's purpose was the dissolution of her marriage, because, on the very next day, in order to secure the promised support of the Lords, she pardoned and recalled Morton and seventy-six other exiles. This was conditional upon them agreeing not to venture within seven miles of the court for two years. Two men were excluded from this general pardon: George Douglas and Ker of Fawdonside,[44] whom Mary considered had committed the worst kind of treason in threatening the lives of herself and her unborn child. Moray, Maitland, Bothwell, Atholl, du Croc and Morton's kinsman, Archibald Douglas, had all been active in procuring the pardon,[45] although, according to a letter written by Bedford to Cecil on 9 January 1567,[46] it was also granted at the request of the English government. Clearly, Mary was paving the way for an amicable settlement of the English succession, but, given the fact that she needed the support of her Lords at this time of crisis, and the pressure that had been applied on her both in England and Scotland, she had really had little choice but to allow the exiles to return.

The timing of the pardon, after the baptism, is significant. Mary must have known that Morton and his fellows had a score to settle with Darnley, the man who had betrayed them after Rizzio's murder. Once they were back in Scotland, Darnley would be in a highly vulnerable position as the target for their vengeance, and he knew it. In allowing them to return to Scotland, Mary was in effect sealing his death warrant. It is hard to believe that she was not aware of this. She also knew that Maitland and Moray had been considering means of ridding her of Darnley, and that Morton and his friends—who had not stopped short of violence when Rizzio became a threat to them—were their allies; they had, moreover, at the very least, agreed to subscribe to the Bond in which the other Lords had resolved to render obedience to Mary but not to her husband. The outcome of such an alliance was almost a foregone conclusion, given that Darnley's offences were much graver, and had had more far-reaching and ruinous consequences than had Rizzio's, and also that, amongst the Scottish nobility, feuds were customarily settled—or prolonged—by the shedding of blood.

But Darnley had behaved in a far worse fashion towards Mary, and had reduced her to such a state of misery, distress and bitterness by his conduct that, as has been noted, she probably no longer cared what became of him, as long as he ceased to trouble her. Mary may have assuaged her conscience with the knowledge that, by insisting that the returning exiles keep well away from court for two years, she had limited the danger they posed to Darnley. The fact that she imposed this condition on them suggests that she was indeed aware of the danger. If, after she had taken such precautions, the Lords managed to take matters into their own hands, she could not be said to be responsible for it, and it could not touch her honour.

The news that his enemies were about to return to Scotland struck terror into Darnley. He was in an isolated position at court, having alienated most of the nobles, and had few supporters. It appears he took desperate measures to redeem himself with the exiled Lords. On 24 December, the same day on which Fawdonside had been expressly excluded from the general remission, a pardon for him passed separately under the Signet,[47] which suggests that it was granted by Darnley without Mary's knowledge and after she had departed from Stirling to spend Christmas at Drummond Castle. That she could not bring herself to forgive Fawdonside for holding a pistol to her pregnant stomach is evident from the fact that she still regarded him as her enemy in 1568. Therefore it is virtually certain that she did not issue this pardon on Christmas Eve 1566. Darnley, moreover, had issued documents under the Signet on other occasions.

The gathering at Stirling broke up on Christmas Eve. Bedford went with Moray to St. Andrews, where he was honourably entertained as his guest for several days.[48] The Queen went without her husband to Drummond Castle near Crieff in Perthshire at the invitation of Lord Drummond. Buchanan later alleged that she there "sought solitude practically alone with Bothwell" and indulged in "filthy wickedness." "They spent about a week in such close accommodation and intimate contact that everyone was bitterly offended by their contempt of reputation . . . In what order they were chambered during their stay, many found fault with, but dared not reprove. How lascivious also their behaviour was, it was very strange to behold." Considering that "everyone" was shocked by their conduct, it is surprising that no other source refers to it. Furthermore, there is evidence that this was not just a private visit, since Mary attended to state business during her stay, and it is likely that she was attended by other Privy Councillors as well as Bothwell.

Meanwhile, William Hiegait had heard from one Cauldwell, a servant of the Earl of Eglinton, that Mary intended to have Darnley "apprehended and put in ward." Hiegait confided this intelligence to the Laird of Minto, Provost of Glasgow, who alerted Lennox to the fact that, "at Craigmillar, the Queen and certain of her Council had concluded an enterprise to the great peril and danger" of his son, "which rested but only on the finishing of the christening and the departure of the ambassadors." Lennox, in turn, warned Darnley, who instructed Hiegait to obtain more information from Cauldwell. According to Casket Letter II, "Minto sent him word that it was said that some of the Council had brought [Mary] a letter to sign to put him in prison and kill him if he did resist." However, she had refused to sanction it.

It will be remembered that, at the time of the Craigmillar conference, there was talk of arresting Darnley for treason, although nothing had come of it. Had Mary really intended to have Darnley put in ward, she would surely have set about it before departing for Drummond Castle, rather than leaving her husband to his own dubious devices. But Darnley was taking no chances. Nor did he remain at Stirling to see if rumour spoke truth. According to Lennox, having received his father's warning, and probably spurred on by his fear of the vengeful exiles, he stole away on Christmas Eve, without taking leave of anyone,[49] and made immediately for the safety of the Lennox heartlands in Glasgow, "being fully resolved to have taken ship shortly after and to have passed beyond the sea."[50]

13

"THE DAYS WERE EVIL"

⌒

D ARNLEY WAS "HARDLY A MILE out of Stirling" when "a violent disorder suddenly struck every part of his body," and when, after what must have been a nightmare journey, he arrived in Glasgow, "livid pustules broke out, accompanied by much pain and vexation in his whole body," and "he was brought so low that nothing but death was expected."[1] According to Buchanan, he had "black pimples all over his body, grievous sweat in all his limbs, and intolerable stink." Herries says that, amongst other symptoms, "his hair fell off." He lay ill for several weeks, wearing a white taffeta mask to cover the blisters. His incapacity effectively wrecked his plan to go abroad[2] and thereby sealed his fate.

The nature of Darnley's disease has been the subject of much debate: Bedford and Nau believed it to be smallpox, which was raging in Glasgow at that time and which usually commences with rigors, headaches, pains in the back and digestive disturbances. Within days, red pustules appear on the skin, mainly on the face and upper body. An attack of smallpox, with its recurring episodes of fever and exhaustion, usually lasts for about three weeks, after which the pustules have dried up and formed scabs that sometimes leave pitted scars, but Darnley was unwell for longer than that, and he had fallen ill before arriving in Glasgow, although he could of course have caught smallpox from one of the Lennox men who came from there—the incubation period is 12–14 days.

Yet it is almost certain that Darnley was suffering from something worse than smallpox. In his memoir of 1568, which was written in French, Bothwell initially asserted that the King had "la petite vérole" (i.e., smallpox), but later amended the last word in his own hand to read "roniole" (rognole), meaning an itch, a colloquial term for syphilis. The *Diurnal of Occurrents* and Lindsay of Pittscottie state candidly that the King was suffering from "a great fever of the pox," which at that time could only mean syphilis. There is, moreover, evidence that he had perhaps had it for some time.

Syphilis is believed to have been brought to Europe by sailors returning from the New World in the late fifteenth century, and in the sixteenth, it swept through Christendom in epidemic form. The primary stage of syphilis is characterised by a painless chancre, or ulcer, on the genitals, which heals itself after a few days, leaving the sufferer with the impression that he is cured; during the secondary stage, which usually occurs after a period without any symptoms, there may be headaches, a sore throat, swollen glands, fever, aches in the bones, a mottled skin rash and sores in the mouth and throat. If syphilis is not treated at this stage, these symptoms may recur. The tertiary stage, which follows after a period of apparent health lasting from five to fifty years, produces more obvious skin lesions, heart disease, paralysis, insanity, blindness or deafness, and death.

It has been suggested that Darnley may have contracted syphilis during one of his early visits to France, when he was free from parental supervision. His attack of measles in 1565 was unusually prolonged and may have been the first manifestation of the secondary stage, while the illness that struck him in late 1566 was probably a recurrence; the eruptions on his face, which some mistook for smallpox pustules, were more likely to have been a rash typical of "the acute inflammatory effects of syphilis when it first became epidemic."[3] There may have been another recurrence in between: in March 1566, Randolph had reported that Darnley was thought to be suffering from leprosy.[4] He was certainly ill at that time, as a blue satin gown was made for him to wear in his sick-bed.[5] Darnley's illness of late 1566 is unlikely to have been tertiary syphilis, as some writers have asserted, because there would have had to have been a gap of at least five years between that and the first symptoms of the second stage, and there is no record of Darnley being ill before the spring of 1565. Furthermore, some historians have claimed that Darnley was doomed to die of syphilis within a short time, but in fact he could have had fifty years or more of life left to him.

The recognised form of treatment for syphilis was mercury, which, when taken in oral form, caused necrosis of the gums, loosening of the teeth and pronounced halitosis. In Casket Letter II—which is probably in substance genuine—Mary refers to Darnley's foul breath, which suggests that he was receiving mercury treatment at that time. Because syphilis was known to be contagious, a series of baths was recommended, and this was part of Darnley's treatment. In 1928, at the request of Dr. Karl Pearson, Sir Daniel Wilson examined what is probably Darnley's skull[6] and found pits in it that must have resulted from a serious disease. Smallpox does not cause such pitting, but an advancing secondary stage of syphilis does. It can also cause inflammation of the cranium, leading to hair loss.[7]

Inevitably, as often happened when royal persons fell ill, there were rumours of poison. Given the general enmity towards Darnley, the sudden onset of his illness and its ominous symptoms, that was hardly surprising. Knox and Buchanan claim that he had been given poison before leaving Stirling, and Buchanan states that Darnley's physician, James Abernethy, a trustworthy doctor "of great skill and experience," on seeing the blisters, "at once pronounced that he had been given poison." Only "the strength of his youth" saved him.[8] According to Melville, it was said that the King "had got poison from some of his servants." Robert Birrel also attributes the illness to poison, while Buchanan is emphatic: "That he was poisoned, it is certainly known." Yet Lennox, surprisingly, makes no allegation of poison, nor is there any mention of it in the depositions of those alleged to have been involved in Darnley's murder. However, in one of the latter, made by Nicholas Hubert, better known as "French Paris," Darnley is described as being eaten up by a loathsome skin disease and a general foulness of body. Given all the evidence, the correct diagnosis is almost certainly syphilis.

It is inconceivable that Mary did not at some stage find out what ailed her husband. She was no innocent in such matters, as her censure of Archbishop Hamilton proves, and she must have been aware of what Darnley's treatment betokened. Such knowledge must have intensified her revulsion against him, not the least because he had uncaringly exposed her and their child to the disease.

. . .

Meanwhile, in London, de Silva had received a disturbing communication from Margaret, Duchess of Parma, Philip II's aunt and his viceroy in Brussels, informing him that de Alava, the Spanish ambassador in Paris, "had advised her that he had news of a plot being formed in Scotland against the Queen."[9]

Coming around the same time as Hiegait's revelations, de Silva's report may well refer to Darnley's plot to overthrow Mary and set either James or himself on the throne, with foreign aid. It should also be considered that information about the Lords' machinations against Darnley, which a perceptive observer could have understood to be a means by which to bring Mary herself to ruin, might have infiltrated diplomatic channels. Whatever the basis of de Silva's warning, Mary was in danger.

In militant mood, the General Assembly of the Church of Scotland convened on Christmas Day and made the Countess of Argyll do penance for participating in the Catholic baptism of the Prince. Two days later, indignant at Mary's temerity at restoring Archbishop Hamilton's powers, and fearful that it might signify her intention to force a Catholic revival, the Kirk petitioned the Council to stay the Queen's warrant to the Archbishop. In response, Mary increased the clergy's stipends, but it was not enough to halt the protests, and Moray warned her that she must comply with the law or risk serious trouble.[10] At the same time, her friends in Europe were warning her not to pursue an annulment for fear of alienating the English Catholics, many of whom viewed Darnley's claim to the English throne as better than hers. Should she discard Darnley, he might become the focus for every plot against her.

Mary must have been in some turmoil when she left Drummond Castle for Stirling on 28 or 29 December.[11] On the 30th, still attended by Bothwell, she visited Tullibardine in Perthshire as the guest of her Comptroller, Sir William Murray, who was not only a friend of Bothwell but also a Lennox man, and had been knighted by Darnley. This visit may well have been made in order to build diplomatic bridges and charm Tullibardine into remaining loyal to his sovereign, whatever her relations with Darnley. Buchanan alleges that Mary and Bothwell openly continued their adulterous liaison at Tullibardine, but they are highly unlikely to have done so in the house of one of the

Lennox affinity. Mary was still at Tullibardine on 31 December,[12] but returned to Stirling with Bothwell on that day or the next.[13]

On 1 January 1567, Moretta finally reached Paris, where he may have conferred with Mondovi and de Alava before pressing on to Scotland. Around this time, Moray and Bedford arrived back at Stirling.

Once Mary was back at Stirling, William Walker came to see her.[14] He told her what Hiegait had revealed to him of Darnley's plot to crown the Prince. As she later told Archbishop Beaton, "At the hearing whereof you may well think we marvelled not a little; and seeing the matter of such importance, could not but insist to have further knowledge of the speakers and authors, that we might better understand the ground and fountain whereof it proceeded." Walker said that Hiegait had "communicated the matter to him, as it appeared, to gratify us, whereupon, we took occasion to send for Hiegait." But once confronted with the Privy Council, both alone and in the presence of Walker, he denied "that he had ever talked with the said Walker on any such subject," and admitted only to having heard from Cauldwell a rumour that Darnley was to be put in ward. Mary ordered her Council to examine Cauldwell also, but he, in turn, denied having said anything at all to Hiegait. Mary was therefore unable to get to the bottom of the matter, and had to content herself with reproving both men for their "groundless talk."[15] Yet her letter to Beaton, written on 20 January, shows that she thought it anything but groundless.

On 2 January, Mary held a Council at Stirling, which was attended by Moray, Huntly, Argyll, Maitland and other Lords, but not by Bothwell, who had left court, probably on that very day, for Dunbar, where he purposed to await the arrival of Morton in Scotland. He had important matters to discuss with him.

Mary remained at Stirling for a few days before visiting Seton.[16] She was eagerly awaiting the conference at which her title to the English succession would, she hoped, be finally acknowledged, and on 3 January, she wrote to her "dearest sister" Elizabeth to thank her for her good intentions towards her in this respect.[17] Bedford left Stirling with this letter on 5 January,[18] and on 5 February, Cecil informed Sir Henry Norris in Paris that Bedford had brought him "good report from the Scottish Queen of her good disposition to keep peace and amity with the Queen's Majesty."[19] It was unlikely that Mary would have prejudiced her hopes in England by plotting to murder Darnley.

On Twelfth Night, 6 January, Maitland and his long-standing sweetheart, Mary Fleming, were finally married, in the chapel royal at Stirling.[20] This marriage to one of Mary's closest attendants served to identify Maitland more closely with the Queen's interests.

Earlier that day, a seemingly innocent incident had taken place. A passport was issued, bearing Mary's signature, permitting one Joseph Lutini, an Italian in her service, to proceed to France on the Queen's affairs.[21] It had been made out and countersigned by her secretary, Joseph Rizzio, who was a friend of Lutini, a fellow Catholic. Rizzio and others also lent Lutini money for his journey. All seemed straightforward and above board, but it was to prove to be anything but, for Lutini's business abroad was nothing to do with the Queen, yet he had managed to coerce Rizzio into forging Mary's signature on the passport. Before that could be discovered, however, Lutini was on his way to Berwick, possibly hoping to meet up there with Moretta.

Unaware of this, Mary was coming to the conclusion that it was unwise to alienate the Kirk. On 7 January, at Moray's urging, she deprived Archbishop Hamilton of his consistorial jurisdiction[22] and, in so doing, said goodbye to any prospect of an annulment of her marriage. The only body in Scotland that now had the power to grant a divorce was the civil—and Protestant—Court of Session. Mary had effectively cut off her one lawful route of escape from her marriage to Darnley. The only honourable option left to her was reconciliation. The other option was murder.

On 9 January, Bedford reported that, although Darnley was full of the smallpox, relations between him and the Queen were "nothing amended." Nevertheless, she had sent her personal physician to him.[23] The *Book of Articles* later maliciously asserted "that she refused to send her mediciner or apothecary to visit him"; Buchanan claimed he had been sent for, "but she herself forbade him to go because she feared that, by his attentions, the sick man might escape death." Not only did Mary send her personal physician, she also gave orders for some of her linen to be cut into ruffs to edge the King's nightshirt.

Darnley sent several messages asking Mary to visit him,[24] but Buchanan says she "daily pretended to be on the point of going to Glasgow, while she awaited news of the King's death." Lennox claims that it was Mary who offered to visit Darnley, but that he replied insultingly, "if she come, it shall be to my comfort and she shall be welcome, but this much you shall declare unto her, that I wish Stirling to be Jedburgh, Glasgow to be the Hermitage, and I the Earl of Bothwell, as I lie here, and then I doubt not that she would be quickly with me, undesired."[25] It should be remembered that Lennox wrote this in 1568 with the intention of proving Mary guilty of Darnley's death, and that his *Narrative* is full of proven errors: this speech sounds very much as if it was invented with the benefit of hindsight.

Ostensibly, Mary did not visit Darnley because she was "very ill, having been injured by a fall from her horse at Seton."[26] This may have been a diplomatic excuse—there is no other record of this fall—for Mary cannot have relished the prospect of seeing Darnley, especially in view of the latest rumours accusing him of treasonable practices and the fact that, to visit him, she would have to go deep into Lennox territory, where she would be vulnerable to attempts to kidnap or kill her. There is evidence in Casket Letter II that she and Darnley were corresponding at this time, but the inference is that these letters were acrimonious.[27] Mary had no reason to believe that a meeting with Darnley would not be too.

That Mary took seriously the rumours that Darnley was plotting to seize young James is evident from her decision to remove her son from Stirling, which was too close to Lennox territory for her peace of mind, and keep him with her in Edinburgh. Another consideration was that, while Mar himself might be loyal, his Countess was of the Lennox affinity, being the sister of Tullibardine. On 10 January, presumably recovered from her fall, Mary set out, having announced, according to Buchanan, that she was moving the Prince to Edinburgh because Stirling Castle was "damp and cold." *The Book of Articles* goes so far as to suggest that Mary thought she could not sufficiently persuade her lover Bothwell of her favour "without she delivered her son also into his hands as a pledge thereof." Yet Bothwell had been away from court since 2 January, and would not return for at least another week; even then he would absent himself again for a time, and there is no evidence that James was delivered into his hands; even if he had been, Bothwell, with his record of staunch loyalty to the Crown, was the ideal choice of guardian, and Mary could have relied on him more than any other to keep her child safe.

On the day the Queen left for Stirling, Morton returned to Scotland, crossing the border at Berwick. From here, he wrote to Cecil, thanking him for his support.[28] The next day, Morton travelled via Wedderburn to Whittinghame Castle in East Lothian, the seat of his cousin, William Douglas. News of his arrival soon reached Bothwell in Dunbar, but it was a week before the Earl rode to Whittinghame, having in the meantime suffered a serious haemorrhage from one of his wounds.[29]

It was probably on Saturday, 11 January that Mary wrote the first of the notorious documents known as the Casket Letters. These letters will be discussed in full later, but the likelihood is that they were genuine letters of Mary's that were later doctored by her enemies in order to prove her guilty, not only of an adulterous relationship with Bothwell, but also of the murder of Darnley. Casket Letter I was almost certainly written to Bothwell, and its text is as follows:[30]

It seemeth that with your absence forgetfulness is joined, considering that at your departure you promised to send me news from you; nevertheless, I can learn none. And yet did I yesterday look for that [which] shall make me merrier than I shall be. I think you do the like for your return, prolonging it more than you have promised. As for me, if I hear no other matter of you, according to my commission, I bring the man [on] Monday to Craigmillar, where he shall be upon Wednesday; and I to go to Edinburgh to be let blood, if I have no word to the contrary.

He is the merriest that ever you saw, and doth remember unto me all that he can to make me believe that he loveth me. To conclude, you would say that he maketh love to me, wherein I take so much pleasure that I never come in there but my pain of my side doth take me: I have it sore today. If Paris doth bring back unto me that for which I have sent, it should much amend me.

I pray you send me word from you at large, and what I shall do if you be not returned when I shall be there; for, if you be not wise, I see assuredly all the whole burden fallen upon my shoulders. Provide for me, and consider well.

First of all, I send this present to Lethington to be delivered to you by Beaton, who goeth to one day of law of Lord Balfour.[31] I will say no more unto you, but that I pray God send me good news of your voyage. From Glasgow, this Saturday morning.

This letter is endorsed, in the hand of Cecil's clerk, "Proves her disdain against her husband." Yet it is unlikely that it refers to Darnley at all—it is far too affectionate, and at variance with the attitude expressed in the much more incriminating Casket Letter II—but to Prince James, who is referred to as "the man," a term of endearment that appears to have been used for children within the Guise family;[32] in other letters, Mary always refers to Darnley as "the King." Nor is this in any sense a love letter, but a complaint that Bothwell had not kept Mary informed of his dealings with Morton, about which she was naturally concerned, for much depended upon Morton's disposition towards both herself and Darnley. With the English succession almost in her grasp, as she believed, she would have wanted nothing to happen that might prejudice her prospects.

The absence of a salutation suggests that Casket Letter I was in fact a postscript to an official letter: Mary was often in the habit of adding such postscripts in her own hand, sometimes without a greeting or signature. This letter bears no signature—none of the Casket Letters does—but is subscribed "From Glasgow, this Saturday morning." This is probably a forged addition, as will be seen. The name of Maitland does not appear in the Scots translation, presumably to avoid incriminating him.

Nicholas Hubert, also known as "French" Paris or "Joachim," was a Frenchman who had once been in Bothwell's service, and later alleged that, for more than six years, he had been bullied, kicked and beaten by his master, although he may have deliberately blackened Bothwell's character, or been induced to under the threat of torture, in order to save his own skin. Paris had also worked for Lord Seton, and was now employed as a *valet de chambre* by the Queen,[33] who sometimes used him as a messenger between herself and Bothwell. Buchanan claims that Paris was "in special trust" with them "touching their secret affairs." It appears that he was more in Bothwell's confidence than Mary's.

In Casket Letter I, Mary instructed Paris to deliver her letter to Maitland, who would give it to either Archibald Beaton (a member of her household who was still in Mary's service in 1568) or John Beaton, Master of the

Queen's Household, to take to Bothwell, leaving Paris free to pick up some medicine for Mary in Edinburgh and return to her with it as soon as possible.

On 12 or 13 January, Mary left Stirling with James, spending the night as the guest of Lord Livingston at his fourteenth-century tower house at Callendar, near Falkirk, on the way.[34] She did not, after all, stop at Craigmillar, but travelled on with the Prince to Holyrood Palace, arriving on 13 or 14 January.[35] On her return, according to Buchanan, "she learned that the King was recovering. Once again, she proceeded to plan his death, and even admitted some noblemen to knowledge of her criminal intent. Some believed this offered a good opportunity for the Queen to summon him and, if he refused to come, openly to put him to death. There were some ready to do the deed. Others recommended that the crime should be committed secretly. All agreed that it should be done in haste before he had fully recovered." Other, more contemporary, evidence, shows that, rather than plotting Darnley's murder, Mary refused to become embroiled in plots against him, as will be seen. Had she really wished to encompass his death, she would have leapt at the chance of others doing the deed for her and taking the blame. In fact, some evidence suggests that, now that his health was improving, it was Darnley who was plotting murder.

On 14 January, on his return from Stirling, Joseph Rizzio received a shock. A member of the royal household called Timothy asked where Lutini's horses and clothes were. Rizzio told him that Lutini's clothes were in his box, but Lutini's servant, Lorenzo Cagnoli, had already informed Timothy that his master had taken everything with him, including his horses, and had told him, "I have properly tricked the Secretary [Rizzio], because he thinks that my clothes are in my box, but there is nothing there." Timothy, who had also lent Lutini money, now angrily turned on Rizzio, saying, "Thus have you tricked me, Mr. Secretary. The Queen shall do me right in this matter." He sought out Sebastien Pagez and made him tell Mary that Rizzio had assured him Lutini had gone to France on her affairs, and that he had lent Rizzio money, "and everyone began to say that there was some knavery afoot," that Rizzio knew of it, and that Lutini had rifled through the Queen's papers. Not wishing to be charged with forgery, Rizzio told Mary that Lutini had taken money from him and had promised to leave him his horses as security. Mary had presumably noticed that some of her bracelets were missing and asked where they were. Rizzio replied that Lutini had taken them with him and that they were in his purse with Rizzio's money. Pagez chimed in that Lutini owed him money also, at which Mary commanded Maitland to write in her name to Berwick, asking Sir William Drury to arrest Lutini and send him back to Edinburgh to face a charge of theft, for "he has lately left his charge" and "fraudulently taken with him the goods and money of divers of his friends and companions."[36] But Drury was away from Berwick just then.

This was certainly no straightforward case of theft, for it was soon to emerge that Rizzio had been acting in concert with Lutini and had lied to Mary and his friends; moreover, Lutini had the temerity to remain in Berwick, where he was almost certainly awaiting the arrival of Moretta, who, incidentally, did not reach London until about 18 January. Other evidence, which will be discussed in the next chapter, suggests that Lutini and Rizzio were working secretly for Darnley and that Lutini had been instructed to liaise with Moretta and, through him, with the King's allies abroad; it appears that, in lying about Lutini, Rizzio was protecting not only Darnley, but his own skin, for forgery was a capital offence.

Maitland had remained with the court since his marriage; he had been at Stirling until 14 January, and was in Edinburgh on the 17th, but soon afterwards left for Lethington. This, as will be seen, was not purely to honeymoon with his bride, for on 18 or 19 January[37] he rode to Whittinghame and met up with Bothwell, Morton and Morton's cousin, Archibald Douglas, a Lord of Session and brother of the Laird of Whittinghame. Douglas, who was a minister of the Kirk but had few virtues to qualify him for this calling, was married to Bothwell's sister, Jean Hepburn. In his time, he would become involved in treason, murder, espionage and forgery.

Bothwell's account of the meeting is succinct and deals only with the official reason for his visit; he says that Morton and Douglas "promised to forget all that was passed by, and, by the good offices of friends, to satisfy those whom they had formerly offended and bore hatred to."[38]

Morton, however, later claimed that Bothwell, "after long communing, proposed to me the purpose of the King's murder, seeing it was the Queen's mind that the King should be taken away. My answer was that I would not in any ways meddle in that matter." He had just been pardoned for one murder and did not wish to become involved in another. "After this, Mr. Archibald Douglas entered into conference with me for that purpose, persuading me to agree to the Earl of Bothwell. Bothwell earnestly proposed the same matter to me again, persuading me thereunto because it was the Queen's mind and she would have it done," whereupon Morton asked him to produce her warrant for the King's assassination. He also sent Archibald Douglas back with Bothwell and Maitland to Edinburgh to sound them out further on the matter, but they proved evasive. Morton later declared that, if the Queen had granted his pardon on condition that he murder Darnley, he would have rejected it out of hand and gone back into exile rather than agree to commit such a foul crime.

Many years later, in 1583, Archibald Douglas wrote his version of events to Mary,[39] stating that Bothwell and Maitland had indeed met Morton at Whittinghame, but "what speech passed between them, as God shall be my judge, I knew nothing at that time, but at their departure I was requested by Morton to accompany them to Edinburgh and to return with such answer as they should obtain of Your Majesty." He added,

It is known to all men, as well by letters passed between [Morton] and [Maitland] when they became in diverse factions, as also a book set forth by the ministers, wherein they affirm that Morton has confessed to them, before his death, that Bothwell came to Whittinghame to propose the calling away of the King your husband, to the which proposition Morton affirms that he could give no answer until such time as he might know Your Majesty's mind therein, which he never received.

It is unlikely, given what happened at Kirk o'Field, that Douglas was telling Mary the whole truth. He was, after all, trying to save his neck at the time. Furthermore, in 1581, Morton "confessed his cousin, Archibald Douglas, came to him with a plan for the murder, to which he neither lent approval or help."[40] It would appear, therefore, that Archibald Douglas had already offered Bothwell his support and that he came to Whittinghame for the specific purpose of persuading Morton to do the same.

There are some grounds for believing that Bothwell produced the Craigmillar Bond at Whittinghame and that Morton and Douglas willingly signed it. It has been claimed that they had a strong motive, besides revenge, for doing so, for in December, Mary would be twenty-five, the age at which Scottish monarchs legally came of age; any grants made by her or in her name during her minority could be revoked at that time. Morton and his kinsfolk had received generous gifts of Crown lands from the Queen over the years, but Darnley was known to disapprove of this, and they feared that his influence would prevail. Yet at this time, Darnley exerted virtually no influence at all over Mary, nor did it look as if he ever would again. In 1581, Morton finally admitted that he had known in advance of the plot to murder Darnley, but that he had refused to become actively involved in it, which was almost certainly the truth; even so, at the time, he lifted no finger to warn his kinsman. This was the vengeance he doubtless felt that Darnley deserved. If others were prepared to exact it for him, there was no reason for him to get blood on his hands.

Darnley's murder was almost certainly discussed at Whittinghame, whoever introduced the subject, although it was not until 1581 that the meeting became public knowledge. Maitland's presence there is proof that he was a part of the conspiracy; he had, after all, initiated it with Moray at Craigmillar.

Bothwell was now a key figure in the plot against Darnley. It is likely that he already had a strong motive for wanting him dead, for, having had time to ponder the consequences of the King's murder, he had almost certainly resolved to marry Mary himself once she was free, and rule Scotland with her, which would explain why he was pursuing his plans so vigorously. According to Melville, he was already "ruling all at court" and had become very friendly with Morton. Bothwell was therefore in a strong enough position to bend men to his will. The evidence, hostile though it is, suggests that he was enlisting support for the plot on the pretext that the Queen had given her approval; whether she had in fact done so is another matter. If they thought she had not, men might not have been so ready to do her such a service.

In his memoir of 1568, however, Bothwell paints himself as an innocent and others as the villains. He says that, after he had helped to obtain a pardon for the exiles, "I thought about retiring to a peaceful life, after the imprisonment and exile I had suffered, and having no more to do with vengeance and strife." He claims that those who had benefited from the pardon "made themselves so obedient and appeared so kindly disposed to everyone that all the nobles and gentlemen of the kingdom were delighted, imagining all quarrels at court to be at an end. But despite this, the conspirators never lost sight of their wicked plans, and plotted night and day for the death of the King." It was more than his life was worth at the time he wrote this to reveal that he had been plotting with them.

Something of what had taken place at the Craigmillar Conference was now known in London. On 18 January 1567, de Silva reported: "The displeasure of the Queen of Scotland with her husband is carried so far that she was approached by some who wanted to induce her to allow a plot to be formed against him, but she refused. But she nevertheless shows him no affection. They ought to come to terms for, if they do not look out for themselves, they are in a bad way."[41] This report corroborates other evidence that Mary was aware of a plot against Darnley. It has been conjectured that Moretta, who arrived in London around the date on which this report was written, was de Silva's informant.

It was probably on 19 or 20 January that Bothwell, Maitland and Archibald Douglas arrived at Holyrood, where Bothwell and Maitland sought Mary's sanction and safeguard for the Bond against Darnley. But, without hesitation, she refused, commanding them to instruct Douglas to "show to the Earl of Morton that the Queen will have no speech of the matter." Douglas "craved that the answer might be more sensible," but Maitland said that Morton "would sufficiently understand it."[42] In 1583, when Archibald Douglas wrote reminding Mary of these events, she did not deny that they had taken place.[43]

Around this time, Mary received an indication that something else was underhand was going on. "A person named John Shaw came to tell the Queen that Andrew Ker of Fawdonside had returned to Scotland from England" and that, although few were prepared to shelter him, he was boasting "that, within fifteen days, there would be a great change in the court, that he would soon be in greater credit than ever, and he would boldly inquire how the Queen was."[44] Given that Fawdonside's pardon had probably been granted by

Darnley, there is every reason to believe that, in return for it, he had agreed to become involved in the latter's traitorous schemes. The reference to Mary's health was almost certainly sinister, but Ker's intentions towards Darnley may have been more sinister still.

Mary now had evidence that two conspiracies were afoot: that of the Lords against Darnley, and that of Darnley against herself. Of the former, she could be in no doubt that the nobles were determined to bring Darnley down and perhaps kill him; nevertheless, she may have felt that her refusal to sanction any move against him would act as a brake upon their designs. Of the latter, she knew only garbled details that were not necessarily linked to each other, but that was enough to set alarm bells ringing in her head. Since Rizzio's murder, she had lived in fear that Darnley would again plot against her.

On 20 January, Mary wrote to Archbishop Beaton in Paris, relating the affair of Walker and Hiegait.[45] It is evident from this letter that she suspected that the rumours of Darnley's activities were true:

> As for the King our husband, God knows always our part towards him, and his behaviour and thankfulness towards us is similarly well known to God and the world; specially, our own impartial subjects see it and, in their hearts, we doubt not, condemn the same. Always, we perceive him occupied and busy enough to inquire of our doings, which, God willing, shall always be such as none report of us anyway but honourably, however he, his father and their faction speak, which we know want no goodwill to make us have ado [trouble], if their power were equal to their minds. But God moderates their forces well enough, and takes the means of execution of their intentions from them. For, as we believe, they shall find none, or very few, approvers of their counsels and devices imagined for our displeasure or misliking.

In view of what was to come, it is important to remember Mary's bitterness towards, and contempt for, Darnley, as expressed in this letter. There is no evidence in it that she was contemplating a reconciliation.

Unable to bear the uncertainty any longer, Mary had decided to go to Glasgow and confront her errant husband. She had resolved to leave on the very day on which she had written to Beaton. It was a courageous decision, for she knew she might be placing herself in grave danger. But Darnley had to be stopped.

Many years later, Melville looked back on this period of mounting crisis with what must have been a shudder. "The days were evil," he wrote; "it was a busy time."

14

"Some Suspicion of What Afterwards Happened"

⌐

M ARY INTENDED NOT ONLY TO confront Darnley, but to bring him back to Edinburgh, where she could keep him under her eye. She must, however, have been aware that, in so doing, she was bringing him into the orbit of men who had signed a bond against him, or who had compelling reasons for seeking revenge on him. Yet she also had evidence that he was conspiring against her, and if that were so, she dared not leave him where he was, at the centre of the Lennox power base.

Mary had the ideal pretext for visiting Darnley for, according to Leslie, he had asked her to do so. Leslie also says that Darnley returned to Edinburgh "by the advice of the nobility and the physicians." It may be that Mary had confided her fears of a conspiracy to her Lords, and that they, having their own secret agenda, urged her to remove the King from Glasgow.

It has often been said that Mary had taken pity on Darnley and genuinely wished for a reconciliation, but this is at variance with the attitude towards him expressed in her letter to Archbishop Beaton and with the other evidence. The time to have taken pity on him was when he had been really ill, but she had now learned that he was getting better.

It has been suggested that Mary wished to bring about a reconciliation, or the semblance of one, in case she became—or already was—pregnant by

Bothwell; Darnley could then be passed off as the father, to avoid scandal. This presupposes that Mary and Bothwell were already lovers, of which there is no satisfactory proof, although she had certainly come to rely on him heavily. It will also be shown, in due course, that Mary is unlikely to have conceived, or been expecting, a child at this time. Finally, Mary's physician must have informed her of the true nature of Darnley's disease; it is hardly likely that she would have wished to resume marital relations with him now, at such risk to herself, and there was no telling how long it would be before he was cured.

The most serious accusation that has been levelled against Mary is that, at Bothwell's urging, she deliberately lured Darnley to Edinburgh to meet his death. Yet the evidence shows that she had already refused on several occasions to sanction any plot against him. Darnley certainly posed a danger to her, and she had every reason for wishing to be rid of him, but she would have had to be a duplicitous character indeed to have consistently rejected all suggestions of assassination, and to have sent her own doctor to him, had she been secretly planning to have him murdered. After all, Bothwell, whom her enemies later claimed had incited her to bring Darnley to Edinburgh, was the same man who had allegedly asked her to sign a warrant authorising Darnley's removal, which she had refused to do. She is hardly likely to have been so inconsistent.

Furthermore, in bringing Darnley to Edinburgh, Mary may have reasoned that she could protect him from those who meant him ill. The last thing she wanted at this time was a scandal that might prejudice the imminent negotiations with England. Without Darnley, her claim to the English throne would have been considerably weakened in the eyes of many of Elizabeth's subjects. She therefore had every reason to keep him alive. It was also imperative that she and he appeared to be on good terms, for the English would not want a queen to whom scandal had been constantly attached, and the very public breakdown of her marriage did not augur well for the future stability of either kingdom. As will be seen, she herself is said to have stated that she intended a reconciliation.

Probably unwittingly, therefore, Mary played straight into the hands of Bothwell, Maitland, Douglas and—almost certainly—Moray. Escorted by Bothwell, Huntly and a party of mounted arquebusiers. Mary left Edinburgh on 20 January for Glasgow;[1] she took with her a horse-litter for conveying her sick husband back to Edinburgh. On the way, she stayed one night with Lord Livingston at Callendar House, and probably sent a summons from there to the Hamiltons to escort her to Glasgow, for, on the 21st, Bothwell and Huntly had to return to Edinburgh;[2] Bothwell had pressing business to attend to in the Borders. The fact that Mary summoned the Hamiltons, who were—as Buchanan correctly pointed out—deadly enemies of the Lennoxes, shows that she had not come to Glasgow in the spirit of reconciliation.

Paris was among those in attendance on Mary; according to his later deposition, which should not be regarded as reliable evidence since it was almost certainly obtained under torture, he carried letters and messages between the Queen and Bothwell at this time.

Archbishop Hamilton,[3] Sir James Hamilton, the Laird of Luss and about forty other gentlemen gathered and, on 22 January,[4] accompanied Mary into Glasgow. Lennox was conspicuous by his absence from the reception party, but had sent Darnley's gentleman, Captain Thomas Crawford of Jordanhill, a staunch Lennox man,

to show her cause why he came not to meet her himself, praying Her Grace not to think it was either for stout stomach [pride] or for not knowing his duty towards Her Highness, but only for want of health, and also that he would not presume to come in her presence until he knew farther her mind, because of the sharp words that she had spoken of him to Robert Cunningham, his servant, in Stirling, whereby he thought he was in Her Majesty's displeasure.

Mary answered "that there was no recipe against fear." Crawford replied "that My Lord had no fear for anything he knew in himself, but only of the cold and unkindly words she had spoken to his servant." Mary retorted that "he would not be afraid [if] he were not culpable," whereupon Crawford said he "knew so far of His Lordship that there was nothing he desired more than the secrets of every creature's heart were written in their face." Clearly angered, Mary asked him if he had any further commission, and when he said no, curtly commanded him to hold his peace.[5]

Glasgow, which lies on the banks of the River Clyde, was then a small city with a cathedral dating from 1175, a famous university that had been founded in 1451, and a concentration of houses, gardens and orchards. Another prominent building was Lennox Castle at Stable Green, which occupied the site of the present Glasgow Royal Infirmary. Since Darnley and his father were both lying ill in the castle, Mary appears to have lodged either in the episcopal palace, which had been unoccupied since 1560, when Archbishop Beaton had been sent as Scotland's ambassador to Paris, or at Crookston Castle, another Lennox stronghold, standing high above the city, which had a central tower and moat and dated from the fifteenth century. It is also claimed that Mary stayed at the Provand's House, or "Lordship," Glasgow's oldest surviving mediaeval house, dating from 1471, but that seems less likely. Wherever it was the Queen lodged, she was guarded by the Hamiltons and her arquebusiers.

On 22 January, du Croc had left Edinburgh for Paris. With him, he took Mary's letter for Archbishop Beaton, and "some suspicion of what afterwards happened"; later, he claimed he had not been "ignorant of the Lord Darnley's death to draw nigh."[6] There is no way of knowing how he came to have these suspicions, and he may have seen some remarks or events as significant only with the benefit of hindsight.

Mary did not visit Darnley on the day she arrived in Glasgow because "he was in so bad a state with the eruptions on his face that he begged her not to see him till he was somewhat better, to which she agreed."[7] The next day, he changed his mind and agreed to receive her.

Mary's interviews with Darnley on 23 January and the following days were recorded both in Casket Letter II and by Thomas Crawford, who claimed that Darnley afterwards told him what had transpired and asked him to report it to Lennox. There is evidence, however, that Crawford's Deposition of 1568 was constructed from Casket Letter II, as there are remarkable similarities between them, and some passages appear to have been copied word for word, one of them 300 words long, which is too much to be coincidental. It may be that Crawford wrote a report at the time and later, at the instance of the Privy Council, improved on it, or amended it, by referring to Casket Letter II.

The Deposition exists in its draft form, with numerous corrections and alterations,[8] and a doctored version was presented as evidence to the English Commissioners in 1568.[9] Because it was produced for propaganda purposes, it should be treated with caution. Some historians believe that the Deposition is a complete forgery but, if so, why does it not refer to Darnley's jealousy of Bothwell? On the contrary, it reflects fairly accurately the tensions between Mary and Darnley.

On the 23rd, Darnley was in a truculent but apparently contrite mood. According to Crawford, after a short conversation, Mary demanded of him why he had complained in his letters "of the cruelty of some. He answered that he complained not without cause, as he believed she would grant herself, when she was well advised." When she inquired about his sickness, he accused her of being the cause of it, adding,

> You asked me what I meant by the cruelty contained in my letters; it is of you only, that will not accept my offers and repentance. I confess that I have failed in some things, and such like greater faults have been made to you sundry times, which you have forgiven. I am but young, and you will say you have forgiven me sundry times. May not a man of my age, for lack of counsel, of which I am very destitute, fall twice or thrice, and yet repent himself and be chastised by experience. If I have made any fail, I crave your pardon and protest that I shall never fail again. I desire no other thing but that we may be together as husband and wife, and, if you will not consent hereto, I desire never to rise forth of this bed. Therefore, I pray you, give me an answer hereunto. God knoweth how I am punished for making my god of you and for having no other thought but on you. And if at any time I offend you, you are the cause for it. When any offendeth me, if for my refuge I might disclose my heart to you, I would speak it to no other; but when anything is spoken to me, and you and I not being as husband and wife ought to be, necessity compelleth me to keep it in my breast, and bringeth me in such melancholy as you see I am.

Illness, it appeared, had wrought a great change in Darnley, but Mary was unsure that it was genuine. She asked him, out of the blue, "why he would have passed away with the English ship. He answered that he had spoken with the Englishman, but not of mind to go away with him, and if he had, it had not been without cause, in respect of the manner how he was used, for he had [money] neither to sustain himself nor his servants, and need not to make further discourse thereof, for she knew it as well as he.

"Then she asked him the purpose of Hiegait. He answered that it was told him. She required how and by whom it was told him. He answered that the Laird of Minto told him that there was a letter presented to her in Craigmillar, made by her own advice and subscribed by certain others, who desired her to subscribe the same, which she refused to do." Clearly, Darnley was well informed, although the facts had become somewhat garbled in the telling. He assured her that "he would never trust that she, who was his own proper flesh, would do him any evil, and if any other would do it, they should buy it dear, except they took him sleeping, albeit he suspected nobody. So he desired her effectuously that she would bear him company, for she found ever some ado to draw herself from him to her own lodging, and would never remain with him past two hours together at once."

It appears Mary was having trouble believing Darnley's protestations of loyalty and devotion, for he had not satisfactorily explained away the allegations of Walker, but had harped on the conspiracy against himself; she remained "very pensive, whereat he found fault." Then abruptly, he said he had heard she had brought a litter with her. She told him she intended to take him back to Edinburgh with her but she had understood that he was not able to ride a horse, so she had brought the litter to have him carried "more softly." Darnley answered "that it was not meet for a sick man to travel that could not sit on a horse, and especially in so cold weather." Mary told him that she was taking him to convalesce at Craigmillar, "where she might be with him and not far from her son." He had little choice in the matter, so he told her that he would go, but only on one condition: "that was, that he and she might be together at bed and board as husband and wife, and that she should leave him no more. And if she would promise him it, upon her word, he would go with her where she pleased, without respect of any danger or sickness wherein he was. And if she would not grant him the same, he would not go with her in no wise."

Mary replied that it was for that that she had come, "and if she had not been minded thereto, she had not come so far to fetch him, and so she granted his desire, and promised him that it should be as he had spoken, and thereupon gave him her hand and faith of her body that she would love him and use him as her husband." Then caution overrode her, and she insisted that, "notwithstanding, before they could be together, he must be purged and cleansed of his sickness, which she trusted should be shortly, for she minded to give him the bath at Craigmillar."

Darnley said "he would do whatsoever she would he do, and would love all that she loved," but "she required him in especial whom he loved of the nobility and whom he hated. He answered that he hated no man, and loved all alike well. She asked him how he liked the Lady Reres, and if he were angry with her." (This seems to have been a later interpolation, inserted after Buchanan's libel naming Lady Reres as Bothwell's procuress had become officially received wisdom.) Darnley merely said "he had little mind of such as she was, and wished of God that she might serve her to her honour."

Then Mary "desired him that he would keep to himself the promise between him and her, and declare it to nobody, for peradventure the Lords would not think good of their sudden agreement, considering he and they were at some words before." Darnley said "he knew no cause why they should mislike of it, and desired her that she would not move any of them against him, like as he would persuade not against her, and that they would work both in one mind, otherwise it might turn to greater inconvenience to them both." Mary replied that "she never sought any way by him, but he was in the fault himself. He answered again that his faults were published, and that there were [those] that made greater faults than ever he made that [he] believed were unknown, and yet they would speak of great and small." Mary asked him "if he might be ready to travel at that time," but his answer is unrecorded.

Several things emerge from this conversation. Firstly, Mary had achieved her stated purpose, which was to persuade Darnley to come to Edinburgh and, although she was uncomfortable in his company, to arrive at a better understanding with him. This is corroborated by a report by a French agent, the Seigneur de Clernault,[10] who stated that entire confidence had been restored between the King and Queen, and by Lennox,[11] Leslie and Nau. It was not out of character for Mary to show such forgiveness to Darnley, since she had done so to the Lords who had been involved in the Chaseabout Raid and the murder of Rizzio. Secondly, her doubts about Darnley's loyalty were unresolved. Thirdly, he was aware that, in leaving Glasgow and the protection of the Lennox affinity, which was certainly against his father's wishes,[12] he might be putting himself in danger. Fourthly, he had almost certainly not been honest with her about his plans for the future; he had meekly agreed to return with her and shown himself unusually trusting of Mary to protect him. Either it suited him to go to Edinburgh, because there he would be better placed to bring his schemes to fruition; or Mary's promise of a resumption of sexual relations heralded, in his mind, his return to power. Lastly, Mary feared the Lords finding out about her reconciliation with Darnley; given their hatred of him, they would be reluctant to accept his restoration to favour and influence, and this might be all that was needed to precipitate the carrying out of their plan to do away with him. It was perhaps not so much for his health as for his own safety that she chose to house him initially at Craigmillar. Given time, and his improved behaviour, his enemies might grow to tolerate him.

After Mary had left, Darnley asked Crawford what he thought of his journeying to Edinburgh. "I answered that I liked it not, because she took him to Craigmillar; for if she had desired him with herself, or to have had his company, she would have taken him to his own house in Edinburgh, where she might more easily visit him than to travel two miles out of the town. Therefore, my opinion was that she took him away more like a prisoner than her husband." Darnley said "that he thought little less himself, and found himself indeed [a prisoner], save the confidence he had in her promise only; notwithstanding, he would go with her, and put himself in her hands, though she should cut his throat, and besought God to have mercy on them both." This passage seems all too contrived: Mary's detractors from Buchanan down have often concluded that she planned to lure Darnley to Craigmillar so that he could be murdered there, and that he feared just this because his enemies had plotted against him there, but in fact the choice of Craigmillar would have been a sensible one, not only because of the healthier air and greater security, but also because Prince James was at Holyrood and Mary did not wish to expose him to any risk of infection.

Mary's enemies later claimed that, while she was at Glasgow, she wrote Casket Letter II to Bothwell. This is by far the longest, most compromising and most controversial of the Casket Letters, and it seems to have been written during at least two sittings, the first of which was allegedly on 23 January.

The composition of the letter suggests that it was an amalgamation of two letters—not necessarily by the same writer—since the tone becomes more emotional and conscience-stricken halfway through and there are unnecessary repetitions. One of these letters was almost certainly a report written by Mary to Moray, Maitland or Bothwell on her interview with Darnley, and the other either a more personal letter to Bothwell—which would be most damning—or a complete forgery. There is no greeting, of course, but Moray's Journal[13] states that at this time Mary was writing letters to Bothwell; and Paris, in his second deposition, claimed that he delivered this letter to Bothwell and carried back an answer the next day, which cannot have reached her before she left Glasgow. Casket Letter II cannot have been written in its entirety to Maitland or Moray because in it they are referred to in the third person. The 3,132-word letter is here quoted at length because of its crucial importance, and the abridged text is as follows:[14]

> Being gone from the place where I had left my heart, it may be easily judged what my countenance was, considering what the body [is] without [the] heart, which was cause that till dinner I had used little talk, neither would anybody venture [to] advance himself thereunto, thinking that it was not good so to do.

There follows the passage recounting Mary's exchange with Crawford and other events relating to her arrival in Glasgow. She adds:

> Not one of the town is come to speak with me, which maketh me to think that they be his [Lennox's], and they so speaketh well of them [the Lennoxes], at least his son.
>
> The King sent for Joachim [Paris] and asked him why I did not lodge nigh to him, and that he would rise sooner, and why I came, whether it were for any good appointment that he came, and whether I had not taken Paris and Gilbert to write, and that I sent Joseph [Lutini]. I wonder who hath told him so much, even of the [coming] marriage of Bastien [Pagez]. This bearer shall tell you more upon that.

This suggests that Darnley had at least one spy at court, and it has been argued that this was Sir James Balfour, which is quite possible. The reference to Bastien's wedding has been seen as sinister, for it was on the night after that wedding that Darnley was murdered. The implication is perhaps that Mary feared Darnley might find out what she and Bothwell had planned for that night, but that is improbable, for at this time the intention was to take him to Craigmillar, not Kirk o'Field, and it is clear that the gunpowder plot was not decided upon until after Darnley had gone to Kirk o'Field. An alternative theory is that Darnley was hoping to use Bastien's wedding as cover for his own treacherous plans, but he could not, at this stage, have predicted Mary's movements on that day. Mary's reference to the wedding is therefore probably innocuous, and merely illustrates her concern that Darnley was so well informed.

The next section of the letter reports the conversation that Crawford recorded, and it will be seen that the two passages have great similarity, although the account in Casket Letter II is more detailed in parts.

I asked him [Darnley] of his letters and where he did complain of the cruelty of some of them. He said that he did dream, and that he was so glad to see me that he thought he should die; indeed, that he has found fault with me that I was pensive.[15]

I went my way to sup. He [Darnley] prayed me to come again, which I did, and he told me his grief, and that he would make no testament but leave all unto me, and that I was the cause of his sickness for the sorrow he had, that I was so strange unto him. "And [said he] you asked what I meant in my letter to speak of cruelty. It was of your cruelty, who will not accept my offers and repentance. I avow that I have done amiss, but not that [which] I have also always disavowed, and so have many other of your subjects done, and you have well pardoned them. I am young. You will say that you have also pardoned me in my time and that I return to my fault. May not a man of my age, for want of counsel, fail twice or thrice and at the last repent and rebuke himself by his experience? If I may obtain this pardon, I protest I will not make fault again. And I ask nothing but that we may be at bed and table together as husband and wife; and if you will not, I will never rise from this bed. I pray you tell me your resolution hereof. God knoweth that I am punished for having made my god of you and had no other mind but of you. And when I offend you sometime, you are cause thereof: for if I thought, when anybody doth any wrong to me, that I might for my resource make my moan thereof unto you, I would open it to no other. But when I hear anything, being not familiar with you, I must keep it in my mind, and that troubleth my wit for anger."[16]

I did still answer him, but that I shall be too long. In the end, I asked him whether he would go in the English ship. He doth disavow it and sweareth so, and confesseth to have spoken to the men.

Afterwards, I asked him of the inquisition of Hiegait. He denied it till I told him the very words, [then he said] that it was said that some of the Council had brought me a letter to sign to put him in prison and to kill him if he did resist, and that he asked this of Minto himself, who said unto him that he thought it was true. I will talk with him tomorrow upon that point. The rest as Willie Hiegait hath confessed, but it was the next day that he came hither.

In the end, he desired much that I should lodge in his lodging. I have refused it. I have told him that he must be purged, and that could not be done here. He said unto me, "I have heard say that you have brought the litter, but I would rather have gone with yourself." I told him that I would myself bring him to Craigmillar, that the physicians and I also might cure him without being far from my son. He said that he was ready when I would, so as I would assure him of his request.

He hath no desire to be seen, and waxeth angry when I speak to him of Walker, and saith that he will pluck his ears from his head and that he lieth. For I asked him before of that and what cause he had to complain of some of the Lords and to threaten them. He denieth it and saith that he had already prayed them to think no such matter of him. As for myself, he would rather lose his life than do me the least displeasure, and then used so many kinds of flatteries so coldly and wisely as you would marvel at. I had forgotten that he said that he could not mistrust me for Hiegait's word, for he could not believe that his own flesh (which was myself) would do him any hurt; and indeed it was said that I refused to have him to subscribe the same.[17] But for the others he would at least sell his life dear enough, but that he did suspect nobody, nor would, but love all that I did love.

He would not let me go, but would have me to watch with him. I made as though I thought all to be true, and that I would think about it, and have excused myself from sitting up with him this night, for he saith that he sleepeth not. You have never heard him speak better nor more humbly, and if I had not proof of his heart to be as wax, and that mine were not as a diamond, no stroke but coming from your hand would make me but to have pity on him. But fear not, for the place [i.e., her love or loyalty] shall continue till death. Remember also, in recompense thereof, not to suffer yours to be won by that false race [probably the Countess Jean] that would do no less to yourself. I think they [Darnley and Jean] have been at school together.

He has always the tears in his eye. He saluteth every man, even to the meanest, and maketh much of them that they may take pity of him. His father has bled this day at the nose and at the mouth—guess what token that is. I have not seen him: he is in his chamber. The King is so desirous that I should give him meat with my own hands, but trust you no more there where you are than I do here.

In sixteenth-century France, bleeding from the nose was believed to indicate fear. Lennox was certainly fearful of Mary, and with good reason, for if Darnley's conspiracy were to be discovered, there would be no mercy for either of them.

This is my first day.[18] I will end [the letter] tomorrow. I write all, how little consequence soever it be, to the end that you may take of the whole that shall be best for you to judge. I do here a work that I hate much, but I had begun it this morning.[19] Had you not list to laugh, to see me so trimly make a lie, at the least dissemble, and to mingle truth therewith.

He hath almost told me all on the Bishop's behalf, and of Sutherland, without touching any word unto him of that which you had told me, but only by much flattering him and praying him, and by my complaining of the Bishop, I have taken the worms out of his nose. You have heard the rest.

"The Bishop" may refer to the Nuncio, Mondovi, with whom there is reason to believe Darnley may have been in contact. The fact that he is not named implies that Bothwell and Mary were already aware of his dealings with Darnley, but it may be that the messenger had instructions to give Bothwell a verbal account of Darnley's dealings with him, as confessed to Mary, which is suggested by the last sentence in the paragraph. Sutherland was a staunch Catholic, and was perhaps one of Darnley's supporters, although there is no evidence that Mary took any reprisals against him for it. The sentence "I have taken the worms out of his nose" means "I have drawn it all out of him," and is a French colloquialism that appears in another letter of Mary's, dated 5 October 1568.[20]

> We are tied by two false races [Lennoxes and Gordons]. The good Devil[21] sunder us, and God knit us together for ever for the most faithful couple that ever He did knit together. This is my faith: I will die in it.
>
> Excuse it if I write ill. You must guess the one half I cannot do withal, for I am ill at ease, and glad to write unto you when other folk be asleep, seeing that I cannot do as they do [i.e., sleep], according to my desire, that is, between your arms, my dear life, whom I beseech God to preserve from all ill, and send you good rest as I go to seek mine, till tomorrow in the morning that will end my note.[22] But it grieveth me that it should let [prevent] me from writing unto you of news of myself, so much I have to write.
>
> Send me word what you have determined hereupon, that we may know the one the other's mind for marring of anything.
>
> I am weary, and am going to sleep, and yet I cannot forbear scribbling so long as there is any paper. Cursed be this pocky fellow [Darnley] that troubleth me thus much, for I had a pleasanter matter to discourse unto you, but for him. He is not much the worse, but he is ill arrayed.[23] I thought I should have been killed with his breath, for it is worse than your uncle's breath, and yet I was sat no nearer to him than in a chair by his bolster,[24] and he lieth at the further side of the bed.

The reference to "your uncle" has been seen as proof that this part of the letter was not addressed to Bothwell, since he did not have an uncle as such; however, the writer may be referring to his great-uncle, the promiscuous Bishop of Moray, who may have been syphilitic, which would perhaps account for his foul breath. Furthermore, this part of the letter is written in more emotional language than the section in which Mary gives an account of her interview with Darnley, and is not likely to have formed part of the report. This reference to "your uncle" is not the only example of the forger's carelessness, as will be seen.

The first section of the letter appears to end at this point, and there follows a list of subjects that the writer has obviously intended as an *aide-mémoire*, to remind her to include them in the letter. They read:

The message of the father, by the way.
The talk of Sir James Hamilton [surname deleted] of the ambassador.
That the Lord of Luss hath told me of the delay.
The questions that he [Darnley] asked of Joachim.
Of my state.
Of my company.
And of Joseph.
The talk that he [Darnley] and I had, and of his desire to please me, of his repentance, and of the interpretation of his letter.
Of Will Hiegait's doing, and of his departure, and of the Lord of Livingston.

Most of these subjects had already been covered; later on, the writer refers to running out of paper and being obliged to use her memo sheet.

The letter then continues:

I had forgotten of the Lord of Livingston, that he at supper said softly to the Lady Reres, that he drank to the persons I knew of, if I would pledge them. And after supper, he said softly to me, when I was leaning upon him and warming myself, "You may well go and see sick folk, yet can you not be so welcome unto them as you have this day left somebody in pain." I asked him who it was; he took me about the body and said, "One of his folks that has left you this day." Guess you the rest.

This day I have wrought till two of the clock on this bracelet, to put the key in the cleft of it, which is tied with two laces. I have had so little time that it is very ill, but I will make a fairer; and in the meantime take heed that none of those that be here do see it, for I have made it in haste in their presence.

Some writers have seen a connection between this bracelet and the ones stolen by Lutini, but there is no evidence of any. What is significant is that Mary warned Bothwell not to let anyone see the bracelet she was making for him, presumably because people might draw conclusions at the sight of such a personal gift.

Mary apparently completed the above section of the letter in the early hours of 24 January. In the morning, she resumed her writing again:

I go to my tedious talk [i.e., with Darnley]. You make me dissemble so much that I am afraid thereof with horror, and you make me almost play the part of a traitor. Remember that, if it were not for obeying, I had rather be dead. My heart bleedeth for it.

After seeing Darnley, Mary continued, opening with a phrase she often used, "summa" or "en somme" (literally "in sum"):

To be short, he will not come but with condition that I shall promise to be with him as heretofore at bed and board, and that I shall forsake him no more; and upon my word, he will do whatever I will, and will come, but he hath prayed me to tarry till after tomorrow.

He hath spoken at the first more stoutly, as this bearer shall tell you, upon the matter of the Englishman, and of his departure, but in the end he cometh to his gentleness again.

He hath told me, among other talk, that he knew well that my brother [Moray] hath told me at Stirling that which he had said there, whereof he denied the half, and specially that he was in his chamber. But now, to make him trust me, I must feign something unto him; and therefore, when he desired me to promise that, when he should be well, we should make but one bed, I told him, feigning to believe his fair promises, that if he did not change his mind between this time and that, I was contented so as he would say nothing thereof: for (to tell it between us two), the Lords wished no ill to him, but did fear lest, considering the threatening which he made in case we did agree together, he would make them feel the small account they have made of him, and that he would persuade me to pursue some of them, and for this respect should be in jealousy if, at one instance, without their knowledge, I did raise the game to the contrary in their presence.

And he said unto me, very pleasant and merry, "Think you that they do the more esteem you therefor? But I am glad that you talked to me of the Lords. I hope that you desire now that we shall live a happy life; for if it were otherwise, it could not be but greater inconvenience should happen to us both than you think. But I will do now whatsoever you will have me do. I will love all those that you shall love, and so you make them to love me also. For so as they seek not my life, I love them all equally." Thereupon I have willed this bearer to tell you many pretty things, for I have too much to write and it is late, and I trust him, upon your word. To be short [summa], he will go anywhere on my word.

Alas! I never deceived anybody, but I remit myself wholly to your will; and send me word what I shall do, and, whatsoever happen to me, I will obey you. Think also if you will not find some invention more secret by physic, for he is to take physic at Craigmillar, and the baths also, and shall not come forth of long time.

In *The Book of Articles*, it is alleged that, whilst at Glasgow, Mary "wrote to Bothwell to see if he might find out a more secret [way] by medicine to cut [Darnley] off." Lennox claims that Mary also wrote in this letter "that Bothwell should in no wise fail to despatch his wife, and to give her the drink as they had devised before," which is what de Silva heard, but there is no evidence of this in the surviving text. It could be that Lennox had seen an early draft of the doctored letter, but if that was so, it was far more logical for any forger to have retained such incriminating evidence than to have edited it out. The conclusion must be, therefore, that Lennox had made up this detail.

The letter continues:

To be short [summa], for that I can learn, he hath great suspicion, and yet nevertheless trusteth upon my word, but not to tell me as yet anything; howbeit, if you will that I shall avow him, I will know all of him; but I shall never be willing to beguile one that putteth his trust in me.

Nevertheless, you may do all, and do not esteem me the less therefor, for you are the cause thereof. For, for my own revenge, I would not do it.

He giveth me certain charges, and these strong, that I fear even to say that his faults be published, but there be [some] that commit some secret faults and fear not to have them spoken of loudly, and that there is speech of great and small. And even touching the Lady Reres, he said, "God grant that she serve to your honour." And that any may not think, nor he neither, that mine own power was not in myself, seeing I did refuse his offers. To conclude [summa], for a surety, he mistrusteth of that that you know, and for his life. But in the end, after I had spoken two or three good words to him, he was very merry and glad.

This passage presumably refers to Darnley's fear of Morton and his reliance on Mary to protect him. She goes on:

I have not seen him this night for ending your bracelet, but I can find no clasps for it; it is ready thereunto, and yet I fear lest it should bring you ill hap, or that should be known if you were hurt. Send me word whether you will have it, and more money, and how far I may speak. Now, so far as I perceive, I may do much with you;[25] guess you whether I shall not be suspected. As for the rest, he is mad when he hears of Lethington and of you and my brother. Of your brother [in law? Huntly?] he sayeth nothing, but of the Earl of Argyll he doth. I am afraid of him to hear him talk; at the last, he assured himself that he [Argyll] hath no ill opinion of him. He speaketh nothing of these abroad, neither good nor ill, but avoided speaking of him. His father keepeth his chamber: I have not seen him.

All the Hamiltons be here, who accompany me very honestly. All the friends of the others do come always when I go to visit him. He hath sent to me and prayeth me to see him rise tomorrow in the morning early. To be short, this bearer shall declare unto you the rest, and if I learn anything, I will make every night a memorial thereof. He shall tell you the cause of my stay. Burn this letter, for it is too dangerous, neither is there anything well said in it, for I think upon nothing but upon trouble[26] if you be at Edinburgh.

Now, if to please you, my dear life, I spare neither honour, conscience nor hazard, nor greatness, taking it in good part, and not according to the intepretation of your false brother-in-law [Huntly], to whom I pray you, give no credit against the most faithful lover that ever you had or shall have.

See not also her [the Countess Jean] whose feigned tears you ought not more to regard than the true travails which I endure to deserve her place, for obtaining of which, against my own nature, I do betray those that could let [prevent] me. God forgive you, and give you, my only friend, the good luck and prosperity that your humble and faithful lover doth wish unto you, who hopeth shortly to be another thing unto you, for the reward of my pains.

I have not made one word, and it is very late, although I should never be weary in writing to you, yet will I end, after kissing of your hands. Excuse my evil writing, and read it over twice. Excuse also that I scribbled, for I had yesternight no paper when [I] took the paper of a memorial. Pray remember your friend, and write unto her and often. Love me always, as I shall love you.

The phrase "my evil writing" is one that Mary often used.

The Scots version ends:

Remember you of the purpose of the Lady Reres. Of the Englishmen. Of his mother. Of the Earl of Argyll. Of the Earl Bothwell. Of the lodging in Edinburgh.

It is this paragraph that has given rise to the theory that there were two letters, for Mary would hardly be reminding Bothwell to remember himself, and it was careless of a forger—if there was a forger—to leave in such a detail. It is significant that the English translator omitted it. It has been put forward that these were directions to the messenger, but that cannot be the case, and the words "remember you" preclude them from forming part of an *aide-mémoire* to the writer, such as appears in the middle of the letter. Furthermore, Bothwell is quite low down in the list of remembrances, which suggests he was not uppermost in Mary's concerns. This paragraph, therefore, must be the end of the report that was perhaps written to Moray or Maitland. Had this letter been genuine in its entirety, it could not have been written to Bothwell. Neither, however, would certain sections of it appear to have been intended for anyone else. As this letter was produced as the most compelling evidence of Mary's collusion with Bothwell, we can only conclude that it had been tampered with or at least partially fabricated.

If genuine, Casket Letter II incriminates Mary not only in an adulterous relationship with Bothwell, but also in helping him to plot Darnley's murder. It offers plausible evidence of the behaviour of two people who were later suspected of being guilty of a murder that certainly took place. But, tampering aside, is the letter in substance genuine?

Let us consider what we know of Mary. She was at a low ebb emotionally, and must have felt panicky and beset by rumours of conspiracies. She had every reason to despise and fear her husband. She had agreed to a reconciliation that may well have been distasteful to her. She was a woman who needed a strong man to lean and rely upon. She had so far refused to become embroiled in plots against Darnley. However, she was now faced with the prospect of resuming sexual relations with her syphilitic husband. The circumstantial evidence against Mary would appear to be strong, but it must be remembered that the overriding objective in her life was the English throne. Marriage to Darnley had strengthened her title to it, and any scandal, such as the murder of her husband or adultery on her part with another man, would seriously prejudice her chances of achieving that objective.

Bothwell, with his long record of service to the Crown, also had every reason to despise Darnley, and was almost certainly plotting to do away with him, in concert with Maitland, Douglas and (probably) Moray. Bothwell was the man who was closest to the Queen, the man on whom she relied implicitly, and he was telling other potential conspirators that she had sanctioned the removal of Darnley. His taste of greatness had bred in him an ambition to seek for higher things and to hope that, once Darnley was out of the way, he might persuade the Queen to marry him. The rapidity with which he put himself forward, after Darnley's murder, as the ideal candidate for Mary's hand, suggests that the desire to be King was the driving force behind his determination to do away with Darnley. Livingston's remark to Mary suggests that he had guessed Bothwell's intentions towards her, but also implies that this was news to her.

It is, of course, quite possible that Bothwell and Mary had already become lovers, as this letter implies. But there is no evidence for it apart from Casket Letter II and the later malicious libels of Buchanan and Lennox.

It has been said that Casket Letter II is a masterpiece in the science of human nature[27] and that this argues its authenticity, but it is possible that anyone with a vivid imagination and the benefit of hindsight could have invented the incriminating passages. As a portrayal of a woman so in thrall to her lover that she is willing to commit murder against the dictates of her conscience for his sake this letter is indeed a masterpiece, and there is evidence that Mary did become in thrall to Bothwell, but only after Darnley's murder. There were several clever men at court with a good insight into the Queen's character and sufficient knowledge of her literary style to reproduce it convincingly—Maitland was one such, Moray another—who could have been the inspiration behind such a forgery.

The fact remains, however, that Casket Letter II has certainly been tampered with—the reference to Bothwell is proof of this. This in itself must cast doubt on the veracity of its contents. The fact that Thomas Crawford copied passages of it almost word for word in order to give evidence against Mary in 1568 is further grounds for suspicion, for if Crawford's testimony was genuine, why could it not have stood alone?

There can be little doubt that the section of the letter reporting the interview with Darnley is mostly genuine—it fits in with all the other evidence and is a convincing portrayal of Darnley's character.

If the rest of the letter was a forgery, it was brilliantly done, with enough seemingly irrelevant detail, such as the memorial in the middle, to make it appear utterly genuine. The forger must have had access to other letters of Mary's in order to imitate her style and, doubtless, her handwriting, which she later claimed was easily copied. It is now impossible to check this, since the original Casket Letters have long since vanished.

As will be seen later, Casket Letter II was produced by Mary's enemies at a time when it was crucial for them to present evidence justifying the action they had taken against her, their anointed sovereign. For that reason alone, it must be suspect. However, the fact that it recounts in convincing detail events that are known to have taken place has led many to conclude that it must be genuine. Yet the reference to Bothwell at the end strongly suggests that it was not entirely so. Given this, and the circumstances in which the letter was produced, it cannot be regarded as reliable evidence of Mary's guilt.

On 23 January, Sir William Drury returned to Berwick to find Joseph Lutini there, who told him he had been dispatched with Mary's "good favour" to France on "certain of Her Grace's affairs," but claimed he was too unwell to proceed on his journey. Drury also found awaiting him the letter from Queen Mary asking him to apprehend Lutini because he had stolen goods and money from his colleagues, and insisting that it was not these that she wished to recover so much as Lutini's person, "for now the Queen mistrusteth lest he should offer his service here in England, and thereby might, with better occasion, utter something prejudicial to her." Drury thought it best to keep Lutini in Berwick until Queen Elizabeth's pleasure was made known to him, and sent a copy of Mary's letter and the forged passport to Cecil.[28]

That same evening, Moretta arrived in Berwick. He was already more than a month late for the christening, which some have seen as suspicious. Moretta certainly met Lutini in Berwick, for Rizzio was to accuse Lutini of divulging to Moretta the fact that he, Rizzio, had been the cause of Lutini's journey. As a result of the meeting, Lutini resolved never to return to Edinburgh for fear of meeting "a prepared death."[29] The evidence suggests that Lutini had been instructed by Darnley, through the good offices of Rizzio, to make contact with Moretta, whom Darnley perhaps hoped might serve as his link with Mondovi and the Vatican in his grandiose scheme to seize power and restore the Catholic faith in Scotland and England. If Casket Letter II is to be believed, Darnley may already have been in contact with Mondovi. Moretta might also be a means of enlisting the support of Spain, Savoy's ally. The fact that Lutini was to go on to France suggests that Darnley may have intended him to make contact with de Alava in Paris.

The hopes invested by the Pope in Mary had been raised by news of the Prince's lavish Catholic baptism, and on 22 January, Pius had written her a joyful letter, praising her for making such a good start and telling her that he was counting on the future salvation of Scotland.[30] But on 24 January (and again on 13 February), Mondovi wrote to him to report the failure of the mission of Father Hay and the Bishop of Dunblane to Scotland. Hay, moreover, had called Mary a sinner for her want of zeal in the Catholic cause.

On 24 January, du Croc, on his way south, met Moretta travelling north from Berwick, and turned back to accompany him to Dunbar, since they were old acquaintances and Moretta was "desirous of the other's company."[31] After staying a night at Dunbar, du Croc resumed his journey to London.

On that same day, Bothwell left Edinburgh for Liddesdale. It was later alleged that, prior to his departure, he had been "overseeing the King's lodging that was in preparing for him,"[32] the implication being that Bothwell had finalised his murder plans. *The Book of Articles* claims that Bothwell went to Kirk o'Field "to visit and consider the house prepared for the King" and was not pleased when others came seeking him out there. But Kirk o'Field had not yet been chosen as a suitable lodging for Darnley: the plan was to take him to Craigmillar. It would have been perfectly logical for Bothwell to have checked that preparations for the King's lodging at Craigmillar were proceeding smoothly before leaving Edinburgh; after all, it was on his way south.

Bothwell remained in the Borders for the next few days, and Mary stayed in Glasgow until 27 January. It will be remembered that Casket Letter I was dated "From Glasgow, this Saturday morning." The only Saturday on which Mary was in Glasgow was 25 January. This letter would scarcely have been sent on this date because the writer is complaining that she has not had news from Bothwell, and had hoped to hear from him "yesterday." But Bothwell had left her only four days earlier and had not yet reached Liddesdale. He had several days of hard riding and a short sojourn in Edinburgh, so would hardly have had time to write, which Mary must have known. Furthermore, "the man" must refer to James: Mary is unlikely to have written so warmly of Darnley at this time. Hence it must be concluded that the postscript "From Glasgow, this Saturday morning" was probably added by a forger to an earlier letter.

Moretta finally arrived in Edinburgh on 25 or 26 January.[33] Father Hay appears to have made himself known to him.[34] According to Buchanan, Moray came to Edinburgh to receive Moretta, and Maitland remained in the city to entertain him.[35] Sir James Balfour lent his house in the Canongate to

Moretta during his stay. Balfour, a Catholic, was a friend of Darnley, and may well have been acting as Darnley's agent.

On the 26th, Moretta had a meeting with Joseph Rizzio, and disclosed details of his conversation with Lutini in Berwick, whereupon Rizzio, in a panic, wrote to Lutini in Berwick, recounting how it had come to the Queen's attention that Lutini had absconded with her bracelets and other people's money, and how Moretta had told him "that you told him that I was the cause that you took this journey. Take heed of what you say, for if you say for whom you have gone, we shall both be in real trouble." Who in Scotland, but Darnley, would have used foreign Catholic agents at court to make contact on his behalf with the Catholic powers in Europe?

Rizzio continued:

I have always said that you had gone because you had taken money, and to let the anger which the Queen had against you die down, and that I had advised you to do so, and that I had lent you money to make this journey, so that you can still say the same. And I said that the money which you have taken from me you would give back when you were returned from France, and thus shall you and I both be excused. And if you do otherwise, you will be the cause of my ruin. For the love of God, act as if I were your son, and I pray you for the love of God and of the good friendship which you have borne me, and I you, to say as I tell you, which is that you are making this journey to bring back your money, and to let the Queen's anger subside and the suspicion which she has of you; and the money which I said you have taken from me, that you have taken it for fear that you should happen to lack in your journey, and that you would restore it when you were returned; and that you are a man of wealth, and that you would not have taken it without returning it to me, because I was always your friend and you would never have thought that I would have made such a fuss of it. And I pray you not to want to be the cause of my ruin.

Rizzio went on to say that the Queen had told him she wanted to speak with Lutini in private, and he urged him to "take care to speak as I have written, and not otherwise" and not let Mary "rattle you with her speech"—evidently Lutini was a volatile fellow. Again, Rizzio begged him, "I pray you to have pity on me and not to be the cause of my death. If you say otherwise than that which I have written, you will be in trouble as well as I." Beneath his signature, he added, "I beg you to burn this letter as soon as you have read it."

It is almost certain that the money that Lutini took with him had been raised by Darnley or stolen on his behalf; it is even possible that it was Darnley who appropriated Mary's bracelets. Rizzio had forged Lutini's passport—a crime for which he could be executed—and was now terrified that the loose-tongued Lutini would betray him. There is no evidence that Lutini received his letter, which seems to have been intercepted by Drury, for it was later found among Cecil's papers. With Lutini now held under guard at Berwick, it is no wonder that Rizzio was frantic with anxiety.

Drury reported on 26 January that, if there was no danger from the cold weather to Darnley's health, Mary would leave Glasgow with him the next day.[36]

Around this time, news of affairs in Scotland was causing some consternation in Paris. On 26 and 30 January, Catherine de' Medici reported to her envoy in Brussels that the Spanish ambassador, Francisco de Alava, had shown "great choler." She charitably put this down to illness, but added that, when he recovered, he would doubtless be more polite. As a precaution, she had had his diplomatic bags searched.

De Alava's irascibility may have been born of anxiety, for it was at this time that he warned Archbishop Beaton that Mary was in danger; it will be remembered that de Alava was reputedly friendly with Darnley, and that he had informed the Duchess of Parma of a Scottish plot against Mary back in December. It seems strange that he had waited until now to get a warning to Mary, but it may be that his new information was sufficiently credible and alarming to prompt him to act. Nor did Beaton waste any time, for, on the 27th, he wrote informing Mary that de Alava had "specially advertised" her "to take heed of yourself." Beaton added that he had "heard some murmuring in like wise by others, that there be some surprise to be trafficked to your contrary." De Alava, he said, "would never let me know of no particular, only assured me he had written to his master to know if by that way he can try any farther, and that he was counselled to cause me haste towards you herewith."

Partly at de Alava's wish, Beaton asked the Queen Mother "if she had heard any discourse or advertisement lately tending to your hurt or disadvantage, but I came no speed [I had no success], nor would she confess that she had got nor heard any such appearance." She said that her ambassadors to Scotland had told her that Mary's affairs "were at very good point"; furthermore, she had heard from Mary's own half-brother, Lord Robert Stewart, that Mary had forgiven Morton, Ruthven and Lindsay, "so she thought there was nothing to be feared." Indeed, she had been glad to hear of the good relations between Mary and her subjects, "and saw nothing that might stop it, except if it were the variance between you and the King, which she desired God to appease." Finally, Beaton humbly beseeched Mary "to cause the Captains of her Guard [to] be diligent in their office, for, notwithstanding that I have no particular occasion whereon I desire it, yet can I not be out of fear until I hear of your news. I pray the eternal God to preserve Your Majesty from all dangers, with long life and good health."[37] The letter was encoded in cipher and entrusted to a Scottish archer, Robert Drury.

What had de Alava heard to make him so anxious for Mary's safety? He probably knew something of Darnley's plotting, but, as he sent Mary a warning, nearly three weeks after Darnley's death, that there was "yet some notable enterprise planned against her," and claimed that he had learned this from the same source, it seems more likely that he had obtained intelligence of the Lords' conspiracy against Darnley and drawn his own conclusions. What seems clear is that King Philip was not involved in any plot against Mary, for he would hardly have sanctioned de Alava's warning if he had intended her any harm. It has been suggested that he was behind Darnley's plot and deliberately sanctioned a warning that would come too late, but at this stage Mary's future movements could not have been predicted, so clearly Darnley's plans did not have the backing of Spain. Yet it seems that de Alava had not revealed all that he knew to Beaton, and it may be that he would have compromised his contacts by giving away too much of what he had heard. Beaton seems to have suspected Catherine de' Medici of knowing more about the "surprise" than she had let on, and indeed she may well have done so, having rifled through de Alava's letters. The fact that de Alava prompted Beaton to question Catherine suggests that he feared what she had discovered, which may account for his "choler" towards her.

Tragically, Beaton's warning was to arrive too late, both for Mary and for Darnley.

15

"ALL WAS PREPARED
FOR THE CRIME"

~

MARY AND DARNLEY LEFT GLASGOW for Edinburgh on Mon-
day, 27 January 1567. Since Darnley, "as yet not whole of his disease,"[1]
was travelling in a litter,[2] progress was slow, and they stopped for the night at
Kilsyth, twelve miles from Glasgow.[3] The *Book of Articles* claims that, "as they
were riding forth the way by Kilsyth, she passed afore, desiring him to follow
her after in the litter. But he, even then suspecting his life, said he would return to Glasgow if she tarried not with him. And she, not willing to spoil the
purpose that was so far brought to pass, returned to him [and] gave him meat
forth from her own hands." There is no contemporary evidence to corroborate this tale.

The King and Queen arrived at Callendar on the 28th.[4] Curiously and,
some thought, ominously, "a raven continually accompanied them" all the
way from Glasgow to Edinburgh.[5] Mary and Darnley spent one or two nights
at Linlithgow Palace on 29, 30 or 31 January, before setting out on the final
sixteen miles of their journey to Craigmillar.[6]

The *Book of Articles* alleges that, while they were at Linlithgow, Bothwell's man, Robert "Hob" Ormiston, came to inform the Queen that Bothwell "was returned to Edinburgh and had prepared all things," but this is a
fabrication because Kirk o'Field had not yet been decided upon as a lodging

for Darnley, and no preparations for the murder were made before then, as Ormiston later testified under interrogation. Moray's Journal claims that Mary waited at Linlithgow until Ormiston brought her news that Bothwell was on his way to Edinburgh.[7] Mary and Bothwell did arrive back in Edinburgh around the same date, but this may have been by coincidence rather than collusion.

On 27 January, Bothwell had ridden out from Jedburgh into Liddesdale, where, to his "great peril," he countered an attack by the vengeful Elliott clan and arrested twelve troublemakers.[8] The next day, he was either at Hermitage or Jedburgh, and on the 29th was on his way back to Edinburgh, which he reached probably on 30 January. Here, he installed himself in his lodgings in Holyrood Palace, which comprised chambers on two floors, connected by a turnpike stair and overlooking the garden.[9] Lord Ruthven had formerly occupied these rooms.[10]

Mary and Darnley approached the outskirts of Edinburgh either that day, 30 January, or on one of the next two days.[11] Bothwell came to meet them and escort them to Craigmillar. But at the last minute, either through fear that he might be imprisoned or murdered behind the castle's stout walls, or because Craigmillar was inconvenient to his own plans, Darnley declared he did not wish to complete his convalescence there,[12] and it was decided that he should go instead to the Old Provost's Lodging at Kirk o'Field, "a country house near the city"[13] and "a place of good air where he might best recover his health."[14] The hasty preparations made for Darnley's reception confirm that this was a last-minute change of plan.[15]

The question of who chose Kirk o'Field is crucial. Darnley's servant, Thomas Nelson, who survived the explosion, later recalled, "It was devised in Glasgow that the King should have lain at Craigmillar, but, because he had no will thereof, the purpose was altered, and conclusion taken that he should lie beside the Kirk o'Field." Nelson expected Darnley to be lodged in the Duke of Chatelherault's mansion at Kirk o'Field, and evidently Darnley did too, "but the contrary was shown him by the Queen, who conveyed him to the other house,"[16] the Old Provost's Lodging, which Darnley "in no wise liked of."[17] This suggests that it was Mary who chose Kirk o'Field, or at least the Old Provost's Lodging. Nelson's account has been questioned on the grounds that it is unlikely that Darnley would have wanted to stay in the house of his family's greatest enemy, but it might have given him a sense of smug satisfaction to think that he could appropriate his adversary's fine mansion: he was the King, and would expect to be lodged in the best house available.

Lennox claims that, when Darnley complained that he "misliked the other [house] that she prepared for him," Mary "took him by the hand and said that, although that house was fairer in his sight, yet the rooms of the other were more easy and handsome for him, and also for her, that there passed a privy way between the palace and it, where she might always resort unto him till he was whole of his disease"; at which Darnley, "being bent to follow her will in all things, yielded to the same, and so entered the house."[18] The "privy way" that Mary referred to was a back route through the grounds of the nearby Blackfriars monastery, which gave access to a lane leading to Kirk o'Field.[19]

"In choosing this lodging," wrote Buchanan, Mary "wished it to appear that her reason was the salubrity of it." He made it appear, however, that she had a more underhand purpose. But there is evidence that Kirk o'Field was not the Queen's choice.

Nau, who may well have got his information from Mary, states that Darnley himself chose Kirk o'Field "on the report of Sir James Balfour," whose brother owned the Old Provost's Lodging, "and some others. This was against the Queen's wishes, who was anxious to take him to Craigmillar, for he could not stay in Holyrood Palace lest he should give the infection to the Prince. On his own account, too, he did not wish anyone to see him in his present condition, nor until he had gone through a course of baths in private." If Balfour was Darnley's accomplice in his treasonous schemes, then—it has been argued—his purpose in suggesting Kirk o'Field may indeed have been a sinister one. It has been seen as significant that Kirk o'Field was chosen after Moretta's arrival; Balfour may have been working in tandem with Moretta, and it is also possible that the treacherous Balfour was conspiring with both Darnley and the Protestant Lords. The fact that Balfour advised the King to go to Kirk o'Field perhaps suggests that he was the driving force behind Darnley's plotting.

In his confession, John Hepburn also claims that Balfour suggested Kirk o'Field.[20] Bothwell states that Darnley's sojourn there "was by common consent of the Queen and her Council, who were anxious to preserve the health of all concerned." This implies that Mary and her Lords consented to a suggestion made by somebody else, probably Balfour. We know that Mary would have preferred Darnley to lodge at Craigmillar, which was not only in a healthy location but was also a fortress where he would be safe from his enemies, and isolated from anyone who was conspiring with him.

Leslie says that Kirk o'Field was decided upon "by the advice of the doctors, as being the most healthy spot in the whole town." This does not preclude Balfour's suggesting it. Having agreed to the King lodging at Kirk o'Field, Mary herself selected the Old Provost's Lodging as the most suitable residence. It had, after all, been used recently by Bedford when he visited Edinburgh for the Prince's baptism. Moreover, it was lying empty, while the Duke's house was at present occupied by Archbishop Hamilton,[21] Chatelherault himself being still in exile in France.

Paris, in his deposition, alleges that it was Maitland who suggested Kirk o'Field. Paris is less likely to be accurate than Nau, but it is not implausible that Mary chose the Old Provost's Lodging on Maitland's advice, perhaps little suspecting that Maitland may have had an ulterior motive in choosing it. Maitland, after all, had been one of the two prime movers in the plot to get rid of Darnley. The house was in a quiet location and could be approached by a back route, and its security would be easy to breach.

Soon after Darnley's murder, Robert Melville went to England and there told de Silva, with regard to Kirk o'Field, that, because of its healthy position, "the King had chosen it."[22] Moretta was to say the same thing to Giovanni Correr, the Venetian ambassador.[23] These reports corroborate Nau and other evidence, and we may therefore safely conclude that it was indeed Darnley who decided that he should stay at Kirk o'Field. We may also conclude that he did not select the Old Provost's Lodging.

Buchanan states that "the place had been made ready for [Darnley's] murder by Bothwell, who, in the Queen's absence, had undertaken that task," but the house at Kirk o'Field was prepared in a hurry after the last-minute decision had been made to change the King's lodgings, so Bothwell could not have had a chance to make ready for the murder. On 20 May following, Servais de Condé, the Queen's steward, stated that the furniture for Darnley was delivered to the house in February.[24] As the King arrived on 1 February at the latest, there must have been a frantic flurry of activity to get the place ready for him.

At Darnley's coming, "the chamber was hung and a new bed of black figured velvet standing therein,"[25] which had been prepared for Bedford. But this was not good enough for a king, so tapestries, hangings, carpets, furnishings and supplies were quickly carted up from Holyrood.[26]

Kirk o'Field lay to the south of Edinburgh, on a hill overlooking the Cowgate; it stood just inside the city wall and three-quarters of a mile from Holyrood Palace, in a semi-rural location, "environed with pleasant gardens, and removed from the noise of the people."[27] The mediaeval conventual church of St. Mary in the Fields had been refounded as a collegiate church in 1510, and stood on a high eminence. East of it, on a rising slope that dropped steeply to the north, there had been erected a range of collegiate buildings around a quadrangle. The church itself had been damaged by the English in 1544 and again by the reformers in 1558, and was now an abandoned ruin.[28]

The main frontage and gate to the collegiate buildings were to the west; in the centre of this range was the New Provost's Lodging, built around 1511–12, which was the residence of Robert Balfour. To the north of this was the Precentor's House, to the south an enclosing wall, and behind it, at right angles to, and lower than, the New Provost's Lodging, was a long hall known as the "Salle" or the Prebendaries' Chamber, which had been built after 1511 and was linked to the Old Provost's Lodging, which stood further down the slope. The latter must have been built before 1510 and parts of it may have dated from the thirteenth century, when the church was originally built by the Austin Friars. Behind the Old Provost's Lodging was a little courtyard and the 21-foot high Flodden Wall, in which there was a postern gate "hard by the house"[29] giving on to a lane called Thieves' Row; beyond lay the walled south garden and orchard, surrounded by open fields known as "the Lands of Bristo," and to the east of the building there were gardens. On the north and east sides of the quadrangle were small, gabled houses that, prior to the Reformation, had accommodated the resident canons, and in the centre was a well. The triple-storeyed Duke's House, where Darnley had hoped to lodge, stood beyond the quadrangle to the north-west; it had been built by Chatelherault in 1554 on the site of the Friars' hospital, or guest house.

Buchanan described the Old Provost's Lodging as "a house not commodious for a sick man, nor comely for a king, for it was both ruined and ruinous, and has stood empty without any dweller in it for divers years before, in a place of small resort between the old falling walls of two kirks, near a few almshouses for poor beggars. And that no commodious means for committing that mischief might be wanting, there is a postern door in the town wall by the house, whereby [the assassins] might easily pass away into the fields." The Old Provost's Lodging had certainly not stood empty for years, and was in no way ruinous. In fact, it was a spacious and well-appointed residence, and Mary herself did not disdain to use it. Nor is there any evidence that Darnley was forced to stay there.

The house's two storeys were connected by a 3-foot-wide turnpike stair in a turret. Darnley's bedchamber was on the first floor, and measured about 16 feet by 12 feet; it had a timber gallery with a window that projected over the Flodden Wall. The wall had a width of 6 feet at the base but tapered to a foot-wide battlemented top; the ground rose steeply at this point, and the drop beyond the wall was no more than 16 feet. When Mary stayed at the house, she slept in a bedchamber directly below Darnley's; her room was six steps up from the main entrance on the ground floor, and had a window overlooking the quadrangle. Each bedchamber had a small anteroom or garderobe, measuring about 7 feet by 12 feet. The single-storeyed Prebendaries' Chamber, or Salle, which measured approximately 45 feet by 15 feet, served as a presence chamber, and was accessed through a passageway and steps from the upper floor. Mary's courtiers would gather here when she visited Darnley.

The kitchen was in the cellar. The low groin-arched vaults below the Prebendaries' Chamber, which were about 6 feet high at the east end and only about 2 feet high at the west end, were connected to the loftier cellars beneath the Old Provost's Lodging, which had a height of between 6 feet and 7 feet. Darnley's house had three outer doors: one, the Fore Entry, opened on to the quadrangle, one led to the garden, and one, in the kitchen, gave on to the little alleyway that led from the quadrangle under the passage between the Prebendaries' Chamber and the Old Provost's Lodging. There may also have been a door nearby giving entry to the vaults of the Prebendaries' Chamber.

Darnley's bedchamber was hung with six tapestries that had been confiscated from the Gordon family after the Battle of Corrichie. It was furnished with a small Turkey carpet, a "high chair" upholstered in purple velvet with three red velvet cushions, a little table covered in green velvet and a chamberpot. A bath was placed by the bed, ready for the King's treatment;

when not in use, it was covered by a door that had been removed from the upper entrance to the turnpike stair on the Queen's orders;[30] it was later implied that she had done this to facilitate the easy access of Darnley's murderers. Darnley did not like the black bed that had been provided for Bedford, so his own violet velvet bed, the one that Mary had given him the previous August, which had previously been owned by Marie de Guise, was brought up from Holyrood.[31]

The Queen's bedchamber had a bed with yellow and green damask hangings. In the Prebendaries' Chamber, a leather chair of estate covered with watered silk of red and yellow, the royal Scottish heraldic colours, was set on a dais beneath a black velvet cloth of estate fringed with silk, and on the walls hung five more Gordon tapestries. In Darnley's garderobe, there was a set of seven tapestries entitled "The Hunting of the Coneys"; the royal close stool had two basins, and a canopy and curtains of yellow taffeta.

During his stay at Kirk o'Field, Darnley was attended by his valet, William Taylor, Thomas Nelson and two grooms, Andrew McCaig and Master Glen. All were lodged in the house, as well as one Edward Symonds and "Taylor's boy," probably the valet's body servant.[32] There was also a cook, Bonkil, who went home when his duties were done. Surprisingly, no mention is made in any source of guards for the King, which seems unusual. Both he and Mary knew that his enemies had been conspiring to take his life, and it is curious that he did not demand guards, nor Mary provide them. The lack of such protection left him dangerously exposed to attack.

After seeing Darnley comfortably installed at Kirk o'Field with his servants, Mary returned to Holyrood. The raven that had accompanied them on their journey from Glasgow remained behind, and was seen on several occasions, perching on the roof of the Old Provost's Lodging.[33]

It seemed that good relations had now been restored between the King and Queen. Mary visited her husband daily,[34] "and used him in every sort as well as he himself could wish."[35] She spent two nights at Kirk o'Field, sleeping in the bedroom below his. They sat up late, sometimes until midnight,[36] talking, playing cards or listening to music, and "many nobles" came with the Queen to divert the convalescent.[37] According to Buchanan, Mary reconciled

Darnley and Bothwell, "whom she wished to be free from suspicion." There were no rows or recriminations. According to Nau, and perhaps Mary, the royal couple were "perfectly reconciled."

"Every man marvelled at this reconciliation or sudden change," wrote Knox, while Buchanan averred that "this pretence of kindness was much suspected by all."[38] It has been regarded by many, then and since, as a deception on Mary's part, calculated to divert suspicion from herself when Bothwell's murder plot came to fruition, and constitutes further circumstantial evidence against her. It is indeed hard to believe that Mary's love for Darnley had flowered anew, but there may be an innocent explanation for her renewed warmth to him. She could have reached the conclusion that she had to make the best of her marriage as there was no honourable way out of it. She may also have been doing her best to gain Darnley's confidence in order to either draw from him details of his conspiracy or persuade him to abandon it; after all, his explanation of the revelations of Hiegait and Walker had been less than satisfactory.

Buchanan claims that, throughout this period, Mary "did not cease to think up every method possible of turning the blame of the crime on her brother James and the Earl of Morton. For when these two, whom she feared and hated, had been eliminated, everything else, she assured herself, would rearrange itself." Since the Craigmillar conference, Mary had been aware that Moray might "look through his fingers" at an attempt to remove Darnley by unlawful means, and she had grounds for believing that Morton would have supported such a move if she had given her consent to it. Buchanan's claim was therefore plausible, even if it might not have been true.

At some point in early February, Mary tried to make peace between Darnley and the Lords, but the latter, already suspicious of what her reconciliation with her husband might portend, refused to co-operate, and warned her that the King would put a knife to her throat and theirs.[39]

Mary spent her first night at Kirk o'Field on Wednesday, 5 February.[40] Darnley had expressed fears for his safety—perhaps on hearing what the Lords had said—and, to reassure him, she had agreed to stay, and sent one of her women to Holyrood to fetch a fur coverlet for her bed. Buchanan later claimed she slept there that night in order to allay the suspicions of those who might later claim that she had plotted to murder her husband.

Two days later, on Friday, 7 February, Darnley had a medicinal bath.

Mary had shown herself so caring towards him that, "being in his bath, [he] would suffer none to handle him but herself."[41] That same day, according to Nelson, the Queen had the King's rich bed removed from the Old Provost's Lodging to avoid it being soiled with dirty water from the bath. The *Book of Articles* also states that the bed and some tapestries were removed on the Friday, and that the bed was replaced by "another worse," because Mary did not want these valuable items destroyed in the explosion. Lennox states that Darnley's bed was moved on Sunday the 9th, the day before the King was due to return to Holyrood, and replaced with a meaner sort of bed hung with purple velvet, Mary telling him that "they should both lie in that rich bed the next night at the palace." Lennox, of course, invested her action with a sinister significance.[42] We know, however, from the list of items lost in the explosion that was drawn up by Servais de Condé, that Darnley's rich bed and all the tapestries were destroyed when the Old Provost's Lodging was blown up. Hence Nelson, Buchanan and Lennox must have been lying.

On 7 February, obviously still suspicious of Darnley's activities, Mary wrote again to Sir William Drury at Berwick, repeating her demand for the arrest of Lutini. Drury sent again to Cecil for instructions, having been told by Lutini that "he doubteth much danger, and so affirmeth unto me that, if he return, he utterly despaireth of any better than a prepared death."[43]

Darnley, whose health was rapidly improving and who was obviously unaware that Mary was still investigating his underhand pursuits, wrote that same day to Lennox of the kindness of the Queen:[44]

My Lord,
I have thought good to write unto you by this bearer of my good health, I thank God, which is the sooner come to through the good treatment of such as hath this good while concealed their good will. I mean my love, the Queen, which I assure you hath all this while and yet doth use herself like a natural and loving wife. I hope yet that God will lighten our hearts with joy that have so long been afflicted with trouble. As I in this letter do write unto Your Lordship, so I trust this bearer can certify the like. Thus, thanking Almighty God of our good hap, I commit Your Lordship to His protection.

From Edinburgh, the VII of February, your loving and obedient son, Henry Rex.

The messenger told Lennox that, when he was summoned to take the letter, he saw the Queen reading it over Darnley's shoulder; visibly touched by it, she put her arm around her husband and kissed him "as Judas did the Lord his Master,"[45] as Lennox put it later.

Had Darnley undergone a genuine change of heart and abandoned his plotting? It would seem so from this letter, which was a private one to his father, who probably knew all about his treasonous plans. It appears his serious illness had made Darnley think again. However, the reference to thanking God for "our good hap" suggests that Darnley believed that his reconciliation with Mary was advantageous in some way to himself and his father, and it may be inferred that he saw it as a stepping stone to gaining the Crown Matrimonial. An alternative explanation is that Darnley did not write this letter at all, but that it was made up by Lennox in an attempt to portray Mary as trying "to remove all suspicion from herself," so that "no shadow of suspicion remained in [Darnley's] mind."[46]

That evening, as Darnley and Mary sat talking, "he promised to give her much information of the utmost importance to the life and quiet of both of them," and reminded her "of the necessity of cultivating a good understanding with each other, and of guarding against those persons who meddled between them (whose names he said he would reveal), and who had advised him to make an attempt upon her life. The designs of these persons tended to the ruin of both of them. He warned her more particularly to be on her guard against Lethington [Maitland], who, he said, was planning the ruin of the one by the means of the other, and meant in the end to ruin both of them, as he could perceive more clearly than ever by their conduct and counsel."[47] As had been made clear to Mary in Glasgow, Darnley was surprisingly well informed, and there can be little doubt that he had heard rumours or talk that Maitland and others were planning to destroy both the Queen and himself, which was partially true. Of course, it took breathtaking audacity for Darnley to occupy the high moral ground in this respect, since he too had been plotting against Mary, and his conspiracies had evolved long before the Craigmillar conference. As had happened after Rizzio's murder, Darnley was trying to shift the burden of suspicion on to others, but in this case he seems to have had good reason for doing so.

Mary spent that Friday night at Kirk o'Field.[48] By now, rumours of a conspiracy against Darnley were spreading. Melville recalled that "many suspected that the Earl of Bothwell had some enterprise against him," but shrank from warning him because he was notoriously indiscreet and would tell all to his servants, "who were not all honest." There was one man, however, who felt compelled to speak out. An English spy in Edinburgh reported to Cecil that, on Saturday, 8 February, a highly agitated Darnley told the Queen that, the previous evening,[49] her half-brother, Lord Robert Stewart, had come to warn him that, "if he retired not hastily out of that place, it would cost him his life."[50] Buchanan claims that Lord Robert told Darnley "of his wife's treachery," on condition "that he kept the knowledge to himself and looked to his own safety."

Mary summoned her brother that Saturday[51] and questioned him about what he had said, in the presence of Darnley, Moray and Bothwell, but he "denied that he ever spoke it."[52] According to Buchanan, this precipitated a violent quarrel between Darnley and Lord Robert, with both drawing their swords, and Mary begging Moray to intervene. There is, however, no evidence before this date that Lord Robert had been conspiring with Darnley, and it is quite possible that he had heard rumours—similar to those that Darnley had heard himself—of the plot to kill the King. His reluctance to say any more may reflect his fear that the conspirators might guess who had warned the King and Queen and take revenge on him accordingly; or he may indeed have heard that Mary herself had approved of the plot, and been reluctant to confront her. Buchanan and Paris later alleged that Mary incited the quarrel in the hope that Darnley would be killed in a duel by Lord Robert, but if this was her intention, why did she ask Moray to intervene?

It has been said that this quarrel could not have taken place because Darnley was a convalescent invalid and too weak to fight. In fact, he was due to complete his treatment the next day with a final medicinal bath, and, as will be seen, was to summon his horses for Monday morning, intending perhaps to ride ten miles to Seton. The likelihood is that he was already up and about by this date.

A letter in Mary's "own hand" was produced in 1568 at the inquiry into her guilt at York; it was said to prove "that there was another mean of a more cleanly conveyance devised to kill the King, for there was a quarrel made betwixt him and the Lord Robert by carrying of false tales betwixt, the Queen being the instrument to bring it to pass; which purpose, if it had taken effect, for they were at daggers drawing, it had eased them of the prosecution of this devilish fact, which, this taking none effect, was afterwards most tyrannously executed."[53] However, this letter was later withdrawn from the documentary evidence, and has never been seen since, which argues that it was almost certainly a bad forgery. Had it been genuine, it is hardly likely that Mary's enemies would have failed to offer such compelling evidence in support of their case.

Casket Letter IV is supposed to have been written by Mary to Bothwell on Friday night, after Darnley had told her of Lord Robert's warning.[54] Buchanan entitled it, "Another letter to Bothwell, of her love to him," and it reads:

I have watched later there above than I would have done, if it had not been to draw out that that this bearer shall tell you, that I find the fairest commodity to excuse your business that might be offered: I have promised him to bring him tomorrow, if you think it give order thereunto.

Now, Sir, I have not yet broken my promise with you, for you had not commanded me to send you any thing or to write, and I do it not for offending of you. And if you knew the fear that I am in thereof, you would not have so many contrary suspicions, which nevertheless I cherish as proceeding from the thing of this world that I desire and seek the most, that is, your favour or goodwill, of which my behaviour shall assure me. And I will never despair thereof as long as, according to your promise, you shall discharge your heart to me. Otherwise I would think that my ill luck, and the fair behaviour of those that have not the third part of the faithfulness and voluntary obedience that I bear unto you, shall have won the advantage over me of the second lover of Jason. Not that I do compare you so wicked, or myself to so unpitiful a person.

The writer is here referring to a tale from Greek mythology, immortalised by Euripides and Seneca. Glauce, the second wife of the hero Jason, was poisoned by his first wife, the famous sorceress Medea, whom he had repudiated. The vengeful Medea also murdered her own two sons by Jason. The inference is supposed to be that Mary feels the same jealousy towards the Countess Jean as Medea did for Glauce, but is not so pitiless as to contemplate poisoning her. If this letter were written to Darnley, however, Mary could be referring to her jealousy of his mistresses. It continues:

> Although you make me feel some grief in a matter that toucheth you, and to preserve and keep you to her whom alone you belong, if a body may claim to himself that which is won by [word illegible, deleted] well, faithfully, yea, entirely loving, as I do and will do all my life, for pain or hurt, whatsoever may happen to me thereby.
>
> In recompense whereof, and of all the evils that you [have] been cause of to me, remember the place hereby. I desire not that you keep promise with me tomorrow, but that we may be together, and that you give no credit to the suspicions that you shall have without being assured thereof. And I ask no more of God but that you might know all that I have in my heart, which is yours, and that He preserve you from all evil, at the least during my life, which shall not be dear unto me but as long as it and I shall please you. I go to bed, and give you good night.
>
> Send me word tomorrow early in the morning how you have done, for I shall think long.

The next sentence has long intrigued historians:

> And watch well if the bird shall fly out of his cage or without his father [deleted by Cecil, who substituted the word "mate"] make as the turtle shall remain alone for absence, how short soever it be.

This was originally meant to imply that Darnley, mourning the absence of his father, might flee from Kirk o'Field.

In the Scots version, this passage is given as:

> Make good watch if the bird escape out of the cage, or without her mate. As the turtle, I shall remain alone for to lament the absence, how short that so ever it be.

Here, the sense and sex of the bird are different; when the bird has flown, the writer will mourn his absence. This is closer to the original French version, which translates as:

Beware lest the bird fly out of its cage, or without its mate, like the turtle dove lives alone to lament the absence, however short it may be.

This implies that it is the writer who will fly away, if driven to do so by her mate, and who will live alone to mourn his absence.[55] This passage may well be based on lines of a sonnet written by Ronsard, a poet favoured by Mary, which read:

> Que dis-tu, que fais-tu, pensive tourterelle
> Dessus cet arbre sec?—Viateur, je lamente.

The letter ends:

That that I could not do, my letter should do it with a good will, if it were not that I fear to wake you, for I durst not write before Joseph and Bastien and Joachim, who were but new gone from I began.

The abrupt opening, which suggests that this letter is only part of a longer one, and the discrepancies between the various translations are perhaps evidence that the original text of the letter has been manipulated to incriminate Mary. In fact, there is very little in it to suggest that she incited the quarrel between Lord Robert and Darnley in order to bring about Darnley's death. Apart from the last two sentences, which may have been added by a forger, this letter could have been written by Mary to Darnley during the first months of their marriage, while they were wrangling about the Crown Matrimonial; this theory is supported by the threat that the writer might fly the cage if provoked too far. Furthermore, the style is reminiscent of that used by Mary in her later letters to the Duke of Norfolk.

Casket Letter III is also said to have been written by Mary to Bothwell at this time, but its opening paragraph shows that this theory cannot be correct:

Monsieur, if the displeasure of your absence, your forgetfulness, the fear of danger so promised by everyone to your so-loved person may give me consolation, can console me, I leave it to you to judge, seeing the unhap [misfortune] that my cruel lot and continual misadventure has hitherto promised me, following the misfortunes and fears, as well of late as of a long time by-past, the which ye do know.

It would have been ludicrous for Mary to write in this vein to Bothwell, since he was in almost daily attendance on her; if this was a genuine letter, then it must have been written at another time.

It continues:

But for all that, I will in no wise accuse you, neither of your little remembrance, neither of your little care, and least of all your promise broken, or of the coldness of your writing, since I am always so far made yours that that which pleases you is acceptable to me, and my thoughts are so willingly subdued unto yours that I suppose that all that comes of your proceeds not be any of the causes foresaid, but rather for such as be just and reasonable, and such as I desire myself. Which is the final order that ye promised to take for the surety and honourable service of the only uphold of my life. For which alone I will preserve the same, and without the which I desire not but sudden death. And to testify to you how lowly I submit me under your commandments, I have sent you, in sign of homage, by Paris, the ornament of the head, which is the chief good of the other members, inferring thereby that, by the seizing of you in the possession of the spoil of that which is principle, the remnant cannot be but subject unto you, and with consenting of the heart. In place whereof, since I have always left it unto you, I send unto you a sepulchre of hard stone, coloured with black, strewn with tears and bones. The stone I compare to my heart, that, as it is carved in one sure sepulchre or harbour of your commandments, and above all of your name and memory that are therein enclosed, as is my heart in this ring, never to come forth, while death grant unto you to a trophy of victory of my bones, as the ring is filled, in sign that you have made a full conquest of me, of my heart, and unto that bones my bones be left unto you in remembrance of your victory and my acceptable love and willing for to be better bestowed than I merit. The enamelling that is about is black, which signifies the steadfastness of her that sends the same. The tears are without number, so are the dreaders to displease you, the tears of your absence, the disdain that I cannot be in outward effect yours, as I am without feignedness of heart and spirit, and of good reason, though my merits were much greater than of the most profit that ever was, and such as I desire to be, and shall take pain in conditions to imitate, for to be bestowed worthily under your regimen. My only wealth receive therefore in all good part the same, as I have received your marriage with extreme joy, the which shall not part forth of my bosom till that marriage of our bodies be made in public, as sign of all that I either hope or desire of bliss in this world. Yet my heart fearing to displease you as much in the reading hereof as I delight me in the writing, I will make end, after that I have kissed your hands with all great affection, as I pray God (O, ye only upholder of my life!) to give you long and blessed life, and to me your good favour, as the only good that I desire, and to ye which I pretend.

I have shown unto this bearer that which I have learned, to whom I remit me, knowing the credit that you give him, as sure does that will be for ever unto your humble, obedient, lawful wife, that forever dedicates unto you her heart, her body, without any change, as unto him that I have made possessor of heart, of which so may hold you assured, yet unto the death shall no ways be changed, for evil nor good shall never make me go from it.[56]

The original French copy of this letter is endorsed "To prove the affections." Mary's enemies offered it as evidence that she was involved in an adulterous relationship with Bothwell. The reference to Paris, which could be an interpolation, indicates that it was sent by Mary to Bothwell, but there are no other clues as to the writer's identity. It was certainly written by a woman to her lover. The couple are engaged in an illicit affair, perhaps a secret marriage since she refers to herself as his lawful wife, and the writer is longing for the time when the "marriage of our bodies" can be made public; in the meantime, she is lamenting her lover's absence and forgetfulness. The tone of the letter is self-abasing and wholly submissive. If not entirely forged, it could have been written by Mary to Darnley, before their marriage, or even by another woman, possibly Anna Throndssen, to Bothwell. It could not refer to Mary's marriage to Bothwell since, from this time onwards, far from being absent, he was constantly in attendance on her. Much of this letter refers to the symbolism in a jewel that the writer has sent to her lover, which represents a tomb, and was probably a *memento mori*, a type of jewel that reminded the wearer of his or her mortality; such jewels were fashionable in the sixteenth century. This jewel has been identified as the black ring set with a diamond that Mary had promised Bothwell in her Will of 1566[57] but, since the writer was also sending "the ornament of the head," which was almost certainly a lock of hair, the jewel is more likely to have been a locket in which her lover could enclose it. The word used in the original French is "bague," which now means a ring or collar, but was used in Mary's Will to describe various jewels.

On Saturday, 8 February, Lennox left Glasgow for Linlithgow. It has been conjectured that he was making his way to Holyrood to greet Darnley on the successful conclusion of the latter's coup against Mary, but Lennox might have been travelling simply with the object of visiting his son, who was now restored to health and favour. He might also have hoped that Darnley would effect a reconciliation between himself and the Queen. According to the Seigneur de Clernault, Lennox was attacked in Glasgow on Sunday evening and was saved from death only by the intervention of Lord Sempill.[58] However, as Lennox was then in Linlithgow, this incident must have happened before he left Glasgow on the 8th, if it happened at all, for Lennox makes no mention of it. There has been conjecture that Clernault was attempting to establish an alibi for Lennox in case Darnley's plans went wrong.

According to de Silva, Darnley had asked to see Moretta, but Mary was still apparently suspicious of Darnley's motives; she had no intention of giving him any chance to liaise with his friends abroad, and had told him that he could not receive Moretta because the latter's master, the Duke of Savoy, still bore resentment towards him, Darnley, because of the murder of his former servant David Rizzio. Moretta, too, had asked to see Darnley, ostensibly to discuss horses, but Mary would not let him.[59]

Mary's chief reason for preventing their meeting may have been to avoid giving any offence to the English that might prejudice her chances of the succession. Darnley had proved himself untrustworthy and had already publicly proclaimed her a bad Catholic to her allies, and she was not entirely sure that he was not still working against her. Her chief preoccupation at this time was the new concord with England, and on 8 February, she announced that she was at last willing to ratify the Treaty of Edinburgh and would be sending Robert Melville to London to open the negotiations; he left the next day.[60] It is hardly likely that, at such a crucial time, Mary would have been contemplating murdering her husband. That night, she dined with Darnley, Bothwell and others at Kirk o'Field.

By 9 February, Sir James Balfour seems also to have left Edinburgh. His departure was perhaps significant. Having seen Darnley installed at Kirk o'Field, at his own suggestion, and Moretta in his Edinburgh house, and having perhaps laid plans with both of them, he may have felt that it was wise to absent himself while those plans came to fruition. Or he was playing a double game with both Darnley and the Lords, and did not wish to stay around to risk betrayal.

Sunday, 9 February was the last Sunday in Lent and therefore a day of carnival and feasting; Mary had a full programme of engagements planned. Darnley began this last day of his convalescence by hearing Mass.[61] Later that morning, Moray came to Mary at Holyrood and told her he had received news that his wife was very ill after a miscarriage[62] and that he must go to her without delay; with the Queen's permission, he left Edinburgh immediately for St. Andrews. In view of what was to happen the next night, it is hard to escape the conclusion that Moray was deliberately absenting himself so as to avoid being implicated, especially since he did not return as soon as his wife had recovered. Nau says that he left "after having matured all his plans necessary for his success in seizing the crown and ruining the Queen." Leslie claims that, on the journey to St. Andrews, Moray told his servant, "This night, ere morning, the Lord Darnley shall lose his life," but it seems that Leslie was trying to fabricate a case against Moray in the absence of other evidence, for this remark is entirely out of character. Moray was normally cautious and highly secretive and it is beyond credibility that he would have let slip such an indiscreet and incriminating remark to a servant.

Meanwhile, Darnley was having his last medicinal bath, and doubtless looking forward to returning to Holyrood the following morning[63] and there resuming full marital relations with Mary.

If Mary's enemies are to be believed, she took time out on this busy day to write Casket Letter V to Bothwell; this is surprising, as he was in almost constant attendance on her that day. The French version[64] is endorsed "Anent the dispatch [dismissal] of Margaret Carwood, which was before her marriage; proves her [Mary's] affection"; Buchanan, in his *Detectio*, entitles the Scots version, "Another letter to Bothwell concerning the departure of Margaret Carwood, who was privy and a helper of all their love." Some writers have identified Margaret Carwood with a maid-of-honour who is known to have incurred the Queen's displeasure at this time by becoming pregnant out of wedlock; this was an embarrassment to Mary because of the severe view that the Kirk took of such matters. However, the letter may not refer to Margaret Carwood at all, for on 8 February Mary granted her a handsome pension, and two days later, on the eve of Carwood's wedding, paid out a lavish sum for a wedding dress for her. She would not have acted thus towards a servant who had incurred her displeasure. Casket Letter V reads:

My heart, alas! Must the folly of one woman whose unthankfulness toward me ye do sufficiently know, be occasion of displeasure unto you, considering that I could not have remedied thereunto without knowing it? And since that I perceived it, I could not tell it you, for that I knew not how to govern myself therein. For neither in that, nor in any other thing, will I take upon me to do anything without knowledge of your will, which I beseech you let me understand; for I will follow it all my life, more willingly than you shall declare it to me. And if ye do not send me word this night what ye will that I shall do, I will rid myself of it, and hazard to cause it to be enterprised and taken in hand, which might be hurtful to that whereunto both we do tend. And when she shall be married, I beseech you give me one, or else I will take such as shall content you for their conditions; but, as for their tongues, or faithfulness towards you, I will not answer. I beseech you that are opinion of other person, be not hurtful in your mind to my constancy. Mistrust me, but when I will put you out of doubt and clear myself, refuse it not, my dear love, and suffer me to make you some proof by my obedience, my faithfulness, constancy and voluntary subjection, which I take for the pleasantest good that I might receive, if ye will accept it, and make no ceremony at it, for ye could do me no greater outrage, nor give more mortal grief.

The likelihood is that this note was sent by Mary to Darnley during his sojourn at Kirk o'Field, and that it concerns the maid who had got pregnant. The letter is written in the spirit of the reconciliation that had taken place between the royal couple. Mary would have had no cause to write to Bothwell on such a matter, for her maid's pregnancy would have been of little interest to him, but Darnley would have been concerned lest it cast a stain upon his wife's honour. Mary is worried because, if he does not tell her what she should do about it, he might not approve if she insists on the maid marrying her lover; if Darnley does not approve of that, however, it might prejudice the good relations between him and Mary, yet he must bear in mind that she is willing to be ruled by him in all things. The letter has an abrupt ending and appears to have been cut in the interests of making it look as if the recipient of such loving sentiments was Bothwell.

Late that Sunday morning, Mary attended the marriage of two of her favourite servants, Sebastien Pagez and Christina Hogg, at Holyrood, and was the guest of honour at the wedding breakfast that began at noon. Before leaving, the Queen promised to attend a masque that Pagez had devised in celebration of his nuptials, which was to be staged late that evening.

By 4 p.m., Mary had arrived at a house in the Canongate[65] where the Bishop of the Isles was hosting a farewell banquet for Moretta, who was returning to Savoy the next day. Bothwell, Argyll and Huntly were among those who accompanied the Queen, and all were attired in the magnificent costumes that they were to wear at the masque that evening; Bothwell's was of black satin fringed with silver.[66]

At around 7 p.m., Mary, "masked"[67] and "accompanied with the most part of the Lords that are in this town,"[68] left the banquet and rode to Kirk o'Field to spend the evening with Darnley. While the Queen chatted to her husband, Bothwell, Argyll and Huntly played at dice with a Catholic Privy Councillor, Gilbert Kennedy, Earl of Cassilis, a brutal young thug who once held a man's legs in the fire to make him give way in a property dispute. Maitland appears also to have been present. Buchanan claims that Mary spoke with Darnley "more cheerfully than usual for a few hours" and "often kissed him." She was doubtless in a convivial mood after the day's festivities. Given the large number of people present, it is likely that they all gathered in the Prebendaries' Chamber, which Darnley was using as a presence chamber: his bedchamber would probably not have been big enough to accommodate them all. There is no reason to believe that he was still confined to bed at this time.

It is not certain how long Mary and her courtiers remained at Kirk o'Field that evening because the sources are conflicting. Both Mary and her Councillors stated, in letters written only a day later, that she left around midnight. Lennox states they stayed until 11 p.m., the Seigneur de Clernault says they left after two or three hours, at either 9 p.m. or 10 p.m.,[69] while de Silva heard that they stayed for three hours.[70] Mary and the Lords were probably correct.

Thomas Nelson, Buchanan and Lennox all claimed that Mary intended to stay the night at Kirk o'Field, and the Lords of the Council, in a letter to Catherine de' Medici, written after Darnley's murder, stated that "it was a mere chance that Her Majesty did not remain there all night." Moretta also told the Venetian ambassador in Paris that Mary intended to stay the night.[71] But Buchanan alleges that, "in the middle of the evening's proceedings, the Frenchman Paris, one of her rascally attendants, entered the King's chamber and placed himself silently, so that he could be seen by the Queen. His arrival was the sign that all was prepared for the crime. As soon as she saw Paris, the Queen pretended that she had just remembered Bastien's wedding, and blamed herself for her negligence, because she had not gone to the masked ball that evening, as she had promised, and had not seen the bride in her bed. With this remark, she rose and went home." Yet Mary had come masked, in costume,[72] ready to attend the masque, so it is highly improbable that she forgot her promise, although she may have left Kirk o'Field later than planned. Lennox does not mention this episode, but offers a different explanation for Mary sleeping at Holyrood, as will be seen.

Darnley certainly expected her to return after the masque and stay the night. He expressed chagrin when, as she made ready to leave for the masque, she apparently changed her mind, possibly in view of the lateness of the hour, and said she would sleep at Holyrood. Bothwell, who had reasons of his own for wanting to keep Mary away from Kirk o'Field, reminded her that she had arranged to ride to Seton in the morning, and added that, in view of the early start she wished to make, it would be more convenient for her to stay at Holyrood.[73] Mary later wrote to Archbishop Beaton that it was "of very chance" that she "tarried not all night, by reason of some masque in the Abbey,"[74] while Leslie recorded, "She returned thanks to God for her preservation from so great a peril, for it looked as though the contrivers of the plot had expected that she would pass the night there with the King, and they planned the destruction of them both." Cecil was informed by one Captain Cockburn that, "were it not for Secretary Lethington and Bastien, Her Grace would not fail to have lain in that same house, and been utterly destroyed."[75] Maitland's role in all this is not clear, but some writers have regarded it as strange that he should have tried to save Mary's life when he had perhaps been plotting her ruin. Yet there is no evidence that Maitland or Moray ever conspired to bring about Mary's death; had that been so, they would have had her executed when they had the power to do so. But there is plenty of evidence that Moray at least wanted the Catholic Queen removed from her throne.

Mary attempted to mollify Darnley by reminding him that, on the morrow, they would be together again on a permanent basis, and promised him that the next night she would sleep with him.[76] As a token of this pledge, she gave him a ring.[77] According to Lennox, she also "called the King to remembrance that David, her servant, was murdered about that same time twelve months."[78] If Mary was conspiring to murder Darnley that night, this seems an indiscreet remark to make.

As Mary mounted her horse in the quadrangle, she espied Paris and, "noticing that his face was all blackened with gunpowder," exclaimed, "Jesu, Paris, how begrimed you are!" He said nothing, and after she had stared at him for a moment, she rode away, having noticed that "he turned very red."[79] As she was observing him by torchlight, this was not surprising, and was probably fanciful thinking on her part, in the light of what she afterwards discovered. Had she been aware that Paris had been helping to shift gunpowder, she would hardly have drawn attention to the fact, so her remark must have been made in genuine innocence. Only later would she have realised the significance of Paris's dirty appearance.

Probably around midnight, Mary and her train of nobles, with Bothwell among them, returned to Holyrood via the Cowgate, Blackfriars Wynd and the Canongate. Lennox claims that Mary had a sackbut, an early form of trombone, sounded as a signal to the waiting assassins, but no other account mentions this. The weather was very cold, with a light frosting of snow, and the night very dark; the new moon would not appear until 6 a.m.

Back at Kirk o'Field, some of Darnley's servants were preparing to leave for the night. One was Alexander, or "Sandy," Durham, Master of the Prince's Wardrobe and the son of Alexander Durham the Elder, silversmith and Argenter[80] of the Royal Household. Sandy Durham features largely in the *Oration*, a treatise by one of Mary's English detractors, Dr. Thomas Wilson.[81] Wilson alleges that Durham made several attempts to obtain leave of absence from Kirk o'Field that night, implying that he knew what was planned and was even a party to the plot; he is said to have been so desperate that he set his bedding alight, a rash thing to do if he was aware that there was gunpowder nearby. In the end, he was given permission to go home. Both Wilson and Buchanan claim that Durham was a spy, planted in Darnley's household by his enemies.

Darnley was by no means alone in the house that night. His valet, William Taylor, was in attendance, as were Nelson, McCaig, Glen, Symonds and Taylor's boy.[82] This gives the lie to Buchanan, who claims that "most" of the King's servants "were gone out of the way, as foreknowing the danger at hand." If this were the case, they might fear reprisals if they warned the King, but why did they not, at the very least, warn their colleagues?

Meanwhile, the Queen had arrived at Holyrood, where she put in a brief appearance at the wedding masque and attended the ceremony of putting the bride and groom to bed.[83] At around midnight, she retired to her apartments. There, she held a private conference with Bothwell and John Stewart of Traquair, the Captain of her Guard. After fifteen minutes, Traquair left, leaving Bothwell and Mary talking alone "for a considerable time." After a while, Bothwell was dismissed and the Queen went to bed.[84]

There is no record of what was discussed on this occasion, and Buchanan no doubt wished to imply that it was Darnley's murder, but there was never any suggestion that Traquair was involved in the Kirk o'Field plot. It has been conjectured that Bothwell and Traquair came to Mary with intelligence that Darnley was plotting to murder her.[85] In his memorial, Bothwell says nothing of this, but merely states that he was in the building, "in that part normally allotted to the guard, on this occasion, fifty strong."[86] In 1568, Bothwell was busily accusing the Protestant Lords of murdering Darnley, and it would not have helped his case to brand Darnley himself a would-be regicide. Of course, there is no proof that Darnley's conspiracy was the subject of this private conversation, but the presence of the Captain of the Guard, the fact that Bothwell was in the part of the palace occupied by the guards, and the late hour of the meeting, all suggest that the matter was urgent and that it was crucial to Mary's security.

Buchanan states that, "after the Queen had gone away, the King talked over the events of the day with the few servants who remained" and recalled "a few words which somewhat spoiled his enjoyment," namely Mary's reminder "that it was about that time last year that David Rizzio had been murdered." Buchanan is here embroidering the almost certainly apocryphal story in Lennox's *Narrative*.

Darnley was planning an early start and did not sit up for more than an hour.[87] An account of his last hours appears in Lennox's *Narrative*, and is apparently based on information supplied by Thomas Nelson, who survived the explosion and was later taken into Lennox's service. Darnley summoned an unnamed servant—who was probably Sandy Durham, as Darnley bade him farewell afterwards—and called for wine. He then "commanded that his great horses should be in readiness by five of the clock in the morning," when he planned to depart for either Holyrood or, more probably, Seton, to join Mary.

Darnley then said to his servant, "Let us go merrily to bed in singing a song before," but declined to accompany them on the lute, saying, "My hand is not inclined to the lute this night." The servant had a book of psalms to hand, and Darnley decided they would all sing the 5th Psalm: "Give ear to my words, O Lord. Hearken unto the voice of my cry: . . . for unto Thee will I pray . . . The Lord will abhor the bloody and deceitful man. But as for me, I will come into Thy house in the multitude of Thy mercy." The rest is a prayer to God to destroy the Psalmist's enemies. It was a highly appropriate text for Lennox's "innocent lamb" to recite in the circumstances, and some writers have wondered if the grieving father deliberately inserted it into his account for good effect, and if Darnley and his servant in fact did sing their "merry song." Drury incorrectly reported to Cecil that Darnley had recited the 55th Psalm,[88] which was even more apposite, and read: "Fearfulness and trembling are come upon me, and an horrible dread hath overwhelmed me . . . It is not an open enemy that has done me this dishonour, for then I could have borne it. It was even thou, my companion, my guide, and my own familiar friend."

Once the singing was done, the King "drank to his servant, bidding him farewell for that night, and so went to bed."[89] After snuffing out the candles, Taylor lay down to rest on a "pallet" bed in Darnley's room. Nelson, Symonds and "Taylor's boy" retired to the gallery that led off the bedchamber, while the two grooms, McCaig and Glen, were to spend the night downstairs.[90]

All was quiet. In a window of the Duke's House, where Archbishop Hamilton was residing, a single light burned, which could be seen "from the highest parts of the town."[91] The raven was still perched on the roof of Darnley's lodging; during the day, portentously, it had "croaked for a very long time upon the house."[92]

16

"Most Cruel Murder"

⁓

SHORTLY BEFORE 2 A.M. ON MONDAY, 10 February 1567, a Mrs.
Barbara Merton, who lived in Blackfriars Wynd, a street that rose from
the Cowgate to the High Street, was awakened by running footsteps; she
looked out and counted thirteen armed men, who had emerged from the gate
of the abandoned Blackfriars monastery to the south and were now hasten-
ing up to the High Street.[1] Around the same time, some women lodging near
the south garden and orchard of Kirk o'Field, "perhaps even in one of the cottages where the ambush was set," heard a man's voice crying desperately,
"Pity me, kinsmen, for the love of Him who had pity on all the world!" Then
there was silence.[2]

Suddenly, "at about two hours after midnight"[3] the air was rent with the
crash of a massive explosion that, according to Buchanan, "shook the whole
town" and was followed by "fearful outcries and the confused cries of the
people." "The King's lodging was, even from the very foundation, blown up
in the air. Several neighbouring houses were shaken, and people who slept in
the furthermost parts of the town were awakened, bewildered and alarmed."[4]
The Queen later wrote that the house was blown up "in one instant."[5] Se-
bastian Davelourt, Keeper of the Ordnance, afterwards likened the sound of
the explosion to thunder, while the Seigneur de Clernault reported that the

"tremendous noise" was equal to a volley of 25 or 30 cannon, "so that every-one awoke."[6] Paris later deposed that, on hearing the "crack," every hair on his head had stood on end,[7] and Herries recorded that "the blast was fearful to all about, and many rose from their beds at the noise."

The Lords of the Council, in a letter to Catherine de' Medici written later that day,[8] concluded that the Old Provost's Lodging and the Prebendaries' Chamber had been "blown into the air by the force of powder, as one might judge by the noise and the terrible and sudden event, which was so vehement that, of a salle, two bedrooms, cabinet and garderobe, nothing remains which was not carried far away and reduced to powder, not only the roof and floors, but also the walls to the foundation, so that not one stone rests on another." In a letter to Archbishop Beaton, also written probably on the 10th, Mary confirmed this, adding that all was "either carried far away or dashed in dross to the very groundstone. It must have been done by the force of powder, and appears to have been a mine."[9] It was said that "great stones, of the length of ten foot and of breadth of four foot, were found blown from the house far away."[10] Clernault reported that the King's lodging was "totally razed."[11]

Just after the explosion, Mrs. Merton and her neighbour, Mrs. Mary Stirling (née Crocket), saw eleven men emerge from Blackfriars gate and run up Blackfriars Wynd. Two of them wore light-coloured clothing. As they passed, Mrs. Merton called after them, "Traitors! You have been at some evil turn!" Mrs. Stirling laid hold of one man by his silk cloak and asked him where the explosion had occurred, but he merely shook her off. She watched as the men split up into two groups: four of them went north towards the High Street, while the other five hastened towards the Cowgate Port in the city wall.[12]

Members of the night watch were soon on the scene at Kirk o'Field, and the first man they saw there was Captain William Blackadder, Bothwell's man, who had conveyed Mary to Alloa after the Prince's birth. Concluding that his presence in the vicinity was suspicious, they promptly arrested him, ignoring his protests that he had been drinking at a friend's house nearby and had come out to see what had caused the explosion. This was probably true, for there is no evidence that he had been a party to the murder plot.

Soon, local people and citizens from further afield, some in their night-clothes, some carrying lanterns, were hurrying towards Kirk o'Field, where they were confronted by a scene of devastation where the south range of the quadrangle had once stood. Their eyes were immediately drawn to the blackened figure of Thomas Nelson, swaying on the top of the Flodden Wall and crying out for help. He had luckily been thrown clear by the blast, and had suffered only superficial injuries. Once he had been rescued, people started digging frantically in the smoking rubble, many with their bare hands, looking for other survivors or bodies. Their search was hampered by the darkness, the biting cold and intermittent falls of snow. But many people were aware that the King had been staying in the house, and they were determined to find him. Soon, there were large crowds at the scene.

Few noticed that, just after the explosion occurred, the candle in the window of the Duke's House had been extinguished.[13] Buchanan placed great emphasis on this, but it could have happened naturally with the force of the blast. But Buchanan, a Lennox man, intended his readers to conclude that Archbishop Hamilton was implicated in Darnley's murder.

At Holyrood, Mary was also awakened by the noise of the explosion, and, thinking it was cannon fire, sent messengers to find out what was happening.[14] Elsewhere in the palace, people were running and screaming in panic, and the royal sentries were asking each other, "What crack was that?" The Queen's messengers "followed the crowd until they came to the King's residence, which they found to be entirely overthrown."[15] The news was quickly conveyed to the palace.

Bothwell was Sheriff of Edinburgh, and it was his responsibility to investigate any crime that was committed there. Since he had not emerged from his lodgings, his servant, George Halket,[16] was sent to wake him up and inform him that Darnley's house had been blown up and that the King was believed killed. Bothwell shot up in bed, crying, "Fie! Treason!"[17] then ordered his own men to go to the scene of the disaster to discover what had happened to the King and the cause of the explosion. That done, he went back to bed with his wife[18] to await news.

Meanwhile, at Kirk o'Field, two mutilated bodies were being uncovered amidst the debris. One of them was Andrew McCaig.[19] The Lords informed Catherine de' Medici that "some" were killed "and some, at God's pleasure, preserved," while Robert Melville informed de Silva that five servants escaped, "who only knew that they had heard the noise."[20] This cannot be correct, since there were six servants in the house at the time of the explosion, and three are known to have died. It is possible that Symonds and Taylor's boy, who were in the gallery with Nelson, also survived, and likely that Glen, who was sleeping on the ground floor with McCaig, was the other man found dead in the rubble. The Lords and Melville may have counted among the survivors guards who are not mentioned elsewhere. There was as yet no sign of Darnley.

At last, at 5 a.m., three hours after the explosion, someone thought to look in the south garden and orchard, beyond the Flodden Wall, and it was there that they found the bodies of the twenty-year-old King and his valet, Taylor, lying "sixty to eighty steps from the house."[21] Both were nearly naked, being clad in short nightshirts, and neither body had a mark on it. Darnley was stretched out on his back, under a pear tree, with one hand draped modestly over his genitals,[22] while Taylor lay a yard or two away, curled up, with his nightshirt rucked up around his waist and his head resting face down on his crossed arms; he had on a nightbonnet and one slipper. Clernault says that the body of "a young page" was also found in the garden, but this is not corroborated by other accounts, nor is a third body shown in the drawing of the scene that is now in the Public Record Office.

Those who saw the bodies were at a loss to know how they had died, for it did not look as if they had perished in the explosion. There were no burns,[23] no marks of strangulation or violence, and "no fracture, wound or bruise."[24] "The people ran to behold the spectacle and, wondering thereat, some judged one thing, some another."[25]

Near to the bodies lay a chair, a length of rope, a dagger, Darnley's furred nightgown and what could have been a quilt or cloak. "The clothes lying near were not only not burned or marked with the powder, but seemed to have been put there, not by force or chance, but by hand."[26] A backless velvet shoe or "mule" was also found in the garden near the corpses; it was later alleged to have belonged to Archibald Douglas, although, as will be seen, he was to deny that it was his.[27]

As soon as the bodies were found, Francisco de Busso, an Italian from Mary's household, hastened to the house of John Pitcairn, a surgeon, who lived in Blackfriars Wynd, and "cried on" him "to come to his master," which Pitcairn did, remaining with Darnley's body for about six hours.[28]

Soon after the discovery of the bodies, Mary was informed of her husband's death. It is not known who brought her the news,[29] but, according to

Nau, "when the Queen was told what had occurred, she was in great grief, and kept her chamber all that day." Bothwell, still in bed with his wife, was told by Huntly of the discovery of the King's body. "I was very distressed at the news, as were many others with me," Bothwell wrote later.[30] Hastily, he dressed, then he and Huntly, together with Argyll, Atholl, Maitland and the Countesses of Atholl and Mar, went to the Queen's room to console her. There, "while the monstrous chance was telling, everyone wondered at the thing."[31]

There is plenty of evidence for Mary's reaction to Darnley's death. The *Book of Articles* states "she was little altered or abashed," but Bothwell told Melville he had found her "sorrowful and quiet" and recalled in his memoirs that she "was greatly affected by it all."[32] Mary herself stated she felt so "grievous and tormented" that she was unable to attend to any business or correspondence, and other sources bear this out. Clernault wrote, "One may imagine the distress and agony of this poor princess at such a misfortune, chancing when Her Majesty and the King were on such good terms." Some writers have suggested that he was drawing conclusions without having seen the Queen, but he also wrote that, when he left her, she was "so much afflicted as to be one of the most unfortunate queens in the world."[33] This is corroborated by Moretta, who reported that he left the Queen deeply afflicted and in great fear of a worse fate.[34] There is no doubt that Darnley's murder left Mary grief-stricken, emotionally shattered and fearful for her own safety. For several months afterwards, she seems not to have functioned normally, and her judgement, never very good at the best of times, utterly failed her.

Scotland was now faced with a major political scandal. At Huntly's suggestion, to which the Queen agreed, fifteen members of the Privy Council met in emergency session at Holyrood to discuss how best to deal with this latest crisis and "deliberate about the means of apprehending the traitors who committed the deed."[35]

At the Queen's command, Bothwell took a company of soldiers to Kirk o'Field "to make a diligent search for the traitors and apprehend them."[36] Argyll accompanied them. Bothwell had Darnley's body carried into "the next house"[37]—the New Provost's Lodging—and placed in the care of Sandy Durham, "under a guard of honour."[38] Bothwell also ordered a thorough search of the area, and he and his men, "in our fury, apprehended some persons suspected of the deed and put them under arrest, until they should render to us a sure account of the place they had been when the murder was committed. Nor did I ever cease making strict search that I might get at the bottom of the whole," Bothwell added, "for I could not imagine that I could ever be suspected."[39] He also "found a barrel or cask in which the powder had been, which we preserved, having taken note of the mark on it."[40] This mark, which is nowhere described, was presumably thought to be a means of identifying the maker or owner of the barrel. It has been suggested by several writers that this barrel was planted at Kirk o'Field with the deliberate intention of incriminating someone.

One of Cecil's agents had already arrived on the scene and begun sketching a plan of the site, including the events of the day as he saw them unfold.[41] His drawing still survives. In it, the pile of rubble marking the area of the demolished buildings can clearly be seen. Darnley and Taylor lie in the orchard to the south, near the items found next to the bodies. To the west, Darnley's body is carried towards the New Provost's Lodging as a crowd of onlookers watch. Further south, Taylor's body is buried, apparently in the churchyard of the ruined St. Mary's Kirk. In the top left-hand corner of the drawing, Prince James sits up in his bed, his hands raised in prayer, and from his mouth there issue the words, "Judge and avenge my cause, O Lord." The drawing was sent to Cecil in London.

According to Buchanan, before dawn broke, someone—the implication is that it was Mary and Bothwell—had sent messengers into England to spread rumours "that the Earls of Moray and Morton were doers of that slaughter." This passage does not appear in the English edition of the *Detectio*. Thomas Wilson also refers to the spreading of slanders, but names no names. If such rumours were actually spread, and that is by no means certain, they may have been the only means available of attaching suspicion to men who had been clever enough to cover their traces.

News of the King's murder spread quickly throughout Edinburgh.[42] People were soon grouping on the streets, fearfully speculating as to the assassins and their motives, then dispersing. They were more startled by the tidings of Darnley's death than they had been by the blast, "whilst the manner of it was no less various censured than reported."[43] Wild rumours began circulating. One was that Lennox had been killed in the explosion,[44] which was, of course, untrue.

. . .

Back at Holyrood, the Queen had proclaimed a period of court mourning and ordered black serge from Florence for a mourning gown, cloak, mules and shoes.[45] She had chosen to follow the French royal custom, whereby a widowed queen remained in mourning for forty days, secluded in her black-draped chambers, which no daylight was allowed to penetrate.[46] Leslie later recalled that she "bemoaned" her husband "a notable time, using none other than candle-light," but Buchanan claimed that Mary's grief was a pretence calculated to "ingratiate herself with the people," and alleged that, whilst she withdrew into seclusion, "the ceremony was evil observed," and "such was her joy that, though she shut the doors, she opened the windows." Paris was among those in attendance in Mary's bedchamber on the morning after Darnley's murder, and he saw that it was already shrouded in black.

The Queen was breakfasting in bed, being waited on by her French governess and other ladies and servants, when Bothwell returned from Kirk o'Field. Paris watched as the Earl entered her room and whispered something in her ear. Buchanan, however, says that Mary only retired to her bedchamber after Bothwell had made his report, at which she "feigned amazement."

A little later, Sir James Melville came to the door of the Queen's apartments to see how she was. Bothwell came out and told him she was "sorrowful and quiet, which occasioned him to come forth." He then privately expressed to Melville his opinion that Darnley's death had been an accident, "the strangest that ever chanced, to wit, the thunder [sic] came out of the sky and had burnt the King's house." This certainly would have been strange, as there had been no storm that night. Bothwell urged Melville to go and see the King's body, expressing surprise that there had, inexplicably, been no marks on it, whereupon Melville dutifully set off for Kirk o'Field.[47]

Buchanan later accused the Queen of "sweetly sleeping" until noon or for most of the day,[48] but this would have been entirely understandable, given that she had had a very disturbed night followed by shocking news. Nau says she was in such grief that she "kept to her chamber all that day," but she seems to have been awake for most of the morning at least, attending to sad but necessary duties that could not wait. The first of these was to summon chirurgeons and apothecaries to carry out a post-mortem examination on

Darnley's body. This took place later that morning, in the presence of the Lords of the Privy Council.[49] During their examination, the doctors discovered that "one rib in the King's body was found broken by the distance of the jump of the fall" and that Darnley had also suffered grave internal injuries.[50] They therefore concluded that he had been blown into the garden by the explosion. Knox claims that the doctors had only said this "to please the Queen," and that "truly he [Darnley] was strangled."[51] If Darnley had been strangled, there would have been evidence of asphyxia and marks around the throat and neck to prove it, but every source states that there were no marks at all on the body.

Once the post-mortem was concluded, the public were allowed in to view the King's corpse. According to Buchanan, "for a long time, the King's body remained a spectacle to a continual crowd of common people,"[52] yet "no one could bring himself to believe that the force of the explosion had thrown him through the roof." Contrary to what Buchanan says, the body did not remain on view for a long time, for when Melville arrived later that morning to see it, it had been moved to an inner chamber and Sandy Durham would not let him enter.[53]

After the post-mortem, the Privy Councillors held a meeting in the Tolbooth under the presidency of Argyll, Lord Justice-General of Scotland. Realising that they must embark upon a damage limitation exercise if Scotland were not to become the scandal of Europe, they wrote a letter giving an account—the first ever account—of Darnley's murder to Catherine de' Medici. This was to be conveyed by her envoy, the Seigneur de Clernault, who had been visiting Scotland and is thought by some writers to have been in league with Moretta and perhaps Darnley, although on the slenderest of evidence. The Lords began:

Madam,
The strange event which occurred in this town last night constrains us to be bold to write briefly to you, in order to give you and yours to understand the miserable deed which has been perpetrated on the person of the King, in such a strange manner that one has never heard tell of a similar affair.

They then described what had happened during the night, before proceeding to offer what was to be the official explanation of events, for the time being at least, an explanation that was based on Mary's own convictions:

> Those that are the authors of this evil only just failed in destroying the Queen by the same means, with a great part of the nobles and Lords who are for the present in her suite, who were there with the King in his room until nearly midnight. And Her Majesty only just failed to remain in order to lodge there all the night, but God has been so kind to us that these assassins were frustrated in half their attempt, He having reserved Her Majesty to take [the] vengeance such a barbarous and inhuman deed deserves. We are engaged in an inquiry, and we doubt not that shortly we shall arrive at a knowledge of those who did it. For God will never permit such a mischief to remain hidden, and, having once uncovered the matter, Your Majesty and all the world shall know that Scotland will not endure that such a cause for shame should rest upon her shoulders, and which would be enough to render her hateful to all Christianity if similar wickednesses should lie hidden and unpunished.
>
> We did not wish to miss making this advertisement to the King's Majesty and yourself by this gentleman, present bearer, the Seigneur de Clernault, who will relate to you all the details, since he is well informed to this end. His sufficience is such that we leave the rest to him, so as not, with a longer letter, to importune Your Majesty.
>
> From Edinburgh, this 10th February.[54]

The letter was signed by Archbishop Hamilton, Argyll, Huntly, Atholl, Cassilis, Bothwell, the Earls of Caithness and Sutherland, Alexander Gordon, Bishop of Galloway, John Leslie, Bishop of Ross, Robert Richardson, the Lord Treasurer, Justice Clerk Bellenden, Secretary Maitland and Lords Livingston and Fleming.

This letter gives the lie to Buchanan's allegation that "there was no mention of an investigation into the murder."

Some time during the morning, Robert Drury arrived from Paris with Archbishop Beaton's letter of warning to Mary, too late for it to be of any use; even if she had received it earlier, there was no hint in it of any threat to Darnley. However, Mary believed that the plot of which Beaton had warned her was the plot that had led to Darnley's death, and that it had been targeted at her also.

A letter, purporting to be from Mary, was sent in response to the Archbishop, giving an account of the murder; this was dated 11 February, but was probably written on the 10th before the results of the post-mortem were known. As it is written in Scots, a language Mary did not normally write in, and is similar in tone and composition to the letter sent by the Lords to Catherine de' Medici, there has been speculation that it was written on Mary's behalf, perhaps by Maitland, as she was too distressed to write herself; on her own testimony, she was unable to attend to her correspondence. The letter probably reflects her views, as expressed to her Councillors, and she may have dictated some or all of it. It begins:

> We have received this morning your letters of the 27th January, containing in one part such advertisement as we find by effect over-true, albeit the success has not altogether been such as the authors of that mischievous fact had preconceived and had put it in execution. And if God in His mercy had not preserved us, as we trust, to the end that we may take a rigorous vengeance of that mischievous deed, which, ere it should remain unpunished, we had rather lose life and all. The matter is so horrible and strange as we believe the like was never heard of in any country.

After outlining the facts, Mary continued:

> By whom it has been done, or in what manner, it appears not yet. We doubt not but, according to the vigilance our Council has begun to already use, the certainty of all shall be used shortly, and, the same being discovered, which we wot [know] God will never suffer to lie hidden, we hope to punish the same with such rigour as serve for an example of this cruelty to all ages to come.

These strong words do not sound as if they came from a woman with a guilty conscience, but as if they were written by someone desperate for vengeance upon those who have done her so great an injury. The letter goes on to voice a strong conviction—one from which Mary was never to depart—that the explosion was meant to destroy her too.

> Always, whoever has taken this wicked enterprise in hand, we assure ourselves it was designed as well for ourselves as for the King, for we lay the most part of all last week in that same lodging, and was there accompanied with the most part of the Lords that are in this town, and had that same night, at midnight, and of very chance, tarried not all night there, by reason of some masque at the Abbey of Holyrood. But we believe it was not chance but God that put it in our head.
>
> We dispatched this bearer upon the sudden, and therefore write to you the more shortly. The rest of your letter we shall answer at more leisure within four or five days by your own servant.[55]

It may not be going too far to say that Mary's distress was caused more by the realisation that she herself might have been the target of the murderers than by her sorrow at Darnley's death. Her feelings of shock and vulnerability could explain her behaviour during the weeks to come, when self-preservation was to be her overriding priority.

Later that day, Darnley's corpse was carried back to Holyrood, where it was embalmed by an apothecary and a surgeon. Buchanan says that, on the Queen's orders, it was borne to the palace by porters on "an old block of form or tree" or "an inverted bench." An account in the Register House in Edinburgh, dated 11 February, gives details of the expenses incurred in "opening and perfuming" the King's body. The receipt was signed by the Queen's apothecary, Martin Picavet.[56]

Buchanan alleges that, when Darnley's body arrived at Holyrood, Mary went to see it. "As she had satisfied her heart with his slaughter, so she would needs feast her eyes with the sight of his body slain. For she long beheld, and not only without grief, the goodliest corpse of any gentleman that ever lived in this age, not only calmly, but even greedily"; elsewhere, he says "she gave no indication of her secret feelings," which is echoed by Knox, who states that she gazed upon the corpse "without any outward show or sign of joy or sorrow." Yet Mary had already gone into seclusion, and kept to her chamber all that day; there is no contemporary evidence that she emerged to look at Darnley's body.

Later that morning, according to Buchanan, "the matter being wondered at, and great execration in the mouths of the multitude" against the assassins,[57] "shame and fear compelled [the Councillors] to do something, and so, shortly before noon, Bothwell and several other conspirators" convened in Argyll's chamber in the Tolbooth to begin an inquiry into the murder.[58] Tullibardine was also present, representing the interests of Lennox. Buchanan implies that the Lords present had a vested interest in keeping the true facts hidden: "at first, they professed ignorance of all that had happened, marvelling at it as a new, unheard of, incredible thing. Then they allowed a very slight examination." Thomas Nelson was the first witness they examined. He and other deponents were "questioned as to the entry of the murderers" and asked "who prepared and ordained that house for the King" and "who had the keys." When Nelson denied that the keys had been in his possession, he was asked, "Who had them, then?" He replied, "The Queen," at which point Tullibardine intervened, saying, "Hold there: he is aground." There were no further questions, and the inquiry was adjourned until the next day.

17

"NONE DARE FIND
FAULT WITH IT"

W HO MURDERED DARNLEY?
    There can be no doubt that he was murdered, but the identity of
the person or persons responsible is surrounded by great mystery, and there
have been so many theories that the subject has become one of the most controversial in history. Was this a political assassination, or a crime inspired by
passion or revenge?

All we can be certain of is that, by early February 1567, some people
were conspiring to murder the King, and that the chief culprits must have
been leading members of the establishment.

For the historian investigating this mystery today, the problems are manifold. As has already been made clear, there is a vast amount of conflicting
and untrustworthy information. Most contemporary sources reflect religious
and sexual prejudices, and much of the source material is suspect because it
was written by people with reputations to protect and a revolution to justify.
Most of the information about Mary's role in the murder comes from her enemies, who had good cause for blackening her name, and whose works are
not strictly contemporary, or from depositions by witnesses who were almost
certainly intimidated into giving the politically correct version of events.
Some of this "evidence" is very compelling and convincing, yet difficult or im-

possible to substantiate through strictly contemporary sources. In recent years, however, thanks to the painstaking work of objective historians and investigators, these hostile accounts have been exposed for the libels they undoubtedly were.

The mystery of Darnley's death was never satisfactorily solved in the sixteenth century: any investigation of the matter was apparently subverted by the desire to protect the guilty and frame the scapegoats, and vital documents, such as the Casket Letters, have since disappeared. There is, it is true, a vast amount of evidence as to what happened on the night of 9–10 February 1567, but most of it lies in the above-mentioned unreliable depositions of suspects and witnesses made behind closed doors, on the orders of the Privy Council, to the Lords of the Secret Council, namely Maitland, Morton, Huntly, Argyll and Balfour, all of whom were probably involved in the plot to murder Darnley. These depositions were attested by Justice Clerk Bellenden, who was not present when they were taken; most of them were not properly witnessed and were perhaps extracted under torture[1] by ruthless and powerful men who had good reasons for wanting the real truth suppressed. Neither were these depositions ever made public nor subjected to any independent examination. History was virtually rewritten to suit the party in power, and rewritten by clever men who knew how to make a forceful case.

The historian's task therefore seems hopeless, and it has been said that it is extraordinarily difficult, if not impossible, to reconcile all the evidence and come up with a credible conclusion. Yet this is not necessarily the case, for amongst the gallons of spilled ink there are plenty of clues.

There were several people, or factions, who might have wanted Darnley dead, or stood to gain from his death. During the two years after his murder, the only two people who were formally accused of it were Bothwell and the Queen, and it was stressed that their motives were an indecent passion for each other and Bothwell's overweening ambition. Mary herself had earlier made it clear that she wished to be rid of Darnley, and not without good reason; furthermore, most ways of doing so were closed to her. However, her accusers, the Protestant Lords, led by Moray and Maitland, had no time for Darnley, who was a constant embarrassment and a threat to their own influence, and they may have seen his murder as an opportunity of ridding themselves of another person who posed such a threat, namely Bothwell, and ultimately seizing power themselves, which was what in fact happened. Nor may their aims have been entirely political, for Morton and several others involved in Rizzio's murder, who had been betrayed by Darnley, had every reason to seek revenge on him. As the years went by, and loyalties shifted, the Lords began accusing each other of the murder, until, in the end, most of the leading nobles of Scotland were among the suspects. There is a more recent theory that Darnley himself plotted the explosion at Kirk o'Field, with a view to killing his wife and most of the Protestant establishment and snatching power for himself, but that something went wrong. Some even pointed the finger at Archbishop Hamilton. There may also have been more than one plot, and more than one culprit or group of persons involved. All of these theories are, on the face of it, plausible.

The chief suspect, however, was Bothwell. Mary herself later came to believe in his guilt and, from 1568, referred to him several times as one of Darnley's murderers. Along with Argyll and Huntly, Bothwell had been brought into the conspiracy against Darnley by Maitland and Moray early in December at Craigmillar. There is evidence that he knew all about the Bond for the King's murder that was probably signed at Craigmillar. It was Bothwell who tried to draw Morton into this conspiracy, and Bothwell who asked Mary to sanction the King's assassination, which Mary later did not deny. Bothwell was almost certainly driven by his ambition to marry the Queen himself and become King, a theory that is supported by his actions subsequent to the murder and by Melville, who states that "the Earl of Bothwell had a mark of his own that he shot at, . . . that he might marry the Queen." That Bothwell acted alone, however, seems unlikely, but at the time, there was so much evidence against him that it appeared he was the prime mover in the plot, which, as we have seen, was not the case.

It is possible that Moray and Maitland, who had long been Bothwell's enemies, planned to use his involvement in the murder as a means of getting rid of him, for not only did they detest him, but they also had good reason to fear that he would usurp their power—he was already far too influential for comfort. Back in August, Bedford had reported that Bothwell was the most hated amongst the Scots nobles and that there was a device to kill him. Since then, his influence had increased, and so had the other Lords' bitter resentment. This would explain why Maitland and Moray brought this unlikely ally into the plot against Darnley. Yet, although Bothwell almost certainly planned Darnley's murder, it is unlikely that he actually killed him.

Much of the evidence against Bothwell lies in the suspect depositions and confessions of his associates,[2] most of whom were certainly his men. As will be seen, these contain improbabilities and irreconcilable discrepancies; more tellingly, there are contradictions in different versions of the same deposition. These inconsistencies may have been the result of confusion on the night of 10 February, or of lapses in memory after the passage of time, but they also support the theory that information given to the interrogators was either manufactured or suppressed in order to isolate and reinforce the case against Bothwell and protect others who may have been involved. There is no doubt that some of these depositions were carefully edited for the same reasons; even Buchanan admits that information was suppressed. There may be an element of truth in these various accounts, for there are several points on which these confessions, obtained from different people at different times, agree, and it is possible that they were not total inventions. Furthermore, their evidence is that of minor players who were acting on the orders of powerful men whose motives and political agenda they were not made privy to and did not fully understand. These depositions were made before men who had no doubt already decided how the official version of events was to be written, and for that reason alone, they should be treated with extreme caution.

The story that these depositions tell is as follows.

Paris claimed that he first came into credit with the Queen on 21 January, when she was at Callendar on her way to Glasgow, and Bothwell was about to return to Edinburgh. Mary gave Paris a purse of money to carry to Bothwell, and when he delivered it, Bothwell said to him, "If you take care what you are doing, the Queen will give you letters to bring to me." It seems strange that Mary should ask Paris to take Bothwell the purse when she could have given it to him herself; they were, after all, staying in the same house.

Three days later, Mary gave Paris letters to carry to Bothwell and Maitland in Edinburgh, and told him to observe their faces as they read them, adding that it was a matter of deciding whether the air was better for the King at Craigmillar or Kirk o'Field. This is an obvious invention, for Kirk o'Field was not suggested as a lodging for Darnley until about a week later. Yet, according to the depositions, Bothwell had been overseeing the final murder preparations at the King's lodging before his departure for Liddesdale on 24 January. Paris states that Mary also told him to tell Bothwell that the King wanted to kiss her, but she did not want him to for fear of his illness.

According to his first deposition, Paris arrived in Edinburgh on 25 January to find Bothwell gone. He claimed to have tracked him down at Kirk o'Field, but this was at a time when, in reality, Bothwell was already in the Borders. Paris says Bothwell read Mary's letter, which is perhaps to be identified with Casket Letter II, then told him, "Commend me to the Queen and tell her that all will go well. Say that Balfour and I have not slept all night, that everything is arranged, and that the King's lodgings are ready for him. I have sent her a diamond. You may say that I would send my heart too, were it in my power, but she has it already." Paris then went to see Maitland, who said that he must tell the Queen to bring the King to Kirk o'Field. Paris's deposition was made at a time when Moray was doing his best to bring about Maitland's ruin; the earlier depositions do not incriminate him. Balfour is also incriminated with Bothwell, because he had recently abandoned Moray's party and voted for the Queen's return.

However, in his second deposition, Paris tells another tale, saying he arrived in Edinburgh on the 25th to find Bothwell dining with Sir James Balfour. Bothwell read Mary's letter, then told Paris to say to Mary that all would be well and that he was sending her a diamond in place of his heart. He then told Paris to go to Maitland "and ask him if he wishes to write to the Queen." Paris found Maitland at the Exchequer House, where Maitland told him that Darnley would be better off at Kirk o'Field. Paris then returned to Glasgow with both messages, arriving before 27 January, which was the day Mary and Darnley departed for Edinburgh.

Having listened to what Paris had to say and asked him many questions about his meetings with Bothwell and Maitland, Mary told him that she intended to appoint her servant Gilbert Curle as valet to Darnley in place of Sandy Durham, whom she did not trust.

Paris rode with the King and Queen towards Edinburgh, and waited with Mary at Linlithgow to hear from Ormiston that Bothwell was on his way back from Liddesdale. When this was confirmed, Mary sent Paris to Bothwell with some bracelets, presumably those referred to in Casket Letter II, which was "discovered" two years before Paris's deposition was obtained; she also sent Bothwell's kinsman and retainer, John Hay, to the Earl with a private message, according to Hay's deposition. John Hay was Laird of Talla in Peeblesshire, and had accompanied Mary on her journey from Glasgow; his mother was a Hepburn. Part of his deposition was suppressed, which suggests that the rest of it is unreliable.

On arrival at Kirk o'Field, Mary became angry with Paris when he had her bed placed directly under where the King's bed stood in the room above, which was, in effect, where Bothwell had decided that the gunpowder was to be lit. Paris had to move the bed to ensure that there was enough space for the barrel in which the powder was to be packed. Lennox claims that the house was already undermined when Darnley arrived there. Neither Paris nor Lennox can be correct, since the decision to use Kirk o'Field was made at the last minute, and, according to John Hepburn's deposition, Bothwell did not decide to use gunpowder until 7 February.

Bothwell allegedly told Paris that, while Darnley was at Kirk o'Field, he himself, through the good offices of Lady Reres, visited Mary's room at Holyrood most nights, while his cousin, John Hepburn of Bolton in East Lothian, kept watch under the palace galleries. Because of this, Bothwell forbade Paris, on his life, to divulge to Mary the fact that his wife was staying with him at Holyrood. This argues either extraordinary forbearance or an unusual lack of curiosity on the part of the Countess, and suggests that Bothwell was using Mary in order to attain his ambitions; allegations to this effect had been made long before Paris made his deposition. Yet although Paris claims that Mary and Bothwell were indulging in regular illicit sex at this time, he also states that the Queen was suffering from pain and weakness, and the Earl from dysentery.

Bothwell was feeling unwell during the Queen's overnight stay at Kirk o'Field on 5 February. After dinner, he told Paris he found himself struck down by his "usual illness," the bloody flux, and asked where he could "do my job." Paris found him a place between two doors, helped Bothwell to undress, and stood watch. As Bothwell relieved himself, he chatted to Paris, but he was obviously brooding over the implications of the reconciliation between Mary and Darnley, and suddenly blurted out, "If the King has ever the advantage over us other Lords, he will want to dominate us, and we do not mean to put up with it. We mean to blow him up in this house with gunpowder. What think you of that?"

Aghast, Paris replied, "You will pardon me if I do not tell you." At this, Bothwell angrily retorted, "What are you saying? Do you want to preach at me?" Paris replied that Bothwell had often been in trouble but no one had helped him. "Now you propose to undertake this big enterprise, far bigger than any trouble you may have had, for they will call down the hue and cry on you." Bothwell snapped that Paris was an utter fool if he thought he, Bothwell, would attempt such an enterprise on his own, and revealed that his chief accomplice was Maitland, "who is considered to have one of the best minds in the country; he is the presiding genius of it all. I have Argyll, Huntly, Morton, Ruthven and Lindsay. I have the signatures of those men, written the last time we were at Craigmillar." Paris asked if Moray was also involved, but Bothwell replied, "The Earl of Moray, the Earl of Moray will neither help nor hinder us, but it is all one." Morton, Ruthven and Lindsay were in favour with Moray when this deposition was made, so the inclusion of their names is interesting, but there is no other evidence that Ruthven and Lindsay, who had just returned from exile, were involved in Darnley's murder.

Bothwell asked Paris to assist in his plans, and when Paris fearfully demurred, rounded on him angrily, demanding, "Why did I put you in the Queen's service if not to help me?" Paris retorted that, during the six years he had been in the Earl's service, Bothwell had known how to make him do his bidding, kicking him in the stomach until he capitulated. Perhaps fearing further violence, Paris reluctantly agreed to help.

The following day, Bothwell approached John Hepburn of Bolton with a proposal to assassinate Darnley "in the fields," which is at variance with Paris's allegation that, two days earlier, Bothwell had already decided to blow up the house. Bothwell assured Hepburn that each of the Lords involved in the plot would send two underlings to assist. Like Paris, Hepburn was initially reluctant to join the conspiracy, but he too gave way to persuasion.

On Friday, 7 February, Balfour apparently first heard of the murder plot, or so he later told the Lords.[3] Paris claimed that Bothwell and Balfour had spent a night at Kirk o'Field on 23/24 January, but, in the suppressed part of his deposition, Hepburn claimed that "my Lord Bothwell sent [him] to Sir James Balfour, desiring that he would come and meet my Lord at Kirk o'Field. To whom Sir James answered, 'Will my Lord come then? If he come, it were better he were quiet.' And yet they met not at that place, then or at no time thereafter, to the deponer's knowledge." Hepburn's knowledge of the plot was, of course, limited.

Morton, in his confession of 1581, stated that he learned of the murder plot "a little before," through Archibald Douglas; this was possibly on Friday, 7 February.

It was on that day, according to John Hay, that Bothwell resolved to carry out the assassination using gunpowder, and informed Hay of his intentions, saying, "John, the King's death is devised. I will reveal it unto you, for if I put him not down, I cannot have a life in Scotland. He will be my destruction." The plan was to place the gunpowder in the Queen's room, immediately below Darnley's bedchamber.

Why Bothwell or anyone else should choose to kill Darnley by the dramatic means of gunpowder, instead of by more common methods of assassination such as poison or suffocation, is a mystery. It may have been designed to ensure that any evidence of his involvement was destroyed, for the Queen had refused to sanction any violence against her husband, and if Bothwell really did wish to marry her, he could not have risked being associated in any way with the crime; yet there were now so many people involved in the plot that discovery was an ever-increasing possibility.

This was the first gunpowder conspiracy against a European prince; it would not be the last, but it was the only one to be carried to its conclusion. There were similar plots to blow up Elizabeth I, the Prince of Parma, the Duke of Florence and James I. As a method of assassination, gunpowder was unreliable. Although it had been used in European warfare for two centuries, it was often of poor quality and unpredictable, and to achieve the destruction of the Old Provost's Lodging, vast amounts of it would have been needed because it was much weaker in strength than it is today, and even then there was no guarantee that it would kill Darnley, let alone destroy the evidence.[4]

Time was running out, as the King's convalescence would soon be at an end. Bothwell's original plan was to kill him on Friday night, but he was obliged to postpone the operation until Saturday because nothing was ready.[5] That Friday, according to Sir William Drury, Bothwell arranged for supplies of gunpowder to be brought from Dunbar Castle.[6] He then summoned Paris and asked if he held a key to the Queen's chamber in the Old Provost's Lodging. Paris said he did not, but he would get one. Bothwell told him, "Do not fail. On Sunday, we will do it." Paris left, his conscience troubling him. He contemplated fleeing abroad, but had no way of chartering a ship, so, after hanging around the docks at Leith, he despondently made his way back to Holyrood. The fact that Bothwell asked Paris, and not Mary, for the keys strongly suggests that Mary was innocent of what was going on.

Meanwhile, Bothwell had persuaded his bailiff, James, Laird of Ormiston in East Lothian—known as Black Ormiston—to join the plotters, overcoming his reluctance by assuring him he "need not take fear, for the whole Lords have concluded the same long since at Craigmillar, all that were there with the Queen, and none dare find fault with it when it shall be done." On that Friday evening, Bothwell outlined the details of his plan to Hepburn, Hay and Ormiston, and told them that, due to lack of time, the murder would now take place on the night of Sunday the 9th. The gunpowder was to be placed in a barrel in the Queen's room, and the lint fuse was to be fed through a hole in the bottom of the barrel.

Ormiston spent all day Saturday in bed in his lodgings in Blackfriars Wynd. It may or may not be significant that Morton's house was in the same street, although Morton, of course, was not in residence, having been forbidden entry to Edinburgh. Bothwell, having learned that Lord Robert Stewart had warned Darnley of a plot against him, hastened to complete his preparations.[7] That evening, Bothwell dined with Mary and Darnley at Kirk o'Field, and afterwards he sought out Paris and again demanded the keys. When the Queen and her attendants had left, Paris slipped the key out of the door to her room and took it to Bothwell, only to be shown a box containing a full set of fourteen counterfeit keys, which, according to a placard that later appeared on the door of the Tron House in Edinburgh, had been cut by one of the city's blacksmiths.[8] Bothwell told Paris to keep the key he had taken.[9] In his other deposition, Paris made the ludicrous claim that he had gone to the Queen and asked her to give him the key to her room because Bothwell wanted to blow up the King with gunpowder!

A great deal of confusion surrounds the subject of the keys to the Old Provost's Lodging. Buchanan states that, before Darnley arrived at Kirk o'Field, the keys were in the possession of the Queen's servants, while Lennox claims that Mary herself held the keys, but neither of these accounts can be correct because, according to Thomas Nelson, who initially received the keys from Robert Balfour, they were held by the King's servants, and when the Queen came to sleep at the house, her room was always kept locked and the keys to it and the postern gate were given into the keeping of the Usher of her Chamber, Archibald Beaton. Bonkil, the cook, kept the key to the door that led from the cellar to the alley. Buchanan says that, "whereas the other keys of the lodging were in custody of the King's servants, Paris, by feigning certain fond and slender causes, had in keeping the keys which Bothwell kept back, of the back gate and the postern." This cannot be correct because there was no lock on the door from the cellar to the garden, although it could be bolted on the inside. The *Book of Articles* states that Paris obtained the key to the Queen's door and the key to the door to the staircase that led to the upper floor; it will be remembered that the door at the top of the stairs had been removed to serve as a cover for Darnley's bath; it may have been rehung after the course of baths was completed.

During Saturday evening, Margaret Carwood sent Paris to Kirk o'Field to fetch the fur coverlet from the Queen's bed. When he reached the house, Sandy Durham asked him to return the key to Mary's bedchamber, but Paris told him that Archibald Beaton had it, and that it was his duty to hand it over.

On Sunday morning, Paris saw Moray taking leave of Mary, then took a walk to Restalrig, a village that lay to the north of Holyrood Palace. On his return, he found the Queen getting ready for Pagez's wedding breakfast. That afternoon, he was amongst her entourage when she attended the farewell banquet for Moretta, and afterwards, as he presented a basin and towel to her, she asked if he had retrieved the coverlet, implying that she was concerned that it would be destroyed when the house was blown up. If that had been the case, she would surely have attempted to rescue the other, far more valuable items that were in the house and were lost in the explosion.

By Sunday evening, two trunks, one of wood, one of leather, containing the gunpowder from Dunbar, had been delivered to Holyrood Palace and stored in the back hall of Bothwell's lodgings. How they were carried past the sentries without arousing suspicion is nowhere explained. In an age in which rooms were lit by candles and flambeaux, and heated by large open fires in winter, Bothwell was risking disaster by keeping such explosive material secretly in his rooms.

Early on Sunday evening, one of Bothwell's men—either William Powrie or George Dalgleish—obtained a yard of lint for a fuse from a soldier of the guard, whose name he did not know. Powrie was Bothwell's porter, Dalgleish his tailor, and while both were enlisted by the Earl to help the conspirators, neither had much inside knowledge of the plot.

Around the same time, according to Hepburn, a servant of John Hay collected a large barrel that Hay had ordered from a merchant at the top of Sandy Bruce's Close[10] and took it to Holyrood. It has been estimated that the barrel was the size of a 54-gallon cask,[11] much larger than a normal, full-size powder barrel, which held 100 pounds and had a diameter of 17 inches, and transporting it through the streets would have been impossible without assistance, but we are not told that Hay's servant had a helper, or a horse.

According to John Hay, from about 4 p.m. until dusk, Bothwell, Hay and Hepburn had been holding a meeting in the room where the powder was being stored. As soon as darkness fell, they walked to Black Ormiston's lodging in Blackfriars Wynd to discuss the final details of the plot with him, and stayed there for over two hours. Ormiston's uncle, Robert "Hob" Ormiston,[12] was also present; until now, he had known nothing of the plan to kill Darnley, but he made no bones about offering his services. After this meeting, from about 8.30 until 10 p.m., Bothwell strolled up and down the Canongate while his henchmen moved the gunpowder to Kirk o'Field, then he joined the Queen and her courtiers there at around 10.15 p.m.

Hepburn told another tale, claiming that Bothwell had stayed at Moretta's banquet until around 7.45 p.m. At around 8 p.m., he called briefly at his mother's house, with Paris, then went on to visit Ormiston. Half an hour later, he left; Hepburn did not know where he had gone, but it was probably to join the Queen at Kirk o'Field.

Ormiston claimed that, as the Queen was riding to Kirk o'Field after the banquet, Bothwell met him and his uncle in the Cowgate in order to check out the route by which the gunpowder was to be transported. After Bothwell had gone, Ormiston went down to the Blackfriars gate, negotiated his way through some ruinous houses, emerged on the other side and opened the gate. Paris, however, states that he and Bothwell went with the Ormistons to the Cowgate, where they met up with Hay and Hepburn. They discussed what was to be done, then Bothwell and Paris went to join the Queen at Kirk o'Field.

The problem with all these stories is that, from about 4 p.m. until Mary returned to Holyrood around midnight, Bothwell was in attendance on her, both at Moretta's banquet and at Kirk o'Field, and conspicuously dressed in masquing costume. He could not, therefore, have been meeting with his fellow conspirators at Holyrood early in the evening, nor could he have visited Ormiston's lodgings, and it is very unlikely that, bent on murder, he made himself so visible by walking in his rich attire up and down the Canongate. Hepburn and Hay may well have met at Holyrood and at Ormiston's house, and were probably coerced by their interrogators into claiming that Bothwell had also been present in order to incriminate him further.

In the evening, William Powrie warned a friend, William Geddes, not to be seen on the streets of Edinburgh that night, a rash comment that would later be used to condemn him. Then, between 8.30 and 10 p.m.,[13] acting on Hepburn's orders, he, Dalgleish and Patrick Wilson, the merchant who had abetted Bothwell in his trysts with Bessie Crawford, transported the barrel and the gunpowder, which was wrapped in leather bags called polks that were packed in the two trunks, openly through the streets from Holyrood to the gate of the Blackfriars monastery, which was about 200 yards from Kirk o'Field. Powrie first claimed that this task was completed in one journey with two horses belonging to Bothwell, but later changed his story and said that they had undertaken two journeys with one horse belonging to the Earl's page, Hermon. This horse carried the trunks on its first journey and the barrel on the next. Powrie made no mention of the barrel in his first deposition. Both tales are suspect because even two horses could not have carried enough gunpowder to cause the explosion that was to follow.[14] Furthermore, the suspicious loads had to be conveyed past the sentries at the palace, two members of the town watch at the Netherbow Port, four near Kirk o'Field, and ten others patrolling the streets.[15]

At the monastery gate, the three men found the other conspirators waiting; Ormiston was wearing a belted nightgown, which was totally unsuitable for the cold night. With them were two cloaked men wearing mules on their feet, whom Powrie, Dalgleish and Wilson did not recognise, and who have never been satisfactorily identified. Both Hepburn and Powrie claimed that Bothwell had left the Old Provost's Lodging and come down to the gate to make sure that the men were speedy at their task. Hepburn says he told them sharply, "Hurry up and finish the job before the Queen comes out of the house, or you will not find it so convenient." It is unlikely he stayed long, for his presence would have been missed.

As it was dark, Hepburn sent Powrie to get candles, which he purchased from a woman in the Cowgate. By the light of one candle, Powrie, Dalgleish and Wilson opened the trunks and carried the polks of gunpowder on their backs through the gate and uphill to the wall surrounding the east garden of the Kirk o'Field quadrangle. At this point, they were forbidden to go further, and Hepburn, Hay and Ormiston carried on with the task of heaving the bags over the wall.

Powrie claimed that this was when he and Wilson made the second journey to Holyrood to collect the powder and the barrel. On the way back to Kirk o'Field, Powrie grumbled, "Jesus! What kind of road is this we are going? I think it is no good." Wilson, well aware of the danger they were in, muttered, "Wheesht! Hold your tongue!" Hob Ormiston was waiting for them at the Blackfriars gate, and he was equally pessimistic. "This is not good," he said. "I do not believe this affair will come about tonight. I will go in and see what they are doing." Then Black Ormiston appeared with Paris, and sent Powrie and Wilson with the empty trunks back to Holyrood. When the latter reached the Blackfriars gate, they found their horses gone, and had to shoulder the trunks and walk.

Soon, the conspirators had carried the barrel and the polks of gunpowder to the back door of the Old Provost's Lodging, which Paris is said to have unlocked. He cannot have done so, however, because it had no lock and was bolted on the inside. The only other doors to the house were the front door, and the door from the cellar kitchen to the alley, to which Bonkil held the key; Paris apparently had a counterfeit.

The Ormistons are said to have gone in first, but the barrel was too large to go through the door and was left in the garden, by the wall. The powder bags were then carried into the house. Paris says he went to the kitchen and asked Bonkil for a candle. Both the back door and the side door opened into the kitchen, and Bonkil, who was not in the plot, must have concluded that something suspicious was going on, if he was in fact still on duty, which is doubtful. It seems strange, too, that Paris should be asking for a candle when Powrie had just bought six.

Paris lit his candle, and by its light, the gunpowder is said to have been emptied into a pile on the floor of the Queen's chamber, directly under the spot where the King's bed stood in the room above. Once this was done, the Ormistons went home, having ascertained that the rest knew how to light the fuse, and Hay and Hepburn remained in the room with the powder. Hay, Hepburn and Buchanan state that this all took place while the Queen and her courtiers were entertaining the King in the room above, but it is more likely that they were in the Prebendaries' Chamber across the passage. However, Bothwell apparently heard muffled sounds, and hastened downstairs.

"My God! What a noise you are making!" he growled. "Everything you do can be heard upstairs."

Apart from attracting attention, there were obvious risks in what the conspirators were supposed to have been doing. At any time, someone—even the Queen herself—could have come into the room to see what was causing the noise, or to fetch something, and found them there with the pile of powder. It is not inconceivable that cloaks were being stored in the Queen's room that evening. Furthermore, the Queen and her Lords would have had with them a number of attendants, who would have been coming and going all evening. Someone surely would have noticed that something odd was going on. Most pertinent of all, had there been so much gunpowder in a heap on the floor, the dust from it would have permeated every part of the room, so that the lighting of even a single candle would assuredly have caused it to ignite.

After Bothwell had gone back to the gathering, Paris is supposed to have made sure that the back door and the door to the stairs were left unlocked. He then locked the door to the Queen's room, left the keys to the downstairs doors with Hepburn, and went upstairs, or into the quadrangle,[16] where he signalled to Bothwell that all was ready. It was then that Mary noticed how begrimed he was.[17] Argyll patted Paris on the back, from which Paris inferred that he too was in the conspiracy; at the time his deposition was made, Argyll had just been forced to submit to the Lords after supporting Mary, so it is not surprising that Paris was allowed to imply his guilt.

The Queen then left Kirk o'Field with Bothwell and her other courtiers.

As Powrie and Wilson emerged from Blackfriars Wynd into the Canongate with the empty trunks, they saw the torches lighting the royal entourage ahead of them.

After his midnight interview with Mary, Bothwell, with the help of Dalgleish, his tailor, changed out of his masquing costume into a canvas doublet, black hose and a thick German soldier's cloak, then, armed with a sword and taking with him Powrie, Dalgleish, Wilson and a very reluctant Paris among others—Lennox says his party numbered sixteen, while the eyewitness, Mrs. Merton, counted eleven—he walked to Kirk o'Field, to supervise the killing of the King.[18]

As he and his men emerged from Holyrood, they were challenged by the palace guards, and said they were "my Lord Bothwell's friends." Finding the Netherbow Port closed for the night, Wilson woke up the porter, John Galloway, and made him open it "to friends of Lord Bothwell's." When the porter asked why they were all abroad at so late an hour, he received no answer. Bothwell then led his men up the High Street and down Blackfriars Wynd, where they knocked at Ormiston's lodgings, only to find he was not at home; Ormiston later claimed that he had gone to the house of his friend, Thomas Henderson. Bothwell and his followers were almost certainly the men whom Mrs. Merton later saw coming up Blackfriars Wynd a short while before the explosion. Lennox claims that they approached Kirk o'Field by "the secret way" that Mary had used, which gave access from the monastery grounds. Once they arrived, Bothwell and Paris climbed over the town wall, the Earl having told the others to wait in the east garden and not stir, regardless of what they heard or saw. Dalgleish was apparently in ignorance of what was to happen, for he later swore before his execution that, "As God shall be my judge, I knew nothing of the King's death before it was done."

One of those who allegedly accompanied Bothwell was a Captain James Cullen, who had served as a mercenary in France, Denmark and Poland. In 1560, he had been an officer of the garrison in Edinburgh Castle, and in February 1567, he was the captain of a band of royal hagbuteers and was described by Cecil as a creature of Bothwell's,[19] but he is more likely to have been answerable to John Stewart of Traquair, the Captain of the Queen's Guard. Moray later referred to Cullen as "one of the very executors" of Darnley's murder, but the part he actually did play in it is uncertain. Captain Cullen is said to have advised Bothwell, before he scaled the wall, "for more surety, to have the King strangled, and not to trust to the train of powder alone, as he had known so many saved." Given what probably happened to Darnley, this tale may have been contrived so as to pin all the responsibility on Bothwell.

In the *Detectio* and the *Book of Articles,* Buchanan claims that only one group of conspirators—Bothwell's—was at Kirk o'Field that night. In his *History,* however, which was written after certain nobles had fallen from favour, he alleges that there were three groups. In fact, there were probably two.

There is little doubt that Bothwell and his henchmen were not the only band of conspirators to converge on Kirk o'Field that night. At some point, armed men of the Douglas faction arrived by stealth on the scene and stationed themselves near the Old Provost's Lodging. Their purpose has been variously debated, one theory being that they were there, on behalf of Morton and the other Protestant Lords, to do away with Bothwell once he had laid the fuse, making it look as if he had perished in the explosion. That way the crime could neatly be attributed to him, and no one else would be implicated. Bothwell was hated by the Lords, but he was useful in his willingness to eliminate Darnley, their common enemy, and he could also be useful as a scapegoat for them all. For that reason, it would be better if he too were eliminated. But this hypothesis is not workable.

Another, more credible, theory is that Archibald Douglas, who had a deadly personal score to settle with Darnley for betraying his kinsman, Morton, was there to ensure that, if by some chance the King escaped the blast, he would not evade death. Thomas Wilson stated that there was "an ambushment before the door, that none should escape" and that the postern in the wall was left open so that the killers could make a quick getaway. Although Morton was not in Edinburgh that night, and had refused to become involved, he may privately have sanctioned this intervention. According to Morton's confession of 1581, Bothwell knew the Douglases were there, for Archibald Douglas had told Morton he was "at the deed doing, and came to the Kirk o'Field yard with the Earls of Bothwell and Huntly." There is no other evidence that Huntly was present that night, but as he was closely associated with Bothwell, it is possible that he was. He had, after all, been one of those taken into the Lords' confidence at Craigmillar. Although one of Bothwell's followers insisted he saw no one beside the Earl's men at Kirk o'Field, "nor knew of no other companies," his evidence was perhaps concocted to protect Morton and his faction.

That Archibald Douglas was at Kirk o'Field that night seems likely. His servant, John Binning, testified under torture in 1581 that Douglas was "art and part" of the murder and "did actually devise and perpetrate it," which is substantiated by Douglas's conduct at Whittinghame. Binning claimed that he and another man accompanied his master when he left Douglas House in St. Mary's Wynd—which ran parallel with Blackfriars Wynd, but lay just outside the Netherbow Port—by the back door and made his way to Kirk o'Field. It was later said that Douglas had left his velvet mule at the scene of the crime, which Douglas denied, but the allegation may be true, for Binning stated that his master was wearing armour beneath his clothes, a steel helmet, and slippers over his boots, as were all his men, as an aid to stealth. Douglas and another man—Binning?—were perhaps the two cloaked men wearing mules whom Powrie had seen earlier at the Blackfriars gate; if so, they were certainly in league with Bothwell.

Hepburn, Hay and Dalgleish all claimed that there were "nine and no more at the deed"—themselves, Bothwell, the Ormistons, Paris, Powrie and Wilson—which became the official line, since it pointed to Bothwell alone as the culprit. Yet there is evidence in diverse sources that there were more than nine men at Kirk o'Field that night. The female witnesses in Blackfriars Wynd saw eleven men before the explosion and thirteen after it. Lennox states that fifty persons surrounded the house that night, of whom only sixteen were in Bothwell's party, although he does not say who the others were. Cecil says there were thirty persons,[20] and Moray later told de Silva he thought thirty to forty persons were involved in the crime.[21] There were certainly more than nine, for this estimate does not take account of Captain Cullen, Huntly (perhaps) and the Douglases. And who were the two cloaked men in mules whom Powrie noticed? It has been variously suggested that they were Huntly and Argyll, Balfour and his brother (of whom more later) or Douglas and Binning.

Further evidence of the Douglases' presence at Kirk o'Field lies perhaps in the testimony of the women living nearby who heard a man crying out to his kinsmen to pity him. However, it is unlikely that it was the Douglases whom Mrs. Merton saw coming up Blackfriars Wynd because they would have had no reason to go along that street.

Moretta later informed Giovanni Correr, the Venetian ambassador in Paris, that "certain women who live in the neighbourhood declare, and from a window perceived, many armed men were round the house."[22] It was later claimed that the Lords had men waiting to ambush Darnley in the cottages that lay in the south garden, adjoining the Flodden Wall. Since the bodies of Darnley and Taylor were found in that garden, it is reasonable to suppose that Douglas positioned some of his men in these cottages. As late as 20 June, Drury informed Cecil that the delay in arraigning those already arrested for Darnley's murder was "for that the three hosts [householders] out either of the which houses there came out eight persons that were all at the murdering of the King, cannot yet be gotten."[23] Nor does it seem that they were ever arrested.

In the English spy's drawing, there appear four mounted men in an alleyway to the south of the south garden. Some writers have thought that their presence is significant. But they are unlikely to have been Douglas men, for they would have gone to ground long before morning, nor is it feasible that these horsemen had anything to do with the murder. They are probably citizens, come from further afield to view the scene of the crime, or they may even represent Bothwell and/or his men coming to investigate the explosion.

According to Lennox, "some said" that Mary herself "was present at the murder of the King, in man's apparel, which apparel she loved sometimes to be in." That Mary enjoyed disguising herself in male attire cannot be disputed, but there is no evidence to substantiate the rumour that she was at Kirk o'Field when Darnley was murdered. Lennox's rumour is at variance with the other libels, which allege that the Queen was in bed when the explosion took place.

According to the depositions, once Paris had unlocked the door to the Queen's chamber, Hay and Hepburn lit the slow-burning fuse,[24] locked the doors through which Darnley might try to escape, and rejoined Bothwell and the others in the east garden, by the Flodden Wall, where they waited for the explosion. After a while, when nothing had happened, Bothwell asked if there was any window through which he could see if the fuse had gone out, for he was determined to check that it had been properly lit. Hepburn, aghast, told him that he would only be able to see that through the Queen's window facing the quadrangle. To his horror, Bothwell began pulling him towards the house, but Hepburn pushed him back, just in time, for at that moment, there was a flash of flame in one of the windows, and in the next instant a great "crack," and they all saw "the house rising" before their eyes.[25] The conspirators scrambled over the wall to where Dalgleish and Powrie were waiting, and ran from the scene, through the precincts of the old Blackfriars monastery and into the Cowgate.

The main problem with this evidence is that, if the door to the Queen's chamber was shut and the other downstairs doors locked, the only window through which the flame could have been seen was that in the Queen's chamber, which looked out on to the quadrangle. There is no way that the conspirators could have seen this from the east garden. Moreover, would Bothwell have been so stupid as to risk going back to the house when it could blow up at any moment?

More pertinently, if gunpowder with weak and unpredictable properties was left in a heap, it might have quickly burnt itself out, or, if it did explode, it would never have destroyed the whole building down to the foundations. The damage would have been limited mainly to the room it was in and the floor above it. Therefore the Old Provost's Lodging could not have been blown up by this means.

Bothwell and his men aimed to scale the Flodden Wall at Leith Wynd, a good way to the north, but it was too high, so they made their way back to the Netherbow Port, brazenly woke the porter and demanded admission, then split up into two groups: Bothwell and Paris went down the Canongate, while the rest returned via St. Mary's Wynd and the Cowgate to the palace. They cannot therefore have been the men whom Mrs. Merton and Mrs. Stirling saw running up Blackfriars Wynd and splitting into two groups; these were probably members of the Douglas party. Why Bothwell and his men chose to go so far out of their way to Leith Wynd is a mystery; they could have got over the wall near the Blackfriars gardens, for a good stretch of it was ruinous there, as the city records testify.

When challenged, Bothwell and his followers gave the Earl's name, not only to John Galloway, but also to the sentries at Holyrood, who also asked them, "What was that crack?," to which they replied, "We know not." In the circumstances, their indiscretion seems staggering, but neither the porter nor the sentries were ever brought forward as witnesses against them. At Holyrood, Bothwell "called for a draught," undressed and went to bed, feigning innocence when he was disturbed half an hour later by George Halket with news of the explosion.[26] Since there was widespread panic in the palace at the time of his return, it is hard to believe that he reached his lodgings without meeting anyone. It is also hard to accept that he walked all the way from Kirk o'Field to Leith Wynd, then back to the Netherbow Port and by the back route to the palace, then prepared for bed, in the time before he was disturbed, and without anybody knowing anything of his movements; most of the city had been aroused by the explosion.

At some point during the return journey, Hay's conscience had begun to trouble him, and he muttered to Paris, "We have given offence to God, but there is nothing to be done save live virtuously and pray."

"Alas!" wailed Paris, whereupon Hay shut him up by threatening him with a pistol. Once he reached Holyrood, Paris lay sleepless on a bed in Bothwell's hall, then left when Hay invited him to spend the night at his house in the Canongate. When he returned to Holyrood in the morning, Paris gave way to terror, but Bothwell assured him that no one would trouble themselves with him when most of the great Lords of Scotland were involved in the plot. But Paris was not reassured, and Bothwell soon lost patience with him.

"Why do you look like that?" he snapped, and pointed out that the other conspirators had "lands, rents and revenues, wives and children, and were willing to give up everything in my service. If you think you have offended God, the sin is not yours but mine."

Later on, still brooding, Paris saw the Queen, but when he told her that people were giving him odd looks, and asked her why she thought this should be, she merely told him not to worry.

That day, Hepburn dropped the counterfeit keys down a hole in a quarry between Holyrood and Leith. Bothwell later gave fine horses to Hay and Hepburn by way of reward for their services, and promised Powrie, Dalgleish and Wilson well-remunerated positions at Hermitage Castle. He assured all his accomplices that, if they held their tongues, "they should never want so long as he had anything."

.   .   .

It is clear that the depositions on which this reconstructed sequence of events is based are so seriously flawed that they cannot be accepted as reliable evidence of what actually happened. All were carefully conjured and doctored so as to attach the responsibility for Darnley's murder exclusively to Bothwell and, later, to Mary and to other persons who had fallen from favour in the interim. What incriminates Bothwell are not these contrived accounts, but the evidence that relates to the conferences at Craigmillar and Whittinghame and the events that took place after Darnley's murder, of which we will shortly be hearing. Although it seems likely that Bothwell and his named followers did engineer the explosion at Kirk o'Field, there is serious doubt as to whether it was carried out in the manner described in the depositions, and as to whether Bothwell was acting alone. He himself told others that the Lords, and even the Queen, were involved in the conspiracy, and whether the latter was true or not, there is good evidence for the former; he must therefore have believed that no one could touch him.

The depositions reveal a plot that was ill conceived, careless and staggeringly amateurish. There was no reason why Hay and Hepburn could not have lit the fuse as soon as the Queen's entourage was clear of Kirk o'Field, or at least as soon as the house was quiet. Nor did Bothwell and the others have any good cause for going back to the house to supervise matters. Going around Edinburgh in a large group at the dead of night and leaving clues to their identity in various places were the acts of fools who seemed to be deliberately trying to attract attention to themselves. Bothwell's past record is one of efficiency and military expertise, and he had demonstrated good qualities of leadership in often difficult situations; it is therefore inconceivable that he had devised this shambles of a conspiracy. Even if he had believed himself so powerful that he did not need to cover his tracks—which does not appear to have been the case—he was certainly aware that he had influential enemies who would seize upon any excuse to destroy him, and that the penalty for regicide was death.

Hence, it is almost certain that Bothwell was not acting on just his own account at Kirk o'Field that night, and that the events that took place there were rather different from those recounted in the depositions.

18

"THE CONTRIVERS OF
THE PLOT"

THE PROTESTATION OF HUNTLY AND Argyll reads: "We judge in our conscience, and hold for certain and truth, that Moray and Lethington were authors, inventors, devisers counsellors and causers of the murder, in what manner and by whatsoever persons the same was executed."

It was Maitland and Moray who first broached the question of the removal of Darnley at Craigmillar, and who took Huntly, Argyll and Bothwell into their confidence. When Mary pointed out that an annulment would impugn her son's legitimacy, Maitland assured her that the Lords would think of other means of freeing her. A bond for Darnley's murder was almost certainly drawn up at Craigmillar, therefore the inevitable conclusion must be that Maitland and Moray were its instigators. Their conversation with Mary suggests that they had thought the whole matter through before involving the other Lords, and the fact that they enlisted the support of their enemy, Bothwell, whose power had become insupportable, probably indicates that he was to be the scapegoat. What they could not have envisaged was the enthusiasm with which Bothwell applied himself to the murder plans, an enthusiasm that derived from his unstated ambition to marry the Queen. Thus he played unwittingly into their hands, enabling them to distance themselves from the actual deed of murder. There is little doubt that he was betrayed into believing that he had their moral support.

Maitland was no stranger to intrigue. He had been at least privy to the plot against Rizzio, for it was he who had warned Cecil that the Italian was about to be murdered. Maitland's cherished political goal was union with England under a Protestant government, and Darnley, with his Catholic pretensions, was an unwelcome obstacle to that. All the sources agree that Maitland signed the Craigmillar Bond; furthermore, his presence with Bothwell at Whittinghame, when Darnley's murder was discussed, proves that he was deeply implicated. There is also some evidence that he chose the Old Provost's Lodging for Darnley, and he may even have prevented Mary from staying there on the fateful night. Darnley had warned Mary, three days before the murder, to be on her guard against Maitland, for he was out to ruin them both. Maitland was undoubtedly involved in the plot, if not its mastermind.

There is no question that most of the Scottish Lords hated Darnley, and even those not directly involved in the plot would have lifted no finger to save him. He had alienated many of them, dishonoured the Queen, intrigued incessantly to disastrous effect and brought scandal upon Scotland, and they were not prepared to tolerate any restoration of his influence. It is no coincidence that the plans that had been laid at Craigmillar were speedily expedited after the Queen and her husband were reconciled.

The evidence against Moray is largely circumstantial, but he certainly had compelling reasons for wanting Darnley taken out. Nau claimed that Moray "had told several Englishmen that it was necessary to get rid of the King, not only because he was a Catholic, but also because he was an enemy to the Queen of England. But there had been private feuds of an old standing between them, both before and after the marriage. The King never forgot the ambuscade before he married the Queen, and wanted to kill him."

Moray was adept at distancing himself from unpleasant events in which he might be implicated and at "looking through his fingers" at what was going on in his absence. His departure from Edinburgh on the eve of the murder is unlikely to have been coincidental, and the contradictory descriptions of his wife's illness suggest that this was a contrived excuse. Nau claimed that Moray left "after having matured all his plans necessary for his success in seizing the crown and ruining the Queen," while Paris said that, when he heard that Moray was leaving Edinburgh, he immediately concluded that the Earl had resolved to be away while the crime was being committed.

Moray had been noticeably silent when the problem of Darnley was raised at Craigmillar: it was Maitland who had done most of the talking. Yet, by his presence, he had made it known that he was involved in the matter. He strongly denied signing the Craigmillar Bond, and the depositions extracted during his regency predictably do not list him among the signatories, but both Leslie and Nau state that he did sign the Bond, and Nau may have got his information from the Queen, who had almost certainly seen it.

Moray took no part in the commission of the murder itself, but there are strong grounds for believing that it had his moral support. According to Paris, Bothwell believed Moray to be neutral, which implies that Moray was aware of what was going on; certainly he made no attempt to save Darnley. Mondovi reported that most people imputed the crime to Moray, "who has always had the throne in view,"[1] while Cecil received an anonymous letter stating that Archbishop Beaton had alleged that Moray was the author of the King's death.[2] Even Moray had to admit to Cecil, "I am touched myself."[3]

Moray had more to gain than anyone else from Darnley's death and the removal of Bothwell. Suited both by bearing and abilities to kingship, only his bastardy had lain between him and the throne. He had been involved in every major plot against his sister, determined to hold on to the political dominance he had come to enjoy, and which had been threatened, in turn, by the ascendancy of unsuitable men promoted by Mary—Rizzio, Darnley and now Bothwell. Some people, including Mondovi, believed that Moray wanted the throne itself, but the evidence suggests that it was power he desired, not a crown. He was also committed to the success of the Protestant Reformation, and would have regarded any means to that end as acceptable. The ultimate consequence of the Kirk o'Field conspiracy was that Moray attained the political supremacy he desired and was able to firmly establish the reformed religion in Scotland.

Buchanan later claimed that, after the murder, "messengers were at once sent to England to spread the report that the King of Scots had been foully done to death by the direct means of the Earls of Moray and Morton"; there is, however, no record of any messenger saying this. Buchanan also asserted that, in Scotland, rumours were "spread by the regicides to the effect that the King had been murdered by the means of Moray and Morton." There certainly were rumours to that effect, and some probably had their basis in truth. After a discussion with Moretta, Giovanni Correr, the Venetian ambassador in Paris, wrote:

> It was widely rumoured that the principal persons in the kingdom were implicated because they were dissatisfied with the King, and above all a bastard brother of the Queen's is suspected because, at the time when she was at variance with her husband, the bastard told her that the King had boasted to him of having had intimacy with her before she was his wife. The Queen, exasperated, asked the King if it was true; the King gave the lie to the bastard, who repeated the accusation to the King's face. From this private quarrel, the report arose that the bastard had desired to revenge himself.[4]

How true this is there is no way of knowing, but there *was* speculation in 1565 that Mary and Darnley had anticipated their marriage, and a puritanical man like Moray would not have relished hearing Darnley boast of it. Indeed, it may have been this that initially caused the rift between Darnley and Moray. But Moray had far more and greater reasons than that for wishing to be rid of Darnley. Of course, Correr could have been referring not to Moray but to Lord Robert Stewart, who had quarrelled with Darnley a day or so before the murder, but that quarrel had had nothing to do with Mary's private relations with Darnley, and there is no suggestion in any source that Lord Robert was involved in the murder.

Correr also claimed that the assassination of Darnley was the work of heretics who had meant to kill Mary too and bring up the Prince in the new faith. Most of this is pretty accurate, but it is unlikely that the murder of the Queen was intended: Maitland had prevented Mary from staying at Kirk o'Field, and Moray later balked at executing her, or doing away with her by other means, even when he had the opportunity.

Mary herself was always to believe that the Protestant Lords had been behind the plot. Nau, whose work almost certainly reflects her views, stated that "it was afterwards made public that [the murder] had been done by the command and device of the Earls of Bothwell and Morton, James Balfour and some others, who always afterwards pretended to be most diligent in searching out the murder which they themselves had committed." Interestingly, no mention is made of Moray and Maitland, who had both died before it was written, but Morton was Regent of Scotland at the time and one of Mary's most virulent enemies. Nau also states that, "if we may judge by the plots, deeds and contrivances of [Bothwell's] associates, it would seem that, after having used him to rid themselves of the King, they designed to make him their instrument to ruin the Queen." Elsewhere, in speaking of the Lords, Nau refers to "the murder which they themselves had committed," and speaks of Bothwell, Morton and Balfour as the guilty parties.

In January 1568, Hepburn and Hay, in their confessions, "accused the greatest and chiefest of [Moray's] Council, who were at that time sitting beside him, especially Morton, Lethington and Balfour, and their own Master the Earl [Bothwell]" of the murder.[5] A report in the secret archives of the Society of Jesus claimed that Maitland was "present at this conference between Moray" and one of the prisoners, who is not named, and, "being very farsighted, he feared that if the criminal were permitted to make [a public] confession, he would name him, or some of his accomplices, for Lethington's conscience accused him of many crimes." Maitland therefore prepared a speech for the condemned man to recite on the scaffold, but to his dismay, the wretch refused, saying "he had reached that frame of mind when threats and compliments are equally worthless, and that nothing should hinder him from saying what his conscience told him to say." Addressing Moray, he said, "Since you, my Lord Regent, occupy the position in which I now find you, of you I will say nothing, and I spare you because of your dignity." Then, turning to Maitland and some others who are not named, he asked, "Who is there among you who either can or dare accuse me of this crime?—a crime of which you are quite as guilty as I am. For you planned what these Lords of mine put into execution, as is attested by the signatures of all of you, which would establish the truth of all my words if they could be produced." At his words, "all were so struck that for a time there was silence."

On the scaffold, "whatever charges he brought openly against the Secretary, the Earls of Morton and Bothwell and James Balfour, whom he affirmed to be the first inventors of this crime, the very same he insinuated sufficiently plainly against Moray. Everyone who knows anything about this affair knows how true is the statement made about him and the others mentioned."[6] The man concerned may have been Hay for, on the scaffold, Hay incriminated Maitland, Bothwell, Huntly, Argyll and Balfour, stating "that Balfour and Maitland were notoriously known as the principal advisers and counsellors," and although he had not seen Morton's signature on the Craigmillar Bond, Bothwell had told him it was there.[7] The report in the Jesuit archives states that the other men executed that day "bore witness not only that the Queen was guiltless of this crime, but that the individuals mentioned above were the authors of the King's murder." Buchanan also says that both Maitland and Balfour, "it is believed, were privy to the plot to murder the King." In his confession, John Binning accused Maitland's brother John of also being involved.

Many believed that Morton had helped to commit the murder,[8] and his indictment of 1581 asserts that he had personally placed the gunpowder "under the ground and angular stones and within the vaults" of Darnley's house, but, in his confession, made that same year, Morton would only admit to having foreknowledge of the murder, not to taking any part in it; he added that nothing had been done to prevent the murder because it was known that the Queen desired it. Morton was not in Edinburgh when it was committed, yet his kinsmen were at the scene of the crime. Possibly Archibald Douglas was there on his own initiative, but his intervention may well have had Morton's blessing. Morton admitted having received Douglas after the murder, even though he knew Douglas had been involved in it. Yet the evidence collectively suggests that, in his confession, Morton was telling the truth. When he was found guilty in 1581 of being "art and part" in the murder, "he showed himself much grieved and, beating the ground once or twice with his staff, said, 'Art and part? God knoweth the contrary.' "[9]

Huntly and Argyll were certainly involved in the conspiracy. According to Morton's confession, Huntly went with Bothwell to Kirk o'Field on the night of the murder, while Argyll was in Edinburgh at the time. He had allegedly patted Paris's shoulder after the preparations for the explosion were completed. There is no reliable evidence to connect any other noble with the murder. Glencairn, Fleming, Kirkcaldy of Grange, Livingston, Melville, Eglinton and Atholl were definitely not involved.

Another man who was to be executed for complicity in Darnley's murder was Archbishop Hamilton. Buchanan was especially eager to condemn him for it. The Archbishop had been in residence in the Duke's House on the night of the murder, and it is from Buchanan that we learn the seemingly ominous detail of the light being extinguished in the window after the explosion. Buchanan claims that

> the good Bishop [*sic*] not only conspired with the Earl Bothwell, but came with the Queen to Glasgow and conveyed the King to the place of his murder, the Bishop being lodged as he was seldom or never before, where he might perceive the pleasure of that cruelty, and help the murderers, and sent four of his familiar servants to the execution of the murder, watching all the night and thinking long to have the joy of the coming of the crown a degree nearer to the House of Hamilton.

The *Book of Articles* alleges that the Archbishop purposely took up residence in the Duke's House to prevent Darnley from lodging there. This is impossible to substantiate, and may be the product of Buchanan's prejudiced imagination, for he was a staunch Lennox man and hated the Hamiltons. Furthermore, in his *History*, Buchanan, having elsewhere alleged that the murder was the work of Bothwell and Mary, asserts that the Archbishop, "when the proposition of killing the King was made to him, willingly undertook it, both by reason of old feuds between their families, and also out of hopes thereby to bring the kingdom nearer to his family. Upon which he chose out six or eight of the most wicked of his vassals and commended the matter to them." In the earlier account there were four vassals, and they were sent to assist the murderers, not do the deed. The Archbishop gave them "the keys to the King's lodgings [and] they then entered very silently into his chamber and strangled him when he was asleep. And when they had so done, they carried out his body through a little gate into an orchard adjacent to the walls, and then a sign was given to blow up the house." In his eagerness to incriminate an old enemy, Buchanan temporarily forgot about Bothwell, and about the depositions of the Earl's accomplices, which he himself had published. But Lennox was Regent at the time this was written, and it was politic to blacken the reputation of the Hamiltons.

It is unlikely that the Archbishop could have seen what was going on at the Old Provost's Lodging from the Duke's House because the north and east sides of the quadrangle stood in the way. Aside from Buchanan's vitriol, there is little reliable evidence to connect Hamilton with the crime. However, he did have every reason to loathe and resent Darnley, and rumours of his guilt were circulating as early as June 1567. Much later, a priest called Thomas Robinson asserted that one John Hamilton, on his deathbed, had confessed to him that he had been present at Darnley's murder on the Archbishop's orders.

That there was a degree of self-interest in the killing is indisputable. It is significant that, in the Parliament held in December 1567, when Mary had reached twenty-five and, had she not by then been deposed, would legally have been able to revoke grants made during her minority, both Moray and Morton were confirmed in their titles and estates, and the earldom of Angus was conferred on Morton's nephew; it had been Darnley's intention to claim it himself.[10]

Most significant of all, Moray and Maitland were soon to be in a position where they could suppress any evidence of their involvement in the crime. That evidence was suppressed we know for a certainty, and we know also that it was manufactured under the auspices of these men. This alone is enough to condemn them, for if the evidence against Bothwell and Mary was sound, why tamper with it or embroider it?

There has been speculation that the Lords who devised the plot had the covert backing of Cecil. Moray and Maitland had striven for years for a closer relationship with their southern neighbour, and it would have suited the English to have a Protestant government in Edinburgh. The Queen of Scots had been a constant thorn in England's side ever since Elizabeth's accession, and her marriage to Darnley had only made matters worse. Despite her fair words, Elizabeth had no intention of naming Mary her successor—she feared her too much for that. The removal of Darnley would therefore remove a potential threat and devalue Mary's claim to the English throne. The French certainly believed that England had been involved in Darnley's murder, and Archbishop Beaton "affirmed that the assassination was controlled from England, where the intention had been to kill the Queen as well."[11] Mary believed this too. In 1581, after Morton's execution, she wrote to Elizabeth and made reference to the secret agents and spies employed by England to bring about her ruin. "I will not at present specify other proof than that which I have gained of it by the confession of one [Morton] who was afterwards amongst those that were most advanced for this good service."

During the twentieth century, another suspect was added to the list of those who might have plotted the explosion at Kirk o'Field: Darnley himself.

As we have seen, there is sufficient evidence to show that, from before the Prince's birth, Darnley had been trying to enlist the support of the Catholic powers for his bid to set himself up as the champion of Catholicism and, with their aid, establish himself as a crusading ruler of Scotland. At one stage, his grandiose plans had also embraced the conquest of England.

There is very little evidence that Darnley actually secured much influential support. Although he seems to have been in contact with Francisco de Alava, King Philip's ambassador in Paris, there are no grounds for believing that the Spanish monarch was interested in his plans. Catherine de' Medici may have known something of them, or may even have encouraged Darnley, and it is possible that he had promised to send Prince James to be brought up in France; nevertheless, Catherine remained noncommittal. Late in 1566, however, Mondovi had informed the Pope that Darnley was just the man to bring about the deaths of the six leading Protestant nobles in Scotland, which Mary had refused to sanction. Once this had been achieved, the Counter-Reformation could proceed apace.

There is no proof, but Darnley may well have fallen in with this plan; indeed, it may have been the reason he intended to return with Mary to Edinburgh. His calumniation of Mary as a dubious Catholic in letters to her European allies had been designed to demonstrate that he, by comparison, was zealous in the faith. But he had his own agenda as well. By the end of 1566, he was apparently planning to overthrow his wife, much as he had intended to do after Rizzio's murder, rule in the name of their son, and re-establish the Catholic faith in Scotland. The murder of the Lords would be a preliminary to this and would remove the chief obstacles in his way. Moretta and Lutini may have been employed as emissaries between Darnley and Mondovi, while de Alava, who had probably shown himself friendly to Darnley until he learned how unreliable and indiscreet he was, realised that something nefarious was afoot and warned Archbishop Beaton. It was probably for this reason that, on 5 April 1567, Sir Henry Norris, the English ambassador in Paris, confided to Sir Nicholas Throckmorton, "As at first I thought, therein I remain not to be removed, that the original of that fact [i.e., Darnley's murder] came from hence [i.e., Paris], for besides that their [the French rulers'] desire is to have the Prince hither, so do I see that all they that are suspected for the same fact make this their chief refuge and sure anchor."[12] Furthermore, Cecil, in a letter to Norris dated 21 March, referred to "the French attempt for the Prince."[13] However, given their mutual animosity, it is entirely predictable that the English should blame the French for Darnley's murder.

At home, Darnley was concentrating on building up support, hence his recall of Ker, and his involvement with Balfour, whom he probably accounted his chief ally; Balfour, after all, owed his political prominence to Darnley's patronage, and he was a Catholic. The younger Anthony Standen was also in Edinburgh at this time. Darnley's staunchest support, however, came from his father, Lennox.

It has been claimed by several recent writers[14] that it was Darnley, with the support of Balfour and Lennox, who plotted the explosion at Kirk o'Field, in an attempt to murder some of the Lords and perhaps the Queen too, then seize the Prince from nearby Holyrood. It would not have been the first time that Darnley had plotted Mary's ruin.

But there are essential flaws in this supposition. Darnley himself had chosen Kirk o'Field, probably at the suggestion of Balfour, yet he could not have guaranteed that the people he wished to destroy would visit him there at all. Moreover, the theory hinges on the fact that Darnley expected the Queen and the Lords to return to Kirk o'Field after the wedding masque on 9 February, so that he could blow them up in the house, but all the evidence shows that Mary had made it very clear that she was not returning, and that there could have been no misunderstanding on Darnley's part. The circumstances in which Darnley was found indicate surprise and haste; furthermore, he had very few servants, no armed support and none of his friends nearby; Balfour had left Edinburgh, and Lennox was in Linlithgow, allegedly on hand to hear of the success of the coup. How was Darnley to consolidate his position after it had taken place?

Buchanan and Wilson claimed that some of Darnley's servants had "gone out of the way as fore-knowing the danger at hand." It has been speculated that Darnley warned them. It is strange, therefore, that he did not warn the servants who intended to stay in the house that their lives were in danger, and far more likely that there was no warning, for if there had been, no one would have dared to stay behind, and we know that six people did. Darnley is said to have left the powder barrel in the garden as a clue that would incriminate the Protestant Lords; just what the connection was is not adequately explained, and in any case, the barrel was probably nothing to do with the murder. Because it was found nearby, an elaborate tale was concocted around it in order to incriminate Bothwell.

Drury later recorded that Ker of Fawdonside was waiting near Kirk o'Field with other mounted men on the night of the murder, his intention being to give aid in that cruel enterprise.[15] It has been suggested that he was there to help Darnley make his escape. Darnley had probably issued Ker's pardon in a bid to buy his forgiveness and gain support, but although Ker seems initially to have played along with this, he had as much reason as Morton to wreak vengeance on Darnley, and, having perhaps been apprised by Douglas or Morton of the murder plot, he may have gone to Kirk o'Field as part of, or in support of, the Douglas contingent. The treacherous Ker also had good reason to hate Bothwell, and perhaps hoped to kill him too.

It has been suggested that the Lords somehow discovered Darnley's plot, which was possibly betrayed to them by either Balfour or Sandy Durham, and that this was what prompted Bothwell's midnight meeting with the Queen and Traquair, at which it was decided that Bothwell should return to Kirk o'Field and turn the tables on Darnley. In fact, the midnight meeting was probably held to discuss the future security of the Prince, now that his father was returning to Holyrood. Given the Queen's busy schedule, there would have been no time to hold this meeting earlier in the day. The matter was almost certainly one relating to James's security, for Traquair was Captain of the Queen's Guard and Bothwell was Captain of the Prince's Bodyguard.

There is no evidence in Mondovi's correspondence that he had pursued his plan for Darnley to bring about the deaths of the Protestant Lords. Of course, Mondovi might have used Moretta as a messenger for intelligence that was too sensitive to commit to paper, but he can hardly have expected Darnley to act when he was still convalescent, nor did Darnley see Moretta whilst he was at Kirk o'Field.

The fact remains that, during the period after Darnley's murder, although there was intensive speculation as to who had committed it, not one person suggested that Darnley himself might have been culpable, despite the fact that several people, including the Queen herself, suspected that he had been plotting to seize power. It was nearly four centuries before anyone suggested that he had been involved.

Sir James Balfour's role in the murder conspiracy is one of the most obscure and mysterious. Balfour was pragmatic as far as religion was concerned. He had early on embraced the Protestant faith, but after being sentenced to the galleys for his part in Cardinal Beaton's murder in 1546, he had turned Catholic in order to buy his freedom. Thereafter he had remained a Catholic, but probably only because it served his interests to do so. He had come to political prominence through Darnley's friendship and patronage, but was soon admitted to the secret counsels of the Protestant Lords. Although he was not involved in the plot against Rizzio, he profited from it, being appointed Clerk Register in place of the disgraced James MacGill in March 1566. By June, however, he was out of favour with the Queen, probably because of his association with her increasingly estranged husband.

In December 1566, Balfour probably drew up and signed the Craigmillar Bond for Darnley's murder, which suggests that he had by then detached himself from the King. At the same time, he may have maintained the pretence of being Darnley's friend. The fact that he lent his house to Moretta may be significant, and may suggest that he was to some degree involved in Darnley's schemes, but only circumstantial evidence supports this theory. We may infer from all this that Balfour was perhaps playing a double game in order to safeguard his own position whoever triumphed. Du Croc, after all, had described him as "a true traitor."

It was almost certainly Balfour who, after Moretta's arrival and the possible revelation of Darnley's plans, suggested that the King stay at Kirk o'Field in a house owned by Robert Balfour. He may have realised that this remote house was suitable for an assassination attempt. Yet by the night of the murder, Balfour had left his Edinburgh house and gone to ground, probably because he did not wish to be associated in any way with the crime, and when he returned he kept a low profile for a time.

However, there is ample testimony that Balfour was involved with his cousin Bothwell—Melville says they "were great companions"—in the Lords' plot to kill Darnley. As we have seen, Hepburn (in the suppressed part of his deposition), Hay, Paris, the report in the secret Jesuit archives, Nau and Buchanan all incriminated Balfour. Buchanan says that both Bothwell and Balfour "were privy to the plot to murder the King" and calls Balfour "one of the chief regicides. He was either the author of, or a participator in" the murder. Balfour was named as one of the murderers in placards that appeared soon after the crime was committed.[16] On 12 March, Lennox accused him of being one of his son's assassins,[17] and on 19 April, Drury reported to Cecil the murder of Balfour's servant, and supposed that the motive had been "very lively presumptions for utterance of some matter either by remorse of conscience or other folly that might tend to the whole discovery of the King's death." De Silva reported to Philip II on 6 September, "It is believed for certain that this man [Balfour] was one of the principal actors in the murder of the King."[18] Later, in 1581, Lord Hunsdon wrote that Balfour was "well known throughout the realm to be one of the principal murderers."[19] Balfour himself would later admit to Sir William Drury that he did know about the murder before it happened, but not until 7 February; later still, he claimed that Mary had asked him to kill Darnley but that he had refused; little credence can be given to either of these stories, which are not borne out by the other evidence and were probably concocted in order to deflect blame from himself.

With his brother owning the Old and New Provost's Lodgings, Balfour would have been able to gain access to Darnley's house in order to position explosives beneath it. Robert Balfour had delivered the keys to the house to Thomas Nelson, but there would almost certainly have been a duplicate set; Hepburn alleged that Balfour had one made. John Binning, Archibald Douglas's servant, later claimed that one of the Balfour brothers was seen at the foot of Thraples or Throplows Wynd (which no longer exists) near Kirk o'Field on the night of Darnley's death. Binning also named Robert Balfour as one of the conspirators. Balfour not only had the opportunity to commit murder, he had a motive, which was the identification of his interests with those of the powerful Lords who were his co-signatories to the Craigmillar Bond.

Morton's indictment of 1581 asserted that he himself had "placed and input" the gunpowder "under the ground and angular [i.e., sloping] stones, and within the vaults in low and secret places," which is at variance with what the depositions and the *Book of Articles* had hitherto claimed, which was that the gunpowder had been placed in the Queen's room, an allegation that was almost certainly invented in order to incriminate her.

On 28 February, Drury informed Cecil that "one from Edinburgh" had affirmed that Balfour had "bought of him powder as much as he should have paid three score pounds Scottish."[20] It has been suggested that this powder was stored in the New Provost's Lodging, and later moved to the house next door. Bothwell claimed that, once the "traitors" had seen that the Old Provost's Lodging "would suit their purpose admirably, they collected a whole lot of gunpowder and stacked it under his [Darnley's] bed," which is what was alleged in the Queen's indictment of 1568. This does not necessarily mean that the powder was placed immediately under the bed, but probably that it was positioned two floors below; Mondovi was told by Clernault that a mine had been "laid under that apartment only where the King slept."[21] Significantly, Bothwell added that "this was done at the dwelling of Sir James Balfour,"[22] which suggests that the powder was stored at Balfour's own house, not the New Provost's Lodging belonging to his brother. At the time Bothwell made this allegation, he had good reason to calumniate Balfour, who had callously abandoned him in order to preserve his own life and career.

In order to bring about the destruction that occurred at Kirk o'Field, it would have been necessary for the gunpowder to be packed into the foundations of the house. A pile of gunpowder loose in a ground floor room would not have had such a devastating effect, and many people were of the opinion that Darnley's house had been mined. On the day after the murder, the Council informed Catherine de' Medici, "It is well seen that this unhappy affair proceeded from an underground mine," while the Queen told Archbishop Beaton that "it must have been done by the force of powder, and appears to have been a mine." Clernault echoed this in his first report of the murder: "It is very clear that this wicked enterprise was occasioned by an underground mine," and later, in Paris, he declared, "Some scoundrels fired a mine, which they had already laid under the foundation of the said lodging. The house was reduced to ruins in an instant." Mondovi refers to a mine exploding,[23] and Moray told de Silva on 19 May that the house had been "entirely undermined."[24] The *Diurnal of Occurrents*, Thomas Wilson and Melville were all of the same opinion, while Lennox claimed that "the place was already prepared with undermines and trains of powder." Buchanan, in his *Detectio*, states that the assassins had retained the key to the lower room, "where they had undermined the wall and filled the holes with gunpowder"; elsewhere he says that the powder was put under the foundations of the house"; this all runs counter to the evidence of the depositions, which Buchanan prints in the English edition of the same work.

It seems fairly certain, therefore, that the house was mined, and that, as Morton's indictment stated, the gunpowder was buried under the ground and packed in between the stones of the vaults; the ceiling was low and the powder was hidden in secret places. Bothwell and Clernault both averred that the powder had been laid beneath the King's bedroom, that is, in the cellar kitchen of the Old Provost's Lodging. This could not have been done until the evening before the murder, for Bonkil and his assistants would have been on duty for much of the time that Darnley was at Kirk o'Field, and there must of necessity have been at least an open fire for cooking, which could have ignited the powder dust at any time. The kitchen staff would probably have left early on the evening of the 9th, having given their master his supper; their services were not needed any further, for the Queen and her entourage would not have required any food, having just attended Moretta's banquet. After Bonkil and his assistants had gone, Bothwell's henchmen would have got speedily and stealthily down to work, conveying the powder from Balfour's house to Darnley's, and putting it in place. This was no doubt how Paris became very "begrimed," as Mary herself noticed, and it was probably the reason why the explosion was delayed for two hours after the Queen's departure.

Because part of the eastern gable wall of Darnley's house was left standing and the back door of the New Provost's Lodging was damaged, it is possible that the vaults beneath the eastern end of the Prebendaries' Chamber, where the ceiling was higher, were also mined, so as to effect the greatest possible damage. The Prebendaries' Chamber was destroyed in the explosion.

For more than four centuries, there has been speculation that Mary, Queen of Scots was a party to her husband's murder, or at least had foreknowledge of it. Even today, the matter is controversial, with Mary's detractors insisting she was guilty and her partisans proclaiming her innocence, much as happened during her own lifetime.

It is indeed possible to construct a convincing case against Mary, even without reference to the Casket Letters and the works of Buchanan and Lennox, for the circumstantial evidence is strong. Mary did want to be rid of Darnley. His treasonable conspiracies were grounds enough to justify his murder. The most telling evidence against Mary is the fact that she took him from the safety of his father's power base at Glasgow to Edinburgh, where he had powerful enemies who had good reason to seek vengeance on him or even kill him; she herself had sanctioned the return of some of these men from exile less than two months earlier. According to the later libels, she was having an adulterous affair with Bothwell at the time, and wanted to marry him, but whether this was true or not, and there is no contemporary evidence to show that it was true, she certainly continued to show favour to Bothwell after he had asked her to sanction the murder of Darnley; Bothwell had earlier told Morton that Mary had given her consent to it.[25] Mary had agreed to a surprising reconciliation with Darnley, which may have been a pretence calculated to divert suspicion from herself. It was perhaps more than coincidence that the syphilitic Darnley was murdered the very night before he had been due to resume carnal relations with his wife. Mary herself had fortuitously—or deliberately—left Kirk o'Field about two hours before the explosion. Finally, she was quite capable of sanctioning the murder of someone who had become inconvenient: there is no escaping the fact that, in 1586, she authorised the assassination of Queen Elizabeth by Anthony Babington and his associates as a preliminary to seizing the throne of England.

On the face of it, this is all pretty damning, but it is not the whole picture. There is no evidence that Mary ever contemplated freeing herself from Darnley by other than legal means. When Maitland suggested that other ways might be found, she insisted that they must not conflict with her honour and conscience. When Mary took Darnley away from Glasgow, she was in possession of compelling evidence that he was plotting against her in order to seize power and rule through their child; she was therefore in some peril, and it would have been unthinkable for her to have left him where he was, with an English ship waiting in the Clyde and his father at hand to raise troops. That Darnley was dangerous was later confirmed by de Alava, who later opined that Mary had had to get rid of him, otherwise he would have killed her.[26] But Mary would hardly have connived at the killing of her husband, who was Queen Elizabeth's cousin, on the eve of the hoped-for settlement of the English succession question. In bringing him back to Edinburgh, however, she unwittingly gave his enemies the opportunity of bringing their plans to fruition.

Mary had indeed recalled the exiles who were out for Darnley's blood, but only after months of being pressured to do so by their friends; she must have known that these men posed a danger to Darnley, but she took measures to prevent them from coming anywhere near him, banning them from court for two years. She may have been lulled into a sense of false security by the fact that Bothwell and other Lords accompanied her on her visits to cheer the invalid at Kirk o'Field.

Mary did continue to show favour to Bothwell after he asked her to sanction Darnley's murder; she also continued to favour Maitland and Moray, even though they had hinted at getting rid of Darnley by underhand means. She was no innocent, and knew the turbulent nature of her nobles. In both cases, she had made it categorically clear that she did not approve of the suggestions put to her, and she doubtless naïvely expected her embargo to be sufficient. Bothwell's loyalty had been proven again and again; she could have imputed his suggestion to an excess of zeal for her welfare, and even if she had taken offence at it, she could not have afforded to alienate him.

With regard to her reconciliation with Darnley, this is in keeping with other evidence that suggests that Mary had come to realise that there was no lawful means of ridding herself of her husband and that, given the imminent hoped-for accord with England, it would be more advantageous to her to stay married: her union with Darnley had greatly strengthened her claim to the English succession, since many members of the English Parliament felt that he had the better claim. Without him, she would have been far less acceptable to Elizabeth's subjects. This apart, it is unthinkable that Mary would have prejudiced these longed-for negotiations by committing murder just as they were about to begin. Instead, she had probably resolved to make the best of her marriage. She had forgiven men who had committed worse crimes against her, so there was no reason why she should not have been reconciled to Darnley. The reconciliation may not have been heartfelt, but Mary may have hoped that, as a result of it, she would be able to wean her husband away from his plotting and prevent him from going abroad, for his abandonment of her at this time would have been a serious embarrassment.

Mary may have left the gathering at Kirk o'Field at a fortuitous time, but she herself would always maintain that she had been the intended victim, and that it was only by a lucky chance that she had not returned to the Old Provost's Lodging to stay the night. In the letters written the day after the murder, both she and the Privy Council stated this belief, and it would be repeated in a report sent to Cecil on 19 March,[27] although soon the official line would change. Mondovi was of the opinion that Mary, by "being too prone to pity and clemency," had become "a prey to those heretics, with danger even to her life."[28] Bishop Leslie, who was in Mary's confidence, later recalled, "She returned thanks to God for her preservation from so great a peril, for it looked as though the contrivers of the plot had expected that she would pass the night there with the King, and they planned the destruction of them both." Even after Mary's death, the belief that she had been the intended victim persisted, as was manifest in the funeral sermon preached in Notre-Dame de Paris by Renauld de Beaulne, Archbishop of Bourges, in March 1587.[29]

As for Mary's capacity for murder, by the time she connived in the plot to assassinate Elizabeth, she had been a prisoner in England for eighteen frustrating and miserable years, during which she had plotted ceaselessly for her release and her elevation to her cousin's throne. She was then an ageing, embittered woman, worn down by injustice and ill health, and a shade of the girl of twenty-four she had been in 1567. In addition, after 1570, the Pope had sanctioned and urged the assassination of Queen Elizabeth as a means of furthering the counter-reformation. Moreover, while there is good evidence of Mary's complicity in the Babington Plot, there is no reliable evidence of it in the Kirk o'Field plot, and prior to 1567, nothing to show that she had the makings of a murderess. She had seen murder and bloodshed at first hand, and been profoundly shocked by it.

There are other good reasons for believing Mary innocent. She did not choose Kirk o'Field as a lodging for Darnley. She had intended that he stay at Craigmillar, where he would be more secure from his enemies. Bothwell allegedly asked Paris, rather than Mary, to bring him the keys to the Old Provost's Lodging; had Mary been in league with Bothwell, it would have been easier, and more logical, for her to supply them. If Mary had been involved in the conspiracy allegedly described by Lord Robert Stewart to Darnley, she would hardly have allowed Darnley to confront Lord Robert. It is also highly unlikely that she would have consented to become involved in a

Protestant plot against a fellow Catholic, because, given Darnley's high-profile protestations of faith, the outcry among her co-religionists would have been great. Furthermore, if Moray and Maitland were behind the conspiracy, which seems almost certain, they would hardly have taken Mary into their confidence; she was certainly in ignorance of it when Maitland warned her not to remain at Kirk o'Field on 9 February. It has been suggested that, as so many people were involved in the plot against Darnley, Mary could not have failed to be aware of it; but even more people were involved in the conspiracy against Rizzio, and she, Bothwell and others had still remained in ignorance of it. With the murder of a king being high treason, the conspirators had even more compelling reasons for maintaining secrecy. Finally, Hay, Hepburn and others had "declared the Queen's innocence" in their confessions,[30] and, in July 1567, her own confessor confided to de Silva that she had had no knowledge of Darnley's murder and was greatly grieved by it.[31]

It is important to remember that almost all the evidence against Mary comes from her enemies and was produced some time after the murder, and that there are serious flaws in much of it, which proves that it was deliberately falsified. The men who were responsible for this evidence—chiefly Moray, Maitland, Morton and Balfour—had to justify the actions they had taken against their Queen and safeguard the continuance of their regime and their own power. They had also to emphasise that the blame lay wholly with Bothwell and Mary, so as to deflect suspicion from themselves, and in so doing they waged one of the most vicious and successful propaganda campaigns in history, the effects of which are still apparent today. These men were certainly clever at covering their traces, but they have left enough clues to condemn themselves. Not only were they guilty of the murder of Darnley, but, in killing a man under the Queen's protection, and pinning the guilt for their crime on Mary, they were also responsible for one of the greatest injustices in history.

So how did Darnley die?

The plot to kill him was masterminded by Maitland and Moray, Maitland being the active partner, Moray the passive one but the ultimate beneficiary. Their motive was to rid Scotland of a troublesome Catholic activist and hopefully implicate their enemy, Bothwell, who had been brought into the plot, with Huntly and Argyll, at Craigmillar. Once Darnley and Bothwell were out of the way, Moray and Maitland would be restored to their former political eminence. Bothwell soon became the leading participant in the plot, having secretly conceived an ambition to marry the Queen once her husband was dead. What with the christening and Darnley's illness, there had been no opportunity for the conspirators to carry out their plans until Darnley returned to Edinburgh. By then, Sir James Balfour had entered the conspiracy, and he suggested that Darnley lodge at Kirk o'Field, which the Lords soon realised was ideal for their purpose.

The Lords had decided to use gunpowder so that all the evidence of the murder would be destroyed, and it would also be easier to pin the deed on Bothwell. Balfour purchased the gunpowder and stored it at his house, whence it was moved to Kirk o'Field on the evening of 9 February. By then, Balfour had apparently left Edinburgh. Once the kitchen staff had gone home, the Old Provost's Lodging was undermined, as perhaps was the Prebendaries' Chamber adjoining it. The men who transported the powder and laid the explosives were those same henchmen of Bothwell's who later made depositions as to their guilt, although these depositions were undoubtedly manipulated by men who had secrets to hide. Bothwell would almost certainly have returned to Kirk o'Field after midnight, and it is possible that Huntly and Balfour were there too. Bothwell must have returned to Holyrood prior to the explosion for, since he was Sheriff of Edinburgh, he could not guarantee that he would not be disturbed when the blast was heard. He could have gone back to the palace over the ruined wall near the Blackfriars monastery, and thence by the gardens along the Cowgate.

Gunpowder being unpredictable, Archibald Douglas and his men, perhaps with Morton's blessing, were on hand to apprehend Darnley should he by any chance escape, which is what appears to have happened. Darnley may have been awoken by suspicious noises outside, which were probably caused by the assassins beating a hasty retreat after lighting the slow fuse(s), or by the "many armed men round the house."[32] Convinced that he was in danger, and fearing that there was no time to lose, Darnley panicked, awoke Taylor—if the latter were not already awake—and begged him to help him get out of the house. Together, by means of a rope and a chair, they climbed out of the window that rested on the Flodden Wall and lowered themselves to the ground about 14 feet below. Darnley took with him a dagger and Taylor his master's nightgown and a quilt or cloak for himself. Before escaping, they may have tried to awaken Nelson and the others who slept in the gallery, but time was against them, and self-preservation uppermost in their minds.

It is possible that, in escaping from the window, Darnley either fell to the ground or jumped, and hurt himself—this would account for the internal injuries discovered during the post-mortem. Birrel speculated that Darnley and Taylor were thrown clear by the explosion then strangled outside, Darnley "with his own garters," although there is no reason to think he was wearing any; being hurtled from the exploding house would also account for Darnley's injuries, but while there is good evidence that a man can be thrown clear from an explosion and left unmarked, it is inconceivable that two men, who were sleeping in different places in the bedchamber, would have been blasted in the same direction and survive without a blemish. It is also inconceivable that several objects and items of clothing would have been found lying neatly beside them. Nau, however, and perhaps Mary, believed that "the King's body was blown into the garden by the violence of the explosion, and a poor English valet of his, who slept in the same room, was there killed." But this would not account for the witnesses overhearing a man pleading with his kinsmen for mercy.

Probably in great pain, Darnley, followed by Taylor, began making his way across the orchard, but Douglas and his men suddenly emerged from the nearby cottages and seized them. Realising that their intent was murderous, Darnley cried to them, "Pity me, kinsmen, for the love of Him who had pity on all the world!"—which is what the women in the cottages heard him say. But the Douglases were out for revenge, and in no way inclined to mercy. They suffocated both Darnley and Taylor, perhaps with the nightrobe and the quilt. Captain Cullen, who apparently later confessed to taking part in the murder, testified that "the King was long a-dying, and in his strength made debate for his life."[33] According to Correr, who had his information from Moretta, Taylor was heard to exclaim, "The King is dead! Oh, luckless night!"[34] After the double murder, the assassins made off towards Blackfriars Wynd, where they were seen by Mrs. Merton and Mrs. Stirling. As soon as they had gone, the house blew up.

This theory of what happened in Darnley's final moments is supported by Moretta, who later told Correr that the King had taken fright at the noise of armed men outside the house, trying the doors, and lowered himself from the window to the garden, where he was surrounded by his murderers; Moretta says they strangled him under the window "with the sleeves of his own shirt," but strangulation would have left marks. After the killing, the assassins blew up the house, hoping people would think Darnley had been killed falling from the window while attempting to escape.[35]

Pietro Bizaro, the Italian visitor to Scotland who had reported Darnley's affair with a lady of the Douglas family in 1565, asserted that the King had been alerted by the sounds of men in the house, and had hidden with Taylor in the cellar. After a while, they emerged into the garden, only to be murdered there. Oddly, there is no mention of them panicking at the sight of the burning fuses in the cellar. Furthermore, there was no entrance to the cellar from the inside of the house.

Clernault had a novel theory which he made known to Mondovi, that the King had been awakened by the smell of the burning fuse(s) but was suffocated by the smoke from the explosion while trying to escape,[36] even though his body was found too far from the house for that to have happened. Melville heard rumours that "the King was brought down to a stable where a napkin was stopped in his mouth, and he therewith suffocated." Lennox claimed that the napkin was soaked with vinegar. Lennox, the *Diurnal of Occurrents*, Herries and Buchanan all asserted, with stunning illogicality, that Darnley and Taylor had been strangled in their beds by murderers who then carried them outside then returned to blow up the house, "to cause the people to understand that this was a sudden fire."[37] If this was the case, why not leave the bodies to be consumed in it instead of going to all the trouble of carrying them to the south garden?

Buchanan claims that the murderers had themselves constructed the postern gate in the town wall in order to remove the bodies to the garden, as if such a breach in the city's defences would not already have attracted attention. Ormiston, who was unaware of Darnley's actual fate, was to declare, "As I shall answer to my God, I knew nothing but that he was blown up," and swore that Hepburn and Hay thought the same. He was adamant that the King had not been handled by any man's hands. Hepburn, before his execution, stated that there had been no more than nine people present at the murder, and if the King were handled by anyone, it was not one of them. Bothwell, when he went to view the bodies the next morning, seemed astonished that there was no mark on them, and was probably not aware at that point that the explosion had not killed them. Whether he ever found out the truth from the Douglases is uncertain and unlikely. Most official versions of the murder, and even Bothwell's own account, which naturally makes no mention of his own involvement, asserted that Darnley had been blown up with the house.

The theory outlined above is grounded in a detailed study of the extensive evidence for Darnley's murder. There can be little doubt that his assassination was a political crime dictated by motives of ideology, self-interest and revenge, and that its aim, and ultimate result, was the securing of power by a faction dedicated to establishing the reformed faith and wielding exclusive influence. But this is not the whole picture. The events that followed the murder also have a bearing on the detection of those responsible, and Mary's subsequent behaviour raises questions that need to be answered.

On 1 March, one Thomas Barnaby wrote from Paris to the Earl of Leicester, "Your letters tell me of the strange and sudden disaster which of late hath happened in Scotland. Pray God the tragedy may have no more acts but one."[38] His prayer was not to be answered.

19

"GREAT SUSPICIONS
AND NO PROOF"

BY DAWN ON 11 FEBRUARY, news of Darnley's murder had reached Berwick,[1] and Drury passed it on immediately to Cecil.[2] Soon, the scandalous tidings would spread throughout Scotland and across Europe, giving rise to universal horror, wild rumours and fevered speculation. Suspicion attached initially to Moray and Maitland,[3] and then, within a short time, to Bothwell. "All Scotland cried out upon the foul murder of the King."[4]

Clernault left for Paris on 11 February, bearing the Council's letter to Catherine de' Medici and Mary's to Archbishop Beaton, the Council having authorised him to answer any questions that the Queen Mother might ask about the murder. That same day, or the next, Moretta left Edinburgh, apparently travelling with Father Hay. With Darnley dead, there was nothing to keep him in Scotland, and Hay's mission had been an abject failure.

On the morning of 11 February, Mary emerged briefly from her black-hung apartments to attend the wedding of her favoured servant, Margaret Carwood, to John Stewart of Tullipowreis in the chapel royal at Holyrood. Two days before Darnley's murder, Mary had paid for black satin and velvet for the bride's wedding gown, and she also paid for the nuptial banquet,[5] although she did not attend it. Her presence at the wedding drew scathing comments from Buchanan, who professed shock that she had emerged from her mourning chamber so soon, and on such a frivolous pretext. Mary may well have been honouring a promise to attend Margaret's wedding, but in doing so, she displayed poor political judgement.

Later that day, on the advice of her Council, who shared her view that the plot had been directed at her, and were concerned for her security, Mary took the Prince to Edinburgh Castle, and retired into seclusion.[6] In her absence, Bothwell took control of the government and acted as the virtual ruler of Scotland. It was Mary's misfortune that she misguidedly placed her trust in a man who had conspired to kill her husband, for, as suspicion attached to him, many people would come to deem her guilty by association. In her conviction that she had been the intended victim, Mary would not have credited that the ever-loyal Bothwell could have been involved in Darnley's murder, but the fact that he and Maitland had broached the matter with her earlier must have given her pause for thought. It is more likely, however, that she suspected Morton, who had had good reason to seek revenge on Darnley. But proving it was another matter.

Nau asserts that "diligent inquiries were made about the murder on all sides, especially by those who were its authors," but, since the latter were in control, evidence was bound to be suppressed. In his memoir, Bothwell innocently claimed that "some Lords of the Council, fearing lest the Queen and myself should make inquiries respecting them, united themselves and manoeuvred against the Queen and the rest of us, in order to prevent our arriving at any certainty." It appears to have been Bothwell, however, who was guilty of this. On the afternoon of 11 February, the Council met again, and questioned several more people, including the only independent witnesses, Barbara Merton, Mary Stirling and the surgeon, John Pitcairn,[7] whose evidence was discounted as mere scandal-mongering. Buchanan refers to Mrs. Merton and Mrs. Stirling as "poor silly women, who, when they had blabbed out something more than the judges looked for, were dismissed again as fools that had indiscreetly spoken." According to Thomas Wilson, "a few poor folks, the next dwelling neighbours to the King's lodging," were so intimidated by their august interrogators that they "neither dared tell what they had seen or heard." The inquiry was then adjourned until the following day.

Atholl, who was a friend of Lennox, had been deeply distressed by Darnley's murder, for, "among other reasons, he had been the chief worker in the marriage."[8] But Atholl had other grounds for distress. On the night after the murder, he and his family had been awakened in their Holyrood apartment by a strange noise, which sounded "as if the foundation of the wall were being quietly undermined." In terror, "they passed the night without sleep," and the next day, "the Earl moved into the town, and shortly afterwards went home, in fear of his life."[9] Tullibardine went with him.[10] Both men's loyalties were with the Lennoxes, and Buchanan says that Bothwell and the other Councillors sitting on the commission of inquiry felt that they were probing too deeply for comfort, and, "perceiving the peril, grudged at Atholl and the Comptroller in such sort that it behoved them, for fear of their lives, to leave the court."

It was probably on 11 February that Lennox, at Linlithgow, received the appalling news of his son's murder. Later on, he would be in no doubt that the person responsible for it was his daughter-in-law the Queen, "this tyrant, who brought her faithful and most loving husband, that innocent lamb, from his careful and most loving father to the place of execution, where he was a sure sacrifice unto Almighty God."[11] We have no record of Lennox's initial suspicions, however.

Mary wrote to Lennox on the day after the murder, promising him justice, and inviting him to Edinburgh to take part in the inquiry.[12] Her letter is lost, as is his reply. The *Book of Articles* alleges that she illegally appropriated the earldom of Lennox for her son, as Darnley's heir, and granted a portion of the lands to Lord Boyd. There is no other evidence for the former, but a gift of the ward of some of the Lennox lands to Boyd appears in the *Register of the Privy Seal of Scotland*. This can only have increased Lennox's undoubted animosity towards the Queen.

On 12 February, Darnley's embalmed body was laid in state before the altar of the chapel royal at Holyrood,[13] and the Councillors resumed their inquiry. Mary later informed her European allies that she "could not but marvel at the little diligence they used, and that they looked at one another as men who wist not what to say or do."[14] She expected them to take a more vigorous approach to tracking down the murderers, but since they already knew who had killed Darnley, there was little point in prolonging the inquiry. Buchanan says "there was in the days following [the murder] more travail for the inquisition of certain money stolen from Margaret [Carwood] nor [than] for the King's murder recently committed." He added that "further examination was postponed, or rather the affair was dropped altogether, for they feared that if they proceeded further, secrets of the court would be revealed to the people."[15]

However, the Council did, on that same day, issue a proclamation in the Queen's name, and perhaps at her behest, offering a handsome reward of £2,000 Scots, "an honest yearly rent" and even a free pardon to anyone identifying Darnley's murderers. "The Queen's Majesty," it read, "unto whom of all others the case was most grievous, would rather lose life and all that it should remain unpunished." The proclamation was signed by Argyll, and fixed to the Mercat Cross of Edinburgh by a herald.[16]

That day, Clernault passed through Berwick. Soon afterwards, Drury sent Joseph Lutini back to Edinburgh. Mary had no further interest in pursuing inquiries into his conduct, so Bothwell gave him thirty pieces of silver and sent him away rejoicing. Three days later, Sandy Durham was awarded a post at court and a pension, payment no doubt for services rendered to Bothwell on the night of Darnley's murder.[17]

In Paris, Mondovi was fretting about the delay in Father Hay's arrival. The Nuncio had not yet abandoned hope of a Catholic revival in Scotland, but the Pope was now insisting that he return to his See, and he wanted to see Hay before he left France. He was also expecting to receive Hay's written account of his visit to Scotland—he could not yet have heard about Darnley's murder—but it had not so far arrived, and may never have done so, for no record of it exists. Mondovi hoped to receive an encouraging report from Hay that would pave the way for he himself to go to Scotland, and it was for this reason that he was reluctant to leave Paris. But on 17 February, Pope Pius, having given up hope that Mondovi's mission would succeed, recalled him.[18]

Robert Melville, having left for London a day or so before Darnley's murder for the purpose of entering into the all-important negotiations concerning the English succession, heard about Kirk o'Field on his way south and immediately returned to Edinburgh to obtain further news and fresh instructions. When he arrived on 13 or 14 February, Mary was "too much distressed" to receive him, "but had ordered him to continue his journey as he had been previously instructed,"[19] so, armed with an official account of the murder furnished him by the Council, he set off again for London at once.

But the news had already reached the English court by means of Cecil's spies, for on 14 February, Mr. Secretary informed de Silva that Queen Elizabeth was aware of Darnley's assassination. De Silva reported, "The Queen expresses sorrow at the death of the King, and she thinks that, although he married against her wish, yet, as he was a royal personage and her cousin, the case is a very grave one, and she signifies her intention to punish the offenders." Soon afterwards, de Silva noticed that Elizabeth, realising that she herself was vulnerable to a similar fate, had ordered the keys to all the doors of her apartments to be removed from the locks and the men guarding her to be vetted.[20]

Moretta, and perhaps Hay, passed through Berwick on 14 February,[21] and it was on this day that Drury reported that Mary had to hand letters and ciphers from the Cardinal of Lorraine and de Alava warning her to take heed of whom she trusted with her secrets and that her husband would shortly be slain. These warnings are similar to that in Archbishop Beaton's letter urging Mary to be on her guard, but Drury was probably reporting garbled rumours, for he could not have had access to Mary's private correspondence, and nor could Moretta.

Late in the evening of 15 February, Darnley was buried in the royal vault of James V in the chapel royal at Holyrood.[22] This was a beautiful sanctuary, with stained glass windows, rich hangings, oak furnishings and a carved, gilded and ribbed ceiling with pendants. But the *Book of Articles* claims that the body was, "without any decent order, cast in the earth without any ceremony or company of honest men," while the *Historie of James the Sext* says that the funeral was conducted "quietly, without any kind of solemnity or mourning." Buchanan also alleges that Mary had Darnley buried beside Rizzio, as she had promised after the latter's murder, but he was in fact buried next to her father. The vitriol in these accounts probably stems from the fact that Darnley was buried according to Catholic rites; Leslie states that his interment was ill-attended because so many of the nobles were Protestants. The *Diurnal of Occurrents* and Birrel both confirm that the funeral was quiet. Custom precluded the monarch attending the obsequies of a consort, so the Queen's absence was not remarked upon.

Lennox and Buchanan claimed that Darnley's "armour, horse and household stuff were bestowed upon the murderers" by the Queen, and Buchanan adds that "a certain tailor [Dalgleish?], when he was to re-form the King's apparel to Bothwell, said jestingly he acknowledged here the custom of the country, by which the clothes of the dead fall to the hangman." Had Mary been guilty of Darnley's murder, she would surely not have been so stupid as to openly reward her partner in guilt in this way, and it seems likelier that she felt that Bothwell was more deserving of these rich perquisites than anyone else.

On 15 February, du Croc reached Dover, where he was overtaken by "an express messenger sent him by the French ambassador with the Queen of England" who informed him of the deaths of Darnley and Lennox and delivered "an urgent commission to use all speed" to return to the French court and be the first to communicate the news.[23] That day or the next, du Croc sailed for France.

Robert Melville, *en route* to London, received word from his brother James that Lennox had left Linlithgow by 16 February and returned to Glasgow. It seems strange that Lennox did not go to Edinburgh to pay his respects to his dead son, but he probably felt he would have been putting himself in danger by doing so. Nor had he any idea how much the Queen or others knew about his involvement in Darnley's plots.

Mary was apparently in no fit state to receive anyone. By 16 February, there was serious concern for her health, and it may be that the reality and horror of Darnley's death and its implications had finally come home to her. Her dreadful illness of October and November was still fresh in everyone's minds, and it was understood that being shut up in black-shrouded rooms was not conducive to her well-being. She herself would have "a longer time in this lamentable wise continued had she not been most earnestly dehorted by the vehement exhortations and persuasions of her Council, who were moved thereto by her physicians' informations, declaring to them the great and imminent dangers of her health and life if she did not, in all speed, break up and leave that kind of close and solitary life, and repair to some good, open and wholesome air, which she did, being thus advised and earnestly thereto solicited by her said Council."[24] Mary's emergence from mourning so soon after her husband's death was later to attract scathing criticism from Buchanan, who asserted that she had "brazenly resisted the comments of the people" in doing so. But this is not borne out by the contemporary evidence.

On 16 February, Mary went to Seton,[25] which had proved a refuge before. She took with her Maitland, Livingston, Archbishop Hamilton and an entourage of one hundred persons, having left the Prince in Edinburgh Castle in the care of Bothwell and Huntly.[26] Captain Cullen is said to have been one of those guarding the Queen at Seton.[27]

Drury, whose source is unknown, reported that Mary led a gay and carefree life at Seton, but his information was probably inaccurate, for he also claimed that the Queen and Bothwell visited Dunbar on 17 February, which is untrue.[28] However, Mary's enemies were later to make up all kinds of scurrilous tales about her visit to Seton. Buchanan and Knox alleged that Bothwell was with her there and "never absent from her side," and that the Queen spent her time "plainly abusing her body with Bothwell" or in going out "to the fields to behold games and pastimes," shoot at the butts and play golf or pell-mell. Buchanan claimed, with vicious irony, that Bothwell was "given a chamber next to the kitchen, yet this was not entirely unsuitable for assuaging their sorrow, for it was directly beneath the Queen's chamber, and if any sudden wave of grief overcame her, there was a stair which was wide enough for Bothwell to get up to console her."[29] Bothwell, of course, was in Edinburgh at the time.

Clernault arrived in London on 16 February, and there wrote his report of Darnley's murder, which concluded, "It has not been discovered, still less is it known, who is the author of it." A copy of the report was left with Cecil, whose clerk endorsed it.[30]

That night, the first of a number of accusatory and defamatory placards was pinned to the door of the Tolbooth in Edinburgh; its anonymous author claimed to have "made inquisition by them that were the doers thereof" and affirmed that "the committers" of Darnley's murder were Bothwell, Balfour, David Chalmers and one Black John Spens, "who was the principal deviser of the murder, the Queen assenting thereto, through the persuasion of the Earl of Bothwell and the witchcraft" of Bothwell's former mistress, Janet Beaton, the Lady of Buccleuch. "And if this be not true, [ask] Gilbert Balfour," brother of James.[31] Drury reported the appearance of this placard to Cecil on 19 February, saying that it was written as if by the Queen and stated, "I and the Earl of Bothwell were doers of the [murder]."[32]

John Spens was the Queen's Advocate;[33] he was later arrested for Darnley's murder, but his role in the conspiracy is unknown. In the "Notes concerning David Chambers" [sic] preserved amongst Cecil's papers at Hatfield, and probably collated by one of his agents during Mary's captivity in England, it is claimed that Chalmers "was a great dealer betwixt the Queen and Bothwell"—it will be remembered that Buchanan claimed they had used his lodging as a trysting place—which "gave cause to my Lord Lennox in his letters to the Queen to accuse David as culpable and participant in the murder of the King his son." On 17 March, Lennox did name Chalmers as a party to Darnley's murder, but there is no other evidence of his involvement.

On 17 February, de Silva informed Philip II of that same murder. He had waited three days since being told the news by Cecil in case word came that the murderers had been apprehended, "but no news has come as to who had been the author of the crime." "The case is a very strange one," he wrote, "and has greatly grieved the Catholics. I think that more must be known than Cecil tells me, because when I sent to ask him if he had any further particulars, he told me he had not but we should soon know more because the Earl of Moray was coming hither, and two gentlemen also whom the Queen of Scotland was sending respectively to France and England, who would no doubt bring further details." That night, Cecil received his spy's drawing of the murder scene at Kirk o'Field.

The two gentlemen whom Mary was sending respectively to London and Paris were Robert Melville and Sebastien Pagez. Pagez left Edinburgh, in the company of M. Dolu, Mary's Treasurer for her French dowry, on 18 February,[34] bearing letters from the Queen to Archbishop Beaton, Mondovi and Queen Elizabeth, although there is no trace of the latter letter or any reply.[35]

Mary was still at Seton when, on 18 February, a letter in Scots was sent in her name to Archbishop Beaton thanking him "heartily" for his letter of warning and touching on various other matters. It was either dictated by Mary or sent by Maitland or her Council. It explained that, when she wrote to the Archbishop immediately after Darnley's death, she had been

so grievous and tormented, we could not make you answer [to] the particular heads of your letter . . . Alas, your message came too late, and there was over-good cause to have given us such warning. Even the very morning before your servant's arrival was the horrible and treasonable act against the King's person, that may well appear to have been conspired against ourselves, the circumstances of the matter being considered; whereupon, at this present, we will be no more tedious, abiding until God manifest the authors to the world. For knowledge thereof, neither we nor our Council shall spare the travail that possibly may be made, wherethrough truth may come to light, and therein is our chief care and study at this present.[36]

On that night, or the next, a second placard appeared in Edinburgh, denouncing three of Mary's foreign servants—Sebastien Pagez, Joseph Rizzio and Francisco de Busso—as Darnley's murderers. Clearly, Mary's presence was needed in the capital, and on the 19th she returned from Seton to Holyrood.[37]

That day, Queen Elizabeth sent Lady William Howard and Mildred Cooke, Lady Cecil to the Tower of London to gently break the news of Darnley's death to his mother,[38] who was still a prisoner. They also, in good faith, told her that Lennox had been murdered with him. Lady Lennox was so overcome with grief that the ladies feared for her sanity, and, within the hour, after hearing their report, the Queen sent her own physician, Dr. Robert Huick, and the Dean of Westminster, to calm the stricken Countess. Later that day, Cecil learned that Lennox was not dead, and sent a messenger to the Tower to convey this news to Lady Lennox, but she remained inconsolable. Cecil told de Silva she "could not be kept by any means from such passion of mind as the horribleness of the fact did require."[39]

Robert Melville arrived in London that night,[40] and was immediately admitted to the Queen's presence so that he could give her the official account of Darnley's murder, which was that the conspirators had planned to kill Mary but that she had, by a lucky chance, avoided death. De Silva sought out Melville and "asked him certain questions to try and get at the bottom of the suspicions as to who had been the author of the crime, but could get nothing definite. Even if the Queen clears herself from it, the matter is still obscure." Clearly there was already speculation in London that Mary had had a hand in Darnley's death, for de Silva added, "The heretics here publish the Queen's complicity as a fact, but they are helped in their belief by their suspicion and dislike for her. The Catholics are divided, the friends of the King holding with the Queen's guilt, and her adherents to the contrary. However it may be, this event will give birth to others, and it is quite possible that this Queen [Elizabeth] may take the opportunity of disturbing the Scots, more for her own ends than for any love she bore the King."[41] In his speculations, de Silva displayed an acute grasp of the situation.

Du Croc arrived in Paris on 19 February,[42] and was the first to convey a report of the murders of Darnley and Lennox to Charles IX, Catherine de' Medici and Mondovi. The next day, Cecil informed Sir Henry Norris, the English ambassador in Paris, that Lennox had not after all been killed.

Buchanan says that the regicides were already disturbed by the accusations that were beginning to be levelled at them, "but the numerous complaints of the Earl of Lennox disturbed them more. He dared not come to court on account of the overweening power and licence of Bothwell, but he bombarded the Queen with letters." The second was sent on 20 February from Houston Castle, Renfrewshire, and read:

Notwithstanding the travail and labour which I perceive Your Majesty takes for the just trial of this last cruel act, and yet the offenders not being known, to my great grief I am therefore forced, by nature and duty, to be so bold as to give Your Majesty my poor and simple advice for bringing the matter to light: which is, to beseech Your Majesty most humbly, for God's cause and the honour of Your Majesty and this your realm, that Your Highness would, with convenient diligence, assemble the whole nobility and estates of Your Majesty's realm, and they, by your advice, to take such good order for the perfect trial of the matter, as I doubt not, with the grace of Almighty God, His Holy Spirit shall so work upon the hearts of Your Majesty and all your faithful subjects, as the bloody and cruel actors of this deed shall be manifestly known. And although I need not to put Your Majesty in remembrance thereof, the matter touching Your Majesty so near as it does, yet I shall humbly desire Your Highness to bear with me in troubling Your Highness therein, being the father to him that is gone.[43]

It might be inferred from this letter that Lennox felt that Mary was not doing enough to seek out and punish the murderers. The reference to her honour is quite pointed.

The distraught Lady Lennox was released from the Tower on compassionate grounds on 21 February, and placed in the house and care of Queen Elizabeth's cousin, Sir Richard Sackville; her surviving son Charles, a boy of about twelve, was allowed to join her there. De Silva heard from Robert Melville that the Countess "used words against his Queen [Mary], whereat I am not surprised, as I told him, because grief like this distracts the most prudent people, much more one so sorely beset. She is not the only person that suspects the Queen to have had some hand in the business, and they think they see in it revenge for her Italian secretary; and the long estrangement which this caused between her and her husband gave a greater opportunity for evil persons to increase the trouble."[44] In the weeks to come, Lady Lennox would not cease to bombard Queen Elizabeth and de Silva with demands for vengeance on the killers of her adored son.

Cecil noted that the news of Darnley's private burial caused great indignation in London: it was felt that, as King of Scots, he had deserved all the pageantry of a state funeral, and the fact that Mary had not accorded him one fuelled people's suspicions.

Not everyone suspected Mary. On 21 February, after speaking with du Croc, Giovanni Correr, the Venetian ambassador in Paris, concluded with great perspicacity that, "until further advices are received, this assassination is considered to be the work of the heretics, who desire to do the same to the Queen, in order to bring up the Prince in their doctrines, and thus more firmly establish their own religion to the exclusion of ours."[45]

By 21 February, Mary was back at Seton,[46] and this time Bothwell was in attendance on her. Buchanan later asserted that "Seton had so many conveniences that they had to go back there, to the detriment of their reputations." When Queen Elizabeth heard an unfounded rumour that Mary was exercising herself in shooting, golf and pell-mell with Bothwell, Huntly and Lord Seton, she refused to believe it, which was probably wise of her, for, according to Robert Melville, who had had the news from his brother James, Mary had gone "to Seton to repose there and take some purgations,"[47] which is evidence enough that she was unwell. Mental stress often had an adverse effect on her physical health.

From Seton, on the 21st, Mary wrote a warm letter in reply to Lennox:

We have received your letter giving us thanks for the accepting of your goodwill and counsel in so good part, in that we did only that which was right. And in showing you all the pleasure and goodwill that we can, we do but our duty and that which natural affection may compel us unto. Always of that ye may assure yourself.

And for the assembly of the estates, it is indeed convenient that such should be, and even shortly before the receipt of your letter, we had caused proclaim a Parliament, at the which we doubt not but you all for the most part shall be present, where first of all this matter, being most dear to us, shall be handled, and nothing left undone which may further the clear trial of the same. And we, for our own part, as we ought, and all noble men likewise, we doubt not, shall most willingly direct all our wits and judgements to this end.[48]

On 22 February, de Silva had an audience with Queen Elizabeth, "principally to speak about Scottish affairs and find out her opinion with regard to them. She spoke of the matter with much apparent sorrow, and said she thought it very extraordinary, but cannot believe the Queen of Scotland can be to blame for so dreadful a thing, notwithstanding the murmurs of the people. I told her I thought the rumours were set afoot by people who desire to injure her and make her odious in this country in respect to this succession, but I agreed with her that the thing was incredible. She tells me she had already taken precautions, by certain signs and words she had used, to exculpate the Queen of Scots."[49]

Two days later, Moretta arrived in London and de Silva took the opportunity of sounding him out about Darnley's death. "His account of the matter is almost the same as that published, although he makes certain additions, which point to suspicion that the Queen knew of, or consented to, the plot. When I asked him what he thought, or had been able to gather as to the Queen's share in it, he did not condemn her in words, but did not exonerate her at all. He thinks, however, that all will soon be known, and even gives signs that he knows more than he likes to say."[50] Had Moretta been hoodwinked by Balfour into believing that Mary knew about the conspiracy? If so, such sensational allegations would certainly have deflected public attention from the real murderers.

It is unlikely that Moretta had a chance to speak with Elizabeth, but she had read Drury's reports, and public opinion in England was becoming so vociferous against Mary that, on 24 February, the English Queen felt she had to offer urgent advice to her sister monarch; she wrote her an unusually frank letter, couched in far more forthright terms than she normally used. Even her customary greeting, "Ma chère soeur," was omitted.

Madam,

My ears have been so astounded, my mind so disturbed and my heart so frightened to hear of the horrible and abominable murder of your late husband and my slaughtered cousin, that I have scarcely spirit to write; and however I would express my sympathy in your sorrow for his loss, so, to tell you plainly, I cannot conceal that I grieve more for you than for him.

O, Madam, I should ill fulfill the office of a faithful cousin or an affectionate friend if I did not urge you to preserve your honour. I cannot but tell you what all the world is thinking. Men say that, instead of seizing the murderers, you are looking through your fingers while they escape; that you will not seek revenge on those who have done you so much pleasure, as though the deed would never have taken place had not the doers of it been assured of impunity.

For myself, I beg you to believe that I would not harbour such a thought for all the wealth of the world, nor would I entertain in my heart so ill a guest, or think so badly of any prince that breathes. Far less could I so think of you, to whom I desire all imaginable good and all blessings which you yourself could wish for. For this very reason, I exhort, I counsel, I beg you deeply to consider of the matter—at once, if it be the nearest friend you have, to lay your hands upon the man who has been guilty of the crime; to let no interest, no persuasion, keep you from proving to everyone that you are a noble princess and a loyal wife. I write thus vehemently not that I doubt, but for affection. You may have wiser counsellors than I am, but even Our Lord, as I remember, had a Judas among the twelve; while I am sure that you have no friend more true than I, and my affection may stand you in as good stead as the subtle wits of others.[51]

The references to Mary not fearing to proceed even against her nearest friend and a Judas among the twelve almost certainly point to Bothwell. Elizabeth was to a degree sincere in her advice to her fellow sovereign, for she was quick to perceive the damage that scurrilous rumours could do to her cousin's reputation. In Elizabeth's opinion, Mary was not taking vigorous enough action to track down the murderers, which was the only way to counteract the gossip. However, Elizabeth's greatest concern was that, if Mary's honour was impugned because of her apparent passivity, the prestige of queens regnant in general would be tarnished, justifying the prejudices of many who believed women unfit to rule. And if Mary's subjects took it upon themselves to depose her, an even more alarming precedent would be set.

Catherine de' Medici took the same view as Elizabeth, and wrote to Mary in a similar vein. Her private opinion was that the Queen of Scots was well rid of her young fool of a husband, but she warned her that she must find and prosecute his killers expeditiously and ruthlessly in order to proclaim her own innocence in the eyes of her subjects. Catherine had never liked Mary, and, unlike Elizabeth, pointedly sent no envoy to express the condolences of the French government on her sad loss.

It is often said that Mary did not heed the wise advice of these two seasoned stateswomen, but it is difficult to see what else she could have done to pursue the murderers, in the absence of any substantial evidence or willing informers. She had entrusted the investigation of the matter to her Councillors (little realising that many of them had a vested interest in preventing the crime being solved), issued a proclamation offering a handsome reward to anyone identifying the murderers, and summoned Parliament to debate the next steps in the inquiry—Melville reported on 26 February that it had been proclaimed for 14 April.[52] It was in the interests of her enemies, however, for people to believe the worst of her.

Reports of Mary's conduct, false though they may have been, did not help matters. On 26 February, according to Drury,[53] she dined at Lord Seton's house at Tranent in East Lothian, "where he and the Earl of Huntly paid for the dinner, the Queen and the Earl Bothwell having, at a match of shooting, won the same of them." Drury may yet again have got his facts wrong, for on the day that Mary was supposed to have been at Tranent she was in fact unwell,[54] but the damage had been done. This was not, people felt, the behaviour expected of a woman who was supposed to be in mourning.

On 26 February, Robert Melville reported to Cecil that Pagez and Dolu had arrived in London with Mary's lost letter to Elizabeth, and said he had

had no word himself from the Queen. He had heard that Prince James had been moved to Holyrood, and that Atholl and Tullibardine had departed to the country but had immediately been recalled to Edinburgh under pain of the penalty for rebellion.[55] Clearly, Bothwell and Maitland were taking steps to prevent them joining forces with Lennox.

That same day, Lennox, who was too agitated to wait for Parliament to meet, fearing that by then any trails would have gone cold, wrote again to Mary with what seemed a very reasonable request:

I render most humble thanks unto Your Majesty for your gracious and comfortable letter. I hear of certain tickets [placards] that have been put on the Tolbooth door of Edinburgh, answering Your Majesty's first and second proclamations, which name in special certain devisers of the cruel murder. I therefore most humbly beseech Your Majesty, for the love of God [and] the honour of Your Majesty and your realm, that it may please Your Majesty not only to apprehend and put in sure keeping the persons named in the said tickets, but also with diligence to assemble Your Majesty's nobility, and then, by open proclamation, to admonish and require the writers of the said tickets to compare [i.e., come forward and confront those named], according to the effect thereof. At which time, if they do not, Your Majesty may, by the advice of your nobility and Council, relieve and put to liberty the persons in the tickets aforesaid. So shall Your Majesty do an honourable and godly act in bringing the matter to such a narrow point, as either the matter shall appear plainly before Your Majesty, to the punishment of those who have been the actors of this cruel deed, or else the said tickets to be found vain of themselves, and the persons who are slandered to be exonerated and put to liberty.[56]

In effect, however, Lennox was asking Mary to arrest people—among them members of her Council and her personal servants—on the highly dubious evidence of persons unknown. His request placed her in an impossible dilemma, for if she did as he wished, she would be violating the law, but if she refused to do so, she would be accused of failing in her duty to pursue her husband's killers.

Balfour returned to Edinburgh on the night of the 26th, accompanied by thirty horsemen. He came furtively and, according to Drury, "when he was near unto the town, he alighted and came in a secret way. He is hateful to the people."[57] Evidently rumours about Balfour's involvement in Darnley's murder were spreading as a result of the first placard, and Balfour must have heard about them. The next day, however, Drury heard that another placard had appeared during the night, "where were these letters written in Roman hand, very great, M.R., with a sword in hand near the same letters; then an L.B. [for Lord Bothwell?] with a mallet near them."[58] Increasingly, Mary's subjects were linking her with Bothwell and Darnley's death. In Scotland, "Bothwell was much suspected of this villainous and detestable murder, and the impression was strengthened by the many evil reports circulated about him."[59] The same thing, to a lesser degree, was happening with Mary, and the favour she had hitherto shown to Bothwell was subject to the most unfavourable interpretations.

On the morning after the placard had appeared, a furious Bothwell appeared in Edinburgh "and openly affirmed, by his oath, that if he knew who were the setters up of the bills and writings, he would wash his hands in their blood. His followers, who are to the number of fifty, follow him very near. Their gesture, as his, is of the people much noted. They seem to go near and about him, as though there were [those] who would harm him; and his hand, as he talks with any that is not assured unto him, upon his dagger, with a strange countenance."[60]

Clernault arrived in Paris on 27 February and delivered his detailed account of Darnley's murder. He also spoke with Mondovi and, that same day, the Nuncio sent to Rome a more accurate account of what had occurred at Kirk o'Field. On the 27th or 28th, Elizabeth dispatched Sir Henry Killigrew once more to Scotland to convey her letter to Mary with letters to the Scottish Council. Ostensibly he had come to express Elizabeth's sympathy on her cousin's loss, but the real purpose of his mission was to gain an insight into the true state of affairs in Scotland. Leslie later referred to him as "a spy, or rather, a traitor, under the guise of an ambassador," and Mahon even suggests that he had come to incite the Scots Lords to rebel against and depose their ineffectual but dynastically dangerous Queen, who was showing such favour to Bothwell, a known enemy to England. It may be significant that little is known of Killigrew's activities in Scotland, and nothing of what he reported to the English government on his return.

Three more placards appeared on church doors, one posted to the door of the Tron House, on the 28th; this referred to a smith who had agreed to testify that he had made the counterfeit keys to Darnley's lodging. Drury, reporting this to Cecil, also mentioned he had been informed "by divers means" that the Countess of Bothwell was "extremely sick and not likely to live. They will say there she is marvellously swollen." The innuendo was clear: Cecil was to infer that the Countess Jean had been poisoned by her husband. Drury added, incorrectly, that Balfour had left Edinburgh after the first placard appeared, but of course he had gone just before Darnley's murder.

According to Drury, Mary had sent twice to Moray, asking him to return to court, for she greatly needed his advice and support at this time, but he, along with Morton and Lindsay, had been meeting secretly with Atholl and Caithness at Dunkeld.[61] This fledgling coalition of Protestants and Catholics is a measure of how strongly opinion was polarising against Bothwell. Mondovi heard later that "the Earl of Moray, having been called by Her Majesty, would not go."[62] Instead, he sent to tell her that "he stayeth himself by my Lady in her sickness."[63] The fact that he had left his wife to go to Dunkeld indicates how sick she actually was.

From late February onwards, the placard and smear campaign gained momentum. Bills were posted to St. Giles's Kirk, the Tolbooth, the Mercat Cross, "the courthouse, on church doors, in the streets, at the crossroads"[64] and even on the gates of Holyrood itself. Some bore crude portraits of Bothwell and the legends, "Who is the King's murderer?" or "Here is the murderer of the King."[65] Another doggerel rehearsed the crimes of "Bloody Bothwell."

Naturally, wild rumours began circulating. One had it that, on the night of the murder, a mysterious figure had flitted through the streets of Edinburgh and aroused four of Atholl's men, supposedly to warn them of the foul deed about to be committed. It was said that a dying man had seen a vision of Darnley being slain, and that one of Bothwell's servants had been secretly murdered after hysterically denouncing his master as the King's killer.[66] "Everybody suspected the Earl of Bothwell, and those who durst speak freely to others said plainly that it was he," wrote Melville, while, according to

Buchanan, "no one now doubted who had planned the crime and who had carried it out." But, wrote de Silva, although grave suspicion attached to Bothwell, no one dared accuse him openly because of his influence and strength.[67]

The gathering intensity of the campaign suggests that it was carefully co-ordinated by a group of people committed to bringing down Bothwell and, ultimately, the Queen herself. The success of this propaganda is evident from the rising groundswell of public opinion against Bothwell and Mary, and the feeling that Darnley's murder had brought "shame to the whole nation." As the people clamoured for justice and retribution, ministers of the Kirk "prayed openly to God that it will please Him both to reveal and revenge, exhorting all men to prayer and repentance."[68] The Queen was alarmed by the libels and rumours, but powerless to stop them, for no one knew for certain who was responsible for them. The placards appeared mysteriously overnight, and their impact on an ignorant populace was immense. "The more they were suppressed, the more the people burst forth in their wrath."[69]

Bothwell himself believed, but could not prove, that "several members of the Council, afraid that the Queen and I might catch up with them, banded together in an effort to obstruct us. They used all manner of trickery, posting up bills and placards at night, casting suspicion on me and my friends."[70] Bothwell may well have been correct in his suspicions, for who else knew for certain of his involvement in the murder? As we have seen, he had probably been earmarked from the start as the scapegoat for it. The fact that Drury received prompt information about each placard as it appeared perhaps suggests that there were those in high places who wanted to keep the English government informed about public opinion in Scotland, and it has even been conjectured that the propaganda campaign was orchestrated from England. The *Book of Articles* claims that "the common people" were responsible for the placards, which is almost certainly an attempt to deflect suspicion from the Lords; some of the placards were undoubtedly written by educated men of letters.

Buchanan was probably correct when he wrote that, "although the conspirators tried to seem contemptuous of these things, they could not hide their uneasiness, so they dropped the investigation of the King's death and, with much more bitterness, set about pursuing the authors of the libels. They prosecuted the search with great severity, sparing neither expense nor labour. All painters and scriveners were summoned to see if they could possibly detect the authors from the pictures and libels."

The smear campaign unnerved Hay, who was then with Bothwell at Seton. According to his dying confession, he sensed that he was being shunned for his association with the Earl, and began to suffer agonising qualms of conscience. One day, when they were in private and discussing Darnley's death, Bothwell asked Hay what he thought "when you saw him blown up."

"Alas, my Lord," Hay replied, "Why do you say that? Whenever I hear such a thing, the words wound me to the death, as they should you."[71] It is interesting to note that Bothwell was still under the impression that the explosion had caused Darnley's death; for obvious reasons, no one had thought to disabuse him of the idea, which strongly suggests that the unlikely coalition of nobles that had formed to bring about Darnley's murder had already disintegrated. Bothwell may not have realised it, but he was on his own now, and politically isolated.

The Queen, however, seemed determined to stand by Bothwell and defy public opinion. Rashly, on 1 March, she bestowed on him further benefits attached to the sheriffdom of Edinburgh and the bailery of Lauderdale.[72] But, contrary to what people thought, Bothwell had not grown rich in her service: the fact that he had just had to dispose of some land to raise funds shows that his financial position was as precarious as ever, and this latest gift was no doubt given in order to avoid him suffering further embarrassment. But the timing of it was disastrous.

On 1 March, in the midst of this clamour, Mary, still at Seton, replied in the most reasonable and accommodating manner to Lennox:

We have received your letter, and by the same perceive that you have partly mistaken our late letter sent you the 23rd of February, in that point that we should remit the trial of the odious act committed to the time of a Parliament. We meant not that, but rather would wish to God that it might be suddenly and without delay tried, for the sooner the better, and the greater comfort to us. And where you desire that we should cause the names contained in some tickets affixed on the Tolbooth to be apprehended and put in sure keeping, there is so many of the said tickets, and therewithal so different and contrary to others in counting of the names, that we wot not upon what ticket to proceed. But if there be any names mentioned in them that you think worthy to suffer a trial, upon your advertisement we shall so proceed to the cognition taking, as may stand with the laws of this realm; and, being found culpable, shall see the punishment as rigorously executed as the wickedness of the crime deserves. What other thing you think meet to be done to that purpose we pray you let us understand, and we shall not omit any occasion which may clear the matter.[73]

Mary was assuring Lennox that she had no intention of deferring the trial of anyone arrested for Darnley's murder until Parliament met. As to his suggestion, there were far too many people named in the placards for it to be realistic for her to apprehend them all, but if he wished to name those whom he believed guilty, and "if he will stand to the accusation of any of them," she would authorise a private prosecution,[74] and if this resulted in a conviction, she would ensure that those convicted would be punished. In no sense can she be said to have been protecting Bothwell, for she must have realised that Lennox would name him. In the absence of any evidence, she herself was powerless to summon any suspect to answer before Parliament.

On the night after Mary wrote this letter, the most notorious and damning of all the placards appeared in Edinburgh. It depicted a bare-breasted and crowned mermaid—a mermaid then being a symbol for a siren or prostitute—holding a whip above a hare surrounded by swords; the mermaid was undoubtedly meant to be the Queen, while the hare was Bothwell's heraldic device. The mermaid was protecting the hare with a whip, but none dared approach it anyway because of the threatening swords. There were two versions of this placard: one is coloured, the other uncoloured with a Latin motto that translates as, "Destruction awaits the wicked on every side." This motto was taken from a book that may well have been given to Darnley by his uncle, John Stuart, Lord d'Aubigny,[75] and its use suggests that adherents of the Lennoxes were involved in the smear campaign.

The contents of the earlier placards were by now notorious in London, and on 1 March de Silva wrote to King Philip: "Every day it becomes clearer that the Queen must take steps to prove that she had no hand in the death of her husband, if she is to prosper in her claims to the succession here."[76] Soon, rumours of Bothwell's guilt had spread to Paris, Madrid and Venice.

Given the mounting crisis, Moray could no longer delay his return to Edinburgh, and he arrived back in early March—certainly before the 8th,[77] and perhaps by the 3rd, when Forster reported to Cecil that Moray had had Balfour imprisoned in Edinburgh Castle. This cannot be correct, as Balfour attended a meeting of the Privy Council on 11 March.[78]

There had still been no reaction from Philip II to Darnley's death. The French ambassador to Spain wrote to the Queen Mother on 3 and 5 March, but said nothing of how the King had received the news, which may indicate that Philip had his own opinions on the matter but did not wish to criticise a Catholic monarch or prejudice Mary's succession in England.

Pagez arrived in Paris early in March and presented Mary's letters to Archbishop Beaton and Mondovi.[79] Soon after his arrival, de Alava reported to King Philip that it was the opinion of many that it was the Queen of Scots who had got rid of Darnley, who would otherwise have killed her. However, de Alava seems not to have believed this, for he had heard from Archbishop Beaton that the murder was controlled from England, where the intention had been to kill the Queen as well.[80]

On 5 March, Killigrew reached Edinburgh with Elizabeth's letter for Mary,[81] who was still at Seton; although she was far from well, she returned to Edinburgh before the 7th in order to welcome him. Buchanan implies that she would not see him immediately because "he arrived too unseasonably ere the stage had been set: the windows open, the candles not yet lit, and all the other apparatus for the play unprepared." Yet it would not have taken too long for Mary's mourning chamber to be prepared in this way, for it had been done very quickly on the morning after Darnley's death, so Buchanan's allegation seems purely malicious, and it is far more likely that Mary was too exhausted by the ten-mile ride from Seton to make the effort to receive an ambassador with the proper ceremony.

The next day, Killigrew was entertained to dinner by Moray, with Huntly, Argyll, Maitland and Bothwell—who had all been involved in Darnley's murder—among the guests, and was afterwards conducted to his audience with the Queen. She received him in a chamber so dark that he could not see her face, "but by her words she seemed very doleful, and accepted my sovereign's letters and message in very thankful manner. I hope for her answer in two days, which I think will gratify the Queen's Majesty."[82] In the event, Elizabeth had to wait rather longer for her answer.

Mahon speculated that someone impersonated Mary on this occasion, but there is no reason to think that, and anyway Killigrew had met her before and would have known her voice. He himself did not question the identity of the woman who received him. The fact that Mary was in a darkened chamber and, according to Buchanan, in bed, is proof that she was still in low spirits and observing her forty days of mourning, and suggests that she had kept the convention whilst at Seton.

In Edinburgh, Killigrew found "great suspicions and no proof, nor appearance of apprehension yet, although I am made believe I shall before I depart hence"; he also detected "a general misliking among the commons and others, which abhor the detestable murder of their King." He met three of Darnley's servants, Anthony Standen, Thomas Nelson and Henry Gwynn, who were hoping to return to England as soon as they could obtain passports. Killigrew also noted that Lennox was still in Glasgow, "where he thinks himself safe, as a man of his told me," among his friends.[83]

Mary's failure, or inability, to deal with the problems confronting her was becoming increasingly manifest. On 8 March, de Silva, who had apparently sent Mary a note warning her of a plot against her—probably the same one that had prompted de Alava to warn Beaton—wrote to Philip II expressing surprise that she had not acknowledged it.[84] Around the same time, Lennox wrote to Cecil asking him to urge Elizabeth to avenge "the shedding of Her Highness's own innocent blood";[85] it was obvious that he had no faith in Mary doing so. By now, having suffered Elizabeth's outrage and Lady Lennox's importunings, Cecil had had enough of the Scottish crisis, and on 11 March he told Drury he desired nothing more than to resign.[86]

Mondovi, however, was still optimistic about Mary. After talking with Pagez, he reported to Rome that the Queen of Scots would now execute the purpose urged on her, which was the deaths of the six leading Scottish Protestant Lords.[87] This was a strange about-turn, and perhaps Pagez was taking rather much upon himself, or Mary had her suspicions as to who was responsible for Darnley's murder. But there is no evidence that she was intending at this time to proceed against anyone for any cause, and it may be that Mondovi had drawn the wrong conclusion from his talk with Pagez.

Certainly Archbishop Beaton was deeply concerned about the rumours linking Mary to Darnley's death, and was moved to unusual frankness and forcefulness in his reply to Mary's letters of 20 January and 10 and 18 February, which displays remarkable prescience. After insisting that he had known nothing of the questionable activities of his servants Hiegait and Walker, he referred to "the horrible, mischievous and strange enterprise and execution of the King's Majesty, who, by craft of men has so violently been shortened of his days," and came straight to the point:

> Of this deed, if I would write all that is spoken here and also in England by [of] the dishonour of the nobility, mistrust and treason of your whole subjects, yea, that yourself is greatly and wrongfully calumniated to be the motive principal of the whole of all, and all done by your command, I can conclude nothing [except] that Your Majesty writes to me yourself, that, since it has pleased God to preserve you to take a vigorous vengeance thereof, that, rather than that it be not actually taken, it appears to me better in this world that you had lost life and all.

As Elizabeth I and Catherine de' Medici had done, Beaton exhorted Mary to

> forth-show, now, rather than ever of before, the great virtue, magnanimity and constancy that God has granted you, by Whose grace I hope you shall overcome this most heavy envy and displeasure of the committing thereof, and preserve that reputation in all godliness you have gained of long, which can appear no ways more clearly than that you do such justice as the whole world may declare your innocence, and give testimony for ever of their treason that has committed, without fear of God or man, so cruel and ungodly a murder, whereof there is so much evil spoken that I am constrained to ask you mercy that neither can I nor will I make the rehearsal thereof, which is ever odious. But alas, Madam, this day, all over Europe, there is no subject in head so frequent as of Your Majesty and of the present estate of your realm, which is for the most part interpreted sinisterly.

Beaton's warning could not have been more candid, and when she got this letter, Mary would know that he had told her the truth and spoken out in her interests. Other letters of his show that he thought her innocent.[88]

The Archbishop added:

I did thank the ambassador of Spain on your behalf of the advertisement he had made you, suppose it came too late, who yet has desired you to remember Your Majesty that yet he is informed and advertised by the same means as he was of before, that there is yet some notable enterprise against you, wherewith he wishes you to beware in time. I write this far with great regret, by reason I can come in no ways to the knowledge of any particular from his master.[89]

De Alava's source was well informed, yet the question must be asked: did the Lords intend any harm to Mary, and how far had they proceeded in their plotting?

It is highly unlikely that Mary had been their intended victim at Kirk o'Field, but almost certain that they had meant to pin the whole responsibility for the crime on Bothwell and thus destroy him. Mary's trust in Bothwell, and her elevation of him to the position of her chief adviser, was anathema to the Lords, especially Moray. The major crises of Mary's reign—the Chaseabout Raid and the murders of Rizzio and Darnley—had arisen as a result of threats to Moray's political dominance, and now here was Bothwell, posing yet another threat. It should not be forgotten that, as well as plotting Rizzio's murder, the Protestant Lords had planned to imprison their Catholic Queen and rule in the name of her child. Mary's continuing refusal or inability to proceed against Bothwell for Darnley's murder, which is what the Lords had probably intended all along, must have gone some way towards sealing her fate, and the mounting public opprobrium against her would have given grounds for a growing conviction that she was not fit to reign.

20

"Laying Snares for Her Majesty"

⁓

Contrary to the perceptions of Archbishop Beaton and others, Mondovi reported on 12 March that most people in Paris imputed Darnley's murder to Moray, "who has always had the throne in view, although he is a bastard. He is persuaded by the [Protestants] that it is his by right, especially as he maintains that his mother was secretly espoused by the King his father."[1] It will be remembered that Mondovi had spoken with du Croc, who believed the murder was the work of the heretics, with Clernault and, more recently, with Pagez. Shortly after Mondovi wrote his report, du Croc was sent back to Scotland by Catherine de' Medici to obtain more information about the political situation there.[2]

In Scotland too, there were rumours that Moray was not entirely guiltless, and on 13 March, Moray himself wrote to Cecil:

However these last accidents have altered many men's judgements, yet, being assured that constant men will mean constantly, I would not [pass by] this occasion to signify the constancy of one thankful heart for the many and large benefits I have from time to time received by your means. And, as I am touched myself, so do I judge of you and all men that feareth God and embraced the life of Christianity and honour, as concerning this late accident so odious and so detestable. Yet am I persuaded discreet personages will not rashly judge in so horrible crimes, but, of honest personages, mean honestly, until truth declare and convince the contrary—neither for particular men's enterprises so ungodly, withdraw their good will from so great a multitude as, I am sure, detests this wild attempt even from their hearts.

Moray also revealed his intention of leaving Scotland in the near future, and asked Cecil to procure "a safe conduct to be sent me in convenient haste."

This is a highly ambiguous letter: although Moray admits he is touched himself by suspicion, he does not actually say he is innocent, but uses rhetoric to imply it. Moray's more important communication was confided verbally to the returning Killigrew, whom Moray had commissioned to carry his letter and speak with Cecil and Sir Nicholas Throckmorton, for "he hath heard or seen more nor I can write."[3] This suggests a close collaboration with the English government in a covert enterprise that almost certainly concerned the downfall of Bothwell, added proof of which may perhaps be found in a letter from Justice Clerk Bellenden to Sir John Forster dated 15 March, stating that he should "never give him trust in time coming if the Earl Bothwell and his accomplices gave not their lives ere midsummer for the King's death."[4] On the same date, in a letter to Cecil, Drury listed Bothwell, Black Ormiston, Hepburn, Hay, Cullen and others including the Laird of Beanston (another Hepburn) and James Edmonstoun as the assassins.[5] Already, the official version of Darnley's murder was being rewritten.

Maitland also wrote to Cecil on the 13th, referring to some candid suggestions made by the latter in two letters that are now lost:

By Mr Killigrew and Mr Melville, I received your letters of 25th and 26th February, and thank you heartily for your frank speech. For my own part, I like your intention, so I know it does not offend such here as have most interest to wish the matter to be earnestly recommended to such as you be; for they mean to demand nothing but right, and that in due time and orderly. For the third mark you wish I should shoot at, to wit, that Her Majesty would allow of your estate in religion [i.e., that she would convert to the reformed faith], it is one of the things in Earth I most desire. I dare be bold enough to utter my fancy in it to Her Majesty, trusting that she will not like me the worse for uttering my opinion in that [which] is profitable for her every way. And I do not despair, but although she will not yield at the first, yet, with progress of time, that point shall be obtained. I pray God it may be shortly.[6]

Unlike Moray's letter, this one is almost certainly connected with the negotiations for the English succession, for it would have been more advantageous for all concerned if Mary became a Protestant. The fact that Maitland thought she would eventually convert suggests that she was not as committed to her faith as the Pope would have liked: certainly her concessions to the Kirk give this impression.

Killigrew left for London with both letters on 14 March.

On that day, after intensive investigation, the Council, namely Moray, Argyll, Huntly and Bothwell, issued a proclamation for the arrest of James Murray of Purdovis (brother of Tullibardine) for treasonably setting up placards "tending to Her Majesty's slander and defamation."[7] James Murray was an enemy to Bothwell and an adherent of the Lennoxes; in 1565, he had been in trouble for alleging that Bothwell intended to murder Moray and had made salacious remarks about the Queen. It is not known what evidence the Lords now held against him, but it seems likely that someone had informed on him. We do know that, after the mermaid placard appeared, the Queen, who was particularly upset by it, had summoned the Minister of Dunfermline "and asked him if he knew the deviser," which he did not. By this time, Murray was already on the list of suspects, and Bothwell asked the Minister if Murray had spoken evil of him. "I have never heard him say well" was the answer.[8]

On learning of this new proclamation, Murray immediately fled into England, after sending a letter to Queen Elizabeth, "begging her favour."[9] Then he wrote to the Scottish Council, offering to come with six men, "armed or naked," to support his allegations in court.

Mary was becoming increasingly uneasy as a result of the clamour over Darnley's death, and decided that the Prince would be safer back in Stirling in Mar's care. On 15 March, Bishop Leslie was sent there to make the necessary arrangements. That day, de Alava reported from Paris that the Queen was so alarmed by the worsening situation in Scotland that she was talking of going to live in France, a prospect that was by no means welcome to her former mother-in-law, Catherine de' Medici, in whose opinion Mary's place was in Scotland and nowhere else.[10] Catherine's disgust at Mary's failure to apprehend Darnley's murderers moved her to write to the Scottish Queen, in the name of herself and King Charles, that, "if she performed not her promise of seeking by all her power to have the death of the King their cousin revenged, and to clear herself, she should not only think herself dishonoured, but to receive them for her contraries, and that they would be her enemies."[11]

Moretta and Father Hay arrived in Paris on 15 March.[12] The next day, having spoken with them both and learned further details of Darnley's death, Mondovi wrote that he was now able

> to understand fully the state of the affairs in Scotland. At this moment, they are in such confusion owing to the death of the King, that there is fear of a very extensive insurrection, for the Earls of Moray, Atholl, Morton and other Lords have joined with the Earl of Lennox, the King's father, under the pretext of avenging his death. The Earls of Bothwell, Huntly and many other men of importance are with the Queen for the same purpose. Both sides are suspicious of each other. Hence it is thought that [Moray], (as I wrote on the 12th instant), aiming at the succession to the throne, desires upon this occasion to murder the Earl of Bothwell, a courageous man, much trusted and confided in by the Queen, with the intention of being afterwards able to lay snares for the life of Her Majesty with greater ease, especially as he can hope, through the slothfulness of the Earl of Lennox, to obtain, by his permission and consent, the governorship of the Prince and, by consequence, the whole realm. If he should gain this, which may God avert, he may be able to accomplish the wicked end he has set before himself, and herein the favour of England will not be wanting. The English Queen is jealous of the Prince as the legitimate heir of both those realms, and will not omit to favour the said Moray, her dependant, being bound to her by many obligations as well as religion.[13]

In this breathtaking indictment of Moray there is no hint of any suspicion of Mary, as Moretta had implied in London, nor is Bothwell linked to Darnley's murder; instead he is referred to merely as an obstacle in the way of Moray bringing about Mary's ruin. Moretta had left Scotland around 11/12 February, but Moray, Morton and Lindsay did not meet up with Atholl and Caithness until after this date, so Moretta must have maintained contact with his very knowledgeable sources in Scotland after his departure, and received new information that made him revise his opinion of the Queen. Apart from his assumption that Moray wanted Mary dead, Moretta's report appears to be a reasonably perceptive summation of the situation, given what was soon to happen.

Mondovi also reported that, according to Father Hay, Mary was anxious that he himself should go to Scotland, but both Hay and Moretta warned him not to. Mondovi could not resist adding that, "if the Queen had done that which was recommended and proposed to her from our side, with promise of all the aids necessary for that most just execution, she would now find herself really mistress of her kingdom."[14]

Moretta saw Giovanni Correr on 20 March; afterwards, Correr reported to the Signory slightly, but not substantially, different details of Darnley's murder from those that Moretta had given Mondovi. Much has been made of these trivial discrepancies, but they may be accounted for by minor inaccuracies or omissions in both reports; in each case, Moretta gave essentially the same story, asserting that Darnley was awakened by suspicious noises and/or frightened by the sight of armed men outside the house, whereupon he fled, only to be strangled in the garden. In one version, Darnley escaped by a gate into the garden, in the other he escaped out of the window; but if he had got out of the window, he would still have had to go through the postern gate into the south garden, so the two stories are not irreconcilable. It was on this occasion that Moretta imputed the murder to the heretics, and in particular to Mary's "bastard-half brother." Correr concluded, "It is widely believed that the principal persons of the kingdom were implicated in this act, because they were dissatisfied with the King."[15]

On 17 March, Lennox replied to the Queen's letter asking him to name those whom he wished to accuse of Darnley's murder:

For the names of the persons aforesaid, I marvel that the same have been kept from Your Majesty's ears, considering the effect of the said tickets, and the names of the persons are so openly talked of: that is to say, in the first ticket, the Earl of Bothwell, Master James Balfour, Master David Chambers [sic] and Black John Spens; and in the second ticket, Signor Francis[co Busso], Bastien [Pagez], John de Bordeaux and Joseph

[Rizzio], David's brother; which persons, I assure Your Majesty, I, for my part, greatly suspect. And now, Your Majesty knowing their names, and being the party as well and more nor I am, although I was the father, I doubt not but Your Majesty will take order in the matter according to the weight of the cause.[16]

Mary was now committed to sending Bothwell and the other men named for trial, but it seems that the decision to do so had not been hers alone. According to Bothwell himself, in a passage in his memoirs headed "My urgent request for a public trial," "as soon as I realised that these [placards] were laying upon me the blame and odium of having committed a crime of which I and all with me were innocent (of which I call God to witness), I prayed Her Majesty and the Council to allow me to stand trial. If, on close inquiry, I were to be found guilty, I would expect to pay the penalty; but if declared innocent (which in all truth I am), such slanderous attacks should cease. This was agreed to."[17]

Leaving aside Bothwell's protestations of innocence, which were crucial to his survival in 1568 when this was written, a trial that would clear his name of the charge of regicide was a highly desirable, if not essential, preliminary to his proposal of marriage to the Queen. Once he was declared innocent, none could accuse him of murdering her husband in order to wed her. As for the trial itself, he must have realised that very little could be proved against him, and that too many people had a vested interest in him keeping his mouth shut. They would have been aware that Bothwell was almost certainly in possession of a copy of the Craigmillar Bond, which would have proved compromising to most of the Queen's leading advisers.

In his letter, Lennox also asked Mary to decide whether or not he should be made guardian of the Prince in place of Mar, a matter that had evidently been referred to in the lost letters that commenced this correspondence.

In fact, Mary had decided that Mar should retain his guardianship of the Prince, and on 19 March, in consequence of this, he reluctantly relinquished his command of Edinburgh Castle and was formally appointed Governor of Stirling Castle instead.[18] Buchanan claims that Mary justified her decision to deprive Mar of the more prestigious post on the grounds that he was ill at the time and that "she could not keep in check the Edinburgh mob, who were then giving trouble, unless she had the castle under her own authority"; however, Nau says that she did it "by the advice of her Council, who considered these trusts too important to be both in the hands of one single individual." It was probably Bothwell who was behind the move, because it was his adherent, Sir James Cockburn of Skirling, who was made Governor of Edinburgh Castle in Mar's place, which effectively placed the fortress in Bothwell's hands. According to the *Diurnal of Occurrents*, the citizens were unhappy about the transference of the governorship.

On 19 March, Argyll and Huntly left with the Prince for Stirling, and on the following day entrusted him to Mar's custody. The fact that the Queen did not travel with her son is perhaps indicative of the state of her health at this time. Had Mary been aware of who her true enemies were, she might well not have entrusted her son to the care of Mar, a leading Protestant, whose wife was the sister of James Murray, the man who was believed to have been behind the placard campaign.

The Countess of Bothwell had now recovered from her serious illness, and on 20 March, she made the first move towards divorcing her husband on the grounds of his adultery with Bessie Crawford:[19] the first procuratory—a document authorising legal action—was signed on this day. What prompted this timely and accommodating gesture on the Countess's part is uncertain. Bothwell's affair with Bessie Crawford belonged to May 1566; why had the Countess waited so long to divorce him for it?

It is possible that Bothwell had told her of his ambitions and secured her agreement to a divorce that would benefit them both. The *Book of Articles* alleges that her brother Huntly persuaded her to it after Mary had restored his ancestral lands, but Parliament did not grant this until 19 April, a month after Jean had applied for a divorce, and Drury reported on 29 March that Huntly misliked the idea of Bothwell divorcing his sister and had only reluctantly agreed to it.

It is also possible that the Countess's action had been prompted by fear for her life. Drury, when reporting that she was thought to be dying, had perhaps implied that foul play had been the cause of her illness, and on 29 March, Sir Henry Norris, the English ambassador in Paris, announced that Lady Bothwell had actually died after being poisoned, and that the marriage of the Earl to Queen Mary would soon follow.[20] It is not beyond the bounds of credibility that Bothwell had tried to poison Jean: he had, after all, plotted Darnley's murder in order to satisfy his ambitions. But the attempt on the Countess's life—if attempt it was—failed, and with public opinion rising fiercely against him, Bothwell may not have dared to try again, for two convenient deaths would have been far too coincidental. According to Leslie, rumour had it that Bothwell had offered his wife the choice of divorce or a cup of poison. Whether he had tried to poison her or not, Jean may have believed he had, and it may have been this that impelled her to give him his freedom.

Accusations against Moray were by now more widespread, and on 21 and 30 March, Drury reported that the Earl had set up two challenges, offering to defend his honour by personal combat against any person defaming him as a regicide.[21] There is no other record of these challenges, so it may be that Drury was again repeating idle gossip.

On 21 March, a Council was held at which Bothwell was present but not Balfour, who appears to have been maintaining a low profile.[22] Two days later, after noon on Palm Sunday, at the Queen's command, a solemn requiem Mass and dirge for the soul of the late King was sung at Holyrood;[23] Mary was present, for this marked the end of her forty days of mourning, but Drury heard that she broke down during the Mass and that many people witnessed it.[24] Buchanan, of course, claims that she was deliberately trying "to placate the popular indignation by simulating grief."

On that day or the next, Mary replied to Lennox, informing him that she had received his letter "naming the persons you greatly suspect," and agreeing to his demands:

For the convention of our nobility and Council, we have prevented [acted in anticipation of][25] the thing desired by you in your letter, and have sent for them to be at us in Edinburgh this week approaching, where the persons nominated in your letter shall abide and undergo such trial as by the laws of this realm is accustomed, and being found culpable in any wise of that crime and odious fact nominated in the tickets, and whereof you suspect them, we shall even, according to our former letter, see the condign punishment as rigorously and extremely executed as that fact deserves. For indeed, as you write, we esteem ourselves party if we were resolute of the authors. And therefore we pray you, be at us here in Edinburgh this week approaching, where you may see the said trial and declare the things which you know may further the same, and there you shall have experience of our earnest will and affectionate mind to have an end in this matter, and the authors of so unworthy a deed really punished.[26]

Had Mary been Bothwell's partner in murder and adultery, it is extremely unlikely that she would have agreed to a private process that carried a high risk of public exposure. Yet she had willingly sought to meet Lennox's demands all along, which gives the lie to Buchanan's claim that she tried to evade them.

It has been said that Mary herself should have initiated the prosecution of Bothwell, yet she had no evidence against him but the accusations in the placards. For the Crown to have brought him to trial on this flimsy pretext might have satisfied public opinion, but would have been a travesty of justice. Nor do the Lords seem to have urged their sovereign to seek out and punish Darnley's murderers; in fact they had abandoned their inquiry as soon as it became clear that it might reveal evidence prejudicial to themselves.

At this time, Queen Elizabeth was telling de Silva that there were "grave suspicions" about Bothwell, and about others near to Mary, but that people "did not dare to proceed against them [i.e., Bothwell and Mary] or make any demonstration in consequence of the influence and strength of Bothwell, both on account of his perpetual office of Admiral, and because the Queen has given him charge of five hundred men who formed her guard."[27] But Mary now had authorised the prosecution of Bothwell, and at his own urging, as Elizabeth would soon find out. De Silva also mentioned that Mary had spoken tentatively to Killigrew of sending the Prince to be brought up in England, which indicates how concerned she was for his safety and her own security in the current political climate. Elizabeth, however, had told de Silva that she was unsure whether she wanted the responsibility of Mary's child, for "it would cause her anxiety, as any little illness it might have would distress her"; on the other hand, "she knew that the French would do their best to take the infant to France," and that she could never allow.[28]

.   .   .

Around 25 March, Clernault apparently arrived back in Edinburgh, carrying letters to Mary from her uncle, the Cardinal of Lorraine. Drury later reported that Mary burned these letters because the Cardinal seemed "much to mislike with her for the death of the King,"[29] but Clernault later told Beaton that Mary had neither read nor paid any attention to any communication he had brought her. According to Drury, Mary "has been for the most part either melancholy or sickly ever since" Darnley's murder; she was unwell on 25 and 27 March, and fainted on both occasions.[30] Yet, on the latter day, which was Maundy Thursday, she insisted on keeping vigil on her knees in the chapel royal from 11 p.m. to 3 a.m.[31]

During that Holy Week, Mary presented Bothwell with some valuable church vestments that had originally come from Aberdeen Cathedral, but had been taken by the 4th Earl of Huntly to Strathbogie for safe keeping after the Reformation, and confiscated by the Crown on his attainder in 1563. These vestments were said to have been made from cloth of gold taken from the abandoned English royal pavilions after Robert the Bruce's victory at Bannockburn in 1314. Mary had a number of these pieces in her possession: three she now gave to Bothwell, and the rest she used to furnish a memorial bed for her husband, which probably replaced the black hangings in her apartments as a symbol of her widowhood.[32] In the circumstances, the gifts to Bothwell displayed a disturbing lack of judgement, but Mary was becoming increasingly dependent on him, and later evidence suggests that she at this time believed him innocent; these gifts may have been made in token of that belief, to sustain him during the trial to come. But some people took great exception to this gift of historic Catholic vestments to a Protestant Lord suspected of murder.

On Good Friday or the day after, the Council, with Bothwell himself among them, but not Balfour, enacted that Bothwell, with those other persons named by Lennox as his accomplices in the murder of the King, be tried on 12 April following. A formal letter of summons, signed by the Queen, was sent warning Lennox and any other accusers he might bring with him to appear in the Court of Justiciary on that day.[33]

According to an Act of James IV passed in 1493, fifteen days had to elapse between citation and trial; forty days were allowed where the accused was charged with treason.[34] In Bothwell's case, only fifteen days were allowed for. This was doubtless arranged so that the trial could take place before Parliament met on 14 April; Buchanan alleged that "the Queen wanted the inquiry settled by that day so that the accused, absolved by the verdict of the court, could be exonerated by the assent of the whole Parliament," but in fact Lennox had told Mary that the matter was too important to be delayed until Parliament met, and she had merely complied with his wishes.

On 29 March, as soon as the Council had concluded its business, Mary set off again for Seton[35] for the sake of her health: on 30 March, Drury reported that she was "troubled this last week with some sickness of which she is not yet all free of." But the rumour-mongers were busy in the wake of news of the Countess of Bothwell's divorce action. On the 29th, Drury wrote that the judgement of the people was that the Queen would marry Bothwell. The next day, Drury informed Cecil that Huntly misliked the idea of Bothwell divorcing his sister, but "has now condescended" to it.[36] The Lords would later accuse Huntly of conniving at Bothwell's marriage to Mary.[37] In Paris, rumour was busy too, and de Alava now voiced a far-fetched suspicion that Darnley's murder had been plotted by Mary and Catherine de' Medici together![38]

Mary had by now replied to Elizabeth's urgent letter, but the reply is lost, and its contents are known only through a report of de Silva, who had discussed the letter with Elizabeth. According to this, Mary's response was disappointing: her letter "only contained lamentations for the troubles she had suffered in her life, and a request that the Queen would pity her, especially in her present grief for her husband, which was greatly increased by the desire of wicked persons to throw the blame of such a bad act upon her. She therefore asked the Queen to help her in her troubles, as she could trust no one else, and begged her not to allow her to be calumniated in [England]."[39]

This pathetic communication was unlikely to impress Elizabeth, who had learned at an early age to deal with adversity, and whose wise advice had been apparently ignored. What it does reveal, though, is Mary's fragile and emotional state of mind, which seems to have affected her physical health and rendered her incapable of decisive action. She had been ill almost continuously since Darnley's death, which incidentally had occurred just eight months after her confinement, and may have triggered postnatal depression. There is plenty of evidence that the loss of her husband had caused her grief, which was no doubt mingled with regret that their life together had been so unhappy. She was also suffering the after-effects of shock and the trauma of realising—as she believed—that the murder plot had been intended for her.

Furthermore, she had to live with the fear that her enemies would make a second attempt, which was why she was contemplating taking the drastic step of sending her baby to England. It must not be forgotten either that Darnley's murder was the climax of a year in which Mary had had to deal with the horrific killing of Rizzio, a difficult childbirth, the disintegration of her marriage, a life-threatening illness, and rumours of plots and conspiracies, and that she had just begun to recover from all this when the tragedy happened.

We may discount the gossip of Drury and Buchanan concerning Mary's activities at Seton as malicious, and even Drury had to concede at length that Mary was suffering from depression and fainting fits and was generally unwell. Her Council had quickly realised that her health might not withstand the rigours of secluded mourning, and since then she had retreated three times to the bracing air of Seton in the hope that it would restore her. There is other evidence that she was not functioning normally. Her voluminous foreign correspondence suddenly ceased, and there is no record of her communicating even with her Guise relatives. Most of the letters sent in her name were in Scots, and therefore not written by her personally but probably by her Council on her behalf, which suggests that she was unable to cope with affairs of state. She was said to be "too grievous and tormented" to reply in full to Archbishop Beaton's letter, and Clernault declared that she had not read or listened to any of the letters he brought her. She had failed to thank both de Alava and de Silva for their warnings of a conspiracy. She had been almost too ill to receive Killigrew, had broken down in public at Darnley's requiem Mass, and had failed to accompany her son to Stirling.

This all suggests a woman racked with shock, grief, stress and anxiety, and it is hardly surprising that some historians have concluded that Mary suffered a nervous breakdown at this time. Certainly she was at the mercy of her emotions and her poor health, which left her incapable of effort and rational judgement and rendered her an ineffective ruler. In this weakened state, she was easy prey for the predatory men who surrounded her. Being a woman who had always needed a strong man to lean upon, it was her tragedy that she now chose to rely on Bothwell, although her letter to Elizabeth suggests that she had doubts about even his trustworthiness. As for her other advisers, to whom she had entrusted the investigation of the murder, most had a hidden agenda and were determined that the truth of the Kirk o'Field conspiracy should remain hidden; Mary later revealed that she had been perturbed at their dilatoriness, but at the time she was probably incapable of calling it into question; because of this, however, it was she who was blamed for it.

From early April, a voice was heard every night in Edinburgh, crying out, "Vengeance on those who caused me to shed innocent blood! O Lord, open the heavens and pour down vengeance on me and those that have destroyed the innocent!"[40] Once again, the Council concentrated its energies on pursuing this minor offender, rather than on investigating the King's murder.

Moray had received his safe-conduct from Elizabeth, and was now—as the crisis deepened and Bothwell grew all-powerful—about to make himself scarce again. "The ostensible reason of his journey was his desire to see [other] countries,"[41] but it was a strange time to be leaving his sister, who now needed his counsel and support more than ever. Buchanan asserts that Bothwell had tried to murder Moray, but this is unsubstantiated, and Moretta had told Mondovi that it was Moray who was plotting to murder Bothwell. But Bothwell was shortly to be tried and might well name Moray as one of his fellow conspirators, and Moray would not have wanted to be in Scotland when that happened.

Moray may also have laid plans, in the event of Bothwell's acquittal, for a coup against him, for he must have suspected where Bothwell's ambitions lay, and if they came to fruition, Moray's position would be untenable; moreover, Bothwell would have the wherewithal to ruin him. Moray said as much to de Silva when he was in London, telling him that the real reason for his leaving Scotland was that

Bothwell, who had always been his enemy, was in so powerful a position, he feared something unpleasant might befall him, particularly as Bothwell had over four thousand men at his disposal, besides the force in Edinburgh and Dunbar, where he says the whole of the artillery and ammunitions are. He said he did not intend to return until the Queen had punished the persons concerned in her husband's death, as he thought it was unworthy of his position to remain in a country where so strange and extraordinary a crime went unpunished. He believes that the truth might certainly be ascertained if due diligence were shown, as it is undoubted that over thirty or forty persons were concerned, and the house where the King was killed was certainly undermined, which could not have been done by one man.[42]

Moray's plans may also have embraced Mary, as Mondovi had concluded on 16 March, after speaking with Moretta. Nau says that "this same Earl, after having matured all his plans necessary for his success in seizing the crown and ruining the Queen, asked her permission to go to France, which she granted, giving him also letters of introduction to her relations, with power to draw money on her dowry." Elsewhere, Nau claims that "the usurpation of the crown had been planned before the departure of the Earl of Moray out of the kingdom." When Moray was in France, Archbishop Beaton warned de Alava that, despite Moray's professions of friendship for Mary, he was in reality her mortal enemy and would show himself to be so on his return to Scotland.[43] Had Moray been innocent of Darnley's murder, or of conspiring against Bothwell and the Queen, there would have been no need for him to leave Scotland.

It was Moray's intention to travel via England to France, Milan and Venice, and on 3 April, he made his Will, appointing Mary the chief guardian of his infant daughter. This document is proof that Moray, that model of moral rectitude, did not believe the gossip about his sister and Bothwell, nor that she was a murderess. The Will is not, however, indicative of his real intentions towards Mary, for it would only come into force if he died abroad before he could realise his ambitions.

It appears that Mary briefly returned to Holyrood from Seton on 4 April, but was back there on the 5th, when a Privy Council was held at Seton.[44] It was later alleged that Mary and Bothwell were betrothed on that day. Amongst the Casket Letters are two marriage contracts. One was undated, in French,[45] and Buchanan alleged that it had been drawn up before Darnley's death, even though it refers to that event. Although it was supposedly signed by Mary, her signature is almost certainly a forgery, and the handwriting bears a resemblance to Maitland's in its letter formation and pressure points.[46] This may be the only original surviving document from the Casket Letters.

The other contract, written in Scots, supposedly in Huntly's writing,[47] but now only known through a copy, was signed allegedly by Mary and Bothwell, witnessed by Huntly and Thomas Hepburn, Parson of Oldhamstocks, and dated at Seton on 5 April 1567. It reads:

> Considering how, by the decease of the King her husband, Her Majesty is now destitute of an husband, living solitary in the state of widowhood; in the which kind of life Her Majesty most willingly would continue, if the weal of her realm and subjects would permit. But, on the other part, considering the inconveniences [that] may follow, and the necessity which the realm has that Her Majesty be coupled with an husband, Her Highness has inclined to marry. And seeing what incommodity may come to this realm, in case Her Majesty should join in marriage with any foreign prince of a strange nation, Her Highness has thought rather better to yield unto one of her own subjects; amongst whom, Her Majesty finds none more able nor endowed with better qualities than the right noble and her dear cousin, James, Earl Bothwell, of whose thankful and true service Her Highness, in all times bypast, has had large proof and infallible experience. And seeing not only the same good mind constantly persevering in him, but with an inward affection and hearty love towards Her Majesty, Her Highness has made her choice of him. And therefore . . . takes the said Earl Bothwell as her lawful husband, and promises that how soon the process of divorce intended betwixt the said Earl and Dame Jean Gordon, now his pretended spouse, be ended by the order of the laws, Her Majesty shall, God willing, thereafter shortly take the said Earl to her husband.

This contract, the wording of which is similar to the unquestionably authentic one drawn up on 14 May, and the Ainslie's Tavern Bond of 19 April (see Chapter 21), was almost certainly forged by Mary's enemies to show that, even before Bothwell's trial and divorce, she, "impatient of the delay," had agreed to marry him.[48] In reality, as will be seen, he had not yet even proposed marriage to her.

Du Croc arrived in Scotland around this time, and went to Seton to present his credentials. Buchanan says he warned Mary how infamous Darnley's murder was abroad, and persuaded her to return to Edinburgh. She arrived in the capital in time to say an emotional farewell to Moray, weeping "at his departure" and "wishing he were not so precise in religion."[49] Moray left for England on 7 April, crossing the border on the 10th,[50] two days before Bothwell's trial and four days before the opening of the Parliament that would have the power to arraign him.

Maitland, the other prime mover in the Darnley conspiracy, whom Nau calls "the chief conductor of all the plots and rebellions" of Moray, remained in Edinburgh with the Queen, keeping a low profile.

On 10 April, Mondovi finally left Paris, having informed the Vatican that Father Hay would be writing an account of his visit to Scotland.[51] It is unlikely he ever did so, for no such account is known to exist. Mondovi's recall signified Rome's admission that Mary was unlikely to promote the Counter-Reformation in Scotland.

On 4 April, Drury had reported that Lennox had besought Queen Elizabeth to request a postponement of Bothwell's trial because he could not gather his witnesses in time and Mary would not grant James Murray immunity from prosecution if he returned from England to testify on Lennox's behalf. Drury added that Lennox believed that those he had accused had entered into bonds against him, but he did not have time "to raise sufficient strength" to defend himself against such dangers as were intended by his enemies towards him.[52]

As soon as she received this letter on 8 April, Elizabeth—who desired nothing more than to see Bothwell found guilty—wrote to Mary, exhorting her, "for the consolation of the innocent," to postpone the trial; "which, if it be denied to them, would make you greatly suspected." Again, she urged Mary to make clear her innocence:

For the love of God, Madam, use such sincerity and prudence in this case, which touches you so closely, that all the world shall have reason to pronounce you innocent of a crime of such enormity, a thing which, if you do it not, you would deserve to fall from the ranks of princesses and, not without cause, become opprobrious to the people; and rather than that should happen to you, I would wish you an honourable burial than a soiled life. You see, Madam, that I treat you like my daughter, and promise you that, if I had one, I should not wish better for her than I desire for you, as the Lord God will bear me witness, Whom I heartily pray to inspire you to do that which will be most to your honour and the consolation of your friends. With my very cordial recommendations as to her to whom I wish the most good that can come to you in the world for the future.[53]

Elizabeth was apparently unaware of Mary's true state, and it was not in the interests of the ruling clique in Scotland to enlighten her: it suited them very well for Mary to be discredited in the eyes of the world because of her evident unwillingness to pursue Darnley's murderers. But Elizabeth's alarm was sincere, for the overthrow of a fellow queen regnant would set a dangerous precedent.

Lennox's letter had alerted Elizabeth to the fact that Bothwell might well escape justice. If, as rumour had it, the Anglophobic Bothwell married Mary, there was a real risk that he would revive the Auld Alliance with France, to England's despite. From now on, therefore, the objectives of Elizabeth and her ministers were simple: they were determined to prevent any marriage between Mary and Bothwell, and they would continue to press for the punishment of Darnley's murderers. To this end, they began to foment disorder in Scotland and inflame public opinion against Bothwell. Bedford, the Governor of Berwick, was ordered to cultivate any man who was disposed "to stand fast for the maintenance of God's honour and for the punishment of the late murder" and was to "comfort" all those "who seem to mislike Bothwell's greatness," and encourage them to unite against him.[54] At all costs, the fragile Anglo-Scots *entente* must be preserved, and any marriage between Bothwell and the Queen prevented.

21

"The Cleansing of Bothwell"

~

THERE IS NO EVIDENCE, APART from the later libels of Lennox and Buchanan, that Mary was involved in an illicit affair with Bothwell at this time. Had she been carrying on so blatantly with him in the way Buchanan described, Drury—ever avid for malicious gossip—would have got to hear of it. Nevertheless, Mary's increasing reliance upon Bothwell, and the favour she had shown to him since Darnley's murder had given rise to speculation that she would marry him. She must have been aware of this speculation, and of the fact that Bothwell's wife had filed for divorce, but that does not mean to say that she meant to marry him, as her enemies later alleged; in fact, events would show rather the opposite.

In the minds of many, Mary's association with the man who was the chief suspect in Darnley's murder, and the rumours of her conduct during what was supposed to be her mourning period, condemned her as being as guilty as he, and her failure to heed the warnings of her friends to bring him to justice and pursue his accomplices had exposed her to growing public opprobrium. That she was ill, both in mind and body, and therefore predisposed to lean upon a strong man who offered her succour and had doubtless convinced her of his innocence, was not widely known. Countless monarchs had connived at murder, but most had played the game by the rules and executed a few scapegoats to appease public opinion. Mary, almost certainly being innocent, did not realise what was required of her, and was too scrupulous to accuse those whose guilt was merely the subject of rumour and calumny, even though it was in her interests to do so.

By contrast, Darnley's reputation—never very good during his lifetime—had been miraculously rehabilitated, as people remembered his youth and his terrible end. The crimes he had committed were forgotten, as was his unpopularity. Ironically, he, a Catholic who had plotted the overthrow of the Protestant establishment in Scotland, became a tragic figurehead in their conspiracy against Bothwell, which is the measure of the success of the propaganda campaign against Bothwell and the Queen.[1] Had Mary acted decisively at this point, she could have saved her reputation and her throne. But she did not, and, for reasons of their own, her chief advisers did not press the matter, and may well have blocked any attempts on the Queen's part to institute a more rigorous inquiry into the murder. Without their support and help, her hands were tied.

Even if Mary was convinced of Bothwell's innocence, as seems likely, she must have realised that Darnley's murder had been planned by people in high places with a vested interest in getting rid of him. There is no evidence that she suspected Morton and the Douglases, but they would have been obvious suspects, since Darnley had betrayed them and Scottish nobles were renowned for their vengeful blood feuds. Neither is there any evidence that, at this stage, Mary believed that Moray and Maitland were behind the murder, although, given what had happened at Craigmillar, she may have had her suspicions. It would have taken a less scrupulous and more ruthless statesman than she to bring any of these Lords to justice, and, lacking any hard evidence against them, Mary was not the person to risk falsely accusing them. It is uncertain anyway that she was capable of decisive action at this time, and her incapacity made it possible for Bothwell and her other Councillors to bend her to their will.

According to Sir John Forster at Alnwick,[2] on 10 April 1567, Lennox, having left Glasgow with 3,000 men of his affinity, arrived at Linlithgow, only to be informed that he was permitted to take just six supporters with him to Edinburgh, where Bothwell's trial was to take place two days hence. This was quite correct: the law allowed the accused to appear at the bar with four attendants, while six were permitted to the accuser. But Lennox had also heard that Edinburgh was already packed with 4,000 of Bothwell's armed supporters, and believed it would be suicide for him to set foot in the city. This is where the Queen's inertia showed to her greatest disadvantage for, had she been in control, she should have ensured that the law applied to Bothwell too. But the indications are that she was by now somewhat intimidated by Bothwell, and powerless, in her weakened state, to gainsay him. Thus she laid herself open to accusations of collusion.

Too late, Lennox appealed to his new ally, Moray, for advice, but Moray had already left for England. Lennox therefore decided to send a protest that he dared not enter Edinburgh for fear of his life, and on the following day, he fell back on Stirling.

From there, he wrote to the Queen, alleging that he was ill and unable to travel to Edinburgh to accuse Bothwell, and asking her to imprison the accused and postpone the trial, that he might have "sufficient time" to obtain such evidence

as the truth shall be known. Otherwise the suspect persons continuing still at liberty, being great at court and about Your Majesty's person, comforts and encourages them and theirs, and discourages all others that would give evidence against them. So that, if Your Majesty suffer this short day of law to go forward, I assure Your Majesty you shall have no just trial.

Lennox also asked Mary to invest him with the power to arrest "such persons as he should be informed were present at the murder of his son."[3] These were entirely unreasonable demands: Lennox had urged an early trial, and was now complaining about it; he was also demanding the imprisonment of men who had not yet been found guilty, and against whom no shred of evidence had come to light, as well as the right arbitrarily to apprehend those whom he, a mere private subject, suspected. Not surprisingly, his requests were ignored, and he had no choice but to retreat to Glasgow.

At 6 a.m. on 12 April, Queen Elizabeth's messenger, John Selby, Provost

Marshal of Berwick, arrived at Holyrood with her letter urging a postponement of Bothwell's trial, only to be informed that Queen Mary was not to be disturbed at this early hour.

He therefore returned between 9 and 10 a.m., "when all the Lords and gentlemen were assembled taking their horses," ready to ride to the Tolbooth. "Then, thinking his opportunity aptest," he tried to enter the palace, only to find that Bothwell's followers had guessed his mission and were bent on denying him entry "in very uncourteous manner, not without some violence offered." Selby, "seeing he could not be permitted to have recourse, as all other persons, whatsoever they were, he requested that some gentleman of credit would undertake faithfully to deliver his letter to the Queen, which none would seem to undertake."

Thomas Hepburn, Parson of Oldhamstocks, presently appeared, "who told him that the Earl Bothwell had sent him with this message, that the Earl, understanding he had letters for the Queen, would advise him to retire him to his ease or about some other his business, for the Queen was so molested and disquieted with the business of that day, he saw no likelihood of any meet time to serve his turn till after the assize." Cockburn of Skirling then came out, and "took occasion to reprehend and threaten" Selby "for bringing English villains as sought to procure the stay of the assize, with words of more reproach."

At that moment, Bothwell emerged with Maitland, and "all the Lords and gentlemen mounted on horseback." Maitland came over to Selby, "demanding him the letter, which he delivered. The Earl Bothwell and [Maitland] returned to the Queen and stayed there within half an hour, the whole troop of Lords and gentlemen still on horseback attending his coming." When they returned, Maitland "seemed willing to have passed by Selby without any speech, but he pressed towards him and asked him if the Queen's Majesty had perused the letter, and what service it would please Her Majesty to command him back again." Maitland answered that, "as yet, the Queen was sleeping, and therefore he had not delivered the letter, and that there would not be any meet time for it till after the assize," and told Selby to wait. Just at that moment, however, a servant of du Croc, who was standing beside Selby, pointed up to where the Queen and Mary Fleming were looking out of a window.[4] Maitland had obviously been lying, but it is unlikely that he showed Mary the letter, for he and Bothwell both had good reasons for wanting the trial to be over before Lennox could track down further witnesses. Nevertheless, the treatment meted out to Queen Elizabeth's emissary had outrageously breached diplomatic niceties, and there was now no chance of any postponement.

"So, giving place to the throng of people that passed, which was great and, by the estimation of men of good judgement, above four thousand gentlemen besides others, the Earl Bothwell passed with a merry and lusty cheer, attended on with all the soldiers, being two hundred, all arquebusiers, to the Tolbooth."[5]

The record of Bothwell's trial is missing from the official archive known as the Books of Adjournal, but a copy survives in the hand of Justice Clerk Bellenden.[6] Argyll presided, as Justice-General, and he and Huntly were the chief judges,[7] being attended by four assessors, Lindsay, Robert Pitcairn, Commendation of Dunfermline James MacGill and a Protestant lawyer, Henry Balnaves.[8] The jury was composed of Andrew Leslie, Earl of Rothes; George Sinclair, Earl of Caithness; Gilbert Kennedy, Earl of Cassilis; Lord John Hamilton, second son of Chatelherault; James, Lord Ros; Robert, Lord Sempill; John Maxwell, Lord Herries; Laurence, Lord Oliphant; John, Master of Forbes; John Gordon of Lochinvar; Robert, Lord Boyd; James Cockburn of Langton; John Somerville; Mowbray of Barnbougle and Lord Ogilvy of Boyne.[9]

Buchanan claims that the judges were "picked out to acquit," but this was hardly a packed jury; according to Bothwell's own account, "there were some who were more enemies than friends." Blackwood says they were all of Moray's faction, but while this is certainly true of Argyll and the assessors, it is an exaggeration in the case of the jury. Rothes, Boyd, Sempill, Forbes and Herries were all at one time or another at odds with Bothwell, or his active enemies, while Hamilton, like Herries, was a staunch Queen's man, and hated Bothwell for his treatment of Arran. Caithness was Moray's adherent. The rest were either friendly towards Bothwell or neutral. Morton had craftily excused himself from the jury on the grounds that the King was his kinsman. Lennox's representative, Robert Cunningham, did not object to any of the jurors.[10]

The trial lasted seven hours, from noon to 7 p.m. The proceedings opened with the Queen's advocates producing her letter of 28 March summoning Lennox to bear witness against the accused, then Bothwell's indictment was read out, accusing him of being "art and part of the odious, treasonable and abominable slaughter" of the King on 9 February last; Buchanan later pointed out that this should have read 10 February, and asserted that the error had been made intentionally in the knowledge that Bothwell could not have been found guilty of a murder committed on the 9th.[11] Bothwell then chose two procurators (attorneys), David Borthwick and Edmund Hay. Lennox was called, but his servant Robert Cunningham appeared in his stead, and, declaring that his master's absence was through fear for his life, lodged a protest that Lennox had not been given sufficient time to prepare his case, and therefore any judgement given by the assize would be in error. Bothwell's procurators answered that Lennox had desired a "short and summary process," and produced his letters to prove it, as well as the Order in Council and the Queen's letter showing that she had complied with this request.

Cunningham produced copies of Lennox's letters to the Queen, including the one naming Bothwell, Balfour and others as the chief suspects. This was the only evidence offered for the plaintiff, and of course it amounted to nothing. Bothwell claims that he "brought forward" his "own sound witnesses to testify where I had been on the night in question," and that their evidence was upheld, but there is no mention of them in the official record. The jury retired from the court, "and after long reasoning had by them upon the said dittay and points thereof, they [returned and] acquitted the said James, Earl of Bothwell of art and part of the slaughter of the King, and by their chancellor [foreman], Caithness, protested that no evidence in its support had been brought by the pursuer." Buchanan states that, despite the verdict, the court had conceded that, "if anyone should later accuse [Bothwell] in proper form and law, this trial would be no impediment."

Despite de Silva's assertion that most jurors refused to vote "as they considered the trial was not free,"[12] Melville later stated that the jurors had acquitted Bothwell, "some for fear, some for favour, and the greatest part in expectation of advantage." In a letter to Sir Nicholas Throckmorton,[13] Robert Melville afterwards expressed the view that Bothwell had overawed the assize at his trial, and Drury alleged that the Earl's arquebusiers "kept the door that none might enter but such as were more for one side than the other."[14] The presence of Bothwell's huge following was certainly intimidating, but even if they had not been there, the outcome would have been the same, for no evidence had been offered against him. Yet the whole affair was undoubtedly a travesty of justice, for had Lennox been granted the time he needed to procure witnesses and evidence, he might well have constructed a better case against Bothwell. But too many people were determined that that should never be allowed to happen. Leslie claims that Morton, Sempill and Lindsay, "with their adherents and affinity, especially procured, and with all diligence laboured, his purgation and acquittal." As only Sempill sat on the jury, this suggests that these three were perhaps behind Bothwell's intimidation of Lennox prior to the trial.

Bothwell walked from the Tolbooth a free man. The Court Recorder wrote that the Earl "was made clean of the said slaughter, albeit that it was heavily murmured that he was guilty thereof,"[15] and the general opinion was that he had not been "cleansed of the crime, but, as it were, washed with cobbler's blacking."[16] According to Buchanan, after "this jolly acquittal," "suspicion was increased and retribution seemed only to be postponed."

Having named Morton, Ruthven, Lindsay, Sempill, Maitland and MacGill as "some who were more enemies than friends," Bothwell states that, "when my enemies and other opponents heard that I had been completely acquitted and had won the day, they at once came round begging me not to proceed against them for all the false charges they had brought against me. But their words did not reflect in any way the thoughts in their hearts, as I have since had reason to know."[17] Their support during his trial, which had been given in the interests of their own self-preservation, had led Bothwell to believe that they were still his allies.

As he left the Tolbooth, Bothwell defiantly "fixed a cartel to the door," on which was written a challenge, "wherein he offered to fight in single contest against any gentleman undefamed that durst charge him with the murder."[18] He then sent a town crier around Edinburgh to proclaim the verdict and had placards and letters bearing his own seal and repeating his challenge posted around the city, daring all comers to meet him in combat to "be taught the truth."[19]

Bothwell claims that "not a man took up my challenge," but in fact, on the following day, he received three anonymous answers: one calling him "the chief author of the foul and horrible murder," while the second named James, Robert and Gilbert Balfour, Archibald Beaton, Spens, Borthwick and Sandy Durham as devisers with him of the murder, and Ormiston, Beanston, Hepburn, Hay, the Blackadders, Cullen, Wilson and four others as active accomplices; at the foot of this were three lines linking Mary with Bothwell in murder and adultery:

> Is it not enough the poor King is dead,
> But the wicked murderers occupy his stead,
> And double adultery has all this land shamed?

The third answer, which was stuck to the Mercat Cross, stated, "There is none that professes Christ and His Evangel that can with upright conscience part Bothwell and his wife, albeit she prove him an abominable adulterer and worse, as he has murdered the husband of her he intends to marry, whose promise he had long before the murder."[20]

Since these answers were all anonymous, there was nothing that Bothwell could do about them.

On 14 April, Parliament met. The Queen was not present on this occasion,[21] but two days later, she made her first public appearance since Darnley's death, going in procession to the Tolbooth, accompanied by Argyll, Morton, Huntly, Bothwell and others, and surrounded by arquebusiers instead of the bailies of Edinburgh, as was customary. Bothwell, as Lord Admiral, rode before the Queen, bearing her sceptre. Melville says that, having been acquitted, Bothwell "remained still the greatest favourite at court," and when Parliament appointed the Lords of the Articles, who were responsible for preparing the business of the Estates, his name was among them, along with those of Morton, Argyll, Huntly and twelve others.[22]

Parliament's business began in earnest on the 17th. Dunbar Castle was formally secured to Bothwell as a reward for his great and manifold service to the Crown, but there is no record of his acquittal being ratified, as he later asserted in his memoirs.[23]

Moray had reached London on 16 April. The next day, according to de Silva,[24] he "was with the Queen for a long time, but I have not been able to learn what passed. It is announced that he will go by Germany to Genoa, or else by way of France, where some people think he will remain." On the 19th,

Moray visited de Silva at his house, and it was on this occasion that he told him that he had left Scotland because he feared "something unpleasant might befall him" through the machinations of Bothwell. He referred disparagingly to the delay in punishing Darnley's murderers, and, "although he did not name any particular person, it was easy to understand by his discourse that he considers Bothwell to be guilty."

De Silva asked Moray

> if the statement about the divorce between Bothwell and his wife was true, and he said it was. As he tells the story, it appears to be a somewhat novel form of divorce, as it is on the petition of the wife. They had been married hardly a year and a half, and she alleges adultery. I asked him whether there had been any ill treatment or quarrel to account for the divorce, to which he replied that there had been none, but that the wife had taken proceedings at the instance of her brother Huntly, who, to curry favour with Bothwell, had persuaded her to do so, and, at Bothwell's request, the Earl was to be restored to his position in the Parliament.

This, of course, is at variance with Drury's earlier report that Huntly misliked the divorce and had had to be persuaded to agree to it.

Moray told de Silva "he had heard that the divorce would be effected in order that the Queen might marry Bothwell, but he did not believe it, considering the Queen's position and her great virtue, as well as the events which have taken place. It really seems improbable, she being a Catholic, and the divorce for such a reason as that alleged." We may infer from this that, despite what was later written about Mary under Moray's auspices, he still had a good opinion of her.

De Silva later discussed the matter with the French ambassador, but the latter was "certain that, if the divorce is effected, the Queen will marry [Bothwell]."

The Scottish Parliament met for its last day of business on 19 April, when the Queen finally ratified the Acts of the Reformation Parliament of 1560; since she had hitherto refused to do so, her capitulation on this issue has been seen as a concession to the Protestant establishment in return for its support for her marriage to Bothwell, but there is no credible evidence that Mary had any intention of marrying Bothwell at this time. Her ratification may well have been the result of Bothwell taking advantage of her weakened state to pressurise her into it, on the basis that—as Buchanan believed—this measure would go some way towards soothing public opinion after the Earl's acquittal.

Parliament also confirmed grants of land and restitutions to Huntly, Sir Richard Maitland, David Chalmers and others, as well as Moray's title to his earldom and Mar's governorship of Stirling Castle. An Act was passed making it a capital offence to set up or even read seditious placards, and eleven forfeitures, including Morton's, were reduced; nine benefited members of the Gordon family.[25] This has been seen as an attempt by Mary to buy support for Bothwell's divorce, but as it had been her intention since 1565 to formally restore Huntly to his lands, she could hardly exempt the rest of his family from the general reversal of attainders.

The distribution of favours by Parliament to several persons implicated in Darnley's murder suggests that Bothwell and the other Protestant Lords were now in control and that the Queen virtually did as she was bidden. Bothwell's word was more or less law, and according to a letter written by Kirkcaldy of Grange to Bedford on 8 May,[26] "the most part of the nobility, for fear of their lives, granted sundry things against their honours and consciences."

On the day Parliament rose, Drury reported that the man who had cried for vengeance in the night had been arrested and "shut up in a prison which they call, for the loathsomeness of the place, the foul thief's pit."[27] He also reported the secret murder and burial of "a servant of James Balfour (who was at the murder of the King), supposed upon very lively presumptions for utterance of some matter, either by remorse of conscience or other folly, that might tend to the whole discovery of the King's death." The implication was, of course, that Balfour had murdered him. Drury added that Balfour, "for some fear he conceives, keeps his house, especially in the night, under great watch and guard."[28] In the wake of the placards that continued to link him to Darnley's murder, Balfour doubtless feared reprisals on the part of a vengeful citizenry.

Bothwell had decided that the time was now ripe to bring his plans to fruition. On the evening of the day when Parliament rose, he gave a supper for the Lords. The venue is disputed, but most accounts state it took place at Ainslie's Tavern in Edinburgh, the site of which is now unknown. The *Book of Articles* asserts that the supper was held in Bothwell's lodging in Holyrood Palace, in an obvious attempt to imply the Queen's collusion, but this was probably not big enough to accommodate such a large company.

The purpose of this supper was not just the celebration of Bothwell's acquittal. When the guests were suitably replete with food and wine, Bothwell produced a bond and asked them to subscribe to it. This bond was to serve as proof of their support for Bothwell against his enemies, and, more importantly, for his marriage to the Queen. The latter part of it read:

> Weighing and considering the time present, and how our sovereign the Queen's Majesty is now destitute of an husband, in the which solitary state the commonwealth of this realm may not permit Her Highness to continue and endure, but at some time Her Highness may be inclined to yield unto a marriage; and therefore, in case the former affectionate and hearty service of the said Earl done to Her Majesty from time to time and his other good qualities and behaviour may move Her Majesty so far to humble herself as preferring one of her native-born subjects unto all foreign princes, to take to husband the said Earl, we, and every one of us undersubscribing, upon our honours and fidelity, promise not only to advance and set forward the marriage with our votes, counsel, fortification and assistance in word and deed at such time as it shall please Her Majesty to think it convenient; but in case any would presume directly or indirectly, openly or under whatsoever colour or pretence, to hinder, hold back or disturb the same marriage, we shall in that behalf esteem, hold and repute the hinderers, adversaries or disturbers thereof as our common enemies and evil willers; and, notwithstanding the same, take part and fortify the said Earl to the said marriage, so far as it may please our Sovereign Lady to allow.[29]

The last sentence suggests that Bothwell's plans hinged upon Mary's consent to the marriage, which had yet to be given. It would have been logical for him to wait until he was cleared of Darnley's murder before approaching her, and he desired the support of the Lords not only as an insurance for the future, but also as ammunition with which to persuade the Queen to the marriage. If it had the consent of her nobility, she might well give serious consideration to it.

The surprising thing is that most of the Lords present at the supper, both Protestant and Catholic, signed the bond. The original bond, on which there were supposed to be 28 or 29 signatures, no longer exists, but the lists of signatories on the surviving copies do not agree, so it is not possible to be absolutely certain as to who the signatories were. The copy attested by Balfour lists Archbishop Hamilton and the Bishops of Ross, Aberdeen, Galloway, Dunblane, Brechin, Orkney and the Isles,[30] the Earls of Argyll, Huntly, Morton, Cassilis, Sutherland, Errol, Crawford, Caithness and Rothes, and Lords Boyd, Glamis, Ruthven, Sempill, Ogilvy, Herries and Fleming. Ruthven, however, is known not to have signed.

The list made by Buchanan's clerk, John Reed, for Cecil in 1568,[31] which was compiled from memory, differs: Moray's name heads the list of earls, although he was out of the country at the time and Mary's confessor later confirmed to de Silva that Moray had not signed the original Bond;[32] Errol, Crawford, Glamis, Ruthven and Fleming do not appear, and Glencairn (who was not in Edinburgh just then), Seton, Sinclair, Oliphant, Home, Ross of Halkhead, Carlyle and Innermeith are added.[33] Home was Bothwell's rival and is unlikely to have signed. Maitland's signature is not included in either list, and Mar's was not sought. Lord Eglinton, a Catholic supporter of the Queen, "subscribed not but slipped away,"[34] while Melville rejected "the large offers made by the Earl of Bothwell when he desired me to subscribe with the rest of his flatterers" and "chose rather to lay myself open to his hatred and revenge."

Bothwell claimed in his memoirs that the Lords "came to me entirely of their own account and did me the honour of offering their support and friendship"; they told him "that they would never agree to [the Queen] marrying a foreigner, [and] said that I was the most worthy of her in the kingdom. They had thought it over and had decided to do all they could to bring about such a marriage." Yet in 1568, the Lords told Elizabeth's Commissioners that they had not signed the bond until Bothwell had produced a warrant from the Queen authorising them to do so.[35]

However, it is more likely that Bothwell persuaded them to sign either by getting them drunk, or by bribery, promises of patronage to come or intimidation. It was alleged that his 200 arquebusiers had surrounded the tavern and could be seen through the windows, but Grange does not mention them, or the Queen's warrant, in a letter sent to Bedford the following day, reporting the events of the evening before.[36] Nau was probably correct when he wrote that "some helped [Bothwell] honestly through friendship, others from fear, being in dread of their lives; others dissembled, meaning through him to carry out their own secret ends and private designs." More sinisterly, though, he claims that the Queen's enemies, "having used [Bothwell] to rid themselves of the King, designed to make [him] their instrument to ruin the Queen"; they had therefore signed the bond to induce her to marry Bothwell "so that they might charge her with being in the plot against her late husband and a consenting party to his death." This later became the accepted Catholic view of the matter, and may not be far from the truth.

The following day, according to Buchanan, some Lords regretted signing the bond and frankly declared that,

if they had not believed that it would please the Queen, they would never have assented. For besides that the business was not very honest, there was always the danger that (as they remembered with her former husband) a quarrel might occur and Bothwell might be thrown aside. Then they themselves might become criminals for having betrayed the Queen and compelled her to enter into an unworthy marriage. Therefore, before the matter was settled, they thought it necessary to ascertain her wishes and obtain a statement signed by her own hand to the effect that what they had done in respect of the marriage was agreeable to her. This was easily obtained, and it was entrusted to the Earl of Argyll.

This account gives the lie to the allegation made in 1568, by Buchanan and others, that the Queen's warrant had been produced the previous evening; furthermore, there is no evidence that Argyll ever had in his possession any statement of approval signed by Mary on 20 April.

On that day, Mary went to Seton for the fourth time since Darnley's death. As she had gone there on the three previous occasions for the sake of her health, it is reasonable to suppose that that was the reason for this visit.

Later that day, she was joined there by Bothwell, Maitland and Patrick Bellenden.[37] Bothwell had with him the Ainslie's Tavern Bond, and when he arrived, he wasted no time in showing it to the Queen and proposing marriage to her.[38] In a letter to the Bishop of Dunblane, she made it clear that this was the first time he had paid suit to her, saying that "he began afar off to discover his intentions to us, and to essay if he might, by humble suit, purchase our good will, to which our answer was in no degree correspondent to his desire."[39]

In rejecting Bothwell out of hand, Mary was taking into consideration the fact that he was married, a heretic and a mere subject, and that their marriage would fatally prejudice future relations with England. More crucially, such a union would, for Mary, be political suicide, for, since Bothwell was still believed by many to be Darnley's chief assassin, she would risk being deemed guilty by association if she married him. Already tongues were wagging about them, and in the present climate she dared not expose herself to further scandal.

Bothwell took the Queen's refusal in good part, and changed the subject, laying forth "his plans to punish the Liddesdale thieves."[40]

Bothwell claims that the Lords "discussed the matter at once with the Queen, to see how our marriage could take place before the solemn assembly of Church and Parliament."[41] Maitland and Bellenden were at Seton on behalf of the Lords and the Council. Maitland, who, under cover of giving Bothwell his support, was possibly engineering his ruin by giving the Lords a pretext to move against him, advised Mary that "it had become absolutely necessary that some remedy should be provided for the disorder into which the public affairs of the realm had fallen for want of a head." This in itself is an admission that Mary herself had lost political control. Maitland informed Mary that the Lords "had unanimously resolved to press her to take Bothwell for her husband. They knew that he was a man of resolution, well adapted to rule, the very character needed to give weight to the decisions and actions of the Council. All of them therefore pleaded in his favour." Significantly, Leslie claims that those who later found fault with the marriage "were then the principal inventors, practisers, persuaders and compassers of the same."

According to Nau, who seems to be exaggerating somewhat, "this poor Princess, inexperienced in such devices, was circumvented on all sides by persuasions, requests and importunities, both in general memorials signed by [the Lords'] hands and presented to her in full Council, and by private letters." Yet Mary remained adamant, even in the face of a second petition by Maitland and Bellenden. "She reminded them of the reports which were current about the death of the late King, her husband," but Maitland

> replied that Lord Bothwell had been legally acquitted by the Council. They who made this request to her did so for the public good of the realm, and as they were the highest of the nobility, it would be for them to vindicate a marriage brought about by their advice and authority. In the end, Her Majesty asked them to assemble the Estates in order that the question might be considered. Thus vehemently urged in this matter, and perceiving that Bothwell was entirely cleared from the crime laid to his charge, [and] suspecting, moreover, nothing more than what appeared on the surface, she began to give ear to their overtures, without letting it be openly seen. She remained in this state of hesitation partly because of the conflicting reports which were current at the time, partly because she had no force sufficiently strong to punish the rebels by whom (if the truth must be told) she was rather commanded than consulted, and ruled rather than obeyed.[42]

Sir William Kirkcaldy of Grange was hailed as the greatest soldier of his day: Nau calls him "a very brave gentleman," while Melville says "he was meek like a lamb in the house, but like a lion in the fields"; yet his heroic reputation belies the fact that he had been a spy in the pay of the English since 1546, and was also dishonest, treacherous and a born intriguer. Grange had been at university in Paris with Thomas Randolph, who had become a long-standing friend, and he had years ago embraced the reformed faith. As a committed Anglophile, he loathed Bothwell—he had been conspicuous by his absence from Ainslie's Tavern—and was hostile towards Mary, although she was unaware of this, and seems to have regarded him as a latter-day knight errant. Grange, for his part, was convinced that Mary had been an accessory to Darnley's murder. Nau later asserted that Moray had "chiefly trusted the Laird of Grange with the execution of [his] designs, and Grange was the tool of Moray and [Maitland]."

Anything written by Grange therefore has to be treated with caution. On 20 April, almost certainly mindful of the instructions left him by Moray, he wrote to Bedford:

> It may please you to let me understand what will be your sovereign's part concerning the late murder among us. Albeit Her Majesty was slow in our last troubles, and lost favour, we bore to her yet; if she will pursue revenge for the murder, she will win the hearts of all honest Scotsmen again. And, if we understand she would favour us, we shall not be long in revenging it.

The next section in the letter relates the business of Parliament, and Grange alleges, incorrectly, that

> the Queen caused ratify in Parliament the cleansing of Bothwell. She intends to take the Prince out of Mar's hands and put him in Bothwell's keeping, who murdered his father. The night Parliament was dissolved, Bothwell called most of the noblemen to supper, to desire their promise in writing and consent to the Queen's marriage, which he will obtain; for she has said she cares not to lose France, England and her own country for him, and shall go with him to the world's end in a white petticoat before she leaves him. Yea, she is so far past all shame that she has caused make an Act of Parliament against all that set up any writing that speaks anything of him. Whatever is unhonest reigns presently in our court.

Grange ended by asking Bedford to have copies of the placards answering Bothwell's challenge printed for distribution on the Continent.[43] Clearly, he and his English paymasters had been actively involved in the smear campaign against Bothwell, and it may well have been Grange who had sent Drury copies of the placards. In August, Bedford was to petition Queen Elizabeth to send Grange "a token of remembrance" for the intelligence he had furnished to the English government.[44]

Grange's letter, with its request for English support, is proof that some design was intended against Bothwell and Mary by the Lords. It is peppered with lies and distortions, and the famous "white petticoat" quote attributed to Mary, of which so much has been made by so many historians, is probably no more than a malicious invention, designed to inflame public opinion in England against a queen whom Grange and his masters wanted overthrown. No one else reported these remarks, and it is highly unlikely that Mary uttered them for Grange's ear alone. The fact that Grange later changed sides and became one of the Queen's stoutest adherents shows that he came in time to understand how badly she had been calumniated by men like himself.

22

"WE FOUND HIS DOINGS RUDE"

MARY RETURNED TO EDINBURGH ON 21 April, but stayed only long enough to sign some papers, then set off immediately to visit Prince James at Stirling.[1] She apparently was beginning to feel more herself at last, and her first priority was to see her son. On her journey, she was accompanied by Maitland, Huntly, Melville and thirty armed horsemen. Bothwell remained in Edinburgh, having told the Queen that, in the next day or so, he would be raising a force to deal with some troublesome Borderers who had just "despoiled" Biggar.[2]

Thanks to the unfounded rumours spread by Grange and others, some people believed that the real purpose of Mary's visit was to remove James from Mar's care and place both him and Stirling Castle in Bothwell's hands. Drury claimed on 27 April that, during the Queen's sojourn at Stirling, Mar prevented her from delivering James into Bothwell's care,[3] while Buchanan stated as a fact:

Bothwell did not consider it to his own security to protect a boy who might one day become the avenger of his father's death; and he wanted no other to stand in the way of his own children in line of succession to the throne. So the Queen, who could refuse him nothing, personally undertook to have the boy brought back to Edinburgh. When she arrived [at Stirling], the Earl of Mar suspected what she was after. He showed her the boy, but in such a way that he was always in his own keeping. The Queen, foiled in her design and unable to take the child by force, made false excuses about why she had come, and set out on her journey home.

Buchanan even claims that Mary's mind "did not shrink" from the crime of infanticide. "She had often been heard to say that the boy would not live long, and that she had been told by a skilled astrologer in Paris that her first child would not live more than a year." No other source mentions this.

Events would show that Mary never contemplated giving her precious son and heir into the custody of Bothwell. After enduring great pain and suffering to give birth to the Prince, she had taken careful measures to protect him, for clearly she was terrified lest someone would harm or kidnap him. Had she entrusted James to Bothwell's care, she could have done so in the knowledge that his loyalty to her and her House was untarnished; he was already Captain of the Prince's Guard, and had been responsible for his safety before, during the Queen's absence. However, by the time Buchanan came to write his libel, people were ready to believe anything of Mary, even that she was ready to facilitate the murder of her own child to make way for her issue by Bothwell.

Some historians claim that Mary rode the thirty-six miles to Stirling in one day, but considering her state of health, and the fact that she had already ridden back from Seton, it is more likely that she stayed the night at Linlithgow, then went on to Stirling on the 22nd. She spent the rest of that day with her ten-month-old baby.

On the evening of 22 April, Mary wrote to Mondovi of the failure of whose mission she was painfully aware; she also knew how her recent ratification of the Kirk in Scotland would compromise her in the eyes of Catholic Europe, and wanted the Pope to know that she had been constrained to it. She therefore begged the Nuncio to keep her in His Holiness's good grace, assuring him that she meant to live and die in the Catholic faith. When her letter later caught up with him, Mondovi observed that, unless the Pope gave her wholehearted support, she might rush precipitately into marriage, even with a heretic like Bothwell, who had been "the Queen's most trusty and obedient adherent."[4]

On 20 May, Drury was to report that, just before she left Stirling on 23 April, Mary tried to poison her son.

> The Prince being brought unto her, she offered to kiss him, but the Prince would not, but put her face away with his hand, and did to his strength scratch her. She took an apple out of her pocket and offered it, but it would not be received by him; but the nurse took it, and to a greyhound bitch having whelps the apple was thrown. She ate it, and she and her whelps died presently. A sugar loaf also for the Prince was brought thither at the same time, and left there for the Prince, but the Earl of Mar keeps the same. It is judged to be very evil compounded.[5]

Although this story was to be repeated as fact by Lennox in his *Narrative*, it was no more than a baseless and vicious slander, for in reality, as Mary took her leave of Mar, she exhorted him to be vigilant and wary that he be not robbed of her son, either by fraud or force.[6] With good reason, she still feared that, if her enemies seized the person of her heir, her reign, and possibly her life, would not long endure.

Lennox, meanwhile, had decided that it was unsafe for him to remain in Scotland, and was even now at Dumbarton, waiting to sail down the Clyde for England; his ship finally left on 29 April. On 23 April, having obtained his information from a well-informed source, he wrote to tell his wife that Bothwell was about to kidnap the Queen.[7]

Lennox's intelligence was correct. Nau says that, having secured the support of the Lords for his proposed marriage, "and seeing the difficulties which would arise from delay, Bothwell resolved by some means or other to seize the person of the Queen, and then, having already gained the consent of all the Lords, to compel her to give hers, in order to bring the negotiations to a conclusion." Bothwell was well aware that he had enemies, and doubtless believed that marriage to Mary would afford him a degree of protection, especially since he had the written backing of the Lords. More to the point, he was an ambitious man, and keen to consolidate the power he already enjoyed.

Whether the Queen was about to collude in her own abduction is another matter.

Given the way that events were moving, it is hardly surprising that, on 23 April, Cecil wrote: "Scotland is a quagmire. Nobody seems to stand still; the most honest desire to go away; the worst tremble with the shaking of their conscience."[8]

On the day Lennox wrote his letter, Mary said farewell to her child, not realising that she would never see him again, and left Stirling for Linlithgow with Maitland, Huntly, Melville and her thirty horse. Four miles out of Stirling, the Queen suffered a severe attack of abdominal pain, and had to rest in a cottage before completing her journey. The royal party did not arrive at Linlithgow Palace until late that night.[9]

That day, Bothwell had ridden twelve miles south-west of Edinburgh to Calder Castle, where he raised a force of 800 horse,[10] ostensibly intending to lead them south to Biggar.[11] At midnight, according to Drury, he visited Huntly at Linlithgow to ask for his assistance in the abduction of the Queen, but a horrified Huntly refused. After an hour of fruitless persuasion, Bothwell left without seeing Mary[12] and when he got back to Calder, he was "in great ill humour."[13] Paris, in his second deposition, claimed that Black Ormiston visited Linlithgow secretly that night, and that he had a long conversation with the Queen.[14] It is more than likely that Paris's story was fabricated in order to make it appear that Mary had colluded in the abduction. If Mary had connived at the abduction, Bothwell would surely have finalised the details with her himself before she left Edinburgh, or when he visited Linlithgow; there was no need to send Ormiston.

The question of whether Mary did in fact collude in the abduction is another matter entirely, but there were those who believed, or affected to believe, that she did. At midnight, while Bothwell was arguing with Huntly, Grange was writing to Bedford:

This is to advertise you that Bothwell's wife is going to part with her husband, and great part of our Lords have subscribed the marriage between the Queen and him. The Queen rode to Stirling this last Monday, and returns this Thursday. I doubt not but you have heard Bothwell had gathered many of his friends, some say to ride in Liddesdale, but I believe it not, for he is minded to meet the Queen this day, Thursday, and to take her by the way and bring her to Dunbar. Judge you if it be with her will or no; but you will hear at more length on Friday and Saturday. I would you tear this after the reading. The bearer knows nothing of the matter. By him that is yours that took you by the hand. At midnight.[15]

The information fed to Lennox and Grange probably came originally from Bothwell himself. It would have been natural for him to confide his plans to one or more of the Lords, who knew of Mary's rejection of his suit and had tried, through Maitland and Bellenden, to persuade her to the contrary. In view of this, Bothwell mistakenly thought he could trust them to support him, but in fact he was playing right into their treacherous hands.

On 24 April,[16] Mary left Linlithgow for Edinburgh with her small retinue. Six miles west of the city,[17] somewhere between the New Bridge over the River Almond at Cramond to the north, and the little bridge over the Gogar Burn to the south,[18] Bothwell was waiting for her with what Mary described as "a great force,"[19] all with drawn swords.[20] As her party drew nervously to a halt, he laid hold of her bridle,[21] as if she were his captive, and told her that she was in danger from a threatened insurrection in her capital, and that he was taking her, for her own safety, to Dunbar, along with Maitland, Huntly and Melville. Mary and her entourage were not convinced by this, and, fearing Bothwell's intentions, "some of those who were with her were about to defend her, but the Queen stopped them, saying she was ready to go with the Earl of Bothwell wherever he wished, rather than bloodshed and death should result."[22] Calmly, she allowed herself to be led away to Bothwell's stronghold at Dunbar, whereupon most of her escort, apart from her personal servants, were dispersed. Robert Melville told Cecil that this "shame done by a subject to our sovereign offends the whole realm,"[23] but Mary's enemies would later condemn her as collusive for offering no resistance.

Before she had been forced to ride off with Bothwell, Mary had sent one of her horsemen, James Borthwick, to Edinburgh to alert the citizens to what was happening to her. The Provost, fearing for the Queen's safety, had the alarm bell rung, summoning the citizens "to armour and weapons," while Skirling, the Governor of the Castle, futilely aimed cannon fire on Bothwell's soldiers as they rode by, half a mile beyond the Flodden Wall and well out of range. When the men of the city had collected their weapons and banded together, they marched through the gates, but they were on foot and had no hope of catching up with Bothwell's mounted force.[24]

After a forty-mile ride, Bothwell and his captives reached Dunbar at midnight,[25] and after they had entered the castle, all its gates were made fast. According to Mary's account of this episode, which she wrote a fortnight later to the Bishop of Dunblane,[26] Bothwell

> asked pardon of the boldness he had taken to convey us to one of our own houses, whereunto he was driven by force, as well as constrained by love, the vehemence whereof had made him to set apart the reverence which naturally, as our subject, he bore to us, as also for safety of his own life.

According to Nau, Mary expressed indignation at the way she was being treated, for it must have been obvious by now that there was no uprising in Edinburgh, as Bothwell had claimed. "How strange we found it of him, of whom we doubted less than any subject we had, it is easy to be imagined," she wrote.[27] But, "in answer to complaints which she made, she was reminded that she was in one of her own houses, that all her domestics were around her, that she could remain there in perfect liberty and freely exercise her lawful authority. Practically, however, all happened very differently, for the greater part of her train was removed, nor had she full liberty until she had consented to the marriage, which had been proposed by the Lords of the Council."[28] Melville says that, at Dunbar, Bothwell "boasted he would marry the Queen, who would or who would not; yea, whether she would herself or not." This was not the sentiment of a man inspired by passion or lust, but that of a man motivated by ambition and the instinct for self-preservation. Mary, however, was in no mood to yield and, for all that she desired no bloodshed, "sent secretly to the Governor of the town of Dunbar to sally out with his troops and rescue her";[29] but she waited in vain for them to arrive.

In the meantime, Bothwell sought her out in private and began, she recorded, to make us a discourse of his whole life, how unfortunate he had been to find men his unfriends, whom he had never offended; how unable he was to save himself from conspiracies of his enemies, whom he might not know, by reason every man professed himself outwardly to be his friend; and yet found he such hid[den] malice that he could not find himself in surety without he were assured of our favour to endure without alteration.

His intentions, he assured her, were entirely honourable.

Other assurance he could not trust to, without it would please us to do him that honour to take him to husband; protesting always that he would seek no other sovereign, but to serve and obey us all the days of our life, joining thereto all the honest language that could be used in such a case.[30]

Mary, however, persisted in her refusal of his suit, even when he again produced the Ainslie's Tavern Bond. Her conduct is hardly consistent with the licentious passion that Buchanan alleged existed between her and Bothwell.

Determined to have his way, Bothwell ignored the Queen's rebuff. According to Melville, who was at Dunbar that night and left the next day, he raped her, laying her open to dishonour and the risk of an illicit pregnancy, with the consequent loss of her reputation. Now, "the Queen could not but marry him, seeing he had ravished[31] her and lain with her against her will."[32] Mary, still in weakened health, "wearied and almost broken," as she herself states in her letter reproduced below, and well aware that she was completely in Bothwell's power, had no choice but to capitulate. Later, in her letter to the Bishop of Dunblane, she wrote of what had happened in less explicit terms, but her meaning was obvious:

Seeing ourselves in his power, sequestered from the company of our servants and others, of whom we might ask counsel, yea, seeing them upon whose counsel and fidelity we had before depended, already welded to his appetite, and so we left alone, as it were, a prey to him, many things we resolved with ourself, but never could find a way out. And yet he gave us little space to meditate with ourself, ever pressing us with continual and importunate suit. In the end, when we saw no hope to be rid of him, never man in Scotland making a move to procure our deliverance, we were compelled to mitigate our displeasure, and began to think upon that he propounded.

Mary was well aware that her troubled realm needed a man's strong hand to restore order and good government, and that she herself was no longer capable of controlling affairs. Such a man could

take pain upon his person in the execution of justice and suppressing their insolence that was rebel, the travails whereof we may no longer sustain in our own person, being already wearied and almost broken with the frequent uproars and rebellions raised against us since we came to Scotland.

It had been made plain to Mary that her Lords would not accept a foreign consort. Bothwell had rendered her loyal service in the past, and she felt that no other of her subjects could equal him,

either for the reputation of his House, or for the worthiness of himself, as well in wisdom, valiance, as in all other good qualities. Albeit we found his doings rude, yet were his words and answers gentle. As by a bravado in the beginning he had won the first point,[33] so ceased he never, till by persuasion and importunate suit, accompanied not the less with force, he had finally driven us to end the work begun, at such time and in such form as he thought best might serve his turn, wherein we cannot dissemble that he has used us otherwise than we would have wished or yet deserved at his hand.[34]

Mary's letter was intended for her envoy to the French court, and she doubtless felt that she had to justify her acceptance of Bothwell's suit whilst at the same time avoiding criticism of the man who was to be her husband, who could not, for the sake of his honour and her own, be openly accused of raping his sovereign. It has also been conjectured by several historians that, after experiencing sexual relations only with immature or callous youths, Mary was surprised to find that intercourse could be very satisfying with a mature man like Bothwell. Yet there is no evidence to support this theory, and her future behaviour does not bear it out.

In July, the Scottish Lords told Sir Nicholas Throckmorton "how shamefully the Queen was led captive, and by fear, force and (as by many conjectures may well be suspected) other extraordinary and more unlawful means, compelled to become bedfellow to another wife's husband."[35]

Lennox, Mary's enemy, and Leslie, her supporter, both claimed that Bothwell used black magic to seduce her, and he is said to have admitted as much in a dubious document known as his Confession, which is almost certainly a fabrication. Throughout his career, Bothwell was frequently accused by his enemies of witchcraft; in a superstitious age, it was an infallible method of character assassination, and even Knox was not immune from such accusations.[36]

Nau does not mention the rape at all. *The Book of Articles*, however, graphically describes how Bothwell "met and ravished" the Queen, "conveying her in haste to Dunbar Castle, where he plainly passed to bed with her, abusing her body at his pleasure, which form of ravishing he practised also to his own advantage, thinking it being a crime of lèse-majesté to take a remission therefor as he did, and under the same crime to comprehend the King's murder in case it might be tried thereafter." This means that Bothwell abducted and raped Mary with a view to securing, amongst other things, a general remission for any treasons he might have committed, which would mean he could never again be tried for Darnley's murder. This assumption may well be correct, for the assize judges had given permission for a retrial in the event of new evidence coming to light, and Bothwell certainly did not want that particular sword of Damocles hanging over him. However, he never got his general remission, merely a pardon for the abduction and rape.

Many years later, Mary informed the Pope, "We were constrained to yield our consent, yet against our will."[37] Leslie states that she took into account her constant fear of imminent danger, and called to mind "the sundry and divers uproars and seditions already made against her, the wretched and most cruel murder of her secretary, the late strange and miserable murder of her husband, the discomfort and desolation wherein she was presently bewrapped, the Earl's activity in martial feats, and the good and faithful service done by him to her mother and to herself." She also feared "some new and fresh stir and calamity if she should refuse her nobility's request." But "though very circumspect and naturally prudent in all her doings," she was "nevertheless a woman, and never to that hour once admonished, either openly or privately after the Earl's acquittal, that he was guilty of the said fact, nor suspecting any thing thereof, yielded to that, to the which these crafty, colluding, suspicious [Lords], and the necessity of the time, as then to her seemed, did in a manner enforce her." She had many good, even compelling, reasons for consenting to marry Bothwell, but the fact remained that most people still believed he had murdered Darnley; by marrying him, Mary would lend credence to the widespread rumours that she had been his willing accomplice, and the consequences would be devastating for her.

Mary had agreed to marry Bothwell as soon as he was free. It is possible, but unproven, that she signed a marriage contract at Dunbar, and it has been suggested that it was possibly one of the two contracts amongst the Casket Letters, but they are probably forgeries.

Buchanan was voicing a belief that had been prevalent at the time when he later asserted that "for coverture of their filthy ways," Bothwell and the Queen "devised a counterfeited ravishing of her person." Even before the abduction, Grange had hinted that it would take place with Mary's consent, and two days afterwards he wrote again to Bedford to say that the Queen "was minded to cause Bothwell to ravish her, to the end that she may sooner end the marriage, which she has promised before she caused murder her husband."[38] At Dunbar, Melville's captor, Captain William Blackadder, told him that the kidnapping "was with the Queen's own consent."[39] On the 27th, Drury reported that "the manner of Bothwell's meeting with the Queen, although it appeared to be forcibly, is yet known to be otherwise."[40] De Silva heard that "all had been arranged beforehand, that the Queen, when the marriage was completed, might pretend that she had been forced to consent."[41]

Mary's enemies believed that she was looking for a way to avoid the public opprobrium that would be sure to follow upon her marriage to Bothwell, and if it could be made to appear that she had been forced into consenting to the union, she might just get away with it. "It seemed to them a marvellous fine invention that Bothwell should ravish and take away the Queen by force and so save her honour," wrote Buchanan. Modern historians often point out that she offered little resistance to Bothwell when he ambushed her, and refused her attendants' offer of help.

Yet there was no reason for staging the abduction as a sop to public opinion, for the Lords and the Bishops had already given their written and verbal approval of the marriage, thereby implying their support against any critics of it. It was Mary's consent that Bothwell needed, and he was prepared to take drastic measures to get it. Moreover, Melville, who was present at Dunbar and knew what was going on, states that Bothwell had lain with Mary "against her will," and his brother Robert, in a letter written to Cecil on 7 May, was in no doubt that the abduction was contrary to her wishes.[42] As for her lack of resistance, how could her small entourage of thirty-three persons have hoped to prevail against Bothwell's 800 armed men? Had Mary permitted them to try, a bloodbath would almost certainly have ensued; instead, she courageously went quietly with her captors. And if the abduction had been staged, why would she send to the Provost of Dunbar for help? The theory of the collusive seizure falls down on the evidence of an Act of Parliament passed against Mary by her enemies on 20 December 1567, in which they refer to her abduction by Bothwell and state: "She suspected no evil from any of her subjects, and least of all from him."[43]

Buchanan says that whether the abduction was with Mary's consent or not "every man may easily perceive by her own letters that she wrote to [Bothwell] by the way as she was in her journey." The letters to which he is referring are Casket Letters VI, VII and VIII, which, along with a love poem from the Casket Documents, are supposed to have been written on 21, 22 or 23 April, during Mary's visit to Stirling.

Casket Letter VI is endorsed by Cecil's clerk, "From Stirling before the ravishment—proves her mask of ravishing." It reads:

Alas, my Lord, why is your trust put in a person so unworthy to mistrust that which is wholly yours? I am wood. You had promised me that you would resolve all, and that you would send me word every day what I should do. You have done nothing thereof. I advertise you well to take heed of your false brother-in-law. He came to me, and without showing me anything from you, told me that you had willed him to write to you that I should say, and where and when you should come to me, and that you should do touching him; and thereupon hath preached unto me that it was a foolish enterprise, and that with mine honour, I could never marry you, seeing that, being married, you did carry me away. And that his folk would not suffer it. And that the Lords would unsay themselves and would deny that they had said. To be short, he is all contrary. I told him that, seeing I was come so far, if you did not withdraw yourself of your self, that no persuasion nor death itself should make me fail of my promise. As touching the place, you are too negligent (pardon me) to remit yourself thereof to me. Choose it yourself and send me word of it. And in the meantime, I am sick. I will differ as touching the matter it is too late. It was not long of me that you have not thought thereupon in time. And if you had not more changed your mind since mine absence than I have, you should not be now to ask such resolving. Well, there wanteth nothing of my part. And seeing that your negligence doth put us both in the danger of a false brother, if it succeed not well, I will never rise again. I send this bearer unto you, for I dare not trust your brother with these letters, nor with the diligence. He shall tell you in what state I am, and judge you what amendment these new ceremonies have brought unto me. I would I were dead, for I see all goeth ill. You promised other manner of matter of your foreseeing, but absence hath power over you, who have two strings to your bow. Dispatch the answer that I fail you not. And put no trust in your brother for this enterprise. For he hath told it, and is all against it. God give you good night.

If this letter was written by Mary to Bothwell, the false brother-in-law to whom she refers can only be Huntly, whom Bothwell is using as a go-between, much to her annoyance, for she does not think that Huntly is to be trusted. She is also angry that her irresolute and apparently incompetent suitor has not been in touch with her on a daily basis, as he promised, to plan the abduction. She fears it will all go wrong, and wishes she was dead.

Huntly, however, had refused to have anything to do with the abduction plot, and had been taken captive along with Maitland and Melville. In the letter, Huntly had told Mary that his family would never suffer her to marry Bothwell, but in fact Huntly had already given his consent to his sister filing for divorce. If Mary had been a party to Bothwell's plans, they would surely have been finalised before her departure on 21 April, when she knew that Bothwell was intending to raise a force. There was therefore no need for him to write to her on a daily basis, as she was only going to be away for three days. Even Buchanan contradicts the "evidence" in this letter, stating that, before she left Edinburgh, Mary had fully arranged with Bothwell the plan and place of the seizure. The inescapable conclusion must be that Casket Letter VI is a forgery.

Casket Letter VII is also written on the premise that Huntly was assisting the abduction plot:

Of the place and the time, I remit myself to your brother and to you. I will follow him and will fail in nothing of my part. He finds many difficulties. I think he does advertise you thereof and what he desires for the handling of himself. As for the handling of myself, I heard it once well devised. Methinks that your services, and the long amity, having the good will of the Lords, do well deserve a pardon, if above the duty of a subject you advance yourself, not to constrain me, but to assure yourself of such place near to me, that other admonitions or foreign persuasions may not let [prevent] me from consenting to that that ye hope your service shall make you a day to attend. And to be short, to make yourself sure of the Lords and free to marry, and that you are constrained for your surety, and to be able to serve me faithfully, to use a humble request joined to an importune action. And to be short, excuse yourself, and persuade them the most you can, that you are constrained to make pursuit against your enemies. You shall say enough, if the matter or ground do like you, and many fair words to Lethington. If you like not the deed, send me word, and leave not the blame of all unto me.

The "importune action" is almost certainly the abduction. From the wording of the beginning of this letter, it would appear that a reply to Casket Letter VI had been received, which would have arrived late on 22 April at the earliest; therefore, if Mary wrote this letter on that day, expecting a reply confirming that Bothwell did indeed intend to proceed with his plans, she was cutting it fine if she expected to hear from him before the 24th. There is no record of Huntly racing back and forth from Linlithgow or Stirling to Edinburgh and Calder with these letters. Moreover, if Mary and Bothwell were in collusion, they could have finalised their plans with Huntly when Bothwell visited Linlithgow. There was no need for this correspondence. Nor is it clear what difficulties Huntly himself had to face. All he had to do was go quietly with the Queen to Dunbar. It was also rather late in the day to advise Bothwell to make sure of the Lords, since he already had their signatures on the

Ainslie's Tavern Bond. Armstrong-Davison thought that Casket Letter VII was a genuine letter from Mary to George Douglas, the man who helped her escape from Lochleven in 1568, which the Lords adapted to suit the abduction plot; if so, then it was added to the Casket Documents a year after their discovery. Otherwise, it must be a forgery.

Mary's enemies claimed that Casket Letter VIII was the third of the series that Mary allegedly sent to Bothwell from Stirling, but it almost certainly relates to a different matter and belongs to a later date, because it refers to Huntly as "your brother-in-law that was," which lends itself to the presumption that the letter must have been sent after Bothwell's divorce.

The 158-line love poem in French from the Casket Documents, often erroneously described as a collection of twelve sonnets, was also alleged by some to have been written by Mary for Bothwell while she was at Stirling. Robin Bell, who edited Mary's collected verse,[44] believes that this poem is consistent with her authenticated style, and that any forger would have attempted to copy her youthful, better known poems, rather than guess how she would write in her maturity. He suggests, however, that the "sonnets" may have been tampered with in order to incriminate Mary: Buchanan claimed that they were composed "(as it is said) while her husband lived, but certainly before [Bothwell's] divorce from his wife." He also says they were written with tolerable elegance, but Brantôme and Ronsard declared that they were in such bad French, and in such an unpolished, fragmented style, that it was ludicrous to attribute them to Mary. It has been suggested that Buchanan himself wrote—or altered—them, since he was one of the few people in Scotland who knew how to compose courtly French verse; furthermore, he knew Mary's style.

During the first night at Dunbar, according to Drury, Huntly quarrelled with Maitland and tried to kill him. Maitland's life was saved only by the intervention of the Queen, who thrust her body in the way of the Earl's drawn sword and warned Huntly that, "if a hair of Lethington's head did perish, she would cause him to forfeit lands and goods and lose his life."[45] Melville also relates this incident, but states that it was Bothwell who attacked Maitland, giving no reason for this apart from the fact that Bothwell was not Maitland's friend. Maitland himself later told Cecil that he had gone in fear of his life since Bothwell, in a fit of ungovernable rage, had tried to kill him, and would have succeeded if the Queen had not hastened to his assistance.

After the attack, Bothwell placed Maitland under guard and kept him a prisoner.[46] The next day, Huntly and Melville were allowed to leave Dunbar. Before Melville left, he told Mary "that those who had advised her [to marry Bothwell] were betrayers of her honour for their own selfish ends, seeing her marrying a man commonly adjudged her husband's murderer would leave a tash [slur] upon her name and give too much ground for jealousy."[47] Mary did not heed his warning.

On 25 April, Queen Elizabeth and her Privy Council, unaware of the dramatic events of the previous day, discussed the situation in Scotland. Elizabeth decided to send Lord Grey de Wilton to Edinburgh to express her displeasure at three things: Mary's failure to bring to justice Darnley's murderers, the favour shown by her to "such as have been by common fame most touched with the crime," and "the contempt or neglect in the burial of the King's body." "So monstrous an outrage" as the Queen's marriage to Bothwell "must be prevented"; but after issuing Grey with his instructions, Elizabeth changed her mind and immediately countermanded them. Instead, she sent another warning to Mary via Bedford, and asked the latter to make inquiries as to the possibility of Prince James being brought up in England.[48] Nau believed—as, most probably, did Mary—that Elizabeth's change of heart had been dictated by the realisation that, if Mary could be persuaded to marry Bothwell, "they might charge her with being in the plot against her late husband."

The next day, Grange wrote again to Bedford, claiming that Mary had caused Bothwell to abduct her so that she could marry him.

The Queen will never cease until she has wrecked all the honest men of this realm. Many would revenge it, but they fear your mistress. I am so suited for to enterprise the revenge that I must either take it in hand or leave the country, which I am determined to do, if I get licence; but Bothwell minds to cut me off ere I obtain it. I pray you let me know what your mistress will do, for if we seek France, we may find favour; but I would rather persuade to lean to England. No honest man is safe in Scotland under the rule of a murderer and a murderess.[49]

On the 26th, Cecil was informed, by one of his agents in Paris, that Archbishop Beaton was openly saying "that the Lord James [Moray] was the author of the King's death, and Lord Lennox is deluded and mocked by him."[50]

Lady Bothwell's suit for divorce came before the Protestant Commissary Court of Edinburgh on 26 April.[51] She "accused her husband, before the Queen's judge, of adultery, which was the only case of divorce recognised by them,"[52] and "therefore requires to be no longer reputed flesh of his flesh."

To the Queen, a Catholic, this Protestant divorce was unacceptable, and on the following day, at the instance of Bothwell, Mary granted Archbishop Hamilton a commission to try the validity of Bothwell's marriage, on the grounds that he and Jean were within the forbidden degrees of kinship and had not been granted a dispensation.[53] This was blatant collusion, for they had indeed received a dispensation, and it had been granted by no other than the Archbishop himself.[54] Furthermore, Hamilton's consistorial powers had been revoked, after protests by the Kirk, in January, and never restored. Technically, therefore, as Buchanan points out, he had no authority to pronounce on matrimonial causes. Strictly speaking, the Queen should have applied directly to the Pope for an annulment, but that would have taken months, and there was no guarantee that he would grant her request, especially if he suspected that she meant to marry Bothwell, a notorious Protestant.

When news of these dubious and collusive proceedings leaked out, many of Mary's loyal subjects turned against her. It was impossible for her to explain that what almost certainly drove her to these desperate measures was the fear of pregnancy and the consequent scandal, which in the present climate might well cost her her throne. She was also a prisoner, and had no choice but to do her captor's bidding.

Mary was still being held at Dunbar, yet so far none of her subjects, Lords or commoners, had attempted to rescue her, which is an indication of how many people believed that she had connived at her own abduction. She herself wrote that she looked in vain for some of her subjects to come to her relief.[55] Only the "highly offended" lieges of Aberdeen offered to help her escape, sending a message on 27 April, desiring to know what they should do "towards the reparation of the matter."[56] Whether Mary received this, or sent an answer, is not known. On 3 May, Robert Melville informed Cecil that Mary had sent asking Elizabeth for help, but had not obtained it.[57]

Drury reported on 30 April that Bothwell had cast off his mourning garments and was now sporting his finest clothes; he had also been seen out walking with Mary at Dunbar, with an escort of arquebusiers, and showing "tokens of mirth"; Mary's response is not recorded.[58] A few days later, Drury reported that she and Bothwell were amusing themselves with archery practice and equestrian exercises, and that the arquebusiers were no longer so much in evidence. The Queen was attended by Bothwell's sister, Janet Hepburn, and by his former mistress, Janet Beaton, and her sister Margaret, Lady Reres, to whom she gave gifts.[59]

On 28 April, Archbishop Hamilton appointed a commission of two bishops and six clerics to inquire into the validity of Bothwell's marriage. The next day, the Countess of Bothwell's divorce suit came before the Commissary Court; as the case was defended, witnesses on her behalf were examined over the following two days; among them were George Dalgleish and Patrick Wilson. Neither of the parties appeared in person, but were represented by lawyers. On 1 May, the court found that Lady Bothwell had established her husband's adultery, and adjourned the case until 3 May.[60]

Bothwell's abduction of the Queen and his obviously collusive matrimonial proceedings had given the Lords the pretexts they needed to move against him, and they now declared their hand. On 1 May, an unlikely coalition comprising Morton, Argyll, Atholl, Mar, Tullibardine and others convened at Stirling and entered into a new bond to strive to the utmost of their power to liberate the Queen from Bothwell's "cruel tyranny and thraldom," preserve the life of the Prince, and bring Darnley's killers, especially "that cruel murderer Bothwell," to justice.[61] This was the first overt move on the part of Bothwell's enemies. Interestingly, despite the fact that public opinion held that Mary had connived at the abduction, the official line was, for the time being, to be that Bothwell had "ravished and detained her" against her will.

According to Nau, "many of the Lords were told that the Queen hindered justice being done for the late King's death." Mar's defection would be particularly hurtful to Mary, but his first loyalty was to the Prince, and it is unlikely that he was aware at this stage of the wider aims of the Lords. Nau says that, "to a certain extent, the Countess of Mar was the cause, a malevolent woman and full of the spirit of revenge." Tullibardine, Lennox's ally, was her brother.

Herries claims that the overthrow of Bothwell, and a plan to place the Queen under restraint, had been decided upon before Moray's departure. As Moray was now in France,[62] and it was undesirable anyway that he should appear involved, Morton was to "manage all." Once the coup had taken place, Moray would return and assume the Regency.[63] De Silva claims that, whilst at Stirling, the Lords "considered the raising of the child to the throne, the government being carried on by them in his name."[64] It is likely that the plot against Bothwell and Mary had the tacit backing of Cecil.

Drury heard that the Lords sent to Mary to ask whether she was held captive against her will, or with her consent, "for if she were held against her will, they would collect a force and rescue her." She replied that "it was true that she had been evil and strangely handled," but that she had since been treated "so well that she had no cause to complain, willing them to quiet themselves";[65] *The Book of Articles* states that she "plainly mocked" them and "showed no signs of discontentation." However, it is unlikely that Bothwell would have allowed the Lords' letter to reach Mary; later, she wrote scathingly of the "profound silence" of her nobles whilst she was at Dunbar.

News of Mary's abduction and rape had now reached the English court. On 1 May, de Silva reported that Elizabeth had informed him of it herself, and that she had been "greatly scandalised" to hear that the Queen had surrendered to Bothwell. "Some say she will marry him, and they are so informed direct by some of the highest men in the country who follow Bothwell. They are convinced of this both because of the favour the Queen has shown him, and because he has the national force in his hands."[66] In Paris, the English ambassadors were alleging that Mary had arranged the assassination of Darnley in order to marry Bothwell.[67]

Early in May, Lennox joined his wife in London, where Elizabeth assured them, in response to their urgent pleas, that she would help them avenge their son's murder. In the meantime, she was hoping to have Prince James brought to England to be raised by his grandmother, Lady Lennox; it may be inferred from this that Elizabeth had ruled out any prospect of the succession going to Mary. However, she was adamant that she would not countenance or approve any rebellion against the Queen of Scots.

Drury reported on 2 May that the Hamiltons, including the Archbishop, were furthering Bothwell's divorce, "hoping to attain the sooner to their desired end."[68] Should Mary be deposed, only the infant Prince would stand in Chatelherault's way to the throne.

Lady Bothwell's divorce was granted by the Commissary Court on 3 May, and on that same day, Archbishop Hamilton's Consistory Court began hearing Bothwell's suit for an annulment.[69] Irritated at the delay, Bothwell sent his henchmen to the chief commissioner, John Manderston, a canon of Dunbar Collegiate Church, with a warning that, if a decision were not given expeditiously, "there shall not fail to be noses and lugs [ears] cut off, and far greater displeasures . . ."[70]

On 5 May, Drury reported that the Lords at Stirling had now resolved that, if the Queen married Bothwell, they would crown the Prince, and that they had sent a warning to her to be careful of her conduct. He added that many of those who had signed the Ainslie's Tavern Bond were now against the marriage.[71] De Silva informed Philip II that, whilst at Stirling, the Lords had diverted themselves with a drama performed by boy players, entitled "The Murder of Darnley and the Fate of Bothwell." The actor playing Bothwell was "hanged" so enthusiastically that "hardly in a long time could life be recovered."[72]

That day, witnesses in Bothwell's suit were examined by John Manderston, sitting alone,[73] while Bothwell, anticipating that he would soon be a free man, left Dunbar with Mary, Maitland and an armed force for Edinburgh. They spent the night at Hailes Castle in East Lothian, which had been a Hepburn stronghold since the fourteenth century.[74] On the 6th, the Countess of Bothwell's procurator appeared on her behalf in the Consistory Court.[75]

Prior to Bothwell's departure, Maitland had been held prisoner at Dunbar; he later told the Lords that an attempt on his part to escape during an archery contest had proved abortive. But the Lords, who were expecting him to arrive any day at Stirling, had already begun to ask themselves if "his constraint of liberty is not altogether against his will."[76] It probably suited Maitland to remain a prisoner, for, if the Lords' coup failed, he could not be accused of disloyalty to his sovereign. Furthermore, whilst working for the downfall of Bothwell, he may well have drawn the line at any treasonable act against Mary, for she was essential to the survival of his Anglo-Scottish policy with its long-cherished aim of political and dynastic union: his behaviour all along would appear to have been dictated by such considerations. His imprisonment enabled him to play for time.

Drury reported on 6 May that Maitland had announced his intention of escaping to join the Lords at Stirling. "The reason why of late he was suspected to have been Bothwell's was for certain letters he was compelled to write, but immediately, by a trusty messenger, he advertised not to give credit to them." But Maitland did not turn up at Stirling; instead, he remained with the Queen. Drury was soon of the opinion that, although he feared Bothwell, he had decided to remain at court until the Lords had increased in strength. In his letter of the 6th, Drury added that Balfour was now installed in a room in Edinburgh Castle and enjoyed equal authority to its Governor, Cockburn of Skirling.[77]

On the evening of 6 May, as the castle guns fired a salute "most magnificently," Bothwell, on foot and respectfully bare-headed, escorted Mary into Edinburgh through the West Port, leading her horse by the bridle as if she were his prisoner;[78] Maitland and Huntly and a "peaceful train"[79] of Hepburn retainers were in attendance. That night, the Queen and Bothwell took up residence in Edinburgh Castle, where Bothwell had 200 arquebusiers stationed outside the Queen's rooms, day and night, so that none might speak with her without his knowledge.[80]

The next day, Archbishop Hamilton granted Bothwell an annulment, stating that his marriage had been "null from the beginning in respect of their contingence in blood, without a dispensation obtained before."[81] Mary cannot but have been aware that this was an outright falsehood, nor that the action had been collusive, and that therefore the annulment was fraudulent and undoubtedly illegal; her doubts are evident from the fact that she asked the advice of "two or three Catholic bishops" before marrying Bothwell.[82] However, both the Catholic Church and the Kirk had now ensured that Bothwell was free to remarry.

On that same day, Bothwell asked John Craig, who had replaced Knox as Minister of St. Giles,[83] to proclaim the banns of marriage for himself and the Queen, but Craig, who was convinced that Mary was being forced into this union against her will, bravely refused to do so, and demanded her written consent and declaration that she had not been constrained by Bothwell. The response was a written order to Craig, signed by the Queen and delivered by Justice Clerk Bellenden that same day, 7 May, ordering him to proclaim the banns and declaring that she had neither been "ravished nor yet detained in captivity." But Craig was not satisfied, and refused to proclaim any banns "without consent and command of the Kirk."[84]

Although Lord Herries had signed the Ainslie's Tavern Bond, he was no friend to Bothwell. Aware of mounting public concern that the Queen would marry the Earl, and, fearful of the consequences, he came to Edinburgh and obtained an audience of Mary. He told her what people were saying throughout the country about her and Bothwell, "requesting Her Majesty most humbly on his knees to remember her honour and dignity and the safety of the Prince, with many other persuasions to show the utter wreck and inconveniences [that] would thereby be occasioned. Her Majesty appeared to wonder how these reports could go abroad, seeing there was no such thing in her mind," whereupon Herries begged her pardon and withdrew.[85] Mary dared not risk a confrontation with Herries, with Bothwell in so volatile a mood, nor would she have wished to alienate a loyal supporter.

Melville was also going to warn Mary about marrying Bothwell, but before he could do so, he received a letter from a Scotsman called Thomas Bishop, who had lived for a long time in England. Bishop "adjured me to show the letter to Her Majesty, declaring how it was bruited that she was to marry the murderer of her husband, who at present had a wife of his own, a man full of all vice; if she married him, she would lose the favour of God, her own reputation and the hearts of all England, Ireland and Scotland." Melville showed Mary this outspoken missive, but, after reading it, she gave it back to him without saying anything, then called Maitland and asked him to read it. When he asked her what it was, she answered accusingly that it was "a device of his own, tending to the wreck of the Earl of Bothwell."

Maitland took Melville aside and asked what had been in his mind that he should show such a letter to the Queen, for "so soon as Bothwell gets notice hereof, as I fear he will shortly, he will cause you to be killed." Melville replied, "It is a sore matter to see that good Princess run to utter wreck, and nobody to be so far concerned in her as to forewarn her of her danger." Maitland told him he had "done more honestly than wisely; and therefore, I pray you, retire diligently before Bothwell comes up from his dinner." Mary herself begged Bothwell to do Melville no harm, but "notwithstanding, I was inquired after, but was flown, and could not be found till his fury was slaked; for I was advertised there was nothing but slaughter in case I had been gotten. Whereat Her Majesty was much dissatisfied, telling him that he would cause her to be left of all her servants, whereupon he renewed his engagements that I should receive no harm."[86] This episode suggests that Bothwell was doing everything in his power to keep from Mary the true extent of the opposition to their marriage until such time as it had been publicly announced; it also reveals that Bothwell had succeeded in turning Mary against Maitland.

Robert Melville informed Cecil on 7 May that the Lords at Stirling wanted English support against Bothwell, even though France had already offered aid (which was subsequently found not to be the case). He had heard that "the Lords have gone to their countries to assemble their friends" and that Bothwell was expected to go to Stirling to seize the Prince, but that Mar was determined not to surrender his charge, and was preparing for a siege. Melville also explained that Mary's sharp response to Elizabeth's letter was due rather to "the counsel of those about her than of herself. For you have experience that Her Majesty behaved herself most moderately when she had liberty to be at her own wise counsel."[87]

It was clear that an armed rebellion was on the point of breaking out, its ostensible aim being the removal of Bothwell; however, its real objective was to place the government in the hands of the Protestant Lords—or the Confederate Lords, as they were now calling themselves. Argyll had ridden to the West to arouse support, Atholl to the North and Morton to Fife, Angus and Kincardineshire, while Mar was holding Stirling and keeping an eagle eye on the Prince.[88]

On 8 May, the General Assembly of the Kirk overrode John Craig and ordered him to publish the banns of the Queen's marriage on the next three Sundays. Buchanan says they "dared not refuse" the Queen's command, but it was Bothwell they really feared, Bothwell, who held all Edinburgh in his grip. A grim Craig demanded to speak his mind in the presence of the Queen and the Earl, "to give boldness to others." That afternoon, he was summoned before Bothwell and the Council to justify his insolence, but instead of craving pardon, he vehemently denounced the marriage: "I laid to his charge the law of adultery, the ordinance of the Kirk, the law of ravishing, the suspicion of collusion between him and his wife, the sudden divorce and proclaiming within the space of four days, and last, the suspicion of the King's death, which his marriage would confirm." Bothwell held his temper and gave a fair answer, but it was "nothing to his [Craig's] satisfaction." The Councillors seemed to him "so many slaves, what by flattery, what by silence, to give way to this abomination."[89] Before Craig went away, Bothwell threatened to hang him if he did not call the banns.

That day, Bothwell, thinking Balfour a trustworthy ally, and perhaps hoping to buy his silence, appointed him Governor of Edinburgh Castle in place of Skirling,[90] who was compensated with the post of Controller of Customs on 1 June. Melville says that Balfour got the governorship because "the Earl and he had been great companions, and he was also very great with the Queen."[91]

The placard campaign was still continuing, and Grange was actively inciting the English against Bothwell. Bedford reported on the 8th that Grange had sent him a placard that had not yet been set up: it named Bothwell, Black Ormiston, Hepburn of Beanston, Hepburn of Bolton, Hay, Cullen and James Edmonstoun as Darnley's murderers. Grange had added that James Murray had offered to prove their guilt according to "the laws of arms."[92] Most of these names had been listed by Drury in his report to Cecil sent on 15 March.[93]

Grange wrote to Bedford on the 8th, informing him that the Lords intended to overthrow Bothwell, and asking for Elizabeth's help. As added inducements, he claimed that the "barbarous tyrant" Bothwell had tried to poison Prince James, and that du Croc had offered French aid against Bothwell and undertaken to join the Confederate Lords, who were about to be joined by Glencairn, Cassilis, Eglinton, Montrose, Caithness, Boyd, Ochiltree, Ruthven, Drummond, Gray, Glamis, Innermeath, Lindsay, Home and Herries—many of whom had signed the Ainslie's Tavern Bond—"with all the West, Merse [the Border area west of Berwick], Teviotdale, the most part of Fife, Angus and the Mearns" (the old colloquial term for Kincardineshire). The Lords' chief concern was to get Bothwell out of Edinburgh Castle and keep him away from Dunbar, "not for fear of him in the field, but besides these two strengths, he has all the [am]munition."

According to Grange, du Croc had tried to dissuade Mary from marrying Bothwell, threatening her with the loss of France's friendship if she went ahead, but "she will give no ear." If true, her refusal must have stemmed either from fear of Bothwell, who had her utterly in his power, or from fear that she was pregnant. Grange also alleged that Mary had Elizabeth's christening font melted down to raise money, but this was untrue. He enclosed letters for Moray and asked Bedford to forward them in haste to the Earl, urging him to come to Normandy and wait in readiness until the Lords sent for him.[94] Clearly, then, Moray knew what was planned. Robert Melville also wrote to Moray via the English ambassador in Paris on 10 May.[95]

In order to still the clamour and speculation, Mary—probably at Bothwell's instigation—issued a proclamation on 8 May, announcing that she had resolved to marry him.[96] The *Book of Articles* points out that, "in all this time, she never required the advice and opinion of her Council and nobility towards her marriage," yet many Lords had signed the Ainslie's Tavern Bond, and the Council had sent Maitland and Bellenden to Seton to urge Mary to marry Bothwell. Nevertheless, Mary could not but have been aware of the increasing opposition to the marriage. The Confederate Lords, meanwhile, wanted the Ainslie's Tavern Bond destroyed.[97]

Early in May, Bothwell, well aware that the Lords were uniting against him, began raising troops and consolidating support in the Borders by offering the Cessford Kers a pardon for the murder of the Abbot of Kelso. Putting a brave face on things, Mary publicly declared that she was content with her nobility, and that, "praise to God," there was "no trouble or insurrection within her realms."[98] On 10 May, she formally pardoned five men who had assisted Bothwell in her abduction;[99] he himself was shortly to receive a public pardon.

On 10 May, Thomas Randolph, who had kept an interested eye on Scottish affairs and was as avid as ever for gossip, informed the Earl of Leicester that Mary was fully resolved to marry Bothwell, and was minded to make

Leith a free burgh named Marienburgh and create Bothwell Duke of Marien-burgh; however, she had fears that he would do away with the Prince or send him to France. The latter would in fact have been a wise move, for it would have put James beyond reach of those who were plotting to depose his mother and rule in his name, but, naturally, Mary would not have wanted him to go so far from her. Randolph stated that Elizabeth was incensed at Grange's "vile" letters, which made Mary sound "worse than any common woman," and was refusing to give any support to the Scottish Lords who had dared to rebel against their anointed Queen.[100]

John Craig duly published the banns of marriage between Mary and Bothwell on Sunday, 11 May at St. Giles, but condemned their union in his sermon, calling upon Heaven and Earth to witness that he "abhorred and de-tested that marriage as odious and scandalous to the world; and, seeing the best part of the realm did approve it either by flattery or by their silence, I desired the faithful to pray earnestly that God would turn to the comfort of the realm that which was done against reason and good conscience."[101] For this, Craig was summoned to appear before the Council two days hence.

Mary moved from Edinburgh Castle to Holyrood Palace on 11 or 12 May.[102] On the 12th, attended by an armed guard, she appeared before the Chan-cellor (Huntly), and the Lords of Session in the Tolbooth and declared that she was marrying Bothwell of her own free will, and that in this marriage she foresaw much peace for the realm. Contradicting her earlier protestations that he had not held her under restraint, she went on to say that, "although at first commoved [angered] against Bothwell, yet, from his good behaviour towards her, from her knowledge of his past, and for a reward of his future services, she freely forgave him for the imprisonment of her person, and be-ing now at full liberty, she intended to promote him to further honours."[103] Under Scottish law, this public pardon, which signified the Queen's acqui-escence, had the effect of nullifying any charge of rape, and was almost cer-tainly granted at Bothwell's instance, for his procurator ensured that the pardon was formally recorded. According to Maitland, a pardon for treason, such as this was, would also have covered the crime of regicide, but this is doubtful; it will be remembered that the *Book of Articles* suggested that the obtaining of a general remission had been one of Bothwell's aims in abducting the Queen.

Later that day, Mary created Bothwell Duke of Orkney and Lord of Shetland, "placing the coronet on his head with her own hands," and knighted four of his adherents, including Black Ormiston.[104]

An undercurrent of anger and discontent was seething in Scotland at the prospect of the marriage. Mary's confessor, Roche Mameret, and some of her other friends warned her against taking Bothwell as her husband, but she would not listen, insisting that "her object in marrying [was] to settle religion by that means."[105] It would appear that she was too deeply in thrall to, and intimidated by, Bothwell to resist his persuasions. All her acts at this time suggest that he had come to dominate her. If worldly nobles went in fear of him, how much more would he overawe the Queen in her weakened state?

On 13 May, John Craig again vehemently defended his position before the Council, but was formally rebuked for his disobedience. "My Lords put me to silence and sent me away," he wrote.[106]

Bothwell's armed forces were increasing in number. On 13 May, Drury reported that the Confederate Lords had sent Mary word that, unless she discharged her soldiers, and paid heed to her nobility, they would not obey her commands. He added that there was friction between Mary and Bothwell because of jealousy on both sides, and that they had engaged in a quarrel lasting half a day. Since Bothwell was the most jealous man alive and would scarcely allow Mary "to look at man or woman," it was believed that they would not long agree after their marriage. "He is offended for a horse which she gave to the Lord of Arbroath [Lord John Hamilton]," while she "much misliked" the fact that Bothwell's former wife was still installed in Crichton Castle.[107]

Despite these tensions, the marriage contract was concluded and signed on 14 May. Huntly, Maitland, Fleming, Lindsay, Bellenden and the loyal Herries were among the witnesses.[108] The contract maintained the fiction that Mary was still her own mistress. It stated that

Her Majesty, being destitute of a husband, living solitary in the state of widowhood, and yet young and of flourishing age, apt and able to procreate and bring forth children, has been pressed and humbly required to yield unto some marriage. The most part of the nobility naming the noble Prince, now Duke of Orkney, for the special personage, Her Majesty has allowed their nomination, having recent memory of the notable and worthy acts and good service performed by him.

Yet while the contract enumerated Bothwell's virtues, it also provided that he should undertake no public business or bestow no gift, privilege or place without the Queen's consent, and that all official documents were to bear either the Queen's signature or joint signatures, but never his alone.

On the eve of his marriage, Bothwell was having doubts about Balfour's loyalty, and with good reason, as events would prove, for Balfour was determined to side with the winning faction. On 14 May, Drury reported that John Hepburn, Laird of Beanston had been appointed Governor of Edinburgh Castle in Balfour's place.[109] Melville says he was "intimately acquainted with Sir James Balfour. I knew how matters stood between Bothwell and him, namely that there were some jealousies arisen." Melville had warned Balfour "that the Earl intended to have the castle out of his hands, for [although] the Earl and he had been great companions, afterwards he [Balfour] would not consent to be present [at Kirk o'Field] nor take part with the murderers of the King, whereby he came in suspicion with the Earl of Bothwell, who would no more credit him, so that he would have had the castle out of his hands." Acting on behalf of the Confederate Lords, Melville "dealt with Sir James Balfour not to part with the castle, whereby he might be an instrument to save the Prince and the Queen, who was so disdainfully handled." Accordingly, Balfour refused to leave his post,[110] and since he had control of the ordnance and the royal treasure, Bothwell had no choice but to leave him in it or risk a bloody confrontation. Alienating Balfour, however, would prove to be his biggest mistake.

Drury also mentioned that the Confederate Lords were beginning to "muse much" on Maitland's prolonged stay with his supposed enemies. Maitland, also, it appears, was waiting to see which faction would emerge victorious. His overriding consideration, however, was the salvaging of his long-cherished plans for the peaceful union of Scotland and England, and it was almost certainly for this reason that he would not, at this stage, abandon the Queen.

On 14 May, on being informed that her Lords would not consent to her marriage unless she ratified the Ainslie's Tavern Bond, Mary formally pardoned all those who had signed it, and promised that neither she nor her heirs would ever "impute a crime or offence to any of the subscribers thereof."[111]

The Queen and Bothwell had now done everything in their power to give a semblance of legality to their marriage and appease their opponents. On the evening of 14 May, with the wedding on the morrow, Melville ventured to return to court, and found Bothwell in a good mood. He even asked Melville to join him and his friends at supper, but after a while, "he fell in discoursing of gentlewomen, speaking such filthy language that I left him, and went up to the Queen, who expressed much satisfaction at my coming." It seemed, however, that she hardly knew what she was doing.

23

"Wantons Marry in the Month of May"

~

Mary was married to Bothwell at 10 a.m. on 15 May 1567 in a Protestant ceremony that was conducted by the groom's adherent, Adam Bothwell, Bishop of Orkney, who was no relation;[1] in his sermon, the Bishop spoke of Bothwell's "penitence" for having been an "evil liver."[2] Mary's agreement to a Protestant ceremony is proof of her complete subjugation to Bothwell's will. Not only was he of the reformed faith, but he doubtless wished to retain the favour of those Protestant Lords who had supported his marriage, and probably convinced the Queen that a Protestant ceremony would go some way towards healing the religious divisions in her kingdom.

Melville, writing decades later, says that the wedding took place in the great hall of Holyrood Palace, but the *Diurnal* claims that it was solemnised in "the old chapel," that is, the abbey church, which was now the parish church of the Canongate. The Queen wore her widow's weeds, as she had done at her marrige to Darnley; her only sartorial concessions to the occasion were to have her black gown trimmed with braid, a yellow gown relined, which was presumably the gown she changed into after the ceremony, although there is no record of this, and a black taffeta petticoat refurbished.[3]

The *Diurnal* states that "there was not many of the nobility of this realm there," yet, although many Lords had joined the Confederates, some did attend, notably Huntly, Maitland, Crawford, Sutherland, Fleming, Boyd, Oliphant, Glamis and Livingston.[4] Archbishop Hamilton and the Bishops of Ross and Dunblane were also present. Nau says these Lords "gave proof that they looked on the union with great satisfaction as greatly tending to the advantage of the kingdom." Nevertheless, "at this marriage there was neither pleasure nor pastime used, as was wont to be used when princesses were married."[5] There was a solemn wedding breakfast, to which the public were admitted; Mary sat at the head of a long table and Bothwell at the foot, and they and their guests ate in silence.[6] Although Mary had laden Darnley with gifts prior to their wedding, her only present to Bothwell was some fur for his nightgown, which had been removed from one of her mother's cloaks.[7]

Mary was soon regretting her heretical nuptials; by participating in them, she believed she had put her immortal soul in peril. "On her return from that unlawful ceremony, the Queen could not help weeping. At once she sent for the Bishop of Ross, and with many tears unlocked the secret of her heart; she showed many clear signs of repentance and promised that she would never again do anything opposed to the rites of the Catholic Church."[8]

That night, a placard appeared on the gates of Holyrood, bearing a Latin quote from Ovid: "Wantons marry in the month of May."

On the wedding day itself, the Bishop of Dunblane was sent to the French court to announce the Queen's marriage, give her version of the abduction and other events that had led up to it, and secure the approval of Catherine de' Medici and Charles IX. He also carried letters from du Croc. The Bishop's instructions were to "make true report of the Duke of Orkney's whole life, and especially of his behaviour and proceedings towards us, [and] that we have been very content to take him for our husband. From his first entering into his estate, he dedicated his whole service to his sovereign." The Bishop was also to say, tellingly, that, from the time of Darnley's death, as Bothwell's "pretences began to be higher, so his proceedings seemed somewhat more strange," and the Queen was "now so far committed to him that we must interpret all things to the best," even though he had displayed "plain contempt of our person and use of force to have us in his power." The Bishop was further to emphasise the fact that the Protestant ceremony had been chosen rather from "destiny and necessity than her free choice," for Bothwell was more concerned with placating his Protestant associates "than regarding our contentation, or weighing what was convenient to us, that has been nourished in our own religion and never intends to leave the same for him or any man on Earth."[9]

It was soon obvious that all was not well between Mary and Bothwell. On the morning after the wedding night, the Queen sent for du Croc, who had diplomatically avoided attending the ceremony on the grounds that he had received no mandate from France to recognise Bothwell as Mary's husband.[10] When he arrived, he found Mary and Bothwell together, but "perceived an estranged demeanour" between them. Mary asked du Croc to excuse her for it, "saying that, if I saw her sad, it was because she could not rejoice nor ever should again, for she did nothing but wish for death."[11] Bothwell must have heard this, but made no comment.

Du Croc also reported, as did Melville, that, the next day, when Mary was alone in her cabinet with Bothwell, "she cried aloud, then sought for a knife to stab herself, or else (said she) I will drown myself." Arthur Erskine and "those who were in the chamber adjoining the cabinet heard her. They think that, if God does not aid her, she will become desperate." Du Croc added, "I have counselled and comforted her the best I could these three times I have seen her. Her husband will not remain so long, for he is too much hated in this realm, as he is always considered guilty of the death of the King."[12] Clearly, the reason for Mary's distress was Bothwell.

Mary's behaviour was hardly that of the woman described by Buchanan, who was so passionately in love and moved by lust that she had been prepared to connive at murder, abduction and rape in order to marry her lover. Had this been the case, she would surely have been ecstatic at the fulfilment of her desires. Instead, she was suicidal. The Protestant marriage ceremony, which she obviously saw as an unforgivable betrayal of her faith, must have had a lot to do with it, but Bothwell's behaviour towards her was also a factor. It is tempting to speculate that he had somehow alienated her on their wedding night; claims that he practised buggery may not have been unfounded, although, as we have seen, they emanated mainly from his enemies. However, Mary's distress had been evident before the wedding night.

Some writers have suggested that, once he was safely married, Bothwell revealed to a horrified Mary his part in Darnley's murder. It is more likely, however, that he kept quiet about it, for there is evidence—as will become clear—that, when he later said a last farewell to her, he gave her a copy of the Craigmillar Bond, revealing the names of the Lords, including himself, who had plotted against Darnley. What her marriage did perhaps, in a very short time, bring home to Mary was that she had both abased and compromised herself by marrying Bothwell.

There is some evidence that Mary's jealousy was aroused by her husband's continuing relationship with his ex-wife. De Silva heard that, after his marriage, "Bothwell passes some days a week with the wife he has divorced."[13] Maitland told Mary that Bothwell had written to Jean more than once, to tell her that he still regarded her as his true wife, and Mary as merely his concubine,[14] and du Croc informed his government: "No one in this kingdom is in any doubt but that the Duke loves his former wife a great deal more than he loves the Queen."[15] Even if there was not much love or affection between Mary and Bothwell, this would have been an inexcusable slight to the Queen.

Such snippets of information and gossip as survive show that it was probably Bothwell's own demeanour that was responsible for Mary's misery. She had been his virtual prisoner for the three weeks before their wedding, and in that time he had taken control of her life. Now that they were married, he revealed himself as a Jekyll and Hyde character, sometimes dour, forbidding and even indifferent, sometimes embarrassingly over-familiar and given to using coarse and even obscene language in her presence. He dictated who might, and who might not, have access to, and speech with, her, and insisted on being present. The Confederate Lords complained that "no nobleman nor other durst resort to Her Majesty to speak with her or procure their lawful business without suspicion, except by him and in his hearing, her chamber doors being continually watched with men of war."[16] Maitland told du Croc that Bothwell "would not let her look at anybody, or anybody look at her, for he knew very well that she loved her pleasure,"[17] and flew into ungovernable rages if she showed the slightest favour to other men, or even to her female friends. The Calvinist in him criticised her for seeking frivolous, worldly diversions, and obliged her to give up the pastimes she so enjoyed,[18] music, card games, hunting, hawking and golf. "In private, he was so beastly jealous and suspicious that he suffered her not to pass a day in patience, without causing her to shed abundance of salt tears";[19] according to Maitland, "from the day of the marriage, there had been no end to the Queen's tears and lamentations."[20]

In public, however, Bothwell's manner towards the Queen was one of "great reverence." Although, as her husband, he had the right to wear his cap in her presence, he made a point of going uncovered, "which it seems she would have otherwise, sometimes taking his cap and putting it on."[21] The royal couple made sure they were seen together as often as possible, and Drury wrote on 25 May that "they now make outward show of great content." They often went riding, but were always surrounded by an armed guard.[22]

It is highly unlikely that Mary was ever in love with Bothwell. Certainly she recognised his strengths and his good qualities, but these had of late been compromised in her eyes by his "rude" conduct towards her; her ambivalent attitude and her resentment towards him are evident in her instructions to the Bishop of Dunblane. To the end of her days, she would maintain that she had married Bothwell for reasons of state. Nevertheless, she was now duty bound to love and obey him, and she may already have suspected that she was pregnant, which, as far as she was concerned, and later declared, represented an insurmountable barrier to her ending the marriage.

On 17 May, Bothwell presided over a meeting of the somewhat depleted Privy Council.[23] Mary was never to bestow on him the title of King, but his actions left no one in any doubt as to who was wielding sovereign power. He himself wrote: "They placed the government of the country in my hands, with the wish that I should bring some order into the country."[24] The indications are that he would have been a strong ruler with a latent talent for diplomacy, but, lacking aristocratic support, he was not to be allowed a chance to prove himself.

On the 18th, du Croc wrote to Charles IX and Catherine de' Medici relating the events of the past few days and enjoining them not to give any credence to the letters he had sent by the Bishop of Dunblane, for they were

merely delusive. You can suppose that I did not entrust to him what I write to you. Your Majesties cannot do better than to make him very bad cheer, and find all amiss in this marriage, for it is very wretched, and is already repented of.

He went on to say that the Queen had summoned the Confederate Lords to attend her, but he did not think they would come. She herself must have suspected as much, for she had begged du Croc to speak to them and persuade them to return to their allegiance. Du Croc believed this would be futile, and although he was prepared to say "all that it is possible for me to say," he thought it more advisable to withdraw and

> leave them to play out their game. It is not fitting that I sit there among the Lords in the name of the King of France, for if I lean to the Queen, they will think in this realm, and in England, that my King had a hand in all that is done. Why, if it had not been for the express command that Your Majesty made on me, I had departed hence eight days before this marriage took place. If I have spoken in a very high tone, it is that all this realm may be aware that I will neither mix myself up with these nuptials, nor will I recognise Bothwell as the husband of the Queen.[25]

Two days later, Drury reported the latest gossip from Edinburgh, stating that "there have already been some jars between the Queen and the Duke," that Mary was distressed by them, and that "the opinion of divers is that she is the most changed woman of face that in so little time, without extremity of sickness, they have seen. It is thought the Queen has long had a spice of the falling sickness [epilepsy] and has of late been troubled therewith." It is more likely that Mary was suffering from fainting fits brought on by stress. Drury added that Balfour was to carry letters to the English court announcing the Queen's marriage.[26] But if Bothwell thought by this means to get rid of Balfour, he was very much mistaken.

Bothwell's influence was soon felt on the political scene. On 22 May, the Privy Council drew up a rota of Councillors who were to be permanently in attendance on the Queen; Morton was among them. A day later, the Council issued a proclamation reaffirming the recent Act of Parliament that had ratified the establishment of the Kirk.

News of the Queen's abduction and marriage had by now reached England. Elizabeth, appalled, expressed "great surprise at these events, and deplores them very much as touching the honour of the Queen."[27] Fearful of the consequences, she was moved to write candidly to Mary with a few home truths:

Madam, it has been always held in friendship that prosperity provideth but adversity proveth friends. Wherefore we comfort you with these few words.

She went on to say that she had learned of her cousin's marriage.

To be plain with you, our grief has not been small thereat: for how could a worse choice be made for your honour than in such haste to marry a subject who, besides other notorious lacks, public fame has charged with the murder of your late husband, besides touching yourself in some part, though, we trust in that behalf, falsely. And with what peril have you married him, that hath another lawful wife, nor any children betwixt you legitimate. Thus you see our opinion plainly, and we are heartily sorry we can conceive no better. We are earnestly bent to do everything in our power to procure the punishment of that murder against any subject you have, how dear soever you should hold him, and next thereto to be careful how your son the Prince may be preserved to the comfort of you and the realm.[28]

Clearly, Elizabeth believed not only that Bothwell had murdered Darnley, but also that he posed a threat to the infant James. She told Randolph that she had "great misliking of the Queen's doing, which she doth so much detest that she is ashamed of her," and confided to him her fear that, Bothwell being "as mortal an enemy to our whole nation as any man alive," he would incite Mary to become her enemy also.[29] Knowing that the Lennoxes were stung by the news of Mary's hasty remarriage, Elizabeth showed great kindness and favour to them at this time, and Cecil told Lady Lennox that the Queen meant to ensure that James was brought to England and placed in her care.[30]

On 24 May, de Silva reported that Mary's marriage had greatly scandalised people in England, "and has caused sorrow to many who see the evils it will bring in its train. It is said here that the cause of the Queen of Scotland's hurry over this marriage is that she is pregnant," which must have been pure speculation, since no one could have known at this early stage that Mary actually was expecting Bothwell's child. De Silva had also heard that the

Scottish Lords were still on the march, "although now that the thing is done, they may come round to it. There is talk of delivering the Prince of Scotland to this Queen to be brought up by his grandmother."[31]

In Scotland, as we have seen, there had been concerned conjecture since before the marriage that Bothwell would seize the Prince and harm him. Buchanan claims that Mary wanted to hand James over to his stepfather, but she had in fact contrived to send Bishop Leslie to Stirling to reiterate her strict injunctions to Mar not to deliver her son into any hands other than her own, under any circumstances. According to Melville, "after the marriage, Bothwell was very earnest to get the Prince in his hands, but my Lord of Mar, who was a true nobleman, would not deliver him out of his custody, alleging that he could not without the consent of the three Estates." But Bothwell would not give up, and after Mar "had made divers refusals," he "made his moan" to Melville, "praying me to help to save the Prince out of his hands who had slain his father, and had already made his vaunt among his familiars that, if he could get him once in his hands, he would warrant him from revenging his father's death. [Mar] desired to know if I could propose any outgait. I answered that he might make this one of his excuses, that he could not deliver the Prince till he should see a secure place to keep him in."[32] It may be that Bothwell's enemies were making too much of his intentions towards the Prince, and that he merely wished to remove the child out of reach of the Confederate Lords, and perhaps send him to France, but no one was taking any chances.

Drury reported on 25 May that Bothwell had secretly warned his followers to be ready for action, and informed Cecil of the contents of the bond drawn up by the Confederate Lords, who were preparing to attack. Lord Home, Bothwell's rival in the south, was to lead a force from the Borders, and Morton one from Stirling. Drury urged Cecil to send military support to Home. He also revealed that Balfour, "doubtful of his entertainment in passing and returning," was not now coming to England; this, however, was almost certainly an excuse contrived to ensure that he stayed in Edinburgh. Drury stated that Bothwell had forbidden Mary to visit James at Stirling—probably from fear that she would fall into the hands of his opponents, since he had also made sure that everywhere she went she was accompanied by an escort of soldiers. Although there were no more nobles at court than had attended the marriage, triumphal entertainments—a masque, a water pageant and a tournament—had been staged there,[33] probably in defiance of a disapproving world.

On 27 May, the Queen and Bothwell both wrote to Archbishop Beaton, explaining the reasons for their marriage. Mary said much the same thing as she had to the Bishop of Dunblane:

> The event is indeed strange, and otherwise nor, we know, you would have looked for. But as it is succeeded, we must take the best of it, and so, for our respect, must all who love us.

She also asked the Archbishop to excuse Bothwell if he seemed unceremonious and lacking in respect; then, revealing her anxiety as to how the marriage would be received at the French court, and showing that she was well aware of the gravity of the matter, prayed for his diligence

> in this case, being no less weighty, but rather of greater consequence, nor any matter we had in hand, that you bestow your study, ingenuity and effectual labours in the ordering of this present message, and in the persuading them to whom it is directed to believe that thing therein which is the very truth.[34]

Bothwell, using the royal plural, wrote to Beaton asking him to assist the Bishop of Dunblane in the exacting task of announcing the marriage to the King and Queen Mother of France and the Cardinal of Lorraine. Of himself and his sudden elevation, he wrote:

> We cannot marvel indeed that this marriage, and the rumours that preceded it, appear right strange to you. The place and promotion truly is great, but yet, with God's care, neither it nor any other accident[35] shall ever be able to make us forget any part of our duty to any noblemen or other our good friends, and chiefly to you, whom we have had good occasion always to esteem with the first of that number. Her Majesty might well have married with men of greater birth and estimation, but, we are well assured, never with one more affectionately inclined to do her honour and service.[36]

That same day, Bothwell also wrote a courteous letter of greeting to Charles IX.[37]

It was Mary's marriage, rather than Darnley's murder, that was the catalyst for her ultimate downfall, and everywhere, reactions to it were worse than she could ever have anticipated. Indeed, it gave rise to an international scandal. Bothwell, wrote Melville, "was at last the Queen's wreck, and the hindrance of all our hopes in the hasty obtaining of all her desires concerning the crown of England."

In Scotland, the Queen's marriage was almost universally condemned as an outrage; many saw in it confirmation of the rumours that she had plotted Darnley's death in order to marry Bothwell, and not a few of her shocked supporters, both Catholic and Protestant, fell away. Broadsheets began circulating in Edinburgh, comparing her with Delilah, Jezebel and Clytemnestra. In England, France and the rest of the Continent, the reaction was much the same: no one believed the explanations offered by Mary and Bothwell. Those who had been Mary's friends and allies no longer wanted anything to do with her. Even Philip of Spain and her Guise relations abandoned her[38]—their silence was deafening—while Catherine de' Medici was of the opinion that it was wrong to attribute to force that which had been brought about "by free will and premeditated determination,"[39] and told Archbishop Beaton that his mistress "had behaved so ill and made herself so hateful to her subjects" that France could no longer offer her aid or counsel.[40]

In the eyes of Catholic Europe, Mary had bigamously married a heretic in an unlawful ceremony, and was consequently damned. In Britain, Catholics who had regarded her as their hope for the future were devastated that she, "without fear of God, or respect for the world, has allowed herself to be induced by sensuality, or else by the persuasion of others, to take one who cannot be her husband, and gives thereby a suspicion that she will go over by degrees to the new fashion," i.e., Protestantism.[41] Giovanni Correr, the Venetian ambassador in Paris, correctly observed that the cause of Catholicism in Scotland had been "deprived of all hope of ever again raising its head."[42] Horrified at what the Queen had done, her confessor, the Dominican friar Roche Mameret, left her service and returned to France.

No allowances were made for Mary's health, her state of mind, the Lords' approval of this union, or the fact that she had been a virtual prisoner when she consented to it; the chain of circumstances leading up to it was sinister enough, in the opinion of many, to condemn her. As for the upstart Bothwell, no one doubted that he had murdered Darnley in order to gain a crown.

Few could believe what Mary had done. The Confederate Lords later explained to Throckmorton, "We thought that, within a short time, her mind being a little settled, and the eyes of her understanding opened, she would better consider of herself."[43] This shows that they were well aware of Mary's state at this time, but of course, they made no attempt to prevent her from making this fatal marriage because it suited them to see her heading for a fall; in fact, they were to exploit public opinion to the full. Nevertheless, Mary's marriage must have convinced them that they were justified in moving against her. Certainly, none of them would have bowed the knee to Bothwell: Nau says that "some joined this party out of jealousy at [his] rapid promotion." For the present, the Lords maintained the fiction that their quarrel was with Bothwell alone. Slowly, but inexorably, Scotland was moving towards civil war.

On 28 May, the Privy Council, in the Queen's name, issued a proclamation summoning the lieges to arms, to convene at Melrose in the Borders on 15 June, with fifteen days' provisions, ostensibly for a raid that Bothwell was to lead against the troublemakers in Liddesdale, but in reality to counter the military threat posed by the Confederate Lords.[44] On 1 June, in an effort to counteract scaremongering rumours, another proclamation was issued, denying that the Queen had any intention of subverting the laws or making changes in religion, and emphasising her love for "her dearest son: of whom shall Her Majesty be careful if she neglect him that is so dear to her, on whose good success her special joy consists, and without whom Her Majesty could not think herself in good estate but comfortless all the days of her life?"[45] On 4 June, in desperation, the Council issued an ordinance complaining that Mary's subjects did not understand her, and denying rumours that Bothwell was trying to gain control of the Prince.[46] It was all futile. By now, most people in Scotland would have believed the Queen capable of anything, even infanticide.

Mary was hoping that the recent *entente* with England could still be maintained, and on 4 June, Robert Melville departed for the English court to officially announce Mary's marriage and secure Elizabeth's approval. With him, he carried a letter for her from the hitherto Anglophobic Bothwell, written in a bid to win her friendship and assure her that he would be "careful to see Your two Majesties' amity continued by all good offices," but it fell on deaf ears, as did a similar letter to Cecil.[47]

At Stirling, around 6 May, the reconvened Confederate Lords, now twenty-six in number, issued a proclamation announcing their intention of delivering the Queen from "thraldom and bondage," punishing Darnley's murderers and protecting the Prince.[48] They also signed a second bond to this effect around this time. These Lords represented a major section of the political establishment, and already they had raised an army of 3,000 men,[49] which, combined with the fact that they were overwhelmingly supported by public opinion, made them a very formidable opposition indeed. Nau says that the Lords had already decided "that Bothwell should be accused of Darnley's murder. All this was done by the advice of Secretary Lethington, with whom Bothwell was on bad terms . . . The Earl of Morton held the first rank among these plotters, as he was in every deadly treason." Maitland, who feared and hated Bothwell, and had probably only stayed with Mary in the hope of salvaging his political ambitions, had now seen the writing on the wall, and was almost certainly in touch with the Confederate Lords.

The rats were deserting. Around 6 June, according to Drury, Huntly requested the Queen's permission to leave court to visit his estates in the north, but she refused to grant it and, "with many bitter words," accused him of plotting treason against her as his father had done.[50]

That same day, Maitland left court without taking leave of Mary,[51] and joined the Confederate Lords, who received him coldly, thinking he had come on the Queen's behalf to spy on them and subvert their cause. He himself later maintained, to Throckmorton and Melville, that he had joined the Lords because he believed that it was the best way to further Mary's interests. It is unlikely that Maitland's motives at this time will ever be fully known. Mary herself always held that, by defecting to her enemies, he had betrayed her under a cloak of loyalty, a belief shared by Morton and Randolph. The *Diurnal of Occurrents* states that Maitland left Edinburgh in fear of his life, which may be partly the truth, for Bothwell had tried to kill him at Dunbar, and, according to Drury, had "used some choler towards Lethington before his departure, wherewith the Queen was somewhat offended."[52] However, the Confederate Lords' victory now seemed certain, and had Maitland stayed with the Queen, he might well have had cause to fear them more than he feared Bothwell.

Argyll, meanwhile, was having second thoughts about joining the Confederate Lords, fearing that his part in Darnley's murder would be exposed if Bothwell were captured and tried. On 6 June, he secretly warned the Queen and Bothwell that the Confederate Lords were plotting their capture and had mustered their forces ready to march on Edinburgh.[53] As Holyrood Palace could not be defended, Bothwell decided that it would be safer for him and the Queen to move into Edinburgh Castle, but Balfour refused to admit them,[54] having decided to throw in his lot with the Lords. He had taken Melville's advice "not to part with the castle," and heeded his warning that, if he did not join the Lords, he would be held as guilty of Darnley's murder as Bothwell was, "by reason of his long familiarity with the Earl." Balfour had certainly had "intelligence with the Morton faction,"[55] and there has also been speculation that he had entered into a secret bond with them which granted him indemnity against prosecution for his part in Darnley's murder, in return for his support. Melville says Balfour had agreed to hold the castle for the Lords on condition "that the Laird of Grange would engage upon his honour to be his protector, in case afterward the nobility should alter upon him."

This was the ultimate betrayal: the loss of Edinburgh Castle was a disaster for Mary and Bothwell, for whoever held the castle held the city. In the circumstances, Bothwell decided that it would be best for them to leave Edinburgh for Borthwick Castle, which lay twelve miles to the south and was owned by the Catholic Lord Borthwick; here they could wait in readiness for their levies to assemble at Melrose, and Bothwell could hopefully rally further support in the Borders.

On 7 June, the Queen and Bothwell left Edinburgh "with artillery and men of war" for Borthwick Castle.[56] In order to raise money for her troops, Mary had had Elizabeth's gold christening font and some of her own plate melted down.[57]

Borthwick Castle, which commanded a valley two miles west of Crichton, was a splendid fortress that had been built around 1420–30. It had a massive U-shaped keep with walls 12–14 feet thick, and was surrounded by a curtain wall with twin corner towers 110 feet high. Inside, there was a lofty vaulted hall with a minstrels' gallery, bedchambers, a chapel and service quarters.[58]

Mary and Bothwell arrived here on 7 June, probably aware that the Lords meant to march on them very soon. Leaving the castle well garrisoned, Bothwell departed immediately with his remaining men for Melrose.[59] It is often stated that he went to Melrose to meet with the lieges who had been summoned on 28 May, yet found the place deserted, but the lieges were not due to assemble there until 15 June. It is more likely that Bothwell made an abortive raid on Home's forces from Melrose;[60] he states in his memoirs that, "when I reached the frontier, I found the enemy in such strength that I could achieve nothing, and returned at once to Borthwick in order to collect a greater force."[61] Mary, meanwhile, had summoned her levies to meet at Muirshead Abbey on 12 June, instead of at Melrose on the 15th, but this "proclamation was not so well obeyed, and so many as came had no hearts to fight in that quarrel."[62]

Mary probably sent Casket Letter VIII to Bothwell when he was at Melrose. Written in what appears to be her style, it reads:

My Lord, since my letter written, your brother-in-law that was came to me very sad, and hath asked me my counsel what he should do after tomorrow, because there be many folks here, and among others the Earl of Sutherland, who would rather die, considering the good they have so lately received of me, than suffer me to be carried away, they conducting me; and that he feared there should be some trouble happen of it, of the other side, that it should be said that he were unthankful to have betrayed me. I told him that he should have resolved with you upon all that, and that he should avoid, if he could, those that were most mistrusted. He hath resolved to write thereof to you of my opinion, for he hath abashed me to see him so unresolved at the need. I assure myself he will play the part of an honest man; but I have thought good to advertise you of the fear he hath that he should be charged and accused of treason, to the end that, without mistrusting him, you may be the more circumspect, and that you may have the more power; for we had yesterday more than 300 horse of his and of Livingston. For the honour of God, be accompanied rather with more than less, for that is the principal of my care. I go to write my dispatch, and pray God to send us a happy interview shortly. I write in haste to the end you may be advised in time.

This letter makes better sense placed in this context, rather than during Mary's sojourn at Stirling before her abuction and Bothwell's divorce. Huntly is known to have been in Edinburgh on 7 June and 10 June, and he was in Edinburgh Castle on the 11th; it is not inconceivable that, on 9 June, the day before the Lords planned to attack Borthwick—which Huntly must have known about—he visited Mary at Borthwick, which was easily accessible from Edinburgh. His visit, and her letter, may be dated to the 9th on the basis of his request to Mary for advice as to what he should do "after tomorrow." The fact that his men arrived with those of Lord Livingston suggests that he had sent them covertly. It is not surprising that he was terrified, in view of Mary's recent accusations of treason, that he would be arrested and charged with it. Relieved that he had come, yet aware that he was still having doubts that he had done the right thing, it would have been natural for Mary to warn Bothwell to treat him with circumspection.

When Mary referred to Sutherland and many other folks being "here," she meant nearby or in the vicinity, which could even mean in Edinburgh. Both Sutherland and Huntly had reason to be grateful to Mary, for she had restored their lands in the recent Parliament. The tone of this hasty letter is dutiful, but in no way loving or passionate; however, Mary must now have known for certain that she was pregnant, and for this reason she had no choice but to fight or fall with Bothwell.

If the letter does date from this time, as seems probable, then it could not have been among the documents in the casket that was discovered by the Lords in Edinburgh on 20 June, for Bothwell never returned to Edinburgh after leaving it on 7 June. In that case, it must have been planted in the casket by the Lords, who later alleged, in order to incriminate the Queen, that it had been written in an entirely different context. This is almost certainly further proof that the evidence against Mary was manipulated.

Bothwell returned to Borthwick on 9 or 10 June, then sent urgent messages to Balfour, Huntly and Archbishop Hamilton to hasten to him with more men. That night, as they had planned, Home, Morton and Mar,[63] with their individual forces, met up at Liberton Kirk, four miles south of Edinburgh, and marched together on Borthwick at the head of 7–800 mounted men armed with muskets.[64] With them were Atholl, Glencairn, Lindsay, Sempill, Ruthven, Tullibardine, Grange, Ker of Cessford and Ker of Fawdonside.[65] At, or before, their approach, Bothwell, knowing that capture would mean certain death, made his escape through a postern gate, leaving Mary to deal with the Lords, presumably relying on them not to make war on a lone woman who was also their sovereign.

The Lords massed their forces before the castle, "discharged several volleys of musketry" and called for Bothwell to come out and take up their challenge.

"Traitor! Murderer! Butcher!" they cried, when he did not appear.[66] Then Mary appeared on the wall to tell them he had gone, and they asked her to return with them to Edinburgh and assist them against her husband's murderers. Knowing they meant Bothwell, she refused. Realising that it was futile to press her further, and knowing that they could not lay siege to the castle since they had no artillery, the Lords shouted a few insults at her, "too evil and unseemly to be told, which the poor Princess did with her speech defend,"[67] then withdrew north to Dalkeith. The Lords later insisted that they had used all courtesy towards the Queen, and had withdrawn as soon as they discovered that Bothwell had left the castle.[68]

As soon as the Lords had arrived, Mary dispatched two messengers to Huntly in Edinburgh, urging him to come to her with armed men, but Morton's men captured them. Later, in the early hours of the morning, they released them before marching off, whereupon the messengers promptly galloped off to the city. Huntly, aided by Archbishop Hamilton, did his best to rouse the citizens against the Lords, but in vain.

At 8 a.m. or earlier, the Confederate Lords entered Edinburgh, to great acclaim, and without any hindrance from Balfour's garrison at the castle.[69] As Bothwell wrote, "the city and castle of Edinburgh had abandoned us and gone over to them."[70] At the Mercat Cross, the Lords told the crowds who had come out to greet them that they had taken up arms only "to pursue their revenge for the murder of the King."[71] Shortly afterwards, they issued a proclamation summoning the citizens to aid them in delivering the Queen from Bothwell.

Huntly and Archbishop Hamilton "took to arming as soon as they saw this change of heart" on the part of the citizens, "in order to defend themselves against the troublemakers, and to save the city. But they were unable to do anything, being greatly inferior in numbers."[72] Huntly was received into Edinburgh Castle on the 11th,[73] but was allowed to leave soon afterwards. Immediately, he fled north to raise troops for the Queen, while Archbishop Hamilton left to rouse support in the south-west.

At midnight on the 11th, Mary, who had no mind to wait until the Lords returned with superior forces, escaped from Borthwick Castle, "dressed in men's clothes, booted and spurred."[74] Tradition says she was lowered to the ground by a rope from a window in the great hall,[75] and thence hastened away through the postern gate. She was met by Bothwell's servants a mile from Borthwick,[76] and joined him at either Hailes Castle or at the fifteenth-century tower known as Black Castle at Cakemuir on nearby Fala Moor, which was the property of the Wauchope family, who were friends of Bothwell.

At 3 a.m. on 12 June, Mary and Bothwell arrived at Dunbar, where they were met by Lords Seton, Yester and Borthwick, and six lairds.[77] Mary had left her wardrobe and personal belongings behind at Borthwick, and had to borrow clothes from a countrywoman: "a red petticoat" that barely covered her knees, "sleeves tied with bows, a velvet hat and a muffler."[78] There was no time to lose, and Bothwell immediately left for the Borders to raise men. At the same time, "a messenger was sent to hasten the coming of the Hamiltons and Huntly, who did not arrive until it was too late."[79]

That day, both Mary and the Confederate Lords summoned the lieges to their banners.[80] Bothwell was to have some success in raising a force of his loyal Borderers, but otherwise comparatively few supporters rallied to the Queen. In their summons, the Lords declared their intention of executing justice on "the murderer of the King and the ravisher of the Queen"; "also, sundry libels were set out in both rhyme and prose, to move the hearts of the whole subjects to assist and take part in so good a cause."[81] These astute measures, combined with the vigorous exhortations of the Protestant clergy, inspired many to join their already formidable army.

Balfour now committed the ultimate treachery. On 13 June, he sent a message to the Queen, advising her

> to take the open field and to march direct to Edinburgh, so as to meet the insurgents on the road. He assured her that they would not keep their ground for a moment, especially when they knew that he had declared against them and would open fire upon their troops. If she did not do so, he would be compelled, he said, to come to terms with them. But he had been won over by the rebels to give this counsel.[82]

This message came before Mary and Bothwell had had a chance to raise sufficient men, but on the strength of it, the Queen decided that the time was ripe for taking possession of the capital,[83] and sent a message to that effect to Bothwell.

The next day, Maitland had an interview lasting three hours with Balfour in Edinburgh Castle,[84] which resulted in Balfour undertaking to surrender the castle to the Confederate Lords and assist them in rescuing the Queen from Bothwell; in return, Maitland promised to support Balfour's claim to retain command of the castle. By now, the Lords had an army of 4,000 men.[85]

On 14 June, Mary left Dunbar with 600 horse and three cannon, and rode to Haddington, where she met up with Bothwell, who had returned from the Borders with a force of 1,600.[86] On the way, the Queen was dismayed to see that "the people did not join as expected."[87] From Haddington, the royal army marched to Gladsmuir, where they proclaimed that "a number of conspirators, under pretext of preserving the Prince, were really trying to dethrone the Queen, that they might rule all things at their pleasure," and that "very necessity compelled her to take up arms, and her hope was in the help of all faithful subjects, who would be rewarded with [the] lands and possessions of [the] rebels."[88] Then they rode to Seton, where, while their soldiers camped at Prestonpans, the Queen and her husband spent what would turn out to be their last night together.[89] They had decided to march on Edinburgh the next day.

On the 15th, Bedford reported to Leicester that the Lords had assured him that they would move against Bothwell alone, but that swift action was necessary because "the Queen is with child."[90] They perhaps feared that, once Mary's pregnancy became evident, the people might not be so willing to rise against her or her husband.

The two armies finally came face to face on 15 June at Carberry Hill, overlooking the River Esk, seven miles east of Edinburgh.[91] The Queen's forces were drawn up on the hillside beneath pennants bearing the Lion Rampant of Scotland and the Saltire of St. Andrew. The Lords were positioned at the foot of the hill, under an emotive white banner portraying the infant James praying before his father's murdered corpse, and bearing the legend, "Judge and avenge my cause, O Lord."[92]

Both sides were reluctant to fight, so the day was spent in fruitless parleying under a hot sun. Glencairn sent the Queen a message stating that the Lords' quarrel was not with the Crown, and if she would abandon Bothwell, they would restore her to her former authority as their natural sovereign; but she angrily refused, saying, "The Lords must yield or try their chances in battle,"[93] adding, with some justice, "It was by them that Bothwell had been promoted."[94]

Bothwell notes that the Lords sent a herald to him "with a written statement of their reasons for taking to the field. These were, firstly, to set the Queen free from the captivity in which I was holding her, and also to avenge the death of the King, of which I had been accused." He replied, somewhat untruthfully, that he "was not holding the Queen in any captivity, but that I loved and honoured her in all humanity as she deserved"; nor had there ever "been any question of my participating in, or consenting to, the murder of His Majesty," but although he had been completely cleared of that charge, he was happy to defend his honour in the field there and then, against any comer.

Du Croc, who had followed the Lords to Carberry Hill, attempted to mediate between the two sides, but to little effect. Bothwell told him that his enemies were merely jealous of the favour he enjoyed: "There is not a man of them but wishes himself in my place." As Mary was by then weeping pitiably, Bothwell challenged one of the Lords to fight him, so that the outcome of the day could be decided by single combat, but when a suitable an-swerer, Lord Lindsay, was finally found, the Queen vetoed the idea, fearing that Bothwell would be killed.

Mary and Bothwell were hoping that reinforcements led by Huntly and the Hamiltons would come to their rescue, but in vain. By the evening, so many of the Queen's men had drifted off home or deserted to the rebels that the outcome of any armed combat was in no doubt. Melville says that "many of those who were with her were of opinion that she had intelligence with the Lords, especially such as were informed of the many indignities put upon her by the Earl of Bothwell since their marriage. [They] believed that Her Majesty would fain have been quit of him, but thought shame to be the doer thereof directly herself." Although Mary's later conduct does not bear this out, it is a good indication of how people at the time perceived her feelings towards Bothwell.

Du Croc was reluctantly impressed by the way in which Bothwell con-ducted himself in this difficult situation: "I am obliged to say that I saw a great leader, speaking with great confidence and leading his forces boldly, gaily and skilfully. I admired him, for he saw that his foes were resolute, he could not count on half his men, and yet was not dismayed. He had not on his side a single lord of note. Yet I rated his chances higher because he was in sole command." But it was now too late. Wishing to avoid unnecessary bloodshed, Mary asked the Lords to state the terms on which she might sur-render. Maitland and Atholl did not want to face her, so they sent Grange to assure her that, if she would consent to place herself in their hands, they would permit Bothwell to leave the field unmolested and go where it pleased him until such time as the matter of his guilt was decided by Parliament.

Bothwell was against this idea; "I knew well what treachery they were hatching: if she did not agree to their demands, I told her, they would take her prisoner and strip her of all authority."[95] He begged her to retreat with him to Dunbar in order to raise another army, but Mary overrode him. The important thing was that her husband should survive. In the meantime, he must lie low until Parliament had debated his case. She told him and Grange that

she owed a duty to the late King her husband, a duty which she would not neglect. Most willingly, therefore, would she authorise everyone to exercise the fullest liberty of inquiry into the circumstances of his death. She intended to do so herself, and to punish with all severity such as should be convicted thereof. She claimed that justice should [also] be done upon certain persons of [the Lords'] party now present who were guilty of the murder, who were much astonished to find themselves discovered.

Only Bothwell could have told her who they were, and it would appear that he had implicated them without revealing his own guilt. Clearly, they were not the principals involved. "In order to attain this [justice]," she told Grange, "she was willing to entrust herself to the good faith of the nobles, thereby to give an authority to whatever they might do or advise."[96]

Then she turned to Bothwell, declaring that, if he were found innocent, "nothing would prevent her from rendering to him all that a true and lawful wife ought to do"; but if he were found guilty, "it would be to her an endless source of regret that, by their marriage, she had ruined her good reputation, and from this she would endeavour to free herself by all possible means."[97]

Bothwell had no choice but to agree to leave Mary in the hands of his enemies. Letting him go was a solution that suited the Lords very well, for he was in possession of dangerous information. They could easily have taken him prisoner, but were reluctant to do so, for then they would have to put him on trial for Darnley's murder, and run the risk that he would incriminate them also. It would be safer to pursue him later and kill him in open combat.

Thus it was agreed that Mary should surrender to the Lords, she "thinking that she could go to them in perfect safety, without fear of treachery, and that no one would dare lay hands on her." According to Bothwell, "it should be clearly understood that the Laird of Grange gave out that he had been sent, at the unanimous request of the rebels, for the sole purpose of offering to the Queen, as their rightful superior, their true allegiance, and to give her a guaranteed safe-conduct to come amongst them. Furthermore, that each single one of them wanted no more than to accord her all honour and obedience in whatever way she wished to command them."[98]

"At parting from the Queen, Bothwell wished to ease his conscience." He told her that Morton, Maitland, Balfour and others "were guilty of the death of the late King, the whole having been executed by their direction and counsel." Then he handed her a copy of the Craigmillar Bond, bearing the signatures of himself, Maitland, Argyll, Huntly and the other nobles, including perhaps Moray and Morton, who had plotted Darnley's murder. If Mary had not suspected or known of it before, the treachery of her Lords was now revealed to her, along with the truth about the man she had married, whose child she was now carrying.[99] This must have come as an unpleasant surprise to her, but Bothwell swore that anything he had done had only been for the good of her realm, and that he had acted on the advice and persuasion of those same Lords who were now opposing him. Before he embraced Mary for the last time and rode off with between twelve and thirty horsemen towards Dunbar, he urged her to "take good care of that paper." However, it was almost certainly taken from her by the Lords soon afterwards and given to Argyll for safe keeping. Not surprisingly, given the names on it, it was never used in evidence against Mary.

Bothwell's motive in giving Mary the bond may not only have been the desire to give her proof of what he had already revealed to her, but also the wish to furnish her with evidence that she could use against the Lords, should the opportunity present itself. However, in giving her a document that incriminated himself, he was also, perhaps deliberately, providing her with an excuse to abandon him, which was undoubtedly in her best interests and would have solved many problems.

"In good faith, and reliance upon the public honour,"[100] the Queen surrendered herself to Grange. A contemporary drawing in the Public Record Office shows him leading her by the bridle to where the Lords waited; she was still wearing the same borrowed clothes she had donned at Dunbar three days previously, which were now spattered with mud.

Morton, Home and the other Lords "used all dutiful reverence" to the Queen as she approached,[101] telling her that she was now in her rightful place among her true and faithful subjects. "For welcome," however, according to Drury, they "showed her the banner with the dead body," which she said "she wished she had never seen."[102] The rebel army stood mute for a few moments, but soon there were cries from the ranks of "Burn the whore! Burn the murderess of her husband!" and Mary was roughly jostled. Grange and some of the Lords "who knew their duty better, drew their swords and struck at such as did speak irreverent language,"[103] but to little lasting effect.

Mary cried, "How is this, my Lord Morton? I am told that all this is done in order to get justice among the King's murderers. I am also told that you are one of the chief of them."

Morton answered, "Come, come, this is not the place to discuss such matters," then he "slunk behind her back" and made himself scarce.[104]

To her horror, the Lords placed Mary under guard like a common criminal. According to Nau, "two very wicked young men were appointed to have the Queen in charge"—one was Ker of Cessford—"both of them most cruel murderers and men of very scandalous life." Du Croc wrote: "I expected that the Queen would have been gentle with the Lords and tried to pacify them, but"—perhaps not surprisingly—"on her way from the field, she talked of nothing but hanging and crucifying them all."[105] To Lindsay, riding beside her, she said, "I will have your head for this, and so assure you."[106]

Weeping, dirty, dishevelled, and so exhausted and faint that she could barely remain in the saddle,[107] Mary was escorted back to Edinburgh, with the fearful Darnley banner carried aloft before her, and the soldiers still yelling insults. Separated from her servants and friends, it was now brought home to her what imprisonment meant.[108] In the city, it became starkly apparent to Mary how her subjects now felt about her. As she rode through the packed streets, the people reviled her as an adulteress and murderess, screaming, "Burn the whore! Kill her! Drown her! She is not worthy to live." The press of bodies was so great that the procession had to slow down to walking pace. By now, Mary was weeping.

At around 11 p.m., at Maitland's suggestion, the Queen was taken to a luxurious fortified and battlemented house known as the Black Turnpike, which stood on the High Street and was the official residence of the Provost, Sir Simon Preston, who had sided with the Lords.[109] Here, she was confined in an upper chamber, still under guard. Outside, the mob relentlessly continued to curse and denounce her. "The women be most furious and impudent against the Queen, and yet the men be mad enough."[110]

Mary's reign was effectively over.

24

"This Tragedy Will End in the Queen's Person"

$\backsim$

M ARY SPENT TWENTY-FOUR DESPERATE hours in the Black Turnpike, with the Darnley banner positioned across the street, level with her window, in silent reproach.[1] The Lords had invited her to join them for supper, but she could eat nothing. Her room was sparsely furnished, and she was denied the services of her female attendants. Instead, there were guards outside the door and two more sitting in her room, who would not leave even when she wished to relieve herself. Exhausted though she was, she found it hard to sleep. Finally, she gave way to despair. On the morning of 16 June, she appeared at the window in an hysterical state, with her bodice undone, her breasts exposed and her tangled hair loose, and with "piteous lamentations" made a distraught appeal for help to the citizens who had gathered below. Some were shocked, some disapproving, some screamed insults, but many were "moved to pity and compassion." Seeing this, the guards pulled Mary away from the window.[2]

Later, the Queen espied Maitland making his way through the crowds. According to one account, when she pleaded with him to come up and speak with her, he would not look at her and pulled his hat down over his eyes; Nau, however, recounts an interview between them, and Maitland himself later told du Croc that he had seen the Queen.

Nau says that, throughout the interview, Maitland was so full of shame that he did not once dare to raise his eyes and look her in the face. He told her that it was suspected and feared that she meant to thwart the execution of the justice demanded on the death of the late King, and that she was [to be] held in custody until everything had been done to authorise this investigation. He told her that the Council would never permit her to return to Bothwell, who, he said, ought to be hanged. Here he discoursed with something more than freedom on Bothwell's habits, against whom he manifested an intensity of hatred.

Having had a whole night in which to think about the bond that Bothwell had given her, Mary now seized her opportunity to confront Maitland. Nau says she was aware of "the false pretexts which the Lords were employing [in] charging her with wishing to hinder justice done for the murder which they themselves had committed. She knew that nothing terrified them so much as the prospect of an investigation." She therefore told Maitland that

she was ready to refute these accusations by joining with the Lords in the inquiry which was about to be made into the murder. As to Bothwell, Maitland knew, none better, how everything had been arranged, he, more than any other person, having been the adviser. She told him that she feared that he, Morton and Balfour, more than any others, hindered the inquiry into the murder, to which they were the consenting and guilty parties. Bothwell had told her so, who swore, when he was leaving her, that he had acted entirely by their persuasion and advice, and showed her their signatures. If she, a queen, was treated merely as one suspected of wishing to prevent the punishment of the criminals, with how much greater certainty could they proceed against him, Morton, Balfour and others, who were the actual murderers? They were all miserable wretches if they made her bear the punishment for their crimes.

The Queen threatened Maitland that,

if he continued to act in conjunction with these noblemen and plot along with them, she would publish in the end what Bothwell had told her about his doings. Seeing himself thus detected, Maitland became exceedingly angry. He went so far to say that, if she did so, she would drive him to greater lengths than he yet had gone in order to save his own life. On the other hand, if she let matters tone down little by little, the day would yet come when he might do her some good service. For the present, he begged she would not ask him to return to talk with her any more. It caused him to be suspected, and did herself no good. If his credit with the nobility were shaken, her life would be in great danger. It had already been frequently proposed that she should be put out of the way, and this he could prevent.[3]

Maitland may have said this partly to frighten Mary and partly to keep her quiet; it was the first intimation she had had that the Lords might not stop at merely imprisoning her. Her threat to use the Craigmillar Bond against him was probably the reason for its seizure by the Lords.

Maitland told du Croc that a weeping Mary had protested against being separated from Bothwell, but he had assured her that the Lords were thinking only of her honour and welfare. He added that she did not know what kind of man Bothwell was, and told her that he could show her a letter proving that the Earl regarded Jean as his true wife and Mary as no more than a mistress; a disbelieving Mary retorted that Bothwell's "letters to her disputed that." Maitland told du Croc, possibly with some exaggeration, that, although Mary had been miserable since her marriage, her passion for Bothwell was still as violent as ever, and that she had declared that she wished only to live and die with him, and that she would most willingly be put on a ship with him, to go where the winds might take them. Naturally, this was impossible, so instead, she proposed that Bothwell be allowed to go into exile, which Maitland agreed would perhaps be the best solution.[4]

Although she was constantly watched, the Lords later alleged that Mary had tried to smuggle out a letter to Bothwell, in which she addressed him as her "dear heart" and swore she would never forget or abandon him. The boy to whom this was entrusted promptly gave the letter to the Lords.[5] Of course, it is unlikely that such a letter ever existed, and almost certain that the Lords had invented it in order to give themselves a pretext for keeping Mary in custody, for their sole stated reason for doing so was to prevent her from communicating with Bothwell. If the letter had existed, it would have been logical for the Lords to keep it as justification for their actions. It would also surely have been mentioned in the *Book of Articles*, which was produced in 1568 on the Lords' behalf, but this claims that Mary had sent Bothwell, not a letter, but a purse of gold.

Despite the Lords' exhortations and promises of restoration to her throne, Mary consistently refused to abandon Bothwell. Drury wrote: "Though her body be restrained, yet her heart is not dismayed; she cannot be dissuaded from her affection to the Duke, but seems to offer sooner to receive harm herself than that he should."[6] Given the unhappy state of her marriage, it is more likely that it was the desire to protect her unborn child's rights, rather than affection for her husband, that dictated Mary's decision. Even though she now knew of Bothwell's complicity in Darnley's murder, she would not denounce her child's father. But, as will be seen, once her pregnancy was behind her, she was ready to renounce him. It suited the Lords, however, to portray their Queen as a woman who was in thrall to a murderer. Buchanan says she told them "that she would willingly endure the worst hardships of ill fortune with him, rather than pass her life in royal magnificence without him."

Clearly, Mary could not remain where she was. The mood of the citizens was generally ugly, and her safety could not be guaranteed while she remained in Edinburgh.[7] Also, there was always the chance that Huntly and the Hamiltons would arrive with an armed force to rescue her, and Bothwell was still at large. Furthermore, she was in possession of very dangerous knowledge and, as her threats to Maitland had proved, she was prepared to use it to her advantage.

The Lords met on 16 June and discussed what was to be done with the Queen. Some of them would have supported her restoration, had she agreed to give up Bothwell, but she had refused to co-operate, so all pretence of restoring her to liberty was abandoned. Du Croc told the nobles that, if they sent her to France, where her guilt had been made manifest, Charles IX would obligingly shut her up in a convent; but if, however, they called on Queen Elizabeth for assistance, the French would take Mary's side. Otherwise, the Lords might do as they pleased with her.[8] This left them with little choice. They dared not put the Queen on trial, in case she incriminated them, nor could they attaint her in her absence because Parliament could be summoned only by the monarch or a legally appointed Regent. Without a conviction, they could not execute her. The alternative was to imprison her in a place where she could do no harm. Grange was against this on the grounds that it contravened his assurances to Mary at Carberry Hill, but he was overruled, and it was at this point that Morton allegedly produced Mary's letter to Bothwell as proof that she was not prepared to keep her word either.[9] At length, the Council issued a warrant for her indefinite detention that was signed by Morton, Glencairn, Home, Mar, Atholl, Lindsay, Ruthven and others. It accused the Queen of "fortifying" Bothwell in his crimes instead of bringing Darnley's murderers to justice, and following "her own inordinate passion, to the final confusion and extermination of the whole realm": this was to be the official line from now on. She was therefore to be isolated to prevent her from communicating with Bothwell,[10] and, of course, to allow the Lords time to establish their own rule. According to Nau, "their one object was the usurpation of the crown, by means of the disastrous and abominable proceedings which had been planned before the departure of the Earl of Moray out of the kingdom." Their decision to imprison the Queen, however, was indisputably high treason.

During the evening of 16 June, Mary was escorted on foot by Morton and Atholl to Holyrood Palace,[11] preceded by the Darnley banner and 200 men, and followed by the other Confederate Lords and 1,000 of their soldiers. The people yelled insults, but Mary shouted back that she was innocent and that they had been deceived by false and cruel traitors. At the palace, much to her relief, she was reunited with Mary Livingston and Mary Seton, with whom she was allowed to relax for an hour or so. As she had hardly eaten for the best part of two days, supper was served to her, but before she could finish it, Morton, who was standing behind her chair, abruptly told her to make ready to leave at once with him. There was no time to pack anything, so all Mary took with her were the clothes she stood up in, a silk nightgown and a coarse brown cloak.[12] Outside, Lindsay and Ruthven were waiting for them, with horses ready saddled. Two chamberwomen and an escort of soldiers accompanied them.

Mary had no idea where they were going, and "Morton gave her to understand indirectly that she was going to visit the Prince."[13] But instead of riding west, they crossed the Forth at Leith, then rode like the wind for Kinross. At Loch Leven, the Queen was bundled into a boat and rowed across the lake to an island about one mile from the shore. On it stood Lochleven Castle; the Lords had decided that this isolated fortress should be the Queen's prison for the foreseeable future.[14]

On her arrival, Mary was in a state of collapse. She was received by the

Laird, Sir William Douglas, and conducted to a room on the ground floor. "The Queen's bed was not there, nor was there any article proper for one of her rank."[15] The next day, Morton left, leaving Mary in the custody of the brutal Lindsay and the hostile Ruthven.[16]

Lochleven Castle, which stands on one of four islands in the loch, lies thirty miles north of Edinburgh. In Mary's day, the castle island was smaller: due to drainage, there was a considerable fall in the water level of the loch during the nineteenth century. Although there had been a fortress on the island since the thirteenth century or before, the square five-storeyed keep dated from the fourteenth and fifteenth centuries, and the round tower and other buildings from the sixteenth. It was in this round tower that Mary would soon be lodged. The castle was owned by the Douglas family, but it had enjoyed quasi-royal status since the fourteenth century, having been visited frequently by successive Scottish monarchs. Mary herself had stayed there with Darnley.[17]

The choice of Lochleven was an obvious one, considering the connections of its owner. Sir William Douglas was Mar's nephew, Morton's cousin and Moray's half-brother. His mother, the formidable Margaret Erskine, Mar's sister, had been mistress to James V before her marriage to Sir Robert Douglas, and was Moray's mother. Euphemia, her daughter by Douglas, was Lindsay's wife. The Dowager Lady Douglas was fond of claiming that she had been married to the King and that her son was legitimate, so she can hardly have felt much warmth towards Mary. However, there is no record of her being spiteful or unkind to her; in fact, Mary was treated with courtesy by all.

Given the family's close connections with the absent Moray, the conclusion is inescapable that the Lords knew they could count on his approval of their imprisonment of the Queen. It is even possible that Lochleven had been chosen before his departure as a possible place of sequestration.

For two weeks after her arrival, Mary allegedly did not eat, drink or speak, "so that many thought she would have died."[18] Then her health and disposition improved somewhat. On 17 July, Bedford reported she was "calmer and better quieted than of late, and takes both rest and meat, and also some dancing and play at the cards, and much better than she was wont to do; and it is said she is become fat."[19] Despite himself, young Ruthven was smitten by her dangerous charm, and became a nuisance; he even promised to set her free if she would become his lover. Mary reacted with great indignation, and Ruthven was speedily removed.[20] After a month, Mary was moved into her new quarters, two rooms on the third floor of the tower, and permitted to walk in the castle gardens. In September, Mary Seton was allowed to join her. However, there was little privacy, for the Dowager Lady Douglas insisted on sleeping in the Queen's room. Fortunately, Mary did not know that Morton had ordered the Laird to kill her if Bothwell or anyone else attempted to rescue her, nor that the Lords had sent Sir James Melville to offer the office of Regent to Moray.

In order to pave the way for her deposition, the Lords were doing everything in their power to incite public opinion against the Queen. Protestant ministers denounced her from their pulpits as a murderess, and broadsheets were circulated emphasising her immorality. In England, Sir Walter Mildmay expressed the opinion that the Queen's fall was "a marvellous tragedy," but it was only what could be expected to befall "such as live not in the fear of God."[21]

The Lords were also systematically despoiling and redistributing Mary's property.[22] Glencairn and his men destroyed the altar and images in the chapel royal at Holyrood. The Queen's jewels were seized and set aside for Moray, who later sold her famous black pearls to Queen Elizabeth and passed on other pieces to his wife. When Mary heard what the Lords were doing, she realised that their intention was not just to keep her in custody until she agreed to abandon Bothwell.

Bothwell, meanwhile, had fled with Seton to the Borders to raise troops, yet met with little success. By 19 June, he was in Dunbar,[23] but left immediately to seek reinforcements, sailing with his followers for Linlithgow, whence he went west to Dumbarton.[24] Soon afterwards, Bedford reported that the Earl was building up a volume of support, and Bothwell himself later claimed that fifty men of rank had rallied to him for the Queen's sake. He claimed they all decided "that it would be advisable to wait for a little" before attacking Lochleven, for the Lords "would naturally be expecting us to mount a rescue attempt. Had we put this into effect, [the Queen's] life would certainly have been in great danger."[25] However, if this support had ever existed, it soon melted away.

For the present, the Lords made no move to take Bothwell, but, true to their promise to pursue and punish Darnley's murderers, they closed in on the lesser fish, Bothwell's henchmen, whose role in the Kirk o'Field conspiracy must have been known to them. By 11 June, they had already arrested Captain Cullen and clapped him in irons,[26] and on the 16th, Lord Scrope reported that, "after some strict dealing"—probably torture—Cullen "hath uttered and revealed the murder, with the whole manner and circumstance thereof."[27] This, however, is unlikely to have been true, as will be seen.

William Blackadder had also been arrested,[28] along with John Blackadder (perhaps his brother), James Edmonstoun and Mynart Fraser, a Swedish sailor, in whose ship the other three had been trying to reach Bothwell at Dunbar. But the vessel was captured, and when the four men were brought ashore at Leith, a mob tried to stone them. All were imprisoned in the Tolbooth.[29]

According to a statement made by Morton on 9 December 1568,[30] on 19 June, while he and Maitland were dining in Edinburgh, they received secret information, probably from Balfour, that three of Bothwell's servants—Thomas Hepburn, Parson of Oldhamstocks, John Cockburn (brother of Skirling) and George Dalgleish—had managed to gain entry to Edinburgh Castle. Buchanan later stated that Dalgleish had been sent by Bothwell to recover "a small silver casket bearing inscriptions which showed that it had once belonged to Francis, King of the French. In this, there were letters, nearly all of them written in the Queen's hand, in which the murder of the King and practically all that followed was clearly revealed. Balfour gave this casket to Bothwell's servant, but first he warned [the Lords]." Buchanan was writing propaganda for the Lords; as has been demonstrated, the authenticity of the letters to which he referred is by no means well founded, nor can there be any certainty that any of them were actually in the casket at this time. Furthermore, it is hardly likely that Bothwell would send his servants to ask Balfour for the casket after the latter had so treacherously betrayed him, especially if it contained anything compromising.[31] Bothwell must surely have heard by now that Balfour had gone over to the Lords, for it was common knowledge.[32]

Morton sent Archibald Douglas, Douglas's brother Robert, James Johnston of Westerrow and about thirteen of his own servants to the castle to search for and apprehend the three men, but when they got there, their quarry had already left, so Morton's men split up into three groups. Archibald Douglas could only find Hepburn's horse, for its master had fled; Cockburn was arrested by Johnston, but afterwards released, as he had no compromising evidence on him; and Robert Douglas tracked down George Dalgleish to a house in Potterrow, near Kirk o'Field itself. With him were found "divers evidences and letters in parchment, viz. the Earl of Bothwell's investments of Liddesdale, of the Lordship of Dunbar, and of Orkney and Shetland, and divers copies," which Robert Douglas brought to Morton with his prisoner.

When questioned, Dalgleish "alleged he was sent only to visit his master's clothing, and that he had no other letters or evidences but those which were apprehended with him; but, his report being found suspicious, and his gesture and behaviour ministering cause of distrust," he was kept under guard overnight and the next day taken to the Tolbooth to be tortured "for furthering of the truth."[33]

Terrified by the sight of the instruments of torment, "and moved of conscience," Dalgleish led Archibald and Robert Douglas back to the house in Potterrow, where he took from "under the foot of a bed" the locked silver casket that had allegedly belonged to Bothwell, which he said he had taken from the castle the day before, and gave it to them. At 8 p.m., it was delivered to Morton, who, "because it was late, kept it all that night." Dalgleish was returned to prison.[34]

That day, 20 June, Drury reported Mary's defeat and incarceration to Cecil, and wrote that the Confederate Lords were awaiting Elizabeth's approval and would not attempt any other enterprise "till they hear how this that they have already done be liked by the Queen's Majesty, at whose devotion it seems they desire to be, to be directed wholly by Her Majesty." He added that Cullen, Blackadder "and others" (among them Powrie, who was arrested around this time) had not yet been arraigned because the authorities had been unable to track down as witnesses the tenants of the cottages at Kirk o'Field, in which they believed these men had been hiding.[35] Meanwhile, the Lords and their acolytes had begun spreading rumours that the Hamiltons were heavily implicated in Darnley's murder. In July, there was speculation that Archbishop Hamilton himself would be charged with it.[36]

On 21 June, the silver casket was forced open in the presence of Morton, Maitland, Atholl, Glencairn, Tullibardine, Archibald Douglas and others, "and the letters within sighted." The Scots word "sicht" then meant "inspect" or "peruse,"[37] so, according to Morton, the letters were read, although many historians have misunderstood the meaning of the word "sichted" and disputed this. Immediately afterwards, the casket and its contents were delivered to Morton for safe keeping, "since which time [he stated in December 1568] I have observed and kept the same box, and all letters, missives, contracts, sonnets and other writings contained therein, surely, without alteration, changing, eking [adding] or diminishing of anything found or received in the said box. This I testify and declare to be the undoubted truth."[38] He was almost certainly lying.

It should be noted that there is no contemporary evidence, apart from Morton's statement, for the discovery of the casket. Had it contained the compelling evidence against the Queen that it was later held to contain—Buchanan says "the whole wicked plot was exposed to view"—it is astonishing that the Lords did not immediately use it against her in order to justify her proposed deposition. Morton's statement, however, merely says that the letters were sighted; it does not even say who wrote them. If letters in the Queen's handwriting had been found in a locked casket belonging to Bothwell, surely the Lords, considering their precarious position, would have seized upon them as evidence to support their coup, and Morton would surely have given some description of them and the shock they engendered. But the fact that Morton made no comment about the Lords' reactions to the letters on the day the casket was opened, and the fact that these letters were not at once made public and used against Mary, suggest that, if such a casket containing documents was found in the manner described, then the documents were of an innocuous nature, and deserving of little publicity.

It might not be stretching credulity too far to suggest that their discovery may have inspired the Lords to seek, or manufacture, letters that *could* be used to incriminate the Queen. Thus, when Buchanan came to compose the *Book of Articles*, which was made public at the same time as Morton's declaration, he could state that, in the casket, "there was found such letters of the Queen's own handwriting direct to [Bothwell] and other writings as clearly testified that, as he was the chief executor of the murder, so was she of the foreknowledge thereof, and that her ravishing was nothing else but a coloured mask."

On the day the casket was allegedly opened, or the day before, Robert Melville was sent to London to explain the Lords' actions to Elizabeth. There is no direct evidence that he took with him secret information about the Casket Letters, although Maitland did write to Cecil stating that the Lords' messenger would explain the reasons why he had taken sides against the Queen. Maitland, however, had taken sides against Mary fifteen days before the alleged discovery of the casket; he also said in his letter that "the best part of the nobility [had] resolved to look narrowly into [Bothwell's] doings, and being by them required, I would not refuse to join me to them in so just and reasonable a cause." He also asked Cecil for English money to finance the Lords' coup.[39]

More than three years later, Randolph was to report that, around this time, another casket was found in Edinburgh Castle. This was said to have been a small coffer covered with green cloth, which contained a copy of the Craigmillar Bond, and it was discovered, probably in Bothwell's apartments, by Balfour and Maitland.[40] Needless to say, this copy of the bond was suppressed.

On 25 June, Drury referred to a casket: "There is [news] here that the Queen had a box, wherein are the practices between her and France, wherein is little good meant to England."[41] Given the timing of this dispatch, it is certainly possible, even likely, that Drury was talking about the silver casket opened by the Lords, which was found to contain only diplomatic documents. If it had contained more contentious matter, the Lords would certainly have informed Drury of it, for they needed to justify their actions to Queen Elizabeth, whose reaction they feared. Drury again mentions this box in a report sent on 29 June, in which he says that the partly coded documents in it have been deciphered.[42] Again, there is no mention of their supposedly dramatic content.

On 21 June, the day the casket was purportedly opened, the Lords sat in Council, but no mention was made in the minutes of the casket or its contents, which is astonishing, given the reputedly sensational nature of the latter. Instead, the Councillors denounced Bothwell for keeping the Queen under restraint, ignoring the fact that they themselves were doing just that, and far more straitly.

That day, in London, de Silva reported that Mary was "five months gone with child,"[43] an obvious error that has nevertheless given rise to all kinds of speculation, since, if it had been true, then the child would have been conceived in the middle of January, when Darnley was ill with syphilis; the natural conclusion might be that Bothwell was the father, which lends credence to the allegations in the libels that Bothwell and Mary were lovers before Darnley's death, and also to the long Glasgow letter. It is more likely that de Silva's informant told him that Mary was five weeks gone with child. When she fell pregnant with James, reports of her condition circulated early, even before it was confirmed—ambassadors kept an eagle eye out for such things. With Mary and Darnley estranged, any hint of a pregnancy would have been scandalous, and thus would attract diplomatic attention, but there are no reports before May that Mary was expecting a child. If she had conceived in January, by late June her condition would have been difficult to conceal, and would soon have been detected by those in charge of her; moreover, her enemies would surely have made political capital out of it.

Mary still had some friends in Scotland. Huntly had remained loyal, and around 21 June, Argyll abandoned the Confederate Lords.[44] Together, they joined the Hamiltons, Lord Crawford and other royalist supporters at Dumbarton, where plans were laid for rescuing the Queen.

From June onwards, in order to exculpate themselves, the Lords did what everyone had urged Mary to do, and ruthlessly pursued a policy of arresting and executing the minor participants in Darnley's murder. There is no doubt that the evidence they obtained from these wretches, which may well have been extracted under torture, and was contained in a series of depositions, was censored, distorted and even invented in order to incriminate Bothwell, and later Mary—neither of whom was in a position to refute the allegations—and divert suspicion from the true culprits, the Confederate Lords themselves, who were now able to have the truth suppressed. Their efforts in this respect produced an official version of the murder that contains many inconsistencies and improbabilities, and can in many respects be proved false, as has been demonstrated. These arrests and executions may have gone some way towards satisfying the public's desire for retribution, but they left many questions unanswered, notably the matter of the Queen's guilt. Furthermore, the material in the depositions has only served to confuse historians, not a few of whom have accepted it as wholly factual, even though there is sufficient evidence to prove the contrary.

From the time they seized power, the Lords were in control of all sources of official information, and there is no doubt that they manipulated such information to their own advantage, for it was essential to justify their conduct towards their anointed sovereign. The chief victim of this policy would, of course, be the Queen.

On 23 June, William Powrie made a deposition describing the conveying of the gunpowder to Kirk o'Field, the details of which were sent by Drury to Cecil four days later; clearly, the Lords were anxious to prove their case to the English. However, on 3 July, Powrie made a second deposition, which contradicted many of the details in the first.[45] Whatever the truth of the matter, something underhand was certainly going on.

Bedford reported on 23 June that the Lords did not wish to imprison their Queen any longer than necessary, but would do as Elizabeth appointed,[46] which suggests that Cecil had all along been aware of their plans. On the 25th, the General Assembly of the Kirk met, and appointed George Buchanan as Moderator. Once Mary's tutor and admirer, Buchanan, a staunch Lennox man, had aligned firmly with the Protestant Lords, and would soon become the Queen's most effectively virulent enemy, spitting out his venom in tract after tract of highly readable propaganda so convincing that much of it is still believed today, flawed though it can be proved to be.

On 26 June, George Dalgleish was brought before the Council and made a deposition about Darnley's murder, in which it was made clear that he had played no active part. Strangely, he did not refer in it to the casket or its discovery, which, together with the fact that his name was not mentioned in connection with them until after he was dead, lends credence to the theory that its original contents were of little import.[47] Had incriminating letters been found, Dalgleish would have been a useful witness to their having been in Bothwell's possession. But it was only after his death, when the Lords had decided to put forward the Casket Letters as evidence against Mary, that the silenced Dalgleish became useful to them as the man who had allegedly led them to the letters.

As Dalgleish was making his confession, Bothwell was back in the Borders, assessing support, and that night he returned to Dunbar, where he no doubt learned of the arrest of his servants. The Lords may have been aware of his return, and, taking no chances, for it was certain that he would try to rescue the Queen and stir up trouble for them, they proclaimed a reward of 1,000 crowns for anyone apprehending Bothwell, and ordered the surrender of Dunbar Castle. Those who helped the Earl would be adjudged "plain partakers with him in the horrible murder."[48] That same day, in an Act of the Privy Council, the Lords announced that they had sufficient proof—"as well of witnesses as of writings"—of Bothwell's guilt, which some writers have understood to refer to the Casket Letters. This is possible, although the reference may be to the depositions. However, it seems likely that, by this time, the Lords had discovered, or forged, some letters that were suitable for their purpose.

Around the 26th, Robert Melville arrived in London with Maitland's letter to Cecil.[49] Certainly, on that day Cecil sent some packets to Moray in France, expressing the hope that he would return at once. Historians have speculated that these packets contained copies of the Casket Letters, but this is unlikely, because in August, Moray revealed to de Silva that he had not actually seen the letters, and seemed to know the contents of only one of them, of which he had heard from a man who had read it.[50]

On 27 June, William and John Blackadder, James Edmonstoun and the Swedish sailor, Mynart Fraser, were summarily tried by a new committee called the Lords of the Secret Council. William Blackadder insisted he was innocent, but he was tortured, found guilty of being "art and part" of Darnley's murder, then hanged and quartered at the Mercat Cross.[51] There is no record of the evidence on which he was convicted. Edmonstoun and John Blackadder were executed the following September, while Fraser was released and allowed to return to his ship.[52]

Around this time, according to Powrie, his friend William Geddes, of whom nothing more is known, made a deposition, but it was afterwards de-

JAMES HEPBURN,
EARL OF BOTHWELL
"A glorious, rash
and hazardous
young man."

JEAN GORDON,
COUNTESS OF
BOTHWELL
She was a woman
of strong character,
"a proper and virtuous
gentlewoman."

HERMITAGE CASTLE
Mary made a 60-mile round trip in a day to visit Bothwell here after he was wounded.

MARY, QUEEN OF SCOTS HOUSE, JEDBURGH
Mary stayed here in the autumn of 1566 whilst she was recovering from her nearly fatal illness.

MARY AND DARNLEY AT JEDBURGH
Contrary to what this picture suggests, Mary accorded Darnley
such a chilly reception that he left the next day.

CRAIGMILLAR CASTLE
It was here that the fateful chain of events that led to
Darnley's murder were set in motion.

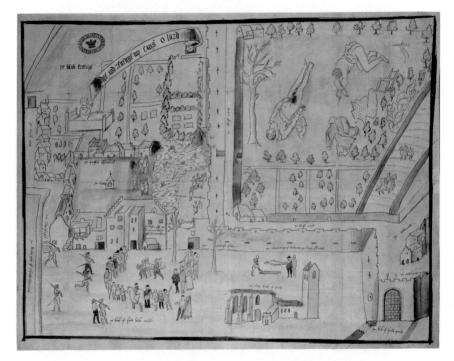

THE MURDER SCENE AT KIRK O'FIELD

The bodies of Darnley and his valet may be seen in the orchard (top right).
The ruins of the Old Provost's Lodging are shown to the left of the centre.
At the bottom (left), Darnley's body is carried away, while (right) his valet is buried.
At the top left, Prince James cries, "Judge and avenge my cause, O Lord."

THE DARNLEY MEMORIAL PAINTING
This vendetta picture was commissioned by Darnley's parents, the Earl and Countess of Lennox, who kneel behind James VI beside their son's tomb. To the right is Darnley's younger brother, Charles Stuart. Inset is a depiction of Mary's defeat at Carberry Hill. The painting is littered with inscriptions demanding divine vengeance on the murderers.

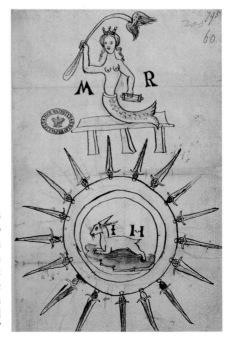

THE INFAMOUS MERMAID PLACARD
It depicts Mary as a prostitute, with Bothwell's hare crest below, and bears the legend, "Destruction awaits the wicked on every side."

DUNBAR CASTLE
Bothwell's power base served as a refuge for Mary after Rizzio's
murder, but was later the scene of her rape.

BORTHWICK CASTLE
After being besieged here by her enemies, Mary made a dramatic
escape dressed in male attire.

MARY IS LED AWAY FROM THE FIELD AT CARBERRY HILL
The Queen surrendered to the Lords, "thinking that she could go to
them in perfect safety, without fear of treachery."

LOCHLEVEN CASTLE
Mary was a prisoner here for ten
months before she escaped and fled to
England.

GEORGE BUCHANAN
"The author of slanderous
and untrue calumnies."

WILLIAM CECIL
"The Queen of Scots is, and always shall be, a dangerous person to Your Majesty's estate."

ELIZABETH I
She told Mary: "Your case is not so clear but that much remains to be explained."

THE CASKET LETTERS MAY HAVE BEEN KEPT IN THIS SILVER BOX
The letters contained "many matters unmeet to be repeated before honest ears." But were they genuine?

stroyed and he was set free.[53] Mary's servants, Sebastien Pagez and Francisco de Busso, were imprisoned in the Tolbooth, but they too were quickly released, as was "Black" John Spens, after he had delivered Bothwell's treasure chest to the Lords. It may be inferred from this that not all these interrogations had to do with Darnley's murder. Possibly through Balfour's good offices, Captain Cullen was also freed, without having made any deposition, which is very strange, considering he had earlier "uttered the whole manner of the murder," and had probably been present at Kirk o'Field. Presumably what he had uttered was in reality of little importance, although it had suited the Lords to declare otherwise.

In Paris, Sir Anthony Standen heard of the fate of the Queen and Bothwell, and of the subsequent arrests, and decided it was safer to spend his life in exile. In the event, "this banishment endured thirty years or more." The younger Standen remained in Scotland, but was imprisoned for a year in Berwick for remaining loyal to the Queen.[54] Black Ormiston and his uncle went into hiding in the Borders; the fate of Robert Ormiston is unknown, but his nephew survived to play a role in the Northern Rising of 1569–70 against Queen Elizabeth.

Du Croc left Edinburgh on 29 June, bearing a communication from the Lords to Charles IX and, it has been suggested, copies of the Casket Letters. The Lords wrote to King Charles that, "of further circumstances and of the whole affair, your ambassador can more fully advise Your Majesty, as we have fully informed him of the justice of our cause." They made no mention of the Casket Letters,[55] but in July, Throckmorton told Elizabeth that "du Croc carries with him matter little to the Queen's advantage, and the King may therefore rather satisfy the Lords than pleasure her,"[56] which has again been interpreted as a reference to the Casket Letters. It is certainly possible that the Lords had furnished du Croc with copies of at least one of the so-called Casket Letters in order to deter the French government from supporting Mary.

On 29 June, Mary's supporters at Dumbarton, notably Huntly, Argyll, Bishop Leslie, Seton, Fleming and the Hamiltons, signed a bond to liberate her.[57]

Such a coalition posed a threat to the Lords, so this would have been the optimum moment to produce the Casket Letters in order to inflame public feeling against the Queen. But the Lords did no such thing.

Queen Elizabeth had been outraged and incensed to hear of Mary's imprisonment. Of the Scottish Lords, she fulminated, "They have no warrant nor authority, by the law of God or man, to be as superiors, judges or vindicators over their prince and sovereign, howsoever they do gather or conceive matter of disorder against her. We are determined that we will take plain part with them to revenge their sovereign, for an example to all posterity. Though she were guilty of all they charge her with, I cannot assist them while their Queen is imprisoned."[58]

In her anger, Elizabeth's first impulse was to declare war, but a horrified Cecil dissuaded her. He and his fellow Councillors were in no way dismayed by what had happened north of the border, and realised that it was to England's benefit to have in Scotland a Protestant government desperate to build friendly relations with its neighbour. Yet Elizabeth had a different agenda. At the end of June, she decided to send that experienced diplomat, Sir Nicholas Throckmorton, to Scotland to bring about Mary's immediate restoration—by persuasion, treaty or force—and a reconciliation between her and her Lords. Once that had been achieved, Throckmorton was to demand that Darnley's murderers be hunted down and tried. At the same time, he was to persuade the Scots to agree to Prince James being brought up in England as Elizabeth's ward. Finally, he was to see Mary and deliver to her an encouraging message from Elizabeth. It was Elizabeth's hope that, in return for her restoration, Mary would ratify the Treaty of Edinburgh.

Not surprisingly, a gloomy and reluctant Throckmorton told Leicester that this was "the most dangerous legation in my life." He knew, all too well, that the Scots would not take kindly to English interference in their affairs.

It is often claimed that, by her intervention, Elizabeth probably saved Mary's life, for, had she given the Lords her support, they might well have executed their Queen. However, as has been noted, they had no legal basis on which they could do so, short of putting her on trial, which carried the risk of her publicly exposing their own guilt. There were, however, other ways of disposing of inconvenient sovereigns, and these Lords had not hesitated when it came to getting rid of Darnley. Throckmorton would soon reach the opinion that they meant to do away with Mary as well. It was the covert assassination of her cousin that Elizabeth almost certainly prevented. Alone of all the monarchs of Europe, the Queen of England, Mary's dynastic rival, was her champion at this time.

Nonetheless, she was shocked to hear reports that Mary was pregnant, for it was obvious that the child must have been conceived out of wedlock. If the reports were confirmed, she declared pessimistically, "It will be thought all was not well before."[59] It is unlikely that Elizabeth had much sympathy with Mary on a personal level. She told Throckmorton she had almost decided "to deal no more with her by way of advice, but look on her as a person desperate to recover her honour."[60] Elizabeth was more concerned to protect the institution of monarchy, and in particular female monarchy, which Mary, by her apparently rash behaviour, had undermined.

Before he left London, Throckmorton saw the Lennoxes. "My Lady wept bitterly, my Lord sighed deeply," he wrote. Lennox was already working in secret for Mary's abdication, and in July, he returned to Scotland. On 1 July, Throckmorton left London in a pessimistic mood, and travelled north with a heavy heart, only to be overtaken by a royal courier, who urged him to make haste.

Meanwhile, on 30 June, the Confederate Lords had issued a summons in Mary's name ordering Bothwell and his accomplices to appear in the Tolbooth on 22 August to answer charges in connection with the King's murder and the abduction of the Queen, or otherwise be "put to the horn," the Scottish term for outlawed.[61]

The next day, Melville informed Cecil that Balfour was now "in daily counsel" with the Council of Confederate Lords, along with James MacGill, the former Clerk Register.[62] Robert Melville had just returned to Scotland, and was sent immediately by the Lords to the Queen at Lochleven, to persuade her to abdicate or divorce Bothwell, but she refused to contemplate either. However, she said she was willing for the Lords to continue pursuing Darnley's murderers.

On 2 July, the Pope, having learned of the Bothwell marriage, broke off relations with Mary. He did not know, he said, which of the two Queens in Britain was the worse, and announced "that it was not his intention to have any further communications" with the Queen of Scots, "unless in times to come he shall see some better sign of her life and religion than he has witnessed in the past."[63]

Five days later, on receipt of Melville's invitation to return to Scotland to assume the office of Regent, Moray promptly left France for England on the first stage of his journey home,[64] having already sent ahead his secretary, Nicholas Elphinstone, to remonstrate with the Lords over their harsh treatment of his sister. Elphinstone passed through London on 8 July.[65] On the 9th, the Lords sent someone, possibly a man called John Wood, with letters from Maitland and Robert Melville for Moray in France.

De Silva made the first direct reference to the Casket Letters on 12 July; in a coded report, he wrote that he had heard from M. de la Forrest, the French ambassador in London, that "the Queen's adversaries assert positively that they know she had been concerned in the murder of her husband, which was proved by letters under her own hand, copies of which were in his [i.e., the ambassador's] possession."[66] The word "letters," in its sixteenth-century context, meant any document with letters in it, so de la Forrest could have been referring to one letter only. He had almost certainly obtained these letters from du Croc, who had arrived in London around 4 July. No further reference is made to these copies, but it is probable that they accounted for the French government's unwillingness to intercede on Mary's behalf. It is unlikely that the French would have publicised the immorality and guilt of one who so recently had been their Queen.

By 13 July, Throckmorton had arrived in Edinburgh to find "the most part of Scotland incensed against the Queen." The next day, he had an interview with Maitland, in which he aired Queen Elizabeth's indignation with the Lords, declaring that she would not endure to have their sovereign imprisoned, deprived of her estate or put in peril; indeed, Mary's offences were as nothing compared with the outrage committed upon her person "by those that are by nature and law subject to her."[67]

Throckmorton found Maitland wise and reasonable, but it soon became clear that the Lords had no intention of allowing him to see Mary, who, he was told, was being "guarded very straitly because she had refused to lend herself to any plans to seek out the murderers of her husband"—which was patently untrue—"or to abandon Bothwell." According to Maitland, she "avoweth constantly" that, if she had to choose between her kingdom and her husband, "she would rather live and die with him a simple damsel; she could never consent that he should fare worse or have more harm than herself." This may also have been a fabrication, but it conformed to the official line that the Lords were taking. "The principal cause of her detention is [that] the Lords, seeing her fervent of affection to him, fear, if put at liberty, she would so maintain him that they should be compelled to be in continual arms against him."

Maitland divulged that Argyll wanted Mary freed from her marriage so that he could marry her to his brother. He confided to Throckmorton that the Lords had no wish "to touch her in surety or honour, for they speak of her with reverence and affection and affirm that, the conditions aforesaid accomplished, they will restore her to her estate." However, she was in great peril of her life by reason of the common people, who were saying that their Queen had no more liberty nor privilege to commit murder or adultery than any private person. Thus the Lords dared not show lenity to the Queen because they feared "the rage of the people." Throckmorton had seen this hostility for himself, and formed the opinion that Mary's life really was in danger. Maitland, however, warned him against meddling, for "a stranger over-busy may soon be made a sacrifice among the people. It were better for us you would let us alone, than neither do us or yourselves good, as I fear in the end it will prove."[68]

That day, or soon afterwards, Nicholas Elphinstone arrived in Scotland, just as John Wood was entering London. As Elphinstone did not return to Moray, he may have had a watching brief in Scotland, and it could have been he, rather than Wood, who communicated details of one of the Casket Letters to Moray.

By 16 July, Bothwell had left Dunbar and sailed north in a further attempt to rally support. He had turned up at Huntly's castle of Strathbogie in Aberdeenshire,[69] but Huntly wanted nothing more to do with Bothwell, so the Earl was forced to withdraw to nearby Spynie Palace, the residence of the licentious Bishop of Moray, his great-uncle. On 17 July, having failed to respond to the Council's summons (when, in fact, he still had until 22 August to appear), Bothwell was declared an outlaw and stripped of all his titles, lands and offices.[70] From then on, his few supporters began to fall away, and royalist resistance to the Lords crumbled. Huntly withdrew to his northern fief, Seton and Fleming abandoned the Queen, and Jean Gordon left Crichton, telling the Countess of Moray she wanted nothing more to do with Bothwell.

Despite the Lords' injunctions, Throckmorton had already managed to make contact with Mary. On the 18th, he reported that he had found means to smuggle to her, in Robert Melville's scabbard, a note letting her know that he had been sent by Queen Elizabeth to help her; in it, he also warned her of "the great rage and fury of the people against her," and urged her, for her own sake, to give up Bothwell. Mary sent back a message that she was in daily fear of her life and in utter despair. Nevertheless, for all her desperate situation, she declared she would rather die than divorce Bothwell for, "taking herself seven weeks gone with child, she should acknowledge herself to be with child of a bastard and to have forfeited her honour" if she had the marriage dissolved. There were no dramatic protestations of love for Bothwell, such as the Lords had described. Throckmorton sighed, "I would to God that she were in case [a position] to be negotiated with."[71]

Throckmorton was in despair, convinced that the Lords would do away with Mary, despite Elizabeth's threats. By 20 July, he had heard that they intended to demand her abdication. Again, he smuggled a message via Robert Melville, urging her to agree to this to save her own life and her unborn child's, since an abdication under duress was illegal and could be rescinded and set aside once she was free. The Lords, however, were growing increasingly resentful of Throckmorton's interference, and on 20 July, Maitland again warned Sir Nicholas not to interfere in Mary's cause. "This is not the time to do her good," he said.[72]

Some time between 20 and 23 July, Mary miscarried of twins and suffered a severe haemorrhage, which left her in a greatly weakened state and bedridden for a time.[73] Throckmorton was told merely that she had had "two fits of an ague."[74]

Historians have long speculated as to the date these twins were conceived. Around 16 July, Mary had said she was seven weeks pregnant, which placed her conception around 28 May, during her month of marriage to Bothwell. Yet less than three weeks later, on 15 June, Bedford had reported, "The Queen is with child." If his report was accurate, then the conception must have taken place before the marriage. On 21 June, de Silva had claimed, probably incorrectly, that Mary was five months pregnant; he perhaps meant five weeks, although that would have been too early, given the limited medical knowledge of the sixteenth century, for a firm diagnosis of pregnancy. If Mary's estimate is followed, then she was eight weeks pregnant at the most when she miscarried. However, twin foetuses could not then have been identified at eight weeks: at 9–10 weeks, a foetus is only 1 inch long. If, however, the babies had been conceived at Dunbar, then the pregnancy would have lasted twelve weeks, and they would have been easily identifiable, for a foetus is 3.5 inches long at three months. Therefore, it seems that Mary either miscalculated, which was common in those days, or, for the sake of her reputation, made out that she had conceived during her marriage, when in fact she had done so soon after her abduction. Bedford's report was therefore accurate, for the pregnancy would have advanced seven weeks by the time he wrote, long enough to be a certainty. Women carrying twins often appear further advanced in pregnancy than those with a single baby, and this probably accounts for the report that Mary had become fat, which Bedford mentioned on 17 July.

De Silva, meanwhile, had spoken with Queen Elizabeth on the subject of the Casket Letters. "I mentioned that I had been told that the Lords had certain letters proving that the Queen had been cognisant of the murder of her husband." Elizabeth replied that "it was not true, although Lethington had acted badly in the matter," from which it may perhaps be inferred that she believed that Maitland had made up the letters. If she saw him, she added menacingly, "she would say something that would not be at all to his taste." It sounds as if Elizabeth knew more than she revealed to de Silva and that her comments were made in the light of intelligence from Scotland that the letters had been fabricated on Maitland's orders.[75]

On 21 July, Throckmorton reported that John Knox had returned in triumph to Edinburgh and was continually thundering from the pulpit against Mary and Bothwell, using his vigorous style of invective to demand that the Queen, that whore of Babylon, that scarlet adventuress, be put to death as a murderess. His violent preaching further inflamed the people's wrath against the Queen, especially when he threatened that God would send a great plague on the whole nation if Mary was spared from punishment. Nothing but the blood of the Queen would satisfy him, wrote Throckmorton.[76] However, even Knox could not persuade Argyll to rejoin the Confederate Lords, although he tried.

Also on 21 July, the Lords gave Throckmorton a document dated 11 July—two days before his arrival in Scotland—which they said was their reply to Elizabeth's demand for better treatment of Mary. In it, they blamed everything on Bothwell, that "notorious tyrant," and insisted they took "no pleasure to deal with our sovereign after this sort, as we are presently forced to do." But they had been forced to imprison her because,

> flat contrary to our expectations, we find her passion so prevail in maintenance of him and his cause that she would not with patience hear anything to his reproach, or suffer his doings to be called in question; but, by the contrary, offered to give over realm and all so she might be suffered to enjoy him, with many threatenings to be revenged on every man who had dealt in the matter. The sharpness of her words were good witnesses of the vehemence of her passion. She would not fail, enduring that passion, so long as any man in Scotland would take up arms at her command for maintenance of the murderer.

The Lords had therefore shut her up

> to sequestrate her person from having intelligence with him, to the end we might have a breathing time and leisure to go forward in the prosecution of the murder.[77]

No mention was made of the Casket Letters, which suggests that the Lords knew they were already on shaky ground where Elizabeth was concerned, and interestingly, the letter stated that Bothwell had imprisoned the Queen "by force": this is at variance with what the Lords were later to allege when they produced Casket Letters VI, VII and VIII, which were all intended to show that Mary had connived at her abduction, and which, if Morton is to be believed, were already in the Lords' possession at this date. It should also be noted that, although Knox and the people were demanding Mary's execution for Darnley's murder, the Lords had hitherto been careful so far not to charge her publicly with it, imputing all the guilt to Bothwell. This may have been because they did not wish to further alienate Queen Elizabeth. But it would not stop them from making threats, as will be seen.

Hearing that Mary was laid low by her miscarriage, the Lords seized their opportunity. On 24 July, Lindsay, Ruthven, Robert Melville and two notaries went to Lochleven with an instrument of abdication for the Queen to sign. Mary was in bed, weak from loss of blood and able to move "only with great difficulty,"[78] but spirited enough to refuse their demands and insist that she put her case before Parliament. At length, when Lindsay manhandled her and brutally threatened to cut her throat if she continued to resist,[79] she took Throckmorton's advice and capitulated, signing away her throne to her thirteen-month-old son on the grounds that she was "so vexed, broken and unquieted" by the responsibilities of her position that she was unable to continue carrying out her duties as Queen. She also signed letters appointing Moray Regent during James's minority, and authorising Morton and the Confederate Lords to govern Scotland until his return.[80] Repeatedly, she protested that she was signing under duress and would not be bound by these documents.[81]

The next day, not having been informed of Mary's abdication, Throckmorton informed Cecil that, according to Maitland, if she did not consent to the Lords crowning James, "they mean to charge her with these three crimes": tyranny, for breach and violation of the laws; incontinency with Bothwell and others, "having, as they say, sufficient proof against her for this crime"; and the murder of her husband, "whereof (they say) they have as apparent proof against her as may be, as well by the testimony of her own handwriting, which they have recovered, as also by sufficient witnesses,"[82] who were probably Bothwell's unfortunate henchmen. Some historians state that Mary was warned of this, and that her capitulation was evidence of her guilt, but it is clear that it was only a contingency plan in case she refused to abdicate. Had they threatened to try her on these charges and thus secured her submission, Lindsay would not have needed to threaten her with death. Throckmorton was pessimistic about the Lords' real intentions towards Mary, and warned, "It is to be feared, when they have gone so far, these Lords will think themselves unsafe while she lives, and take her life."[83]

On 26 July, Throckmorton pressed for his recall. "I see no likelihood to win anything at these men's hands," he told Cecil, and in another letter, confided to Leicester: "It is to be feared that this tragedy will end in the Queen's person as it did begin in the person of David the Italian and the Queen's husband."[84]

25

"False Calumnies"

MARY'S CONFESSOR, ROCHE MAMERET, HAD by now arrived in London, and on 26 July, de Silva reported an interview with him, in which Mameret had said that, until the question of Mary's marriage to Bothwell was raised, he had never seen a woman of greater virtue, courage and uprightness. He insisted that she had had no knowledge of Darnley's murder and that she was greatly grieved by it. Mameret disapproved of the collusive suits that had made the Bothwell marriage possible, which (he told de Silva) made it illegal, and also the Protestant nuptials, but said that Mary had sworn to him that she had married Bothwell with the hope of settling religion by that means. He assured the ambassador that "those who had risen against the Queen had not been moved by zeal to punish the King's murder, as they had been enemies rather than friends of his; nor [had they been moved] in consequence of the marriage, as they had been all in favour of it and had signed their names to that effect; but their sole object had been a religious one, as they thought the Queen, being a Catholic, might settle religion in a way not to their liking."[1] Mameret's view was somewhat narrow, for religion, of course, had not been the Lords' only motivating factor.

Having read Throckmorton's reports, an enraged Elizabeth defied Cecil and her Council, and wrote back on 27 July that she would not negotiate with the Scottish Lords while Mary was in prison, and that she was not impressed by the Lords' "colourable defences" of their actions. She told him to threaten war if they dared to depose or execute their mistress. That day, he reported that the Lords were undecided as to what to do with Mary.[2]

Wasting no time, the Lords hurriedly crowned the Prince, as James VI, at Stirling, on 29 July. For the first time in Scottish history, the ceremony was conducted according to Protestant rites. Knox preached the sermon, Mar carried the young King in his arms, and Morton and Home took the oath on James's behalf; but only thirteen peers were present, and the Hamiltons were excluded. Throckmorton, naturally, declined to attend. The ceremony was performed by Adam Bothwell, Bishop of Orkney—he who had married Mary and Bothwell—but the crown was too large for the baby's head, and had to be held above it. In the church, Lindsay and Ruthven took an oath that Mary had resigned her throne voluntarily. There were joyful celebrations in Edinburgh, and also at Lochleven, where Mary was made painfully aware of the reason for them.[3]

At the end of July, according to Throckmorton, Bothwell was still staying with his uncle at Spynie Palace. It would be fortunate, Sir Nicholas observed, if Bothwell were executed "or died by God's hand."[4] Soon afterwards, Bothwell was betrayed to his enemies by the Bishop of Moray's bastard sons, and was obliged to flee further north to Orkney, taking with him 200 followers.

Melville was making overtures to the Hamiltons, trying to induce them to join the Lords, but after being slighted at the coronation, the Hamiltons were in no mood for reconciliation. Years later, Melville wrote that he, Maitland and Grange were "secret favourers of the Queen" at this time, and "judged it fit that the whole country should be joined together in quietness, fearing that, in case civil war [broke out], it might endanger Her Majesty's life." Yet Maitland's behaviour towards Mary, as reported by Throckmorton, argued otherwise. On 31 July, Throckmorton declared to Leicester that he himself had saved the Scottish Queen's life, though to what continuance was uncertain.[5] His mission, after all, had not been entirely in vain, even if it had not achieved what Elizabeth wanted.

Moray had arrived in London on 23 July, and left on the 31st.[6] During his stay, he had meetings with Queen Elizabeth and de Silva; the latter reported that Moray had expressed sorrow for the conduct of the Lords towards the Queen, and "said he could not fail to strive for her liberty because, beside being her brother, he was much beholden to her; but still, Bothwell's business and the King's murder had much grieved him and had caused him to leave the country. He returned now to see what could be done in these troubles, although he feared they would be difficult to mend. Many of those concerned in the Queen's detention were his closest adherents," and if Bothwell liberated her by force, she might try to avenge herself on them. "He would therefore find some means by which she should remain Queen, but without sufficient liberty to do them any harm, whilst punishing at the same time the authors of the King's murder." De Silva "told him that the business might be remedied if Bothwell were put where the Queen is; and if he were captured, it might be easy to settle things. He thought so too, as he said, because they could kill him, and the Queen would then be free of him, and they would be safe."

Not knowing that Mary had already abdicated, Moray had said he hoped to avoid her deposition, but that the discovery of the Casket Letters made that unlikely. He had been sent from Scotland details of one of the letters by a man who had read it—perhaps Elphinstone—and told de Silva something of its contents, which he said "proved beyond doubt" that the Queen had been "cognisant of the murder of her husband." He added that he had not even told Elizabeth about it, "although she had given him many remote hints on the subject" of the Casket Letters.

The letter Moray described was said to have been written in Mary's handwriting on three sheets of paper, and to have been signed by her and sent to Bothwell. It said that he was

> not to delay putting into execution that which had been ordered because her husband [Darnley] used such fair words to deceive her and bring her to his will that she might be moved by them, if the other thing were not done quickly. She said that she herself would go and fetch him [Darnley], and would stop at a house on the road, where she would try to give him a draught, but if this could not be done, she would put him in a house where the explosion was arranged for the night upon which one of her servants was to be married. He [Bothwell] was to try and get rid of his wife, either by putting her away or poisoning her, since he knew that

she [Mary] had risked all for him, her honour, her kingdom, her wealth which she had in France, and her God, contenting herself with his person alone.[7]

Even allowing for details becoming garbled in the telling, and a couple of vague similarities to the text of Casket Letter II, this letter cannot be identified with any of the Casket Letters as they are known today. To begin with, it was signed by Mary; none of the Casket Letters bear signatures. Secondly, it was allegedly written before Mary went to Glasgow to fetch Darnley; the first of the known Casket Letters was meant to have been sent from Glasgow. Thirdly, it mentions poison as the preferred method of killing, which Mary is going to administer herself; in Casket Letter II, there is only a reference to "a more secret invention by medicine" that Bothwell is to find, while the blowing up of the house is not referred to in any of the letters. Fourthly, it shows Mary urging Bothwell to divorce or poison his wife—again, this is not mentioned in the letters that survive, although Buchanan refers to it appearing in a letter Mary wrote to Bothwell from Glasgow. Fifthly, how could Darnley be using fair words to Mary if he was absent in Glasgow? Relations between them had been so bad before his departure that Mary could in no way have anticipated that he would speak to her so movingly.

This all suggests that the letter of which details were sent to Moray was an early attempt by the Lords at forgery or manipulation that was later rejected in favour of something more subtle. Buchanan certainly knew of this letter, and so did Lennox, as will be seen. If it had been genuine, then it would have provided prima facie evidence against Mary that would have bolstered the Lords' case; but it was never used against her, which argues its spuriousness. Why it should have been rejected in favour of other letters that were less explicit is a mystery, for subtlety was not a feature of the Lords' propaganda campaign against Mary. The only explanation can be that, when it came to producing this letter in public as evidence, the Lords realised that there was something in it that betrayed its dubious authenticity.

Moray told de Silva that the worst thing Mary had done, in his opinion, was to pet and fondle Darnley only hours before he was murdered with her connivance. He was appalled by it, and "grieved for the honour of his father's House." The perceptive de Silva was not taken in by Moray's protestations of goodwill towards Mary. "By his manner of speech and the difficulties he raised, it seemed to me that, although he always returned to his desire to help the Queen, this is not altogether his intention. I gather that the Lords can depend on him better than his sister can, although he says he will do his best for her. I am more inclined to believe that he will do it for himself, if he finds a chance."[8]

By 5 August, Throckmorton was more optimistic about gaining Mary's consent to a divorce: now that she had miscarried, there was nothing to bind her to Bothwell any more, apart from the hope that he would rescue her. Throckmorton reported that all his efforts were now directed towards saving her life rather than restoring her to the throne.[9] Two days later, the news of Mary's abdication reached London, and an enraged Elizabeth's first reaction was to recall Throckmorton and snarl about declaring war on the Lords.[10] Her plan was either to send English troops to Scotland, or to bribe the Hamiltons to rise against the Lords on Mary's behalf, but Cecil warned her that her intervention might cost Mary her life. Elizabeth furiously accused him of being lukewarm in Mary's cause, but, as they were arguing, Throckmorton's letter arrived, which lent weight to Cecil's warning and made Elizabeth pause. Four days later, she changed her mind and decided not to make war on the Scots. Instead, she ordered Throckmorton to stay at his post and promote the Regency of Moray, which seemed the best guarantee of Mary's safety; however, if the Lords harmed Mary in the meantime, Throckmorton was to threaten them in the strongest terms with England's vengeance. However, by 9 August, Throckmorton had managed to wring a promise from Maitland that Mary "shall not die any violent death unless some new accident chance"; he was now, more than ever, convinced that he had saved her life.[11]

Bothwell had just arrived in the Orkney Isles in the far north, where he made an attempt to raise more men, but was thwarted by the machinations of Balfour's brother Gilbert, Bailiff of Orkney, who prevented him from establishing a secure base on the islands. He and his followers therefore took to piracy, harrying English and Danish shipping from the four men-of-war that, as Lord Admiral of Scotland, he had commandeered before sailing north.[12]

The Lords were now determined to pursue Bothwell and kill him, and on 10 August, the Dundee authorities were ordered to fit out four ships for an expedition against him, which was to be led by Kirkcaldy of Grange and Tullibardine. That day, Grange wrote to Bedford: "Although I be no good seaman, I promise he [Bothwell] shall either carry me with him, or else I shall bring him dead or quick to Edinburgh."[13]

Moray returned to Edinburgh on 11 August, to a rapturous welcome on the part of those who regarded him as their Protestant saviour, and immediately took control of the government.[14] Some of the Lords feared that Moray would be too lenient with his sister, while Argyll, Boyd, Livingston and others tried to negotiate with him for her release, with no success. Tullibardine urged her death, on the grounds that, if freed, she might marry again and have issue, which was a thing to be feared. Again, Throckmorton begged the Lords not to execute Mary, and warned that her death might provoke the Hamiltons to attempt the throne. Maitland replied smoothly that he had heard from Archbishop Hamilton that the Hamiltons, who had hitherto supported Mary, were in favour of her being executed, for then all the nobles would be able to come together without fear of the future.[15]

The Hamiltons had, until Mary's abdication, been plotting a marriage between her and Lord John Hamilton, Chatelherault's second son, which they hoped would follow her mooted divorce from Bothwell, and which would ensure a Hamilton succession. Now they were ready to betray her, having realised that only the life of an infant lay between them and the throne. That this was their motivation is clear from the fact that, as a condition of their support for the Lords, they insisted that Darnley's brother, Lord Charles Stuart, be excluded from the succession. Throckmorton was disgusted that noblemen "could have such double faces and such traitorous minds."[16]

By 13 August, Balfour had resigned his governorship of Edinburgh Castle to Grange,[17] in return for "a large grant of money" and church lands, an acquittance of all concern in Darnley's murder—which would not have been necessary had he not been involved—and Moray's priory of Pittenweem in Fife.[18] Throckmorton says he left "on good composition" with the Lords,[19] but Grange was obviously the better man for the job. Later, Balfour was made President of the Court of Session.

On 15 August, Moray visited Mary at Lochleven. She greeted him with "great passion and weeping," but he was "cold and reserved." It was a painful meeting, in which he caused her great distress by his reproaches for her conduct, and gave her "such injurious language as was likely to break her heart. The injuries were such as they cut the thread of love betwixt him and the Queen for ever." Mary insisted she was "innocent of all that could be laid to her charge" and that God would in the end "manifest her innocence," but after she had objected to Moray being appointed Regent, he left her with "nothing but the hope of God's mercy."[20]

When he returned the next day, his mood was more conciliatory. He told Mary that he could not obtain her liberty, but "would assure her of her life and, as much as lay in him, the preservation of her honour" by preventing the publication of her letters, but if she made trouble and persisted in her inordinate affection for Bothwell, her life would be in peril and he would not be able to save her. However, if she lamented her past sins, "so as it might appear she detested her former life and intended a more modest behaviour," and if she showed abhorrence for Darnley's murder and "minded no revenge to the Lords and others who had sought her reformation," she might "one day be restored to the throne." Believing this, Mary kissed Moray and begged him to accept the Regency.[21]

In London, later that month, Lady Lennox told de Silva that "the Queen of Scots admitted to her brother that she knew the conspiracy for her husband's murder."[22] Moray, however, made no mention of this in his account to Throckmorton. Lady Lennox was naturally happy to spread any calumny about the woman who, she believed, had murdered her son.

Moray returned to Edinburgh on 19 August. After speaking with him, Throckmorton reported that Moray meant to have obedience to the young King's government if it cost him his life. However, he was not disposed to execute Mary, or keep her in perpetual prison. It was clear to Throckmorton that, rather than sympathising with Mary, Moray concurred with the Lords, "yea, and as seriously as any one of them."[23]

By 14 August, Bothwell and his fleet had arrived in the Shetland Isles, where he hired two more ships.[24] Five days later, Grange and Tullibardine embarked with nine warships to seek him out. They sailed first to Orkney, then, finding he was not there, pressed on to Shetland.

Moray was proclaimed Regent on 22 August.[25] Scotland now had a

Protestant government, swept to power on a platform of public virtue, and committed to bringing Darnley's murderers to justice. Moray proved a popular ruler and a good administrator. He restored order to the troubled kingdom, and peace in the Borders—in January 1568, Drury was to report that that troublesome region had not been quieter for forty years.[26] The Hamiltons, however, did not welcome Moray's appointment.

Moray trusted Maitland no more than Mary did, suspecting—possibly with good reason—that the Secretary was a secret supporter of the Queen, although Melville says that all who found fault with the Regent's harsh attitude towards his sister "lost his favour." From the first, Moray banned Maitland from his counsels, and thereafter, the former colleagues were on increasingly bad terms.

Elizabeth, not surprisingly, refused to recognise either Mary's abdication or James VI's title and Moray's Regency, and recalled Throckmorton immediately (he left on 30 August). In response, a sanguine Moray wrote with some insight to Cecil: "Although the Queen's Majesty your mistress outwardly seems not altogether to allow the present state here, yet doubt I not but Her Highness in her heart likes it well enough."[27] For the time being, as if to confirm the truth of this, Elizabeth—having realised that the French did not intend to interfere in Scotland—made no serious efforts to restore Mary or overthrow Moray. Although diplomatic relations between England and Scotland had been officially broken off, Moray and Cecil continued to correspond in private. And while Moray told Cecil that his new office was neither welcome nor pleasing,[28] there is no doubt that the change of government suited both very well.

Grange's ships reached the Shetlands at the beginning of September, but Bothwell narrowly evaded capture and was driven by gales towards Norway with two men-of-war and 140 men; among them, perhaps, was Paris.[29] Bothwell's other ships were taken, however, and Hay, Hepburn and Cullen, being found on board, were placed under arrest before being conveyed back to Edinburgh, where they were thrown into prison. When interrogated, Hay initially told his captors that Bothwell and Huntly had murdered the King.

Bothwell later claimed that his plan was to go to France by way of Denmark, "where I could make arrangements for the dispatch of troops and naval forces to Scotland." He felt sure that Mary would approve of this move, "but to make certain of this, I managed to get details of this plan to her. In her opinion, [it] was excellent, and she begged me to put it into effect as soon as possible."[30] Bothwell does not reveal his means of communication with Mary, but it is clear that some people at Lochleven were becoming increasingly sympathetic towards her, and one of them may have smuggled messages. A holograph letter from Mary was later found on Bothwell's ship: in it, she complained of the treatment meted out to her by the Lords, and lamented that no friends had stood by her, so it must have been written after she was confined at Lochleven.[31] It is unlikely, given that Mary was constantly watched while she was in the Black Turnpike, that she had managed to get out a letter to Bothwell from there, as the Lords claimed she had tried to do.

But Bothwell's scheme did not work out as he had planned. On 2 September, his ship sailed into Bergen, where it was his misfortune to be recognised by Anna Throndssen, the woman he had jilted after promising to marry her, and various other creditors, who took their complaints to Frederick II, King of Denmark and Norway.[32] As a result, at the end of September, Bothwell was placed in honourable confinement in Copenhagen Castle while Frederick decided what was to be done with him.[33] It did not help that there had also been found on Bothwell's ship a copy of the proclamation branding him as the murderer of the King and an outlaw with a price on his head; nor that, during his short rule in Scotland, Bothwell had shown himself friendly towards Sweden, with whom Frederick was at war. Nevertheless, his imprisonment was not entirely punitive, for the King was well aware of Bothwell's importance as a useful political hostage.

On 5 September, Bedford reported that Hay had made a deposition revealing "the whole device of the murder, declaring who were the executioners of the same, and went so far as to touch a great many, not of the smallest."[34] Drury informed Cecil that Hay was being spared until the great personages he had accused could be arrested.[35] But this did not happen. Obviously Hay had "touched" far too many people, for on 13 May, he made a second deposition, accusing only Bothwell.[36] The other names had evidently been suppressed.

Sandy Durham was also in the Tolbooth at this time, but there is no record of what happened to him. On 15 September, Moray, reporting the return of Grange and Tullibardine with their prisoners, commented that few of those taken were "notable men, excepting Cullen, who chanced by God's provision in our hands, and being his chamberchild and one of the very executors, he may make us clear in the whole action as it proceeded."[37] Moray's meaning is obscure: was Cullen Bothwell's cabin-mate on board ship, and did the Regent hope to get from him an account of how Bothwell had managed to escape? Or, which is more likely, had Cullen been Bothwell's protégé (the word "chamberchild" may have homosexual connotations) and one of the "executors" of Darnley's murder, and was Moray hoping that he would give details of it to the Lords? If so, why did Moray not rely on Cullen's earlier testimony, in which he had revealed "the whole manner and circumstance" of the murder? He may have desired to hear it for himself, having been out of Scotland in July, or he may have wanted it put into the form of a deposition, none having been taken before. What is more likely, however, is that Cullen had revealed nothing useful during his earlier interrogation, but that Moray believed that he was able to do so. When this proved not to be the case, Cullen was released. He was next heard of in 1570–1 as an officer of the Edinburgh garrison. Hepburn did not make a deposition until 8 December.[38]

It seemed that Mary's cause was hopelessly lost. On 15 September, Argyll and Huntly came to terms with Moray, and Argyll was given a place on the Regency Council.[39] But the Hamiltons were determined to overthrow Moray, and had formed their own confederacy for this purpose. At a meeting in September, they announced their appointment of Lord John Hamilton (acting for the exiled Chatelherault), Argyll and Huntly as regents, and stated that the aims of their confederacy were to pursue Darnley's murderers and liberate Mary. But their embryonic coup was easily suppressed by Moray, whose rule was rapidly gaining popular support.[40] On 1 October, Dunbar Castle, which had been held for Bothwell by his adherent Patrick Hay of Whitelaw against the Lords since the Earl's flight, finally fell (the Lords had it destroyed in 1568). The only fortress left in royalist hands was the mighty stronghold of Dumbarton in the west which was being held by Lord Fleming for the Queen. Also on 1 October, a long list of sixty-two Summonses of Forfeiture for the murder of the King was drawn up by the Council. Naturally, there were some significant omissions: none of the Douglases, for example, were mentioned. Soon afterwards, Lord Herries, who had supported the Queen, submitted to Moray, although he privately remained loyal to Mary. By the middle of October, Moray was able to tell Cecil that Scotland was quiet.[41] Even Elizabeth had come to terms with the fact that she could do nothing to change the situation there.

On 11 November, Moray appointed Morton Chancellor in place of Huntly. That month, the Lords acquitted Bothwell's uncle, the Bishop of Moray, of complicity in Darnley's murder, which was absurd, considering that the Bishop had never been implicated in it. This may, however, have been a politic exercise to demonstrate the fairness and impartiality of the Lords, who were prepared to acquit Bothwell's partisans as well as condemn them.

At the end of September, Drury had reported that Mary had put on weight and, "instead of choler, makes a show of mirth." In October, Bedford wrote: "The Queen is as merry and wanton[42] as at any time since she was detained," and had "drawn divers to pity her, who before envied her, and would her evil." Now, on 28 November, Drury gleefully reported "a suspicion of over-great familiarity" between the Queen and eighteen-year-old George Douglas, brother of Sir William, which had increased "more and more, and [is] worse spoken of than I may write."[43] In December, Drury wrote that Mary had asked Moray to consent to her marriage to Douglas, once she was free of Bothwell—whom she was no longer refusing to abandon—but that Moray had told her that Douglas "was overmean a marriage for Her Grace."[44] Mary may have seen Douglas as a means of escape, but Cecil claimed that Douglas had fallen into "a fantasy of love" with her. Nau, however, gives the impression that his affection for Mary was chivalrous and platonic, but whatever its nature, he was still sent away from Lochleven. Furthermore, the rumours reported by Drury gave rise to the later bruit that Mary had borne Douglas a child.

Drury also reported on 28 November that the Lords had met to discuss the documents in the silver casket. He revealed that "the writings which did comprehend the names and consents of the chiefs for murdering of the King are turned to ashes," but that evidence incriminating Mary had been "kept to be shown"[45] at the Parliament that had just been summoned to meet in December. The "writings" that had been destroyed almost certainly included the copy of the Craigmillar Bond that Bothwell had entrusted to Mary, which Argyll must have surrendered to Moray. The destruction of the Craigmillar

Bond is proof of the Lords' awareness that it incriminated them in Darnley's murder and that they could not therefore use it against Bothwell. It has been claimed that they would hardly have informed Drury of its destruction, but there were among the Lords a growing number of those who secretly supported Mary, and his informant may well have been one of them.

On 4 December, emboldened by the success of their coup and the support of the people for their government, the Lords framed an Act of Council formally charging Mary with Darnley's murder, and also with an intent to murder her son. The Act stated that "the cause and occasion of the taking of the Queen's person on 15 June last was in the said Queen's own default, inasfar as by divers her privy letters written and subscribed with her own hand, and sent to James, Earl of Bothwell, chief executioner of the horrible murder, it is most certain that she was privy, art and part, and of the actual devise and deed of the murder of the King, her lawful husband." The document was signed by Morton, Maitland and Balfour, all of whom had been implicated in the murder, and twenty-seven others. This was the first official reference to the Casket Letters, and the first occasion on which the Lords formally accused Mary of Darnley's murder. They had realised by now that they were unlikely to lay hands for some time on their first scapegoat, Bothwell, so they had decided to bring Mary to justice instead, for several reasons. They had to justify their continuing imprisonment of her now that she had abandoned Bothwell, satisfy the people's thirst for vengeance, damn the swelling wave of sympathy for the imprisoned Queen by a timely reminder of her misdeeds and crimes, and at the same time remove a possible focus for rebellion. Above all, they needed to justify their deposition and imprisonment of the Queen in Parliament, and thereby safeguard themselves from charges of treason. For many days, the Lords had debated what to do about the Casket Letters before coming to the conclusion that the only course to take was to "open and reveal the truth of the whole matter from the beginning, plainly and uprightly, which, insofar as the manifestation thereof may tend to the dishonour of the Queen, they are most loath to enter in."[46] Nevertheless, they were going to do it.

Attention should be drawn to the fact that, in the Act, the Lords stated that the reason they had taken the Queen into custody on 15 June was the proof of her guilt that was evident from the Casket Letters, yet these letters were not in fact discovered until nearly a week later. Furthermore, the Act is known to us through a copy sent to Cecil; it is not mentioned in the record of the Council's proceedings for 4 December 1567 that is preserved in the Register House in Edinburgh.

On 8 December, Mary reached twenty-five, the age at which Scottish sovereigns were deemed to have attained their majority, and at which they could rescind any grants of land bestowed during their minority. Aware that Parliament was soon to assemble, she wrote to Moray on that day, begging to be allowed to appear before Parliament to "vindicate her innocence" and

> answer the false calumnies which had been published about her since her imprisonment. She would submit herself to all the rigour of the laws, according to which she earnestly desired that proceedings should be taken for the punishment of all persons who might be found guilty of the murder of the late King. There was no law which permitted anyone to be condemned outright without his cause having been heard, if it touched but the welfare of the least of her subjects. It was much more reasonable, then, that justice should be done to her, their Queen, in a matter which touched her honour, which was dearer to her than her life.

Moray sent back a brisk refusal.[47] There was a high degree of self-interest involved in his decision, as well as political considerations. Too many of the Confederate Lords had received grants from Mary, and they were determined that she should never have the opportunity of cancelling them.

Nau claims that, at this time, Moray was scheming to make himself King, taking the view that he "could presently rid himself" of young James. "Many of his party were now earnest with him to declare himself King. With these views, Moray had employed various persons to discover how he might establish his legitimacy by proving the marriage which he was now advised to assert as having been secretly contracted between King James V and his mother, although she was then married to another man. This proposition was then abandoned, for Moray saw there was faint hope of the success which he had expected."

Parliament met on 15 December, and passed an Act declaring that Mary's abdication, James's coronation and Moray's Regency were all "lawful and perfect." Another Act ratified "the retention of our Sovereign Lord's mother's person" and stated that the conduct of the Lords had been fully justified by her actions, "inasmuch as it was clearly evident, both by the evidence from divers her privy letters written wholly with her own hand to the Earl of Bothwell, and her marriage to Bothwell, that she was privy, art and part, of the actual devise and deed" of Darnley's murder. The Act had effectively tried and condemned Mary without her being heard. There were objections from Huntly, Herries and others, but they were speedily overruled.[48]

Some historians have made much of the fact that the words "and subscribed," which appeared in the Act of Council of 4 December, do not appear in the Act of Parliament. None of the Casket Letters that were later produced in evidence against Mary was signed, and it may be that the Lords noticed their error in the Act of Council and were quick to amend it in the Act of Parliament. It has also been suggested that the Act of Council found among Cecil's papers is a forgery,[49] but why such a document should have been counterfeited is a mystery. In addition it has been claimed that the signatures and addresses were removed from the Casket Letters between 4 and 15 December.[50] Yet the discrepancy may be due to simple error: after all, Bothwell is referred to as "James, Earl of Bothwell" in the Act of Council, and as "James, sometime Earl of Bothwell" in the Act of Parliament.

A declaration by the Queen's loyal nobles issued at Dumbarton in 1568 stated that "Her Majesty's writing" was "produced in Parliament";[51] in this document, the "writing" is constantly referred to as "it," which suggests that only one piece of writing was produced. Yet there is no mention of this in any other source. If one or more of the Casket Letters were indeed produced in Parliament, no one questioned their veracity. There were too many vested interests involved and too many reputations to protect.[52]

Between 15 and 20 December, Parliament re-enacted the legislation of the Reformation Parliament of 1560, and restated the Protestant Confession of Faith, which was the cornerstone of the reformed Kirk. It also repeated the Act of 1564 that declared Mary of age, so that no one could say that the Lords had forced a minor to abdicate. On 20 December, Parliament ratified the forfeiture of Bothwell's titles and estates and declared him guilty of treason. This Act stated that the Queen had "suspected no evil from any of her subjects, least of all from him," which appeared to exonerate her of the crimes of which she had just been declared guilty.[53] On the day this Act was passed, Caithness protested, on behalf of all the jurors at Bothwell's trial, that the evidence had not been adequate to justify his condemnation.[54]

On 6 February 1568, Archbishop Beaton reported that Moray had been determined to prosecute Archbishop Hamilton in Parliament "on the plea that he had a hand in the murder, which is only a calumny." If the report was true, Moray stayed his hand, but Lennox and his supporters certainly believed in the Archbishop's guilt, which would have serious consequences for him later on.

When Mary heard of the Acts passed against her, she was horrified at these terrible slurs upon her honour, and fearful that she was in danger of death. In desperation, she appealed to both Elizabeth I and Catherine de' Medici for help, but neither responded. In fact, each was more concerned to outbid the other for Mary's black pearls, which, as has been noted, Moray finally sold to Elizabeth.

Around this time, Moray, Morton, Balfour and others visited Mary at Lochleven, but they showed her "such contempt and disdain that the breach ever afterwards grew wider. Moray could never bear her to insist, as she did earnestly and continually, that she ought to be discharged of the crimes imputed to her, about which she was much more solicitous than for her life and the re-establishment of her authority." Mary showed herself particularly contemptuous of Balfour, who had betrayed her and Bothwell twice in June, and called him an "arch traitor" to his face, which caused him to hide himself behind the other Lords, "reddening excessively."[55]

By 22 December, only seven of the sixty-two persons summoned for Darnley's murder remained at liberty: the Ormistons, James Murray, Patrick Wilson, Paris and two others. Wilson had disappeared, and was never caught. The Ormistons were still hiding out in Liddesdale, in the house in which Ker of Fawdonside was being held under arrest. Murray was in exile in England, and Paris was probably in Denmark with Bothwell.

Argyll, Huntly and Herries formally recognised Moray as Regent on 29 December,[56] but although it seemed that Mary's former supporters had one by one fallen away, by the end of that fateful year of 1567, public opinion was changing in her favour.

The new year of 1568 began with a public spectacle in Edinburgh, calculated to satisfy the demands of the people for justice and retribution. On 3 January, Hay, Hepburn, Powrie and Dalgleish were tried for treason and condemned, then immediately hanged and quartered at the Mercat Cross. According to their depositions, neither Powrie nor Dalgleish had done anything to merit death, but these depositions may not reflect the real truth, and anyway the Lords were not concerned with such niceties. The dismembered corpses of the executed wretches were displayed on pikes above the gates of Glasgow, Hamilton, Dumbarton, Ayr and other western towns, where support for Mary was strongest.

Drury claimed that, on the scaffold, Hepburn had declared that Huntly, Argyll and Maitland had all signed the bond for Darnley's murder,[57] and the *Diurnal of Occurrents* claims that Hay also named Bothwell, Balfour and "divers other nobles of the realm" and said that "Balfour and Maitland were notoriously known as the principal advisers and counsellors"; but this dying testimony was never offered in evidence against any of those named. Archbishop Beaton informed the Cardinal of Lorraine that all four of the condemned "confessed that they had amply deserved the punishment of death, yet declared the Queen's innocence, and accused the greatest and chiefest on [the] Council, who were at that time sitting beside [them], especially Morton, Lethington and Balfour, and their own master, the Earl."[58] This testimony gave rise to uncomfortable rumours in Edinburgh that the servants were being made scapegoats for the masters, as well as demands that the Lords named "should suffer for their demerits," and a fresh series of placards and broadsheets began to appear. One was posted outside Moray's town house, and another to the very wall of the Council Chamber in the Tolbooth, which asked, "why John Hepburn and John Hay were not compelled openly to declare the manner of the King's slaughter, and who consented thereto?" This whispering campaign served to bolster the Queen's cause, especially when it became known that the nobles named by the condemned men had "incontinently departed" from Edinburgh, "which [made] the charge against them all the more probable."[59]

The Lennoxes were still convinced that Bothwell and Mary were the sole authors of their son's slaughter, and in January 1568, they commissioned a memorial picture to proclaim to the world the deep sense of injustice they felt. Painted by a Dutchman, Livinius de Vogelaare, it shows Darnley's mourning parents and younger brother kneeling before his armour-clad effigy in the chapel royal at Holyrood. In front of them kneels Darnley's son, the infant James VI, and in the corner is a vignette of Mary's defeat at Carberry

Hill. The picture is littered with inscriptions, but most have been obliterated by time and clumsy restoration; one reads, "Arise, Lord, and avenge the innocent blood of the King my father." The memorial was painted in London, and therefore does not give an accurate impression of Darnley's real tomb, but its real impact was meant to be as a piece of powerful political propaganda, intended to provoke Queen Elizabeth to demand the ultimate penalty for Mary and the extradition of Bothwell, who was to suffer the same fate. Elizabeth's petition to Frederick II to send Bothwell back to Scotland to face trial failed, and the Lennoxes did not live to see the execution of Mary on the English Queen's orders, but *The Memorial of Lord Darnley* survives in the Royal Collection at Holyrood Palace as a searing testimony to their terrible and vengeful grief.[60]

In faraway Denmark, having just been transferred to Malmoë Castle, on the opposite shore of the Sound to Copenhagen, Bothwell was also stating his case, but in a different manner. On 5 January, he dictated his memoirs, in French, to a Danish secretary appointed by Frederick II; Bothwell himself wrote the subheadings that appear in the margin. These memoirs were later published as *Les Affaires du Conte de Boduel*. Naturally, this was a highly sanitised version of events, for it was written in the hope of securing Bothwell's release, and its aim was to present its author in the best possible light and his enemies as utter villains. It named, as "the leaders and principal authors of all this trouble and sedition," Moray, Atholl, Glencairn, Morton, Mar, Lindsay, Maitland, Bellenden, MacGill, Home, Ruthven, Tullibardine, Preston and Balfour, amongst others—just about all of the ruling élite in Scotland. Bothwell concluded: "I have been falsely accused, detained without justification, and prevented from going about the business I have in certain kingdoms with various princes and noblemen for the freeing of my Princess."[61]

On 13 January, Bothwell wrote to Frederick II explaining the factional strife in Scotland; it is clear from this letter that he was still corresponding with Mary, for he says that she has authorised him to offer Frederick the Isles of Orkney and Shetland in exchange for troops and ships. None of these letters between Bothwell and Mary has survived. It would appear that Mary was hoping that Bothwell would return at the head of an army and rescue her. But Frederick did not take up Bothwell's offer—he was in fact hoping to get the Scottish government to give him Orkney and Shetland in exchange for his prisoner. In the meantime, "the Scottish King" was quite comfortably housed and allowed visitors and other privileges.

On 11 February 1568, Drury reported that Mary had been severely ill with "a disease in her side and a swelling in her arm, of whose sickness there ariseth divers bruits and reports in Scotland."[62] Because this illness occurred nine months after her abduction by Bothwell, there was talk that the Queen had secretly given birth to his child; her miscarriage the previous July was not common knowledge.

In 1659, Le Labourer, Louis XIV's almoner, who edited and annotated the memoirs of the French diplomat, Michel de Castelnau, Sieur de la Mauvissière,[63] claimed in a footnote—without citing his source—that Mary "was brought to bed of a daughter at Lochleven, who, being privately transported to France, became a nun in the convent of Soissons." In the nineteenth century, the writer Charlotte Mary Yonge wrote a novel about this child (whom she called Bride), entitled *Unknown to History*; in this version, the ship carrying the little girl to France is wrecked, but Bride is rescued by a kinsman of the Earl of Shrewsbury who later marries her to his son, Sir Humphrey Talbot.

Since's Nau's account of the Queen's miscarriage of twins could only have come from Mary herself or her physician, it must be reliable. Even if the miscarriage story had been invented in the 1570s in order to protect the identity of the unknown Princess at Soissons, Mary's pregnancy would never have advanced to full term without being detected by her gaolers. Furthermore, Mary later referred to James VI as "my only child." Her illness of January/February 1568 was without doubt a recurrence of the old pain in her side, which was almost certainly caused by a gastric ulcer exacerbated by stress. Bishop Gilbert Burnet, in his *History of My Own Time* (1724–34), claimed, without any foundation, that Mary had borne a son to George Douglas.

By March 1568, relations between England and Scotland were warmer, but there was dissension amongst the Lords, who were beginning to be divided in their attitude to Mary. Maitland in particular was becoming strongly disaffected, and secretly sent the Queen a ring in token of his support. M. de la Forrest, the French ambassador in London, was of the opinion that two-thirds of the people in Scotland would rise against Moray if an opportunity arose, for it was felt "that the said Regent and his chief supporters should clear themselves of the murder of the late King—a thing much to be desired, for, for a long time, it has been confidently asserted that these men were ac-complices in the said murder."[64] Taking advantage of the increasing upsurge in the Queen's popularity, Seton and the Hamiltons openly declared for her, and in April, encouraged by the way things were going, Mary herself formu-lated plans for escape.

Alarmed in case the growing clamour should prejudice the thawing rela-tions with England, Moray sent Nicholas Elphinstone to London with a copy of the Act of Parliament that had pronounced Mary guilty of the murder of Darnley, along with the black pearls that Elizabeth had so much coveted, at a reduced price.[65] But Elizabeth refused to become embroiled in Scottish af-fairs.

On 25 March, Mary made an abortive attempt to escape from Lochleven. Soon afterwards, Moray visited her to upbraid her for her folly, only to be confronted by a woman in fighting spirit who angrily castigated him for passing the Act of Parliament that had authorised her detention.

Five weeks later, Mary did succeed in escaping.

26

"I Am No Enchantress"

W ITH THE ASSISTANCE OF GEORGE Douglas, Lord John Hamilton, and an orphaned kinsman of George's, William Douglas, who stole the Laird's keys, a disguised Mary got out of Lochleven on 2 May 1568, while the household was diverted by a May Day pageant. She was met on the further shore of the loch by Lord Seton, Alexander Hepburn, Laird of Riccarton, who was Bothwell's cousin, and Lord Claude Hamilton (another of Chatelherault's sons) and taken to Seton's castle at Niddry,[1] two miles north of Broxburn in West Lothian. From there, she sent Riccarton to recapture Dunbar Castle from the Lords, and dispatched two messengers, one to Archbishop Beaton in Paris, informing him of her liberation, and the other to Frederick II to demand Bothwell's release.[2]

Moray was in Glasgow when the news of Mary's escape was brought to him. "Sore amazed," he immediately issued a proclamation summoning the lieges to arms.[3] Sir William Douglas was suicidal, but after bungling an attempt to fall on his dagger, pulled himself together and began raising troops to send in pursuit of his prisoner.

On 3 May, Mary led her growing force west to Cadzow Castle near Hamilton, the chief seat of the Hamilton family,[4] where she was joined by several nobles. Here, Archbishop Hamilton helped her to draft a strongly worded proclamation repudiating her abdication, reasserting her lawful sovereignty, and condemning the "ungrateful, unthankful and detestable tyrants and treasonable traitors" who had deposed and imprisoned her, "whom no prince, for their perpetrated murders, could pardon or spare." The proclamation also named the Hamiltons Mary's next heirs after Prince James. The Hamiltons had masterminded her rescue, and she was now dependent on them; they were determined to wring every advantage from it, and in the event of this restoration succeeding, they expected to be the power behind the throne. Mary was well aware of this, and because she was unwilling to burn her boats and bind herself to them, she never made the contentious proclamation public. Instead, she gave the Hamiltons to believe that she was considering a marriage with Lord John Hamilton.

Mary now wrote to Moray, demanding that, as she had abdicated under duress, he must resign as Regent forthwith. When he refused to negotiate, she concentrated her efforts on gathering an army and, with the help of the Hamiltons and other supporters, raised 6,000 men. As her forces grew, so did the Queen's optimism and Moray's alarm; before his troops were at full strength, he decided to march on the royalists. Meanwhile, Argyll had joined Mary and been made Lieutenant of her army; Huntly soon followed. When Queen Elizabeth heard the news of Mary's escape, she sent a message of congratulation, offering help and support; but Mary was never to receive it.

On 8 May, Mary's chief supporters—who now numbered nine earls, nine bishops, 18 barons, 14 commendators (receivers of ecclesiastical revenues) and 90 lairds—signed the "Hamilton Bond," in which they undertook to help her regain her throne. The Queen felt that the best course was to seek an armed confrontation rather than lay the issue of her sovereignty before Parliament, and decided to lead her army west to relieve Dumbarton, which was being held by her supporters against the Lords.

But the Queen's hopes were suddenly extinguished when, on 13 May, Moray's army of 4,000 men led by the invincible Kirkcaldy of Grange inflicted a crushing defeat on her less ably commanded force at the Battle of Langside, just outside Glasgow. It did not help matters that, at a crucial moment, Argyll had withdrawn his troops, claiming he had suffered an epileptic fit, which few believed. His retreat demoralised the royalist soldiers, who soon began fighting amongst themselves and deserting. Seton was captured,[5] as was Bishop Leslie, and 100 of the Queen's men were killed. Some, like David Chalmers, escaped into exile.

Believing that her cause was lost, Mary fled from the field with Herries, Fleming, Livingston and a dozen other supporters, and rode south-west to Dumfries and Galloway. During her flight, she shaved her head, so as not to be recognised, and was forced to sleep on the ground and subsist on a diet of sour milk and oatmeal.[6] Her friends tried to persuade her to make for France, where she had lands and an income, but Mary made the fateful decision to flee to England because she was convinced, in the light of Elizabeth's recent championship of her cause, that her cousin would do everything in her power to help her regain her throne. By the end of August, she told her supporters, she would be back in Scotland at the head of an English army.

Mary spent her last night in Scotland at the twelfth-century Dundrennan Abbey, a little way south-east of Kirkcudbright. The next day, 16 May, she set sail from Abbeyburnfoot (near Port Mary) with her companions, and crossed the Solway Firth to England. She would never see her kingdom again.

Mary's boat put in at Workington on the shores of Cumberland. The next day, she wrote to Queen Elizabeth, outlining her troubles and asking for help. In this letter, she accused the Confederate Lords of devising, "subscribing to and aiding" Darnley's murder,

> for the purpose of charging it falsely upon me, as I hope fully to make you understand. I, feeling myself innocent, and desirous to avoid the shedding of blood, placed myself in their hands. They have robbed me of every thing I had in the world, not permitting me either to write or speak, in order that I might not contradict their false inventions.[7]

Arriving in a strange land as a distressed sovereign who had come to place herself under the protection of a neighbouring monarch, Mary had little understanding or appreciation of the political problems that her presence in England would cause her cousin Elizabeth. In her simplistic view, she believed that her "dear sister" would unhesitatingly grant her military and financial aid, and speed her back on her victorious way to Scotland.

But the situation was not as straightforward as Mary thought. As a Catholic and a dynastic rival for Elizabeth's throne, who had never ratified the Treaty of Edinburgh withdrawing her claim, she represented a dangerous threat to the English Queen's security, for there were many in Christendom who regarded Mary as the rightful sovereign of England. As a Catholic in a Protestant country, Mary would be a focus for every Catholic agitator and dissident, especially in the north, where the old religion had its greatest following. With her legendary beauty and charm, she might inspire rebellion on both dynastic and religious grounds, and her presence in England would be a magnet to Philip of Spain and the rest of Elizabeth's foreign enemies.

There was another disturbing aspect, in that Mary had been condemned by the Scottish Parliament for Darnley's murder, and many believed her to have been an adulteress and fornicator also. Whatever Elizabeth's personal feelings on the matter, it would be inappropriate and unwise for her, Darnley's cousin, and a virgin queen with a reputation to protect, to receive someone as notorious as Mary.

Yet Mary was a crowned queen, whose abdication Elizabeth had refused to recognise, and by the laws of blood, hospitality and rank, was entitled to be treated as such. She had also been dealt with appallingly by her own subjects. On the other hand, she was too dangerous a person to be permitted to move about freely in England, nor could she be allowed to go to France, in case the French should send an army to Scotland to restore her, which was the last thing Elizabeth wanted. It was small wonder that, when Elizabeth learned of Mary's arrival, she was plunged into an agony of perplexity over what to do with her. Mercifully, she was unaware that the political crisis that the Scottish Queen's coming had precipitated would not be resolved for nearly nineteen years.

Mary had expected to be escorted to London for talks with Elizabeth, but on 18 May, as soon as the local authorities received news of her arrival, she was taken instead to Carlisle Castle, where she was courteously received into what she would soon realise was protective custody. She was deferred to with all the respect and dignity due to a queen, but kept vigilantly under guard, pending instructions from Westminster.

The news spread fast. Two days later, Drury informed Moray of Mary's flight to England,[8] by which time Lennox, who had fought for the Lords at Langside, had already heard of it. When an express messenger reached London on 20 May, Queen Elizabeth summoned an emergency meeting of the Privy Council, at which, with a view to getting rid of Mary as quickly as possible, she declared her wish to receive her honourably and discuss her restoration. This was immediately opposed by Cecil, who had no wish to see the Protestant government in Scotland overthrown. Reminding Elizabeth that Mary had been plotting against her for years, he was all for sending her back to face her fate, but Elizabeth refused to contemplate this on the grounds that she would be sending Mary to her death. On the other hand, she really did not want to embroil herself in a war with Scotland. In the end, it was decided that the Queen of Scots should be kept in honourable custody as her guest until the "vehement presumption" of her complicity in Darnley's murder was resolved. Elizabeth would be the unwilling arbiter between Mary and her subjects; if innocent, Mary should be restored, if not, some accommodation might be reached whereby she could still remain Queen but Moray would rule. "Our good Queen has the wolf by the ears," observed Matthew Parker, the Protestant Archbishop of Canterbury.

Elizabeth sent orders to Sir Francis Knollys and Lord Scrope to go to Carlisle to formally welcome Mary, take charge of her, and explain that it would be impossible for her to be received by their mistress until "the great slander of murder" had been "purged."[9] In London, the French ambassador was expressing the opinion that Elizabeth would never let Mary come near her.[10]

In order to show herself impartial, Elizabeth requested Moray to stop harassing Mary's supporters. Cecil, who had his own agenda, ordered Drury to keep in close touch with Moray, and when Drury received these instructions on 25 May, he at once informed Moray of them.[11] They may have included an adjuration to the Regent to present as convincing a case as possible against Mary.

Cecil was greatly in favour of an investigation into Mary's guilt, but English courts had no jurisdiction over foreign princes, and as this particular crime had been committed in Scotland, it was clear from the first that the Queen of Scots could not be put on trial; the only course open to the English was to hold an inquiry into her conduct. If Mary's guilt could somehow be established, and her reputation publicly destroyed, Elizabeth would be justified in keeping her in custody, and her supporters would hopefully abandon her; thus the threat she posed would be neutralised. The first priority, therefore, was to convince Mary that an inquiry was in her best interests.

As soon as Moray received Drury's message, which was around 26/27 May, he began to prepare his case. He was, of course, concerned to justify the continued existence of his government, and his own political survival, by proving Mary's guilt. If she were found innocent, his position in Scotland, and that of his fellow Lords, would become untenable. It was therefore imperative that he use all the resources at his disposal to establish her guilt. Once again, the Scottish propaganda machine swung into action, this time in a deliberate campaign to blacken Mary's name.

Moray had already sent John Wood to London on 21 May, "to damage the cause of Mary with Queen Elizabeth and the English nobility."[12] Wood arrived in London before 27 May, and Nau says that, after Elizabeth had heard what he had to say, her kindness towards Mary diminished somewhat. Moray also dispatched at this time a mercenary soldier, Captain John Clerk, to Denmark to take Bothwell dead or alive.

On 21 or 22 May, Cecil had asked Lennox, who was visiting his wife at Chiswick, to demand justice against Mary for Darnley's murder. Lennox needed no further prompting, and immediately set to work on a "Supplication," which would later form the basis of the three versions of his *Narrative*;[13] he used as his chief sources Thomas Crawford and Thomas Nelson, with whom he had no doubt discussed Darnley's murder on several occasions. The resulting text, which was completed between 26 and 28 May, was a masterpiece of character assassination, in which authentic details blended with falsehoods and distortions. For example, Nelson had testified that Mary initially meant to take Darnley to Craigmillar in January 1567, but Lennox does not mention Craigmillar; instead, he states that Darnley was taken to a place "already prepared with undermines and trains of powder," which cannot be true. In some respects, the "Supplication" is contradicted by the evidence in the depositions, which had been kept secret. In the later versions of the *Narrative*, some of these discrepancies have been amended. Lennox is also at variance in many respects with the propaganda of Buchanan. One example is his claim that Mary's adultery with Bothwell began before the birth of the Prince; Buchanan states it began about three months afterwards.

Curiously, Lennox refers to only one of the Casket Letters; he says it was "written to Bothwell from Glasgow" before Mary left with Darnley for Edinburgh, and sent

> to let him understand that, although the flattering and sweet words of the King her husband had almost overcome her, yet she, remembering the great affection which she bare unto [Bothwell], there should be no such sweet baits dissuade her or cool her said affection from him, but would continue therein, yea, though she should thereby abandon her God, put in adventure the loss of her dowry in France, hazard such titles as she had to the crown of England and also the crown of her realm. Wishing him then presently in her arms, [she] therefore bade him go forward with all things according to their enterprise, and that the place and everything might be finished as they had devised, against her coming to Edinburgh And for the time of execution thereof, she thought it best to be the night of Bastien's marriage. She also wrote in her letter that Bothwell should in no wise fail in the meantime to dispatch his wife, and to give her the drink as they had devised before.[14]

In most respects, this was the letter that Moray had described to de Silva. Lennox had either been shown it, or told about it, while he was in Scotland, or he had got his information from the ambassador in London. Lennox presented his "Bill of Supplication" to Elizabeth on 28 May.

The evidence suggests that, until Moray heard from Cecil on 26/27 May, he had intended to use just one of the Casket Letters against Mary, if need be. None of the other letters had ever been referred to individually, but they probably did exist at this time: although the word "letters" was used in both singular and plural contexts, there had been several references to "copies" and "writings." Most of these other letters were probably genuine letters of Mary's that were to be used out of context (possibly Casket Letters I, part of II, III, IV, V and VIII); they were perhaps considered insufficiently incriminating or convincing, and had only been kept for use as a last resort. It was probably at this time, therefore, that they were tampered with and that Casket Letters VI and VII, the marriage contracts and the sonnets, were forged. Moray was now prepared to use every weapon at his disposal against Mary.

On 22 June, Moray told Cecil that Wood had in his possession copies of the Casket Letters in Scots.[15] It has often been assumed that they were sent to him in a packet that Drury speedily forwarded from Moray on 30 May, but, on the assumption that the decision was taken on 27 May to produce more incriminating letters, that would have given the Lords three days at the most to doctor and forge their evidence. It is more likely that the copies were sent to Wood later in June, and that they included a revised version of the letter referred to by de Silva and Lennox, which was probably Casket Letter II as we know it. It would be safe to assume that all the letters received by Wood were in their final form.

On 27 May, Moray commissioned George Buchanan, that staunch Lennox man, to prepare an indictment against Mary. This indictment was written in Latin in the closing days of May, and later formed the basis for Buchanan's *Detectio* and his *History*. Again, it was a *tour de force* of vitriolic anti-Marian propaganda, calculated to discredit Mary in English eyes as a monster of moral depravity and thus destroy Elizabeth's sympathy for her. That it was based on second-hand knowledge, and was flawed, distorted and grossly inaccurate in parts, mattered little at a time when so much hung on it making a deadly impact on those who heard it. Masked by such powerful rhetoric, its inconsistencies went unnoticed.

Balfour may have assisted Buchanan in collating evidence. On 11 July, Drury reported that he was in confidential relations with Moray and employed on the most secret affairs of the state.[16]

Buchanan's indictment was completed at the beginning of June. He himself refers to the haste with which it had been written, which is testimony to the sense of urgency felt by the Lords with regard to the amassing and production of evidence.

On 28 May, Knollys and Scrope saw Mary at Carlisle and told her that she could not be received at the English court until she had been acquitted of Darnley's murder, and that that could only be achieved by submitting to Elizabeth's judgement. Mary reacted by bursting "into a great passion of weeping," and averred that no one but God "could take upon them to judge princes." She asked that she might be permitted to state her case before Elizabeth, and insisted that the charges against her had been a mere pretext. She had, she added, counter-accusations to make. Firstly, Morton and Maitland had assented to the murder of Darnley, "as it could well be proved, although now they would seem to persecute the same." Furthermore, the real cause of the Lords' rebellion was the desire of the rebels "to keep by violence that which she had given so liberally, since by her revocation thereof within full age, they could not enjoy it by law."[17] This was to be refuted by Wood in writing, at Cecil's instigation, on 5 June.[18]

Knollys was impressed by Mary's sincerity. In his report to Elizabeth, he wrote that everyone in the north of England was convinced of her innocence.[19] After Knollys and Scrope had left, Mary wrote to Elizabeth, complaining of her detention and offering to appear before her to purge herself of the calumnies of her enemies. Herries took the letter to London.

Knollys saw Mary again on 30 May, and discussed her forced abdication. She bitterly condemned Moray's conduct, but Knollys pointed out that, if princes could lawfully be deposed for insanity, they could also be deposed for murder, "for the one is an evil humour proceeding of melancholy, and the other is an evil humour proceeding of choler; wherefore the question is whether Your Grace deserved to be put from the government or not, for if Your Grace should be guilty of any such odious crime, then how should they be blamed that have deposed you?" In tears, Mary protested again that she was innocent, only to be told once more that the only way to be purged of any crime was in submitting to Elizabeth's judgement. His Queen, he added, would be "the gladdest in the world" to see Mary declared innocent.[20]

On 8 June, Elizabeth sent an envoy, Throckmorton's cousin Henry Middlemore, to Scotland, with instructions to stop at Carlisle on the way and deliver her reply to Mary's letter of 28 May. In it, Elizabeth promised that she would restore Mary to her throne if she would permit her to hold an official inquiry to establish her innocence. However, she could not receive Mary until that had been done.

"Oh, Madam," she protested, "there is no creature living who wishes to hear such a declaration more than I. But I cannot sacrifice my reputation on your account. To tell you the truth, I am already thought to be more willing to defend your cause than to open my eyes to see the things of which your subjects accuse you." However, Mary could rest assured that she would be as careful of Mary's life and honour as Mary herself was, and that, "once honourably acquitted of this crime, I swear to you before God that, among all worldy pleasures, [receiving you] will hold the first rank."[21]

Elizabeth also sent a letter to Moray, accusing him of "very strange doings" against a sovereign prince. Rather stretching the truth, she told him that Mary was "content to commit the ordering of her cause to us," and insisted that he inform her of his defence "against such weighty crimes as the Queen has already [objected], or shall hereafter, object against you."[22] Her letter was entrusted to Middlemore.

On 11 June, John Wood visited Lennox at Chiswick. That day, he wrote a letter on Lennox's behalf to Moray, asking rather belatedly for certain information about Darnley's murder, and in particular about the activities of Archbishop Hamilton. Lennox, however, still held the Queen to be the chief culprit, for, referring to the Casket Letters, he observed that "there is sufficient evidence in her own handwriting to condemn her." Lennox also sent to Crawford, Robert Cunningham and another of his henchmen, John Stewart, ordering them to use every means to obtain further evidence against Mary. This all suggests that he did not think his "Supplication" went far enough, and that he was preparing a stronger case to lay before the inquiry.

By the summer of 1568, there was growing support in Scotland for the Queen's party. Huntly and the Hamiltons were still staunch in their loyalty, and her adherents numbered both Catholics and Protestants. A recent convert to her cause was Kirkcaldy of Grange, who had never been comfortable with the Lords' treatment of Mary. As its Governor, he now held Edinburgh Castle for her. Maitland had also had a change of heart, and was now working in secret with Atholl for her restoration.

Bishop Leslie had now joined Mary at Carlisle, and early in June, she sent him to London, where he and Herries were to seek an audience with Queen Elizabeth and plead their mistress's case.[23] Knollys reported on 11 June that Mary showed a great desire to be revenged on her enemies. The next day, Wood reported to Maitland that Mary had accused him and Morton of Darnley's murder, and warned them against attending the inquiry in England, in case Mary made her accusations public.[24] Maitland took this warning very much to heart.

On 13 June, Middlemore arrived at Carlisle and delivered Elizabeth's letter to Mary. After reading it, she burst out passionately that she was an absolute prince and only God could judge her, and that there were things that she would reveal only to Elizabeth, face to face. Why could Elizabeth not summon Maitland and Morton to London, and let them debate the matter with her in Elizabeth's presence?[25]

When Middlemore had gone, Mary wrote to Elizabeth, telling her to remove from her mind the notion that she had come into England for the preservation of her life. On the contrary, she had come

> to clear my honour and obtain assistance to chastise my false accusers; not to answer them as their equal, but to accuse them before you. Being innocent, as—God be thanked—I know I am, do you not wrong me by keeping me here, encouraging by that means my perfidious foes to continue their determined falsehoods? I neither can nor will answer their false accusations, although I will with pleasure justify myself to you voluntarily as friend to friend; but not in the form of a process with my subjects.[26]

Herries and Leslie saw Elizabeth and her Council around 14 June. They protested that Mary was innocent, and solemnly affirmed that the Confederate Lords, "who, under the pretext of this crime, wished to deprive their sovereign of her life and dignity, were the very men by whose most wicked plots and devices this crime was perpetrated, a crime of which she was wholly ignorant. Already, it was well understood by the larger portion of her nobility," and her supporters were so "strong in their conviction, they had risked their lives and all that they possessed in defending the innocence of their sovereign." The Council promised that Herries and Leslie would have an answer to their complaints in three days.[27]

On the 17th, Elizabeth saw Herries in private and told him that she was still waiting for a favourable answer from Mary to her letters, to which he replied that there would be no other reply than that which she had already received. Mary was "entirely guiltless, and will prove her innocence very clearly, not only to Your Majesty, but also to all the other sovereigns of Christendom." Elizabeth undertook to summon Moray and try to ascertain what had induced him to treat Mary "contrary to all law and justice." If, she said, after hearing his side of the matter, Mary's accusations still seemed justified, "I will defend her cause just as I would defend my own." Otherwise, she would do her best to bring about a reconciliation between Mary and her subjects. However, she would not act as a judge in the matter. Herries believed that she was playing for time, and that Mary "had little to hope for in that quarter."[28]

The Council met on 20 June and declared its support for Elizabeth's refusal to receive Mary. The Queen, they declared, could not in honour aid or restore her cousin, or suffer her to depart from the realm "before her cause be honourably tried." It was decided at this meeting that Mary should be moved from Carlisle in case she tried to escape.[29]

Fleming had now joined Herries in London, and on 22 June, Elizabeth saw them both and "made her final reply," declaring that she would defend Mary in every way, but in so doing she had to have "due regard to her own good name and dignity." She could therefore do no less than inquire into the truth of the accusations, and intended to summon Moray and his friends into her presence, and to entrust the inquiry to her Councillors; and if there was no truth in the charges against Mary, she would defend her cause. Otherwise, she would try to place Mary "on a good footing with her subjects."

But Herries was not deceived by her fair words. "For whatever the Queen of England might pretend, her real intentions towards her cousin were clearly proclaimed by her actions. She has been boasting in private of the great captive she has made without having incurred the expenses of a war."[30] Herries had also learned that James MacGill was on his way to London with "certain pretended Acts of Parliament," which declared that Mary had voluntarily abdicated. Herries had secured Elizabeth's agreement that MacGill should not be received at court, but she received him anyway.[31]

When Middlemore reached Scotland and delivered Elizabeth's letter to Moray, he found the Scottish Lords anxious to stress Mary's guilt. But Moray was perturbed by Elizabeth's demand that he justify his actions to her, and on 22 June, he told Middlemore that he had specifically sent John Wood to London with matter he trusted would resolve the Queen's doubts. Because the case was to be aired in public, he was "most loath" to make any accusations against Mary, "for all men may judge how dangerous and prejudicial that should be." Therefore, "it were most reasonable we understood what we should look to follow thereupon, in case we prove all that we allege; otherwise, we shall be as uncertain after the cause concluded as we are at present. And therefore we pray Her Highness in this point to resolve us."

He then turned to the matter of the Casket Letters. "It may be that such letters as we have of the Queen that sufficiently, in our opinion, proves her

consenting to the murder of the King, shall be called in doubt by the judges."
Since Wood had copies of the letters in Scots,

> we would earnestly desire that the said copies may be considered by the
> judges that shall have the examination of this matter, that they may re-
> solve us this far, in case the principal [originals] agree with the copy, that
> then we prove the cause indeed. For when we have manifested and
> shown all, and yet shall have no assurance that it we send shall satisfy
> for probation, for what purpose shall we either accuse, or take care how
> to prove, when we are not assured what to prove, or, when we have
> proved, what shall succeed?[32]

What Moray was asking was, in effect, that the commissioners (who had not
yet been appointed) would comment on the veracity of his evidence before
it had been submitted to the inquiry, which was outrageous, considering that
he was an interested party. He also wanted to know what would happen if
the Lords proved their case, for, if he accused Mary of murder, he was burning his boats as far as reaching a compromise with her was concerned. He
was also well aware that, whether Mary was guilty or not, Elizabeth, for political considerations, might attempt to restore her at any time, with fearful
consequences for himself. Both his requests reveal his awareness of the enormity of the charges he was laying against his sovereign. If his evidence had
been genuine, it is unlikely that he would have betrayed such anxiety. But,
as has been demonstrated, it was not, it was essentially flawed and corrupt,
and he knew that there was a risk of discovery. This is why he was asking for
guarantees.

Moray received no direct answer from Elizabeth. But towards the end of
June, Cecil told Wood, off the record, that no matter what was being said in
public, the English government had absolutely no intention of restoring Mary
to her throne, whatever the outcome of the inquiry. Clearly, this was not to
be an impartial investigation, but a charade held for purely political reasons.

On 30 June, Elizabeth wrote to Mary, expressing the wish that, her innocence being such as she hoped, she would not refuse to answer questions
put by any noble personage sent to her by herself; this would not be a judicial inquiry, but one carried out for Elizabeth's own satisfaction. "I assure you

I will do nothing to hurt you, but rather honour and aid you," she added reassuringly.[33]

But before this reached Mary, some letters from Wood to Moray fell accidentally into her hands. Reading that her letters were to be used against her in evidence induced symptoms of shock, for she had had bitter experience of how ruthless the Lords could be in their own interests; as she herself wrote to Elizabeth, "these letters, so falsely invented, have made me ill."[34] Would she have admitted to them making her ill if she were guilty?

Between May and October, Mary bombarded Elizabeth with over twenty letters urging a meeting between them. "I am no enchantress," she wrote, "but your sister and natural cousin." It was all to no effect. Elizabeth observed that Mary's obvious fear arose from "guiltiness," but Cecil crossed this out, and wrote "doings."[35]

By the beginning of July, Elizabeth was growing weary of Mary's importunings, and begged her to "have some consideration of me instead of always thinking of yourself." Historians have also taken a generally dim view of Mary's constant protestations of innocence and repeated demands for an interview, but, if innocent, as the evidence strongly suggests, she cannot be blamed for her insistence, since it must have appeared to her that no one was listening.

On 13 July, Moray, having received Cecil's assurances, formally agreed to take part in an inquiry.[36] However, he was not pleased to learn that he would in fact be a defendant, for the inquiry was to be based on Mary's charges against her subjects. Even now, despite what Cecil had said, Moray feared that Elizabeth would insist on Mary's restoration. He was also determined to prevent Bothwell from being extradited by the English and called to give evidence, and to this end sent an urgent message to Captain Clerk in Denmark to expedite matters.

Around 13–15 July, Mary was moved, under protest, to isolated Bolton Castle in Yorkshire, which had been chosen because it was as far from Scotland as from London. Here, with Sir Francis Knollys as her "host," she kept great state as a queen, and was allowed to go hunting under escort; the fiction was maintained that she was Elizabeth's honoured guest. But the restrictions on her liberty greatly distressed her, and Knollys had to cope with tears and reproaches. He also had to bear in mind Cecil's reminder that, "besides the vehement presumption against her of the horrible murdering of her husband, other things were known; and these might become known to the whole world."[37]

Both Elizabeth and Cecil wanted Mary kept in captivity, but they needed a pretext for doing so, which it was hoped that the inquiry would provide. But first, Mary had to be persuaded to agree to the inquiry. During July, Elizabeth saw Lord Herries and informed him that Moray had agreed to take part in an inquiry into the conduct of the Confederate Lords, but that no formal judgement would be given. Then, laying her bait, she said that, if Mary would "remit her case to be heard by me, as her dear cousin and friend, I will send for her rebels and know why they deposed their Queen. If they can allege some reason for doing so, which I think they cannot, I will restore Queen Mary to her throne"—by force, if necessary—"on condition that she renounces her claim to England and abandons her league with France and the Mass in Scotland, receiving the [Book of] Common Prayer after the manner of England." If the Lords' evidence against Mary proved sufficient, then she would be restored with conditions, but whatever the findings of the inquiry, the Lords were not to be punished for their actions and were to "continue in their state and dignity."[38]

On 22 July, Elizabeth informed Moray that she had told Herries of his willingness to appear, and warned him that, during the inquiry, "nothing will be done or intended in any way" to Mary's prejudice.[39] Two days later, Herries arrived at Bolton with Elizabeth's promise of restoration. Tempted as Mary was to agree to the inquiry, there were too many conditions attached, and she was particularly disturbed about the requirement to abandon the Mass. For four days, she agonised over what she should do. Then, on 28 July, she capitulated, and agreed to "submit her cause to Her Highness in thankful manner," believing that Elizabeth's offer was genuine. Thereafter, she was in a buoyant mood, confident of success, for Elizabeth had made it clear that she would be restored whatever the outcome of the inquiry. Immediately, Mary ordered her supporters in Scotland to lay down their arms, provided that Moray's men had done the same.

Few people at Elizabeth's court were deceived by the Queen's fair words. That month, both the French and Spanish ambassadors reported that the English meant to keep Mary in prison.[40] On the 29th, Lennox wrote to Wood to say he was glad to hear his opinion that Mary would agree to the inquiry, and asked to be informed of the time and place. His letter also revealed that he had been in regular contact with Moray.[41]

Mary was anxious to be seen to be keeping her part of the bargain. From 8 August onwards, Knollys was writing optimistically of her flirtation with the Protestant faith. She accepted the ministry of an Anglican chaplain, and willingly listened to his sermons, even one in which he denounced popery to her "attentive and contented ears."[42] But Moray had no intention of being so conciliatory. On 16 August, in what can only be seen as a provocative move, he proclaimed in Parliament the forfeiture of the Hamiltons, Herries, Fleming, Leslie and other royalist supporters.[43]

During August, Elizabeth and her advisers made preparations for the inquiry—or conference, as it was to be called—that was to be held at York early in October. Commissioners were to be appointed by Mary, Moray and Elizabeth, and it would be the task of the English commissioners to listen to the evidence and report their findings to Elizabeth, who would then act upon them. Although the stated purpose of the conference was to compel the Lords to account for their conduct against their sovereign, the real issue to be debated was whether Mary was guilty of complicity in Darnley's murder. No judgement would be given because Elizabeth had no authority to judge the Queen of Scots, neither did she wish to see her found guilty. Her aim was to keep her in captivity, not only as a political bargaining counter in England's future negotiations with the Scots, but also to give Elizabeth a good excuse for interfering in, and manipulating, Scottish affairs to her own advantage. Moray, for his part, wanted Mary branded a murderess and adulteress before the world and kept in prison in England, so that he could continue to rule Scotland unhindered. Although Moray was anxious about the evidence he was to submit, the outcome of the conference would be decided on political considerations alone.

Lennox was beginning to be a nuisance. On 18 August, he reminded Cecil that he had sent Elizabeth the "Supplication" asking for justice, to which he had not had a response, and urged that, as he was "the party whom the matter toucheth nearest," his appearance at the inquiry "may be thought necessary."[44] A week later, Elizabeth refused him leave to attend the conference at York.

Moray now began pressing Frederick II for Bothwell's extradition to Scotland so that he could be tried for Darnley's murder. He even asked Frederick to permit Captain Clerk to execute Bothwell and send his head to Edinburgh. Both demands were refused.

On 29 August, Elizabeth named her commissioners. Thomas Howard, 4th Duke of Norfolk, premier peer of the realm and a Protestant widower of thirty, was to act as chairman. Assisting him would be Thomas Ratcliffe, 3rd Earl of Sussex, and Sir Ralph Sadler, a seasoned diplomat with wide experience of Scottish affairs. Aware of Moray's reluctance, the Queen instructed her commissioners to do everything in their power to make him produce all his evidence against Mary. They were told that, if the case against the Queen of Scots was "plainly proved," Elizabeth would deem Mary "unworthy of a kingdom"; but if it were not proved, then she would restore her. Of course, Mary had been told that she would be restored whatever the outcome, and Moray had been reassured that she would not be restored at all.

On 6 September, Moray was issued a safe-conduct by the English government.[45] Shortly afterwards, Mary announced that she would not be appearing in person at York because she did not recognise the right of any tribunal to try her; however, she was willing for her commissioners to represent her there, and announced that she had chosen Leslie, Herries, Livingston, Boyd, Gavin Hamilton, Commendator of Kilwinning, Sir John Gordon of Lochinvar and Sir James Cockburn, the Laird of Skirling, to act for her. Some of these men were Protestants yet had remained loyal to the Queen, but none of them had the subtlety and cunning of Moray and his associates. Mary ordered them to treat Moray and her other "disobedient subjects" only as defendants who were appearing to answer the charges she had made against them, and wrote to Elizabeth: "I will never plead my cause against theirs unless they stand before you in manacles."

In her formal instructions to her commissioners, written on 9 September, Mary denied writing the Casket Letters:

In case they allege to have any writings of mine which may infer presumptions against me, ye shall desire that the principals be produced, and that I myself may have inspection thereof, and make answer thereto;

for ye shall affirm in my name I never wrote anything concerning that matter to any creature, and if any such writings be, they are false and feigned, forged and invent[ed] by themselves, only to my dishonour and slander; and there are divers in Scotland, both men and women, that can counterfeit my handwriting, and write the like manner of writing which I use as well as myself, and principally such as are in company with themselves; and I doubt not, if I had remained in my own realm, I should before now have discovered the inventors and writers of such writings, to the declaration of my innocence and the confusion of their falsehood.

Mary may have been implying that the letters had been forged by Maitland, who later admitted to Norfolk that he could imitate her writing, or by Archibald Douglas, who later gained a reputation as a notorious forger. She was never to deviate from her insistence that the Casket Letters were forgeries.

Even though Mary had announced that she would not appear at the York conference, she was dismayed to learn that she was not to be permitted to attend anyway. Elizabeth was determined not to give her the opportunity publicly to declare her innocence and deny writing the Casket Letters, because her beauty and charm might sway the commissioners and prejudice the desired outcome of the inquiry. Elizabeth was also aware of Moray's reluctance to produce the Casket Letters, and must have guessed that, if Mary was allowed to scrutinise them, she might find in them enough flaws to seriously undermine his case. Mary was not only the complainant in this case, she was also, effectively, the accused, and to deny her the right to appear in person to defend herself was a flagrant breach of justice.

In Scotland, the Queen's nobles assembled at Dumbarton on 12 September and, aware that the Casket Letters were going to be Moray's most important pieces of evidence, declared that the letters produced by the Lords in Parliament the previous December were forgeries. "And if it be alleged that Her Majesty's writing should prove Her Grace culpable, it may be answered that there is no place mention[ed] in it by the which Her Highness may be convicted, albeit it were her own hand-writ, as it is not. And also, the same is devised by themselves [the Lords] in some principal and substantious clauses, which will be clearer near the light of day." This supports the theory that the Casket Letters were in part genuine letters of Mary's that had been tampered with and augmented. The nobles also declared that "there was nothing done in their [the Lords'] Parliament that could prejudice the Queen's honour in any sort, Her Grace never being called nor accused. It is against all law and reason to condemn any living creature without first hearing them in their defence."[46] Whereupon these royalist Lords, those same Lords who had signed the Hamilton Bond in May, subscribed to a new bond to support the Queen against her enemies.

Moray and his friends were underterred. On 16 September, as the Regent was preparing to leave for England, Morton entrusted the Casket Letters to his safe keeping, and received in return a receipt for "a silver box overgilt with gold" containing "missive letters, contracts or obligations for marriage, sonnets or love ballads, and all other letters contained therein," which were stated to have been kept by Morton "without any alteration, augmentation or diminution thereof in any part or portion."[47] If the "missive letters" were the eight that we know today, what then were all the "other letters"? As will be seen, there were probably more than eight letters in the casket.

Two days later, a commission was issued in the name of King James, authorising Moray, Morton, Lindsay, Adam Bothwell, Bishop of Orkney, and Robert Pitcairn, Commendator of Dunfermline, assisted by Maitland, James MacGill, the Protestant lawyer Henry Balnaves (who hated Mary), and Buchanan, as secretary, to meet Queen Elizabeth's commissioners at York, and to declare the causes why the Lords had taken up arms against their sovereign lady.[48] Relations between Moray and Maitland were now frosty, but Moray had decided to take the Secretary, that "necessary evil," with him because he feared it would be unsafe to leave him in Scotland. As for Maitland, he was determined to do all in his power behind the scenes at York to protect Mary's interests. In the furtherance of a future dynastic union with England, for which he had worked for years, he hoped to bring about a reconciliation between the Regent and Mary that would lead to the latter's restoration. In this, he had an ulterior motive, for, fearful that his own role in Darnley's murder would be exposed, he wanted to avoid a close examination of the evidence by the commission. But neither Mary nor Moray trusted him: both regarded him as treacherous. However, if Maitland could turn matters around in the Queen's favour at York, she might forgive him and be more amenable to reaching some composition with Moray.

On 20 September, Elizabeth wrote a private letter to Moray, assuring him that, although it had been reported that she intended to restore Mary even if she were found guilty, this was not in fact the case,[49] and this was reiterated by Cecil in a letter sent on the 25th. Meanwhile, Elizabeth had learned, through Knollys, that Mary had told her Catholic friends that her interest in Protestantism was merely opportunistic.[50] Proof of this is to be found in a letter Mary wrote in September 1568 to the Queen of Spain, claiming that, with King Philip's help, she would "make ours the reigning religion" in England. Already, she was scheming to seize Elizabeth's crown. But since her marriage to Bothwell, Philip had ceased to support her. Late in September, fearful that her co-religionists were being alienated by her dabbling in Protestantism, Mary publicly reaffirmed her devotion to the old religion before a large gathering of Catholics at Bolton Castle. But on 29 September, her instructions to her commissioners contained an undertaking that she would consider embracing religious conformity with England after her restoration.[51] In her desperation to regain her throne, Mary was trying to be all things to all people, and learning to be duplicitous in the process.

Moray and his colleagues left Edinburgh for York on 25 September. They took with them the English translation of Buchanan's indictment, called the *Book of Articles*, which significantly contained more detailed references to the Casket Letters than the original. Mary's commissioners arrived at York on 2 October, Moray's and Elizabeth's on the 3rd. Sir Ralph Sadler was probably not alone in feeling unhappy and perplexed about the outcome of the conference that was to open on the morrow. As for Norfolk, he had little faith in Mary's commissioners, and believed that she had better friends on Moray's side than on her own.[52]

27

"These Rigorous Accusations"

⁓

THE YORK CONFERENCE OPENED ON 4 October 1568. The first four days were taken up with preliminary formalities: on the 5th, Moray and his colleagues agreed to the form of the oath to be sworn by the commissioners, but this was objected to on the next day by Mary's commissioners, Herries saying he was willing to swear to nothing but what was just and true, but not to swear to all he knew to be true:[1] in other words, he was prepared to tell the truth, but not the whole truth. Some historians have inferred from this that he did not believe Mary to be innocent, but it may be that she did not wish her commissioners to disclose intimate information that might touch her honour. Nor might they have wanted to reveal unpalatable truths about Bothwell that might compromise Mary's position. In the event, they did swear an oath on 7 October, but affirmed as they did so that Mary was a sovereign princess who acknowledged no judge; they also referred to Elizabeth's promise to them to restore Mary. In turn, Moray and the other Scottish commissioners swore to declare the cause why they had taken up arms against their Queen and deposed her.

As Mary was the plaintiff, her commissioners were heard first. On 8 October, they laid her complaints against Moray and the Confederate Lords, accusing them of taking up arms against their lawful sovereign, deposing and incarcerating her, usurping the Regency and compelling her to seek justice from her royal cousin. Furthermore, they had ruined her reputation by "feigned and false reports." In answer, Moray claimed that the Lords had been intimidated into signing the Ainslie's Tavern Bond by the presence of Bothwell's armed retainers; that Mary had relinquished sovereign power to the traitor Bothwell; and that after Carberry Hill, she had rigorously menaced all who had taken part against Bothwell, which had left the Lords with no option but to imprison her until Darnley's murderers had been brought to justice. He insisted that she had abdicated voluntarily, which was a blatant lie, and that his Regency had been ratified by Parliament.[2]

The next day, Mary's commissioners restated her case in writing, in what became known as the Book of Complaints. When this was submitted, Moray asked for time in which to frame a reply. His own complaint was submitted in writing on 10 October.

Between sessions, there was a great deal of "off the record" discussion between the various commissioners; Norfolk, as chairman, had made it his business to sound out all the principals. On 9 October, Moray privately asked him if the English commissioners had the authority to pronounce on Mary's guilt, and, if she were found guilty, whether she would be delivered up to the Scots for punishment or kept in prison in England. He said that, until the present, he had preferred to conceal Mary's infamy—regardless of the fact that he had sent Elizabeth a copy of the Act of Parliament accusing his sister of Darnley's murder—but before he took the irrevocable step of charging her with murder and producing his evidence, he must know how, if he proved his charges, he and his colleagues would be protected from Mary's vengeance. Consequently, he would not accuse her until he had a written guarantee that, if found guilty, she would not be restored, and Elizabeth would recognise the government of King James.

Norfolk should have informed Mary's commissioners of Moray's concerns, but instead he secretly forwarded the Regent's requests immediately to London, then adjourned the conference in order to give Elizabeth and her Privy Council time to consider them. Clearly, Moray did not want to produce the Casket Letters if there was any chance of Mary returning to Scotland.

The next day, the English commissioners sent a report to Queen Elizabeth, informing her that the Regent had as yet said nothing publicly about Darnley's murder, since he was was waiting for her reassurance that his evidence was sufficient to condemn Mary; again, Moray was trying to secure a judgement before presenting his evidence. To this end, Maitland, MacGill, Buchanan and Wood had privately, and most irregularly, shown the English commissioners "such matter as they have to condemn the Queen of Scots of the murder of her husband," viz. a copy of the Ainslie's Tavern Bond and a warrant allegedly signed by Mary on 19 April 1567 approving it, the two marriage contracts from the Casket Documents, Mary's two letters (Casket Letters VI and VII) apparently consenting to her abduction, Casket Letter I, Casket Letter II—"one horrible and long letter of her own hand, containing foul matter and abominable to be either thought of or to be written by a prince"—"divers fond ballads" and another letter that purportedly proved that Mary had incited the quarrel on 8 February 1567 between Darnley and Lord Robert Stewart, in the hope that Stewart would kill Darnley; no copy of this letter has survived. As for Casket Letter II and the love "sonnets," they did, according to Norfolk,

> discover such inordinate love between [Mary] and Bothwell, her loathing and abhorrence of her husband that was murdered, in such sort as every good and godly man cannot but detest and abhor the same.

The Lords had sworn and affirmed that these letters and poems were all written by Mary's hand. Much swayed by the evidence, the English commissioners observed that

> the matter contained in them [was] such as could hardly be invented or devised by any other than by herself, for that they discourse of some things which were unknown to any other than to herself and Bothwell; and it is hard to counterfeit so many, so the matter of them, and the manner how these men came by them, is such, as it seemeth, that God, in Whose sight murder and bloodshed of the innocent is abominable, would not permit the same to be hid or concealed.

Norfolk and his colleagues enclosed for their sovereign's perusal a paper on which they had noted the chief and special points of the said letters, written, as they say, with her own hand, to the intent it may please Your Majesty to consider of them, and so to judge whether the same be sufficient to convict her of the detestable crime of the murder of her husband, which, in our opinions and consciences, if the said letters be written with her own hand, is very hard to be avoided.[3]

Copies of these documents should also have been made available to Mary's commissioners, but political considerations took priority over legal niceties throughout this inquiry, and the Lords were determined that Mary should not have the opportunity to comment on their evidence before Elizabeth had seen it. Moreover, this evidence was so contentious that the English commissioners dared not draw any conclusions until they knew what Elizabeth's view would be. Although they had professed to be shocked by the letters, they had made it clear that any condemnation of Mary would depend upon whether the letters had in fact been written by her.

This was a crucial point. The paper that was sent to Elizabeth by her commissioners survives in the Cotton MSS. in the British Library, and contains extracts in Scots from Casket Letters I and II. Therefore the letters shown to Norfolk, Sussex and Sadler must have been in Scots. However, the Lords were ready "to swear and take their oaths" that these letters were the originals in Mary's own hand.[4] As she normally wrote in French and was not very proficient in Scots, and as there is technical evidence (such as errors in translation) that the original Casket Letters were in French, these letters in Scots could not have been written by Mary.

Moray had also taken the trouble to send copies of the Casket Letters to Cecil, and later noted that these were delivered to the Secretary on 15 October.

Moray was not the only one to indulge in underhand practices. By 11 October, Maitland had leaked a copy or copies of at least one of the Casket Letters to Mary, perhaps with the help of his wife, Mary Fleming, and sent a note asking how he could best assist her. She replied that he should pacify Moray, speak a word in her favour to Norfolk, look upon Leslie as her friend, and use all his influence to "stay these rigorous accusations."[5] Maitland, more than most people, must have known the truth about the Casket Letters. Had they been genuine, it is unlikely that he would have wished to help Mary. But he himself was probably implicated heavily in Darnley's murder, and his conscience now seems to have been troubling him. He would have sent the letters to Mary so that she could prepare her defence against them. Mary, for her part, naturally did not want such shocking and defamatory accusations against her to be made public.

Maitland also made it his business to warn Mary's commissioners that the Lords had shown their evidence to Elizabeth's commissioners.

On 12 October, Mary's commissioners asked the English commissioners for time to frame a reply to Moray's response to the charges. Then they rode off to Bolton to tell Mary what Maitland had told them. That day, Norfolk wrote to the Earl of Pembroke, giving him to believe he thought the letters to be genuine. But Norfolk, for reasons of self-interest, did not want them to be made public: Elizabeth was childless, and if she died, Mary might well become Queen of England. She would not readily forgive those who had helped to publicly brand her an adulteress and murderess.

When Herries and his colleagues returned to York on 13 October, Norfolk asked them to apply to Mary to have their remit extended, so that they could "treat, conclude and determine of all matters and causes whatsoever in controversy between her and her subjects." The next day, Moray reiterated his answer to the Book of Complaints, reserving his right to "eik" (add to or amplify) his statement.

Meanwhile, Mary had been complaining to Sir Francis Knollys of the clandestine proceedings at York, and told him that, if the Lords "will fall to extremity, they shall be answered roundly and to the full, and then we are past all reconciliation." On 15 October, Knollys warned Norfolk that Mary was aware of what was going on behind her back.

On the 16th, Mary's commissioners delivered their formal written reply to Moray's written complaint of 10 and 14 October. They said that, if Bothwell was the murderer of the King, that circumstance had been unknown to Mary at the time of their marriage, and that the Lords who afterwards accused him of that crime had urged her to marry him; furthermore, the marriage had taken place after his acquittal. Later, these same Lords had never made any serious attempt to apprehend Bothwell. At Carberry Hill, misled by Grange's fair words, Mary had entrusted herself to the honour and loyalty of her Lords, but had been miserably deceived. It was stressed that she had abdicated only after being threatened with execution.

This, of course, was the truth, and it complicated matters. That day, Norfolk wrote to Cecil that this cause was

the doubtfulest and dangerest that ever I dealt in; if you saw and heard the constant affirming of both sides, not without great stoutness, you would wonder! You shall find in the end [that] as there be some few in this company that mean plainly and truly, so there be others that seek wholly to serve their own private turns.

Norfolk himself would shortly be numbered among the latter. Later that day, whilst hawking at Cawood, Maitland sought him out in private and informed him that the Casket Letters had almost certainly been forged, since many people could imitate Mary's handwriting; he had even occasionally done it himself. This revelation, startling as it was, was but a preamble to the real purpose of the meeting. For Maitland had thought of a solution to the present impasse, and suggested to a highly receptive Norfolk that it might be to his advantage to consider marriage with the Queen of Scots; he was certain that, if she married the premier English Protestant peer, the Lords would be willing to restore her to her throne. Later on, Mary, or her heir, might inherit the English crown, Maitland's dream of an Anglo-Scottish dynastic alliance would become reality, and he himself would prosper under a grateful sovereign, having expunged his earlier crimes.

The fact that Norfolk was prepared to contemplate such a marriage—or was dazzled by the prospect of the crown of Scotland and also, perhaps, that of England—suggests that he was not as shocked by the Casket Letters as some historians have believed. He was possibly reassured by Maitland's revelation that they had been forged; on the other hand, he may not have cared too much, given what he stood to gain by this proposed union. Indeed, he would give everyone cause to believe he still thought Mary guilty.

However, Norfolk was also aware that there was a clause in his commission that threatened anyone contemplating marrying Mary with a traitor's death. It was this that held him back from giving Maitland a final answer. However, he did reveal that Elizabeth had no intention of restoring Mary or finding her guilty; all she desired, he told Maitland, was an excuse to keep the Queen of Scots a prisoner in England. Then, if in the future she wished to restore her, there would be no bar to her doing so. Maitland told Norfolk he should inform Moray of Elizabeth's intentions, for if Moray thought there was any chance of Mary's restoration, he would not dare to produce any evidence against her. This would have suited Maitland very well.[6]

Maitland saw to it that a rumour of the proposed marriage was disseminated amongst the commissioners at York, and one morning a hopeful Leslie presented himself at Norfolk's lodging, asking the Duke to confirm the bruit that he bore a certain goodwill towards Queen Mary. Around this time, Norfolk—who now had a very good reason for wanting Mary cleared of murder—took Maitland's advice and told Moray that, "albeit the Queen had done, or suffered harm to be done, to the King her husband," for the sake of her son, he did not wish to see "our future Queen," accused or dishonoured. He said that, although he had been sent to hear Moray's accusation, neither he nor Elizabeth would pass any sentence on her, and he urged Moray not to use the Casket Letters as evidence. Moray told no one of this except Maitland and Melville;[7] he was now more uncertain than ever as to whether he dared produce the Casket Letters before the commission.

Elizabeth was becoming increasingly unhappy about the way things were going at York. There were too many intrigues behind the scenes, which were causing unnecessary delays. Moray, although he was determined to keep Mary out of Scotland, seemed reluctant to produce any evidence against her. By 16 October, Elizabeth was thinking of adjourning the conference to Westminster, where she and Cecil could keep a close watch on things, and on that day, she sent orders to Norfolk to adjourn the proceedings so that she could lay the issues he had raised before the Privy Council; she also summoned representatives of each party to London "to resolve her of certain difficulties that did arise" between them. She also wanted to find out why Moray and his colleagues forbore "to charge the Queen with guiltiness of the murder." Three days later, the Queen's orders and summons reached York, and it was agreed that Maitland, MacGill, Leslie and Kilwinning should go to London. They left on 22 October.

Mary, meanwhile, had been telling Knollys that she "would not greatly mislike" a marriage with a kinsman of Elizabeth. Knollys reported this to Cecil on 20 October, so Mary must have heard from her commissioners of the rumours about Norfolk, who was Elizabeth's kinsman on her mother's side. Knollys added that, in his opinion, the Queen could not detain Mary with honour "unless she be utterly disgraced to the world, and the contrary party maintained." Knollys was now spending many pleasant hours teaching Mary English, and despite his puritanism, was obviously becoming ensnared by her charms.

On 20 and 21 October, the commissioners discussed whether or not Moray should have the Regency, Herries and his friends arguing that the office should have gone to Chatelherault (who was then in London), as heir presumptive after James and the nearest to Mary in blood. Moray retorted that it was for Parliament to choose a governor.[8] Fearful of the political consequences of his prolonged absence from Scotland, he also urged that the proceedings of the commission be expeditiously concluded.

Mary had now abandoned the idea of a reunion with Bothwell, and on 21 October, authorised her commissioners to consent to the dissolution of their marriage.[9] At the same time, messengers were sent to Denmark to obtain Bothwell's agreement to this. Mary had quickly decided that marrying Norfolk would be a sensible solution to her problems, and had already begun to correspond with him. Despite the danger, he was willing to be persuaded, and before long they were addressing each other in very affectionate terms.

After the representatives had left for London, Sussex wrote to Cecil with an incisive summation of the unavoidable outcome of the inquiry:

This matter must at length take end, either by finding the Scotch Queen guilty of the crimes that are objected against her, or by some manner of composition with a show of saving her honour. The first, I think, will hardly be attempted for two causes: the one, for that, if her adverse party accuse her of the murder by producing her letters, she will deny them, and accuse most of them of manifest consent to the murder, hardly to be denied, so as, upon trial on both sides, her proofs will judicially fall best out, as it is thought. I think the best in all respects for the Queen's Majesty [Elizabeth], if Moray will produce such matter as the Queen's Majesty may find judicially the Scotch Queen guilty of the murder of her husband, and therewith detain her in England at the charges of Scotland.

Therefore Mary must either be found guilty, "or the matter must be huddled up with a show of saving her honour."

Sussex went on to say that, if Mary would confirm Moray's Regency, the Regent would forbear to accuse her and repeal the Act of Parliament declaring her guilty of Darnley's murder. He added that the Hamiltons wanted her restored because they hated Moray.

> Thus do you see how these two factions, for their private causes, toss between them the crown and public affairs of Scotland, and care neither for the mother nor child, but to serve their own turns.

In short, Sussex was disgusted by "the inconstancy and subtleness of the people with whom we deal."[10]

Sussex was in effect saying that, even though he (and no doubt most other people) knew that the Scottish Lords were guilty of Darnley's murder, and that Mary's testimony would probably demonstrate this, it would be better for Elizabeth if Moray were to produce his letters and give her an excuse to keep Mary in custody. It was really immaterial whether or not Mary was innocent: English interests must be protected. It was therefore imperative that Mary should not be given a chance to appear before the commission to state her case. Clearly, Sussex had little faith in the authenticity of the Casket Letters. Yet, if his summation was correct, it mattered little whether they were genuine or not.

At the same time, Mary was writing to Elizabeth to say that she hoped presently to see a good end to the inquiry, "whereof we may be perpetually indebted to you."[11] A day later, she wrote to inform her supporter, the Earl of Cassilis, in Scotland, of "the good proceedings" at York, where nothing had as yet been proved against her. But, unknown to Mary, Elizabeth's attitude towards her was toughening. On 24 October, Cecil reported that she would not allow the Queen of Scots to be advanced to greater credit than she deserved. It may well be that Elizabeth had heard the rumours about the Norfolk marriage, which she would certainly have seen as a threat to herself; moreover, Norfolk was supposed to be impartial, and should not be inviting accusations of treason by courting the Scottish Queen. As for Mary, this was proof that she would not scruple to plot against Elizabeth. Norfolk himself told Moray he had heard that Elizabeth regarded the continued existence of Bothwell as a useful safeguard against Mary remarrying. Norfolk's duplicity was probably the deciding factor in Elizabeth's revoking of the conference to Westminster.

A further sign of her displeasure came on 30 October, when her Council agreed that Moray should be given the assurance he required, in order to make him press his charges against Mary. Confident of success, the Council decided that Mary should be imprisoned in Tutbury Castle once the conference was over. They also agreed that the English commission should be enlarged.

The representatives of both parties had now arrived at Hampton Court. It had been decided that Elizabeth would see Herries and Kilwinning first and make vague promises of desiring "some good end" to the inquiry. Then she would see Maitland and MacGill and tell them that, if they brought a charge of murder against Mary, and "if it may certainly appear to Her Majesty and her Council that the said Queen was guilty, then Her Majesty will never restore her to the crown of Scotland, but will make it manifest to the world what she thinketh of the cause."[12]

Leslie, no fool, had already guessed Elizabeth's intentions, and informed Mary that her cousin's "determined purpose" would be to wait until Moray and his colleagues had uttered "all they could to your dishonour, to the effect to cause you to come in disdain with the whole subjects of this realm, that ye may be the more unable to attempt anything to her disadvantage." He warned her that, when the Lords had produced their evidence, Elizabeth would not pass any judgement, but would "transport you up in the country and retain you there till she thinks time to show you favour, which is not likely to be hastily, because of the fear she has herself of your being her unfriend." Mary's optimism now began to fade.

In Denmark, Captain John Clerk had been doing his best to gain access to Bothwell, but without success; he also had a commission to arrest Paris, and on 30 October, was lucky enough to track him down, along with one William Murray, Mary's former Chamberlain. On that day, Clerk gave Bothwell's keeper, Peter Oxe, a receipt for the two men, whom he planned to take back with him to Scotland to face trial and punishment.[13] On 20 November, Clerk wrote to inform Cecil of the arrest of Paris, so clearly his arrest was considered to be of the greatest importance. Here was a key witness to Darnley's murder, who could give evidence before the commissioners. Yet Paris was never called upon to do this. In fact, he was not brought home to Scotland until long after the inquiry had ended. The inference must be that Paris knew too much about the Lords' involvement in Darnley's murder.

Elizabeth had certainly heard the rumours about Norfolk's plan to marry Mary[14] when, on 3 November, she informed him that, "to take away the delay of time," the next session of the inquiry would be held at Westminster[15] with the Privy Council and the principal peers of the realm being required to attend. Mary was told that the adjournment had been made so that "her restitution may be devised with surety to the Prince her son and the nobility that have adhered to him." For all that, it would be to Mary's disadvantage to have the inquiry moved 250 miles away from Bolton.

When Norfolk arrived at court soon afterwards, Elizabeth played a game of cat and mouse, quizzing him about the rumour that he hoped to marry the Queen of Scots. Lying in his teeth, he denied it, saying "he never meant to marry such a person, where he could not be sure of his pillow"—a reference to Darnley being suffocated—and would rather go to the Tower.[16] But Elizabeth was not deceived. However, she bided her time, waiting to see what the Duke would do.

Moray arrived at Hampton Court around 13 November, and was received in private by Elizabeth, a privilege that had been denied to his accuser, Mary, as her commissioners were not slow to point out to her. With Moray lodged at Kingston-upon-Thames, Elizabeth was to remain at Hampton Court throughout the inquiry, monitoring the proceedings from a tactical distance. On 21 November, Cecil wrote in a private memorandum that "the best way for England, but not the easiest," was for Mary to "remain deprived of her crown and the state continue as it is."

On 22 November, Mary instructed her commissioners to complain to Elizabeth of the manifest unjustness of admitting Moray to her presence, and not herself. She told them that, if Elizabeth would not consent to receive her in person in the presence of the English nobility and the foreign ambassadors, and give her the chance to answer all that "may or can be alleged against us by the calumnies of our rebels," they must "break the conference and proceed no further therein."[17]

The next day, Chatelherault descended on Hampton Court and protested that the Palace of Westminster was a judicial venue, "where causes civil and criminal used to be treated." Elizabeth told him that she had no intention of acting as a judge, and that the Painted Chamber, in which the conference was to be held, was not a place where judgements were given.

The additional English commissioners, whose names were announced on 24 November, were Cecil, the Earls of Leicester, Warwick, Arundel, Pembroke, Essex and Bedford, William Parr, Marquess of Northampton, Sir Nicholas Bacon, Keeper of the Great Seal, Sir Walter Mildmay and the Lord High Admiral, Edward Fiennes, Lord Clinton. All were Protestants and hostile to Mary, but the Catholic Earls of Northumberland and Westmorland were also summoned to attend.

The enlarged commission reconvened at Westminster on 25 November. Before the commissioners were sworn and their complaints resubmitted, Leslie declared that his Queen would not be bound by any judgement as she was a sovereign princess. The English commissioners assured him that they did not intend to proceed judicially.

Nevertheless, their attitude towards Mary was noticeably harsher. On that day or the next, they saw Moray in private and told him that, after all the evidence had been presented, they would report to their mistress what they found to be true, and that she would then pronounce what appeared to her to be true. They also gave the Regent a formal undertaking that, if he produced his proofs, and if Mary was found guilty, Elizabeth would recognise James as King of Scotland, and himself as Regent, and would either hand Mary over to the Scots for trial, or keep her securely in England.

Armed with this, Moray at last ventured to make his sensational allegations in public. On 26 November, protesting that he was acting only under necessity and most unwillingly, he presented his "Eik," or amplification, in which he declared, "Whereas in our former answer we kept back the chiefest cause and grounds whereupon our actions and whole proceedings were founded, seeing our adversaries will not content themselves, but by their obstinate and earnest pressing, we are compelled for justifying of our cause to manifest the naked truth." It was a dramatic moment that must have held everyone in the Painted Chamber spellbound, waiting for what would come next.

Moray went on:

It is certain, as we boldly and constantly affirm that, as James, sometime Earl of Bothwell, was the chief executor of that horrible and unworthy murder perpetrated in the person of King Henry of good memory, so was she [Mary] of the foreknowledge, counsel, device, persuader and commander of the said murder to be done, maintainer and fortifier of the executors thereof, by impeding and stopping of the inquisition and punishment due for the same according to the laws of the realm, and consequently, by marriage with the said Bothwell, universally esteemed chief author of the murder. Wherethrough they began to use and exercise an uncouth and cruel tyranny in the whole state of the commonwealth, and (as well appeared by their proceedings), intended to cause the innocent Prince, now our Sovereign Lord, [to] shortly follow his father, and so to transfer the crown from the right line to a bloody murderer and godless tyrant. In which respect, the estates of the realm of Scotland, finding her unworthy to reign, discerned her demission of the crown.

This last contradicted what Moray had said at York: that Mary had abdicated voluntarily.

The Eik was presented on a Friday, just before the commissioners were due to leave for Hampton Court for the weekend, which would give them time to digest and ponder its shocking contents. Yet although they saw Elizabeth at Hampton Court, Friday's dramatic event was not discussed.

The commissioners met again at Westminster on Monday, 29 November, when Moray again recited his accusations, and his Eik was delivered in writing to Mary's commissioners, who immediately withdrew to discuss it. When they returned, they said they thought it strange that Moray and his colleagues should make such accusations in writing against their Queen, who had always been so generous to them, and asked for time in which to consider their answer. At this point, Lennox presented himself before the commission, in defiance of Elizabeth's orders, and submitted "in writing, briefly but rudely, some part of such matter [against Mary] as he conceived to be true, for the charging of the Queen of Scots with the murder of his son," which the English commissioners did not think worthy of much consideration.

The next day, Mary's commissioners asked for yet more time in which to prepare an answer to Moray's Eik. Herries presented this on 1 December, asserting that it was not the punishment of Darnley's murder that had moved the Lords to rebellion, but the desire to usurp their sovereign's authority before she could revoke the grants she had made to them in her youth. After reading his statement, Herries asked the English commissioners to consider how dangerous it was for subjects to bring false accusations against their sovereign, and told them that it would soon appear that some of those who were now accusing Mary were themselves privy to the making of bonds for the murder of Darnley. In making these accusations, Herries was exceeding his brief, for Mary had told him and his colleagues merely to demand that she be allowed to appear in person and, if this was refused, to withdraw from the conference. Herries concluded by saying that he and his fellow commissioners could say no more until they had received further instructions from their Queen, and both he and Leslie protested that, as Moray was allowed to appear at the conference, Mary should not only be allowed to attend, but also be permitted to defend herself in person against Moray's accusations before Queen Elizabeth, her nobility and the foreign ambassadors.

Some of the English commissioners went to Hampton Court on 2 December to see Elizabeth. They returned with a summons for Mary's commissioners to attend the Queen there the next day. Herries and his team duly presented themselves, and gave Elizabeth a written request for Mary to appear in person at the conference, repeating the protest they had made the previous day about the inequitable treatment of their mistress and the Regent. Elizabeth told them she would give them an answer on the following day.

On 4 December, Elizabeth told Mary's commissioners that she agreed it was "very reasonable that [Mary] should be heard in her own cause," but she insisted that, "for the better satisfaction of herself," the Regent must first present his proofs. Before she could answer their request "on every point," therefore, or decide where, when and in whose presence Mary should testify, she had to confer with the Scottish commissioners. That same day, Elizabeth told her own commissioners and the Privy Council that she would not receive Mary as long as she was defamed by accusations.

Herries and Leslie were so pessimistic about the outcome of Elizabeth's discussion with the Lords that they began to think that the best way to bring the inquiry to a conclusion without further damaging Mary's reputation was to negotiate a compromise, or "appointment," with the Lords. Rashly, without waiting for Mary to sanction such a course, they saw Elizabeth again in private and suggested it to her, offering to come to terms with Moray. Elizabeth told them sternly that, now that Moray had laid such charges against Mary, their proposal was inconsistent with their mistress's honour. It should have been clear to them that an obvious desire on their part to avoid responding to the charges would be interpreted as proof that the Queen of Scots was guilty. It would be far better to have Moray's evidence subjected to public scrutiny and seen to be unfounded, then he and his accomplices could be punished for "so audaciously defaming" their sovereign. Herries and Leslie thereupon withdrew, stressing to Elizabeth that the idea of a compromise came not from their mistress but was only "of their own consideration, partly gathered of the desire they had to have things quietly ended, partly also upon [Mary's] disposition that this whole cause should be ended by the Queen's Majesty with some appointment."

Within hours of this interview, Mary's commissioners were summoned back to see the Queen and her Privy Council, and were told by Elizabeth that she did not think Mary's honour was sufficiently endangered to justify her appearing in person to defend herself. After all, no proofs had so far been shown against her (although Elizabeth well knew they soon would be), and she did not wish unnecessarily to subject Mary to a 250-mile journey in driving snow. Of course, Elizabeth did not want Mary winning hearts and minds by her charms and her protestations of innocence, for that would undermine Moray's attempt to present the Casket Letters as credible evidence.

Elizabeth warned Mary's commissioners that, if they were not allowed to answer on their Queen's behalf, or failed to do so, it might be thought that the charges against her were not without foundation. Furthermore, she feared it might be degrading for Mary, as a sovereign princess, to have to deny such charges, and anyway, she herself thought that Moray's case would not stand up to scrutiny, and that Mary's name would be cleared without there being any need to resort to such desperate measures. Herries and Leslie, much dismayed, insisted that it would be better for Mary to appear in person, but Elizabeth adamantly refused to allow this.

When the conference reconvened on 6 December, the English commissioners were preparing to convey to Moray Elizabeth's misliking of the accusations he had made against Mary, but before Moray had even arrived, Mary's commissioners, belatedly following their instructions, announced that they were formally withdrawing from the inquiry on the grounds that Elizabeth had rejected Mary's plea to be heard in person. Before leaving, they made a formal protest to the English commissioners that, "in case Your Lordships proceed in the contrary, then whatever has been, or shall be done hereafter, shall not prejudge in any way our sovereign's honour, person, crown and estate; and we, for our part, dissolve and discharge this present conference, having special command thereto by our said sovereign."

As Mary was no longer represented, the inquiry should have immediately been terminated, but it was enabled to continue by virtue of a calculated objection on the part of the English commissioners to the form of protest offered by Mary's commissioners, which they said did not reflect Elizabeth's true meaning. This objection, which was the inspiration of Cecil and was not entered into the Journal of the conference, gave Moray time in which to produce his evidence. Mary's commissioners were not even aware as yet that the inquiry was continuing in their absence.

After Herries and company had left the Painted Chamber, Lord Keeper Bacon told Moray that Queen Elizabeth thought it strange that he should accuse his sovereign of "so horrible a crime," and told him that the commission was ready to hear his answer. This was the cue for Moray, with a display of reluctance, to exhibit his proofs. He produced the Book of Articles, the depositions of some key witnesses, the Act of Parliament condemning Mary, and Lennox's *Narrative*, and left all these documents, except the Book of Articles,[18] for the English commissioners to digest overnight. Given the falsehoods, distortions and inconsistencies in these "proofs," Moray must have known he could count on the complacent discretion of the English Lords, who had no doubt received their instructions from Cecil.

The next day, 7 December, the Book of Articles was read out to the depleted commission. Afterwards, Moray appeared with his colleagues, and said he trusted that the English commissioners were now satisfied that the Lords were not guilty of the crimes with which they had been charged. Obviously testing the water, he said he also "required to know whether Your Lordships were not now satisfied with such things as they had seen; and if they were not, that it would please them to show if in any part of those Articles they conceived any doubt, or would hear any other proof, which they trusted needed not, considering the circumstances thereof were notorious to the world."

To Moray's dismay, the English commissioners made it clear that they did not intend to offer any opinion on his evidence, which made it appear that the proofs offered so far were probably insufficient for their purpose. After a hurried discussion in private, the Scottish commissioners, "with fresh protestations of loyalty and affection" to Queen Mary, produced documentary evidence of Bothwell's trial and acquittal, and finally, the silver casket itself, the two marriage contracts, one in Scots, one in French, and Casket Letters I and II, both in French. There is no evidence that these were left for the English commissioners to peruse overnight.

On the 8th, Moray offered in evidence the remaining Casket Letters and the love poem, all in French, a journal of events from the birth of Prince James to the Battle of Langside, now known as Moray's Journal, and the depositions of Hay, Hepburn, Powrie and Dalgleish. The English commissioners had copies made of the Casket Letters, compared them to the originals to ensure they were properly transcribed, then gave the originals back to Moray, who had now concluded his evidence. There is no record of the reactions of the English commissioners to these documents.

In publicly producing the Casket Letters, Moray had taken an irrevocable step that precluded any future reconciliation or compromise with Mary, which is what Cecil had been aiming at all along. The Regent and Elizabeth now shared a common determination to prevent the restoration of the Queen of Scots.

28

"Pretended Writings"

THE CASKET LETTERS NO LONGER exist. They disappeared in
1584, during Mary's lifetime. After the Westminster conference, Moray
took them back to Scotland, then entrusted them to Morton for safe keeping, but after the latter's death in 1581, they were given by his bastard son to
William Ruthven, 1st Earl of Gowrie,[1] who repeatedly thwarted Queen Elizabeth's attempts to gain possession of them; she wanted them in order to justify keeping Mary in custody. In 1584, after conspiring against the
eighteen-year-old James VI, Gowrie was arrested and executed, and with his
forfeiture, the Casket Letters presumably came into the King's possession.
They were never seen again.

Of course, Gowrie himself could have destroyed the letters, but this is
unlikely. In 1584, James VI was determined to rehabilitate his mother's reputation; it was at this time that Buchanan's condemnatory works were
banned by Parliament. James may have felt that it would serve no purpose to
rake up old scandals by exhibiting the Casket Letters as forgeries; furthermore, there were then very few people left alive who could have testified that
the letters *were* forgeries. Therefore James may well have feared that their existence would compromise his policy of rehabilitation. It is unlikely that he
would have been so zealous to restore the reputation of his mother had he

believed that the Casket Letters were genuine, for that would have been to acknowledge that she had connived at the murder of his father. Moreover, if James destroyed the letters in the belief that they were authentic, then he would also have got rid of the highly damaging deposition of Paris, which nevertheless survives.

James probably concluded that no purpose would be served in keeping such contentious reminders of the tragedy that had cost his mother her throne: if the letters were declared forgeries, then her supporters might try to use them to claim that she had been wrongfully deposed and was still the rightful Queen of Scots, which would compromise his own position. The best course therefore was to destroy the letters.

Theories that the Casket Letters were in existence after 1584 are based on slender evidence. One is that James VI gave them to his favourite, James Stewart, Earl of Arran, which would explain why the silver casket that had allegedly held them came into the possession of the Hamilton family, since Arran held their estates for a time.[2] Goodall referred to an unnamed historian who, having researched Charles II's restoration of 1660, asserted that the Casket Letters were at that time in the possession of James Douglas, Marquess of Douglas. Goodall, writing in 1754, claimed that the letters had since been seen at Hamilton, which had passed to Douglas's son William through his marriage to Anne, daughter and heiress of the first Duke of Hamilton. There is no other evidence for the Casket Letters having been at Hamilton, although it is possible that the casket itself was there at one time, as will be seen. Another historian, Gabriel Naudé, claimed to have seen the letters at Rome, but again, there is nothing to corroborate his statement.

Unfortunately, the disappearance of the Casket Letters has meant that historians have never been able to give a conclusive verdict on their authenticity. Neither the first Scottish translations from the original French, nor a set of copies made in Scotland in 1571, has survived.[3] All that remains are the French copies and English translations taken and made at the Westminster conference, and printed versions of the letters in Latin, Scots, English and French, all dating from the 1570s.[4]

Of the copies made at Westminster, all but one are in the secretary script used by the same English clerk. Each letter has a heading, written either by Cecil or the clerk, stating what the letter allegedly proved. Casket Letter VI is the only one in an Italianate hand, which is not dissimilar to Mary's handwriting in her earlier years, but has been corrected by another hand. This has led to theories that it is one of the original Casket Letters, left by Moray in England by mistake, but it is clearly not in Mary's writing, and Cecil himself endorsed it with the word "French," which makes it almost certain that it is just a copy.[5]

The Journal of the commission states that, after the copies of the Casket Letters had been made, they "were read in French, and a due collation made thereof, as near as could be by reading and inspection, which the Earl of Moray required to be redelivered, and did thereupon deliver the copies being collationed."[6] This suggests that the copies made in French were exact transcriptions of the originals, and if this is so, then the originals are unlikely to have been written by Mary because her customary orthographic idiosyncrasies are nowhere evident in the surviving copies of Casket Letters III, IV, V and VI.[7]

Mystery surrounds the casket itself, as well as its contents. The Journal of the commission describes a "little coffer of silver and gilt, not fully one foot long, being garnished in many places with the Roman letter F, set under a royal crown."[8] This suggests that the casket had once belonged to Francis II, and that Mary had brought it back with her from France. A silver casket purporting to be this one is now on display at Lennoxlove in East Lothian; it was bought by the Marchioness of Douglas after 1632, but sold on her death, and was later repurchased by her daughter-in-law, Anne, Duchess of Hamilton. Of French origin, it is 8 inches long, dates from the fifteenth or early sixteenth century, and is decorated with scrollwork and the Hamilton arms, the latter being engraved on the orders of Anne, Duchess of Hamilton. Yet it does not correspond in every respect to the description of the casket produced by the Lords, for there are no crowned Fs to be seen, and this box has a key. The Lords' casket had no key, and had had to be forced open. There is, however, evidence that the lock of the Lennoxlove casket had been broken at some stage; furthermore, the Hamilton arms may have obliterated the crowned Fs, although they are said to have been "in many places."[9] In 1889, a silver casket of the right size, marked in two places with the letter F, but denuded of gilding and other ornaments, was said by Henderson to have been at Hamilton Palace. This is certainly not the casket at Lennoxlove, and disappeared when Hamilton Palace was demolished in 1927.

We have seen that the original contents of the casket were almost certainly harmless diplomatic dispatches; Herries insisted that it had contained the Craigmillar Bond between Bothwell and the Lords, but other evidence makes this unlikely. Whatever the Confederate Lords later planted in the casket, there were certainly more documents than have survived in copy form today. When, in 1571, Morton gave Lennox a receipt for the Casket Letters, he specified that the casket contained "missive letters, contracts or obligations for marriage, sonnets or love ballads, and other letters, to the number of 21."[10] Today, we have copies of eight letters, two marriage contracts and a love poem, totalling eleven documents in all. It has been suggested that Morton meant that there were twenty-one pieces of paper, but the wording of the receipt indicates that he was referring to twenty-one separate documents. Among them must have been ten documents of which copies have not survived. We know that, at York, Moray produced a letter that he claimed had been written by Mary, which referred to the quarrel she had incited between Darnley and Lord Robert Stewart. This letter was not amongst those presented in evidence at Westminster, and no longer exists even in copy form. Nor does Mary's alleged warrant, urging the Lords to sign the Ainslie's Tavern Bond, which was also produced at York, but not at Westminster.[11] It may therefore be inferred that there were probably other documents that were never used in evidence.

It has been made abundantly clear in this narrative why the Casket Letters are untrustworthy as evidence against Mary. Yet, for nearly 450 years, controversy has raged, and scholars have argued over them, and today there are still those—some of them eminent historians—who believe in their authenticity. Leslie, like many of Mary's partisans both then and since, held that, even if the letters were genuine, they actually proved very little against her, for they did not contain "any express commandment of any unlawful act or deed to be committed and perpetrated," but only "unsure and uncertain guesses, aims and conjectural supposings," which did not constitute "any good and substantial proof." Indeed, there is plenty of circumstantial evidence against Mary without the Casket Letters—people suspected her of involvement in Darnley's murder weeks before they were discovered, and long before they were made public—although, as has become evident, much of this evidence can be discounted on closer analysis. Nevertheless, as far as Moray and his colleagues were concerned, the Casket Letters were the cornerstone of their evidence.

It has been argued that, if the authenticity of the letters were to be undermined, that would not prove Mary's innocence, only that the Lords were determined to make doubly sure of her conviction. However, without the Casket Letters, the Lords' case rested on the highly dubious *Book of Articles* and some depositions that have since been shown to have been falsified in the most important particulars. Had they had a genuine case against Mary, they could have brought forward sound witnesses and veracious evidence. But they did not. They produced the Casket Letters, which they—and the English government—calculated would have a catastrophic effect on Mary's already sullied reputation. Thus the Casket Letters are of crucial importance in determining her guilt, for they are the only evidence of her alleged adultery with Bothwell and therefore offer a motive for her complicity in Darnley's murder.

It is essential to examine the reasons why so many people have accepted the Casket Letters as genuine. Firstly, and perhaps most importantly, they appeared to corroborate the circumstantial evidence. Secondly, it has been said that Atholl, who was present at the opening of the casket, later came to support Mary, but never at any time protested that the letters were not genuine; Atholl, however, was a faint-heart who had fled from Edinburgh after Darnley's murder, in the belief that he too was about to be assassinated, and was now living temporarily in retirement. It is unlikely he would have wanted to prejudice his close friendship with Lennox by undermining the Lords' case at this time, and it was only after Lennox's death that he began actively to oppose Morton. Furthermore, while neither Huntly nor Herries spoke out in the Parliament of December 1567 against the Act condemning Mary on the evidence of her privy letters, both hastened to join her when she escaped from Lochleven, which suggests that, in December, they had been too intimidated by Moray and the other Confederate Lords to speak out on her behalf.

It is often claimed that it would have been virtually impossible for a forger to produce the letters in the five days between the Lords' coup and the opening of the casket on 21 June 1567. This presupposes that it was the Casket Letters as we know them today that were "sighted" on 21 June, when in fact the evidence suggests that the documents seen that day were of an innocuous nature. There seems to have been no hurry to produce the letters: some may not have been written in their final form until a year after their alleged discovery. This factor demolishes many of the arguments in favour of the letters' authenticity.

It is also asserted that the destruction of the Casket Letters by James VI is proof of their authenticity, although it has been shown that he had other compelling reasons for getting rid of them. Furthermore, it is argued that Moray would not have risked producing forgeries in evidence, nor would Elizabeth have countenanced it. This theory does not take account of the fact that, during the inquiry, the Casket Letters were only shown to a restricted number of individuals who had been carefully selected by the English government and who were aware of the conclusions they were meant to reach, nor of the fact that the English government and the Scottish Lords shared a common aim and were effectively acting in collusion.

It has been pointed out that the letters are too long to be forgeries, are packed with authentic details and idioms that no forger could have known about or imitated, and would have been more incriminating if forged. It has been noted, however, that the evidence strongly suggests that the Lords had cunningly decided to manipulate genuine letters, or use them out of context; after Mary's deposition, they had access to all her papers, and it appears that they found suitable material among them. Probably only two letters had to be forged. Thus the letters had the appearance of genuineness. Buchanan, Mary's former tutor, who should have known what he was talking about, claimed that the Casket Letters were in her handwriting, but he was not only a Lennox man but also a fanatical supporter of Moray, and he was responsible for some of the most notorious lies about Mary, so cannot be relied upon.

It has also been alleged that Mary and her supporters remained silent on the matter of the Casket Letters, which argues her guilt, yet this is to ignore the fact that, at Dumbarton, in September 1568, her Lords publicly protested that she had not written them, and that she herself, and her commissioners, repeatedly condemned the letters as forgeries. It has also been said that no one at the time claimed that the letters were forged, but Mary and her supporters certainly did, and Maitland—who was in a position to know—seems to have done so too; he later became one of her staunchest supporters, which is perhaps significant in itself.

Mary's detractors argue that she also denied writing the fatal but undeniably genuine letter authorising Anthony Babington to proceed with the assassination of Queen Elizabeth in 1586, but this does not necessarily mean that she lied about the Casket Letters. There is a great deal of corroborative evidence against her denial of 1586, and plenty of evidence to support her declaration that she did not write the Casket Letters.

Some have argued that Casket Letter II supports Crawford's deposition, but, as has been noted, the two documents are so similar that one must have been copied from the other, which supports the manipulation theory. Furthermore, Casket Letter II is almost certainly by two different hands.

Jenny Wormald, one of Mary's most virulent detractors, states that it would not have made sense for the Lords to forge the letters and then been reluctant to use them as evidence, but in fact the letters had originally been used as justification of the deposition of the Queen, at a time when the Lords could not have envisaged that they would be required to produce them publicly in evidence against her. In 1568, Moray had no guarantee that Mary would not be restored, and producing such evidence against a sovereign who might be in a position to punish him for it was a very serious step indeed, hence his reluctance.

It was also useless for the English commissioners to conclude that there were things in the letters that were known only to Mary and Bothwell, for neither Mary nor Bothwell was ever given a chance to see the letters and corroborate this. The Lords could have made up anything they liked to put in the letters. The omission of signatures, addresses and dates may argue the furtiveness of genuinely illicit letters, but may also have been a deliberate ploy on the part of the forger; it should be remembered, however, that the letters were originally said to have been signed by Mary. It is significant that the mere addition of a place and day to the genuine Casket Letter I, thereby placing it in what was almost certainly a different context, proved highly advantageous to the Lords.

Forgery was a flourishing political industry in the sixteenth century, an age in which ambassadors commonly numbered among their suites men who were experts at counterfeiting or ciphering. It would not have been difficult for the Lords to find someone capable of manipulating their evidence to the required standard.

As has been seen, there is plenty of evidence that the Casket Letters were either forgeries or genuine documents that had been tampered with. It is surely no coincidence that they had conveniently come to light at a time when the Lords most needed them, and when Mary was safely confined at Lochleven. The Lords certainly had compelling motives for fabricating them: they needed to justify their sensational deposition of their anointed sovereign in an age in which monarchy was virtually sacrosanct, and they were critically aware that they were safeguarding their political survival and also, when it came to it, their lives. It seems that the letters were also fabricated in order to make it appear that the motive for Darnley's murder was purely domestic, in order to deflect public interest from the Lords' political aims. There is no doubt that, without the Casket Letters, Moray's case would have been extremely weak.

It is significant that, before December 1567, the Lords aimed their accusations solely at Bothwell. As soon as he had passed beyond their reach, they looked to Mary as the nearest available scapegoat. However, they were supposed to have had in their possession letters proving her guilt six months earlier; certainly their failure to use such compromising evidence when it would have been to their advantage to do so is highly suspicious. Had it been genuine, it would have enabled them to get rid of Mary once and for all. It was only later, when they had to justify themselves before the world, that the Lords reluctantly produced the letters. Furthermore, Moray's anxiety to have them accepted as reliable evidence prior to the inquiry suggests he was worried that someone might challenge their authenticity.

Strangely, during the months leading up to the inquiry, one of the Casket Letters seems to have undergone some metamorphosis: early descriptions of it by de Silva and Lennox do not correspond to any of the final versions exhibited to the commission. Had such a damaging letter existed, the Lords would have been mad not to use it against Mary, but instead, it was apparently replaced with the far less compromising Casket Letter II. This suggests that the Lords had first experimented with complete forgeries, but had later decided that it was safer to base their evidence on genuine letters.

Herries admitted that a casket had been found, but insisted that Morton had later exchanged the original documents in it for false ones, which corroborates the evidence of Drury. Herries also claimed that, had the letters been genuine, the Lords would have happily used them to convict Mary and put her to death.

Then there is the technical evidence, revealed through study of the translations, that the original letters were unlikely to have been written by Mary. Although there was a definite attempt to imitate her characteristically elegant style, there are clumsy discrepancies. Hundreds of her genuine letters have survived, but none in which there appear the kind of "coarse" sentiments that feature in Casket Letter II. Furthermore, computerised comparisons of orthographic patterns have revealed that the letters were not all by the same hand. A few writers subscribe to the recent unsubstantiated theory that some were by an unknown mistress of Bothwell; Gore-Browne even suggested that they were written by Anna Throndssen, but she is unlikely to have been able to write good French, and as she was in Norway from 1563, is also unlikely to have written of her jealousy of Jean Gordon; neither could her handwriting ever be mistaken for Mary's. Both Ronsard and Brantôme dismissed the abysmal, unpolished love poem as a fabrication, and declared it could not possibly have been written by Mary. There is no escaping the fact that every single letter poses a problem, whether in sense, style or timing.

It is enormously telling that neither Moray nor Queen Elizabeth wanted Mary or her representatives to see the Casket Letters. Nor, despite the latter's insistent pleas, were they ever allowed to do so. Of course, Mary had secretly been sent copies, but she could not reveal that; all she could do was protest that she had not written the letters, and offer to prove that they were forgeries and accuse the Lords of being the "principal authors." But she was given no opportunity to do so.

Had the letters been genuine, Moray could triumphantly have challenged Mary's commissioners to find fault with them; yet he did no such thing. Nor did he produce the witnesses, Dalgleish and Paris, who could have testified to the discovery of the casket and the sending of the letters: conveniently, Dalgleish was dead, and Paris detained in Denmark.

At York, the Lords swore that the Scots copies of the Casket Letters that they showed privately to the Lords were the originals; yet at Westminster, they affirmed that the French copies that they produced in evidence were the originals. They were either lying in the former case, or their meaning was misunderstood by the English commissioners.

Elizabeth herself, on seeing the Casket Letters, professed to be shocked and declared that they "contained many matters unmeet to be repeated before honest ears, and easily drawn to be apparent proof against the Queen."[12] Yet she took care never to express an opinion on their authenticity, and showed regret that Moray had so rashly produced them in public. But Elizabeth's considerations were political, not moral, and her main preoccupation was the security of her throne and kingdom; there was also a strong feeling in England that Mary was guilty, which she dared not ignore. Her priority was to find an excuse to keep the Scottish Queen under lock and key, a course with which the Lords heartily concurred. Thus, given the political agenda of the inquiry, the Casket Letters were never subjected to any independent scrutiny.

After the inquiry, Leslie, who had had plenty of dealings with the English commissioners, claimed that "the nobles of England that were appointed to hear and examine all such matters as the rebels should lay against the Queen, have not only found the said Queen innocent and guiltless of the death of her husband, but do fully understand that her accusers were the very contrivers, devisers, practitioners and workers of the said murder, perfectly knowing her innocency." As for modern assertions that Norfolk believed in Mary's guilt, Elizabeth herself said, "The Queen of Scots will never want an advocate so long as the Duke of Norfolk lives."[13]

There is no escaping the fact that much of Moray's other evidence—the Book of Articles, the depositions, the Lennox *Narrative*—was deliberately falsified in order to deflect suspicion from his own party and lay it on Mary. It is also true that the Confederate Lords had broken every one of their promises made to Mary at Carberry Hill. They were men without honour, capable of deception and duplicity, and would certainly not have scrupled at counterfeiting some letters in their own interests. On the other hand, there is no evidence that Mary falsified any evidence, either before or after Darnley's murder. As for her actions after the murder, it has been demonstrated that she was ill, mentally and physically, and had consequently, by her own admission, lost control of her affairs. The Lords had taken full advantage of this.

Lady Reres features as Mary's confidante in Casket Letter II, and also as her bawd in the *Detectio*, the *Book of Articles* and the deposition of Paris. Yet, although she was in attendance at the birth of James VI, there is no other evidence that Lady Reres was especially close to Mary: she was not listed as belonging to the Queen's household,[14] nor was she remembered in Mary's Will.[15]

As to who may have forged and manipulated the letters, many writers point the finger at Maitland, who himself admitted that he was easily able to counterfeit Mary's handwriting. But Maitland was in bad odour with the Lords from before Carberry Hill, and later became Mary's man; he also warned Norfolk that the letters were possibly forged. A more likely forger is Morton's kinsman, the unscrupulous Archibald Douglas, who, as has been seen, was almost certainly the man who had murdered Darnley, and who therefore had every motive for pinning the blame on Mary. Douglas had spent time in France and presumably learned the language, but, more pertinently, was accused in 1581 of forging letters from Bishop Leslie to Esmé Stuart, Duke of Lennox, favourite of James VI. Were these the first damning letters he had counterfeited?

In the light of all the evidence, it is impossible to resist the conclusion that the Casket Letters were fabrications. As far as the commission was concerned, however, their importance lay not so much in their contents as in their usefulness.

29

"MUCH REMAINS TO BE EXPLAINED"

O N 9 DECEMBER—TOO LATE to prevent the Casket Letters from being offered in evidence—the protest of Mary's commissioners was received in its amended form by Cecil. Having now discovered what had happened in their absence, Leslie and his colleagues made a further objection against the travesty of justice whereby such dramatic evidence was produced at hearings at which they had not been present, and demanded the summary arrest of those who had laid such charges against their sovereign. When this was refused, they again withdrew from the conference, which should, of course, have immediately been terminated.[1]

When they had gone, the English commissioners proceeded as if nothing had happened, and continued to read and peruse the Casket Letters, which had now been translated into English, and the other evidence presented by Moray. Morton gave, on oath, his account of the discovery of the Casket Letters, which was based on a written declaration he had given to Cecil the previous day.[2] Many writers have given credence to Morton's words, but they can be proved inaccurate in at least one respect, for he claimed that Dalgleish was caught with Bothwell's patent of creation as Duke of Orkney on him; Bothwell in fact had this with him when he arrived in Norway. Finally, Thomas Nelson and Thomas Crawford appeared in camera as witnesses for the Lords, Crawford offering a revised version of his earlier testimony as to what passed between Mary and Darnley at Glasgow.

The next day, the Lords swore on oath that the Casket Letters were "undoubtedly" in Mary's handwriting. The commissioners then adjourned for the weekend, but on Monday, 12 December, examples of Mary's handwriting were exhibited to them, allowing them to make comparisons with the calligraphy of the Casket Letters. Leslie, hearing of this, protested that these comparisons constituted no legal proof of Mary's authorship, but merely reflected the opinions of the commissioners.

On the 13th, another deposition by Thomas Crawford was produced, this time recounting what Hepburn and Hay had said to him from the scaffold nine months before. That day, Elizabeth decided to further enlarge her commission: to avoid any accusation of partiality, she summoned her remaining Privy Councillors and six more earls to view the evidence; among them were the Catholic Earls of Northumberland and Westmorland, who had not arrived in time for the opening of the Westminster conference.

The enlarged commission met at Hampton Court for the final session of the conference, which lasted from 14 to 15 December. During it, the proceedings of the inquiry were read out, and the commissioners were given the chance to study and consider the evidence, including the Casket Letters. Afterwards, the English nobles expressed gratitude to the Queen for revealing to them the particulars of the inquiry, "wherein they had seen such foul matter as they thought truly in their consciences that Her Majesty's position was justified." They agreed that Mary's guilt was, "upon things now produced, made more apparent," and said that "they could not allow it as meet for Her Majesty's honour to admit the said Queen to Her Majesty's presence, as the case now did stand." De Silva, however, heard that the peers were not unanimous in their conclusions, and that, at the last meeting of the conference on the 15th, some had the courage to check the unseemly violence of Cecil's attitude towards the Queen of Scots.[3]

Elizabeth had nevertheless achieved her aim: the evidence against Mary had been aired before the most influential men in the kingdom, yet the Scottish Queen had never been heard in her own defence. Furthermore, the blame for this could be laid squarely on the shoulders of Mary and her commissioners, who had seemingly boycotted the inquiry, from which it might be inferred that there was no defence that they could offer. It was in this climate that Elizabeth declared the conference at an end.

Wishing to be seen as fair-minded, Elizabeth made a point of seeing Mary's commissioners on 16 December, and, "with many expressions of sympathy" for their mistress, reminded them that the Regent's evidence constituted "very great presumptions and arguments to confirm the common report against the said Queen." She told them that she was willing to reopen the inquiry if Mary agreed to answer Moray's charges, either through her commissioners, or in writing, or to a delegation of English nobles. Leslie and Herries wrote to Mary at once, urging her to compromise, so that she would not be assumed guilty "of such horrible crimes only for lack of coming into Her Majesty's presence," adding that Elizabeth had said that, if Mary refused all three options, "it will be thought as much as if she were culpable."

But Mary ignored their advice. On 19 December, she angrily rejected all Elizabeth's proposals, declaring that she could hardly be expected to answer charges based on evidence that she had not been allowed to examine, nor would she "answer otherwise than in person" before Elizabeth. Instead, she instructed her commissioners to ask for copies of all the writings produced against her, commanding that they themselves must see the originals. Then, "by God's grace, we shall make such answer thereto that our innocence shall be known to our good sister and to all other princes."

In the same letter, Mary belatedly drew up a list of her own charges against Moray, declaring that, in his Eik, he and his fellows had "falsely, traitorously and miscreantly lied, imputing to us the crime whereof they themselves are authors, inventors, doers and executors," a crime of which she now formally accused them. She expressed outrage at the Lords' accusation that she had plotted the death of her own child, which "calumny should suffice for proof and inquisition of all the rest, for the natural love of a mother towards her bairn confounds them." She referred back to the murder of Rizzio, when the Lords themselves would have "slain the mother and the bairn both when he was in our womb." Lastly, she condemned Moray's Regency as manifestly unlawful.[4]

This letter had not yet reached London when, on 21 December, despite heavy snow, Elizabeth sent some of Mary's commissioners to Bolton to give her a detailed report of the inquiry. With them, they carried a letter from the English Queen, informing Mary that

> as we have been very sorry of long time for your mishaps and great troubles, so find we our sorrows now double in beholding such things as are produced to prove yourself cause of all the same; and our grief herein is also increased in that we did not think at any time to have seen or heard such matters of so great appearance and moment to charge and condemn you. Nevertheless, both in friendship, nature and justice, we are moved to stay our judgement before we may hear of your direct answer thereunto. We cannot but, as one prince and near cousin regarding another, as earnestly as we may, require and charge you not to forbear answering.[5]

Elizabeth had seemingly forgotten her earlier declarations that she would pass no judgement on Mary's case; she was now more concerned with the fact that Mary could not be found guilty unless she had put forward a defence. She ended her letter by telling Mary that she would be "heartily glad and well content to hear of sufficient matter for your discharge." Yet, on the day after this was written, Cecil drafted a memorandum that envisaged Mary's detention in England as the ideal outcome of the inquiry; it would be best, he wrote, if she was "to remain in the realm and not depart until she has repaired the wrong done by her claim to the crown." This was the crux of the matter. Moreover, Cecil was of the opinion that, even if Moray and the Lords had been accessories to Darnley's murder and the Bothwell marriage, Mary was probably guilty too. But regardless of whether she was guilty or not, England's security was paramount.

Leslie and Herries were not optimistic about the outcome of the inquiry. They realised that, if Mary would not answer the Lords' case, her position would be perilous indeed. Again they tried to bring about a compromise, in the interests of preserving Mary's honour. They suggested three alternatives: firstly, Mary could ratify her abdication and live out her life in retirement in England; secondly, she and James could rule Scotland as joint sovereigns, while Moray retained the Regency; thirdly, she could remain Queen of Scots, but live in seclusion in England while Moray ruled in her name as Regent. Moray rejected the last two suggestions, but urged that Elizabeth press Mary to agree to the first. Elizabeth naturally favoured this course, since it would remove the need for her to pronounce judgement, and accordingly, she wrote to Knollys on 22 December, ordering him to suggest to Mary, "as if from yourself," that, in view of her refusal to answer the charges, her wisest course would be to accept Moray's government, commit her cause "to perpetual silence," and live in England as a private person for the rest of her life. Leslie, who had suggested this course, urged Mary to take it.[6]

On 22 December, having learned that Herries and Leslie were planning to accuse the Scottish Lords of the murder of Darnley, Lindsay wrote to Herries and challenged him to a duel. Herries replied: "That you were privy to it, Lord Lindsay, I know not; and if you will say that I have specially spoken of you, you lied in your throat." He added that he was willing to take up a challenge from the "principals" in the murder, which was probably a reference to Moray, Maitland and Morton.

Herries and Leslie met with the English commissioners on Christmas Eve and informed them that they had been authorised by Mary to charge the Regent and his colleagues with Darnley's murder. The next day, they presented to Elizabeth Mary's list of charges against the Scottish Lords, and asked to see the writings produced against their Queen. Elizabeth said she thought this a "very reasonable" request, and said she was glad to hear that "her good sister would make answer in that manner for the defence of her honour."

Meanwhile, at Bolton, Knollys had been urging Mary to answer the accusations of her enemies. Upon receiving Elizabeth's letter of 22 December, he told Mary that she stood "in a very hard case," and if she would not answer the charges, she would "provoke" Elizabeth "to take you as condemned, and to publish the same, to your utter disgrace and infamy, especially in England. And after this sort [he continued] I began to strike as great terror into her as I could. She answered stoutly as she would make all other princes know how evil she was handled, coming upon trust into this realm, and saith, 'I am sure the Queen will not condemn me, hearing only mine adversaries, and not me.'" Knollys answered, "Yet she will condemn you if you condemn yourself by not answering." He told her that the best way of saving her honour and consigning all the accusations against her to oblivion was to resign her crown to her son and "remain in England a convenient time."

"The judgement of the world would in such a case condemn me," Mary replied. Knollys suggested she "think better on it at her pleasure," and left. He warned Elizabeth he did not believe that Mary would ever be brought to answer the charges against her without being assured beforehand that judgement would be given in her favour, "unless your Council would take a short answer for a sufficient answer: that is to say, that the accusations of her adversaries are false because that she, on the word of a prince, will say that they are false." It was unreasonable, of course, for the English to expect Mary to answer Moray's accusations without seeing the evidence, or being allowed to defend herself in person; she told Knollys that she could easily overturn the Lords' case, but had never had any intention of answering it before anyone other than Elizabeth, her equal. It is hardly surprising that, in these circumstances, Mary expected judgement to be given in her favour, yet it was perhaps rash of her to stand on her dignity as a sovereign ruler and refuse to answer the charges of her subjects, when, as Knollys had so succinctly pointed out, she stood in such a hard case.

At long last, Mary was beginning to perceive that the English were in collusion with Moray, and that Elizabeth's fair words had all along masked a steely determination to maintain the present state of affairs. Around this time, Mary wrote to Mar, begging him to guard James and not allow him to be brought openly to England or taken by stealth.[7]

On 28 December, Mary's commissioners met again with the English commissioners, and were disturbed to learn that the latter were almost to a man convinced of the soundness of the Scottish Lords' case, "notwithstanding our reasons to the contrary." Things now looked very dismal indeed for Mary.

At Bolton, on 1 January 1569, Lord Scrope added his persuasions to those of Knollys, urging a doubtful Mary to abdicate. Mary said she would think on their advice and give them her answer in two days. Afterwards, Knollys and Scrope reported to Elizabeth that she would never yield.[8]

Mary must have felt isolated and friendless. Leslie's efforts to reach an honourable compromise had almost amounted to a betrayal. She could trust no one, for there was no one who did not have an ulterior motive. They were all urging her to abdicate, as if she were guilty, but if she did as everyone urged, she would virtually be acknowledging her guilt. This made her mind up. On 3 January, she told Knollys that her resolution was unalterably fixed, and that she would prefer death to the ignominious terms proposed by her enemies.[9]

Back at court, the Earl of Arundel told Elizabeth plainly on 4 January that one who had a crown could hardly persuade another sovereign to leave her crown because her subjects would not obey her. "It may be a new doctrine in Scotland, but it is not good to be taught in England." However, Elizabeth's course was set, and she was impervious to arguments.

Mary was trying to gather evidence against the Lords. On 5 January, she sent Huntly the famous written declaration of what had taken place at Craigmillar in December 1566, which she required him and Argyll to sign as a true record of events, and which implied that Maitland and Moray were the instigators of the plot against Darnley. The two Earls were to affirm that, "the murder of the said Henry Stuart following, we judge in our consciences that the said Earl of Moray and Secretary Lethington were authors, inventors, devisers, counsellors and causers of the said murder, in what manner or by whatsoever persons the same was executed."[10] As has been argued, this was probably the truth, but Huntly and Argyll were also implicated in the murder, although Mary may not have been aware of this. Unfortunately for her, this document was intercepted by English spies, and was in Cecil's hands by 19 January, for it was on that date that Moray wrote his answer to it, for Cecil's benefit.

As they had been instructed, Mary's commissioners saw Elizabeth on 7 January, and demanded that, pursuant to their sovereign's resolve to charge Moray and the Lords with Darnley's murder, she "desired the writings produced by her rebellious subjects, or at the least the copies thereof, to be delivered unto them, that their mistress might fully answer thereto, as was desired." Elizabeth said she would give them an answer in two or three days. When she suggested that it would be better all round if the Queen of Scots abdicated, Leslie protested that Mary would prefer death, and that as this was her final resolution, he could not write to her again on the subject, as Elizabeth wished. Even as this meeting was taking place, the English government was drawing up a paper assessing the possibilities of keeping Mary in England, securely held but with all the courtesies due to a queen, without Elizabeth having passed any judgement on her.

An embittered Mary had ceased to believe in Elizabeth's assurances and goodwill, and, with little understanding of the true extent of Catholic support for her cause in England, now embarked on the first of many intrigues against her royal cousin. On 8 January, she sent a message to Philip of Spain, via the Spanish ambassador, telling him that, with his help, she herself could be Queen of England in three months, and Mass would once more be celebrated all over the country.[11] But Philip was not ready to commit any resources to such a hazardous undertaking; he also feared that, if Mary did win the English crown, she would ally herself with France, Spain's enemy.

It is clear that, from January 1569 onwards, Mary was more interested in claiming the English throne than in regaining the Scottish one. After all, the one might be a springboard to the other. To this end, she was to be implicated in a relentless series of plots against Elizabeth, becoming the focus and figurehead of Catholic intrigues that were all centred upon restoring the ancient faith in England. "My last breath shall be that of a queen," she was to declare.[12]

On 9 December, Mary's commissioners told the English Lords at Hampton Court that their mistress would never abdicate. The next day, Elizabeth formally ended the inquiry with her long-awaited pronouncement, in which she declared that nothing had been sufficiently proved, against either Mary or Moray, and that she "saw no cause to conceive an ill opinion of her good sister of Scotland." When it came to the point, Elizabeth had after all declined to pass judgement, not wishing to make it appear that a reigning sovereign was subject to the jurisdiction of any tribunal.

In giving this ruling, Elizabeth had reserved all her options. The evidence offered against Mary had given her a pretext for keeping her in custody, since she dared not set her at liberty; yet, as Mary had not been found guilty of any crime, and the evidence had been kept secret, Elizabeth could choose to restore her to her throne whenever it suited her. Mary was the trump card in her hand, to be played whenever Elizabeth wished to manipulate Scottish affairs to her own advantage. Her verdict made sound political sense, for she had shown herself helpful to both sides, and thereby avoided offending either the Scots or Mary's Catholic supporters. Furthermore, it ensured the continuance of a friendly Protestant regime in Scotland, and bound England and Scotland together in long-term amity for the first time in history. It had also left Mary tainted by suspicion, with her innocence in question.

On the day Elizabeth gave her verdict, Cecil told Moray that Elizabeth, hearing of "the unquiet state and disorder of the realm of Scotland now in his absence, thinketh meet not to restrain any further the Earl and his adherents' liberty, but suffer him and them at their pleasure to depart, till she hear further of the Queen of Scotland's answers to such things as have been alleged against her."[13] It was pretty safe to assume that Mary would never condescend to answer Moray's charges, and that he would not need to be recalled.

On the 11th, in an attempt to prevent Moray's return to Scotland, Mary's commissioners told Cecil, in the presence of the Regent, that they had been instructed by Mary to accuse Moray and his adherents of Darnley's murder, but were still awaiting copies of the "pretended writings given in against their mistress, which they have divers times required of the Queen's Majesty and her Council, but they have not as yet obtained; and how soon they received the copies thereof, she would answer thereto in defence of her innocence." Cecil made no answer. It would appear that both he and the Lords were aware that Mary would be able to demolish their case, and that he was determined that she should not have the opportunity to do so. On 12 January, therefore, Moray was granted formal licence to return to Scotland, even though Mary had charged him with regicide.

Mary's commissioners were informed by Cecil, on 13 January, that Elizabeth would not deny the Queen of Scots sight of "true copies" of the Casket Letters, but before they were delivered to her, she required "a special writing sent by the Queen of Scots, signed with her own hand, promising that she will answer to the things laid to her charge without exception"; then the matter would be subject to trial, and she would be judged innocent or guilty. Elizabeth warned her to think seriously about the consequences of a guilty verdict, for then "the Queen's Majesty can never with her honour show her any favour." Mary's commissioners reiterated that, "whatsoever thing was produced by the Queen's rebels was but invented slanders and private writings, which could not prejudice her in any wise." They also claimed that Mary, like Moray, should be given licence to return to Scotland, but Cecil answered that Moray had promised to return at any time if Elizabeth required his presence; "in the meantime, the Queen of Scotland could not be suffered to depart, for divers respects." With their worst fears confirmed, Herries and Leslie made vehement protests, but Cecil would not say any more.

Moray left London around 19 January, enriched by a large loan from Elizabeth, which was to be used to crush the Marian party in Scotland. Before he left, he had told Norfolk that, "so far from not loving his sister, she was the creature upon Earth that he loved the best. He never wished her harm. Her own pressing was the occasion of that which was uttered to her infamy." He also discussed the prospect of a marriage between Norfolk and Mary, and departed under the impression that Elizabeth looked kindly upon it, when in fact she had warned Norfolk to put all thoughts of this marriage out of his head. Moray had also been granted a farewell audience with Elizabeth, who promised to maintain him in his Regency.

After Moray had gone, the French ambassador, at Mary's instance, interceded with Elizabeth on her behalf, expressing the hope that Her Majesty would not permit the Queen of Scots to be oppressed by her rebellious subjects, and would furnish Mary's commissioners with copies of the evidence against her. Elizabeth looked profoundly moved, and promised that this would be done the very next day. But she did not keep her word. On 20 January, she wrote coldly to Mary:

> It may be, Madam, that in receiving a letter from me, you may look to hear something which shall be for your honour. I would it were so, but I will not deceive you. Your case is not so clear but that much remains to be explained.

There were no further pronouncements on Mary's future. It was obvious to most people that Elizabeth intended keeping her a prisoner.

30

"THE DAUGHTER OF DEBATE"

~

MARY WAS MOVED TO TUTBURY Castle in Staffordshire on 26 January 1569, and placed in the custody of its owner, George Talbot, Earl of Shrewsbury. For the next eighteen years, she would remain Elizabeth's prisoner. It is often claimed that, throughout that time, she maintained her silence over the Darnley murder, yet it is almost certain that her version of events formed the substance of Claude Nau's *Memorials*, written in 1578 while he was employed as her secretary.[1]

On 31 January, Mary's commissioners were allowed to depart for Scotland. Lord Fleming returned at once to Dumbarton Castle, which he thereafter helped to hold in the Queen's name against the Lords in power. Herries united with Chatelherault and the Hamiltons to plot a revolt against Moray, but in April 1569, after refusing to acknowledge James as King, they were imprisoned by the Regent.

As the years passed, Mary was confined in several different houses, notably Wingfield Manor and Chatsworth House in Derbyshire, and Sheffield Castle in Yorkshire. Her existence in captivity was not unduly onerous to begin with, but as it became clear that she was increasingly becoming the focus of plots against Elizabeth's throne, security was tightened and further restraints were placed on her. Although keeping Mary under restraint had seemed the best solution in 1568, Elizabeth was to find that her presence in England was a constant source of anxiety, for there was always the risk that she might either escape, incite Elizabeth's Catholic subjects to rebel, or inspire attempts on Elizabeth's crown or her life.

Nevertheless, Mary was housed in some luxury and deferred to as a queen. Amongst her possessions, she kept miniatures and portraits of Francis II and Darnley, but none of Bothwell.[2] Although she was only twenty-six when she was moved to Tutbury, she aged rapidly in captivity, and took to wearing wigs to hide her greying hair, while her health, never particularly robust, declined over the years, making her a martyr to rheumatism. Yet poor health did not deflect her from her ambition to seize the English throne and be revenged on her enemies.

Her brief flirtation with Anglicanism over, she became increasingly pious, as became the rightful Catholic Queen of England. With a conscious display of religiosity, she cultivated a new and successful image as a martyr who had suffered for her faith at the hands of heretics, which was calculated to enlist the sympathy and support of the Pope and the Catholic powers, and obliterate the false and unfair stigma of murderess and adulteress.[3] As time went by, many Catholics forgot the scandals that had touched Mary's past, and thought of her only as the dynastic hope of their religion, and the Catholic powers in Europe came to espouse her cause with increasing—and, to Elizabeth, alarming—fervour. Yet for Scottish and English Protestants, she remained the evil woman who had killed her husband in order to marry her lover.

After the imprisonment of Herries and Chatelherault, Leslie returned to England to work for Mary's restoration, and was told by Elizabeth that she fully intended to bring this about "without making any mention of the murder of her husband or any part of the rest of the heinous crimes."[4] Leslie was also hoping to bring about the marriage between Mary and Norfolk, which he believed would be to the advantage of both Queens. He had been working for some time on a written defence of Mary, in response to the calumnies of Buchanan, and this spirited work was published abroad in May 1569, although, significantly, it was suppressed in England and made an indignant Elizabeth think again about restoring Mary. Of Mary, Leslie wrote: "Her person and the whole trade of her godly and virtuous life past do far repel and drive away all suspicion and conjectural presumptions." After the *Defence* was published in France in 1571, copies of it were smuggled into England.

Moray was still trying to justify his position, and on 13 May 1569, published a proclamation accusing Mary afresh of Darnley's murder.[5] Around the middle of June, Paris was brought back to Scotland.

Mary was still making plans for a marriage with Norfolk, which she regarded as a means of escaping from captivity. In June, at her instigation, Bothwell authorised Lord Boyd to procure an annulment of his marriage to Mary,[6] and she herself commanded Boyd to ask Moray and the Lords for a written mandate to institute "an action for divorce" in Scotland, on the grounds that, when their wedding took place, Bothwell was already contracted to another wife and had not been lawfully divorced from her. Mary may also have applied to the Pope for an annulment. By 8 July, Norfolk himself was negotiating with Moray to secure the annulment of the Bothwell marriage, with a view to marrying Mary and thereby uniting England and Scotland.[7] In this enterprise, he had Maitland's support, as well as that of Philip of Spain and the powerful Catholic Earls of Northumberland and Westmorland. The Catholics' agenda differed, in that they saw the Norfolk marriage as a means to Elizabeth's overthrow and the re-establishment of the ancient religion in England.

But, at a congress of the Scottish Lords at Perth on 25 July, forty of the forty-nine nobles present dismissed Mary's request for an annulment on the grounds that it was impious; in truth, they feared that any man she married now would take up arms in her cause. They also publicly avowed that they would never allow her to return to Scotland, either as Queen or co-regent, or even as a private person. Balfour, surprisingly, was among the nine who voted for Mary's restoration:[8] he had already fallen foul of Moray, and perhaps feared exposure for his part in Darnley's murder. Maitland, who had also declared for Mary, publicly opined that it was very strange that those who had so lately taken up arms against their Queen expressly for the purpose of separating her from Bothwell, should now have so entirely changed their minds.[9] Relations between Moray and Maitland were now, understandably, icy. The Secretary, having "seen that the scales had turned," had long since secretly begun "to traffic for the Queen's return to Scotland,"[10] and now he was making his position clear. It was, unfortunately, too late for either himself or Mary.

Argyll had also voted in favour of Mary, but soon afterwards submitted to Moray and was reconciled to the Lords.

Three days later, the Scottish Lords rejected Norfolk's request, pointing out that, if the Queen of Scots wanted her freedom, she only had to ask King Frederick to chop off Bothwell's head. Mary was greatly grieved that her proposals had been rejected out of hand, while her supporters in Scotland gave more serious thought to the notion of restoring her by armed force.

On 9 and 10 August, in his prison at St. Andrews, Paris made two depositions. In the first, apparently voluntary, one, he made no accusations against Mary; but in the second, which was almost certainly extracted under torture, the interrogation being supervised by (among others) Buchanan and John Wood, Paris charged the Queen directly with Darnley's murder. Significantly, and probably correctly, he also implicated Maitland, Balfour, Huntly and Argyll in the crime. Of course, the aim of this, in the light of recent events, was to undermine the Queen's party, but these depositions were never made public because the testimony in them was greatly at variance with that in the earlier depositions, and much of it was obviously contrived. Even Buchanan omitted to publish them, although he included the depositions of Hay, Hepburn and Dalgleish in his Detectio.

There is no record of Paris being put on trial. He was summarily hanged and quartered for his part in Darnley's murder on 16 August. Six days too late, Elizabeth wrote to Moray requesting that he be sent to London for interrogation, her purpose being to discover the extent of Moray's involvement in the crime. But Moray had already ensured Paris's silence. Instead, he sent Paris's depositions to London, trusting that they would be "found so authentic as the credit thereof shall not seem doubtful."[11] But even the wily Cecil could find no use for such obviously flawed documents, and they were consigned to oblivion.[12]

Moray now set out to destroy Maitland. At the beginning of September, he enticed him to Stirling and caused Thomas Crawford to accuse him in Council of Darnley's murder.[13] As a result, Maitland was placed under house arrest, where, "seeing that his life was in immediate danger, [he] began with increased activity to organise a party for his own security" and continued to plan Mary's restoration, negotiating "with every member of her party."[14] He secured as allies Grange, Atholl and Seton.

Balfour, another turncoat, was also arrested at this time and accused of the murder of Darnley, but was freed on condition that he agree to answer a summons to trial when required, which, for "secret causes" between him and the Lords, he never was.[15] This may refer to the indemnity about which several historians have speculated.

Moray's intention was to imprison Maitland in the fortress of Tantallon, a castle on the East Lothian coast that was owned by Morton, but while he was being conveyed there, he was rescued by Kirkcaldy of Grange and carried off to Edinburgh Castle, which Grange was holding for Mary. Maitland was only too pleased to join him. This coalition between Scotland's greatest politician and her greatest soldier was a blow to Moray, but he had not the resources to besiege the mighty fortress of Edinburgh.

In England, that September, Elizabeth found out that Norfolk was scheming to marry Mary, and her rage was such that Moray's government became more secure overnight. By 11 October, Norfolk was a prisoner in the Tower of London. That month, in retaliation, a rising broke out in the north of England, orchestrated by the Catholic Earls; its aims were to depose Elizabeth and set up Mary in her place, bring about Mary's marriage to Norfolk, and thereby return England to the Church of Rome. The King of France was supporting the rebels, King Philip was sympathetic, and a Florentine banker and papal agent, Roberto Ridolfi, was funding the enterprise. This was the most dangerous threat to her security that Elizabeth had encountered since her accession.

Although Mary did not support the rebellion, Cecil warned Elizabeth that "the Queen of Scots is, and always shall be, a dangerous person to your estate," and said, with some prescience, that, if she were found guilty of her husband's murder, "she shall be less a person perilous; if passed over in silence, the scar of the murder will wear out, and the danger [will be] greater." Elizabeth's Councillors were urging her to have Mary executed, and for a time she gave serious thought to their pleas; she even allowed them to draw up a death warrant. Then she backed down, realising that the execution of an anointed queen would set a very dangerous precedent indeed. She did, however, write reminding Charles IX that Mary's husband had been "foully murdered" and that she had married "the principal murderer."[16]

In November, as the northern rebels marched south towards Tutbury, Mary was moved to Coventry; at this point, the rebellion began to collapse. By 20 December, it had been ruthlessly suppressed by Elizabeth's forces. But Mary was still cherishing hopes of marrying Norfolk, and in December and January, sent passionate letters to him in the Tower.

By 1570, many nobles had become disaffected from Moray's rule, and the Hamiltons were openly voicing suspicions that he was plotting to seize the throne, which they themselves claimed as next heirs after James VI. On 23 January, a nephew of Archbishop Hamilton,[17] James Hamilton of Bothwellhaugh, assassinated the Regent as he rode through the streets of Linlithgow. There can be little doubt that the Archbishop himself was implicated in the murder. Bothwellhaugh escaped to France.

Moray was buried in St. Giles's Kirk, Knox having preached his funeral sermon, in which he called upon God to remember the Regent's foolish pity for Mary and the other murderers of Darnley. "He is at rest, O Lord, and we are left in extreme misery!" he cried. It was true, for the death of "the good Regent," as the people were now calling him, plunged Scotland into chaos.

When Mary heard of her half-brother's death, she wrote to Archbishop Beaton "that she was the more indebted to the assassin," but "that he had acted without her instigation." In a letter to Moray's widow, she declared that the murder had been done against her will. Nevertheless, she awarded Bothwellhaugh a pension.[18]

She had much to thank him for, because after the Regent's death, her party grew in strength, which weakened the position of the Protestant Lords, whose unofficial leader was Morton. This led to civil war in Scotland. The Lords began attacking Grange in Edinburgh Castle, but with little success. It seemed at one point that the Marian party might emerge triumphant, for Huntly was holding the north-east and the Hamiltons the west, Chatelherault and Herries having been released after Moray's death. The King of

France had offered them his support. It would be easy for him to land an army at Dumbarton, which commanded the estuary of the Clyde and was held by Lord Fleming for the Queen.

As the crisis deepened in Scotland, Pope Pius V, having learned of the ruthless suppression of the Northern Rising, precipitately excommunicated Queen Elizabeth, exhorting her subjects to rise against her and set Mary in her place. The English government feared that, armoured with this papal sanction, Catholics might be encouraged to plot against the Queen, and from this time they were regarded less as heretics than as traitors. Further restrictions were placed upon them, and security around Mary was tightened. Most Catholics in England ignored the Bull of excommunication, but the government could afford to take no chances.

Elizabeth was determined that the next Regent of Scotland should be someone who was friendly towards England. She chose Lennox, and forced the reluctant Scots to accept him. He was elected Regent on 12 July 1570, although his wife and son Charles were made to stay in England as hostages for his good behaviour. At this time, both Elizabeth and Mary were independently scheming to have James brought to England and placed in the care of his grandmother, Lady Lennox. Mary's mother-in-law had always condemned her as Darnley's murderess, but on 10 July, in the interests of her son, Mary swallowed her pride and wrote an aggrieved letter to the Countess, expressing the hope that her innocence would be made manifest to her:

Madam, if the wrong and false reports of rebels, enemies well known for traitors to you, and alas! too trusted of me by your advice, had not so far stirred you against mine innocency (and, I must say, against all kindness, that you have not only condemned me wrongfully, but so hated me, as some words and open deeds have so testified to all the world, a manifest misliking in you against your own blood), I would not thus long have omitted my duty in writing to you, excusing me of those untrue reports made of me. But hoping, with God's grace and time, to have my innocency known to you, as I trust it is already to the most part of all indifferent [impartial] persons, I thought it not best to trouble you for a time, till such a matter is moved that touches us both, which is the transporting your little [grand]son and my only child in this country. I would be glad to have your advice therein, as in all other matters touching him. I have borne him, and God knows at what danger to him and me both, and of you he is descended. So I mean not to forget my duty to you in showing herein any unkindness to you, how unkindly soever ye have dealt by me, but will love you as my aunt and respect you as my mother-in-law. Your natural good niece and loving daughter, Marie.[19]

Mary may have hoped, by bringing Lady Lennox over to her side, to have some future contact with the son she had not seen for over three years. She had sent gifts and later wrote letters to him, but it is doubtful he was allowed to receive any of them. Nor would the Scots consent to him being taken out of the country, so Mary's scheming came to nothing. Her letter to Lady Lennox was doubly in vain, for that lady refused to revise her implacable opinion of her daughter-in-law, and when, the following September, Elizabeth was toying with the idea of restoring Mary to her throne, Lady Lennox begged her to reconsider:

The knowledge thereof is to me of no small discomfort, considering that, notwithstanding the grievous murder which, by her means only, was upon my son, her husband, executed, divers persons in this realm doth yet doubt, and a great many doth credit that, since her coming hither, she is found clear and not to be culpable of that fact.[20]

Lady Lennox also sent Mary's letter on to Lennox, who responded:

What can I say but that I do not marvel to see her write the best [she] can for herself. It will be long time that is able to put a matter so notorious in oblivion, to make black white, or innocency to appear where the contrary is so well known. The most indifferent, I trust, doubts not of the equity of your and my cause, and of the just occasion of our misliking. Her right duty to you and me were her true confession and unfeigned repentance of that lamentable fact. God is just and will not in the end be abused.[21]

As Regent, Lennox espoused the Protestant cause with fervour, but met constant opposition from his old rivals, the Hamiltons, and the rest of the Marian party, who refused to recognise his Regency. Never popular in Scotland, he made himself even more hated by his grim determination to avenge Darnley's murder. On 16 July, he wrote to his wife that he was still assured of Mary's guilt, having been convinced by the Casket Letters, "the confessions of men gone to the death, and other infallible experience."[22]

Maitland, who had felt it safe to leave Edinburgh Castle after Moray's death, had gone to Atholl, and was now acknowledged the leader of the Queen's party, despite having been struck down of late with a wasting disease: he could no longer walk and was so weak that even to sneeze was painful.[23] Grange had remained at his post, determined to hold Edinburgh Castle for Mary. Balfour had also stayed loyal to Mary, if only out of self-interest, for Lennox was out for his blood. In August, Lennox defeated Huntly at Brechin, and Elizabeth brought about a truce between the two parties, which was, however, broken early in 1571 by the Hamiltons.

Under Lennox's auspices, George Buchanan was appointed tutor to the four-year-old King, a post he would hold for eight years. Buchanan saw to it that James was well educated, but he brought the child up to believe in his mother's guilt, and accordingly subjected him to a severe Calvinist regime. Years later, James would reject and suppress Buchanan's views, and would also condemn Moray as an unnatural rebel, but by then he had been so indoctrinated that, not remembering Mary, he could never love her, but saw her chiefly as a threat to his throne.

Lennox made renewed efforts to secure Bothwell's extradition, and sent one Thomas Buchanan to Denmark to demand it. This envoy became aware that Bothwell and Mary were still corresponding freely, and protested that this should be stopped and that the couriers concerned—an English spy called Horsey and Bothwell's Danish page, Herman—should be imprisoned. Mary was also in contact with Hepburn of Riccarton, Bothwell's cousin, who doubtless provided another channel of communication. After reading Thomas Buchanan's report, Cecil expressed concern that Bothwell could so easily make contact with Mary. None of the letters between the couple has survived.

In the summer of 1570, Elizabeth demanded that Frederick have Bothwell executed, reminding him that it did him no honour "that a regicide should wander free to live unpunished."[24] Again, in March 1571, she urged that the Earl be released for trial in Scotland or England, which was the last thing the Scottish Lords wanted: they were pressing for Bothwell's summary execution. But Frederick demurred; he still regarded Bothwell as a useful political pawn, and it was by no means uncertain that Mary would regain her kingdom. Furthermore, Bothwell had consistently denied any involvement in Darnley's murder.[25]

There is little doubt that the English establishment knew very well who Darnley's true killers were. In a letter to Cecil dated 15 October 1570, Thomas Randolph wrote from Scotland that he minded not "to name such as are yet here living," who were "most notoriously known to have been chief consenters to the King's death; only I will say that the universal bruit cometh upon three or four persons which subscribed a bond promising to concur and assist each other in doing the same."[26] These persons were almost certainly Maitland, Huntly, Argyll and Bothwell (Moray being dead), and Cecil must have already known or guessed who they were.

In November 1570, Sir Henry Norris, the English ambassador in Paris, incorrectly reported that the Pope had annulled Mary's marriage to Bothwell on the grounds of rape.[27] No documentation of this exists in the Vatican archives, and the report is proved false by the fact that Mary again raised the question of nullity in 1575. In January 1571, Mary sent Master Horsey with a message to King Frederick, urging "that Lord Bothwell be not delivered up to punishment,"[28] and in June that year, the French government echoed her request, fearing that, if Bothwell were put on trial, his revelations might be damaging to her. The next month, Lennox informed Frederick that he was content to postpone Bothwell's case until another day.

Norfolk's release from the Tower in August 1570 signalled the inception of what became known as the Ridolfi Plot, the aim of which was to place Mary and Norfolk on the English throne with Spanish help. The Florentine Ridolfi was to act as agent and financier, and Bishop Leslie was one of the brains behind the plot.

In January 1571, Ridolfi offered to act as Mary's representative in the courts of Europe, where he would be well placed to enlist support for her cause. He later claimed that she agreed to this, but none of her written credentials survives, nor do any of the incriminating letters he alleged she had written. In one of these, dated 8 February, she outlined the plot to Norfolk and invited him to join the conspiracy, much to his alarm; but he had been won over by 10 March.

At the end of March, Thomas Crawford, crying "A Darnley! A Darnley!," captured the seemingly impregnable Dumbarton Castle from the Queen's supporters, depriving them of a strategically valuable fortress, and bringing the West under the control of the Regent. Fleming escaped to France (he died in September 1572), but one of those taken was Archbishop Hamilton, who was to feel the full force of Lennox's vengeance. The Regent was convinced that the Archbishop had helped to murder Darnley, and also knew him to be the man who had masterminded Moray's assassination. On 7 April, without bothering with the formality of a trial, he had him hanged in his ecclesiastical vestments, and then quartered, at Stirling.[29] To the last, the Archbishop protested his innocence. Afterwards, Buchanan wrote the account of Darnley's murder that imputed it to Hamilton, which, as has already been noted, was at variance with his earlier allegations; but it was now necessary to provide justification for Lennox's tyrannical and unprecedented execution of the Primate of Scotland.

The Archbishop's death provoked Grange into publishing an act of defiance against Lennox, and led to an intensification of the civil war. Grange was now holding Edinburgh Castle against what would become known as the "Lang Siege," and was joined there by Maitland and Rothes. In June 1571, Captain Cullen, who had been in Edinburgh Castle with Balfour, was captured by Morton and promptly executed, "to the end that [Morton] might the more freely enjoy the favour of his fair wife."[30] Thereafter, Morton lived in open adultery with Mrs. Cullen.

Herries, believing that Mary's cause was hopeless, sought a reconciliation with Morton in August 1571. But the Hamiltons were not giving up without a fight. On 4 September, in revenge for the murder of Archbishop Hamilton, they and their allies attempted a coup, and Lennox was assassinated in the process, being shot during an attack on Stirling Castle. His title was inherited by his sixteen-year-old son, Charles, and the moderate but ailing Mar, Elizabeth's candidate and Morton's puppet, replaced him as Regent the following month.

The English government had now received secret intelligence of the Ridolfi Plot. On 7 September, Norfolk was arrested on a charge of high treason, and sent to the Tower of London. When questioned, Mary admitted having dealings with Ridolfi, but denied being involved in any conspiracy. Bishop Leslie was also sent to the Tower, on 24 October, and that same week, an outraged Elizabeth, convinced that Mary had connived at her assassination, finally authorised the publication in London of Buchanan's *Detectio*, which included transcripts of three of the Casket Letters in an appendix and Thomas Wilson's *Actio contra Mariam* (known in English as *The Oration*), a venomous attack on Mary modelled on the *Detectio*, but with even more errors. A Scots edition of the *Detectio* was also published in London (and again in Scotland in 1572), which included all eight of the Casket Letters. Now, for the first time, the people of England and Scotland could read the evidence for Mary Stuart's complicity in the murder of her husband, and, unsurprisingly, these works became bestsellers. In January 1572, Elizabeth at last recognised James VI as King of Scots, and thereby made the Scottish government aware that she had no further intention of restoring Mary.

On 3 November, under interrogation by Thomas Wilson, Master of the Court of Requests, and in fear of the rack, Leslie broke, and made the first of several statements that were highly damaging to Mary, attributing the Northern Rising to a plot between her, Norfolk and the northern Earls. Three days later, he said that "the Queen his mistress was not fit for any husband," for she had "poisoned the French King, as he credibly understood," consented to the murder of Darnley, then "matched with the murderer," Bothwell, and brought him to Carberry Hill in the hope that he too would be killed. Now she was planning to marry Norfolk, who Leslie believed would not survive long. In the circumstances, little credence can be given to this statement, although some writers have relied on it as evidence that Leslie believed in Mary's guilt. Dr. Wilson himself was shocked by it, and observed, "Lord, what a people are these! What a Queen, and what an ambassador!"[31]

Two days later, Leslie was made to write to Mary to tell her that he had been forced to confess all he knew about the plot, since her letters had been produced before the Council.[32] Mary also received a copy of Buchanan's book, which Elizabeth had pointedly sent her; she promptly denounced it as "the lewd work of an atheist." Her detractors have pointed out that she did not specifically comment on the Casket Letters or disclaim authorship of them, but as they were part of the book, and she had denounced it in its entirety, there was no need for her to do so.

Norfolk was condemned to death for high treason on 16 January 1572. For some months, Elizabeth could not bring herself to sign the death warrant. She also resisted the insistent pleas and demands of her government to put Mary to death also, despite having been warned that, until the Scottish Queen was dead, neither her crown nor her life would be secure. It was probably at this time that Elizabeth wrote her famous poem about Mary:

The daughter of debate, that aye discord doth sow,
Shall reap no gain where former rule still peace hath taught to know.

On 26 May, aware that public feeling against Mary was intensifying, the English Parliament drew up a Bill of Attainder listing the Scottish Queen's offences and depriving her of her claim to the English throne, but it never became law because Elizabeth vetoed it. Instead, she threw Norfolk to the wolves. On 2 June, he was beheaded.

The following August, the St. Bartholemew's Day Massacre took place in France, and hundreds of French Protestants were mercilessly slaughtered. Any remaining sympathy that the English may have felt for Mary was extinguished in the ensuing anti-Catholic backlash, and again there were demands for her execution. The English ambassador in Paris did his utmost to persuade the French government that Mary was guilty of multiple adultery, the murder of two husbands, and bigamy. Yet even now, Mary was continuing with her secret intrigues, which moved Charles IX to comment with acute foresight that "the poor fool" would never cease until she lost her head.

In September 1572, in an attempt to shift the problem of what to do with Mary on to the Scots, the English government asked Mar to demand that she be returned to Scotland to face trial for the murder of Darnley, a trial that would almost certainly lead to demands for the extreme penalty. Although Mar personally felt that Mary's death was "the only salve for the cures of this commonwealth," the Scottish Lords in general were not in favour of the idea, not wishing to take responsibility for the execution of a queen. Morton said they would agree to the proposal if Elizabeth was prepared to send English troops to stand around the scaffold. Naturally, Elizabeth would not agree to this: she could not be seen to be sanctioning the beheading of a fellow sovereign, so the plan was abandoned.

Once Elizabeth's resolve not to restore Mary became known in Denmark,

Bothwell lost his value as a political prisoner, and King Frederick withdrew his privileges. With them went Bothwell's hopes of ever regaining his freedom.

Mar died suddenly, "regretted by many," on 28 October 1572. According to Melville, he became violently ill after dining with Morton at Dalkeith. "Some of his friends and the vulgar suspected he had gotten wrong at his banquet."[33]

A month later, on 24 November, the day Knox died urging Elizabeth "to apply the axe to the root of evil,"[34] Morton was elected Regent of Scotland, being the fourth man to hold the office since Mary's deposition. Morton was one of Mary's most implacable enemies, and he was determined to crush her party; he was to prove an effective, if ruthless and avaricious, regent, and restored relatively stable rule to Scotland whilst maintaining very friendly relations with Elizabeth. Argyll had now established his loyalty to the Lords, and was made Lord High Chancellor by Morton; he died in 1574. Balfour also came to terms with the new Regent, professed the Protestant religion and obtained the reversal of his forfeiture.[35] However, he proved something of an embarrassment to Morton, for many were offended that he "should enjoy the benefit of pacification,"[36] so in 1573 he went to France and Spain, where he tried to raise funds and support for the restoration of the Catholic faith in Scotland.

Since Lennox's death, Lady Lennox had undergone a change of heart towards Mary. She no longer believed her guilty of Darnley's murder. Proof of this may be found in a letter from Mary to Archbishop Beaton, dated May 1578, in which Mary states that "this good lady was, thanks to God, in very good correspondence with me these five or six years bygone," which places the reconciliation around 1572/3. Mary revealed that Lady Lennox had

confessed to me, by sundry letters under her hand, which I carefully preserve, the injury she did me by unjust pursuits which she allowed to go out against me in her name, through bad information, but principally, she said, through the express orders of the Queen of England and the persuasion of her Council, who also took much solicitude that she and I might never come to good understanding together. But how soon she came to know of my innocence, she desisted from any further pursuit against me; nay, went so far as to refuse her consent to anything they should act against me in her name.[37]

We do not know how Lady Lennox came to be convinced of Mary's innocence, but it is easy to believe that she had been the tool of Elizabeth and her Council. Therefore, she must have had sound reasons for resisting their demands that she continue to spread slanders about Mary.

Under Morton, the last bastions of Marian resistance were destroyed. Blackness Castle, which had been held by Lord Claude Hamilton for a year, fell to the Regent on 10 February 1573. Until now, Chatelherault had remained faithful to the Queen's cause, but on 23 February, at the entreaty of Elizabeth, he and the rest of the Hamiltons, along with Huntly, were reconciled to Morton at what became known as the Pacification of Perth. This would lead shortly to the final collapse of Mary's cause in Scotland and the end of the civil war. According to the terms of the Pacification, the lands of the Hamiltons and Gordons were restored, and Archbishop Hamilton was posthumously rehabilitated. Chatelherault retired to Hamilton and died there on 22 January 1575. Huntly died the following year.

Morton was now free to concentrate his efforts on taking Edinburgh Castle, which was the only fortress left in the hands of Mary's supporters. But Grange had so far successfully resisted his besiegers. In April, at Morton's invitation, an English army led by Sir William Drury arrived in Edinburgh with its siege guns to boost the Regent's forces. On 29 May, after thirteen days of massive bombardment that had virtually reduced it to ruins, the once-mighty stronghold fell to Morton, and Mary's party was finally crushed. Even Seton made his peace with the Regent, and was soon afterwards admitted to the Privy Council.

Grange, Maitland and Lord Home were taken prisoner. Grange was hanged on 3 August at the Mercat Cross.[38] Home was imprisoned in Edinburgh Castle and died there, still a captive, on 11 August 1575. Maitland, who was so ill that he had been carried down to the vaults during the siege, was imprisoned at Leith,[39] and would no doubt have met the same fate as Grange had he not either died from a stroke on 8 or 9 June, or taken his own life by poison: Melville claimed that he had committed suicide "after the old Roman fashion." Morton had his decomposing body brought to trial in its coffin so that he could be condemned as a traitor, an outrage that provoked angry protests from Elizabeth. At her intercession, Morton had the body decently buried.

Shrewsbury reported that, after hearing of Maitland's death, Mary made "little show of grief, and yet it nips her near."[40] Perhaps she had come to realise that Maitland had, in his latter years, been a true friend to her.

Bothwell was first reported to be mad in March 1573. "A man lately out of Sweden reported that the Earl Bothwell was stark mad and had long been so."[41] It was probably for this reason that, on 16 June that year, Frederick had him transferred to close captivity in "a much worse prison," the formidable Dragsholm Castle.[42] In the sixteenth century, insanity was not understood and lunatics were usually kept under lock and key, often in rigorous conditions. Bothwell was now of little use to Frederick, so his immurement had no political consequence.

Dragsholm was a grim thirteenth-century Romanesque fortress situated on the north-west coast of Zealand: in Bothwell's time, the sea lapped its 8-foot-thick walls, but has since receded. The castle was often used as a state prison, many of its inmates being lodged in rooms in the great north-eastern tower.[43] Bothwell may have been kept there, but once he disappeared behind the walls of Dragsholm, very little information about him seeped out. Herries, whose source is unknown, wrote: "The King of Denmark cast him in a loathsome prison, where none had access to him, but only those that carried him such scurvy meat and drink as was allowed, which was given in at a little window." That he was badly treated is confirmed by a French envoy, M. de Thou, who said he had been "thrust into the severest confinement at Dragsholm." Spottiswoode described it as "a vile and loathsome prison," and speaks of Bothwell "falling in a frenzy," which, if he were not obliviously insane already, would surely have been provoked by the rigours of his incarceration, which would have been unbearable for such an active and intelligent man.

In June 1574, Morton made a final attempt to have Bothwell extradited,[44] as well as the mercenary, John Clerk, who had also been imprisoned at Dragsholm for making a nuisance of himself. But Frederick refused to let either man go.

Late in 1573, the Regent's spies tracked down and arrested Black Ormiston, who was tried and sentenced to death. On 13 December, before he left his prison in Edinburgh Castle for the scaffold, he made a formal confession of his part in Darnley's murder to John Brand, Minister of the Canongate Kirk. Some writers believe that Ormiston's confession is unreliable as evidence, and in some respects this is almost certainly true, for it incorporates glaring errors that make it obvious that Brand was doing his poor best to keep to the official version of events, yet it nevertheless frequently manages to contradict the depositions of Hay, Hepburn, Powrie, Dalgleish and Paris. Seemingly, both Ormiston and Brand had become confused with the passage of time. However, the confession contains no attempt to incriminate the Queen: Ormiston declared that he had never spoken with her about the murder and that when, afterwards, he told her that people were saying he had been present at the scene, she said nothing.[45] If she knew nothing, she would have been unable to comment. It seems, moreover, that Brand was more concerned to extract information that would incriminate Maitland, who was dead, and Balfour, who had become disaffected from the Regent. Ormiston was executed later that day.

In December 1573, Queen Elizabeth appointed Sir Francis Walsingham her chief Secretary of State in place of Cecil, who had been made Lord Treasurer. Walsingham was a Puritan and an implacable enemy of the Queen of Scots, whom he called "that bosom serpent," and he would from now on make it his mission in life to bring her to justice. To this end, he set up an efficient and powerful network of spies in order to counteract the Catholic plots that centred upon Mary.

By 1574, Jesuit seminary priests were infiltrating England, their purpose being to undermine Elizabeth's rule and the Anglican Church, and to work under cover for the re-establishment of the Catholic faith. Soon, there were rumours that Philip of Spain was planning to invade England with the intention of overthrowing Elizabeth and replacing her with Mary, rumours that would alarmingly prove not to be unfounded.

In such a climate, anyone showing themselves sympathetic to Mary's cause was automatically under suspicion. In September 1574, Lady Lennox was asked by Elizabeth if the rumours of her reconciliation with Mary were true, but she prudently denied it, and wrote to Cecil, now Lord Burghley,

> I asked Her Majesty if she could think so, for I was made of flesh and blood, and could never forget the murder of my child; and she said nay, by her faith, she could not think that ever I could forget it, for if I would, I were a devil.[46]

On 4 November 1575, after yet another spell in the Tower, this time for marrying off her son Lennox without the Queen's permission,[47] Lady Lennox wrote to Mary the letter that is proof of their reconciliation and the ongoing correspondence between them:

> It may please Your Majesty, I have received your token, both by your letter and other ways, much to my comfort, especially perceiving that most zealous care Your Majesty hath of our sweet and peerless jewel in Scotland [James]; I have been no less fearful and careful as Your Majesty of him, that the wicked Governor [Morton] should not have power to do ill to his person . . . I beseech Your Majesty, fear not, but trust in God that all shall be well; the treachery of your traitors is known better than before. I shall always play my part to Your Majesty's content, willing God, so as [He] may tend to both our comforts. And now must I yield to Your Majesty my most humble thanks for your good remembrances. Almighty God grant to Your Majesty long and happy life. Your Majesty's most humble and loving mother and aunt, M.L.[48]

It is evident from this letter that Lady Lennox had become convinced of the guilt of Morton and his colleagues, hence her fears for James's safety. Unfortunately, the letter never reached Mary: it was intercepted by spies and sent to Cecil.

That same month, Mary published her Will, in which she bequeathed her claim to the English succession in turn to Elizabeth, then young Lennox, and the rights to the earldom of Angus to Lady Lennox, in defiance of Morton's claim, which she declared had been invalidated by "his secret understanding with our enemies and rebels that made the enterprise against [Darnley's] life, and also took up arms and bore banners displayed against me."[49] Lennox died in April 1576, leaving his claim to the throne to his infant daughter, Arbella Stuart, but the Scottish Parliament refused to allow her to inherit her father's title and lands, arguing that these should pass by right to Darnley's heir, James VI. After the death of her only surviving son, Lady Lennox suffered a "languishing decline."[50]

In 1575, Mary made another attempt to have her marriage to Bothwell annulled, on the grounds that he had not been properly divorced from his first wife, and that he had taken Mary by force. Leslie, recently released from the Tower, was sent to Rome to present evidence in support of her suit.[51] In August 1576, several depositions from key witnesses were transcribed in Paris.[52] This evidence is still in the Vatican Library, but there is no record of an annulment having been granted.

This was perhaps because, from late 1575 onwards, there were several false reports of Bothwell's death. On 24 November, Cecil wrote: "There came news out of Denmark that the Earl Bothwell and Captain Clerk were dead in prison. Howbeit, since that, the death of Captain Clerk is confirmed, and that Bothwell is but great swollen and not dead."[53]

But the rumours persisted—Bothwell was again reported dead late in 1577—and it was also said that, prior to 1573, the ailing Earl, believing himself to be on his deathbed, had made a written testament in which he confessed that he had killed Darnley with the connivance of Moray, Maitland and Morton, and "testified by his soul['s] salvation to [Mary's] innocence." Hearing these rumours, Mary naturally desired to gain possession of this testament, and on 1 June 1576, wrote to Archbishop Beaton asking him to make inquiries on her behalf. At the end of July, Beaton regretfully informed her that, although he had sent a courier to Denmark to find out more, it would prove too expensive (probably in bribes to courtiers, officials and gaolers) to investigate the matter. On 6 January 1577, Mary informed Beaton that Frederick had sent a copy of the testament to Elizabeth, who naturally kept it secret.

Mary and Nau continued to believe in the testament's authenticity, but it can now be established from the abstracts that are extant that, if it existed at all, it was a forgery. Two of those listed as witnesses were already dead when they were supposed to have signed it, and it contains far-fetched allegations that Grange, Boyd and Lord Robert Stewart were among the murderers. It was probably the work of a well-meaning but misguided supporter of the Queen, who was zealous to proclaim her innocence.

On 9 March 1578, Lady Lennox died, having been seized with violent pains only hours after dining with Leicester. There was talk that he had poisoned her, but unfounded popular rumour credited him with the deaths of several other people, among them his first wife: several unproven allegations appear in a scurrilous tract entitled *Leicester's Commonwealth*, which was published in 1584. Lady Lennox had been ailing for some time, and it has been claimed that Leicester would have had no motive for killing her.[54] That is not quite true. Leicester was staunchly loyal to Elizabeth, and it was well known in court circles that Lady Lennox, that inveterate intriguer, was in regular correspondence with Mary, which would certainly have aroused suspicions and anxieties in Elizabeth. After the Countess's death, Leicester took her steward, Thomas Fowler, into his service, probably in order to gain access to her papers, of which Fowler apparently had custody. Leicester may have believed that among those papers was to be found the evidence for Lady Lennox's change of heart towards Mary, which, if it got into the wrong hands and were made public, could seriously compromise Elizabeth's policy of keeping Mary in custody. So there were good reasons for murdering Lady Lennox, even though it can never be certain that Leicester did so.

The Countess was buried in Westminster Abbey in a splendid tomb surmounted by her painted effigy and adorned with kneeling figures of her eight children. The statue of Darnley is distinguished by a crown suspended above the head and an ermine mantle, denoting his royal but uncrowned status. Her son Lennox was interred with her.

Three days after Lady Lennox's death, Atholl and the new Earl of Argyll brought off a coup against their old enemy, Morton, and forced him to resign from the Regency. Having gained control of the eleven-year-old James VI, they had him declare himself of age. Real power, however, would remain in the hands of a regency Council headed by Atholl, who was appointed Chancellor of Scotland on 29 March. But Morton had no intention of relinquishing power. At the beginning of June, he effected a counter-coup and regained control of the King and the Regency, conceding that Atholl and Argyll should assist him in the government. When Atholl died unexpectedly, in April 1579, Morton was suspected of poisoning him, although this was never proved.

At Dragsholm, the crazed Bothwell had been held in increasingly vile conditions. It is often stated that he was chained to a pillar in such a way that he was unable to stand upright, but there is no contemporary evidence for this allegation, which rests on a local tradition that was related to the Earl's biographer, Gore-Browne, when he visited Dragsholm in 1935.[55] But many of Bothwell's contemporaries testify to his insanity, notably Herries, Buchanan, Melville, the French envoy de Thou, and Maitland's brother John, who, during a visit to Copenhagen in 1590, heard how Bothwell had become "distracted of his wits or senses." Herries also says that the Earl was "overgrown with hair and filth." Buchanan states that he "was driven mad by the filth and other discomforts of his dungeon." The cessation of entries relating to expenses for Bothwell in the castle accounts in the spring of 1576 gives credence to these reports.

In the end, this cruel treatment claimed its victim. Bothwell "died miserably"[56] on 14 April 1578. What was almost certainly his body was embalmed and placed in an oak coffin and buried beneath the nave of Faarvejle Church, twenty miles from Dragsholm. In 1858, the coffin was opened and the body found to be in a good state of preservation, having been naturally mummified by the salty sea air; the head had become detached, and lay below the shoulder; it was taken away and placed on a writing table in the castle for a time. Thereafter, the mummy was displayed under glass in a shallow crypt until 1970, when, at the instigation of the future Queen Margrethe II of Denmark, it was buried in Riis's Chapel, an annexe to the church. Although there is no inscription on the coffin, this body was obviously that of a nobleman, since it rested on a white satin cushion and was shrouded in fine linen and silks, so it is unlikely to have been that of Captain Clerk, as has been suggested.[57] The body measured about 5 feet 6 inches long; in the nineteenth century there were traces of red and silver hair on the skull, and in

1935 Gore-Browne observed a faint white scar on the temple, probably the result of the wound dealt by Jock Elliott in October 1566. In 1976, a move to have the body returned to Scotland ended in failure.[58]

There is no record of Mary's reaction to the death of Bothwell. In 1580, in liaison with the Spanish ambassador in London, she embarked on a fresh round of dangerous plotting against Elizabeth. That year, Pope Gregory XIII ruled that whoever sent the English Queen out of the world "with the pious intention of doing God service, not only does not sin, but gains merit." In Mary's eyes, this would have justified all her future conspiracies against Elizabeth.

In March, Mary learned that Balfour, then in the Netherlands, was offering to provide evidence to incriminate Morton in the murder of Darnley in return for permission to re-enter Scotland unmolested and the restoration of his Scottish estates, an offer that was to be enthusiastically taken up by Morton's enemies, who were again looking for an excuse to topple him. Balfour was doubtless hoping to ensure that he would not be in danger of prosecution if he returned to Scotland; of all those who had been involved in Darnley's murder, most were dead, but Morton was not only still alive but in power, and must be neutralised. Mary also had an interest in Balfour's evidence, and on 18 March asked Archbishop Beaton to secure possession of it, especially the murder Bond that Morton was supposed to have signed.[59] In response, Balfour sent Mary such evidence as he had, but it apparently did not amount to much, and it certainly did not include the Bond. In May, Mary told Beaton that they should play along with Balfour, evidently hoping that more documents could be extracted from him.

Balfour spent several months negotiating the terms of his return with King James and Morton's enemies, and on 12 December 1580, he arrived in Edinburgh and was granted a private audience with the young King. James was now heavily reliant on his handsome but ruthless French-born cousin, the pro-Catholic Esmé Stuart, Count of Aubigny: having conceived an adolescent passion for Stuart, he had created him Earl of Lennox on 5 March 1580. Lennox was ambitious and wanted Morton ousted from power, and it was he who headed this new conspiracy against the Regent, which was backed by Ochiltree's son, Captain James Stewart, another royal favourite who was soon to be created Earl of Arran by James. Lennox was aware of Balfour's Catholic sympathies and confident that his testimony would bring down the Regent, for Balfour had assured Lennox that he did indeed hold the murder Bond, and that Morton's signature was on it.

On 31 December 1580, in front of the King and his Council, Captain Stewart fell on his knees, denounced Morton for having conspired in Darnley's murder, and demanded his arrest. Morton contemptuously denied the charge, insisting that it was well known that he had punished with the utmost rigour every person who had been involved in the late King's death.

"It is false!" cried Stewart. "Where have you placed your cousin, Archibald Douglas? Does not that most infamous of men now pollute the bench of justice with his presence,[60] instead of suffering the penalty due to the murderer of his sovereign?"[61] At this, Morton drew his sword, but he was seized and, with the other Lords present loudly supporting the charge, placed under arrest and confined in Edinburgh Castle, the King making no move to save him. In January, Morton was transferred to a prison cell in Dumbarton Castle.[62] Elizabeth, meanwhile, was making frantic but fruitless efforts to save him, which suggests that she was perhaps fearful of what might be revealed at his trial, but his other "friends" had abandoned him, "for he was loved by none and envied and hated by many, so they all looked through their fingers to see his fall."[63]

Sir William Douglas, Archibald Douglas and other members of Morton's family were also summoned to answer charges. Sir William was banished beyond the Firth of Cromarty in the far north. The Laird of Whittinghame, Archibald's brother, revealed under interrogation that Archibald had forged letters in an attempt to bring down Lennox;[64] as has been noted, these may not have been the first incriminating letters that he had forged. Furthermore, it was almost certainly he who had actually struck down Darnley. But Douglas, alerted by the Regent's apprehension, had already fled to England, and thus managed to evade arrest, for Elizabeth adamantly refused to deliver him up to James VI. In his absence, his lands were declared forfeit, and his servant, John Binning, was arrested.

Morton's removal from power left Scotland in the hands of a clique that was sympathetic to Mary, and paved the way for schemes for her restoration as joint ruler with her son. But, while Elizabeth affected to support such schemes, they never reached a satisfactory conclusion because there were so many conflicting interests involved. Even though the truth about Darnley's murder was now well known, Mary was still being punished for it.

On 30 January, Balfour asked Mary to produce an affidavit containing everything that she knew about the Darnley murder. This, of course, did not amount to much. In March, Thomas Randolph, the English agent, informed Lords Hunsdon and Huntingdon: "I spoke again of the Bond in the green box, containing the names of all the chief persons consenting to the King's murder, which Sir James [Balfour] either hath or can tell of."[65] But Balfour had still not shown anyone the Bond.

Morton's trial took place at the Edinburgh Tolbooth on 1 June. He was accused of having been "art and part" of Darnley's murder, and in answer to the charge, "granted that he was made privy thereto, but had no hand in devising thereof."[66] Balfour testified against him, but failed to produce the murder Bond; he had probably never had it in the first place. Morton was found guilty of treason, declared forfeit, and condemned to be hanged and quartered the very next day, but King James commuted the sentence to decapitation.

Before his execution, Morton made a confession to John Brand and two other ministers of the Kirk, which was first published in the 1587 edition of Raphael Holinshed's *Chronicles of England, Scotland and Ireland*. This is not the full text of the original, since Holinshed admitted that he had omitted sensitive passages that mentioned "great persons now living," who may have included Queen Elizabeth herself, and possibly Mary: anything favourable to Mary would have been unwelcome in the political climate that prevailed in England at the time. There are manuscript copies of the confession extant, but they too may have been censored. In his confession, Morton admitted that he had with others foreknown the crime, but that nothing had been done to prevent it because it was known that the Queen of Scots desired it, which is what he had been told by Bothwell and Maitland. He also confessed to meeting with those men at Whittinghame and to receiving Archibald Douglas after the murder.

Morton was beheaded on 2 June 1581 in the Grassmarket in Edinburgh on a guillotine known as "the Maiden," which he himself had introduced from Halifax as a more humane method of execution. "He died resolutely" with his hands untied, and his head was set up on a spike above the Tolbooth, where it remained until December 1582.[67] Mary professed herself "most glad" at his passing.[68]

The next day, John Binning, Archibald Douglas's servant, was put to the torture, and revealed Douglas's part in Darnley's murder. He was tried and condemned,[69] then hanged and quartered at the Mercat Cross that same day. In 1582, another of Archibald Douglas's men, George Home, Laird of Sprott, was tried for complicity in Darnley's murder but acquitted.

On 19 June 1581, James VI reached the age of fifteen, and assumed personal rule. He had done with regents, preferring to rely on the counsels of Esmé Stuart, who was created Duke of Lennox in August 1582. That month, hard-line Protestants led by William Ruthven, now Earl of Gowrie, kidnapped the King and forced Lennox to flee to France, where he died in 1583. James escaped from his captors in June 1583 and reasserted his authority as King.

Meanwhile, there had been a new conspiracy to place Mary on the throne of England, hatched by the Guises, the Pope, Philip of Spain and the Jesuits. In October 1582, Walsingham discovered that Mary was communicating in cipher with her foreign allies, and her correspondence was thereafter vetted and she herself kept under closer surveillance. At this time, Elizabeth again taxed Mary with the murder of Darnley. Mary demanded to have any charges put in writing before she answered them, but this was never done, exposing Elizabeth's words as an idle threat. In the wake of Morton's execution, Elizabeth would have been on very tenuous grounds had she formally accused Mary of murdering Darnley. On 21 November, an aggrieved Mary wrote a scathing letter to Elizabeth, accusing her of bringing about her downfall:

> By the agents, spies and secret messengers sent in your name into Scotland while I was there, my subjects were corrupted and encouraged to rebel against me, and to speak, do, enterprise and execute that which has come to the said country during my troubles. Of which I will not at present specify any proof, than that which I have gained of it by the confession of one who was afterwards amongst those that were most advanced for their good service.[70]

Mary was apparently referring to Morton.

Balfour, who had almost certainly been a leading player in the Darnley murder, died in his bed in 1583. He "had served with all parties, had deserved all, yet had profited by all."[71] Mary called him "a traitor who offered himself first to one party and then to the other."[72] Yet, of all those who had been involved in the Darnley conspiracy, he was one of the few who met a peaceful end.

Between April and November 1583, Archibald Douglas, now in France, was doing his best to ingratiate himself with Mary in the hope that she would be a suitor to James VI on his behalf. On 12 November, Mary wrote to Castelnau that she had promised to do her best for Douglas, but desired to know "the main cause of his banishment, for if he is in any way connected with the death of the late King my husband, I will never intercede for him."[73] Soon afterwards, Douglas wrote to her, stating that in 1566, Moray, Atholl, Bothwell, Argyll and other Lords had entered into a bond with the then exiled Lords to have nothing to do with Darnley as King, and to sue for the return of the exiles; this, he said, had been discussed at the Craigmillar Conference. Douglas naturally made no mention of the murder Bond. He added that he had been chosen as the intermediary between the Lords and the exiles.

Around this time, the plot to place Mary on the English throne was revealed to the English government by one of its participants, Francis Throckmorton, who was later executed. Mary was heavily implicated, as was the Spanish ambassador, who was expelled. Elizabeth was urged to bring Mary to justice, but refused out of hand.

In May 1584, after he had again been discovered conspiring against James VI, the Earl of Gowrie was executed; it was at this time that the Casket Letters came into the possession of the King. Neither James nor his mother had any reason to love the Ruthven family, and when, in 1600, the Earl's sons were involved in another treasonable plot, Parliament ruled that the name of Ruthven be abolished for all time. The last of the line died in the Tower of London in 1652, nearly a century after Patrick, Lord Ruthven had burst into Mary's supper chamber at Holyrood and demanded that Rizzio leave it.

Mary was gratified by the punishment meted out to Gowrie, and soon afterwards sent a messenger to James to demand the head of Lindsay also, which she had sworn she would have after Carberry Hill. James, however, contented himself with imprisoning Lindsay at Tantallon Castle. Lindsay died in 1589.

Walsingham still feared that Mary was plotting against Elizabeth, and in August 1584, he tightened the security net around her. The next month, he showed Elizabeth a letter that convinced her that Mary was again conspiring to overthrow her. This led in October to the famous Bond of Association, whereby thousands of English gentlemen pledged themselves under oath to take up arms and destroy Mary if it became known that, knowingly or otherwise, she was the focus of any plot against the Queen's life. The principles of this bond were enshrined in the Act of Association, passed by Parliament in February 1585. The following month, King James wrote to his mother to tell her that it was impossible to ally himself with her because she was "captive in a desert"; in truth, he was anxious not to jeopardise his hopes of the English succession by favouring one who was regarded with such deep suspicion by the English. In May, he concluded a treaty with Elizabeth that made it clear that he had abandoned all ideas of sharing sovereignty with his mother and implied that Mary was to remain in captivity. For Mary, this was a devastating betrayal that marked the end of her long-cherished hopes of freedom and restoration. Deeply embittered, she resolved to bequeath her crown and her dynastic claim to England to Philip of Spain, effectively disinheriting her son.

Increasing demands that Mary be kept under stricter surveillance led in April 1585 to the appointment of the sternly puritanical disciplinarian, Sir Amyas Paulet, as her custodian. Under his rule, Mary was allowed no visitors and no correspondence.

In May 1586, nearly twenty years after the event, Archibald Douglas was at last tracked down and tried for the murder of Darnley. The trial—which was the last of those related to the crime—was a farce, since Douglas had in his possession evidence of collusion between the English and Scottish governments, and Elizabeth bribed James to ensure a favourable verdict, even though most people now knew that Douglas was the man who had killed Darnley. Of the nineteen chosen jurors, ten deemed it unwise to put in an appearance, and their places were filled by ten others "who happened to be at the bar," amongst them Douglas's man, George Home. The court was packed with the Douglases and their supporters.

The depositions of Ormiston, Hay, Paris and Binning were offered in evidence, despite the fact that there was no reference to Douglas in any of them. No witnesses were called to testify against the accused. In his defence, Douglas stated he could not have lost his velvet mule at Kirk o'Field because he was not wearing it, since the road that led there from his house was too rough for a man in armour to walk on in slippers. At the end of the day, he was pronounced "clean and acquit of being in company with Bothwell, Ormiston, Hay and Hepburn in committing the crime."[74] Douglas's rehabilitation led to his being restored to his lands and appointed ambassador to England.

Douglas's acquittal and the treachery of her son may have been factors in Mary's decision, made in July 1586, to approve the plan of a young Catholic gentleman, Anthony Babington, to assassinate Elizabeth and replace her with the Scottish Queen. Mary was unaware that Walsingham was being sent all her letters and had in fact set up the means by which she was able to smuggle them out to her friends, and she walked straight into his trap when, against Nau's advice, she approved in writing Babington's treasonable conspiracy. After nineteen years in unjust captivity, she was desperate for freedom and the opportunity to win by force that which she believed to be hers by right. She was so detached from reality that she had little idea that she was hated and feared by the majority of Elizabeth's subjects.

Elizabeth reacted to news of the plot with panic, and had the cousin whom she referred to as a "wicked murderess" arrested on 9 August. The English government could now proceed against Mary under the Act of Association. Under questioning, Nau admitted sending her letter and did not refute its contents. Mary saw this as a betrayal, but it was no more than the truth.

Babington and his associates were tried and condemned on 13 September, and executed a week later with horrific barbarity. On 25 September, Mary was moved to mediaeval Fortheringhay Castle in Northamptonshire to await trial. Thirty-six commissioners appointed by Elizabeth assembled there on 11 October, but Mary insisted that no court was competent to try her since she was "a queen and sovereign" and not one of Elizabeth's subjects. But when Elizabeth wrote that it was her will that Mary answer the charges "as if I were myself present," Mary capitulated, although she continued to refuse to acknowledge the court's jurisdiction.

Her trial took place on 15 and 16 October. Although Mary put up a spirited defence and denied all the charges, its outcome was a foregone conclusion, for the evidence was incontrovertible. But just as the commissioners were about to give their verdict, Elizabeth's messenger arrived, proroguing the court to the Star Chamber at Westminster, to meet again in ten days' time. There, on 25 October, Mary was pronounced guilty. Four days later, Parliament ratified the verdict and pressed for "a just sentence"; in their view, there could only be one just sentence.

Elizabeth embarked on her usual stalling tactics, but Parliament was determined to resolve the problem of the Queen of Scots for good. On 12 November, it petitioned Elizabeth to have Mary executed. Elizabeth was plunged into an agony of indecision. Mary was undoubtedly guilty and had increasingly menaced Elizabeth's security ever since the latter's accession in 1558. On the other hand, Elizabeth knew that executing an anointed queen would establish a dangerous precedent and undermine the whole institution of monarchy, which she held as sacred, and she feared the reaction of Catholic Europe, and her Catholic subjects, if she took such a drastic step. Over the years, it had been Elizabeth, with her hatred of bloodshed, who time and again had intervened to save Mary's life, even when Mary had plotted against hers; now she was being pressurised to kill her. Understandably, she refused. But the demands of Parliament and her Council for justice grew ever more insistent. At last, on 1 February 1587, Elizabeth gave way and signed Mary's death warrant, which was immediately sent by her Councillors to Fotheringhay. Later, she would deny that she had authorised its dispatch and punish those concerned.

The warrant arrived on 7 February, and Mary was told to prepare for death on the morrow. That night, she wrote her last letter, to Henry III of France,[75] in which she protested that she would meet death "innocent of any crime": as a devout Catholic, she would not have counted the assassination of the heretical Elizabeth as a crime because the Pope had sanctioned and urged it, but she was almost certainly also referring to the murder of Darnley. She further asserted that "the Catholic faith and the assertion of my God-given right to the English crown are the two issues on which I am condemned."[76] In her own eyes, she was dying as a martyr for her faith.

The following morning, she walked calmly to the scaffold in the great hall of the castle, and there, before a large concourse of people, removed her black gown to reveal a kirtle of red, the Catholic colour of martyrdom. It took three strokes to sever her head, but she was probably unconscious after the first. Afterwards, her body was sealed in a lead coffin and stored in the castle until late July, when Elizabeth authorised its burial in Peterborough Cathedral. There was a solemn funeral with the banners of Mary, Francis II and Darnley hung on the pillars of the nave; Bothwell's was deliberately omitted. In his funeral sermon, the Protestant Dean of Peterborough could not resist raking up old scandals and portraying Mary's execution as divine retribution: "The day [of the execution] being very fair did, as it were, show favour from Heaven and commended the justice; the eighth day of February, that judgement was repaid home to her, which the tenth day of the same month, twenty years past, she measured to her husband."[77]

But Mary's courageous demeanour on the scaffold obliterated for many—as it still does—the earlier image of her as an adulteress and murderess, and led to perceptions of her as a tragic heroine rather than a fallen woman.

When Elizabeth I died on 24 March 1603, James VI of Scotland succeeded her as James I of England, and Mary's and Maitland's vision of the union of the crowns was fulfilled. However, this was a Protestant union, and Mary's hopes of the two kingdoms being returned to the Church of Rome were never to be realised.

Although James had loudly condemned his mother's execution, he did not allow it to prejudice his friendship with Elizabeth nor his hopes of the English succession. But his conscience remained disquieted, and in 1612, to ease it, he translated Mary's remains to a magnificent tomb in Westminster Abbey, in the opposite side chapel of the Henry VII Chapel to that where Elizabeth lay. Mary's tomb is next to that of Lady Lennox, and bears a beautiful effigy of white marble. She lies among the English monarchs, whose throne she so coveted in life but was destined never to occupy.

It is said that James also ordered the demolition of Fotheringhay Castle, but in fact he sold it off. It was already decaying and was described as ruinous in 1635, ten years after James's death. It was later dismantled and its stones used for local buildings. The staircase down which Mary walked to her execution is now in the Talbot Hotel at Oundle, which was built in 1626.

All that remains of Fotheringhay today is the grassy mound on which it once stood and a single block of masonry.

Most of those who had been involved in one way or another in Darnley's murder had now died or come to a violent end. Only Archibald Douglas, the actual murderer, survived in prosperity.

Given the nature of the circumstantial evidence against Mary, it is not surprising that so many writers have concluded, with the Dean of Peterborough, that her execution was a just punishment for one who had killed her husband. But it can be demonstrated again and again—and has been in this text—that the bulk of the evidence against Mary is flawed. Apart from the notorious Casket Letters and the highly dubious deposition of Paris, there is no documentary evidence of an adulterous relationship with Bothwell, nor is there any contemporary evidence that Mary plotted Darnley's death. Leaving aside the later libels and the claims of her enemies, who had powerful motives for constructing a case against her, there is nothing but the often ill-informed opinions of historians to condemn her. The arguments for her innocence are many, and have been well rehearsed in the foregoing chapters. Taken together, they constitute a strong case in her defence.

It is easy to see why Mary's detractors consider her guilty. Even after extensive research, I believed, as I began to write this book, that Mary was guilty. But when I came to analyse the source material in depth, it became increasingly obvious that such a conclusion was not possible. Mary's own reluctance to answer the Lords' charges against her has been seen as suspicious, but it clearly arose from her conviction that she was not answerable to anyone but her equal, Elizabeth, rather than from a wish to evade awkward questions. It has been said that she never directly refuted the charges, but, as we have seen, that is not so.

Mary's poor judgement repeatedly served her ill. Her imprudent marriage to Darnley, her rash favour shown to Rizzio and her utterly foolish decision to flee to Protestant England rather than Catholic France, and to ask for succour from a queen whose throne she had laid claim to, all contributed to her ruin. Yet she had no control over the events that overtook her, the plotting that led to Darnley's death, and her own frail health which prevented her from responding to his murder as her contemporaries expected. Nor, as an inexperienced Catholic female sovereign, could she halt the reformist movement in Scotland, of which her removal from power was a natural progression. Instead, in an age that did not understand religious tolerance, she followed a policy of conciliation whilst making the right noises to the Pope about the restoration of Catholicism, and consequently lost credibility with both sides. Her tragedy was that she was in many respects innately unsuited for the role to which she had been born. Compared with her cousin Elizabeth, she was a political innocent, and as such she was thrust into a situation in which a seasoned, hard-headed male ruler might have floundered.

No court of law would today convict Mary of the charges laid against her by the Lords. The integrity of her character is well attested by the opinions of those who faithfully served her over a period of many years. That she was the object of an extended campaign of character assassination is beyond doubt. Furthermore, since so much of the evidence of her enemies has been discredited, doubt must be cast on the rest. Mary paid a high price for the ambitions of others: she paid for it in the loss of her throne, the long years of captivity, separation and alienation from her only living child, and her own violent death. In the circumstances, she must, with justice, be regarded as one of the most wronged women in history.

POSTSCRIPT

Six years ago, when I wrote my biography of Elizabeth I, I did a great deal of background research on her rival, Mary, Queen of Scots. Until that time, my knowledge of Mary had been superficial at best, and I was unaware of the depth of controversy that surrounded her role in the murder of her second husband, Lord Darnley. Nor did I realise that the conclusions that I finally, and in good faith, reached would be so contentious. Unsurprisingly, and quite rightly, they were edited out of *Elizabeth I*.

Yet I remained intrigued by the mystery surrounding Darnley's murder, and when I suggested to my publishers that I write a book investigating Mary's possible involvement in it, they readily agreed. I had little idea then of what I was letting myself in for. Firstly, reams had been written on the subject since the sixteenth century; secondly, most of the evidence was contradictory or hopelessly prejudiced—indeed, at least three-quarters of the original source material had been written by Mary's enemies; and thirdly, to judge by the modern literature on the subject, many people still hold strong opinions as to whether or not Mary was guilty. Yet the last full-scale investigation was printed as long ago as 1967, so a reappraisal of the matter was long overdue.

It therefore became my mission to amass as much evidence as possible. In order to do so, I consulted numerous works, and in the process gathered more information than has ever appeared in any other work. Having transcribed tens of thousands of pieces of research, I numbered each one and entered it in sequence on a vast chronological plan that ran to 103 pages. I had thought that the book plan for my previous book, *Henry VIII: The King and His Court*, was complicated, but that ran to only 40 pages.

Using a strictly chronological plan had worked well for a book that I wrote twelve years ago on another royal murder mystery, *The Princess in the Tower*, and produced astonishing results—but that was a picnic compared to solving the puzzle of Darnley's murder.

My objective was to assess the evidence objectively, and to strip away centuries of political, religious, and romantic bias. But even so, with my research completed and my plan drawn up, I had little idea of what conclusion I was going to draw: was Mary guilty, or was she innocent? On the face of it, it would have been possible to write two books with different outcomes, each supported by contemporary evidence. In the event, considering what I had read so far, and after much deliberation, I decided to base my theory on what appeared to be compelling circumstantial evidence. It was not until I had actually written a substantial part of the book, and come to analyse the evidence for the plot against Darnley, that I realised that my original conclusion was flawed; and it was at this point that I came round full circle to the opposite opinion.

Mary, Queen of Scots, is one of the most intriguing and controversial figures in history. Born in 1542, she was the daughter of James V, King of Scots, by his French wife, Marie de Guise. Mary succeeded to the throne when she was only a week old, and immediately became the focus of Henry VIII's ambition to marry her to his son, the future Edward VI, and thus unite England and Scotland under Tudor rule. But the Scots had no wish to give up their independence, so Mary was sent, at the age of five, to be brought up at the French court, where she received a good education and learned every feminine accomplishment. In 1558, the fifteen-year-old Mary, now an acknowledged beauty, was married to the Dauphin Francis, son and heir of Henry II, King of France.

Later that year, the Catholic Queen Mary I of England died, and was succeeded by her Protestant half-sister, Elizabeth I. In the eyes of Catholic Europe, Elizabeth was a heretic, a bastard, and a usurper, and the rightful Queen of England was her Catholic cousin, Mary, Queen of Scots. Immediately, Henry II had Mary proclaimed Queen of England, much to Elizabeth's fury and the consternation of the English government. But Henry II had too many other preoccupations to invade England on his daughter-in-law's behalf. Mary later dropped the title Queen of England, but continued to press for her right to be designated Elizabeth's successor, a demand that Elizabeth was to frustrate at every turn. The acquisition of the English throne would remain the driving ambition of Mary's life, dominating her policies as Queen of Scots and permanently souring her relations with Elizabeth I.

In 1560, the young King Francis died, and the following year a grieving Mary reluctantly left the luxurious French court and returned to her more spartan native land to take up the reins of government. She was eighteen years old and received a generally warm welcome from her subjects.

But Mary's position as a Catholic Queen in a land that had recently undergone a hardline Protestant revolution was never going to be easy, and the problems she faced would have been daunting even for a strong, experienced male ruler. Her conciliatory policy with regard to religion was neither understood nor approved of in that dogmatic age, and she was only tolerated by the Protestant establishment as long as she remained in tutelage to the ruling clique, the so-called Lords of the Congregation, who were headed by her bastard half-brother, the Earl of Moray. All went relatively well until Mary tried to shake off that tutelage and act independently, as she did over her second marriage.

Mary was a highly desirable bride and did not lack for suitors, but she was initially determined to make a grand marriage with Don Carlos, the heir to Phillip II of Spain. When Don Carlos was found to be insane and Phillip terminated the negotiations, Mary's thoughts turned to her cousin, Henry Stuart, Lord Darnley, who was regarded by many as having a stronger claim to the English throne than she did herself. The uniting of two such claims posed a serious threat to Queen Elizabeth; nor did the Scottish Lords want their Queen to marry the reputedly Catholic Darnley. Nevertheless, in 1565, the eighteen-year-old Darnley traveled north to Scotland to woo the Queen, and Mary rapidly became infatuated with him.

Ignoring the vociferous opposition, Mary married Darnley with almost indecent haste. The honeymoon was spent quelling a rebellion on the part of the Scottish Lords.

Mary was soon to regret her hastiness. Despite his good looks, Darnley was weak, vicious and promiscuous, certainly with women and possibly with men also. Within weeks, the royal marriage was on the rocks.

The situation only grew worse during the ensuing months, as Mary turned to her Italian secretary, David Rizzio, for companionship, giving rise to scandalous rumors—which Darnley believed—that she was betraying her marriage vows. Indeed, if she was not having an affair with Rizzio, her behavior certainly gave the impression that she was.

Despite the growing rift between the royal couple, Mary became pregnant. Darnley continually pressed her to grant him the Crown Matrimonial, which would give him the right of succession in the event of her death, but she adamantly refused. Early in 1566, Darnley, his jealousy at the boiling point, entered into an unlikely alliance with the Protestant Lords to remove the hated Rizzio, their mutual enemy. But even those hardened nobles were shocked when Darnley insisted that the hated Italian be slain in Mary's presence, in the apparent hope of inducing a miscarriage and possibly the Queen's death; the Lords had cunningly promised him the Crown Matrimonial, so that he could rule in her stead, but of course they had no intention of keeping their promise to the young fool. Without Mary, Darnley would be nothing in Scotland.

After Rizzio's murder, Mary was shut up in her apartments by the Lords. Yet despite her shock and horror, she was able to persuade Darnley that he had been used by the treacherous nobles, who would soon certainly turn on him. Together, Mary and Darnley managed to escape from the Lords, and with the help of the loyal Earl of Bothwell, Mary was able to reestablish her authority as Queen.

Those Lords who had taken part in Rizzio's death were exiled, but in order to wreak revenge upon Darnley, who had deserted and betrayed them, they wrote to the Queen revealing the true part he had played in the conspiracy. This was something Mary could not forgive, and for a long time afterwards, she and Darnley were virtually estranged. However, in view of the scurrilous rumors about the paternity of her unborn child, the Queen dared not risk alienating her husband too greatly, in case he denied that he was its father; when her son James was born in June 1566, she made Darnley publicly acknowledge the infant as his own. "He is so much your son," she said, "that I fear it will be the worse for him."

Relations between the royal couple now went from bad to worse; Darnley continued to plot against Mary and to defame her reputation in the eyes of Catholic Europe. When Mary became seriously ill in the autumn of 1566, her advisors blamed her broken health on the emotional strain she was suffering because of Darnley. At this time, she told those about her that she wanted to die, for she saw no way out of her miserable marriage.

In December 1566, at a conference held in Craigmillar Castle near Edinburgh, Mary's Lords discussed the problem of Darnley with her. An annulment was ruled out because it would impugn the legitimacy of Prince James, and Darnley could not be arraigned for treason because he was King of Scots and in Scotland a king could not technically be guilty of treason. The Lords told Mary to leave the problem with them, and then "Your Grace shall see nothing but good and approved by Parliament." Mary had insisted, however, that Darnley must not be got rid of by any means that touched her honor or the legitimacy of her child. In return for their support, the Lords pressured her into agreeing, much against her will, to the return of the Lords who had been exiled for Rizzio's murder; but they were pardoned only on condition that they did not approach within seven miles of the court for two years. This suggests that Mary must have guessed that they would be out for Darnley's blood. What she may not have known was that, at Craigmillar, the Lords she had consulted with had privately drawn up a bond for Darnley's murder.

On the day the exiled Lords returned to Scotland, Darnley fled to Glasgow, his father's power base. On the way, he fell seriously ill. It was given out that he had smallpox, but all the evidence suggests something rather worse.

Meanwhile, Mary had received the disturbing intelligence that Darnley had been plotting to seize her throne. She dared not leave him where he was, and reluctantly rode to Glasgow with the intention of bringing him back to Edinburgh. After some straight talking, there followed a reconciliation that many have viewed as suspicious. Was Mary luring Darnley to his death? Or did she genuinely intend to be reconciled to him, having realised that there was no honorable way out of their marriage?

Mary's intention was that Darnley should complete his convalescence within the securely fortified Craigmillar Castle, but Darnley himself chose to lodge in the collegiate quadrangle at Kirk o'Field, south of Edinburgh. Here, the Queen and her courtiers visited him daily, and Darnley wrote to his father that "my love the Queen" could not do enough for him. He made rapid progress and it was decided that he should return to Holyrood, and resume married life with Mary, on Monday, 10 February 1567. Mary spent the evening of the 9th with him, then—all too conveniently, some believe— she left with her courtiers to attend a wedding masque at the palace. At two o'clock the following morning, Darnley's lodging was completely destroyed in an explosion that shook the city of Edinburgh; three hours later, his unmarked body was found in a garden some way from the house. There was no doubt that he had been murdered.

Soon, with very good reasons, the finger of public suspicion pointed at the ambitious Bothwell as Darnley's murderer, and when it became apparent that the Queen was doing very little to track down the killers, that finger pointed at her also. Yet few of her subjects were aware that she had suffered a mental and physical breakdown after Darnley's death.

It was the government that should have initiated proceedings against Bothwell, yet it was left to Darnley's father, the Earl of Lennox, to bring a private prosecution against the Earl. But the law permitted Lennox to bring only six followers into Edinburgh with him; it did not, however, prevent Bothwell from packing the city with four thousand of his armed followers. Not surprisingly, Lennox deemed it prudent to stay away, and without the only witness for the prosecution, Bothwell was acquitted.

With his name cleared, Bothwell coerced the nobles into supporting his suit to the Queen, but when he proposed marriage to Mary, she turned him down. When, less than three months after the murder, Bothwell abducted and almost certainly raped Mary, some said that it had been done with her collusion. Their necessary marriage followed soon afterwards, but it was a union that the Scottish Lords and people were not prepared to tolerate. Many now believed that Mary and Bothwell had been involved in an adulterous affair and had conspired to kill Darnley so that they could marry. A month after the marriage, at a bloodless confrontation at Carberry Hill near Edinburgh, Mary was taken prisoner by the Scottish Lords, then placed in the island fortress of Lochleven and forced, by threats of violence, to abdicate in favor of her thirteen-month-old son, whom she was never to see again.

The rest of her story is well known. After ten months in captivity, she escaped to England, begging for military aid from Elizabeth. But Mary, with her claim to the English throne and her dubious past, was a dangerous and embarrassing guest, and Elizabeth, for her own security, had little choice but to keep her a virtual prisoner for nineteen long years. In 1569, an English inquiry into Mary's complicity in Darnley's death reached no certain conclusion, despite her repeated protestations of innocence; it was here that the incriminating Casket Letters, said to have been written by Mary to Bothwell, were produced by the Scottish Lords as evidence that the guilty lovers had plotted Darnley's death. Mary firmly denied that she had written these letters, but she was never allowed to see them, nor to appear in person to defend herself. As the letters disappeared in 1584, and are known only through copies, historians are unable to pronounce conclusively on their authenticity. Nevertheless, there are good reasons for questioning their veracity and genuineness.

It is at this point in Mary's story that we can see how various different perceptions of her have evolved. It was in the interests of the Scottish Lords who deposed her to disseminate convincing propaganda portraying her as an adulteress and murderess, a view that many people would still agree with today. Yet during her years of captivity in England, Mary, as the focal point of several plots to place her on Elizabeth's throne, began to be revered as a Catholic icon, an image she herself consciously fostered. Even after being found guilty, on good evidence, of having plotted Elizabeth's assassination, she appeared on the scaffold wearing red, the liturgical color of Catholic martyrdom, with the intention of announcing to the world that she was dying for her faith.

The emotive image of the Catholic martyr Queen had such a powerful impact on her followers that it wholly blotted out any memory of her previously dubious reputation, and gave rise to a long-standing tradition of semi-hagiographic historical writing that still has echoes in modern biographies.

That last tragic scene on the scaffold also inspired the romantic tradition of the tragic heroine, an image of Mary that was to flower in the art and literature of the romantic era, and that would later find expression in countless narrative paintings, historical novels, and films.

It was not until the late twentieth century that historians began to paint a new picture of Mary, showing her as a failed monarch who was unique in making her claims to another throne a priority over the country of which she was already Queen. Her choices of husbands were disastrous, and her religious policy inconsistent and unrealistic. In all, she was the architect of her own downfall. In fairness to Mary, it could be said that her downfall was inevitable, given the revolution that had taken place in Scotland; yet it was she herself who, unwittingly or not, provided the Lords with the means of bringing it about.

Thanks to these different views of Mary, her character remains elusive, obscured by the preconceptions and prejudices of many who have chosen to tell her story. The controversy still rages. Lady Antonia Fraser, in her definitive biography of the Queen, published in 1969, believed Mary innocent of complicity in Darnley's murder, but there are several historians today who disagree with that view. They prefer to believe the so-called libels put about by Mary's enemies, on the basis that these seemingly corroborate the circumstantial evidence against Mary. The moral outrage expressed by earlier writers hostile to Mary has been replaced by a creeping cynicism. Yet who is right? And can there ever be any certain verdict?

Guilty or not, the story of Mary Stuart reads like a Shakespearean tragedy. It is not surprising that Hamlet is said to have been partly based on it. This is a dark tale of vicious intrigue, ambition, lust, violence, and murder, all enveloped in mystery. At the center is this enigmatic woman, on whom rivers of ink have been spilt throughout four centuries, and on whom I have just managed to spill quite a lot more. Was she a murderess, or at least an accessory to murder? Having read my conclusions, you, the reader, must decide if you agree with them.

ABBREVIATIONS USED IN THE
NOTES AND REFERENCES

Full titles are given in the Bibliography; all other titles may be easily accessed from the Bibliography.

Anderson	*Collections*	
	Collections relating to the History of Mary . . .	
CSP Domestic	*Calendar of State Papers, Domestic Series*	
CSP Foreign	*Calendar of State Papers, Foreign Series*	
CSP Scottish	*Calendar of State Papers relating to Scotland . . .* , ed. Bain et al.	
CSP Spanish	*Calendar of Letters . . . relating to Negotiations between England and Spain*	
CSP Venetian	*Calendar of State Papers . . . in the Archives of Venice*	
Jebb	*De Vita et Rebus Gestis . . . Mariae*	
Labanoff	Mary, Queen of Scots: *Lettres, instructions . . .*	
Pitcairn	*Ancient Criminal Trials in Scotland*	
Teulet	*Relations politiques . . .*	

NOTES AND REFERENCES

INTRODUCTION
1 Bothwell

1. THE THREE CROWNS
1 Knox
2 *Diurnal of Occurrents*
3 Knox. Knox's quotation was altered in the 1570s by the chronicler Robert Lindsay of Pittscottie into the more famous version of King James's words, "It cam wi' a lass, and it will gang wi' a lass."
4 *Diurnal of Occurrents*
5 *CSP Scottish*
6 *The Letters of Henry VIII*, ed. Muriel St. Clair Byrne, London, 1936
7 Lindsay of Pittscottie
8 State Papers in the Public Record Office
9 Raphael Holinshed: *Chronicles* (London, 1577)
10 Cited by Bingham: *The Making of a King*
11 Spottiswoode
12 Cited by Woodward
13 Cited by Thomson: *The Crime of Mary Stuart*
14 Melville
15 For a fuller discussion, see Smailes and Watkins
16 *CSP Foreign*
17 Cited by Woodward
18 *CSP Scottish*; Knox; Antonia Fraser. Mary never mastered Gaelic, the language spoken in the Scottish Highlands.
19 Brantôme
20 Ibid.
21 Melville; Jebb
22 Tytler: *History of Scotland*
23 *CSP Scottish*
24 Ibid.
25 Herries
26 *CSP Scottish*
27 Cited by Gore-Browne
28 Blackwood
29 Cited by Gore-Browne
30 Ibid.

31 If the mummified skeleton at Faarvejle Church in Denmark is his, as seems probable.
32 Melville
33 *CSP Scottish*
34 Anderson: *Collections*
35 *CSP Scottish*
36 "A Declaration of the Lords' Just Quarrel," in *Satirical Poems*
37 *CSP Venetian*
38 *CSP Spanish*; see Antonia Fraser: *Mary, Queen of Scots* for a full discussion of the matter.
39 Fraser: *The Lennox*
40 Ibid.
41 Cited by Bingham: *The Making of a King*
42 Bothwell
43 *CSP Venetian*
44 *CSP Scottish*
45 *CSP Venetian*
46 Ibid.; *CSP Foreign*

2. "The Most Beautiful in Europe"
1 Fraser: *The Lennox*; *CSP Foreign*; *CSP Scottish*; *CSP Spanish*
2 Cited by Black: *Reign of Elizabeth*
3 Melville
4 *Diurnal of Occurrents*
5 Brantôme
6 Cited by Steel
7 Cited by Watkins
8 After James VI became James I of England in 1603 and moved south, Holyrood Palace was rarely used. In 1650, following a serious fire, Oliver Cromwell ordered his troops to repair it. After 1671, Charles II completed James V's original plan and built the other three sides of the main quadrangle, as well as the South Tower, which was designed to match the North Tower, in which larger sash windows were installed. James V's chapel royal was dismantled at this time, along with other 16th-century state rooms; they were all replaced by new royal apartments. Under Charles II, the abbey church became the chapel royal, but in 1768 the roof collapsed, leaving the abbey in the ruinous condition in which it remains today.

At the time of the 17th-century restoration, the old King's Lodgings on the first floor of the North Tower were remodelled and became the Queen's Apartments, although their layout remains much as it was in Mary's day. During the 18th and 19th centuries, Mary's former rooms were occupied by the Dukes of Hamilton, and for a long time it was erroneously believed that the furniture in them had once been Mary's. By the early 19th century, these rooms were ruinous, and they were not fully restored until 1976. The Jacobean frieze in the bedchamber, discovered in the early 20th century, dates from about 1617, when the initials of Mary and James VI were added to the original oak ceiling.

After George IV's visit to Scotland in 1822, Holyrood Palace regained favour as a royal residence; since then, it has again become the official Scottish residence of the sovereign.

9 Cited by Erickson
10 *CSP Scottish*
11 *CSP Venetian*
12 *Lennox Narrative*
13 *CSP Scottish*
14 Ibid.
15 Ibid.
16 Ibid.
17 Ibid.
18 Ibid.
19 Cited by Mahon, Hosack and Goodall; *Lennox Narrative*
20 Maitland was often incorrectly referred to by his contemporaries as Lethington, a title that in fact belonged to his father.
21 Cited by Black: *Reign of Elizabeth*
22 Cited by Skelton: *Maitland*
23 Cited by Stevenson
24 Bothwell

3. "Powerful Considerations"

1 Bothwell
2 Knox
3 Blackwood
4 Bothwell
5 Knox
6 *CSP Scottish*
7 Ibid.
8 Ibid.
9 Lord John Stewart died in 1563, aged only 31. Mary grieved deeply for him, saying that God always took from her those she loved best. Lord John left one son, Francis, who was created Earl of Bothwell in 1581 by James VI. He was a notorious sorcerer and troublemaker, and died in exile in 1612.
10 *CSP Scottish*; Knox
11 Bothwell
12 Ibid.; State Papers in the Public Record Office; Pitcairn
13 *CSP Scottish*
14 Ibid.
15 Ibid.
16 State Papers in the Public Record Office
17 *CSP Spanish*
18 Ibid.
19 *CSP Scottish*
20 *CSP Domestic*

21 *Diurnal of Occurrents*; Pitcairn; Knox
22 Bothwell
23 State Papers in the Public Record Office
24 Bothwell
25 Ibid.; *CSP Scottish*
26 Cited by Sitwell
27 *CSP Spanish*
28 Ibid.
29 Ibid.
30 *CSP Scottish*
31 Strickland: *Lives of the Queens of England (Elizabeth I)*
32 Knox
33 Brantôme
34 *CSP Spanish*
35 *CSP Venetian*
36 *CSP Spanish*
37 Teulet
38 Melville
39 *CSP Scottish*
40 Ibid.
41 Report on the state of Scotland during Mary's reign, sent in 1594 by Jesuit priests to Pope Clement VIII, and cited by Stevenson in his edition of the *Memorials* of Claude Nau
42 *CSP Scottish*
43 Ibid.
44 Ibid.; *Diurnal of Occurrents*
45 *CSP Scottish*
46 Melville
47 Ibid.
48 Ibid.
49 The Lennox Jewel was purchased by Queen Victoria and is now in the Royal Collection at the Palace of Holyroodhouse, Edinburgh.
50 Cited by Gore-Browne
51 Bothwell
52 *CSP Foreign*
53 Melville
54 *CSP Scottish*
55 Melville
56 Cited by Keith
57 *CSP Spanish*
58 Teulet. Knox and Buchanan also took the view that Elizabeth supported a marriage between Mary and Darnley, a belief that was widely prevalent in European diplomatic circles. See *Papal Negotiations* and *CSP Scottish*.
59 *Diurnal of Occurrents*
60 *CSP Scottish*

4. "A Handsome, Lusty Youth"

1 The first Henry Stuart, Lord Darnley, had been born in March 1545 at the Palace of Stepney, which had been granted by Henry VIII to the Lennoxes, and died on 28 November that year. He was buried in the Parish Church of St. Dunstan, Stepney.

2 *Papiers d'Etat*, ed. Teulet

3 See Bingham: *Darnley*

4 The names of the four girls and one other boy who died young are nowhere recorded, so they must have died before baptism. The number of children, and their sex, are known only from the weepers on their mother's tomb in Westminster Abbey.

5 Teulet

6 Pearson

7 *Lennox Narrative*; cf. Darnley's own letters in various sources, chiefly Bingham: *Darnley*

8 *CSP Scottish*

9 Knox

10 *CSP Spanish*

11 *CSP Scottish*

12 *Historie of James the Sext*

13 Nau

14 *Historie of James the Sext*

15 Melville

5. "Most Unworthy to Be Matched"

1 Melville

2 *Lennox Narrative*

3 *CSP Scottish*

4 Labanoff

5 Cited by Donaldson

6 *CSP Scottish*

7 Melville

8 *CSP Scottish*

9 Bothwell; *CSP Scottish*

10 *CSP Scottish*

11 Ibid.

12 Ibid.; Keith

13 Keith

14 Bothwell

15 *CSP Spanish*

16 Melville

17 *CSP Scottish*

18 Melville

19 Buchanan

20 Cited by Sitwell

21 *CSP Scottish*
22 Ibid.
23 *CSP Spanish*
24 *CSP Scottish*
25 Ibid.
26 Leslie: *Defence*; Anderson: *Collections*
27 Additional MSS.; Bannatyne MSS.
28 *CSP Scottish*
29 Ibid.; Keith
30 *CSP Scottish*
31 Ibid.
32 Ibid.
33 *CSP Spanish*
34 *CSP Scottish*
35 Pitcairn
36 Teulet
37 Labanoff
38 *CSP Scottish*
39 Ibid.
40 Ibid.
41 Ibid.
42 Ibid.; Throckmorton noticed Mary's coldness towards Maitland.
43 *CSP Scottish*
44 Ibid.; *Register of the Privy Council*
45 Bothwell
46 Ibid.; *Diurnal of Occurrents*
47 Cotton MSS. Caligula
48 *CSP Scottish*
49 Ibid.
50 Ibid.; Buchanan
51 *CSP Scottish*
52 Ibid.
53 Ibid.
54 Ibid.
55 Ibid.
56 Ibid.
57 Ibid.
58 Teulet
59 *CSP Scottish*
60 Ibid.
61 Randolph to Cecil, cited by Keith
62 Keith
63 *CSP Scottish*
64 Ibid.
65 Melville
66 *CSP Scottish*

67 Knox
68 Ibid.
69 Bothwell
70 The Moray plot is well attested: see Randolph to Cecil, 4 July 1565, in Keith; *CSP Spanish*; Melville; Leslie; Knox; Labanoff; Lindsay of Pittscottie; Blackwood. Buchanan dismisses the alleged plot of his patron Moray against the Queen as existing only in her imagination, and asserts that Moray had been warned by Ruthven of a plot by Mary and Darnley to murder him at Perth, which was the reason why he had stayed away. This differs from Randolph's contemporary account of events, which alleges that Darnley and Rizzio were plotting against Moray; Buchanan's version is obviously an attempt to blacken Mary's name.
71 *CSP Scottish*
72 Seton Palace was extended in the 17th century but largely demolished in 1789–90, when the present Seton Castle, designed by Robert Adam, was built. Only the vaulted ground floor remains from Mary's time. The apartments she occupied were on the first floor. Seton Collegiate Church, which dates from c.1434 and stood beside the palace, still remains in the grounds.
73 *CSP Scottish*
74 Melville
75 Pollen: "Dispensation"
76 *CSP Scottish*
77 Keith
78 *CSP Spanish*

6. "THE CHASEABOUT RAID"
1 *Diurnal of Occurrents*
2 Melville
3 Randolph to Leicester, in *CSP Scottish*
4 *Inventaires*
5 Randolph to Leicester, in *CSP Scottish*
6 Household Expenses for 29 July 1565, in the Scottish Record Office
7 Randolph to Leicester, in *CSP Scottish*
8 *CSP Scottish*
9 A silver medal commemorating the marriage and showing both Mary and Darnley crowned and bearing the legend in Latin "Whom God hath joined together, let no man put asunder," is in the Scottish National Portrait Gallery; there are only two surviving examples of the "Henricus et Maria" silver ryal coin: one is in the British Museum, and another, in better condition, is in a private collection.
10 *Book of Articles*
11 *CSP Scottish*
12 Melville
13 *CSP Scottish*
14 Melville
15 Ibid.
16 *Lennox Narrative*
17 Knox

18 *Register of the Privy Council*
19 *CSP Spanish* .
20 Teulet
21 *CSP Scottish*
22 Ibid.
23 *Register of the Privy Council; Diurnal of Occurrents*
24 *CSP Scottish*
25 Teulet
26 Keith
27 *CSP Scottish*
28 Ibid.; *Diurnal of Occurrents*
29 Knox
30 Buchanan
31 *CSP Scottish; Diurnal of Occurrents*
32 Teulet
33 *CSP Scottish*
34 Ibid.
35 Buchanan; *Register of the Privy Council*
36 *Papal Negotiations*
37 Labanoff
38 *CSP Scottish*
39 *Register of the Privy Council*
40 Buchanan
41 *CSP Scottish*
42 *CSP Foreign*
43 Letter cited by Strickland in *Lives of the Queens of Scotland*
44 Labanoff
45 Teulet
46 Nau
47 Teulet
48 *CSP Scottish*
49 Ibid.; *Diurnal of Occurrents*
50 Cited by Wright; *CSP Scottish; CSP Foreign*
51 *CSP Scottish*
52 *Papal Negotiations*
53 *CSP Scottish*
54 Ibid.
55 Ibid.
56 Teulet
57 *CSP Scottish*

7. "There Is a Bait Laid for Signor David"
1 Randolph, in *CSP Foreign*
2 *CSP Scottish*
3 *Lennox Narrative*
4 Keith

5 Herries
6 Ibid.
7 *CSP Spanish*
8 *Register of the Privy Council*
9 *CSP Scottish*
10 *Papiers d'Etat*, ed. Teulet.
11 *Cecil Papers*
12 *Lennox Narrative*
13 *CSP Spanish; CSP Scottish*
14 Labanoff
15 *CSP Scottish*
16 Ibid.
17 *Cecil Papers*
18 *CSP Scottish*
19 Ibid.; *CSP Foreign*. The new coins had on the obverse a design of a tortoise, representing Darnley, climbing a crowned palm tree, representing Mary. An example may be seen in the National Museums of Scotland. See Stewart: *Scottish Coinage*.
20 *Register of the Privy Council*. Randolph and Buchanan are incorrect in claiming that Darnley's name was placed second on all documents. In all the Acts of the Privy Council, only one, that authorising the change of coinage, has the Queen's name appearing first. It also appears first on documents on which Darnley's sign manual was obviously added later.
21 *CSP Scottish*
22 *Inventaires*
23 *CSP Scottish*
24 Ibid.
25 Keith; Strickland
26 *Register of the Privy Seal*
27 *CSP Scottish*
28 Melville
29 McCrie
30 *Papal Negotiations*
31 *CSP Scottish*
32 *CSP Spanish*
33 Melville
34 *CSP Spanish*
35 Gore-Browne
36 *CSP Scottish*
37 Ibid.; Bedford later informed Cecil that this rumour was baseless.
38 *CSP Foreign*
39 Buchanan
40 Melville
41 State Papers in the Public Record Office: Domestic, James I. The elder Anthony Standen was a minor player in the Gunpowder Plot of 1605.
42 Ruthven: Narration
43 Melville

44 Ruthven: Narration
45 Melville; Bothwell
46 Bothwell
47 Ruthven: Narration; *Cecil Papers*; Wright
48 *Cecil Papers*
49 Melville
50 Ibid.
51 *CSP Scottish*
52 *Cecil Papers*
53 Ruthven describes his illness as "an inflammation of the liver and a consumption of the kidneys"; it could have been cancer, or perhaps the consequence of heavy drinking.
54 Ruthven: Narration
55 Melville
56 Blackwood
57 *CSP Scottish*; Ruthven: Narration; Keith; Labanoff; Knox; Buchanan
58 Melville
59 *CSP Scottish*
60 Harleian MSS.
61 Knox
62 *Diurnal of Occurrents*
63 Keith; Tytler: *History*; MSS. in the National Library of Scotland
64 Keith
65 Ibid.
66 *CSP Scottish*
67 Melville
68 *CSP Scottish*
69 *Inventaires*
70 A document alleged to be this dispensation is preserved at Dunrobin Castle, but may not be authentic.
71 Knox
72 In 1599, Jean married Ogilvy as her third husband.
73 *CSP Scottish*
74 Ibid.; Ruthven: Narration; Keith; Buchanan; Knox
75 *Diurnal of Occurrents*
76 *CSP Scottish*; Miscellany of the Maitland Club (3 vols., 1833)
77 *CSP Scottish*
78 Ibid.; Cotton MSS. Caligula
79 Knox
80 *CSP Spanish*
81 Knox; Buchanan
82 Knox

8. "THIS VILE ACT"

1 Strickland: *Lives of the Queens of Scotland*
2 There are several accounts of the events that followed. Two were by eyewitnesses:

Mary's version appears in two similar letters, one to Archbishop Beaton (2 April 1566, in Labanoff, hereinafter referred to as Mary to Beaton) and the other to Charles IX and Catherine de' Medici (*CSP Venetian*, hereinafter referred to as Mary to Charles IX).

Lord Ruthven wrote his account in his 6,000-word Narration, which, after being edited by Cecil, was completed on 30 April 1566 in England (hereinafter referred to as Ruthven). It was written for the benefit of the English Privy Council and is obviously an attempt to portray Ruthven and his accomplices in the best possible light.

On 11 March, in Berwick, Randolph wrote an account of Rizzio's murder (additional MSS., hereinafter referred to as Randolph), based on information given him by one Captain Carew, an English spy in Edinburgh, who had spoken with Mary, Darnley and others involved.

On 27 March, Randolph and Bedford wrote a joint letter to Cecil describing the recent shocking events (Cotton MSS. Caligula; Wright, hereinafter referred to as Randolph and Bedford).

In the 1570s, Claude Nau compiled a detailed account of the murder, based probably on Mary's own reminiscences; it gives details that only she could have known.

Melville's memoirs are those of someone who was well informed but was not actually an eyewitness, although he was at Holyrood at the time of the murder; his record of events is succinct and probably accurate.

There are very few discrepancies in all these accounts, and together they provide what is probably the truth about the events of 9–12 March, 1566.

 3 Randolph
 4 Ruthven; Randolph and Bedford
 5 *Register of the Privy Council*; Keith; Pitcairn; Ruthven; Gore-Browne
 6 Melville
 7 Ibid. Mary gives the time as 7 p.m.
 8 Ruthven. Mary gives a similar account of this conversation, although less detailed.
 9 Mary to Beaton
10 Ruthven
11 Mary to Beaton
12 Ruthven
13 The full text is given by Gore-Browne.
14 State Papers in the Public Record Office: Domestic, James I
15 Ruthven
16 Ibid.; Randolph and Bedford
17 Melville
18 Birrel
19 Randolph and Bedford
20 Ruthven; Mary to Beaton
21 Randolph and Bedford
22 Herries says Morton struck the first blow; Paul de Foix (*Papiers d'Etat*, ed. Teulet) says it was George Douglas.
23 *CSP Scottish.* On 23 March, Drury reported to Cecil that one of Ruthven's fol-

lowers had arrived in Berwick with his arm bound up—he had been wounded whilst attacking Rizzio.

24 Ruthven; Randolph and Bedford

25 Ibid.

26 Mary to Beaton

27 Ibid. Randolph and Bedford say there were 60 wounds on the body. From 1722 onwards, a supposedly indelible bloodstain was said to denote the place where Rizzio was murdered, a myth that was still current in the 19th century. Today, a plaque marks the spot. In the 18th century, a richly inlaid dagger was discovered hidden in the rafters of Queen Mary's Bath House; it may have been hidden there by one of Rizzio's murderers.

28 *CSP Scottish*

29 Ruthven

30 Randolph and Bedford

31 Mary to Beaton

32 Herries

33 Ruthven

34 Mary to Beaton

35 Ibid.; Nau

36 Mary to Beaton

37 Randolph

38 Mary to Beaton

39 Nau

40 Melville

41 Ibid.; Bothwell; Ruthven; *Papiers d'Etat*, ed. Teulet

42 Melville

43 Mary to Beaton

44 Nau

45 Ibid.; Ruthven

46 Melville

47 Nau

48 Ibid.

49 Ibid.

50 Ibid.

51 Ibid.; Leslie

52 Nau

53 Ibid.

54 Randolph

55 Nau

56 Mary to Beaton. It must have been Darnley who informed her of this.

57 Nau

58 Cited by Sitwell

59 Nau

60 Ibid.

61 Ibid.

62 Ibid.

63 Ruthven; Randolph and Bedford
64 Ruthven; Keith
65 Melville
66 Mary to Beaton
67 Nau
68 Mary to Beaton; Randolph and Bedford
69 Ruthven
70 Ibid.
71 Ibid.
72 Mary to Beaton
73 Cited by Sitwell
74 Ruthven
75 *Diurnal of Occurrents*
76 Nau
77 Ibid.
78 Cited by James Mackay
79 Nau
80 Ruthven
81 Ibid.; Melville
82 Ruthven
83 Mary to Charles IX
84 Bothwell
85 Nau
86 Melville
87 Nau
88 Ibid.; Ruthven
89 Nau
90 *Lennox Narrative*
91 Nau. In her letter to Charles IX, Mary states that she and Darnley were attended by Traquair, Erskine and "two other persons only," one of whom was Standen and the other, according to Randolph, "one gentlewoman," who was probably Margaret Carwood, one of the Queen's favourite maids-of-honour. Later that year, Mary got Darnley to knight Standen for his loyal service.
92 Nau
93 Armstrong Davison
94 Nau
95 Randolph
96 Memoir to Cosimo de' Medici, in Labanoff

9. "As They Have Brewed, So Let Them Drink"

1 Because of its infamous associations with Bothwell, Dunbar Castle was dismantled on the orders of Parliament in 1568. Only ruins remain.
2 Bothwell
3 Mary to Charles IX
4 Randolph to Cecil, State Papers in the Public Record Office
5 Nau

6 *Register of the Privy Seal; CSP Scottish*
7 *CSP Scottish;* Labanoff
8 *CSP Venetian*
9 Nau
10 *Register of the Privy Council; Diurnal of Occurrents;* Ruthven
11 Ruthven
12 Nau
13 Melville
14 Ibid.
15 Mary to Charles IX
16 Melville
17 Randolph to Cecil, State Papers in the Public Record Office
18 Melville
19 Ibid.
20 Randolph says she lodged on the High Street.
21 Randolph and Bedford; Nau; *Diurnal of Occurrents*
22 *Lennox Narrative*
23 Mary to Charles IX
24 Buchanan
25 *Register of the Privy Seal*
26 Nau
27 Melville
28 Cited by Gore-Browne
29 *CSP Spanish; Papiers d'Etat,* ed. Teulet; *CSP Foreign;* Keith
30 Mary to Beaton
31 Mary to Charles IX
32 *Diurnal of Occurrents; Papiers d'Etat,* ed. Teulet; Buchanan
33 State Papers in the Public Record Office
34 *CSP Scottish*
35 Cited by Bowen
36 *CSP Scottish*
37 Cited by Prebble
38 State Papers in the Public Record Office
39 *CSP Spanish*
40 Ibid.
41 *CSP Venetian*
42 *CSP Scottish*
43 Ibid.
44 Bothwell
45 *CSP Scottish*
46 *Register of the Privy Council; Diurnal of Occurrents;* Pitcairn; Keith; Bothwell
47 *CSP Scottish*
48 Melville
49 *Lennox Narrative*
50 *Register of the Privy Council.* Darnley continued to sign documents, or they were stamped with his sign manual, but he had no say in the formulation of policy.

51 From "Lord Bothwell," in *English and Scottish Popular Ballads*
52 Nau; *CSP Foreign*
53 *Register of the Privy Council*; Nau
54 During the siege of 1573, King David's Tower was destroyed. In 1578, the Regent Morton refortified Edinburgh Castle and built the Half Moon Battery on the site of David's Tower. In 1615–17, the royal lodgings were remodelled for James I, at which time painted decorations were added to the tiny room in which he was born; the panelling was not installed until 1848. The initials of James's parents were probably placed over the doorway in 1617; they may have come from elsewhere. In 1650, Oliver Cromwell dismantled much of the castle's fortifications. Since the Act of Union of 1707, Edinburgh Castle has been kept in good repair. The Scottish Crown Jewels and the Stone of Destiny are housed in the former royal lodgings.
55 *CSP Scottish*
56 Nau
57 Teulet; *CSP Scottish*
58 *CSP Scottish*
59 *Lennox Narrative*
60 Labanoff
61 *CSP Spanish*
62 *Original Letters*
63 *Inventaires*
64 *CSP Foreign*
65 Randolph, in *CSP Foreign*, 13 May 1566
66 *Diurnal of Occurrents*
67 Nau
68 *CSP Foreign*
69 Nau
70 Melville
71 Nau
72 Ibid.
73 Ibid.
74 Melville
75 *Lennox Narrative*
76 *CSP Scottish*
77 *CSP Spanish*, 18 May 1566
78 Nau
79 *CSP Scottish*; Nau
80 Maitland to Randolph, in Cotton MSS. Caligula; *CSP Spanish*
81 *CSP Spanish*; *CSP Scottish*
82 Barberini MSS., Barberini Library, Rome
83 *Papal Negotiations*
84 *CSP Spanish*
85 Ibid.; *Papal Negotiations*
86 Egerton MSS.
87 *Papal Negotiations*

88 This had been Pius's own See prior to his elevation to the Papacy.
89 Leslie
90 *Papal Negotiations*
91 *CSP Scottish*
92 Ibid.
93 Knox
94 Additional MSS., Bodleian Library
95 *Calendar of the Manuscripts at Hatfield House*
96 *Lennox Narrative*; Hume: *Love Affairs*
97 Nau
98 Buchanan alleges that Mary ignored Darnley in her Will and that Bothwell not only featured prominently but was also appointed Governor of her child and of the realm. Mary's Will was perhaps destroyed so that the lies in the libels would not be exposed. Moray, under whose auspices Buchanan wrote, must have been aware of the Will's true contents, as he was to have been a beneficiary.
99 *Inventaires*. Mary's Will does not survive, but a testamentary inventory of the jewels she meant to bequeath, annotated by herself, still exists in the Register House in Edinburgh.
100 Clerk of Penicuik MSS., Register House in Edinburgh
101 State Papers in the Public Record Office; Chalmers
102 *CSP Scottish*
103 Nau
104 Melville
105 Nau
106 *CSP Scottish*; Calderwood
107 Nau

10. "AN UNWELCOME INTRUDER"
1 Melville
2 *Bannatyne Miscellany*. She was the wife of Sir Arthur Forbes of Reres.
3 Nau
4 Herries says he was born between 9 a.m. and 10 a.m.; Melville had the news from Mary Beaton between 10 a.m. and 11 a.m. and claims he was the first to be informed. Nau and the *Diurnal of Occurrents* state that the Prince was born between 10 a.m. and 11 a.m. Buchanan says he was born a little after 9 a.m.
5 Cited by William Robertson
6 *Diurnal of Occurrents*; Nau
7 Herries
8 Strickland
9 See Gent, and Antonia Fraser.
10 Nau
11 *CSP Scottish*
12 Ibid.
13 Bothwell
14 *CSP Scottish*
15 Ibid.

16 Ibid.
17 State Papers in the Public Record Office: Domestic, James I
18 *CSP Spanish*
19 Ibid.
20 *CSP Scottish*
21 Nau
22 *CSP Scottish*
23 Ibid. James's cradle is now at Traquair House, Innerleithen.
24 *CSP Spanish*
25 Teulet
26 *CSP Foreign; Cecil Papers*
27 *CSP Spanish*
28 *CSP Foreign; Cecil Papers*
29 *CSP Scottish*
30 Ibid.
31 Ibid.
32 *CSP Spanish; CSP Scottish*
33 Nau says she was at Alloa on 28 July.
34 *Selections from Unpublished Manuscripts*
35 Ibid.
36 *Register of the Privy Council*
37 *Register of the Privy Seal*
38 Buchanan
39 Ibid.
40 *CSP Scottish; Nau*
41 Knox
42 Alloa Tower is still owned by the Erskines, but is substantially altered from what it was in Mary's day. In the early 18th century, it was remodelled to match a nearby mansion, and in 1800, a serious fire damaged the roof and consumed many of the family heirlooms, among them what was said to be the only portrait of Mary painted while she was in Scotland. The Tower was restored in the 1990s and re-opened by Queen Elizabeth II in 1997.
43 *Lennox Narrative*
44 *Selections from Unpublished Manuscripts; CSP Scottish*
45 *CSP Spanish*
46 Nau
47 Melville
48 Cotton MSS. Caligula; *Selections from Unpublished Manuscripts; CSP Foreign*; Keith; *Illustrations of the Reign of Queen Mary*
49 *CSP Foreign*
50 *Lennox Narrative*
51 Nau
52 *CSP Scottish*
53 Leslie
54 Ibid.
55 Ibid.

56 *Papal Negotiations*
57 Raumer
58 Keith
59 *Inventaires*
60 *CSP Scottish*; Nau
61 The peel tower in which Mary stayed is the oldest part of Traquair House, and is now attached to the north end of the main block, which was built in 1642. At the end of the 17th century another wing was added. In the King's Room is a bed slept in by Mary when she stayed with Lord Herries at Terregles Castle in 1568, just prior to her flight to England; this bed was brought to Traquair in 1890. Also at Traquair are a rosary, crucifix, reticule and purse said to have belonged to Mary, and a document dated 1565, bearing her signature and Darnley's.
62 Nau
63 Ibid.
64 *Papal Negotiations*
65 *CSP Spanish*
66 *CSP Foreign*
67 Keith
68 Nau
69 Ibid.
70 Cited by Gore-Browne
71 *CSP Foreign*

11. "No Outgait"
 1 *Cecil Papers*
 2 *CSP Scottish; CSP Foreign*
 3 Du Croc to Archbishop Beaton, in Keith
 4 *Papal Negotiations*
 5 The Privy Council to Catherine de' Medici, in Keith
 6 Du Croc to Archbishop Beaton, ibid.
 7 The Privy Council to Catherine de' Medici, ibid.
 8 Ibid.
 9 Ibid.
10 Ibid.; du Croc to Archbishop Beaton, in Keith; *Papiers d'Etat*, ed. Teulet
11 Du Croc to Catherine de' Medici, in Keith; *Papiers d'Etat*, ed. Teulet; Labanoff
12 Nau
13 The Privy Council to Catherine de' Medici, 8 October 1566, in Keith; Teulet
14 Ibid.
15 Leslie; Keith
16 *Papal Negotiations*
17 *Register of the Privy Council*
18 Melville
19 *Register of the Privy Council*
20 *Lennox Narrative*
21 "The Answer of Moray," 1569, in Keith
22 Archibald Douglas to Queen Mary, ibid.

23 *Diurnal of Occurrents*
24 Bothwell had shot Elliott in the leg with a pistol before being wounded himself. There are conflicting reports as to Elliott's fate: some claimed he died of his wounds, but Sir John Forster stated that he escaped and recovered (Additional MSS., British Library). There is some evidence that he continued to pursue his lawless existence until 1590, when he may have died.
25 Buchanan
26 Cited by McKechnie
27 Nau
28 Keith
29 Cited by Gore-Browne
30 Teulet
31 *CSP Scottish*
32 Keith; *Papiers d'Etat*, ed. Teulet
33 Labanoff
34 Du Croc to Catherine de' Medici, in Keith; *Papiers d'Etat*, ed. Teulet; Labanoff
35 Report of 12 November, in *Papal Negotiations*
36 Keith; Teulet
37 Cotton MSS. Caligula
38 *Diurnal of Occurrents; CSP Foreign; Register of the Privy Seal*; Tytler: *Scotland*
39 Hermitage Castle still stands today, its courtyard in ruins but its outer walls intact. Although extensively restored in 1820, it is perhaps the best preserved example of a Border fortress.
40 *CSP Scottish*; Nau
41 A French 16th-century pocket watch and case were unearthed by a mole and found on this spot by a shepherd in the early 19th century. Both are now on display at Mary, Queen of Scots' House in Jedburgh.
42 *Lennox Narrative*
43 Chalmers; Tytler: *Scotland*
44 Nau, writing in the 1570s, states she fell ill on the day after her ride to Hermitage, i.e., on 16 October; on 18 October 1566, the Council informed Beaton that the illness came on two days after the ride, i.e., on 17 October. As their account was written only a day later, the Council are more likely to be correct.
45 Nau
46 Ibid.
47 *CSP Venetian*
48 Ibid.
49 Nau
50 Ibid.
51 Keith
52 *CSP Spanish*
53 Buchanan
54 *Register of the Privy Council*
55 Bishop Leslie to Archbishop Beaton, in Keith
56 Ibid.
57 Cited by Tytler: *Scotland*

58 Bishop Leslie to Archbishop Beaton, in Keith
59 Nau; *CSP Spanish*. Mary's instructions are in the archives of Edinburgh University.
60 *Register of the Privy Council*
61 Leslie; Nau
62 Nau; Leslie
63 Nau; Leslie
64 Bishop Leslie to Archbishop Beaton, in Keith; *Diurnal of Occurrents*
65 Keith
66 *Diurnal of Occurrents*
67 The building known today as Mary, Queen of Scots' House was greatly altered and extended in the 17th and 19th centuries, but was restored largely to its 16th-century state in 1986–87.
68 *CSP Scottish*
69 *CSP Foreign*
70 Teulet
71 *Papal Negotiations*
72 De Silva states he had learned about what followed in a letter from Mary "dated the 1st instant" (*CSP Spanish*). Buchanan incorrectly states that Mary received the letter from or about Darnley on 5 November when she was on her way to Kelso, but she did not leave Jedburgh until 9 November, and her messenger, Stephen Wilson, had left for England with news of the Darnley letter around the 8th. Mary must therefore have received the letter on or shortly before 1 November while she was still at Jedburgh.
73 Buchanan says the letter was from Darnley but it is hardly likely that Darnley would have himself divulged to Mary the information that de Silva states was in it. Armstrong Davison speculated that it had come from the Comte de Brienne, but he did not arrive in Scotland until 2 or 3 November.
74 *CSP Spanish*
75 Ibid., 17 February 1567
76 *CSP Spanish*
77 Labanoff; *Papal Negotiations*
78 Fr. Edmund Hay, SJ, to Francis Borgia, Father General of the Society of Jesus, in the archives of the Society of Jesus
79 Keith
80 Sir John Neale: *Elizabeth I and her Parliaments* (2 vols, London, 1953–7)
81 *CSP Foreign*
82 *CSP Scottish*
83 *CSP Spanish*
84 *CSP Foreign*
85 *CSP Scottish*
86 *Papal Negotiations*
87 Melville
88 Buchanan: *Detectio*. A slightly different version appears in the *Book of Articles*, where it is said that Lady Reres's purpose was "not altogether unknown to such as attended in the Queen's company."

89 *Diurnal of Occurrents*; Keith
90 Keith

12. "UNNATURAL PROCEEDINGS"

1 *Book of Articles*
2 Du Croc to Archbishop Beaton, 6 December 1566, in Keith
3 *Papal Negotiations*
4 Keith
5 Du Croc to Archbishop Beaton, 6 December 1566, in Keith
6 Cotton MSS. Caligula. The full text is in Keith, Goodall and Mumby: *Fall of Mary Stuart.*
7 It was not unusual for two people of the same sex to share a bed when space was at a premium.
8 Although restored to his title and earldom, Huntly had yet to recover his estates.
9 Goodall
10 It was actually drawn up two months before, not three, but after six years it would be natural for Ormiston to be a little inaccurate as to dates. Elsewhere in his confession, Ormiston quotes Bothwell as saying that the matter had been concluded at Craigmillar.
11 Pitcairn
12 *Register of the Secret Seal; Inventaires; Register of the Privy Seal*
13 The official record is in Cambridge University Library.
14 Moray's Answer, dated 19 January 1569 and written by Moray and Cecil in London, is pasted to the back of the Protestation.
15 *CSP Foreign*
16 Nau
17 Du Croc to Archbishop Beaton, in Keith
18 Sir John Forster to Cecil, 11 December 1566, in *CSP Foreign*
19 Melville
20 *Register of the Privy Council*
21 *Lennox Narrative*
22 Casket Letter II, in *CSP Scottish*
23 *Lennox Narrative*
24 *CSP Spanish*; Teulet
25 *Register of the Privy Council*; Keith
26 *Papal Negotiations*
27 Du Croc to Archbishop Beaton, in Keith
28 Keith; *CSP Venetian; Diurnal of Occurrents*
29 Du Croc to Archbishop Beaton, in Keith
30 *Inventaires*; Cotton MSS. Caligula; *CSP Foreign*. Buchanan later referred only to Mary providing clothing for Bothwell: "The Queen did her best to make Bothwell appear the most magnificently dressed of all her subjects and guests." He meant to emphasise that she was singling Bothwell out for special favour because he was her lover. This is a typical example of how Buchanan massaged the facts in order to support his denunciation of Mary.
31 Nau

32 Ibid.

33 Du Croc to Archbishop Beaton, in Keith

34 Buchanan

35 Knox

36 Du Croc to Archbishop Beaton, in Keith

37 The Elizabethan historian William Camden says that Bedford had been instructed not to acknowledge Darnley as King.

38 Cotton MSS. Caligula; Nau

39 Du Croc to Archbishop Beaton, in Keith

40 Mary to Archbishop Beaton, 20 January 1567, in Labanoff

41 Ibid.

42 *Register of the Secret Seal; Register of the Privy Seal*

43 Antonia Fraser

44 *CSP Scottish*

45 Ibid.; Bothwell; *Bannatyne Miscellany; CSP Foreign*

46 *CSP Scottish*

47 *Register of the Privy Seal*

48 *CSP Scottish*

49 Morton's confession of 1581, in Holinshed. Buchanan alleges that Darnley left Stirling because his rival Bothwell had been "set up to his face as an object of universal respect," but this is not corroborated by the other evidence.

50 *Lennox Narrative*; Mary to Beaton, 20 January 1567, in Labanoff

13. "The Days Were Evil"

1 Knox; Buchanan

2 *Lennox Narrative*

3 Pearson

4 *CSP Scottish*

5 *Inventaires*

6 The skull, which had been removed in 1768 from the vandalised royal vault at Holyrood, is now in the Royal College of Surgeons, London.

7 Pearson

8 Knox

9 *CSP Spanish*

10 Keith

11 Ibid.

12 *Register of the Secret Seal*

13 Ibid.; Keith; Buchanan

14 This interview must have taken place in the New Year, after Darnley had left Stirling and Mary had returned from Tullibardine. This would have been the first opportunity that Walker had had to speak with her.

15 Mary to Archbishop Beaton, 20 January 1567, in Labanoff

16 *CSP Scottish*

17 Labanoff

18 *CSP Scottish*; Keith

19 *Cabala*

20 *Inventaires*

21 Labanoff

22 *CSP Foreign; CSP Scottish*; Keith

23 State Papers in the Public Record Office; *CSP Foreign*

24 Nau

25 *Lennox Narrative*

26 Nau

27 Buchanan says Mary had tried to lull Darnley's suspicions "by her frequent loving letters," but this seems unlikely in view of the other evidence.

28 *CSP Scottish*

29 Teulet

30 Throughout this book, I have quoted the modern English translations of the Casket Letters, except where there are discrepancies in the Scots, French and Latin versions.

31 *CSP Scottish*

32 Mahon: *Lennox Narrative*

33 Buchanan

34 Keith

35 Birrel says the 13th, the *Diurnal of Occurrents* the 14th. These two sources often show a discrepancy of one day.

36 *CSP Scottish*

37 The date of the meeting at Whittinghame is not recorded, but it must have been after Maitland left Edinburgh on 17 January. As it was reported by Drury on the 23rd, it must have taken place around 18 or 19 January. For the Whittinghame episode, see *CSP Scottish*; Morton's confession of 1581 in Holinshed; Archibald Douglas's letter to Mary of 1583 in *Inventaires*; *Diurnal of Occurrents; Bannatyne Miscellany*; Calderwood

38 Bothwell

39 *Inventaires*

40 *CSP Scottish*

41 *CSP Spanish*

42 Holinshed

43 *Inventaires*

44 Nau; his account is corroborated by a letter from Drury to Cecil dated 13 August 1575.

45 Labanoff

14. "SOME SUSPICION OF WHAT AFTERWARDS HAPPENED"

1 *Diurnal of Occurrents*. Birrel; Anderson: *Collections; Book of Articles*; Moray's Journal, in Cotton MSS. Caligula

2 Moray's Journal, in Cotton MSS. Caligula; Anderson: *Collections; Book of Articles*

3 Buchanan

4 Drury reported she had arrived on the 22nd (*CSP Scottish*).

5 Crawford's Deposition, original MS. in Cambridge University Library, edited copy in *CSP Scottish*

6 *CSP Spanish; CSP Foreign*

7 *CSP Spanish*

8 Cambridge University Library

9 *CSP Scottish*; Goodall. After this was read out, Crawford said that the words quoted in his deposition were "the same in effect and substance as they were delivered by the King to him, though not perhaps in all parts the very words themselves."

10 *CSP Scottish*; Labanoff

11 *Lennox Narrative*

12 Ibid.

13 Moray's Journal, in Cotton MSS. Caligula

14 The English version is among the State Papers in the Public Record Office. The only parts omitted here are a few minor irrelevancies. The letter appears here with corrected translations.

15 The last four words appear only in the Scots, Latin and French versions.

16 It will be seen that these passages are very similar to Crawford's Deposition.

17 The original letter, which was in French, has disappeared, but it is clear from the Scots, French and Latin versions that the English translator has made errors. This has been mistranslated in the English version as "to let blood."

18 Another mistranslation: "journée" means "day" in French, not "journey," which appears in the English version.

19 The last part of this sentence only appears in the English version.

20 Labanoff

21 Probably mistranslated. The word appears as "Devil" in the Scots version and as "yeere" in the English.

22 Given as "bible" in the English version, which is probably a mistranslation of "billet."

23 An obvious mistranslation. It is probably a reference to Darnley's skin eruptions.

24 The other versions state that the writer was sitting at the foot of the bed.

25 This last part of the sentence has next to it in the margin a translation from the original French in Cecil's own hand, since the English translator has made an error. This sentence does not appear in the Scots version, and may well have caused problems for the Scottish translator also.

26 In the English version, this word is given as "grief"; all the other versions give "trouble."

27 Lang

28 *CSP Scottish*

29 Cited by Mahon: *Lennox Narrative*

30 *Papal Negotiations*

31 *CSP Scottish*

32 Moray's Journal, in Cotton MSS. Caligula

33 *CSP Venetian*

34 Maitland to Cecil, 8 February 1567, in *CSP Scottish*

35 *CSP Spanish*

36 *CSP Scottish*

37 Keith; Teulet

15. "All Was Prepared for the Crime"

1 *Lennox Narrative*
2 Drury to Cecil, 26 January 1567, in *CSP Scottish*; *CSP Venetian*; Buchanan
3 *Book of Articles*
4 Moray's Journal, in Cotton MSS. Caligula; *Lennox Narrative*; *CSP Scottish*
5 Nau
6 *Book of Articles*
7 Cotton MSS. Caligula
8 Lord Scrope to Cecil, 28 January 1567, in *CSP Scottish*
9 Thomson: *Crime of Mary Stuart*
10 Buchanan
11 Moray's Journal states 30 January, Birrel 31 January, and the *Diurnal of Occurrents* 1 February.
12 *Lennox Narrative*
13 *CSP Venetian*
14 Melville
15 *Inventaires*
16 Pitcairn; Goodall; Anderson: *Collections*. Thomas Crawford made a similar deposition (Cambridge University Library).
17 *Lennox Narrative*
18 Ibid.
19 Mahon: *Lennox Narrative*
20 Pitcairn
21 *Book of Articles*
22 *CSP Spanish*
23 *CSP Venetian*
24 *Inventaires*
25 Nelson's deposition, in Pitcairn, Goodall and Anderson: *Collections*
26 *Inventaires*; Leslie
27 Records of the Burgh of Edinburgh, cited by Gore-Browne
28 The buildings and topography of Kirk o'Field were extensively researched by Mahon for his book *The Tragedy of Kirk o'Field*, a work to which many authors, including myself, are deeply indebted. There is also a contemporary plan of Kirk o'Field, which was drawn up by one of Cecil's agents hours after Darnley's murder on 10 February 1567, which is now in the Public Record Office.

 The collegiate buildings at Kirk o'Field were later converted into the College of King James and a house for its Principal, and in the late 18th century, the central quadrangle of Edinburgh University and its Hall of the Senate, designed by Robert Adam, were built on the site.

 None of the original collegiate buildings remains, but the site of the Prebendaries' Chamber and the Old Provost's Lodging lies just inside the right angle created by South Bridge Street and South College Street. Tour guides in the city vaults point out what they say are the remains of the cellars of Darnley's house and an adjacent close, the cellars being distinguished by Gothic arches, but these are not in the correct location.

29 Buchanan
30 Nelson's deposition in Pitcairn, Goodall and Anderson: *Collections*
31 Details of all the furniture and hangings in the Old Provost's Lodging are in *Inventaires*. Thomas Nelson is the source for the changing of Darnley's bed (Pitcairn; Goodall; Anderson: *Collections*).
32 Nelson's deposition, in Pitcairn, Goodall and Anderson: *Collections*
33 Nau
34 *CSP Spanish*; Leslie
35 *Lennox Narrative*
36 Leslie
37 Ibid.
38 Knox
39 Nau
40 Nelson's deposition, in Pitcairn, Goodall and Anderson: *Collections*
41 *Lennox Narrative*
42 Ibid.
43 William Tytler
44 *Lennox Narrative*
45 Ibid; cf. Buchanan
46 Buchanan
47 Nau
48 Nelson's deposition, in Pitcairn, Goodall and Anderson: *Collections*
49 Buchanan says "three days before the murder."
50 Melville
51 The Indictment of 1568 states Saturday afternoon, the *Book of Articles* and Paris's deposition Saturday morning.
52 Melville
53 *CSP Scottish*; Goodall
54 The English translation appears to be a copy from the original French, and is among the *Cecil Papers* at Hatfield House. Moray's Journal, in Cotton MSS. Caligula, states that Mary's confrontation with Lord Robert and Darnley "conform[ed] to her letter written the night before."
55 See Armstrong Davison
56 The original French copy is in the Public Record Office. This English translation is taken from the Scots version in *CSP Scottish*.
57 *Inventaires*
58 *Papal Negotiations*
59 *CSP Spanish*
60 *CSP Scottish*
61 *Papal Negotiations*; reported by Father Hay to Mondovi.
62 In the *Detectio*, Buchanan says she had smallpox during pregnancy; in his *History*, he claims she had a miscarriage.
63 *Lennox Narrative*; *CSP Venetian*. Lennox states that Mary had decided that Darnley should return to Holyrood on 10 February.
64 In the Register House in Edinburgh.

65 This house was owned by Mr. John Balfour (*Book of Articles*), not Sir James Balfour, as is sometimes stated.

66 *Inventaires; Book of Articles*; Mondovi to Alessandria, 27 February 1567, in *Papal Negotiations*

67 Mondovi to Alessandria, 27 February 1567, in *Papal Negotiations*

68 Labanoff. Buchanan says she had a "fairly large" or "a numerous attendance." Clernault (*Papal Negotiations*) states she was accompanied by "all the principal Lords of her court."

69 *CSP Scottish*

70 *CSP Spanish*

71 *CSP Venetian*

72 Clernault's report, in *Papal Negotiations*

73 *Lennox Narrative*

74 Keith

75 *CSP Scottish*

76 *CSP Venetian*; Giovanni Correr, the Venetian ambassador in Paris, was informed of this by Moretta.

77 *CSP Venetian* (Moretta to Correr); *Book of Articles; Lennox Narrative*; Nelson's deposition, in Pitcairn, Goodall and Anderson: *Collections*; Crawford's deposition in Cambridge University Library; Buchanan: *History*; untitled ballad on the death of Darnley by Robert Lekprevik of Edinburgh, in *CSP Scottish*; *CSP Spanish*—de Silva says Mary gave Darnley "a jewel."

78 *Lennox Narrative*; Buchanan repeats this in his *History*

79 Nau

80 Collector of the Queen's rents.

81 Thomas Wilson

82 Nelson's deposition, in Pitcairn, Goodall and Anderson: *Collections*

83 *CSP Scottish*

84 Buchanan; Thomas Wilson

85 Mahon: *Tragedy of Kirk o'Field*

86 Bothwell

87 Nelson's deposition, in Pitcairn, Goodall and Anderson: *Collections*

88 *CSP Scottish*

89 *Lennox Narrative*

90 Nelson's deposition, in Pitcairn, Goodall and Anderson: *Collections*

91 Buchanan

92 Nau

16. "Most Cruel Murder"

1 Additional MSS.; *CSP Venetian*

2 Mondovi to Cosimo de' Medici, in Labanoff; Mondovi to Alessandria, 15/16 March 1567, in *Papal Negotiations*. Mondovi had received this information from Moretta.

3 The Privy Council to Catherine de' Medici, 10 February 1567, in the Sloane MSS.

4 Buchanan

5 Mary to Archbishop Beaton, 10/11 February 1567, in Keith; cf. the Seigneur de Clernault in State Papers in the Public Record Office, *CSP Scottish* and *Papal Negotiations*

6 State Papers in the Public Record Office; *CSP Scottish*; *Papal Negotiations*

7 Pitcairn

8 Sloane MSS.

9 Ibid.; Keith

10 *Historie of James the Sext*

11 State Papers in the Public Record Office; *CSP Scottish*; *Papal Negotiations*

12 Additional MSS.

13 Buchanan

14 Clernault, in State Papers in the Public Record Office, *CSP Scottish* and *Papal Negotiations*. According to Buchanan, "the Queen, in great expectation of success, how finely she played her part it is marvellous to tell: for she not once stirred at the noise of the fall of the house, which shook the whole town, nor at the fearful outcries that followed." Lennox states that, "upon the crack and noise, which the Queen waited for to hear, she went to bed" (*Lennox Narrative*). Buchanan says much the same thing elsewhere, and in the *Book of Articles* claims that the explosion "neither feared nor moved the Queen."

15 Clernault, in State Papers in the Public Record Office, *CSP Scottish* and *Papal Negotiations*

16 *Book of Articles*

17 Deposition of William Powrie, in Pitcairn

18 Bothwell

19 Pitcairn

20 *CSP Spanish*

21 Clernault, in State Papers in the Public Record Office, *CSP Scottish* and *Papal Negotiations*

22 Buchanan. See the sketch of the murder scene in the Public Record Office for the positions of the bodies.

23 Herries; Knox

24 Buchanan; *CSP Spanish*

25 Knox

26 Buchanan

27 Pitcairn

28 Additional MSS.

29 The *Book of Articles* states that it was Bothwell, but it is more likely that Mary would have been informed of Darnley's death before Bothwell was.

30 Bothwell

31 Buchanan

32 Bothwell

33 Clernault, in State Papers in the Public Record Office, *CSP Scottish* and *Papal Negotiations*

34 *CSP Venetian*

35 Bothwell

36 Ibid.; Knox

37 Knox. The *Book of Articles* alleges that Darnley's body was "left lying in the yard [*sic*] where it was apprehended the space of three hours" before "the rascal[ly] people transported him to a vile house near the room where before he was lodged." This is obviously a distortion of the truth.

38 Bothwell

39 Ibid.

40 Ibid.

41 Now in the Public Record Office.

42 Nau

43 Crawfurd: *Memoirs*

44 *Papal Negotiations*

45 *Accounts of the Lord High Treasurer*, 15 February 1567

46 In his *Detectio*, Buchanan wrote that this was the custom in Scotland also, and de Silva reported that Robert Melville had left Mary "confined to her chamber, with the intention of not leaving it for forty days, as is the custom of widows there" (*CSP Spanish*). However, there is no evidence that either of the two previous widowed Queens, Margaret Tudor, wife of James IV, and Marie de Guise, wife of James V, ever observed this custom.

47 Melville

48 In his *Detectio* and *The Book of Articles*, Buchanan states that Mary slept till noon, but in his *History*, he claims that she slept most of the day. This is another example of the inconsistencies in his narratives.

49 Nau

50 Mary herself reported this in a letter written on 16 February 1567 to Mondovi, who in turn reported it to Alessandria (*Papal Negotiations*).

51 Knox

52 The *Book of Articles* states that Darnley "remained 48 hours as a gazing stock," but this cannot be true. His body was laid in state on 12 February, and it would have taken a day or so for the embalming processes to be completed.

53 Melville

54 Sloane MSS.

55 Keith

56 Keith; *Accounts of the Lord High Treasurer*

57 *Book of Articles*

58 Buchanan; *Book of Articles*; *CSP Scottish*

17. "None Dare Find Fault with It"

1 Adam Blackwood, a Catholic supporter of Mary whose work was published in 1581 in France, is the only source to mention torture. He states that these deponents "had been extraordinarily racked" and beaten with hammers "to draw some one word against their mistress," but they refused to say anything to condemn her.

2 The texts of the depositions quoted in this chapter are to be found in Pitcairn, Anderson: *Collections*, and Goodall. Three modern works that have proved very useful for this chapter are Mahon: *Tragedy of Kirk o'Field*, which is the result of ten years' research and sets out to show that Darnley was responsible for the explosion, a theory that is now largely discredited; Gore-Browne: *Bothwell*, which

reaches the same conclusion; and Thomson: *Crime of Mary Stuart*, which attempts to reconstruct the murder from the depositions.

3 *CSP Scottish*

4 For a fuller discussion of 16th-century gunpowder, see Mahon: *Tragedy of Kirk o'Field.*

5 *Book of Articles*

6 *CSP Scottish*

7 Melville

8 *CSP Scottish.* Hepburn says that Bothwell had 14 counterfeit keys; Ormiston mentions only 13. The lockable doors were as follows:

  1 Front door from quadrangle

  2 Side door in alley leading to cellar/kitchen

  3 Downstairs door to stairs

  4 Door to Queen's garderobe

  5 Door to Queen's bedchamber (2 keys)

  6 Door to downstairs passage to garden

  7 Door to passage leading to Prebendaries' Chamber

  8 Door to Prebendaries' Chamber

  9 Upstairs door to stairs (used as cover for Darnley's bath)

 10 Door to King's garderobe

 11 Door to King's bedchamber

 12 Door to postern gate in Flodden Wall

    N.B. There was no lock on the back door, which was bolted on the inside. Allegations that the conspirators had two keys to this door are spurious.

    There were therefore 13 keys to the house.

9 In one deposition Paris says this incident took place on Friday, in the other, on Saturday. The latter is more likely to be correct. Paris made his deposition more than two years later, so an allowance must be made for a lapse in memory.

10 This close no longer exists; it led off the Grassmarket, which lies to the south of Edinburgh Castle and the Royal Mile.

11 Mahon: *Tragedy of Kirk o'Field*

12 The *Book of Articles* states incorrectly that Hob Ormiston was Black Ormiston's father.

13 Hay claimed that Bothwell was walking up and down the Canongate while the powder was being transported, which took place between 8 p.m. and 10:15 p.m., but Powrie claimed that he did not begin shifting the powder until 10 p.m.

14 Mahon: *Tragedy of Kirk o'Field*

15 Gore-Browne

16 Nau; Lennox says nothing about Paris giving a signal.

17 Nau

18 The accounts by Hay, Hepburn, Powrie and Dalgleish of Bothwell's return journey to Kirk o'Field are almost identical.

19 Mahon: *Tragedy of Kirk o'Field; CSP Scottish*

20 *CSP Scottish*

21 *CSP Spanish*

22 *CSP Venetian*

23 *CSP Scottish*

24 It was later alleged that Bothwell himself had lit the fuse, but there is no evidence that he went into the house.

25 *Calendar of Letters and State Papers . . . in Rome*. This story was told by Hepburn just before his execution, to another prisoner, Cuthbert Ramsay, who repeated it in 1576 in Paris as evidence in support of Mary's plea for an annulment of her marriage to Bothwell.

26 Buchanan

18. "The Contrivers of the Plot"

1 *Papal Negotiations*

2 *CSP Scottish*

3 Ibid.

4 *CSP Venetian*

5 Sloane MSS.

6 Cited by Mahon: *Tragedy of Kirk o'Field*

7 *CSP Scottish; Diurnal of Occurrents*

8 *CSP Scottish*; Melville

9 Spottiswoode

10 *Acts of the Parliaments of Scotland*

11 Teulet

12 State Papers in the Public Record Office; *CSP Scottish; CSP Foreign*

13 *Cabala*

14 Notably Mahon: *Tragedy of Kirk o'Field*, and Gore-Browne.

15 *CSP Foreign*

16 *CSP Scottish*

17 Keith

18 *CSP Spanish*

19 *CSP Scottish*

20 State Papers in the Public Record Office; Tytler

21 *Papal Negotiations*

22 Bothwell

23 *Papal Negotiations*

24 *CSP Spanish*

25 Morton's confession, in Pitcairn

26 *CSP Spanish*; Teulet

27 *CSP Foreign*

28 *Papal Negotiations*

29 Gore-Browne

30 Sloane MSS.

31 *CSP Spanish*

32 *CSP Venetian*

33 Report of Sir William Drury, in *CSP Scottish*

34 *CSP Venetian*

35 Ibid.

36 *Papal Negotiations*

37 *Diurnal of Occurrents*
38 Pepys MSS.

19. "Great Suspicions and No Proof"
  1 Buchanan
  2 *CSP Foreign*
  3 Buchanan; Camden
  4 Melville
  5 *Inventaires*
  6 Keith
  7 *CSP Scottish; The Book of Articles* is in the Hopetoun MSS. in the Register House, Edinburgh
  8 Buchanan
  9 Ibid.
 10 *Book of Articles*
 11 *Lennox Narrative*
 12 Drury to Cecil, 19 February 1567, in *CSP Scottish*; Moray's Journal, in Cotton MSS. Caligula. Mary's surviving letters from this correspondence with Lennox are all in Scots, which suggests that they were not written by Mary herself but by her Council on her behalf.
 13 Keith
 14 Labanoff
 15 Buchanan
 16 *CSP Spanish*
 17 *Inventaires*
 18 *Papal Negotiations*
 19 *CSP Spanish*
 20 Ibid.
 21 Drury to Cecil, *CSP Scottish*; Drury does not mention Hay.
 22 *Diurnal of Occurrents*; Clernault, in *Papal Negotiations*. Knox claimed incorrectly that Darnley was buried in Holyrood Abbey.

  Under Charles II the chapel royal was demolished and the royal remains removed to a new vault in Holyrood Abbey, which was now designated the new chapel royal. During the Glorious Revolution of 1688, a mob vandalised the abbey and forced open the royal vault but did not disturb the bodies. When the abbey roof collapsed in 1768, the vault was opened again and Darnley's skull was removed along with that of Madeleine of France, first wife of James V.

  Darnley's skull was examined in 1798 and found to bear the marks of syphilis. After three changes of ownership, it was presented to the Royal College of Surgeons in 1869. See Bingham: *Darnley.*

  By the 19th century, the royal vault was in a ruinous condition, and several of Darnley's bones were removed; one was advertised for sale in a Harrogate newspaper. The vault has since been restored.
 23 *Papal Negotiations*
 24 Leslie
 25 *Diurnal of Occurrents*

26 Ibid.
27 Mahon: *Tragedy of Kirk o'Field*
28 State Papers in the Public Record Office
29 Buchanan; *Book of Articles*
30 Report of the King of Scots' Death, in *CSP Scottish*
31 Keith
32 *CSP Scottish*
33 Antonia Fraser
34 *CSP Scottish*. Drury recorded that he passed through Berwick on 19 February.
35 Mahon: *Tragedy of Kirk o'Field*
36 Labanoff
37 *Diurnal of Occurrents*
38 Cecil to Sir Henry Norris, 20 February 1567, in the *Cecil Papers*
39 *CSP Spanish*
40 *CSP Foreign*
41 Ibid., report of 22 February 1567
42 *Papal Negotiations*
43 Anderson: *Collections*; Keith
44 *CSP Spanish*
45 *CSP Venetian*
46 Labanoff
47 Robert Melville to Cecil, 26 February 1567, *CSP Scottish*
48 Anderson: *Collections*; Keith; Labanoff
49 *CSP Spanish*
50 Ibid.
51 State Papers in the Public Record Office; *CSP Scottish*. There are several translations of this letter from the original French, which accounts for the various versions in different books. I have largely followed Froude's translation
52 *CSP Scottish*. The *Diurnal of Occurrents* claims that it was also proclaimed on 27 February.
53 Letter of 28 February 1567, in *CSP Foreign*
54 Leslie
55 *CSP Scottish*
56 Keith; Sir Henry Killigrew to Cecil, 8 March 1567, *CSP Scottish*
57 Tytler
58 Drury to Cecil, 27 February 1567, *CSP Foreign*
59 Nau
60 Drury to Cecil, 28 February 1567, *CSP Foreign*
61 *CSP Foreign*
62 *Papal Negotiations*
63 Drury to Cecil, 28 February 1567, *CSP Foreign*
64 Bothwell
65 *CSP Scottish*; for the placard campaign, see also *CSP Foreign*; Birrel; Anderson: *Collections*
66 *CSP Scottish*
67 *CSP Spanish*

68 Killigrew to Cecil, 8 March 1567, *CSP Scottish*
69 Buchanan
70 Bothwell
71 Pitcairn; Anderson: *Collections*; Goodall
72 *Register of the Privy Seal*
73 Labanoff
74 Killigrew to Cecil, 8 March 1567, *CSP Scottish*
75 Bingham: *Darnley*; *CSP Scottish*. The two mermaid placards are now in the Public Record Office.
76 *CSP Spanish*
77 *Register of the Privy Council*
78 Ibid.
79 *Papal Negotiations*
80 Teulet
81 *Diurnal of Occurrents*
82 Killigrew to Cecil, 8 March 1567, *CSP Scottish*
83 Ibid. Anthony Standen had returned to England by 15 March, when Mary, or her Council, wrote to Robert Melville in London, asking him to seek the favour of the English government on Standen's behalf (Labanoff).
84 *CSP Spanish*
85 *CSP Scottish*
86 Ibid.
87 *Papal Negotiations*
88 *Selections from Unpublished Manuscripts*
89 Ibid.; Keith

20. "Laying Snares for Her Majesty"
1 *Papal Negotiations*
2 Ibid.
3 For Moray's letter and communication with Killigrew, see *CSP Scottish*
4 *CSP Foreign*
5 State Papers in the Public Record Office; *CSP Scottish*
6 *CSP Scottish*
7 *Register of the Privy Council*; Anderson: *Collections*
8 Drury to Cecil, 20 March 1567, *CSP Foreign*
9 Drury to Cecil, 29 March 1567, ibid.
10 Teulet
11 Drury to Cecil, 30 March 1567, *CSP Foreign*
12 *Papal Negotiations*
13 Ibid.
14 Ibid.
15 *CSP Venetian*
16 Keith
17 Bothwell
18 *Acts of the Parliament of Scotland*; *Diurnal of Occurrents*

19 Drury incorrectly states that Janet Beaton, the Lady of Buccleuch, was cited as co-respondent (*CSP Foreign*).
20 *CSP Venetian; CSP Foreign*
21 *CSP Scottish*
22 *Register of the Privy Council*
23 Birrel
24 Drury to Cecil, 29 March 1567, *CSP Foreign*
25 The word "prevent" did not acquire its present meaning until the 17th century.
26 Labanoff
27 *CSP Spanish*
28 Ibid.
29 *CSP Foreign*
30 Ibid.
31 Drury to Cecil, 29 March 1567, *CSP Foreign*
32 Ibid.; *Inventaires*
33 *Register of the Privy Council*; Keith; Anderson: *Collections*
34 Hosack (see *Book of Articles*)
35 Labanoff
36 *CSP Foreign*. Cecil was aware of the divorce suit by 3 April.
37 *CSP Scottish*
38 Teulet
39 *CSP Spanish*
40 *CSP Foreign*
41 De Silva to Philip II, 21 April 1567, *CSP Spanish*
42 Ibid.
43 Teulet
44 Keith
45 Cotton MSS. Caligula
46 Mitchell
47 *Book of Articles*
48 Ibid.
49 *CSP Foreign*
50 Ibid.; de Silva to Philip II, 21 April 1567, *CSP Spanish*
51 *Papal Negotiations*
52 *CSP Foreign*
53 William Robertson: *History of Scotland*
54 Gore-Browne

21. "THE CLEANSING OF BOTHWELL"

1 Knox did not take part in this campaign; after Darnley's murder, he had retired from Edinburgh to work on his *History of the Reformation*.
2 Letter to Cecil, 15 April 1567, *CSP Foreign*
3 Goodall; Keith; *CSP Scottish*
4 Drury to Cecil, 15 April 1567, in Tytler: *Scotland*
5 Ibid. James Anthony Froude, the eminent but biased 19th-century historian, had

no time for Mary and was not above inventing evidence against her. He alleges that she was seen to give Bothwell a friendly nod from her window as he rode off to the Tolbooth, and also asserts that Bothwell was riding Darnley's horse. These details do not appear in contemporary sources but have been frequently repeated by other writers.

6 *CSP Scottish*
7 *CSP Foreign*
8 Anderson: *Collections*
9 Keith
10 Buchanan
11 Keith
12 *CSP Scottish*
13 10 May 1567, *CSP Scottish*
14 *CSP Foreign*
15 *Diurnal of Occurrents*
16 *CSP Foreign*
17 Bothwell
18 *CSP Scottish*
19 *CSP Spanish*
20 *CSP Scottish*. Drury sent a copy of one of these answers to Cecil on 19 April (*CSP Foreign*).
21 Keith
22 Ibid.; Gore-Browne
23 Leslie and Nau also claimed that Bothwell's acquittal was ratified by Parliament.
24 De Silva to Philip II, 21 April 1567, *CSP Spanish*
25 *Acts of the Parliament of Scotland*
26 *CSP Scottish*
27 The word "pit" meant "prison" in Scots.
28 *CSP Foreign*
29 For copies of the Ainslie's Tavern Bond, see Cotton MSS. Caligula; Keith; Anderson: *Collections; CSP Scottish*
30 Buchanan says the Bishops added their signatures the following day.
31 Cotton MSS. Caligula
32 *CSP Spanish*
33 Both lists are in Keith.
34 Keith
35 *CSP Scottish*
36 Ibid.
37 Nau
38 Ibid.
39 Labanoff. This gives the lie to Throckmorton's claim, made on 30 April in a letter to Leicester, that Mary and Bothwell had been married at Seton before she went to Stirling (*CSP Foreign*).
40 Forster to Cecil, 24 April 1567, *CSP Scottish*
41 Bothwell
42 Nau

43 State Papers in the Public Record Office; *CSP Scottish*
44 *CSP Scottish*

22. "WE FOUND HIS DOINGS RUDE"

1 *Diurnal of Occurrents; CSP Scottish*
2 *Cecil Papers*; Lang
3 *CSP Foreign*
4 *Papal Negotiations*; Labanoff
5 *CSP Scottish*
6 Cited by MacNalty
7 The letter was sent via Drury.
8 Cited by Plowden: *Two Queens in One Isle*
9 Buchanan
10 Estimates of the number of Bothwell's men vary. Nau says there were 1,500, the *Diurnal of Occurrents* 800, Buchanan 600 and de Silva 400. The *Diurnal* is the most likely to be correct.
11 Gore-Browne
12 *CSP Foreign*
13 *Calendar of Letters and State Papers . . . in Rome* (Cuthbert Ramsay's evidence, 1576)
14 Pitcairn; Anderson: *Collections*; Goodall
15 State Papers in the Public Record Office; *CSP Scottish*. Some historians wrongly ascribe this letter to Lennox, claiming it was the one he wrote to his wife on 23 April.
16 *Register of the Privy Council; Diurnal of Occurrents*
17 De Silva to Philip II, 1 May 1567, *CSP Spanish*
18 *Diurnal of Occurrents; CSP Scottish*; Melville; Gore-Browne. The exact location of the abduction has not been fully established. In an Act of Parliament of 1567, the place is referred to as being "near the bridges, commonly called Foulbriggs" (or Foulbridge), which Strickland identified with Fountainbridge, but this is only just south of the West Port and nowhere near the River Almond. The *Diurnal* says the abduction took place "between Kirkliston and Edinburgh at a place called The Bridges." In the 17th century, there was a farm called The Bridges at the village of Over Gogar, which has now been swallowed up by Edinburgh's suburban sprawl. Buchanan and Herries state that the location was "Almond Bridge," while a pardon of October 1567 says "near the Water of Almond." Birrel claims it was at "Cramond Bridge," on the road between Edinburgh and South Queensferry. The likeliest location is a little way to the south of Cramond, in the area referred to in the text. (See Gore-Browne.)
19 Letter to the Bishop of Dumblane, in Labanoff
20 *CSP Spanish*
21 Melville
22 De Silva to Philip II, 1 May 1567, *CSP Spanish*. De Silva had got his information from Cecil and from the messenger who brought the news to London.
23 Robert Melville to Cecil, 7 May 1567, *CSP Scottish; Calendar of Letters and State Papers . . . in Rome* (Cuthbert Ramsay's evidence, 1576)

24 Robert Melville to Cecil, 7 May 1567, *CSP Scottish*

25 *CSP Spanish*

26 Labanoff

27 Ibid.

28 Nau

29 *CSP Spanish*

30 Labanoff

31 At this date, the word "ravish" meant "abduct" or "kidnap," as well as "rape," and was more commonly used in the former context; cf Moray's Journal: "He met her upon the way, seemed to ravish her, and took Huntly and the Secretary prisoners." The different meanings of the word have led to some confusion on the part of historians.

32 Melville

33 This probably refers to the Ainslie's Tavern Bond.

34 Labanoff

35 *CSP Scottish*

36 The confession is printed as an appendix to Bothwell.

37 Labanoff

38 State Papers in the Public Record Office; *CSP Scottish*

39 Melville. Blackadder had been freed by the authorities after being arrested for Darnley's murder, probably through the good offices of Bothwell.

40 *CSP Foreign*

41 Letter to Philip II, 3 May 1567, *CSP Spanish*

42 *CSP Scottish*

43 *Acts of the Parliament of Scotland*

44 *Bittersweet Within My Heart*

45 Drury to Cecil, 6 May 1567, *CSP Foreign*

46 Drury to Cecil, 2 May 1567, ibid. Somehow, Maitland was managing to smuggle out messages to Drury.

47 Melville

48 *CSP Foreign; CSP Scottish*

49 State Papers in the Public Record Office; *CSP Scottish*

50 *CSP Scottish*

51 Stuart: *Lost Chapter*. The documents relating to the case are in the Bodleian Library, Oxford. The Commissary Court had replaced the old Catholic Consistory Court in dealing with matrimonial causes.

52 Buchanan

53 Stuart: *Lost Chapter*

54 A document purporting to be this dispensation is preserved at Dunrobin Castle in Sutherland, Jean's home after her second marriage, but its authenticity has been questioned.

55 Hosack (see *Book of Articles*)

56 *Maitland's Narrative*

57 *CSP Scottish*

58 *CSP Foreign*

59 Drury to Cecil, 4 and 6 May 1567, *CSP Foreign*

60 Stuart: *Lost Chapter*
61 Robert Melville to Cecil, 7 May 1567, *CSP Scottish*; Grange to Bedford, 8 May 1567, ibid.; *Register of the Privy Council*
62 He arrived there by the end of April.
63 Keith
64 De Silva to Philip II, 11 May 1567, *CSP Spanish*
65 *CSP Foreign*; Buchanan; *Book of Articles*
66 *CSP Spanish*
67 De Alava to Philip II, 3 May 1567, Teulet
68 State Papers in the Public Record Office
69 *Diurnal of Occurrents*; Stuart: *Lost Chapter*
70 *Calendar of the Manuscripts at Hatfield*
71 De Silva to Philip II, 11 May 1567, *CSP Spanish*
72 Ibid.
73 Stuart: *Lost Chapter*
74 Hailes Castle, which is 1.5 miles south-west of East Linton, was built before 1300 and was the original seat of the Hepburns. Now a ruin, it is one of the oldest surviving stone castles in Scotland. It was partly dismantled by Parliamentary forces in 1650, during the Civil War. The chapel dates from the 16th century.
75 Stuart: *Lost Chapter*
76 *Calendar of Letters and State Papers . . . in Rome* (Cuthbert Ramsay's evidence, 1576)
77 *CSP Scottish*
78 *Diurnal of Occurrents*
79 Buchanan
80 The Scottish Privy Council to Throckmorton, 11 July 1567, Keith
81 Stuart: *Lost Chapter*. Jean Gordon was given valuable estates as part of her divorce settlement, and held them until her death in 1629 in the reign of Mary's grandson, Charles I. She married secondly Alexander Gordon, 12th Earl of Sutherland (d. 1594), then thirdly her former suitor, Alexander Ogilvy of Boyne (Keith).
82 *CSP Spanish*
83 *The Book of Articles* incorrectly refers to him as the Reader of St. Giles. A reader was an unordained assistant to the Minister (Donaldson).
84 Keith
85 Melville
86 Ibid.
87 *CSP Scottish*
88 Grange to Bedford, 8 May 1567, *CSP Scottish*
89 Knox
90 *Diurnal of Occurrents*
91 Melville
92 *CSP Scottish*
93 Ibid.
94 Ibid.
95 Ibid.
96 Stuart: *Lost Chapter*

97 *Book of Articles*
98 Cited by Gore-Browne
99 *Register of the Privy Seal*
100 Keith. Elizabeth's condemnation of Grange's letters is also mentioned by Nau.
101 Anderson: *Collections*
102 *Calendar of Letters and State Papers . . . in Rome* (Cuthbert Ramsay's evidence, 1576)
103 Drury to Cecil, 20 May 1567, *CSP Foreign*; Keith; Anderson: *Collections*; Buchanan; *Book of Articles*
104 *Register of the Privy Seal; Diurnal of Occurrents.* The others were James Cockburn of Langton, Patrick Hay of Whitelaw and Patrick Hepburn of Beanston. Although, strictly speaking, Bothwell should from henceforth be referred to as Orkney, for the sake of clarity I have continued to refer to him as Bothwell.
105 *CSP Spanish*
106 Keith
107 *CSP Foreign*
108 Labanoff; Goodall
109 *CSP Foreign*
110 Melville
111 Cotton MSS. Caligula; Anderson: *Collections; Book of Articles*

23. "WANTONS MARRY IN THE MONTH OF MAY"

1 *Diurnal of Occurrents*; Melville. The *Diurnal* states that the marriage took place at "ten hours afore noon." De Silva, who got his information from Cecil, says incorrectly that it was "at four o'clock in the morning." (Letter to Philip II, 24 May 1567, *CSP Spanish*)
2 Drury to Cecil, 20 May 1567, *CSP Foreign*
3 *Inventaires*
4 This gives the lie to de Silva, who had heard from Cecil and Leicester that "there were only three persons of rank at the marriage."
5 *Diurnal of Occurrents*
6 *Calendar of Letters and State Papers . . . in Rome* (James Curl's evidence, 1576)
7 *Inventaires*
8 Leslie; Keith
9 Labanoff; Anderson: *Collections*
10 Teulet; Keith
11 Du Croc to Catherine de' Medici, 18 May 1567, Teulet; Anderson: *Collections*; Keith
12 Keith; Melville
13 *CSP Spanish*
14 *CSP Foreign*
15 Teulet
16 Keith
17 Ibid.
18 Ibid.
19 Melville

20 Teulet
21 Drury to Cecil, 27 May 1567, *CSP Foreign*
22 Drury to Cecil, ibid.
23 *Register of the Privy Council*
24 Bothwell
25 Teulet
26 *CSP Foreign*
27 *CSP Spanish*
28 *CSP Scottish*
29 Tytler: *Scotland*
30 *CSP Spanish*
31 Ibid.
32 Melville
33 *CSP Foreign*
34 *Selections from Unpublished Manuscripts*; Teulet
35 In 16th-century usage, the word "accident" merely meant "something that happens."
36 *Selections from Unpublished Manuscripts*; Teulet
37 Teulet
38 Buchanan
39 *CSP Venetian*
40 Cited by Plowden: *Two Queens in One Isle*
41 Cited by Black: *Reign of Elizabeth*
42 *CSP Venetian*
43 *CSP Scottish*
44 *Register of the Privy Council*; *Diurnal of Occurrents*; Keith
45 Keith
46 *Register of the Privy Council*; Wormald
47 Labanoff; *CSP Scottish*
48 Keith
49 Melville. The second bond is undated but was drawn up after the Bothwell marriage.
50 *CSP Foreign*
51 Ibid.
52 Letter to Cecil, 7 June 1567, ibid.
53 Buchanan
54 Leslie
55 Teulet
56 Gore-Browne
57 Drury to Cecil, 7 June 1567, *CSP Foreign*
58 Borthwick Castle was only slightly damaged during its bombardment by Cromwell's forces in 1650, after which it was abandoned. It was restored in 1890 and is now one of the best preserved castles in Scotland, and remains very much as it was in Mary's day. The castle is now a hotel, and guests may stay in the actual chambers used by Mary and Bothwell.
59 Teulet; *Diurnal of Occurrents*; *CSP Foreign*

60 Keith
61 Bothwell
62 Melville
63 Keith
64 Nau
65 Keith
66 Nau; Drury to Cecil, *CSP Foreign*
67 Drury to Cecil, *CSP Foreign*
68 For the events at Borthwick, see the *Diurnal of Occurrents*, a letter from an eye-witness, John Beaton, to his brother, Archbishop Beaton, in the Sloane MSS., and the narrative of the Captain of Inchkeith, in Teulet. Estimates of the strength of the Lords' forces vary from 7–800 to 1,000 or 1,200.
69 John Beaton, in Sloane MSS.; *Diurnal of Occurrents*; *CSP Scottish*
70 Bothwell
71 Cited by Sitwell
72 Bothwell
73 Knox
74 *Diurnal of Occurrents*; Teulet; John Beaton, in Sloane MSS.
75 The window through which Mary is said to have escaped can still be seen today.
76 John Beaton, in Sloane MSS. *The Book of Articles* states that Ormiston was one of those sent to meet Mary.
77 Nau
78 *CSP Foreign*; Teulet
79 Nau
80 *Diurnal of Occurrents*
81 Melville
82 Nau
83 Ibid.
84 John Beaton, in Sloane MSS.
85 Nau
86 Teulet; *Diurnal of Occurrents*. Nau incorrectly gives the strength of the royal forces as 4,200. Reports that the two armies were of roughly equal size are therefore incorrect.
87 Cited by Antonia Fraser
88 Cited by Gore-Browne
89 Nau
90 *CSP Scottish*
91 For the Battle of Carberry Hill, see Bothwell; *Diurnal of Occurrents*; Nau; Melville; du Croc's account, in Teulet; *Book of Articles*.
92 *CSP Scottish*. A coloured drawing of the Darnley banner is in the Public Record Office.
93 Cited by Sitwell
94 Cited by Prebble
95 Bothwell
96 Nau
97 Ibid.

98 Bothwell
99 Nau
100 Ibid.
101 Melville
102 Letter to Cecil, 10 June 1567, *CSP Foreign*
103 Melville
104 Nau
105 Du Croc to Catherine de' Medici, 17 June 1567, Teulet
106 Drury to Cecil, 18 June 1567, *CSP Foreign*
107 Calderwood
108 Nau
109 *Diurnal of Occurrents*; Teulet. The Black Turnpike was demolished in 1788. An erroneous tradition claims that it was located opposite the Mercat Cross, where the offices of Edinburgh City Council now stand, but it has been established that it probably stood on the north side of the High Street, on the site of the entrance to Cockburn Street (*Proceedings of the Society of Antiquaries of Scotland*, cited by Gatherer, editor of Buchanan).
110 Cited by Neale

24. "THIS TRAGEDY WILL END IN THE QUEEN'S PERSON"

1 Drury to Cecil, 18 June 1567, *CSP Foreign*; Buchanan
2 Teulet; John Beaton, in Sloane MSS.
3 Nau
4 Du Croc to Catherine de' Medici, 17 June 1567, Teulet
5 Melville. In 1573, Robert Melville stated that he had refused to smuggle out a letter from Mary to Bothwell, so the Queen had burned it in anger.
6 *CSP Foreign*
7 This was also Drury's opinion (ibid.).
8 Teulet
9 Melville
10 Bothwell
11 *Diurnal of Occurrents*; Nau
12 Nau; Leslie
13 Nau
14 *CSP Scottish*
15 Nau
16 Ibid.
17 Lochleven Castle is now a ruin. However, Mary's chamber in the south-east tower and the chapel have been identified.
18 Nau
19 *CSP Foreign*
20 Nau
21 Cited by Brigden
22 Nau; Calderwood
23 *CSP Scottish*
24 Bothwell

25 Ibid.
26 John Beaton, in Sloane MSS.
27 *CSP Scottish*
28 *CSP Foreign*
29 Pitcairn; Keith
30 Morton's account was read out to the Westminster Commission on 9 December 1568. It is entitled: "The true declaration and report of me, James, Earl of Morton, how a certain silver box overgilt, containing divers missive writings, sonnets, contracts and obligations for marriage betwixt the Queen, mother to our Sovereign Lord, and James, sometime Earl of Bothwell, was found and used." (Additional MSS., hereinafter referred to as Morton's Statement)
31 Leslie
32 *Diurnal of Occurrents*; *CSP Scottish*
33 Melville states incorrectly that Dalgleish was arrested in September 1567 in Orkney.
34 Morton's Statement
35 *CSP Foreign*
36 *CSP Scottish*
37 See Henderson
38 Morton's Statement
39 *CSP Scottish*
40 Randolph to Cecil, 15 October 1570, *CSP Foreign*
41 *CSP Foreign*
42 Ibid.
43 *CSP Spanish*
44 *CSP Scottish*; Teulet
45 Pitcairn; Anderson: *Collections*; Goodall
46 *CSP Scottish*
47 Pitcairn; Anderson: *Collections*; Goodall
48 *CSP Scottish*
49 Ibid.
50 *CSP Spanish*
51 The Scottish penalty for treason was hanging and quartering, which was less barbaric than the English equivalent, which also involved castration and disembowelling.
52 Pitcairn; Keith
53 Pitcairn
54 CSP Domestic, James I, in the Public Record Office
55 Melville
56 *CSP Scottish*
57 Ibid.; Spottiswoode
58 *CSP Scottish*
59 Cited by Somerset
60 *CSP Scottish*
61 Ibid.; Keith
62 *CSP Scottish*

63 *Papal Negotiations*
64 *CSP Foreign*
65 Keith
66 *CSP Spanish*
67 *CSP Scottish*; Keith
68 *CSP Scottish*
69 Ibid.
70 Ibid.
71 Ibid.
72 Ibid.
73 Nau
74 *CSP Scottish*
75 De Silva to Philip II, 21 July 1567, *CSP Spanish*
76 *CSP Scottish*
77 Ibid; *Selections from Unpublished Manuscripts*; Keith
78 Nau
79 Ibid.
80 *Register of the Privy Council; Diurnal of Occurrents; CSP Scottish*
81 Nau
82 Keith
83 Ibid.; *CSP Foreign*
84 *CSP Scottish*

25. "False Calumnies"
 1 *CSP Spanish*
 2 *CSP Scottish*
 3 Ibid.; *Diurnal of Occurrents*
 4 *CSP Scottish*
 5 State Papers in the Public Record Office
 6 *CSP Foreign*
 7 De Silva to Philip II, 2 August 1567, *CSP Spanish*
 8 Ibid.
 9 *CSP Scottish*
10 Ibid.
11 Ibid.
12 Ibid.; *Register of the Privy Council*
13 *CSP Scottish*
14 Ibid.
15 Ibid.
16 Ibid.
17 Melville
18 *Historie of James the Sext*
19 *CSP Scottish*
20 Ibid.; Keith; Nau; *CSP Spanish*
21 *CSP Scottish*
22 *CSP Spanish*

23 Throckmorton to Cecil, 20 August 1567, *CSP Scottish*
24 *CSP Scottish*; Bothwell
25 *CSP Scottish*; *Register of the Privy Council*; *Diurnal of Occurrents*
26 *CSP Foreign*
27 Cited by Marshall: *Elizabeth I*
28 *CSP Scottish*
29 *CSP Foreign*. In two reports, dated 15 June and 1 July 1567, Drury reported that Paris had drowned, yet it is clear from later evidence that he was with Bothwell in Scandinavia. Because it was generally believed he was dead, no one thought to ask for his extradition.
30 Bothwell
31 This letter no longer exists.
32 Frederick's daughter Anne (1574–1619) was married in 1589 to Mary's son, James VI.
33 *CSP Scottish*
34 State Papers in the Public Record Office
35 Ibid.
36 Pitcairn; Anderson: *Collections*; Goodall
37 *CSP Scottish*
38 Pitcairn; Anderson: *Collections*; Goodall
39 *CSP Scottish*
40 Ibid.
41 *CSP Foreign*
42 The word "wanton" could then mean "capricious" or "revelling in luxury," as well as "promiscuous."
43 *CSP Foreign*
44 Wright
45 *CSP Foreign*
46 Goodall; *Cecil Papers*; *CSP Scottish*
47 Nau
48 *Acts of the Parliament of Scotland*; *Diurnal of Occurrents*; Nau; Goodall
49 Hosack (see *Book of Articles*)
50 Schiern
51 Goodall
52 This notorious Act was later expunged from the parliamentary record and is only known today because it was printed in 1568.
53 *Acts of the Parliament of Scotland*
54 Ibid.; *CSP Scottish*
55 Nau
56 Goodall
57 Drury to Cecil, 4 January 1568, *CSP Foreign*
58 Archbishop Beaton to the Cardinal of Lorraine, 6 February 1568, Sloane MSS.
59 *Diurnal of Occurrents*
60 A slightly later copy of the picture is in the collection of the Duke of Richmond at Goodwood House, and was engraved by George Vertue in the 18th century.

61 Bothwell. The original manuscript was preserved in the collection of the Comtes d'Esneval at Château Pavilly in France, but was apparently lost in the destruction of the library during the Second World War. A copy of the MS. was once in the royal library at Stockholm, but is also missing. It is only known through a copy made in 1828.

62 *CSP Foreign*

63 Castlenau; Jebb. These memoirs were first published in 1731.

64 Teulet; Labanoff

65 Ibid.

26. "I Am No Enchantress"

1 Niddry Castle was built around 1511. It is today in ruins, but has recently undergone some restoration.

2 Tytler

3 *Diurnal of Occurrents*; Nau

4 The ruins of Cadzow Castle, which lie to the south of the town of Hamilton, are now in a dangerous state, and may only be viewed from outside.

5 Seton was imprisoned in Edinburgh Castle until 1569. After his release, he continued to work actively on Mary's behalf.

6 Nau

7 Mumby: *Fall of Mary Stuart*

8 *CSP Foreign*

9 *CSP Scottish*

10 Teulet

11 *CSP Foreign*

12 Nau

13 Now in Cambridge University Library. The Narrative is 14 pages long. The first page and part of the second are in Lennox's handwriting; the rest was probably dictated to a clerk, suggesting that a degree of urgency was involved.

14 *Lennox Narrative*

15 *CSP Scottish*; Goodall

16 *CSP Foreign*

17 *CSP Scottish*

18 Ibid.

19 Ibid.

20 Ibid.

21 Ibid.

22 Ibid.

23 Nau

24 *CSP Scottish*

25 Ibid.

26 Mary, Queen of Scots: *Letters*, ed. Strickland

27 Nau

28 Ibid.; Teulet

29 Cotton MSS. Caligula

30 Nau; Herries to Mary, 23 June 1568, Teulet
31 Herries to Mary, 23 June 1568, Teulet
32 *CSP Scottish*; Goodall
33 *CSP Scottish*
34 Ibid.
35 Cotton MSS. Caligula; Perry
36 Moray to Elizabeth, 13 July 1568, *CSP Scottish*
37 *CSP Scottish*
38 Ibid.
39 Ibid.
40 *CSP Spanish*; Teulet
41 Additional MSS., British Library
42 *CSP Scottish*
43 The proclamation was repeated on 17 November.
44 *CSP Scottish*
45 Ibid.
46 Goodall
47 *Register of the Privy Council*; Goodall
48 Goodall
49 *CSP Scottish*
50 Ibid.
51 Goodall
52 *CSP Scottish*

27. "These Rigorous Accusations"

1 *Cecil Papers; CSP Scottish*; Goodall
2 *CSP Scottish*; Goodall. The records of the York and Westminster conferences are preserved in *CSP Scottish* and Goodall. Unless otherwise stated, all references in this chapter come from these sources.
3 *CSP Scottish*; Goodall; Anderson: *Collections*; Cotton MSS. Caligula
4 Ibid.
5 *Cecil Papers*. This was revealed by Leslie under interrogation in the Tower of London in 1571.
6 *Cecil Papers; CSP Scottish*; Melville
7 Melville
8 *Cecil Papers*
9 Labanoff
10 *Calendar of the Manuscripts at Hatfield*
11 Labanoff
12 Goodall; *Cecil Papers; Calendar of the Manuscripts at Hatfield*
13 This document was found by Schiern in the Danish archives at Roskilde.
14 She had heard it from the French ambassador.
15 *Cecil Papers*
16 Ibid.
17 Labanoff
18 It is not amongst the companion documents in the Public Record Office or the

Cotton MSS., but is to be found in the Hopetoun MSS. in the Register House, Edinburgh.

28. "PRETENDED WRITINGS"

1 Goodall claimed incorrectly that Morton left the Casket Letters to his nephew and heir, Archibald Douglas, Earl of Angus and Morton.
2 Henderson
3 *CSP Scottish*; Goodall
4 The texts of the Casket Documents can be found in the appendix to *CSP Scottish*.

Of the copies made during the Westminster conference in 1568, the following survive:

In the Public Record Office: Casket Letters I, II and V in English, and Casket Letters III and V in French.

Among the *Cecil Papers* at Hatfield: Casket Letters IV and VI in French and English.

A copy of the French marriage contract is in Cotton MSS. Caligula.

There are no contemporay copies of the other documents.

Casket Letters I, II and IV were printed in the Latin edition of Buchanan's *Detectio* (1571).

All eight letters were printed in the Scots edition of the *Detectio* (1571) and in Thomas Wilson's English edition of 1572.

Seven of the letters, omitting Casket Letter III, were printed in the French edition of 1573.

Casket Letters VII and VIII, the love poem and the marriage contract in Scots exist only in printed form.
5 Henderson
6 *CSP Scottish*; Goodall
7 Armstrong Davison
8 *CSP Scottish*; Goodall
9 Lang; Antonia Fraser; James Mackay
10 *CSP Scottish*; Goodall
11 *CSP Scottish*; Goodall
12 *CSP Scottish*; Goodall
13 *CSP Scottish*
14 Teulet
15 *Inventaires*

29. "MUCH REMAINS TO BE EXPLAINED"

1 Unless otherwise stated, all references in this chapter come from *CSP Scottish* and Goodall.
2 Morton's original declaration has been lost; it is known through a copy in Additional MSS.
3 *CSP Spanish*
4 Labanoff
5 Cotton MSS. Caligula

6 *Calendar of the Manuscripts at Hatfield*
7 Labanoff
8 Cotton MSS. Caligula; *Cecil Papers*
9 State Papers in the Public Record Office
10 Keith
11 *CSP Spanish*
12 Cited by Bowen
13 Leslie

30. "THE DAUGHTER OF DEBATE"
1 Nau's original Latin manuscript is in the Vatican Archives.
2 Watkins
3 The Catholic martyr image was well developed by the time Leslie published his Latin history of Scotland in 1578 in Rome; his work emphasises Mary's sufferings for her faith.
4 Cotton MSS. Caligula
5 State Papers in the Public Record Office
6 Chalmers
7 *Cecil Papers*
8 They included Atholl and Huntly.
9 Tytler
10 Nau
11 Laing
12 Paris's original depositions are in the Public Record Office; copies are in Cotton MSS. Caligula. They were first published in Anderson's *Collections* in 1725.
13 *CSP Scottish; Historie of James the Sext*
14 Nau
15 *CSP Scottish*
16 Cotton MSS. Caligula
17 Buchanan
18 Labanoff
19 Cited by Robertson: *History of Scotland*
20 Cited by Froude
21 Cited by Robertson: *History of Scotland*
22 Cited by Mahon: *Lennox Narrative*
23 *CSP Scottish*
24 Teulet
25 Ibid.
26 State Papers in the Public Record Office
27 *CSP Foreign*
28 *CSP Scottish*
29 Herries
30 *CSP Scottish*
31 *Calendar of the Manuscripts at Hatfield; Cecil Papers*
32 Ibid.
33 Melville

34 Knox was buried in St. Giles's Churchyard in Edinburgh, the site of which is now occupied by the Law Courts. Knox's grave is marked by a slab in the car park, which is marked "I.K. 1572." His young widow married Ker of Fawdonside.

35 *Register of the Privy Council,* 8 January 1573

36 Spottiswoode

37 Keith

38 A plaque in Edinburgh Castle now commemorates Grange's gallant defence of it.

39 He is said to have been imprisoned in a vault under Leith parish church (Bingham: *Making of a King*).

40 *CSP Scottish.* Maitland's burial place is unknown.

41 Cited by Gore-Browne

42 Gore-Browne

43 In the late 17th century, parts of Dragsholm Castle were destroyed during a war between Denmark and Sweden. The castle was partially rebuilt in 1694–7, although large parts of the mediaeval building survive. Nowadays, Dragsholm is surrounded by woodland and farms.

44 *Register of the Privy Council*

45 Pitcairn

46 *CSP Domestic Edward VI, Mary and Elizabeth*

47 Lennox was married in December 1574 to Elizabeth Cavendish, daughter of Bess of Hardwick, Countess of Shrewsbury. Their only child was Arbella Stuart (1575–1615), who inherited Darnley's claim to the English throne.

48 *CSP Scottish*

49 Robertson: *History of Scotland*

50 Cited by Ashdown

51 *CSP Foreign.* Mary's undated instructions to Leslie are in Cotton MSS. Caligula.

52 *Calendar of Letters and State Papers . . . in Rome*

53 State Papers in the Public Record Office

54 Ashdown

55 For a fuller discussion of this local tradition, see Gore-Browne.

56 Melville. Buchanan says that Bothwell "ended his life in well-deserved misery." Spottiswoode says he "made an ignominious and desperate end." For evidence for the date of his death, see Gore-Browne.

57 Cheetham suggested that the head was Bothwell's and the body Clerk's, but this theory was based on the erroneous assumption that they died in the same week. Clerk had already been dead for over two years.

58 See, chiefly, Lang: *Mystery of Mary Stuart*, and Gore-Browne.

59 Labanoff

60 Archibald Douglas had been a judge or Lord of the Court of Session since 1565.

61 Spottiswoode

62 Melville

63 Ibid.

64 *CSP Scottish*

65 Tytler

66 Melville

67 Ibid.

68 Labanoff
69 Pitcairn. The record of his trial is incomplete and may have been deliberately destroyed in part.
70 CSP Scottish
71 Cited by Thomson
72 Nau
73 Jebb
74 Pitcairn; Gore-Browne
75 He had succeeded his brother Charles IX in 1574.
76 This letter is in the National Library of Scotland in Edinburgh.
77 Cited by Neale

BIBLIOGRAPHY

Primary Sources

The Accounts of the Lord High Treasurer of Scotland, Vol. XI: 1559–66, and Vol. XII: 1566–67 (ed. T. Dickson and Sir James Balfour Paul, H.M. General Register House, Edinburgh, 1877–1916)

Accounts of the Masters of Works, Vol. I, 1529–1615 (ed. H.M. Paton, HMSO, Edinburgh, 1957)

Accounts and Papers relating to Mary, Queen of Scots (ed. D.J. Crosby and John Bruce, Camden Society, 1867)

The Acts of the Parliaments of Scotland (12 vols, ed. T. Thomson and C. Innes, Edinburgh, 1814–75)

Acts of the Privy Council of England (32 vols, ed. John Roche Dasent et al. HMSO, London, 1890–1918)

Acts and Proceedings of the General Assemblies of the Kirk of Scotland (ed. T. Thomson, Bannatyne Club, 1839, Maitland Club, 1839)

Additional MSS. (Bodleian Library Oxford)

Additional MSS. (British Library)

Ailsa Muniments: Inventory (Historical Manuscripts Commission, Vol. III Supplement, 1431–1599)

Ancient Criminal Trials in Scotland from AD 1488 to AD 1624, embracing the entire reigns of James IV and V, Mary, Queen of Scots and James VI. Compiled from the Original Records and MSS., with Historical Notes and Illustrations (3 vols, ed. Robert Pitcairn, Bannatyne and Maitland Clubs, Edinburgh, 1833)

Anonymous: Life of Queen Mary (Cotton MSS. Caligula, British Library)

Argyll Papers (Inverary Castle, Scotland)

Ashmole MSS. (Bodleian Library, Oxford)

Baker, Richard: *Chronicles of the Kings of England* (London, 1643)

Ballatis of Luve: The Scottish Courtly Love Lyric, 1400–1570 (ed. John MacQueen, Edinburgh, 1970)

Bannatyne, George: *The Bannatyne Manuscript, written in time of Pest, 1568* (MSS. II, Bannatyne Club, Edinburgh; ed. W. Tod Ritchie, Scottish Text Society, Edinburgh and London, 1934)

Bannatyne Miscellany, containing Original Papers and Tracts, chiefly relating to the History and Literature of Scotland (Bannatyne Club, Edinburgh, 1827)

Barberini MSS. (Barberini Library, Rome)

The Bardon Papers: Documents relating to the Imprisonment and Trial of Mary, Queen of Scots (ed. Conyers Read, Camden Society, 3rd Series, XVII, 1909)

Birrel, Robert: *The Diary of Robert Birrel, Burgess of Edinburgh, containing Divers Pas-*

sages of State and Other Memorable Accidents, 1532–1605 (printed in Fragments of Scottish History, listed below)

Bittersweet within My Heart: The Collected Poems of Mary, Queen of Scots (trans. and ed. Robin Bell, London, 1992)

Blackwood, Adam: Apologia pro Regibus (Poitiers, 1581)

Blackwood, Adam: History of Mary, Queen of Scots: A Fragment (trans. anon., Maitland Club, Edinburgh/Glasgow, 1834)

Blackwood, Adam: Martyre de la Royne d'Escosse (Paris, 1587; Edinburgh, 1588)

Blackwood, Adam: La Mort de la Royne d'Escosse (Paris, 1588)

The Book of Articles (Hopetoun MSS.; ed. John Hosack in Mary, Queen of Scots and her Accusers—see below)

Bothwell, James Hepburn, 4th Earl of: Les Affaires du Conte de Boduel, l'an MDLXVIII (published 1586; ed. H. Coburn and T. Maitland, Bannatyne Club, Edinburgh, 1829)

Bouille, René de: Histoire des Ducs de Guise (Paris, 1850)

Bourgoing, D.: Marie Stuart, son procès et son exécution d'après le journal de Bourgoing, son médecin (ed. M. Regis Chantelauze, Paris, 1874)

Brantôme, Pierre de Bourdeille, Seigneur de: Vies des Dames Illustriés (6 vols, Leyden, 1665–6; trans. Katharine Prescott Wormesley as The Book of the Ladies: Illustrious Dames, with Elucidations of Some of those Ladies by C.A. Sainte-Beuve, London, 1899)

Brantôme, Pierre de Bourdeille, Seigneur de: Oeuvres complètes (ed. Bouchon, Paris, 1823)

A Brief History of the Life of Mary, Queen of Scots, and the Occasions that brought her and Thomas, Duke of Norfolk, to their Tragical Ends (London, 1681)

Buchanan, George: Detectio Mariae Reginae: Ane Detection of the Doings of Marie, Queen of Scots, touching the Murder of her Husband and her Conspiracy, Adultery and Pretensed Marriage with the Earl Bothwell, and a Defence of the True Lords, Maintainers of the King's Majesty's Action and Authority (Edinburgh, 1571, 1572); published as The Detection of the Doings of Mary, Queen of Scots (London, 1582; trans. by "a Person of Honour of the Kingdom of Scotland," London, 1721)

Buchanan, George: Georgii Buchanani Opera Omnia (ed. Thomas Ruddiman, Edinburgh, 1715, 1727)

Buchanan, George: Indictment of Mary, Queen of Scots (Cambridge University Library)

Buchanan, George: De Jure Regni apud Scotos (Edinburgh, 1579)

Buchanan, George: Rerum Scoticarum Historia (Edinburgh, 1582; Frankfurt, 1584; Amsterdam, 1643; Edinburgh, 1700; ed. James Man, Aberdeen, 1762; trans. James Aikman as The History of Scotland, Translated from the Latin of George Buchanan: with Notes and a Continuation to the Union in the Reign of Queen Anne, 4 vols, Glasgow, 1827)

Buchanan, George: The Tyrannous Reign of Mary Stewart (Books XVII–XIX of Rerum Scoticarum Historia and Detectio Maria Reginae Scotorum) (trans. and ed. W.A. Gatherer, Edinburgh, 1958)

The Buik of the Kirk of the Canongait (ed. Alma B. Calderwood, Scottish Record Society, Edinburgh, 1961)

Cabala, sive scrinia sacra: Mysteries of State and Government in Letters of Illustrious Persons (London, 1654)

Calderwood, David: *The True History of the Church of Scotland from the Beginning of the Reformation unto the End of the Reign of King James VI* (Rotterdam, 1678; ed. T. Thomson and D. Laing, 8 vols, Woodrow Society, Edinburgh, 1842–9)

Calendar of Letters, Despatches and State Papers relating to Negotiations between England and Spain, preserved in the Archives at Simancas and Elsewhere (17 vols, ed. G.A. Bergenroth, P. de Goyangos, Garrett Mattingly, R. Tyler et al., HMSO, London, 1862–1965)

Calendar of Letters and State Papers relating to English Affairs, preserved principally in the Archives of Simancas, Vol. I: Elizabeth, 1558–1567 (ed. Martin A.S. Hume et al., Public Record Office, 1892–9; reprinted 1971)

Calendar of Letters and State Papers relating to English Affairs, in Rome, 1558–1587 (ed. J.M. Rigg, London, 1916–26, reprinted 1971)

Calendar of the Manuscripts of the Most Honourable the Marquis of Salisbury, . . . preserved at Hatfield House (23 vols in 19, Historical Manuscripts Commission, London, 1883–1976)

Calendar of State Papers, Domestic Series, of the Reigns of Edward VI, Mary and Elizabeth, 1547–1603 (12 vols, ed. Robert Lemon and Mary Anne Everett Green, 1856–72)

Calendar of State Papers, Domestic Series, of the Reign of James I (ed. Mary Anne Everett Green, London, 1857)

Calendar of State Papers, Foreign Series, of the Reign of Elizabeth, Vol. VIII: 1566–68, preserved in the State Paper Department of Her Majesty's Public Record Office (ed. Allan James Crosby, London, 1871)

Calendar of State Papers, Foreign Series, of the Reign of Elizabeth I, 1558–89, preserved in the State Paper Department of Her Majesty's Public Record Office (23 vols, ed. Joseph Stevenson, W.B. Turnbull et al. 1863–1950)

Calendar of State Papers and Manuscripts relating to English Affairs preserved in the Archives of Venice, Vol. VII: 1558–1580 (ed. Rawdon Brown and G. Cavendish-Bentinck, HMSO, London, 1864–98)

Calendar of the State Papers relating to Scotland, 1509–1603 (ed. M.J. Thorpe, 1858)

Calendar of State Papers relating to Scotland (Edinburgh and Glasgow, 1889–1979)

Calendar of the State Papers relating to Scotland and Mary, Queen of Scots, 1547–1603. Preserved in the Public Record Office, the British Museum and elsewhere in England (12 vols, ed. Joseph Bain, W.K. Boyd and M.S. Giuseppi, HM General Register House, Edinburgh, 1898–1969)

Camden, William: *Annales Rerum Anglicarum et Hibernicarum Regnante Elizabetha, or The True and Royal History of the Famous Empress Elizabeth* (London, 1594, 1615; trans. from the Latin by Abraham Darcie, London, 1625, and by R. Norton, London, 1635, and by Thomas Hearne, London, 1717)

Castelnau, Michel de, Seigneur de Mauvissière: *Memoires de Michel de Castlenau* (ed. Le Labourer, Paris, 1731)

Catherine de' Medici, Queen of France: *Lettres de Catherine des Medicis* (ed. M. de la Ferrière, Paris, 1880–1919)

Caussin, N.: *L'Histoire d'incomparable Reyne Marie Stuart* (Paris, 1645)

The Cecil Papers: A Collection of State Papers relating to Affairs in the Reigns of King Henry VIII, King Edward VI, Queen Mary and Queen Elizabeth, to the Year 1596, left by William Cecil, Lord Burghley, and now remaining at Hatfield House (15 vols, ed. Samuel Haynes and William Murdin, London, 1740–59)

Chambers, David: *Discours de la légitime succession des femmes aux possessions de leurs parens* (Paris, 1579)

Chronicles of the Families of Atholl and Tullibardine (ed. 7th Duke of Atholl, Edinburgh, 1908)

Clerk of Penicuik MSS. (Register House, Edinburgh)

A Collection and Abridgement of Celebrated Criminal Trials in Scotland (ed. Hugo Arnot, Advocate, Edinburgh, 1758)

Collections relating to the History of Mary, Queen of Scotland (4 vols, ed. James Anderson, Edinburgh, 1725–8, London, 1729)

A Complete Collection of State Trials (ed. D. Thom, William Cobbett and T.B. Rowel I, 1809–98, reprinted 1972)

Conn, G.: *Vitae Mariae Stuartae* (Rome, 1624)

Cotton MSS. Caligula and Vespasian (British Library)

Craig, Sir Thomas, of Riccarton: *Henrici Illustrissimi Ducis Albaniae, Comitis Rossiae etc. et Mariae Serenissimae Scotorum Reginae Epithalamium, 1565* (trans. Wrangham in *Epithalamia Tria Mariana*, listed below)

Crawford, Thomas: *History of the University of Edinburgh* (Edinburgh, 1640)

Dépenses de la Maison Royal (Register House, Edinburgh)

A Diurnal of Remarkable Occurrents that have passed within the Country of Scotland since the Death of King James the Fourth till the Year MDLXXV, from a Manuscript of the Sixteenth Century in the Possession of Sir John Maxwell of Pollock, Baronet (ed. T. Thomson, Bannatyne Club, XLV Edinburgh, 1833)

Early Views and Maps of Edinburgh, 1544–1852 (Royal Scots Geographical Society, n.d.)

Edinburgh, Records of the Burgh (Scottish Burgh Records Society, Edinburgh, 1875)

Egerton MSS. (British Library)

Elizabeth I: *The Letters of Queen Elizabeth* (ed. G.B. Harrison, London, 1935, reprinted 1968)

Elizabeth and Mary Stuart (ed. Frank A. Mumby, 1914)

English and Scottish Popular Ballads (ed. James Francis Child from his own collection; ed. Helen Child Sargent and George Lyman Kittredge, London, 1905)

Epithalamia Tria Mariana (ed. Revd Francis Wrangham, Chester, 1837)

d'Ewes, Sir Simonds: *The Journals of all the Parliaments during the Reign of Queen Elizabeth* (revised and published by Paul Bowes, 1682 and 1693)

Fragments of Scottish History (ed. Sir John Graham Dalyell, Edinburgh, 1798)

Frarin, Peter: *An Oration against the Unlawful Insurrections of the Protestants of our Time under Pretence to Reform Religion* (Antwerp, 1566)

Fuller, Thomas: *The Church History of Britain* (1655; ed. John Gough Nichols, 1868)

The Hamilton Papers: Letters and Papers illustrating the Political Relations of England and Scotland in the XVIth Century. Formerly in the Possession of the Dukes of Hamilton, now in the British Museum (ed. Joseph Bain, Edinburgh, 1890–92)

Harleian MSS. (British Library)

Herries, John Maxwell, Lord: *Historical Memoirs of the Reign of Mary, Queen of Scots, and a Portion of the Reign of King James the Sixth* (ed. Robert Pitcairn, Abbotsford Club, Edinburgh, 1836)

Historical Records of the Family of Leslie, 1067–1869 (ed. C. Leslie, 1869)

The Historie and Life of King James the Sext (author unknown; ed. T. Thomson, Bannatyne Club, Edinburgh, 1825; ed. Malcolm Laing, Edinburgh, 1904)

The History of Mary Stuart (ed. Joseph Stevenson, Edinburgh, 1883)

Holinshed, Raphael: *The Chronicles of England, Scotland and Ireland* (London, 1587; 6 vols., ed. Sir Henry Ellis, London, 1807–8).

Illustrations of the Reign of Queen Mary (Maitland Club, XXV, Glasgow, 1837)

Index to the Principal Papers relating to Scotland in the Historical Manuscripts Commission's Reports (ed. C.S. Terry, 1908)

Inventaires de la Royne d'Escosse, Douairière de France: Catalogues of the Jewels, Dresses, Furniture, Books and Paintings of Mary, Queen of Scots, 1556–1569 (ed. Joseph Robertson, Bannatyne Club, Edinburgh, 1863)

Jeney, Thomas: *Master Randolph's Phantasy* (in *Satirical Poems*, below)

Keith, Robert: *History of the Affairs of Church and State in Scotland from the Beginning of the Reformation to 1585* (3 vols, ed. J.P. Lawson and J.C. Lyon, Spottiswoode Society, Edinburgh, 1844, 1845, 1850)

Knox, John: *The History of the Reformation of Religion in Scotland* (London, 1587; Edinburgh, 1732; ed. William McGavin, Glasgow, 1831; revised and ed. Cuthbert Lennox, Edinburgh, 1905; ed. William Croft Dickinson, London, 1949)

Knox, John: *The Political Writings of John Knox* (ed. Marvin A. Breslow, The Folger Shakespeare Library, Washington, London and Toronto, 1985)

Knox, John: *The Works of John Knox* (includes *History of the Reformation in Scotland* and Knox's correspondence) (6 vols, ed. David Laing, Bannatyne Club, Edinburgh, 1846–64; reprinted New York, 1966)

Lansdowne MSS. (British Library)

The Lennox Narrative (Cambridge University Library MSS.; ed. Reginald Henry Mahon in *Mary, Queen of Scots: A Study of the Lennox Narrative in the University Library of Cambridge*, Cambridge, 1924).

Leslie, John, Bishop of Ross: *A Defence of the Honour of the right high, mighty and noble Princess Marie, Queen of Scotland* (London, 1569; revised edition under the pseudonym Philippes Morgan, Liège, 1571)

Leslie, John, Bishop of Ross: *The History of Scotland from the Death of King James I in the Year 1436 [sic] to the Year 1561* (ed. T. Thomson, Bannatyne Club, XXXIX, Edinburgh, 1829/30; 2 vols, trans. James Dalrymple and ed. E.G. Cody and William Murison, Scottish Text Society, Edinburgh, 1895)

Leslie, John, Bishop of Ross: *De Origine, Moribus et Rebus Gestis Scotorum* (Rome, 1578)

Leslie, John, Bishop of Ross: *Paralipomena ad historiam, comitia et annales Scotiae Joanis Leslei, episcopi Rossensis, eodem auctore* (Secret Archives, Vatican Library, Rome)

Letters and Papers, Foreign and Domestic, of the Reign of Henry VIII (ed. James Gairdner and R.H. Brodie, HMSO, London, 1901–2)

Letters of Queen Elizabeth and James VI of Scotland (ed. J. Bruce, Camden Society, 1849)

Letters of Royal and Illustrious Ladies (ed. Mary Anne Everett Wood, London, 1846)

Lettres de Catherine de' Medicis (ed. H. de la Ferrière-Percy, Paris, 1880)

Lettres de Charles IX à M. de Fourquevaux (ed. R. de Rouer)

Libraries of Mary, Queen of Scots and James VI (Maitland Club Miscellany, Glasgow, 1834)

Lindsay of Pittscottie, Robert: *The History and Chronicles of Scotland* (ed. J.G. Dalyell, 1824; 2 vols ed A.J.G. Mackay, Scottish Text Society, Edinburgh, 1899–1911)

Maitland's Narrative (Ipswich, 1833)

Maitland, Sir Richard: *Poems* (Maitland Club, 1830)

Mary, Queen of Scots: *Letters of Mary, Queen of Scots, and Documents connected with her Personal History, now first published* (ed. Agnes Strickland, 3 vols, London, 1842–3)

Mary, Queen of Scots: *Lettres inédites de Marie Stuart* (ed. Prince Alexandre Labanoff, Paris, 1839)

Mary, Queen of Scots: *Lettres inédites de Marie Stuart* (ed. A. Teulet, Paris, 1859)

Mary, Queen of Scots: *Lettres, instructions et mémoires de Marie Stuart, Reine d'Ecosse* (7 vols, ed. Prince Alexandre Labanoff, Paris, 1844–5), trans. into English as *Letters of Mary Stuart, Queen of Scotland* (trans. William Turnbull, 7 vols, London, 1844–5) (Casket Letters not included)

Mary, Queen of Scots: *Lettres de Marie Stuart* (ed. Alexandre Teulet, Paris, 1859) (includes Casket Letters)

Melville, Sir James of Halhill: *Memoirs of his own Life, 1549–93* (London, 1683; ed. D. Wilson, London, 1752; ed. Thomas Thomson, Bannatyne Club, Edinburgh, 1827, reprinted 1872; ed. A. Francis Steuart, London, 1929; ed. Gordon Donaldson, The Folio Society, 1969)

Memoirs of the Reign of Queen Elizabeth (ed. T. Birch, 1764)

Memorials of Transactions in Scotland (ed. R. Bannatyne, Bannatyne Club, Edinburgh, 1836)

Miscellanea Antiqua Anglicana, or a Select Collection of Curious Tracts Illustrative of the History of the English Nation (London, 1816)

Miscellaneous Papers principally illustrative of Events in the Reigns of Queen Mary and James VI (Maitland Club, Glasgow, 1834)

Miscellaneous State Papers, 1501–1726 (ed. the Earl of Hardwicke, 1778)

Miscellany of the Scottish History Society, Vol. II (Scottish History Society, Edinburgh, 1904)

Narratives of Scottish Catholics under Mary Stuart and James VI (ed. W. Forbes-Leith, Edinburgh, 1885)

The National MSS. of Scotland (3 vols, London, 1867–73)

Nau, Claude, Sieur de Fontenage: *Memorials of Mary Stuart, or The History of Mary Stewart from the Murder of Riccio until her Flight into England, by Claude Nau, her Secretary* (BL Cotton MSS.; ed. Revd Joseph Stevenson, SJ, with *Illustrative Papers from the Secret Archives of the Vatican and other Collections in Rome*, Edinburgh, 1883)

Original Letters illustrative of English History (ed. Henry Ellis, London, 1824–46)

Papal Negotiations with Mary, Queen of Scots, during her Reign in Scotland, 1561–67, Edited from the Original Documents in the Vatican Archives and Elsewhere (ed. John Hungerford Pollen, Scottish Historical Society, XXXVII, Edinburgh, 1901)

Papers relating to the History of Mary Stuart, including "Maitland's Narrative" of the Principal Acts of the Regency (ed. W.S. Fitch, privately printed, Ipswich, 1842)

Papiers d'Etat, pièces et documents inédits ou peu connus relatifs à l'Histoire de l'Ecosse au 16e siècle (ed. Alexandre Teulet, Paris, 1852–60; Bannatyne Club, Edinburgh, 1852–60)

Pepys MSS. I & II (Historical Manuscripts Commission, Magdalene College, Cambridge)

Perlin, E.: *Description d'Angleterre et d'Ecosse* (1558)

Phyllips, T.: *A Commemoration of the Right Noble and Virtuous Lady Margaret Douglas's Good Grace, Countess of Lennox* (1578)

Proceedings and Ordinances of the Privy Council of England (ed. H. Nicholas, Records Commissioners, London, 1834–7)

The Register of the Great Seal of Scotland, 1546–80 (ed. J.M. Thompson, Edinburgh, 1886, reprinted Edinburgh, 1984)

The Register of the Privy Council of Scotland, Vol. I: 1545–1569 (ed. John Hill Burton et al., HM General Register House, Edinburgh, 1877)

The Register of the Privy Seal of Scotland (ed. M. Livingstone et al., Edinburgh, 1908, 1957, 1963)

The Register of the Secret Seal of Scotland, Vol. V (same as preceding)

Registrum Honoris de Morton: A Series of Ancient Charters of the Earldom of Morton with other Original Papers (Bannatyne Club, Edinburgh, 1853)

Relations politiques de la France et de l'Espagne avec l'Ecosse au XVI siècle (ed. Alexandre Teulet, Paris, 1862)

Remarks and Collections (ed. Thomas Hearne, Oxford Historical Society, 1898)

Ronsard, Pierre de: *The Works of Ronsard* (ed. Prosper Blanchemain, Paris, 1857)

Royal MSS. (British Library)

Ruthven, Patrick, Lord: Narration (in MS. Oo 7(47), Cambridge University Library); published as *A Relation of the Death of David Rizzi*, London, 1699; also in R. Keith's *History of the Affairs of Church and State in Scotland down to 1567*, ed. J.P. Lawson, Spottiswoode Society, 1844; ed. Goldsmid, 1891)

Sadler, Sir Ralph: *The State Papers and Letters of Sir Ralph Sadler, Knight-Banneret* (2 vols, ed. Arthur Clifford, Edinburgh, 1809)

Sanderson, William: *A Complete History of the Lives and Reigns of Mary, Queen of Scotland, and her Son and Successor, James the Sixth* (London, 1656)

Satirical Poems of the Time of the Reformation (ed. J. Cranstoun, 2 vols, Scottish Text Society, 1891–3)

Scottish Historical Documents (ed. Gordon Donaldson, Edinburgh and London, 1974)

Selections from Unpublished Manuscripts in the College of Arms and the British Museum, illustrating the Reign of Mary, Queen of Scotland, 1543–68 (ed. Joseph Stevenson, Maitland Club, XLI, Glasgow, 1837)

Sempill, Robert: *Ballads* (in *Satirical Poems*, above)

The Silver Casket, being Love Letters and Love Poems attributed to Mary Stuart, Queen of Scots, now Modernised and Translated, with an Introduction (ed. Clifford Bax, 1912, 1946)

Sloane MSS. (British Library)

Spottiswoode, John, Archbishop of St. Andrews: *The History of the Church and State of*

Scotland, beginning the Year of our Lord 203, and continued to the End of the Reign of King James the VI of ever blessed Memory (London, 1655; 3 vols, ed. M. Russell and M. Napier, Bannatyne Club and Spottiswoode Society, 1847–51)

State Papers in the Public Record Office

Statutes of the Realm (11 vols, ed. A. Luder et al., Records Commissioners, London, 1810–28)

Stranguage [Udall], William: *The History of the Life and Death of Mary Stuart, Queen of Scotland* (London, 1625)

"A Temple Newsham Inventory, 1565" (ed. F.W. Crossley, *Yorkshire Archaeological Journal*, 25, 1918–19)

Udall, William (see Stranguage)

De Vita et Rebus Gestis Serenissimae Principis Mariae Scotorum Reginae Franciae Dotoriae (ed. Samuel Jebb, 2 vols, London, 1725)

The Warrender Papers (ed. Annie I. Cameron and R.S. Rait, Scottish Historical Society, 3rd Series, XVII, Edinburgh, 1931–2)

Wilson, Thomas: *The Oration: Actio contra Mariam* (Edinburgh, 1571)

SECONDARY SOURCES

Alford, S.: *The Early Elizabethan Polity: William Cecil and the British Succession Crisis, 1558–69* (Cambridge, 1998)

Andrews, Allen: *Kings and Queens of England and Scotland* (Leicester, 2000)

Anonymous Elder of the Church of Scotland: *Mary, Queen of Scots: A Narrative and Defence* (1889)

Arbuthnot, Mrs. P. Stewart-Mackenzie: *Queen Mary's Book* (London, 1907)

Armstrong Davison, M.H.: *The Casket Letters: A Solution to the Mystery of Mary, Queen of Scots and the Murder of Lord Darnley* (London and Washington, 1965)

Armstrong Davison, M.H.: "The Maladies of Mary, Queen of Scots and her Husbands" (Scottish Society of the History of Medicine: *Report of Proceedings*, 1955–6)

Armstrong, Robert Bruce: *The History of Liddesdale* (Edinburgh, 1883)

Arnot, Hugo: *The History of Edinburgh* (London, 1788)

Ashdown, Dulcie M.: *Tudor Cousins: Rivals for the Throne* (Stroud, 2000)

Ashley, Maurice: *The Stuarts in Love, with some Reflections on Love and Marriage in the Sixteenth and Seventeenth Centuries* (London, 1963)

Ashley, Mike: *British Monarchs* (London, 1998)

Atholl, John, 7th Duke of: *Chronicles of the Atholl and Tullibardine Families* (privately printed, 1908)

Bailey, Helen: *Borthwick Castle: Its Place in History* (Galashiels, undated)

Baillie-Hamilton, Lady: "A Historical Relic" (*Macmillan's Magazine*, 90 undated)

Balfour, Sir James: *The Scots Peerage* (Edinburgh, 1905)

Barbe, Louis A.: *In Byways of Scottish History* (Edinburgh, 1912)

Barbe, Louis A.: *Kirkcaldy of Grange* (Edinburgh and London, 1897)

Baring, M.: *In my End is my Beginning* (London, 1931)

Barwick, G.F.: "A Sidelight on the Mystery of Mary Stuart: Pietro Bizari's Contemporary Account of the Murders of Riccio and Darnley" (*Scottish Historical Review*, 31, 1924)

Beckinsale, B.W.: *Elizabeth I* (London, 1963)

Begg, Robert Burns: *The History of Lochleven Castle* (Edinburgh, 1890)

Bekker, E.: *Maria Stuart, Darnley, Bothwell* (Giessener Studien aus dem Gebiet der Geschichte, 1, 1881)

Bentley-Cranch, Dana: "Effigy and Portrait in Sixteenth Century Scotland" (*Review of Scottish Culture*, 4 1988)

Bertière, Simone: *Les Reines de France au temps les Valois* (Paris, 1994)

Bingham, Caroline: *Darnley: A Life of Henry Stuart, Lord Darnley, Consort of Mary, Queen of Scots* (London, 1995)

Bingham, Caroline: *James VI of Scotland* (London, 1979)

Bingham, Caroline: *The Kings and Queens of Scotland* (London, 1976)

Bingham, Caroline: *The Making of a King: The Early Years of James VI and I* (London, 1968)

Bingham, Caroline: *The Poems of Mary, Queen of Scots* (Royal Stuart Papers, X, The Royal Stuart Society, 1976)

Bingham, Madeleine: *Mary, Queen of Scots* (London, 1969)

Bingham, Madeleine: *Scotland under Mary Stuart: An Account of Everyday Life* (London, 1971)

Black, J.B.: *Andrew Lang and the Casket Letter Controversy* (Edinburgh, 1951)

Black, J.B.: *The Reign of Elizabeth, 1558–1603* (Oxford, 1959)

Blake, William: *William Maitland of Lethington, 1528–1573* (Studies in British History, XIX, Lampeter, 1990)

Bold, Alan: *Scotland's Kings and Queens* (Andover, 1992)

Bourciez, Edouard: *Littérature de cour sous Henri II* (Librairie Hachette, Paris, 1886)

Bowen, Marjorie: *Mary, Queen of Scots, the Daughter of Debate* (London, 1934; reprinted London, 1971)

Breeze, David J., and Donaldson, Gordon: *A Queen's Progress. An Introduction to the Buildings associated with Mary, Queen of Scots, in the Care of the Secretary of State for Scotland* (HMSO, Edinburgh, 1987)

Bresslau, Harry: *Die Kassettenbriefe der Königin Maria Stuart* (Historisches Taschenbuch, 6th Series, 1, 1882)

Brigden, Susan: *New Worlds, Lost Worlds: The Rule of The Tudors, 1485–1603* (London, 2000)

Brown, P. Hume: *History of Scotland* (3 vols, Cambridge, 1908–12)

Brown, P. Hume: *John Knox: A Biography* (2 vols, London, 1895)

Brown, P. Hume: *Scotland in the Time of Queen Mary* (London, 1904)

Burns, E.: *Scottish Coins* (London, 1887)

Burton, J. Hill: *The History of Scotland* (8 vols, Edinburgh, 1873–4)

Callendar House: Guidebook (Falkirk Museums, undated)

Campbell, Hugh: *The Love Letters of Mary, Queen of Scots, with her Love Sonnets* (London, 1824)

Cannon, John, and Griffiths, Ralph: *The Oxford History of the British Monarchy* (Oxford, 1988)

Capper, Rosi: *Mary, Queen of Scots' House and Visitor Centre, Jedburgh, Roxburghshire* (Jedburgh, 1997)

Carruth, Revd J.A.: *Mary, Queen of Scots* (Norwich, 1988)

Castles of Scotland (Andover, 1988)

Chalmers, George: *A Detection of the Love Letters Lately Attributed to Mary* (London, 1825)

Chalmers, George: *Life of Mary, Queen of Scots* (2 vols, London, 1818)

Chambers Biographical Dictionary (ed. Magnus Magnusson, Edinburgh, 1990)

Chauvire, Mons. Roger: *Le Secret de Marie Stuart* (Paris, 1937)

Cheetham, J. Keith: *On the Trail of Mary, Queen of Scots* (Edinburgh, 1999)

Cherry, Alastair: *Princes, Poets and Patrons: The Stuarts and Scotland* (Edinburgh, 1987)

Chronicle of the Royal Family (ed. Derrik Mercer, London, 1991)

Cochran-Patrick, R.W.: *Catalogue of the Medals of Scotland: From the Earliest Period to the Present Time* (Edinburgh, 1884)

Coventry, Martin: *The Haunted Castles of Scotland* (Edinburgh, 1996)

Cowan, Ian B.: *The Enigma of Mary Stuart* (London, 1971)

Cowan, Ian B.: *Mary, Queen of Scots* (Edinburgh, 1987)

Cowan, Ian B.: *The Scottish Reformation: Church and Society in Sixteenth Century Scotland* (London, 1982)

Cowan, Ian B., and Shaw, Duncan: *The Renaissance and Reformation in Scotland* (Edinburgh, 1983)

Cowan, Samuel: *The Last Days of Mary Stuart and the Journal of Bourgoing, her Physician* (London, 1907)

Cowan, Samuel: *Mary, Queen of Scots, and Who Wrote the Casket Letters* (2 vols, London, 1901)

Crawford, Thomas: *The History of Mary, Queen of Scots* (Edinburgh, 1793)

Crawfurd, David: *Memoirs of the Affairs of Scotland* (London, 1706; Edinburgh, 1753)

Creighton, Mandell: *Queen Elizabeth* (London, 1899)

Crouther Gordon, Revd T.: *A Short History of Alloa* (London, 1986)

Cust, Lady Elizabeth: *Some Account of the Stuarts of Aubigny in France, 1422–1672* (privately printed, London, 1891)

Cust, Lionel: *Notes on the Authentic Portraits of Mary, Queen of Scots* (London, 1903)

Dalrymple, Sir David, Lord Hailes: *Annals of Scotland* (3 vols, London, 1797)

Dalrymple, Sir David, Lord Hailes: *Miscellaneous Remarks on "The Enquiry into the Evidence against Mary, Queen of Scots"* (London, 1784)

Dawson, Jane E.A.: "Mary, Queen of Scots, Lord Darnley and Anglo-Scottish Relations in 1565" (*International History Review*, 8, 1986)

Dickinson, W. Croft: *A New History of Scotland, Vol. I* (London, 1961)

Dickinson, W. Croft; Donaldson, Gordon, and Milne, Isobel: *A Source Book of Scottish History, Vol. II* (Edinburgh, 1958)

Dictionary of National Biography

Donaldson, Gordon: *All the Queen's Men: Power and Politics in Mary Stewart's Scotland* (London, 1983)

Donaldson, Gordon: *The First Trial of Mary, Queen of Scots* (London, 1969)

Donaldson, Gordon: *Mary, Queen of Scots* (London, 1974)

Donaldson, Gordon: *Scotland: Church and Nation through Sixteen Centuries* (Edinburgh and London, 1972)

Donaldson, Gordon: *Scotland: James V to James VII* (Edinburgh and London, 1965)

Donaldson, Gordon: *Scottish Kings* (London, 1967)

Donaldson, Gordon: *The Scottish Reformation* (Cambridge, 1960)

Donaldson, Gordon, and Morpeth, Robert S.: *Who's Who in Scottish History* (Oxford, 1973)

Douglas-Irvine, Helen: *Royal Palaces of Scotland* (London, 1911)

Drummond, Humphrey: *Our Man in Scotland: Sir Ralph Sadler, 1507–1587* (London, 1969)

Drummond, Humphrey: *The Queen's Man: James Hepburn, Earl of Bothwell and Duke of Orkney 1536–1578* (London, 1975)

Dunbar, John G.: "The Palace of Holyroodhouse during the First Half of the Sixteenth Century" (*Archaeological Journal*, 120, 1964)

Dunbar, John G.: *Scottish Royal Palaces: The Architecture of the Royal Residences during the Late Mediaeval and Early Renaissance Periods* (East Linton, 1999)

Duncan, Thomas: "Mary Stuart and the House of Huntly" (*Scottish Historical Review*, 4, 1906/7)

Duncan, Thomas: "The Queen's Maries" (*Scottish Historical Review*, 2, 1905)

Duncan, Thomas: "The Relations of the Earl of Murray [*sic*] with Mary Stuart" (*Scottish Historical Review*, 6, 1909)

L'Ecole de Fontainebleau (Exhibition Catalogue, Grand Palais, Paris, 1972)

Edwards, Francis: *The Dangerous Queen* (London, 1964)

Edwards, Francis: *The Marvellous Chance* (London, 1968)

Elton, G.R.: *England under the Tudors* (London, 1965; revised edition, 1969)

Erickson, Carolly: *The First Elizabeth* (New York, 1983; London, 1999)

Evans, Joan: *A History of Jewellery, 1100–1870* (London, 1953)

Eyre-Todd, George: *The History of Glasgow, Vol. II* (Glasgow, 1931)

Falkland Palace and Royal Burgh (The National Trust for Scotland, Edinburgh, 1995)

Fawcett, Richard: "The Early Tudor House in the Light of Recent Excavations" (at Temple Newsham) (*Leeds Arts Calendar*, 70, 1982)

Fawcett, Richard: *The Palace of Holyroodhouse* (Royal Collection, London, 1992)

Fawcett, Richard: *Stirling Castle* (Edinburgh, 1983)

Fleming, David Hay: *Mary, Queen of Scots: From her Birth to her Flight into England: A Brief Biography with Critical Notes, and a Few Documents, hitherto Unpublished, and an Itinerary* (London, 1897)

Forst, H.: *Maria Stuart und der Tod Darnleys* (Bonn, 1894)

Francis, Grant R.: *Scotland's Royal Line: The Tragic House of Stuart* (New York, 1929)

Fraprie, S.A.: *The Castles and Keeps of Scotland* (London, 1908)

Fraser, Lady Antonia: *Mary, Queen of Scots* (London, 1969)

Fraser, Lady Antonia: *Mary, Queen of Scots and the Historians* (Royal Stuart Papers, VII, the Royal Stuart Society, 1974)

Fraser, William: *The Book of Douglas* (4 vols, Edinburgh, 1884/5)

Fraser, William: *The Lennox* (2 vols, Edinburgh, 1874/6)

Freebairn, James: *Life of Mary Stewart* (Edinburgh, 1725)

Froude, James Anthony: *The History of England from the Fall of Wolsey to the Defeat of the Spanish Armada* (12 vols, London, 1856–70)

Gauthier, Jules: *Histoire de Marie Stuart* (2 vols, Paris, 1875)

Gent, Frank: "The Coffin in the Wall: An Edinburgh Castle 'Mystery' " (*Chambers' Journal*, September and October 1944)

Glasford Bell, Henry: *Life of Mary, Queen of Scots* (2 vols, Edinburgh, 1828, 1831)

Glen, John: *Early Scottish Melodies* (Edinburgh, 1900)

Goodall, Walter: *An Examination of the Letters Said to be Written by Mary, Queen of Scots, to James, Earl of Bothwell; shewing by Intrinsic and Extrinsic Evidence that they are Forgeries; also, an Enquiry into the Murder of King Henry* (2 vols, Edinburgh and London, 1754)

Goodman, Jean, in collaboration with Sir Iain Moncrieff of that Ilk: *Debrett's Royal Scotland* (Exeter, 1983)

Gore-Browne, Robert: *Lord Bothwell: A Study of the Life, Character and Times of James Hepburn, 4th Earl of Bothwell* (London, 1937)

Gow, Ian: *The Palace of Holyroodhouse* (Royal Collection, London, 1995)

Grant, I.F.: *The Social and Economic Development of Scotland* (Edinburgh, 1930)

Great Dynasties (ed. Arnoldo Mondadori, Milan, 1976)

Great Scots (Scottish National Portrait Gallery, Edinburgh, undated—1990s)

Grierson, Elizabeth Wilson: *Edinburgh Castle, Holyrood and St. Giles' Cathedral* (London, 1908)

Hamilton, Angus, Duke of: *Maria R.: Mary, Queen of Scots, the Crucial Years* (Edinburgh and London, 1991)

Handbook of British Chronology (ed. Sir F. Maurice Powicke and E.B. Fryde, London, 1961)

Hannan, Thomas: *Famous Scottish Houses: The Lowlands* (London, 1928)

Hannay, R.K.: "The Earl of Arran and Queen Mary" (*Scottish Historical Review*, 18, 1920)

Harris, Stuart: *Mary, Queen of Scots, and Sir Simon Preston's House, Edinburgh* (Edinburgh, 1983)

Harrison, John: *The History of the Monastery of the Holy Rude and of the Palace of Holyroodhouse* (Edinburgh, 1919)

Henderson, T.F.: *The Casket Letters and Mary, Queen of Scots* (Edinburgh, 1889; Edinburgh and London, 1890)

Henderson, T.F.: *Mary, Queen of Scots: Her Environment and Tragedy* (2 vols, London, 1905)

Henderson, T.F.: "Mr. Lang and the Casket Letters" (*Scottish Historical Review*, 5, 1904)

Henderson, T.F.: *The Royal Stewarts* (Edinburgh and London, 1914)

Heritier, Jean: *Marie Stuart et le meurtre de Darnley* (Paris, 1934)

Hibbert, Christopher: *The Virgin Queen: The Personal History of Elizabeth I* (1992 edition)

Hind, A.M.: *Engraving in England in the 16th and 17th Centuries* (2 vols, Cambridge, 1952, 1955)

Hosack, John: *Mary, Queen of Scots, and her Accusers* (2 vols, Edinburgh and London, 1870, 1874; Edinburgh, 1969)

Howard, Maurice: *The Early Tudor Country House: Architecture and Politics, 1490–1550* (London, 1987)

Hume Brown, P.: *Early Travellers in Scotland* (Edinburgh, 1891)

Hume Brown, P.: *George Buchanan, Humanist and Reformer* (Edinburgh, 1890)

Hume Brown, P.: *Scotland in the Time of Queen Mary* (Edinburgh, 1904)

Hume, David: *History of England under the House of Tudor* (2 vols, London, 1759; with a continuation by Tobias Smollett, 3 vols, London, 1824)

Hume, David: *The History of the House and Race of Douglas and Angus, Vol. II* (Edinburgh, 1748)

Hume, Martin A.S.: *The Love Affairs of Mary, Queen of Scots: A Political History* (London, 1903)

Hunter, John: *Mary Stuart* (Edinburgh, 1996)

Hurstfield, Joel: *Elizabeth I and the Unity of England* (London, 1960)

Ireland, William: *Effusions of Love from Chatelar to Mary, Queen of Scots* (London, 1805)

Jauncey, James: *Blair Castle* (Atholl Estates, 1999)

Jenkins, Elizabeth: *Elizabeth the Great* (London, 1958)

Johnson, Paul: *Elizabeth I: A Study in Power and Intellect* (London, 1974)

Keith, Robert: *The History of the Affairs of Church and State in Scotland from the Beginning of the Reformation to the Retreat of Queen Mary into England, anno 1568* (Edinburgh, 1734; ed. J.P. Lawson, 3 vols, Spottiswoode Society, 1844–50)

Kendall, Alan: *Robert Dudley, Earl of Leicester* (London, 1980)

Knecht, R.J.: *Catherine de' Medici* (London and New York, 1998)

Laing, David: *Collegiate Churches of Midlothian* (Bannatyne Club, 1861)

Laing, Malcolm: *The History of Scotland from the Union of the Crowns on the Accession of James VI to the Throne of England, to the Union of the Kingdoms in the Reign of Queen Anne. With a Preliminary Dissertation on the Participation of Mary, Queen of Scots, in the Murder of Lord Darnley* (4 vols, London, 1819)

Lamartine, Alphonse de: *Mary Stuart* (Edinburgh, 1859)

Lamont-Brown, Raymond: *Royal Murder Mysteries* (London, 1990)

Lane, Henry Murray: *The Royal Daughters of England* (2 vols, 1910)

Lang, Andrew: "The Casket Letters" (*Scottish Historical Review*, 5, 1904)

Lang, Andrew: *History of Scotland* (4 vols, London, 1900–7)

Lang, Andrew: *The Mystery of Mary Stuart* (London, 1901; revised editions 1904 and 1912)

Lang, Andrew: *Portraits and Jewels of Mary Stuart* (Glasgow, 1906)

Law, Thomas Graves: "Mary Stewart" (in *Cambridge Modern History*, Vol. III, Cambridge, 1904)

Leader, J.D.: *Mary, Queen of Scots, in Captivity, 1569–1584* (London, 1880)

Lee, David John: *The Secrets of Niddrie Castle* (Thornhill, 1984)

Lee, Maurice: *James Stewart, Earl of Moray: A Political Study of the Reformation in Scotland* (New York, 1953)

Lehmberg, S.E.: *Sir Walter Mildmay and Tudor Government* (Austin, Texas, 1964)

Lettenhove, Baron Kervyn de: "Marie Stuart d'après les documents conservés au Château d'Hatfield" (*Bulletin de l'académie royale de Belgique*, 2nd series, 34, 1872)

Levine, Mortimer: *The Early Elizabethan Succession Question, 1558–68* (Stanford, California, 1966)

Lindsay, Ian G.: *Old Edinburgh* (Edinburgh, 1944)

Linklater, Eric: *Mary, Queen of Scots* (Edinburgh, 1933)

Livingstone, M.A.: *Guide to the Public Records of Scotland* (1905)

Lockie, D.M.: "The Political Career of the Bishop of Ross, 1568–90" (*University of Birmingham Historical Journal*, 1953)

Lynch, Michael: *Edinburgh and the Reformation* (Edinburgh, 1981)

Lynch, Michael: "Queen Mary's Triumph: The Baptismal Celebrations at Stirling in December, 1566" (*Scottish Historical Review*, 69, no. 187, April, 1990)

Lynch, Michael: *Scotland: A New History* (London, 1991)

MacAlpine, Ida, and Hunter, Richard: *Porphyria, a Royal Malady* (British Medical Association, London, 1968)

MacCunn, Florence A.: *A Life of John Knox* (London, 1895)

MacCunn, Florence A.: *Mary Stuart* (London, 1905)

MacDonald, Alasdair A.: "The Bannatyne Manuscript—a Marian Anthology" (*Innes Review*, 37, no. 1, Spring 1986)

Mackay, James: *In my End is my Beginning: A Life of Mary, Queen of Scots* (Edinburgh, 1999)

Mackay, Moira: "The Mystery of Kirk o'Field" (*Scottish Memories*, March 1998)

MacKenzie, Agnes Mure: *The Scotland of Queen Mary* (London, 1936)

MacKie, Charles: *The Castles, Palaces and Prisons of Mary of Scotland* (1849)

Mackie, J.D.: "The Will of Mary Stuart" (*Scottish Historical Review*, 11)

MacNalty, Sir Arthur Salusbury: *Mary, Queen of Scots: The Daughter of Debate* (London, 1960)

Mahon, Reginald Henry: *The Indictment of Mary, Queen of Scots as derived from a Manuscript in the University Library at Cambridge, hitherto unpublished* (Cambridge, 1923)

Mahon, Reginald Henry: *Mary, Queen of Scots: A Study of the Lennox Narrative in the University Library of Cambridge* (Cambridge, 1924)

Mahon, Reginald Henry: *The Tragedy of Kirk o'Field* (Cambridge, 1930)

Marshall, Rosalind K.: *Elizabeth I* (HMSO, London, 1991)

Marshall, Rosalind K.: *Mary of Guise* (London, 1977)

Marshall, Rosalind K.: *Queen of Scots* (HMSO, Edinburgh, 1986)

Marshall, Rosalind K.: *Virgins and Viragos: A History of Women in Scotland from 1080 to 1980* (London, 1983)

Martine, Roddy: *Royal Scotland* (Edinburgh, 1983)

Mary, Queen of Scots: The Scottish Setting (National Galleries of Scotland, Edinburgh, undated—1980s–90s)

Mary Stewart: Queen in Three Kingdoms (ed. Michael Lynch, Oxford, 1988)

Matheson, C.: *Catalogue of the Publications of Scottish Historical Clubs and Societies and of the Volumes relative to Scotland published by the Stationery Office &c.* (1928)

Mathew, Archbishop David: *James I* (London, 1967)

Mathieson, W.L.: *Politics and Religion: A Study in Scottish History from the Reformation to the Revolution, 1550–1695* (2 vols, Glasgow, 1902)

Maxwell, Sir Herbert: *A History of the House of Douglas, from the Earliest Times down to the Legislative Union of England and Scotland* (1902)

Maxwell Stuart, Peter and Flora: *Traquair* (Norwich, 1986)

McCrie, Thomas: *The Life of John Knox* (2 vols, Edinburgh, 1831)

McKechnie, W.: *Mary, Queen of Scots in Jedburgh, 1566* (Selkirk, 1978)

McKenzie, Dan: "The Obstetrical History of Mary, Queen of Scots" (*Caledonian Medical Journal*, 15, 1921)

McLaren, Moray: *The Shell Guide to Scotland* (London, 1967)

Michael of Albany, HRH Prince: *The Forgotten Monarchy of Scotland* (Shaftesbury, 1998)

Michel, Francisque: *Les Ecossais en France* (Paris, 1862)

Mignet, Francis A.: *Histoire de Marie Stuart* (2 vols, Paris, 1851; published as *The History of Mary, Queen of Scots*, 2 vols, London, 1851)

Millar, A.H.: *Mary, Queen of Scots: Her Life Story* (Edinburgh, 1905)

Millar, A.H.: *Traditions and Stories of Scottish Castles* (Edinburgh and London, 1947)

Millar, Oliver: *The Tudor and Stuart and Early Georgian Pictures in the Collection of Her Majesty the Queen* (London, 1963)

Miller, Joyce: *Mary, Queen of Scots* (Edinburgh, 1996)

Mitchell, C. Ainsworth: *The Evidence of the Casket Letters* (Historical Association Pamphlet, London, 1927)

Mitchison, Rosalind: *A History of Scotland* (London, 1970)

Morris, Christopher: *The Tudors* (London, 1955)

Morrison, N. Brysson: *Mary, Queen of Scots* (London, 1960)

Muir, Frank: *John Knox* (London, 1929)

Mulvey, Kate: *Mary, Queen of Scots: An Illustrated Historical Guide* (Norwich, 2001)

Mumby, Frank Arthur: *The Fall of Mary Stuart: A Narrative in Contemporary Letters* (London, 1921)

Mumby, Frank Arthur: *Mary, Queen of Scots and Queen Elizabeth: The Beginning of the Feud* (Boston, 1914)

Mure Mackenzie, Agnes: *The Scotland of Queen Mary and the Religious Wars* (London, 1936)

Neale, John E.: *Queen Elizabeth I* (London, 1933, reprinted 1998)

Norris, Herbert: *Tudor Costume and Fashion* (London, 1938; reprinted New York, 1997)

The Oxford Illustrated History of Tudor and Stuart Britain (ed. John Morrill, Oxford, 1996)

Parry, His Honour Sir Edward: *The Persecution of Mary Stewart: The Queen's Cause: A Study in Criminology* (London, 1931)

Pearson, Dr. Karl: "The Skull and Portraits of Henry Stewart, Lord Darnley, and Their Bearing on the Tragedy of Mary, Queen of Scots" (*Biometrika*, July 1928, University College, London, July, 1928; bound as a single volume, Cambridge, 1928)

Percy, Eustace: *John Knox* (London, 1937)

Perry, Maria: *Elizabeth I: The Word of a Prince* (London, 1990)

Perry, Maria: *Sisters to the King* (London, 1998)

Petit, J.A.: *History of Mary Stuart, Queen of Scots* (trans. Charles de Flandre, 2 vols, Edinburgh, 1873)

Philippson, Martin: *Histoire du regne de Marie Stuart* (3 vols, Paris, 1891–2)

Phillips, James Emerson: *Images of a Queen: Mary Stuart in Sixteenth Century Literature* (Berkeley and Los Angeles, 1964)

Plowden, Alison: *Elizabethan England* (London, 1982)

Plowden, Alison: *The House of Tudor* (London, 1976; revised edition, Stroud, 1998)

Plowden, Alison: *Tudor Women: Queens and Commoners* (London, 1979)

Plowden, Alison: *Two Queens in One Isle: The Deadly Relationship of Elizabeth I and Mary, Queen of Scots* (Brighton, 1984)

Plumb, J.H.: *Royal Heritage* (London, 1977)

Plumptre, James: *Observations on "Hamlet" . . . as an Indirect Censure on Mary, Queen of Scots* (1796)

Pollen, J.H.: "The Dispensation for the Marriage of Mary Stuart with Darnley and its Date" (*Scottish Historical Review*, 4, 1907)

Pollen, J.H.: *Mary, Queen of Scots and the Babington Plot* (Scottish History Society, 1922)

Prebble, John: *The Lion in the North: One Thousand Years of Scotland's History* (London, 1971)

Pringle, Denys: *Craigmillar Castle* (Historic Scotland, Hawick, 1996)

The Private Lives of the Tudor Monarchs (ed. Christopher Falkus, The Folio Society, London, 1974)

Puttfarken, Thomas; Hartley, Christopher; Grant, Robert; and Robson, Eric: *Falkland Palace and Royal Burgh* (National Trust for Scotland, 1995)

Rait, Sir Robert Sangster: *Mary, Queen of Scots, 1542–1587: Her Life and Reign* (London, 1899)

Raumer, F. von: *Elizabeth and Mary Stuart* (London, 1836)

Read, Conyers: *Mr. Secretary Cecil and Queen Elizabeth* (London, 1955)

Read, Conyers: *Mr. Secretary Walsingham and the Policy of Queen Elizabeth* (3 vols, Oxford, 1925)

Rich, D.C.: *European Paintings in the Collection of Worcester Art Museum* (1974)

Ridley, Jasper: *John Knox* (Oxford, 1968)

Robertson, H.: *The History of Scotland* (1791)

Robertson, Thomas: *The History of Mary, Queen of Scots* (Edinburgh, 1793)

Robertson, William: *The History of Scotland during the Reigns of Queen Mary and of King James VI till his Accession to the Crown of England, with a Review of Scottish History previous to that Period, and an Appendix containing Original Papers* (3 vols, London, 1759)

Rogers, Charles: *History of the Chapel Royal in Scotland* (Grampian Club, 1882)

Ross, Josephine: *The Tudors* (London, 1979)

Rossaro, Massimo: *The Life and Times of Elizabeth I* (Verona, 1966)

Roulstone, Michael: *The Royal House of Tudor* (St. Ives, 1974)

Routh, C.R.N.: *Who's Who in Tudor England* (London, 1990)

Royston, Angela: *Mary, Queen of Scots* (Andover, 2000)

Russell, E.: *Maitland of Lethington, the Minister of Mary Stuart* (London, 1912)

Sanderson, Margaret: *Mary Stewart's People* (Edinburgh, 1987)

Scarisbrick, Diana: *Tudor and Jacobean Jewellery* (London, 1995)

Schiern, Frederik: *The Life of James Hepburn, Earl of Bothwell* (trans. from the Danish by Revd David Berry, Edinburgh, 1880)

Scott, J.: *Bibliography of Works relating to Mary, Queen of Scots, 1544–1700* (Edinburgh Bibliographical Society, II, 1896)

Scott, Mrs. Maxwell: *The Tragedy of Fotheringhay* (London, 1895/1905)

Scott-Moncrieff, George: *Edinburgh* (Edinburgh, 1965)

The Scots Peerage (9 vols, ed. J. Balfour Paul, London, 1904)

The Secret History of Mary Stuart (trans. from the French by Eliza Haywood (Edinburgh, 1725)

Semple, David: *The Tree of Crocston: Being a Refutation of the Fables of the Courtship of Queen Marie and Lord Darnley at Crocston Castle under the Yew Tree* (Paisley, 1876)

Sepp, B.: *Maria Stuart und ihre Anklager zu York, Westminster und Hampton Court (1568–9)* (Munich, 1884)

Sepp, B.: *Tagebuch der unglücklichen Schottischen-Königen zu Glasgow* (Munich, 1882)

Seton, G.: *History of the Family of Seton* (London, 1896)

Shire, Helena M.: *Song, Dance and Poetry of the Court of Scotland under James VI* (Cambridge, 1969)

Simmonds, Edward: *The Genuine Letters of Mary, Queen of Scots, to James, Earl of Bothwell* (Westminster, 1726)

Sitwell, Edith: *The Queens and the Hive* (London, 1962)

Skelton, Sir John: *The Impeachment of Mary Stuart* (Edinburgh, 1876)

Skelton, Sir John: *Maitland of Lethington and the Scotland of Mary Stuart* (2 vols, Edinburgh, 1887–8)

Skelton, Sir John: *Mary Stuart* (London, 1893)

Smailes, Helen, and Thomson, Duncan: *The Queen's Image: A Celebration of Mary, Queen of Scots* (Edinburgh, 1987)

Somerset, Anne: *Elizabeth I* (1991)

Speedy, Tom: *Craigmillar and its Environs* (Selkirk, 1892)

Starkey, Dr. David: *Elizabeth* (London, 2000)

Steel, David and Judy: *Mary Stuart's Scotland: The Landscapes, Life and Legends of Mary, Queen of Scots* (London, 1987)

Steuart, A. Francis: *Seigneur Davie: A Short Life of David Riccio* (London and Edinburgh, 1922)

Stevenson, Joseph: *Mary Stuart* (Edinburgh, 1886)

Stewart, A.F.: *The Trial of Mary, Queen of Scots* (Edinburgh, 1923)

Stewart, I.M.: *Scottish Coinage* (London, 1955)

Strickland, Agnes: *The Life of Mary, Queen of Scots* (2 vols, London, 1888)

Strickland, Agnes: *Lives of the Queens of England* (London, 1840–8)

Strickland, Agnes: *Lives of the Queens of Scotland and English Princesses connected with the Regal Succession of Great Britain* (8 vols, Edinburgh and London, 1850–9)

Strickland, Agnes: *Lives of the Tudor Princesses* (London, 1868)

Strong, Sir Roy: *The English Icon: Elizabethan and Jacobean Portraiture* (London, 1969)

Strong, Sir Roy: *Hans Eworth: A Tudor Artist and his Circle* (Leicester Museums and Art Gallery, 1965)

Strong, Sir Roy: *Tudor and Jacobean Portraits* (2 vols, London, 1969)

Strong, Sir Roy, and Oman, Julia Trevelyan: *Mary, Queen of Scots* (London, 1972)

Stuart, Gilbert: *History of Scotland* (London, 1782)

Stuart, John: *A Lost Chapter in the History of Mary, Queen of Scots Recovered: Notices of James, Earl of Bothwell and Lady Jane Gordon and of the Dispensation for their Marriage; Remarks on the Law and Practice of Scotland relative to Marriage Dispensations; and an Appendix of Documents* (Edinburgh, 1874)

Tabraham, Chris: *Edinburgh Castle* (Historic Scotland, 1995)

Tabraham, Chris: *Stirling Castle* (Historic Scotland, 1999)

Tait, Hugh: "Historiated Tudor Jewellery" (*The Antiquaries' Journal*, 42, 1962)

Tannenbaum, S.A. and D.R.: *Marie Stuart: Bibliography* (3 vols, New York, 1944–6)

Temple Newsham Guidebook (Leeds City Art Galleries, 1989)

Terry, Charles S.: *A History of Scotland* (Cambridge, 1920)

Thirlestane Castle Guidebook (Banbury, undated)

Thomson, Duncan; Marshall, Rosalind K.; Caldwell, David H.; Cheape, Hugh, and Dalgleish, George: *Dynasty: The Royal House of Stewart* (Edinburgh, 1990)

Thomson, George Malcolm: *The Crime of Mary Stuart* (London, 1967)

Tranter, Nigel: *The Fortalices and Early Mansions of Southern Scotland, 1400–1650* (Edinburgh and London, 1935)

Trinquet, Roger: "L'Allegorie politique au XVI siècle dans le peinture française—ses Dames au Bain" (*Bulletin de la Société de l'histoire de l'art française*, 1967)

Turner, Sir George: *Mary Stuart: Forgotten Forgeries* (London, 1933)

Tytler, Patrick Fraser: *An Account of the Life and Writings of Sir Thomas Craig of Riccarton* (Edinburgh, 1823)

Tytler, Patrick Fraser: *The History of Scotland* (8 vols, Edinburgh, 1841–5)

Tytler, William: *An Inquiry, Historical and Critical, into the Evidence against Mary, Queen of Scots* (2 vols, Edinburgh, 1760)

Villius, H.: "The Casket Letters: A Famous Case Reopened" (*Historical Journal*, 28, 1985)

Watkins, Susan: *Mary, Queen of Scots* (London, 2001)

Weir, Alison: *Britain's Royal Families* (London, 1989)

Weir, Alison: *Elizabeth the Queen* (London, 1998)

Weir, Alison: Margaret Douglas, Countess of Lennox (unpublished research, 1974)

Whitaker, John: *Mary, Queen of Scots, Vindicated* (3 vols, Edinburgh, 1787/1793)

Williams, Neville: *Elizabeth I, Queen of England* (London, 1967)

Williams, Neville: *The Life and Times of Elizabeth I* (London, 1972)

Williamson, David: *Brewer's British Royalty* (London, 1996)

Willson, David Harris: *King James VI and I* (London, 1956)

Wilson, Derek: *Sweet Robin: A Biography of Robert Dudley, Earl of Leicester, 1533–1588* (London, 1981)

Woodward, G.W.O.: *Mary, Queen of Scots* (Andover, 1992)

Wormald, Jenny: *Court, Kirk and Community: Scotland 1470–1625* (London, 1981)

Wormald, Jenny: *Lords and Men in Scotland: Bonds of Manrent, 1442–1603* (Edinburgh, 1985)

Wormald, Jenny: *Mary, Queen of Scots: A Study in Failure* (London, 1988; reprinted as *Mary, Queen of Scots: Politics, Passion and a Kingdom Lost*, London, 2001)

Wright, T.: *Queen Elizabeth and her Times* (London, 1838)

Zweig, Stefan: *The Queen of Scots* (London, 1935)

HOUSE OF STEWART

James IV
King of Scots
1473-1513   1. m.

(by Isabella   (by Margaret
Stewart)   Drummond)

Johanna   Margaret   Marie de Guise   m.   James V
d.1560/3   m.   1515-1560   King of Scots
m.   John,   1512-1542
Malcolm   Lord Gordon
3rd Baron   d.1517
Fleming
d.1547

John   Mary   Margaret   George   Francis II,
5th Baron   Fleming   m.   Gordon,   King of France
Fleming   1542-aft. 1581   John   4th Earl   1544-1560
c1536-1572   m.   Stewart,   of Huntly
↓   Sir William   4th Earl   1514-1562
                 Maitland   of Atholl
                 of Lethington   c1518-1579
                 c1528-1573   ↓
                 ↓

                                   (by Margaret   (by Elizabeth
                                   Erskine)   Carmichael)

George   Sir John   Jean   James   John
Gordon,   Gordon   Gordon   Stewart,   Steward,
5th Earl   d.1562   m.   Earl of   Prior of
of Huntly   James   Moray   Coldingham
c1535-1576   Hepbern,   1531?-1570   1532?-1563
                            4th Earl   m.   m.
                            of Bothwell Agnes Keith   Jean
                            c1535-1578 ↓   Hepburn
                            div.1567   ↓

Henry VII   m.   Elizabeth of York
King of England   1466-1503
1457-1509

Margaret   m. 2.   Archibald Douglas   Henry VIII
Tudor   Earl of Angus   King of England
1489-1541   1490?-1557   1491-1547

Margaret   m.   Matthew
Douglas   Stuart,
1515-1578   Earl of Lennox
1516-1571

1. m. Mary,   m. 2.   Henry Stuart,
Queen of Scots   Lord Darnley,
1542-1587   King of Scots
1546-1567

3. James Hepburn,
4th Earl of Bothwell
c1535-1578

(by Euphemia   (by Elizabeth   Edward VI   Mary I   Elizabeth I
Elphinstone)   Beaton)   1537-1553   1516-1558   1533-1603

Robert   Jean
Stewart,   Stewart
Earl of   m.   James VI, King of Scots
Orkney,   Archibald   (James I, King of England)
Prior of   Campbell,   1566-1625
Holyrood   5th Earl   m.
1533-1591   of Argyll   Anne of Denmark
           1530-1573   1574-1619
           div. 1573

Royal House of Stuart

THE DYNASTIC CLAIMS OF THE LENNOXES AND THE HAMILTONS

James II
King of Scots
1430-1460

m.

Mary of Gueldres
1433-1463

James III
King of Scots
1452-1488

m.

Margaret of Denmark
c1456-1486

James IV
King of Scots
1473-1513

1. m.

Margaret Tudor
1489-1541

m. 2.

Archibald
Douglas,
6th Earl of
Angus
1490?-1557

Marie de Guise
1515-1560

m.

James V
King of Scots
1512-1542

Margaret
Douglas
1515-1578

m.

Matthew
Stewart/Stuart
4th Earl of
Lennox
1516-1571

Mary,
Queen of Scots
1542-1584

m.

Henry
Stuart,
Lord Darnley
1546-1567

Charles
Stuart,
5th Earl of
Lennox
1556?-1576

m.

James VI
King of Scots
1566-1625
(James I of England)

Arbella
Stuart
1575-1615

Mary 1451?-1488   m.   James, 1st Lord Hamilton 1398?-1479

Elizabeth d. aft. 1531   m.   Matthew Stewart, 2nd Earl of Lennox d. 1513   James Hamilton, 1st Earl of Arram 1475?-1529   m.   Janet Beaton d. c1522

John Stewart, 3rd Earl of Lennox d.1526   James Hamilton, 2nd Earl of Arram, 1st Duke of Chatelherault 1515-1575   John Hamilton, Archbishop of St. Andrew's d.1571

Robert Stewart, Bishop of Caithness d.1586   John Stewart/Stuart 5th Lord of Aubigny d.1567

Elizabeth Cavendish d.1582   Esmé Stuart, 1st Duke of Lennox d.1583   James Hamilton, 3rd Earl of Arram c1537-1609   Lord John Hamilton, 1st Marquess of Hamilton c1539-1604   Lord Claude Hamilton, 1st Baron Paisley c1544-1622

ILLUSTRATION CREDITS

Second Section

James Hepburn, 5th Earl of Bothwell: artist unknown, 1566, Scottish National Portrait Gallery

Jean Gordon, Countess of Bothwell: artist unknown, 1566, Scottish National Portrait Gallery

Hermitage Castle: Scotland in Focus/M. Moar

Mary, Queen of Scots' House, Jedburgh (Stockscotland)

Mary, Queen of Scots and Darnley at Jedburgh: painting by Alfred W. Elmore, 1877, courtesy of Astley House—Fine Art

Craigmillar Castle: Scotland in Focus/M. Moar

The Murder Scene at Kirk O'Field: drawing made the morning after Darnley's murder, Public Record Office Image Library (SP52/13)

The Darnley Memorial Picture: painting by Livinius de Vogelaare, 1568, The Royal Collection © 2002, Her Majesty Queen Elizabeth II (photo: A. C. Cooper)

Mermaid placard: Public Record Office Image Library (SP52/13 no. 60)

Dunbar Castle: Scotland in Focus/M. Moar

Borthwick Castle: Scotland in Focus/M. Moar

Meeting of the Lords with Mary, Queen of Scots at Carberry Hill, 1567; artist unknown, Public Record Office Image Library (SP52/13)

Lochleven Castle: Scotland in Focus/Willbir

George Buchanan: artist unknown, 1581, Scottish National Portrait Gallery

William Cecil: by or after Arnold van Brounckhorst, c. 1560–70, by courtesy of the National Portrait Gallery, London

Elizabeth I: artist unknown, c. 1560, by courtesy of the National Portrait Gallery, London

"The Queen Mary Casket," in the collection at Lennoxlove House, Haddington

INDEX

MARY, QUEEN OF SCOTS, AND THE MURDER OF LORD DARNLEY

Alison Weir

A Reader's Guide

Reading Group Questions and Topics for Discussion

1. The author describes four views of Queen Mary: the adulteress and murderess, the Catholic martyr, the romantic heroine, and the inept woman with poor judgement. How true is each view? And how much have these images obscured our view of the real Mary? What was the real Mary like?

2. In the author's view, Mary made two fatal errors that blighted her life. What were these? Would you say that Mary was the victim of circumstance and unscrupulous men, or of her own poor judgement?

3. Who was the most guilty: Elizabeth I for keeping Mary prisoner for nineteen years and then having her executed? Or Mary, for seeking aid from Elizabeth, whose crown she coveted, and for ceaselessly plotting her ruin?

4. Some people think it incredible that Mary could not have known of the plot against Darnley, given that so many people were involved. Yet she had certainly not known of a similarly orchestrated plot against Rizzio. Do you think that, after the conference at Craigmillar, she should have realized that Darnley's life might be in danger?

5. How do you account for Mary's inertia after Darnley's murder? Does the author make a convincing case for it being due to a physical and mental breakdown?

6. Did Mary collude in her own rape by Bothwell? What evidence is there that she was forced into marriage with him?

7. Suppose Elizabeth had sent Mary back into Scotland with an English army in 1568 and it proved victorious in winning her back the throne, what do you think the consequences might have been?

8. This question was asked by a reader at an event: Did Darnley have any good points? The author, at a loss for an answer, mentioned his youth and his good looks! Is there anything you think she could have added?

9. Has Mary ever been well-portrayed on screen? How would you rate the performances of Katharine Hepburn (*Mary of Scotland*, 1936), Vanessa Redgrave (*Mary, Queen of Scots,* 1971), Vivian Pickles (*Elizabeth R,* 1971), Clémence Poésy (*Gunpowder, Treason and Plot,* 2004), Barbara Flynn *(Elizabeth I,* 2005), and Samantha Morton (*Elizabeth: The Golden Age,* 2007)? Do you think that Scarlett Johansson is a good choice for the role in the forthcoming film?

10. Having read the book, do you agree with the author's conclusions?

Read on for a preview of

MISTRESS OF THE MONARCHY
by Alison Weir

INTRODUCTION

This is a love story, one of the greatest and most remarkable love stories of medieval England. It is the extraordinary tale of an exceptional woman, Katherine Swynford, who became first the mistress and later the wife of John of Gaunt, Duke of Lancaster, one of the outstanding princes of the high Middle Ages.

Katherine Swynford's story first captured my imagination four decades ago, when I read Anya Seton's famous novel about her, *Katherine*. This epic novel made a tremendous impact on me as an adolescent, and still has the power to move me today. And I am not alone, because it has hardly been out of print since its first publication in 1954, and ranked ninety-fifth in the top one hundred favorite books voted for by the public in BBC TV's "The Big Read" in 2003. (Interested readers will find more about this novel in the Appendix.)

It would not be an exaggeration to say that I have wanted to write this book for forty years. But even when I became a published author in the late eighties, no publisher would have contemplated commissioning a biography of this relatively obscure woman. And that remained the situation for many years, until the recent explosion of interest in all things historical, which inspired me to seize the chance to make my longstanding secret dream come true.

Katherine Swynford deserves a biography for many reasons. First and foremost, she was romantically linked to John of Gaunt, one of the most charismatic figures of the fourteenth century, and their passionate and ultimately poignant love affair is both astonishing and moving. Katherine was clearly beautiful and desirable, not to say enigmatic and intriguing, and some of her contemporaries regarded her as dangerous also. Her existence was played out against a vivid backdrop of court life at the height of the age of chivalry, and she knew most of the great figures of the epoch. The renowned poet Geoffrey Chaucer, author of *The Canterbury Tales*, was her brother-in-law. She lived through the Hundred Years War, the Black Death, and the Peasants' Revolt, knew passion, loss, adversity, and heartbreak, and survived them all triumphantly. Her story gives us unique insights into the life of a medieval woman.

Yet Katherine was unusual in that she did not conform to many of the conventional norms expected of women in that age, and in several respects her story has relevance for us today. Feminist scholars are now beginning to see her from a new perspective, as a woman who was an important personage in her own right, a woman who—in a male-dominated age—had remarkable opportunities, made her own choices, flouted convention, and took control of her own destiny. Katherine was intelligent, poised, and talented, and fortunate enough to move in circles where these qualities were valued and encouraged in women. Among the choices she faced were ones that would be familiar to women today, although her modern counterparts would not have to endure the moral backlash that at one time rebounded on Katherine and probably wrecked her life. Yet they would identify with her as a woman who coped brilliantly with the sweeping, and sometimes devastating, changes of fortune that befell her.

Above all, Katherine Swynford occupies an unprecedented position in the history of the English monarchy; dynastically, she is an important figure. She was the mother of the Beauforts, and through them the ancestress of the Yorkist kings, the Tudors, the Stuarts, and every other British sovereign since—a prodigious legacy for any woman. Without her, the course of English history would have been very different.

* * *

Writing a biography of Katherine Swynford poses its own particular problems, however, for her voice has been silenced forever: No letter survives, no utterance of hers is recorded. None of her movable goods are extant, and we have barely any details of the clothes she wore, so we cannot determine her tastes in art, literature, or dress. Her will is lost, and with it any insights it might give us into her feelings for John of Gaunt, her moral outlook, her family relationships, or her charities. She is one of the most important women in late fourteenth-century England, and yet so much about her is a mystery to us. She is famous but, paradoxically, she is little known.

Furthermore, the contemporary sources to support a biography of Katherine Swynford are meager and fragmentary at best. She rates barely a mention in the chronicles of the period, and such references as there are, usually reflect monastic prejudice against a woman who was regarded as "a she-devil and enchantress." The best evidence for her life lies mainly in the dry entries in John of Gaunt's *Register*, the *Calendar of Patent Rolls*, the *Duchy of Lancaster Records* in the National Archives, and the civic and clerical records of Lincoln, Leicester, and other places. The rest is largely inference. Yet there is a wealth of evidence on which to base those inferences, as will be seen. There is monetary evidence, and archaeological evidence. Much remains of the many castles and manor houses owned by John of Gaunt, in which Katherine would often have resided, not the least of which is his magnificent range and great hall at Kenilworth, which she would have known well. Houses in which she herself lived for long periods—Kettlethorpe Hall in Lincolnshire, and the Chancery and the Priory in the close of Lincoln Cathedral—also survive in part. There is, in addition, much surviving documentation on John of Gaunt's fabulous but long-lost Savoy Palace, so it is possible to place Katherine and her prince in the context of vividly recreated authentic settings.

So although there is a great deal that is not known about Katherine Swynford, and the tantalizing glimpses of her that appear in the sources often raise more questions than they answer, there is enough to justify a long overdue biography. This book therefore represents a quest to discover the truth about this most intriguing of royal ladies. It has led to the most fascinating historical investigation I have ever undertaken, affording unique opportunities for original research, which has encompassed delving into numerous contemporary sources (and in some cases having them retranslated), following up significant clues—sometimes into unexplored territory—examining the remains of the houses in which Katherine lived, interpreting intriguing allusions in stained glass and ancient manuscripts, and studying a wealth of pictorial evidence.

In drawing up a detailed chronological framework for Katherine's life, then piecing together the myriad pieces of information I had gathered and analyzing them within the context of that framework, I was surprised by the interesting revelations that emerged, some of which challenge the received wisdom about my subject, or lend weight to existing theories. Time and again I was surprised at what I have been able to infer from my research. It is, above all, my hope that what will unfold in the pages that follow is a convincing and challenging portrayal of a most fascinating—but elusive—woman.

ALISON WEIR
CARSHALTON, SURREY
APRIL 2007

Spring 1378

I n March 1378, putting aside "all shame of man and fear of God," John of Gaunt, Duke of Lancaster, the mightiest subject in the realm of England, was to be seen riding around his estates in Leicestershire "with his unspeakable concubine, a certain Katherine Swynford." Not only was the Duke brazenly parading his beautiful mistress for everyone to see, but he was "holding her bridle in public," a gesture that proclaimed to all his possession of her, for it implied that the rider thus led was a captive, in this case one who had surrendered her body, if not her heart. And as if this were not shocking enough, the fact that the Duke was flaunting his mistress "in the presence of his own wife" created a scandal that would soon spread throughout the length and breadth of the kingdom and beyond. Even today, echoes of that furor still reverberate in the pages of history books.

John of Gaunt's conduct in that long distant spring led disapproving contemporaries to conclude that he had "made himself abominable in the eyes of God," and that Katherine Swynford was "a witch and a whore." Thus was born the legend of the "famous adulteress" who occupies a unique place in English history. There can be no doubt that in her own lifetime she was the subject of great scandal and notoriety, for she was closely linked to John of Gaunt for a quarter of a century before they married, and had already known him for many years before he wed the desirable young wife who was so openly insulted on that tour of Leicestershire in 1378. Years later, after John's wife had died and he married Katherine, controversy and criticism surrounded their union, for she was far below him in status, morally unacceptable, and considered highly unsuitable in many respects. But she confounded her critics and gradually came to be tolerated and even respected.

Indeed, all the evidence suggests that Katherine Swynford was no lightly principled whore, which is what hostile chroniclers would have us believe; on the contrary, she was one of the most important female figures of the late fourteenth century, and more likely to have been a woman deserving of our admiration and esteem. Her partner in adultery—later her husband—was the son of King Edward III of England and one of the epoch's most famous and celebrated paragons. From her is descended every English monarch since 1461, and no fewer than five American presidents.

The truth about Katherine Swynford has been obscured by people down the centuries accepting at face value the calumnies that were written about her by a few disapproving contemporaries; and too because nearly every aspect of her story is shrouded in mystery, exaggerated by debate, or simply obliterated by time. Nearly everything about her is controversial. When and where was she born? What did she look like? How many children did she bear? When did she become John of Gaunt's mistress? What influence did she have? And what was the nature of their relationship over the years? Above all, did she really deserve all the moral opprobrium heaped upon her after her lover paraded her in public on that fateful spring day?

We will never know the whole truth about Katherine and John, for only echoes of their voices and their deeds have come down to us, but one thing is certain, and it shines forth from nearly every source: These two were lovers, and their love endured through prosperity and adversity, war and endless separations, time and distance. Love and destiny brought them together, sealing their fate and changing the course of English history itself. So this is, essentially, a love story.

ONE

Panetto's Daughter

Katherine Swynford, that "famous adulteress,"[1] was set on the path to notoriety, fame, and a great love at the tender age of two or thereabouts, when she was placed in the household of Philippa of Hainault, wife to Edward III of England. This would have been around 1352, and Katherine's disposition with the popular and maternal Philippa was almost certainly due to her father, Sir Paon de Roët, having rendered years of faithful service to the Queen and the royal family of Hainault.

Katherine possibly had noble or even royal connections through her mother, but claims that she was closely related through her father to the aristocratic lords of Roeulx cannot be substantiated. The Roeulx were a great and powerful Hainaulter family that could trace its descent from the ancient counts of Flanders and Hainault, who were themselves descended from the Emperor Charlemagne, and from England's famous King Alfred. William the Conqueror had married a princess of that house, Matilda of Flanders, and by her was the founder of the ruling dynasties of England, the Norman and Plantagenet kings. Since the twelfth century the lords of Roeulx had prospered mightily.[2] Their landholdings centered mainly on the town of Le

Roeulx, which lies eight miles northeast of Mons, but their name is also associated with Roux, forty miles east of Mons, and Fauroeulx, twenty miles to the south.

That Katherine shared a close kinship with the lords of Roeulx is doubtful on heraldic evidence alone—or the lack of it.[3] Her family was relatively humble. The chronicler Jean Froissart, a native of Hainault, who appears to have been quite well informed on Katherine Swynford's background, states that Jean de Roët, who died in 1305 and was the son of one Huon de Roët, was her grandfather. Neither bore a title. Yet it is possible that there was some blood tie with the Roeulx. Paon de Roët, the father of Katherine Swynford, whose name appears in English sources as Payn or Payne,[4] and is pronounced "Pan," was almost certainly baptized Gilles, a name borne by several members of the senior line of the Roeulx, which is one reason some historians have linked him to this branch of the family.[5] Of course, the similarity in surnames suggests a connection—in that period, the spellings of Roeulx and Roët could be, and were, interchangeable—as does the fact that both families are known to have had connections with the area around Mons and Le Roeulx. But discrepancies in arms would appear to indicate that Paon was at best a member of a junior branch of the House of Roeulx; all the same, it is possible that the royal blood of Charlemagne and Alfred the Great did indeed run in Katherine's veins.

The arms of the town of Le Roeulx were a silver lion on a green field holding a wheel in its paw;[6] this is a play on words, for "wheel" in French is *roue*, which is similar to, and symbolic of, Roeulx. It was a theme adopted by Paon's own family: His arms were three plain silver wheels on a field of red; they were not the spiked-gold Katherine wheels later used by his daughter.[7] On the evidence of heraldic emblems on the vestments given by her to Lincoln Cathedral, Katherine Swynford used not only her familiar device of Katherine wheels, which she adopted after 1396, but also her father's device of three plain silver wheels.[8]

If Jean de Roët was his father, as seems likely, then Gilles alias Paon was born by 1305–06 at the very latest. Thus he did not marry and father children until comparatively late in life. The references in the *Cartulaire des Comtes de Hainaut* to "Gilles de Roët called Paon or Paonnet" imply that the name Paon was almost certainly a nickname, although it was the name by which Gilles became customarily known, and it even appeared on his tomb memorial. In French, *paon* means "peacock," which suggests that Paon was a vain man who liked dressing in brightly colored, fashionable clothes, possibly in order to impress the ladies. However, in the form *pion*, it means "usher,"[9] a term that may be descriptive of Paon's duties at court.[10]

John of Gaunt's epitaph states that Katherine came from "a knightly family," and Paon's knighthood is attested to by several sources,[11] although we do not know when he received the accolade. In 1349 he is even referred to as a lord, and his daughter Elizabeth as "noble,"[12] which reflects his landed status and probably his links to aristocratic blood. This is also evident in his ability to place his children with royalty,[13] which suggests—in the case of his daughters, at least—that there was the prospect of some inheritance that would ensure they made good marriages.[14] We know Paon held land in Hainault, because in 1411 his grandson, Sir Thomas Swynford, Katherine's son, was to pursue his claim to lands he had inherited there from his mother.[15] Paon is unlikely, however, to have owned a large estate and was probably not a wealthy man[16] since he was to rely heavily on royal patronage to provide for his children's future.

Paon had first come to England in December 1327 in the train of Philippa of Hainault, who married the young King Edward III on January 24, 1328, in York Minster. Paon perhaps served as Philippa's usher, and may have been present in that capacity at the royal wedding, which took place in the as yet unroofed minster in the midst of a snowstorm.

After Philippa's nuptial celebrations had ended, nearly all her Hainaulter servants were sent home. Apart from a handful of ladies, only Paon de Roët and Walter de Mauney, her carving squire, are known to have been allowed to remain in her retinue,[17] a mark of signal royal favor, which suggests that Paon was highly regarded by both the young king and queen, and was perhaps a kinsman of Philippa, possibly through their shared ancestry.

That kinship may also have been established, or reinforced, through marriage. No one has as yet successfully identified Katherine's mother, for the name of Paon's wife is not recorded in contemporary documents. The slender evidence we have suggests he perhaps married more than once, that his first marriage took place before ca. 1335, and that his four known children, who were born over a period of about fifteen years or more, may have been two sets of half siblings; in which case Katherine was the child of a second wife, whom he possibly married in the mid–late 1340s. We know he maintained links with Hainault, probably through the good offices of Queen Philippa and other members of her house, so it may be that at least one of his wives was a Hainaulter.[18]

It is also possible that Katherine's mother herself was related to the ruling family of Hainault,[19] and while this theory cannot be proved, it is credible in many respects. If Paon was linked by marriage, as well as by blood, to Queen Philippa, that would further explain his continuing links with the House of Avesnes and the trust in which he and his family were held by the ruling families of England and Hainault. It would explain too why all his children received royal patronage and why Queen Philippa took such an interest in them; and it was possibly one reason why John of Gaunt may have felt it was appropriate to ultimately marry one of them.

But there is unlikely to have been a close blood tie.[20] If Paon's wife was related to the House of Avesnes, it must have been through a junior branch or connection. Had the kinship been closer, we would expect Paon to have enjoyed more prominence in the courts of England and Hainault. There have, of course, been other unsubstantiated theories as to who Katherine's mother could have been,[21] but this is the most convincing.

Whether Paon was related by marriage to Queen Philippa or not, he was evidently held in high regard by her, and he played his part in the early conflicts of the Hundred Years War, which broke out in 1340 after Edward III claimed the throne of France. For a time Paon served Queen Philippa as Master of the House,[22] and in 1332 there is a record of her giving money to "Panetto de Roët de Hanonia";[23] this is the earliest surviving reference to him. His lost epitaph in Old St. Paul's Cathedral describes him as Guienne King of Arms,[24] and it may have been through Philippa's influence that he was appointed to this office in ca. 1334,[25] Guienne being part of the Duchy of Aquitaine and a fief of the English Crown.

By the mid-1340s, Paon was back in Queen Philippa's service as "one of the chevaliers of the noble and good Queen."[26] In 1346 he fought at Crécy under Edward III. That same year, "Sir Panetto de Roët" was present at the siege of Calais, and in August 1347 he was Marshal of the Queen's Household, and one of two of her knights—the other was Sir Walter de Mauney—assigned to conduct to her chamber the six burghers who had given themselves up as hostages after Calais fell to Edward III, and whose lives had been spared thanks to the Queen's intercession.[27]

Philippa, however, never courted criticism by indiscriminately promoting her compatriots, which may explain why Paon, although well thought of and loved by the Queen because he was her countryman,[28] never came to greater prominence at the English court[29] and why he eventually sought preferment elsewhere.

By 1349, the year the Black Death was decimating the population of England and much of Europe, Paon had apparently returned to Hainault. From that year on, there are several references to him in the contemporary *Cartulaire des Comtes de Hainaut*, the official record of service of the counts of Hainault.[30] The first reference concerns a "noble adolescent, Elizabeth de Roët, daughter of my lord Gilles, called Paonnet, de Roët," who, sometime after July 27, 1349, was nominated as a prebendary, or honorary canoness (*chanoinness*),[31] of the chapter of the Abbey of St. Waudru in Mons by Queen Philippa's elder sister, Margaret, sovereign Countess of Hainault and Empress of Germany. The choice of a convent in Mons, so close to the former Roeulx estates, reinforces the theory that Paon was connected to that family and that his lands were located in this area.

Girls were not normally accepted into the novitiate before the age of thirteen, so Elizabeth de Roët, who was described as being "adolescent" at the time of her placement, was probably born around 1335–36 at the latest. St. Waudru was a prestigious and influential abbey, and it was an honor for a girl to be so placed by Countess Margaret; it further demonstrates the close ties between the Roëts and the ruling family of Hainault, and suggests yet again a familial link between them. It was unusual for the eldest girl of a gentle family to enter the cloister, but given the fact that Paon's daughters were both to offer their own daughters as nuns, we might conclude that giving a female child to God was a Roët family custom.

Paon also had a son, Walter de Roët, possibly named after Sir Walter de Mauney,[32] who in 1355–56 was in the service, in turn, of Countess Margaret and her son, Duke Albert, and Edward III's eldest son and heir, Edward of Woodstock, Prince of Wales, popularly known to history as the "Black Prince." As Walter was a Yeoman of the Chamber to the Prince in 1355, and probably fought under his command at Poitiers in 1356, he is likely to have been born no later than 1338–40.

Between 1350 and 1352 there are seven references to Paon in the *Cartulaire des Comtes de Hainaut*. For example, on May 11, 1350, he is recorded as preparing to accompany Countess Margaret's sons—Duke Albert, Duke William, and Duke Otto—on a pilgrimage to the church of St. Martin at Sebourg near Valenciennes to make their devotions at the shrine of the twelfth-century hermit, St. Druon. It was probably in that year that Paon's famous daughter was born.

ABOUT THE AUTHOR

ALISON WEIR published her first book, *Britain's Royal Families*, in 1989, and has since written many other historical works, among them *The Six Wives of Henry VIII*, *The Life of Elizabeth I*, *Eleanor of Aquitaine*, *Henry VIII: The King and His Court*, *The Princes in the Tower*, and *Mistress of the Monarchy* as well as two novels, *Innocent Traitor: A Novel of Lady Jane Grey* and *The Lady Elizabeth*. She lives in Surrey, England, with her husband.